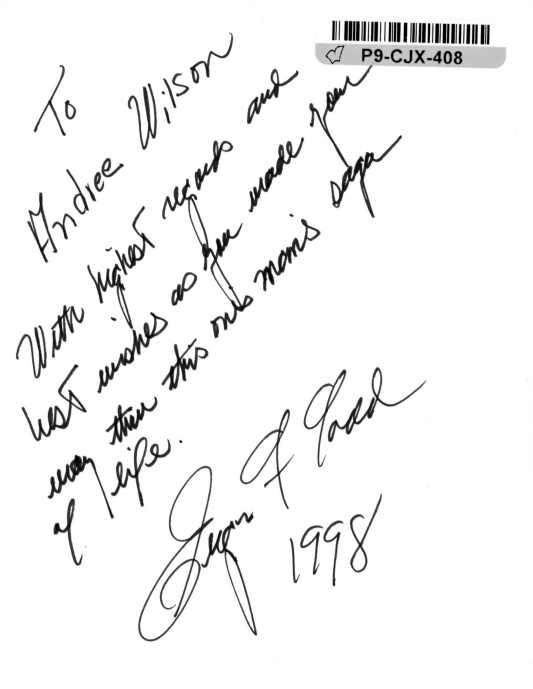

To
Andree Wilson

With highest regards and
best wishes as you wade your
way thru this one man's saga
of life.

Eugene F. Gadd
1998

Tales

&

Irreverencies

of a

Country Parson

Tales

&

Irreverencies

of a

Country Parson

Eugene F. Todd

Western Americana Publishing

First printing in 1997.

Although the author and publisher have made every effort to ensure the accuracy and completeness of information contained in this book, we assume no responsibility for errors, inaccuracies, omissions, or any inconsistency herein. Many personal names have been deliberately changed to protect the identities of individuals. Any slights of people, places, or organizations are unintentional.

Book manufactured by BookCrafters, Inc., Chelsea, Michigan
Printed and bound in the United States of America
Design: Becky Milmoe
Production and Graphics: Barbara Mabray
Publishing Consultant: Jody Berman
Editor-in-Chief: Monroe Billington
Back cover photograph by Peterson Studio, Cheyenne, Wyoming

Library of Congress Card Number: 96-61212
ISBN (cloth): 0-9654090-7-4

Western Americana Publishing
P.O. Box 20444
Cheyenne, Wyoming
82003-7011
FAX 307-632-0629

Gene Todd's gifted talent as a storyteller has such an irresistible way of drawing you into his life that putting his book down is virtually impossible. It's like taking one last peanut from the dish — just one more chapter, then I'll go to bed.

His unusual description, whether it be the characters who entered his life, such as Elmer Hicks (a burly brute who drove a delivery truck), his first college roommate, or the description of the Todd cattle ranch at Ucross, Wyoming, where he grew up (a place used squarely in the story, as if you were there yourself), grips your attention from the very beginning. It's as if you are looking through the window observing the unfolding of a truly fascinating life in all its intimate details.

Tales & Irreverencies of a Country Parson is definitely not irreverent. On the contrary, the honesty and integrity with which this exceptional storyteller spins the tale of a life lived to the fullest, brings you to a holy place in which you see Gene Todd not so much as a writer or an Episcopal priest — but a delightful old friend you love having around.

I know you will enjoy *Tales & Irreverencies of a Country Parson* as much as I did.

The Right Reverend William Jerry Winterrowd
Episcopal Bishop of Colorado

To my wife, Rosemary, and all my extended family:
Past, Present, and Future. Echoing Browning's couplet:

Grow old along with me, the best is yet to be,
The last of life for which the first was made.

Contents

FOREWORD
by Monroe Billington

I first met Gene Todd in September 1955. My very pregnant wife and I had arrived in Vermillion, South Dakota, a couple of weeks previously in preparation for my first full-time teaching position. A native of Oklahoma with a fresh Ph.D. from the University of Kentucky, I had been appointed as an assistant professor of history at the University of South Dakota.

On the last Sunday in August my wife and I worshipped at the University Baptist Church at which time we learned that the new minister and his very pregnant wife were due to arrive within a few days and that he would lead the worship service the next Sunday. We attended that service and met the Todds. From that meeting blossomed a friendship between Gene and me which has lasted exactly forty years as I write these words in 1995.

Gene and I spent a great deal of time together during the five years he lived in Vermillion. A bond of love, understanding, and emotional support evolved, going far beyond the original attractions, including common interests, shared intellectual pursuits, and psychological similarities. After he moved away and after I later relocated to New Mexico State University, we continued our friendship by regularly sending each other cassette tapes rather than writing letters.

Recently I had occasion to mention to a small group that I have corresponded with a dear friend via tape recordings for forty years. One person expressed incredulity. Another person responded, "We all have friends who are important to us, but most come and go. You are very fortunate to have had a good friend over a long period of time. Most people go through a lifetime without experiencing the joy of having a really special longtime friend."

That person was affirming what I already knew: that Gene Todd and I have developed a profoundly special friendship. Over the years we have shared our most intimate feelings and thoughts without fear of vulnerability. Each has given emotional support to the other as we have dealt with events and struggled with decisions concerning careers and families. We have shared emotional highs and lows, not necessarily "giving advice" but always "being there" when we were needed.

When Gene told me that he was considering writing his autobiography, I urged him to do it. As the work progressed, I continued to give him encouragement. I knew that his story would be of interest not only to his progeny, but also to many others beyond his family, since his life has been inextricably bound with the history of this nation.

His childhood in northern Wyoming, his schooling in Denver, his years in South Dakota and his long career in Cheyenne coincide with the history of the American West throughout the last three-quarters of the twentieth century. His life was an integral part of the development of the western region of the United States. That he was a clergyman does not diminish his life story; rather it adds another and oftentimes unusual dimension to the history of his native region of the nation.

Gene has said that he did not think his life story was particularly interesting. I disagree with him, but he and I very much agree on another point: that the stories he has told about many of the varied and interesting people he has met in his lifetime are worth telling. He has chosen to use his own life story as a common thread to tie together the human interest stories he includes here. The result is a unique autobiography which emphasizes his interrelationship with a number of truly fascinating individuals — not to say characters.

Whether Gene Todd was a "typical" minister or whether he was an exception to the rule (as implied in the title of this work) is not particularly relevant. The point is that his life experiences are a part of a larger whole, and his relating them here adds to the totality of the history of the Rocky Mountain West. And since he is a longtime student of history with a deep and genuine love for and understanding of the American West, he tells his story with proper emphasis on fact and perspective.

Finally, Gene has a wonderful sense of humor. Indeed, among the many attractions which pulled me to him early on was this characteristic, and it has continued to be a magnet during the many years of our friendship. Gene has the uncanny ability to see the humor of a situation and enjoy a good laugh, sometimes in the midst of sadness or even trauma. You will discover numerous examples of this delightful humor, often directed at himself, on almost every page that follows.

And so, as you read, share with Gene his successes and failures and his joys and sorrows but most of all his humor and his irreverencies. If you will do that, he will know that his telling his story was worth it.

ACKNOWLEDGMENTS

I'm grateful to family and friends who encouraged me to write this book after my promising or threatening to do so for many years before I started it. I cannot thank typists for laboriously wading through countless manuscript revisions, as most authors do, because I typed and retyped every word of it on my Macintosh computer.

But I am especially grateful to my dear friend Dr. Monroe Billington, a successful author and historian, who edited every page with professional skill and patient advice, but whose friendship was such that he never deleted one word or sentence without first consulting me. He was the first person to read the developing manuscript and encouraged me to keep it up. Without his approval, I probably would have trashed it.

Dr. Charley Arehart, Diarmid Campbell, and Mari Galereave read selected chapters and gave me valuable advice. Patti Hunton Joder, of pioneer Wyoming stock, was the first person in Cheyenne to whom I anxiously entrusted the manuscript for critical review. Her sense of humor runs on the same bizarre track as mine, and I needed to know whether my description of Wyoming and its colorful people, including many who were mutual friends of hers, was both historically accurate and socially acceptable. Her absolute assurance that it was proved to be most helpful.

And then there was Larry Borowsky, a professional publishing editor and literary surgical technician, who helped me slice away at every sentence and page to tighten it up for publication. Although half my age and of the Jewish faith, his critical commentary on the theological manifestations of practical Christianity and the comedy of church politics was both provocative and refreshing. And not too different from that of a typical Jewish synagogue.

Thanks for the memories shared by Jena Carey, Shirley Flynn, Winifred Read, and Florence Esmy Howar who personally knew, or certainly knew a lot about, many of the historical Cheyenne characters about whom I have written in this book. And I am forever grateful to my former church secretary and capable administrative assistant at St. Mark's Episcopal Church, Bobbie Parrish, who graciously supplied me with historical data from the parish register — which I was constantly requesting by phone from Colorado, where I did all of my writing.

And to my loving wife, Rosemary, who endured my persistent tenacity, which she called stubbornness, to get the project finished — I owe a special debt of gratitude.

The fascinating world of publishing became a new revelation to me. I am indebted to the professionals at the prestigious University Press of Colorado who encouraged me to cut the manuscript by one-third for successful marketing. Perhaps I will be sorry that I didn't follow their expert advice and go with them in the publication of this book. Don and Barbara Mabray, publishers of Denver's classy and glossy *Relocation Guide*, introduced me to the marvelous wonder of electronic publishing. They allowed me to sit beside them at work on their powerful computers to watch my written text and photographs digitally transformed before my eyes from CD-ROM discs onto the printed page of this book. I didn't know anything about talented book designers until I met Becky Milmoe who demonstrated how essential they are to the publishing business. Not only did she design the overall presentation of this book — but her artistic cover design, all done by computer-driven electronic imaging, was astonishing.

Of course, every author needs a professional publishing consultant and an overall editorial supervisor who manages the writing project from start to finish — from raw manuscript to the final product of a hardcover printed volume. This person was Jody Berman of Boulder, Colorado. Her many years of professional experience in the publishing business, along with her perfectionistic editorial skill and personal encouragement to a bumbling writer, made her absolutely invaluable to this country parson.

BookCrafters, Inc., of Chelsea, Michigan, prides itself in operating one of the largest and most modern book manufacturing plants in the world, printing for the major publishing houses of America. They can also boast of a gracious and considerate staff.

I need to remind the reader that in writing this autobiographical saga, I tried hard to avoid violating pastoral confidentiality. For this reason alone, I could not include many tales I wanted very much to tell. Conseqently, in this book, I frequently changed the names or slightly altered the circumstances to protect the identities of a few people from whom I could not, for a variety of reasons, receive permission to include their sensitive stories in the narrative. However, those persons accurately named (using actual names) generally are characters of such repute that changing their names would not conceal their public identities at all. You can rest assured that the basic drama and trauma of the story as a whole, along with the wonderful human characters who became a part of my life's journey, are as real to life as I can possibly portray them. Reality is so much greater than fantasy. Fictional writing is not my forte.

PROLOGUE

Don't read this book if you want to read theology. I am not a theologian. If you're interested in theology, go to the library and check out the classical works of Aquinas, Calvin, Hooker, Temple, Tillich, Neibuhr, and Bonhoffer — to get you started.

Don't read this book if you're in the mood to read something about Christian sainthood. There hasn't been much saintliness in my life. Read the Lives of the Saints or the Confessions of Augustine.

Don't read this book if you're hoping to find inspiration for your own spiritual journey. This book is not my private spiritual journal, nor is it a manual for yours. Go to any Christian bookstore and you'll find dozens of testimonial publications, vividly describing the author's rapturous salvation after bingeing too long on sensuous sin.

Don't read this book if you're looking for a manual on how to attain peace of mind. There's nothing more stressful than another frantic search for peace of mind in our age of anxiety. I have found a reasonable balance between peace and anxiety within my struggling life, I think, but I wouldn't pretend to suggest how to achieve it in yours.

Don't read this book if you think it's primarily the story of my life or of my Christian ministry, because neither has been that unique or interesting.

Then why read this book at all? What's it all about?

Primarily, it is about the human interest stories of many people I've met during my life and ministry — ordinary people whose ordinary lives have become entwined with mine during the ordinary living of life. My rather dull life becomes the basic skeleton of the narrative, while the stories of others become the flesh and blood. Naturally, there is a sprinkling of theology, inspiration, and spirituality through it all — and a lot of devilish stuff sandwiched in between. So it is with anyone's life.

The title of the book came from an auspicious occasion in Cheyenne, Wyoming, when U.S. District Judge Ewing Kerr; the Most Reverend Hubert Newell, Catholic bishop of Cheyenne; and I were invited to speak at a banquet, sharing a few humorous personal anecdotes. The three of us found it enjoyable, poking fun at ourselves to the amusement of all. I thought it a most unusual and delightful format, a pleasant departure from what normally is asked of after-dinner speakers.

But the master of ceremonies took his job very seriously. Before we took our places at the head table, he diligently inquired from each of us precisely how we should be properly introduced.

"I want my introductions of you three honored guests to be absolutely perfect," he said.

I told him that, as an Episcopal priest, I could be formally introduced as either the Reverend Eugene Todd or just as Father Eugene Todd. And thereafter I could be called simply Father Todd or the Reverend Mr. Todd.

"Please make certain," I added, "since you're wanting to be absolutely perfect, that you don't introduce me as Reverend Todd, because the word Reverend by itself is not grammatically correct as a formal title for a clergyman."

The master of ceremonies had good reason to be very pleased with his own performance. His introductions and courtesy references to Judge Kerr, Bishop Newell, and me were flawless, technically correct in every way. In fact, at the conclusion of the evening's activities he decided to thank the three of us again — this time off-the-cuff, just to demonstrate his newly acquired proficiency with honorary prefix titles.

He started out perfectly, "In conclusion, once again I want to thank our esteemed guests: His Honor, U.S. Federal District Judge Ewing Kerr; His Excellency, the Most Reverend Bishop Hubert Newell; and, sitting between the two, His . . ." He stammered, then panicked when he blanked out on the proper prefix (there is none) for a simple village priest. Remembering my caution not to call me just plain *Reverend* as a title, he blundered forward with, "And sitting between the two is — His Irreverency, Father Eugene F. Todd!"

The banquet room exploded with laughter and applause.

Had he let it pass as an intended pun, it would have been a brilliant finale to a lighthearted evening. But the poor guy didn't know what mistake he had made and was bewildered at the uproar. He leaned over and asked Bishop Newell what it was he had mistakenly said, but the mild-mannered bishop was laughing too hard to tell him. Muddled, with an expression of total confusion on his face, he stood there at the podium wringing his hands until his wife ran to his rescue, whispering the *faux pas* in his ear. And then the poor fellow literally turned every color of the rainbow — which only added to the hilarity of it all.

The next day, he personally called on me offering another apology for what he considered to be his humiliating goof. I assured him that I took no offense, and went on to congratulate him on a job well done. "The slip of your tongue was so ingeniously appropriate to the festivity of the evening we were all enjoying, that if ever I write a book on my life, I will somehow incorporate that new word into its title. Hence, *Tales & Irreverencies of a Country Parson.*

I've been in too much mischievousness in my life to be called reverent — in spite of the fact that I'm an ordained Episcopal priest. One might wish my life was conspicuously more religious, but then it would run the terrible risk of becoming sanctimonious and boring — even to me. I contend it is a mortal sin to bore people.

I'm far more concerned about the *relevancy* of my life and ministry among the people I've met along the way than I am about its *reverency*.

So this book becomes the autobiographical story and irreverency of a Wyoming ranch kid who struck out on his own to find relevance in a world far removed from the peaceful hills of his boyhood home.

How well I succeeded or failed is for the reader alone to decide.

Eugene F. Todd

Chapter 1

My earliest memory is one of drowning.

I was two years old and distinctly remember that although the gate leading out of the fenced yard around the house was securely tied with a rope, still I could wiggle my little body through. Once I had done that, I was free to explore the wide-open world of a typical Wyoming ranch, with its barns, sheds, and corrals — all filled with animals. I walked down past the large cottonwood trees to the watering hole, where the little colts would prance and frolic in the rippling waters. I wanted to do the same as they.

That's how I got myself into the floodwaters of Piney Creek, which ran directly behind our ranch house.

At first the water was cool and refreshing. The leather shoes protected my tender feet from the sharp rocks of the creek bed, which made it easier for me to play at the water's edge. I moved out into the swifter current and felt it push against my legs. When my feet slid out from under me, I lunged out to grab a large, slippery rock and there hung for dear life. I don't remember screaming. I couldn't regain my footing and soon lost hold of the slippery anchor.

The creek swept me about twenty yards away into a slow-moving whirlpool, swirling over the summer swimming hole, where the water was eight feet deep. The proximity of the whirlpool to the house was the first thing that saved my life; otherwise I most certainly would have been swept downstream, around the bend behind the barn, long before I was discovered missing back at the yard.

The second thing that saved me was that I floated on my back, which enabled me to keep breathing as my body slowly spun in the gigantic whirlpool. When the water washed over my face, instead of strangling, I vividly remember swallowing it . . . swallowing . . . swallowing.

My Aunt Della heard me screaming and shouted the alarm. Everyone came running toward the swimming hole. And there they spotted me, still floating on my back, in the whirlpool. My mother forgot her lifelong

1

hydrophobia and waded into the water up to her shoulders, then held onto the legs of my twelve-year-old cousin, Evelyn Sampson, who reached out with a stick and snagged my coveralls and pulled me ashore.

My mother held me up by my feet, and water came gushing out of my stomach and lungs. I was unconscious but still breathing. She wrapped me in a blanket, carried me into the living room, and cradled me in her arms until late afternoon. One can well imagine the horrors my poor mother must have endured during that long period of my unconsciousness. In those days, on an isolated cattle ranch, there was nothing more she could do but wait. I suddenly awakened, slid down off her lap, asked for a cookie, and went outside to play. Obviously, it was no big deal for me. But for my panic-stricken mother this marked the beginning of a lifelong commitment to damage control.

I'm quite certain that when I graduated from the University of Denver twenty years later, my mother and father, who attended the ceremony, must have felt especially elated that this brain-damaged son somehow managed to con his way through college in spite of his drowning.

✧

My birth on July 1, 1928, marked the beginning of what my parents could only have called their worst of times.

My father, Fred J. Todd, came to northern Wyoming in 1901 as a stow-away on a railroad immigrant car and became a working cowboy on large cattle spreads in Sheridan and Johnson counties. He was only nineteen years old. Shortly thereafter, the whole Todd family migrated from Iowa to this latest frontier of the American West.

He took out a homestead, like many young settlers of the early West, married an attractive schoolteacher named Gladys Wilcox, bought a ranch on lower Piney Creek, and began raising a family: three sons — George, born in 1910, Luther, in 1912; and Roger, in 1917 — and one daughter, Edna, born in 1921.

Things went well, times were good, and ranching was prosperous. They expanded their operation and built a wonderful new home along the banks of the creek. The horse barn was connected to the cow barn, and both were constructed of thick stone walls with stone quarried on site from the ranch. Dad was the first rancher on Piney Creek to buy a gasoline-driven Ford car — which he called his "exploding gas tank." I find this astonishing in view of the fact that if you asked him how else could a Ford be powered except by a gasoline engine, he would have answered, "Much better with a good team of fast horses." The irony was, he preferred horses over auto-mobiles, tractors, and power-driven machinery and established himself as a successful horse breeder of beautiful saddle horses as well as Clydesdale draft animals. It was truly the best of times for the Fred Todd family.

Their good fortune was soon to make a drastic change. One year after my birth the blue skies turned black along upper Piney Creek and that evening, at bedtime, a neighbor galloped his horse three miles down the valley and shouted his warning across the river that a flood was coming. My parents had only minutes to spare in a desparate run for their lives. Grabbing a few blankets and scooping me up into their arms, they ran to higher ground above the road. They huddled on the hillside in the darkness of the night with their children, a hired man, and one horse and waited out a horrendous thunderstorm. Lightning flashes illuminated the scene below — and all they could see was water. They heard the pathetic squealing of horses, milk cows, and pigs confined to their pens — and then it stopped. Lightning continued to flash, and now they saw large objects floating in the roaring floodwaters — haystacks, roofs, furniture.

It was all over for them. They tramped through the mud for several miles across the rain-drenched hills to the nearest neighbor. Early the next morning, Dad rode his horse to the mesa overlooking the valley below, and, he later said, "The sun sank at sunrise."

Miraculously, my parents' new ranch house was still standing, along with the stone barns, but everything else they had worked twenty-three years to accumulate was gone. Everything would need rebuilding: bridges, corrals, irrigation headgates, roads, telephone lines — everything. The livestock that drowned in the deluge would have to be replaced. Had they known at the time that the rebuilding would take twenty years, they probably would never have started. It was June 1929.

The following October, the stock market crashed. It couldn't have happened at a worse time. My folks had borrowed to the hilt to recover their losses from the once-in-a-century flood. Now the Great Depression descended upon them with all its tragic fury, which made payment of bank loans a virtual impossibility. The monumental economic calamity was bad enough for my parents. They didn't need a two-year-old drowning himself in the river to make things worse. My father already was forty-five and my mother forty-three when I was born in 1928. In spite of that, two years later my younger sister, Sadie, was prematurely born. She was so tiny that they cribbed her in a shoebox behind the kitchen stove, where the warmth served as an incubator. In 1932 a younger brother, Lewis, came along.

Mom always referred to the last three of her seven children as her second family. It was a second family she didn't need, because things couldn't have been worse on the ranch — or anywhere in America, for that matter — from 1929

No photos exist showing Dad and Mom with all seven adult children. This rare picture shows six of the seven of us with the folks. Seated (left to right): George, Dad, Mom, and me. Standing (left to right): Luther, Sadie, Edna, and Roger. Missing is my youngest brother, Lewis.

to 1940. Consequently, I don't remember my folks as being the kind of ideal parents often depicted today. How could they have been? They already had to finish grooming their first set of children before turning them loose on the world. My oldest brother, George, was already fixing to get married when I was born. The Depression slammed Americans to their knees — including my parents and all their Piney Creek ranching neighbors. To top it off, a series of droughts struck northern Wyoming in the early 1930s. The parched land dried up, and the topsoil blew away like dust in a relentless whirlwind.

The awesome backdrop of the Great Depression colored the world I knew as a young child. It was a dark ominous cloud that hung over the first ten years of my life. My memories of these years cannot help but reflect the sense of doom and gloom that generally prevailed. I remember hopping off the school bus as a child of six, walking to the corrals behind the barn, and, in absolute horror, witnessing the brutal slaughter of all our farm animals. Government workers, as part of the New Deal's solution to livestock overproduction (Agricultural Adjustment Act — AAA), were wrestling sheep to the ground and methodically smashing in their skulls with sledgehammers, then skinning off the woolen pelts and tossing the carcasses into large dump trucks. Next the hogs and their little pigs went, squealing as they dropped from the rifle shots. Then the cattle — including almost all our milk cows and their calves.

I stood there, alone and speechless, still clutching my little lunch bucket, paralyzed with fear. The ranch dogs were as traumatized as I, hiding and quivering in fright back down under the kitchen porch, where I soon crawled to join them. We offered what comfort we could to one another as we heard the bleating of the sheep and squealing of the pigs amid the sporadic rifle shots and loud shouting of the men. It was as if we were escaping the whole-sale massacre of an invading army.

I never asked why the brutal slaughter occurred and don't ever remember getting a voluntary explanation. I'm sure I wouldn't have understood had someone tried. This violent and bloody incident of my childhood had to be repressed into the dark abyss of my unconscious — hopefully to be forever forgotten. If the gruesome killing was hard on me as a child, I can only imagine how difficult it must have been for Dad, a rancher dedicated to the breeding and nurturing of livestock. But the relentless drought made it impossible to feed and care for them, and overproduction of livestock had reduced meat prices to nothing. It makes no more sense to me today, as an adult, than it did to me as a child. The emotional strain was so severe for my parents that they couldn't even discuss the incident among themselves, much less us kids, who they thought were oblivious to the horror of it all.

The Great Depression threw millions of Americans into abject poverty, and the Todds on Piney Creek were no exception. Fortunately for us kids, we were poor but didn't know it, because everyone else was in the same boat. Our poverty was probably not as bad as that experienced by most Americans. In the first place, we were well fed. Mom's huge vegetable garden provided a year's supply of all the canned food we needed. Our chicken house was always filled, which provided us abundantly with fresh eggs and fried chicken dinners. Still a succulent delicacy for me is the enticing aroma of chicken slowly frying in a large black skillet. Our cows provided fresh milk, sweet cream for the table, and hand-churned butter — with first dibs on the glass of buttermilk which gushed from the churn once the wooden plug was pulled.

The folks did all their own butchering right on the ranch premises. Huge wooden barrels were filled with an abundant supply of sugar-cured pork and slabs of salted bacon. Beef steaks and pot roasts, always cooked well done, were our daily diet. Potatoes were harvested each fall, stored in the cool potato cellar and served at every meal three times a day, every day of the year. We were well fed during the Great Depression because we produced almost all our food right there on the ranch. Trips to Sheridan for grocery staples were few and far between.

Mom sewed almost all our clothing, which included a heavy winter coat every new school year, one set of good overalls and shirts for school and dress-up occasions, and a ragged old pair to wear the rest of the time. I don't remember any luxuries at all. No movies. No ice cream unless we cranked it out ourselves. No goodies from a soda fountain (although once in awhile we'd be treated to the sweet taste of little candies, which Mr. Dorman, who operated the general store in Ucross, would toss in the return milk jar when the folks brought him cream). No electricity. For refrigeration we used a wooden cooler-chest supplied with ice cut from the frozen waters of Piney Creek each winter and stored under several feet of sawdust in the ice house behind the barn. At night, the ranch house seemed dark and shadowy from the dim light of smoky kerosene lamps that we carried from room to room. Lanterns used in the barns were so dim that you could scarcely see at all.

During the depths of the Great Depression, it seemed as if everyone plodded onward in perpetual slow motion, dulled by a state of gloomy desperation. I can recall the folks struggling to survive in the ranching business and forever arguing over whether they should carry on or call it quits. The never-ending hard times, terrible droughts, and devastating invasions of Mormon crickets and grasshoppers were taking their toll on us all. I vividly remember a constant parade of highway tramps begging for food at Mom's kitchen door and men pleading with Dad for a job as a hired hand — even trading their labor for room and board.

✧

Again I must remind myself that this general mood of unhappiness of my earliest childhood must be viewed against the awful backdrop of the Great Depression. But I don't want the reader to conclude that these are the only memories I have. Quite the contrary. The overall impression of long cold winters, hot dry summers, miserable hard times and grim desperation for survival which consumed my parents is punctuated with flashbacks of intermittent pleasantries associated with joyful sights and experiences which come flooding back to me now.

A pleasant memory is one of attending political rallies with my parents at the dance hall above Dorman's general store in Ucross. For some strange reason, as a child I took real interest in these candidates and listened intently to what they promised the voters. The politicians would bribe the women inside the hall with candy and men outside the hall with free whiskey. Pure country politics. An ol' fashioned country dance would follow. It was fun watching all the grownups that I knew in the ranching valley enjoying themselves out on the swaying and sagging dance floor. It seems that all personal scores among the men were settled outside — either with the exchange of friendly drinks or flying fists. We neighborhood kids were old enough to run freely outside and watch these nocturnal activities, including peeking in on young lovers in the parked cars.

Back at the Todd ranch, I remember that my drowning hole in Piney Creek was also a swimming hole in the summer and a wonderful ice-skating pond in the winter which we tremendously enjoyed although we never had swimsuits or ice skates. That really didn't matter because we kids became quite adept at improvising. Besides, it was more fun sledding on the ice.

More flashbacks. The horse barn was always a special place for us kids. Its thick stone walls made it cool in the summer and warm in the winter. Inside was the pungent smell of leather, hay, straw, and horse manure. There were always several saddle horses stabled there. Harnesses and saddles were hung along the wall opposite the heavy timbered stalls — stalls reserved mainly for Clydesdale draft horses which provided the raw horse-power on a working family ranch.

Accurate detailed painting of the Todd ranch at Ucross, Wyoming, showing Piney Creek flowing directly behind the ranch house and barns, with Lookout Mountain in background with prehistoric Indian ruins on top.

As a child, my younger sister, Sadie, and I would play in the barn with the young foals of these huge working mares. With their mothers out in the field, these colts would romp and play inside the barn, and we joined them. We'd affectionately hug them, scratch their necks, nuzzle their soft noses, and they would seek out our attention by coming to us for more affection. They became like tame kittens and were already considered "broke" long before halters and harnesses were ever placed on them — so accustomed had they become to growing up with us kids.

The loft above the barn was always jammed full of summer and winter feed, with its wooden floor smooth as polished glass from all the hay that was pushed across it. It was fun to slide down the huge mounds of stacked hay, or swing, tarzan style, from ropes attached to the rafters high above.

There were ponies to ride, always bareback. Kids' ponies they were called, tame and gentle, but stubborn and headstrong enough to know that while riding them, they could stop and graze for awhile and there wasn't much a barefoot kid could do with bridle jerks, or flopping your legs, to make them do otherwise. But they were always gentle enough that five or six of us kids could straddle any one of them all at one time, or play circus by standing up on their backs or crawling under their bellies. They were good creatures of the earth. Ol' Red Wing is the one I especially remember who produced a beautiful sorrel colt every summer, and her colts provided the pool of saddle horses used regularly on the ranch.

✧

I remember the Todd ranch as more of a small rural village than anything else. It was never to me an isolated lonely place as many Wyoming ranches would later become. There were always several families living on the ranch at any one time: hired men in the bunk house, groups of Filipino men or migrant Mexican families, with children, who worked the sugar beet fields, sheepherders coming in from the hills for supplies, cattlemen and cowboys drifting in and out — always trout fishermen along Piney Creek and deer hunters in the fall. The place was constantly alive with people, a beehive of activity. During fall roundups huge herds of cattle would stop overnight on our ranch while being driven to a railroad terminal in Ucross for shipping to Omaha, Sioux City, and Chicago. The cowboys would unroll their bedrolls in the bunkhouse and then drift over into the dining room of our ranch house, where Mom had prepared a delicious pot-roast dinner. Overnight arrangements had all been worked out by these cattlemen in advance with my parents, and Mom was paid for the extra meals she served. Dad was paid for the extra feed to the cattle and horses. It was exciting to watch all this frenzied activity reminiscent of the Old West. The foreman would assign one or two cowboys to ride herd during the night to make sure the cattle didn't drift over into the fields or mix with our stock.

One of these cattlemen, Billy Grubb from Story, Wyoming, was a bachelor rancher, and we kids especially enjoyed him because he would play card games with us after the dishes had been cleared from the dining table and the oilcloth wiped clean. He was a most unusual person because he really seemed to enjoy kids and would seek us out, preferring to spend fun time with us rather than with his crew of cowboys in the bunkhouse.

Neighbors often used Dad's blacksmith shop. I usually ended up cranking the blower to fan the coals white-hot while horseshoes, branding irons, and other tools were pounded into final shape on the anvil, then dipped into a barrel of cold water and tossed out onto the earthen floor to cool. I still occasionally hear in my sleep the ring of hammers on that anvil.

It was common for total strangers to appear at our house at mealtimes. It was an unwritten social custom of the Old West to feed anyone who came around at dinnertime because it could be a long ride to the next ranch. Dad made much of this custom in his book, *Recollections of a Piney Creek Rancher*, in which he claimed it was an act of downright hostility to refuse to offer such an invitation to any cowboy horsebacking through the wide open range — even if you didn't like him or the outfit he worked for.

Mom was an excellent cook, and the Todd ranch was known for its gracious hospitality to friends and neighbors. People didn't even ask if they could eat with us. If they were anywhere in the neighborhood at mealtime they would simply walk into the dining room and draw up a chair to the table. They could expect the same generosity if they needed a place to stay all night. If the bunkhouse was full they would sleep in the hayloft. I remember Mom saying she never knew how many she'd be cooking breakfast for until they showed up in the kitchen ordering their eggs over easy.

Of course, this kind of hospitality was made possible only because of the stable food supply on any Wyoming ranch at that time. Again I must say, there was always plenty of meat in the pork barrel, beef in the ice house, potatoes in the cellar, and home-canned goods in the basement. Mom's bread loaves were nearly ten inches high and sixteen inches long, and she baked twelve loaves at a time — twice a week. Obviously, there were a lot of hungry mouths to feed at the Todd ranch.

During the winter, when I was around twelve years old, I began trapping muskrats and mink, which thrived in Piney Creek. I would set the traps along the banks where the long grasses would bend down toward the water, thereby creating little runways, or private corridors, where the critters could scamper unseen by man or their natural enemies. I had to conceal the traps under the water to hide any scent of myself and then constantly move them a few inches each evening. I had to check them at the crack of dawn each morning before school. I learned that muskrats would literally chew off their legs to free themselves from the metal traps, leaving only a severed foot for me to find the next morning.

Once I found a live mink in my trap. I had to kill the poor thing by clubbing it too death, because a bullet wound would damage the precious fur pelt. Watching it desperately trying to defend itself from my clubbing, with its broken legs gripped in the steel clamps of the trap, was simply too much for me to bear. I felt a companionship with that desperate animal fighting for its life in a world created for us both, and I knew it had as much right to live in this world as I did. Somehow I sensed that we shared a common kingdom. Where this little bit of philosophical insight came from I will never know, because I don't ever remember hearing it from anyone else.

I continued to monitor my trap line every morning and evening, but, unknown to everyone, I had sprung the traps. Philosophically, I had come to believe that humanity involved something more than inflicting death and pain on others in the animal kingdom. But I would continue tramping along the creek banks daily looking now for fresh footprints in the snow and on the ice and along their private corridors covered over by the grass and bushes along the water's edge. It was exciting for me to discover this secret world of theirs, and I wished them well.

In the summer, that same Piney Creek also had another special attraction to me. I knew every nook and cranny of its many bends as it snaked back and forth across the floor of our beautiful ranch valley. It teemed with wildlife. The beavers worked feverishly on their marvelous dams. They would flap their broad tails against the water before diving out of sight whenever I approached. The muskrats and mink were always there, silently swimming across the deeper pools. Wild geese spent their summers all along Piney Creek, and cranes fished along the shores, maintaining their silent vigil as they stood on one leg, their necks bent downward, waiting for their catch. When startled by my approach they would loudly flap their huge wings, slowly lift from the water and barely become airborne as they sailed off down the river. Their graceful flight was like poetry in motion.

I explored most of the many little islands along Piney Creek. Some were only a few feet wide and not much longer. Others were much larger, with outcroppings of rock and little green interior gardens of wildflowers hidden in the thick willows. Each island had a distinctive character and charm of its own. Because they were constantly irrigated from the flowing stream on both sides, these islands formed a lush green ribbon all summer. They were the first to show signs of life in the springtime with the budding pussy willows, then the dense foliage of the cottonwoods and spruce, with knee-high grass so thick you could hardly walk through it. And in late October, again because of constant watering, these island trees were aglow with the fall splendor of splashed gold and orange, crimson and vermillion. They shone like jewels reflected in the water.

I even made a deal with Dad for personal ownership of these islands, which I thought of as my island kingdom. No one else claimed or made good use of them. I could slip off my shoes, roll up my pant legs, and wade out across the sharp rocks through the cold rapids to most of them. Sometimes the water was so cold my leg muscles would ache for hours. Many birds nested on these islands; ducks paddled along the water's edge, and beautiful pheasants would nest within the outcroppings of rock and sagebrush.

One island was surrounded by water too deep for wading. I lashed two cottonwood trunks together, about two feet thick and several feet long, and floated out to them — pretending to invade like a pirate. I would anchor my homemade raft with a rope to the nearest tree when I returned to the opposite bank. At this age I read *The Adventures of Tom Sawyer* and fantasized what it would be like to live someday on a hidden island like this. Years later I realized just how tiny these islands actually were. But they were immensely special to me in the lonely and secret world of my own imagination.

Lonely, yes, but never lonesome.

The Wyoming hills held a special mystery for me as well. They rose up suddenly from the irrigated fields scattered along the alluvial floor of our Piney Creek ranching valley and ascended to a myriad variety of peaked and rounded shapes, each with a special character of its own. The deep ravines between them were filled with wild bushes of plum, buffaloberry, and chokecherry. In the springtime the color and fragrance of their colorful blossoms were the most wonderful things a kid could imagine.

The bottoms of these long draws, several miles long, were filled with a continuous series of springs. Some were nothing more than muddy seepholes, but in other places the water would trickle down over the rocks into miniature pools from which the animals drank. The constant supply of water made these hills a natural refuge for wild game and a marvelous grassland for the cattle and horses that Dad pastured there.

The ravines feeding down into the deeper draws were filled with little grassy rooms, opening up to the sun from within the crush of thick bushes, not visible from the outside unless you crawled through the underbrush to reach them. No wonder this was good country for the deer. Here fawns were completely hidden from potential predators. Each of these little secluded pockets was special to me, and I knew every one of them as part of my fabulous collection of private retreats from the world.

There were interesting geological formations of sandstone and lava rock (clinkers from underground coal-bed burns millions of years ago) up along these draws and gullies — made ever-colorful by the greenery and sagebrush clinging to every crevice and drooping down across the face of the stony surfaces. Particularly interesting was a petrified tree stump rolled up inside a ball of rock, resting on its side, exposing the tree at its center. Obviously, the tree became rolled under by some primeval geological formation that pushed across the face of the earth, probably a glacier during the ice ages, accumulating the mass of rocky material around itself until finally it petrified and was left abandoned and deposited on the lofty hillside behind our ranch house.

Animal trails wound their way up and down these draws and hillsides like well-traveled roadways. Horses, cattle, and wild game traveled them constantly. No doubt ancient buffalo and Indians preceded them. They would eventually lead to the summit of these hills, if you learned which ones to take, like the well-marked interstate highways of today. Along these well-worn trails you would spot the tepee rings of prehistoric Indians, who would have camped there close to water, protected from the wind by the hills, with the bushes in the draws below teeming with wild game. No wonder this land was sacred to the Crows, Arapahos, and Sioux who claimed it as their favorite hunting grounds. Many centuries before these latecomers, prehistoric people camped and hunted here.

When you reached the highest peaks of these hills, the view was always breathtaking. Below would be the full spread of the Todd ranch, with the creek winding back and forth between the checkered fields. The ranch buildings nestled within the large cottonwoods always looked like miniature boxes when viewed from the distant hilltops. Your eyes would follow Highway 14 as it wound its way up the valley past neighboring ranches until it rounded out of sight. Depending on the wind, which usually was nonexistent in Sheridan County, you could hear the occasional drone of traffic until it seemed to fade away into total silence.

Beyond the sagebrush hills on the opposite side of the valley was the panoramic sweep of the majestic Big Horn Mountains, their high, snow-covered peaks glistening white all summer long. One could not avoid stopping for just a minute to absorb the spectacular magnificence of the view, regardless of how many times you had seen it before. This was Wyoming country in all its natural glory.

This was the world into which I was born and raised — the world I came to know and love as a kid growing up on a family operated cattle ranch in Sheridan County, along the banks of a little mountain stream we called Piney Creek, near a tiny hamlet of a town named Ucross. The spaciousness of the open land made an indelible impression on me, both for good and bad, as you shall see.

But I must repeat, it was also a world invisibly marked with the darkness of the Great Depression, which wrapped itself around the life of every person who experienced it. As if it were a gigantic octopus, this monster sucked away the joy of life from too many who survived it — including children. I will not say it robbed us of our childhood, but it certainly diminished it. Pervasive hardship and uncertainty invariably spawned a gloom that hung heavy over every endeavor. It's a delusion to think that children were oblivious to this pollution of the human spirit, though we wish it were otherwise.

During these critical years of our infancy, I don't remember Dad ever playing with Sadie, Lewis, and me, as fathers should and normally do. I don't fault him for this. After all, we were children of the *second family;* by that time in his life he had grandchildren nearly our age. But it wasn't the ravages of old age that consumed him. It was his struggle to rebuild a ranch that a disastrous flood had washed away and to cope with the demands of an era that reduced all economic enterprise to ashes.

Dad and Mom wrapped the tattered strands of their life around their cherished family — and with incredible effort and extreme personal sacrifice held body and soul together as we survived the Great Depression. They did the best they could with what they had at the time — and you cannot ask or expect more than this from anyone.

✧

Somehow I always knew I was different from most other kids my age. I was certainly different from my younger siblings. My sister Sadie was a born farm and ranch girl. My father made a tragic mistake in channeling too much of his resources in getting my brothers established in the ranching business. Had he concentrated on Sadie instead, today she would surely own the largest ranching operation in northern Wyoming. Mom worried that she might never domesticate this tomboy.

My younger brother Lewis was a good athlete and later became a skilled construction craftsman after he discovered, in less than one month, that college was not his cup of tea.

I tended to escape into an inner world of fantasy to soothe the isolation and loneliness I so keenly felt during childhood. My fragile health was made all the more painful for me by a physical affliction I apparently inherited from my mother — severe headaches. Fifty years later, when I was professionally treated at a prestigious headache clinic in Atlanta, these early childhood episodes were officially diagnosed as migraines.

The Atlanta doctors probed my childhood, and I was flooded with memories of trying to calm the excruciating pain of these terrible headaches. I described going off by myself to a quiet place — along an isolated creek bank, or in the hayloft, or under the bushes in a draw leading up into the hills. I always went someplace cool and shady, preferably dark, and there I would lie perfectly still with my eyes tightly closed, not moving a muscle for hours at a time. The headache specialists of Atlanta, mostly psychiatrists, stated that this pattern of self-treatment was one of the surest signs of migraine headaches.

I never asked for an aspirin because I never knew they existed. I don't ever remember Mom having analgesics of any kind around the house, nor did she ever suggest pain medication. Consequently, I tried to conceal these migraine attacks from my family, desperate to deny the existence of pain altogether. But occasionally they became so debilitating I could no longer quietly endure them. That there was something specifically wrong with me never registered in my consciousness. I simply wondered why I couldn't endure suffering as well as other kids. I wondered, Why couldn't I measure up and be like them? If it was the human condition to hurt and be sick, then why couldn't I cope with it as well as others? So I succumbed to the migraines' misery in lonely isolation.

Hence, out of raw necessity, I was compelled to escape into a fantasy world of my own making. Dad surely worried about me, his only son who didn't naturally take to ranching. I think my mother instinctively knew that my destiny in life was elsewhere.

Another thing that set me apart from others my age was that I loved school at a time when no country kid was supposed to like it. But school brought rich meaning into my life at a very early age.

The school we were bused to was only four miles away at Ucross. This wide place in the road consisted of nothing more than the school, two filling stations, and a general store with a post office. It didn't even have a busted-down beer tavern, which in Wyoming meant it didn't qualify as a bona fide town. The name Ucross came from the cattle brand (U-cross) of a huge ranching enterprise that thrived in the late 1890s. The operation's owner, a wealthy Chicagoan named Joe Leiter, enhanced his considerable fortune by marriage into the famous Woolworth family. He would visit his ranch in a private railroad car. The little town of Ucross scratched itself into existence on land previously owned by the Leiter estate.

Ours was a two-room school with a "teacherage" attached to the back. (The teacherage had formerly been the Todd school located on our family ranch.) Country schools have many recreational advantages over city schools. We had a barn on the premises for those who rode horses to school, and a barn is always an incredible place in which to play. In addition to playing the usual games of hide and seek and softball, we could also frolic like Indians in the bushes along the banks of Clear Creek — and occasionally cut our own willow fishing poles and fish there. In the wintertime we sledded on the ice. It's a wonder there were no drownings.

I was fortunate to have a few good teachers in the little country school at Ucross. Three I remember particularly. Rose Fowler was my first-grade teacher and taught me how to read. At an earlier time, before I was born, she boarded with my parents while teaching at the Todd school, where she met and married our hired man, John Fowler. She lived all her life in our ranching community, and to this day we consider her a part of the Todd family and address her affectionately as Aunt Rose.

Minnie Moore, my teacher during fifth and sixth grades, desperately tried teaching me arithmetic in spite of my total inability to comprehend it, even to this day.

We never had teachers entirely to ourselves in one grade level, alone, as in most schools today. Like all teachers in country schools back then, ours had to teach more than one grade. While working on my fourth-grade assignment, for example, I could watch Aunt Rose phonetically sounding out the alphabet to the first-graders. And while working on my fifth-grade reading assignment I couldn't help but listen to Minnie Moore reading an English lesson to the seventh-grade students.

I give special credit, however, to Nan Newenswander, who took charge of my eighth-grade education and inspired me to pursue a lifetime of study and intellectual pursuit. It wasn't until the eighth grade that someone gave me permission to feel okay about these natural instincts. Nan was a person of tremendous influence at a critical time in the formative years of my life. She taught me that it was all right, not abnormal, to love books and learning.

This self-revelation was important, because I truly loved reading. A brand new book was a wondrous thing to me, with its fragrant leather binding and tidy printed pages. But an old leather-bound volume was equally important, with its faded yellow paper and brittle pages. Books became treasures that were never to be thrown away. More enthralling was the power of words and language. I marveled at how an elusive idea or emotion could be transformed into a powerful expression of thought and feeling through carefully crafted words.

Our school library consisted of an old set of encyclopedias known as the *Book of Knowledge*. I could spend hours with these dusty old volumes, which everyone else ignored. But the teachers regularly supplied our school with books borrowed from the Carnegie Library in Sheridan. I remember reading every book in a long series about a fantasy forest inhabited by imaginative animals — rabbits, skunks, mink, coyotes, beavers, and the wise ol' owl, all of which lived along the banks of Piney Creek and in my private island kingdom.

But I generally preferred nonfiction. I don't remember reading many novels. I was terribly attracted to biographies of famous people, particularly political figures. I also read history, stories about life in foreign countries, and books about law and government. Like many youngsters, I became especially fascinated with Abraham Lincoln. When my teachers told me I had read all the Lincoln books in the Sheridan library, I began reading them through a second time. Then I switched to Thomas Jefferson, Theodore Roosevelt, and Franklin Delano Roosevelt.

Inevitably, I moved from reading to writing. I began going beyond my class assignments, composing extra little stories and poems for the teachers to read and grade. I wrote a poem about Abraham Lincoln and slavery but remember only the first stanza of it now:

A tall sad-faced man in the White House stood
The slaves to be freed, he knew he could
He looked to the slaves with sad smiling face
They looked to him for the freedom of their race.

Even then, I knew I wouldn't make it as a poet, so I began writing other things. I collected tablets and loose-bound notebooks and filled their pages with my thoughts, feelings, ideas, dreams, and aspirations — but always in secrecy. Much of the writing was done up in the hills, where I wouldn't be seen or disturbed. I even hid some of my tablets there. When these little notebooks accumulated I would burn them in the furnace. I was fearful that they would fall into the hands of those who not only would mock what I had written, but would jeer the fact that I was writing at all. I didn't know which fate was worse. On that account I destroyed almost everything I wrote. I could not afford the risk of discovery.

My writing became part of a more general secrecy in which I shrouded myself, as shameful as the migraine headaches that plagued me.

Perhaps the obsessive need to hide this part of myself contributed to the headaches. In my journals I tried to understand the pain these headaches inflicted and the meaning of suffering — but in vain. I would have vigorously denied the headaches and journal writing had someone asked me about either subject. For some reason, and to this day I do not understand why, I felt that both were unacceptable forms of human behavior.

When I was in sixth grade, I secretly began submitting articles I had written to newspapers. Most of them were never published, but some were.

I wrote a little story about my Aunt Nettie, who lived alone in a little home-stead house on our ranch. Actually, she was my father's elderly aunt, my grandfather's sister, which made her my great-aunt. But she was the only grandmother rolemodel I ever had.

I wrote about the time she invited me to spend the night with her so that we could watch the deer at her kitchen door early the next morning. Dad loaned her a salt block, normally used for cattle, which she placed only twenty feet away from her cottage doorway. At dawn the deer, as they migrated from the fields at night to the daytime hills, would grace-fully leap over the fence into her yard to lick the salt. She instructed me to stand behind her as she softly spoke to them — telling the mothers to take their fawns up into the protection of the hills. She had done this for so many years that they seemed totally unafraid of her, as if charmed by her familiar lilting voice.

I sent the story to the publisher of the little weekly newspaper she sub-scribed to at Elliott, Iowa, where she used to live, and he published it. Aunt Nettie was horrified when she read about herself, and Mom cautioned me never to do that again.

In seventh grade I began writing weekly news stories about neighbors and social events in the Ucross community and sent them to the *Sheridan Press* in Sheridan, Wyoming. The paper printed them under the heading "Ucross." The newspaper did this regularly with correspondents from a num-ber of surrounding rural communities. But, again, I did it secretly. It was easy to pick up news about our neighbors along the Piney Creek ranching valley simply by being a student at the Ucross school. School kids revealed a lot of information about what was going on, and I listened conscientiously. I intently read other local news columns from places such as Big Horn, Banner, Clearmont, Dayton, and Ranchester. These local reporters would describe things such as dinner parties, family reunions, picnics, deaths, and people away on trips. I carefully constructed my news stories accordingly, only adding my own descriptive adjectives for flair and style.

It became a community mystery as to who was writing this weekly col-umn. Not even my parents knew. I never hinted it was me. They found out after about six months, but only by accident. I happened to be in Sheridan one day and I dropped my Ucross news column off at the offices of the *Sheridan Press*. When I handed it to the receptionist she told me the edi-tor wanted to see me. I was terror-stricken. Now my cover would be blown and I would be revealed and prosecuted, maybe end up in jail, for crimi-nal impersonation of a newspaper reporter. Instead, the editor graciously welcomed me into his office. Obviously he had sensed from my handwriting, and surely the contents of my columns, that I was not an adult but a young counterfeiter. But rather than expressing the scorn I expected, he complimented me on my efforts and encouraged me to continue writing. Then he told me that although they didn't pay local correspondents, they did provide them with a free subscription to the *Sheridan Press*. He said he would write my parents telling them they no longer had to pay for delivery of the daily newspaper. I couldn't dare tell him that my folks had no inkling that I was the mystery Ucross reporter.

I was much relieved when the folks got the letter. They weren't angry, and Mom even offered to help me write the weekly column. What she really wanted, of course, was the right of censorship to make certain no libel suits were filed against the Todds. I would write the column, and she'd make appropriate suggestions and pencil in grammatical corrections. Eventually she even called neighbors for news scoops on the single-line rural telephone system.

Once the editor invited his rural correspondents to visit the office to see how a daily newspaper was published and to be his guest for lunch. Only one older woman and I showed up. I was thrilled to see how our columns were handled once approved for publication. I watched the Linotype operator, sitting at a noisy clanking machine filled with molten lead, type the news items from my hand-scribbled manuscript, then saw my written words transformed into hot melted slugs, each containing a single line of type that slid down a chute into a mold, which later was transferred to the cylinders of the rolling presses. It was a fascinating process.

Besides my growing fascination with reading and writing, another medium captured my imagination at this time. And this was the spoken word — on radio.

It all began when I was six years old, as a first grader, when I witnessed the erection of the Ucross school's very first radio receiver. Half a dozen men did the work. First they snapped a heavy copper wire to the rope on the flagpole and hoisted it to the top. (What an ingenious way to string up a radio antennae.) The other end drooped down through the school window. Another crew of men dug a manhole and buried heavy steel rods attached to a ground wire. They poured gallons of water into the hole before filling it in with dirt. Then they carried in the radio itself. The detachable speaker was pulled to the front of the room as far as its speaker cable would allow. Then in came a large wooden crate filled with heavy wires and dozens of tubes. The men spent the rest of the afternoon arguing over the diagram as to how they were to connect a series of batteries. By four o'clock, when school let out, they had them all hooked up — except the *big one,* a freshly charged wet car battery, which was to appear later. (Remember, this was before the days of rural electrification.)

That evening I sat with my parents in the one room of our country school. Someone turned on the master switch and in stone silence we watched a man named Carl slowly manipulate a series of dials. After a few minutes, we heard the noise of electromagnetic static crackling forth from the front speaker. Everyone applauded the noise, because this meant the receiver was correctly hooked up.

"The signal is a little weak," Carl explained, "because it's got a long ways to go to get here."

Finally, the noisy static quieted as the channel cleared — and we heard the clarion voice of Franklin Delano Roosevelt. The roll of his voice, its cadence and pitch, made him sound like the Almighty God. I will never forget the look on the faces of those ranchers, tenant farmers, and laborers as they sat there in stony silence, in the flickering shadows of the dim kerosene lantern, intently listening to every word as if their lives depended upon it — which they did.

Simple souls they were, mostly poor, hardworking people, frightened to death in the midst of the Great Depression, listening to the sonorous voice of their president repeating his common theme that they had nothing to fear but fear itself. The United States of America was their country, and it wouldn't let them down. There would be food. There would be jobs. The banks would be secure. Hang on, don't despair. There was hope.

I remember watching the wife of a desperately poor itinerant laborer, exhausted from raising several children in an abandoned shack while her husband was away looking for work. She turned her face to the wall and quietly wept, as if she had been given the courage to try hanging on for just one more day — one day at a time. This was 1934, before the days of public welfare, Social Security benefits, and unemployment compensation. Unless this dirt-poor woman had a garden, a milk cow, and some chickens there would be nothing to feed her children but dandelion greens in the summer — and the unreliable charity of neighbors in the winter.

As a six-year-old, I honestly thought the president of the United States, from the White House, was speaking directly to her at the Ucross school. Now I know that, in a sense, he really was. I was too young to understand the content of the message, but I was caught up in the heavy emotion that filled the schoolroom. For the first time in my life, I witnessed the power of the spoken word to people whose spirits were broken — and desperate to hear a word of hope.

In addition, I was spellbound by the medium of that message — radio. I went outside to see where the sound was coming from. I peeked inside the speaker to see if there was a miniaturized man in there. I got behind the table holding the contraption and, looking through the maze of batteries, wires, and glowing hot tubes, tried to figure out how the sound got there.

"From the wires?" I asked.

No, not really, I was told. It comes from the air. From top of the mountains and out over the hills — down into the valley below — came the voice of someone who spoke directly to a group of people huddled in a room hundreds, even thousands of miles away. A copper wire reaching high into the sky and grounded deep in the earth brought words of life to people grasping for hope.

The miracle of it all.

I was hooked on radio for the rest of my life. Later the folks purchased a battery-operated radio for our ranch home. This was still before the days of rural electricity. The speaker was incorporated into a beautiful wood cabinet, which contained all the equipment to make it work. But since battery power gradually weakened if used for more than one hour at a time, we had to conserve energy by listening sparingly — and turning the radio off during commercials.

It was about this time, around 1935 or 1936, that a radio station was crowded into a back room of the second floor of Carroll's Furniture store in Sheridan. KWYO was owned and installed by Bob Carroll, who also owned the furniture store. From that time on, whenever the folks went to town, I headed straight for that radio station. It was a very simple arrangement. One room served as a studio, and a second room was used as an office and doubled as a second studio. There I would sit hour after hour, watching the operation of this primitive radio station.

Every afternoon there was a live broadcast of a cowboy singer named Rambling Bob. His guitar playing and singing were awful, everyone said, but he played requests in response to cards and letters. There he would sit in the sweltering heat of the second-floor studio with all the windows closed to keep out noise, and with sweat pouring off his face he would thump on his guitar and belt out his songs for several hours at a time. Alone, outside the soundproof window, I maintained my solitary watch. He invited me to come inside his cramped quarters, into the stifling heat, and he'd share with me his bottle of warm soda pop and a few bites of his melting candy bar. It was obvious he appreciated this fan club of one.

I was totally mesmerized with it all. My early obsession with radio broadcasting would become a lifelong passion.

✧

In addition to the written and spoken word, another manifestation of the word made itself present to me during the formative days of my youth. And this time I will capitalize it as the Word.

The Word of God has come to have special interpretations to many people. Generally speaking, when they refer to the Word of God they mean quite literally the Bible — which is not what I necessarily mean when I use the word within a religious context. Be that as it may, somewhere in the formative years of my youth there slowly evolved a vague awareness of a power beyond myself — an omnipresent other — toward which I was irresistibly drawn with an undefinable spiritual yearning. I've never been able to describe this inner yearning, nor decide from whence it came. The Todd family didn't attend church because there was no established church in our ranching community. Sheridan and Buffalo were too far away. Besides, there were too many Sunday morning chores on a working family ranch for church attendance. Laypeople occasionally tried to get a community Sunday school organized, but these never materialized into anything substantial. I don't think I attended Sunday school more than a dozen times before I went away to college.

Baptist laymen did drive out from Sheridan to conduct Sunday evening services in the Ucross schoolhouse. However, these would last no more than a few months at a time, only to be abandoned for lack of interest. However, one layman by the name of Norman Cook endured for several years before giving up and moving on to another field of evangelistic endeavor.

My general impression of these preaching services was negative. In the first place, I think, they consisted of evangelistic tirades that neither edified or converted. Nonetheless, I commend the dedication of the laypeople who did the best they could to save the lost and wayward souls of our ranching valley. The kindest thing I can say about these religious endeavors is that they were well intended — but a dreadful bore. And I think it's a sin to bore people in the name of religion.

My harshest criticism is that I felt compelled to repudiate everything these laymen preached. They were forever haranguing us to condemn the evil world, along with all lusts of the flesh, and to embrace a God who either would save us for heaven or condemn us to burn eternally in hell. I know today what they probably meant theologically and were trying to preach, but it didn't come across that way to me as a kid. What they said about the love of Christ was lost in their torrent of words about the vengeance of an angry God. I refused to accept their deity of fire and brimstone.

The preachers particularly harped on dancing. Maybe that was because this was the one sin which they could safely rail against since the open mention of sex was dreadfully too taboo for public discussion. They also knew dancing was the one sin which all ranching communities cherished — a social event which most often brought all the people together for fun and relaxation. It was always a family event. Parents brought along their babies and children and bedded them down in quilts in a spare room, or under the wooden benches along the wall. Historically, it was here that cowboys met the school moms who later became their wives. Everyone danced with everyone else. It was common for women to dance with one another — specialized dances, like the schottische, that men didn't always know the steps to. Even men danced with men before women were available on the frontier. We all heard these stories. Country dances were the social glue that held the community together.

I heard the contorted wrangling of the preachers as to what dancing might lead to. In that case, even as a kid, I reasoned that surely logic prevailed and they would make exceptions for husbands and wives dancing with one another. But to no avail — this, too, was morally wrong. Therefore, I concluded, again as a youngster with limited logic, that sex was wrong only because it might lead to dancing.

But as a junior high kid, I had already decided that dancing was something I fully intended to do and would thoroughly enjoy — and if sex was a necessary prelude to it — then sex simply became a magnificent bonus that the good Lord tossed in on the way toward the real thing.

The preachers actually seemed to enjoy telling us how dreadful the eternal punishment was going to be for all the sinners. I remember thinking to myself that good decent people wouldn't threaten this holocaust on their worst enemies, much less on friends whose souls they were trying to save. Obviously, the preachers meant well, and this was the only way they knew to convey their fervent message, but that kind of evangelism simply didn't score well with this ten-year-old skeptic. Such preaching left the opposite impression of what they intended. I remember one preacher exercising great rhetoric in describing the rapture that would occur when all Christians, in one gigantic flash, would blast off into the heavens with Jesus. He told of passengers inside a streamliner railroad Pullman car, fast asleep in their comfortable beds, who were completely unaware that the rapture had come like a thief in the night and snatched away the Christian engineer at the throttle of the mighty steam engine. Totally unbeknownst to these passengers, the midnight train, roaring down the tracks through the darkness at ninety miles per hour, would soon crash into one horrendous explosion of fire and steam and smoke!

I had not yet taken my first train ride, but I was enthusiastically anticipating it. Consequently, I decided right then and there that when that great moment came in my life, I would pray to God that the engineer wasn't a Christian. Any old pagan would do — just as long as he got me through my first great train ride.

Clearly this kind of fundamentalist evangelical preaching just didn't register well with me. It seemed irrelevant to the country life I knew and was too violent and threatening. Its only intent was to save souls. As worthy as that goal may be, I wondered, what happens after your soul gets saved? Not one word was spoken that I can remember about how you lived the Christian life once you were saved. Or how one coped with failure and disappointment, or with death and sorrow, or with personal rejection and pain, or with conflict and the crises of momentous decisions. Nothing.

They would rave about the joy of believing, but I never saw it on their faces or in their personal lives. I asked myself, *If they are as redeemed as they say they are, how come they never look or act like it? How come I never see them having a good time — if not on the dance floor?*

With a negative religious beginning like that, it's a wonder I went on to devote forty years of my life to the ministry of Jesus Christ. What changed?

These negative experiences of the Christian Church, at the hands of mortal men who are flawed and sometimes wrong, were not my true religious beginning. In fact, the natural beauty and wonder of the good earth that surrounded me, my contemplation of its glory and my childhood interaction with it, are what pointed me toward a Creator God. Only God could create something this powerful and this beautiful and this wonderful. Renouncing this natural universe, as I thought the preachers were encouraging us to do, was the most illogical and sacrilegious thing I could ever imagine.

The formative years of my youth, the secret places of my world of quiet solitude, cultivated an inquiring mind and a discerning heart. My mother must have been influential, because she always peeled away the veneer of religious fanaticism that was so apparent among the preachers we knew and heard. Her love of good books, sound learning, and a search for knowledge made an indelible impression on me. To her much credit is due.

A vague but ever-present spiritual quest for the omnipresent other permeated the world I knew as a child. Where it came from, I do not know. It remains elusive even to me. But it slowly evolved in the countless hours of my youth when I was alone, splashing out to my island kingdom in Piney Creek, watching the teeming wildlife as if I were one in communion with it; seeking out my secret places for quietude and studied reflection, hiking to the summit of the highest hills to be surprised anew by the glory of the view below; searching out my thoughts and writing them down in notebook journals; and reading books, which I concealed under my coat and carried wherever I went.

And praying. Praying to a Creator God who created the beauty of the earth and the goodness of life and said it was good. A God who transcended all the trivial and mean-spirited things attributed to him by those who are his spokespersons and preachers.

Although I did a lot of reading, amazingly I read very little from the Bible — except the Psalms. I discovered Psalm 8 and memorized it. The psalmist's expression of awesome wonder at God's universe and man's role in relation to it attracted my attention as much then as it does today. It reads, in part:

> *O Lord, our God, How excellent is thy name in all the earth,*
> *Thou hast set thy glory above the heavens.*
> *. . . When I consider thy heavens, the work of thy fingers,*
> *The moon and the stars which thou hast made,*
> *What is man that thou art mindful of him?*
> *And the son of man that thou hast visited him,*
> *For thou hast made him a little less than the angels*
> *And crownest him with glory and honor.*

If the Lord was the God of *excellent glory* above the heavens and in all the earth, as the psalmist proclaimed and which I had come to believe, then he ought to be worshiped in the beauty of holiness. It would have to be a religion of mystical communion that reverenced and reflected the awesome splendor of the Lord's living spirit pulsating throughout the universe. The Word of God.

But I did not experience this religious dimension in the preaching services to which I was exposed in my youth.

When I was about twelve years old I accompanied my parents to a Catholic funeral in Buffalo, Wyoming. It was my first exposure to liturgical worship, and I liked it because it lifted up for me a semblance of this intangible thing for which I had been religiously searching: the fragrance of incense, an altar laden with flowers, the swish of beautiful vestments, the liturgy chanted in a language I could not understand (Latin) — but, primarily, an overall sense of holiness that seemed suspended between heaven and earth. But the foreign evils of Catholicism were too well known to everyone in the Todd family at that time, so I immediately dismissed whatever subliminal attractions I may have initially felt toward it.

My spiritual search would have to lie elsewhere, but I had no idea where. In fact, I wasn't even certain that I should pursue it any farther. Because it seemed so intensely personal and prone to fanciful imagination, I finally decided that the search would have to pursue me instead of my pursuing it. Only then could I momentarily let go of it. And I did — abandoning it altogether in high school and not resuming it again until college.

✧

As a junior high youngster I was far from totally preoccupied with intellectual and spiritual pursuits. Life plodded on with the steady pace of everyday chores and tasks common to every kid growing up on a Wyoming ranch.

Milking cows was always a major part of any ranch operation in those days. Dad always maintained six to a dozen milk cows on the place. These cows provided all the dairy products our family consumed: milk, home-churned butter, rich buttermilk, and sweet thick cream, which Mom used abundantly in all her cooking.

During winter it was my chore to clean out the cow barn every night after school. Our milk cows were kept overnight in their stanchions. This meant the place was a terrible mess the next morning. After a little snack and a change of clothes, I'd buckle up my overshoes and head out for the cow barn. If you know anything about cattle, you know that cow manure is sloppy. I would scoop the slop down the long troughs on both sides of the center aisle and heave the stuff outside into a large pile, which in the spring would be hauled away in a manure spreader to the fields as fertilizer. This was the worst part of the miserable job.

The better part came later. After the barn was cleaned, I would scatter bedding straw about a foot deep across the whole area for the cows that night. I would fill their mangers with hay tossed down from the loft above and then push it back with my hands to make room for a gallon can of ground grain for each cow. All of these chores would take an hour or more. Impatiently waiting outside was the herd of dairy cows, who earlier had wandered in from feeding out in the wintry fields.

It was always a special pleasure to open the barn door and watch these bovines rush out of the cold and snow into a nice warm barn made especially inviting with bedding straw beneath their feet. They'd make their way directly to their own individual stanchion and begin feeding on the feast of hay and grain I had prepared for them. I could sense the sheer delight this experience brought these critters every night.

Then I'd begin the milking. Each cow had her own name and her own personality. The barn cats and ranch dogs would congregate under the bucket shelf for their daily serving of warm whole milk, which they lapped up with loud gulps. Usually Dad would arrive about then and help me finish the milking and carry the heavy cream cans to the house, where the cream was separated from the skim milk. This was my evening routine for over six years, until I graduated from high school and left home.

When spring and summer arrived, Dad would move the cows to their own pasture across the highway, and with this new supply of nutrient grass they no longer required feeding in the cow barn. In the warmth of summer they could now spend the night out in a dry corral. I no longer had the daily job of cleaning out the barn.

But now I had a new job — riding out into the pasture every night after school to herd in the milk cows. This was a special treat for me. I rode a little sorrel pony for whom I had great affection. His name was Snake. He was a young gelding with white stocking feet. We should have called him Boots.

As I entered the horse barn he would lift his head above his stall and call out to me with a greeting nicker, in a low gentle way, clearly saying, "I'm here. Come on . . . let's go!"

Sometimes I'd throw a saddle on him, but usually not. He wasn't large, so it was easy for me to leap up on him bareback. After being cooped up in the barn all day, he was anxious to get going.

When we passed through the gate into the cow pasture, he knew it was time for the run of his life. I'd lean forward and reach around his neck, Indian style, and off we would go. He would open up and run as hard as his feet could carry him, and it seemed that we literally flew across the landscape. The whizzing sagebrush became a grayish blur. He knew every twist and turn along the hillside path, dodging boulders and trees, then hurdling across ravines and gulches so wide that we were airborne much of the time. The rhythmic sound of his hooves beating the ground beneath us sounded at first like an airplane motor revving up, then became a steady musical drone in my ears. I would tighten my grip around his neck as we approached a deep washout ahead because I never quite knew how he would negotiate the gigantic leap off the lip of the embankment — soaring out into space while I could feel his muscles tense for the landing below. One false slip and it would have broken both our necks.

As we sped across the face of the earth with the wind whistling past my face, pressed tightly up against his neck and mane, my imagination would go wild with fantasies of Snake and me escaping a thundering herd of 1000 Sioux Indians, armed to the teeth. Every night we would do this. It was the only time in my life on the ranch that I felt such a rapport with a horse, that rider and horse merged as one in body and spirit. The vivid memory of these daily runs served me well for many years to come. Later in life, when I became the rector of a large Episcopal church and felt that the wardens and vestry and even the bishop were in hot pursuit and closing in upon me, I would conjure up that childhood memory. In my imagination I would tighten my hold around the neck of ol' Snake and away we would thunder, leaving everyone far behind in our dust.

✧

During these teen years I came into possession of a young bum lamb, which I bottle fed until it was too old to drink from the nipple anymore. That lamb was my special pet and practically lived in the cow barn. When it was about nine months old it started to mature as a full-sized ewe with a heavy fleece of wool. I got her a collar, attached a very small bell, and appropriately named her Tinker Belle.

By this time she had become a fond and devoted friend to me. I could lead her anywhere by simply crooking a finger around her collar. If I let go of the collar, she would trot along beside me like a dog. When I took her with me into an open meadow she and I would play. She would run in large circles around me and then zip past me, daring me to try catching her. If I dropped to my hands and knees during our playtime together, she would gallop full speed in a half-circle and then come at me like a dive bomber and leap right over the top of me. Then she would hunker down while I repositioned myself for a repeat performance. I'm certain the reason she acted this way was that she didn't know how to be a sheep. After all, she had never seen one. I'm convinced that she figured out that she wasn't human and thought herself a dog.

Since she hung out in the cow barn, a daily ritual developed between the two of us every evening when I entered the barn to do my chores. The moment she saw me, she would start bleating, jump to her feet, and come leaping toward me with the frolic of a little lamb. I would hug her, and rub cheeks with her while she affectionately nibbled on my ear. Then she would rise up on her hind legs, like a goat, while I held out a handful of Wheaties or Grape Nuts which she gobbled up. Then I would reach my arms around her shoulders and we would whirl — round and round we would go, with her head resting on my shoulder, dancing cheek to cheek.

As I went about my chore of cleaning out the cow barn, she would follow me around and periodically yank on my sleeve with her teeth indicating it was time again for me to give her a little personal attention. I would fondly stroke her head while we rubbed cheeks and she nibbled on my ears again. Or maybe we'd do another dance. Every evening I would give her a drink of warm milk and a little of the ground grain which I fed to the milk cows.

And, of course, she could munch on the hay and would sleep on the fresh bed of straw. She was fattening out and becoming a beautiful animal. No question, she had a good life in the sheltered environment of that cow barn.

One evening I went out to the barn with my handful of Grape Nuts and found her dead. She had foundered from overeating, which is typical for sheep. I tried frantically to revive her, but she was gone. I remember burying my face in the fleece of her wool and sobbing inconsolably. She had become my very affectionate friend and playmate, a joy and a comfort.

I placed her body on a sled and pulled it into an isolated wooded area in the bend of the creek about a mile away and buried her in a snowbank, heaping the snow into a frozen pyramid above her.

In my spiral notebook journal that night I tried expressing my heartfelt grief. I concluded that it was possible for man and animal to have a bond of affection greater than that possible between animals — and perhaps between humans as well. This rapport of understanding transcended all other relationships, giving us yet another glimpse of the greater love that existed between God and man. I tried to explore the meaning of this in my journal — and wonder now what I wrote. But that journal, like all other spiral notebooks before it, was carefully destroyed.

✧

I desperately wanted a bicycle when I was about twelve years old. My parents couldn't afford a luxury of this magnitude, so I volunteered to thin beets to earn the money. The standard pay for migrant beet workers was nine dollars per acre, and I finished three acres of the backbreaking fieldwork, thus earning more than what a new bike would cost. My folks still opposed my juvenile extravagance, so I settled on a secondhand model that cost only ten dollars. But again Dad and Mom seemed terribly disappointed in my frivolous self-indulgence, even though I had earned the money myself. My guilt became so overwhelming that I finally gave up on it entirely and let them keep the money I had earned.

Instead I built a crude wooden rack, into which I mounted a single bicycle wheel, a warped one that somehow ended up on the ranch. I used to push that contraption for miles through the fields and up into the hills, running behind it as fast as my legs could carry me — just to watch the wheel spin. Strangely, I became quite content with this pathetic substitute for the real thing.

To this day, I have never owned my own bicycle, although a few abandoned clunkers came into my temporary possession as an adult. I will feel forever too guilty to buy one for myself. But I made certain that all of my children had a bike of their own — usually before they were ready to ride it.

✧

A pivotal moment in my life occurred when I was about twelve years old. It was a cold Christmas Eve, and I was herding the milk cows to the barn for our evening chores. (As I recall, we didn't make much of Christmas Eve fifty years ago on the ranch. Our celebration was reserved for Christmas Day.) It was dark, and I was trudging along behind the cows across a frozen beet field toward a grove of willow trees directly ahead. As always when I'm out in the cold, I was shivering, and while stumbling through the snow a revolutionary thought flashed through my mind — *I can decide my own destiny!*

I thought — *I need not plod on and on into oblivion, into whatever unchosen set of circumstances may engulf me. I do not have to surrender my identity and talents and succumb to becoming a rancher, a hired hand, a coal miner, a sheepherder, a ditch digger, or anything I do not want to become. I, alone, can become whatever I feel called to do.*

And I will.

How inconsequential that sudden realization may seem today. But my short life had been lived under the foreboding cloud of the Great Depression. The overwhelming focus of that era was one thing — mere survival. You didn't have the luxury of doing with your life what you may have wanted or chosen. People survived by grabbing hold of any job they could scrounge in a world of the desperately unemployed, with no public welfare or social relief. People who had a job, any kind of a job, no matter how miserable, considered themselves fortunate. The fearful alternative was a tragic fate of abject destitution beyond all comprehension today — but all too familiar to those who scrabbled through the horror of the Great Depression.

Somehow, I realized that I had the power to make of my life whatever I chose. I need not be a passive victim to the limited choices handed out by others. My life would generally be what I determined it to be. The decision was up to me. I didn't have to trudge on and on like a clod into a void of nothingness.

On that Christmas Eve, around 1940, I gave myself the most incredible gift a child could ever give oneself — the freedom to become whatever my talents in life directed me to fulfill.

Of course, at this point in my life I had no idea where that might ultimately lead me. As I stumbled across the rows of frozen beet tops behind the sauntering cows, I asked myself for the first time, *What will be your choice in life?* I recall saying to myself, *Remember forever this night and the questions you have raised. Whatever professional career you may someday choose as an adult, answer the question this boy is asking of you tonight: Is this really what you wanted to become?*

Many years later on every Christmas Eve, I would celebrate the Holy Eucharist at St. Mark's Episcopal Church, Cheyenne — using the medium of the written word (biblical), the spoken word (preaching), and the liturgical word of God (faith). There I would stand behind the beautifully decorated altar covered with lovely white linens and polished silver chalices, surrounded with the fragrance of incense and the choral sounds of Christmas music coming from a wonderful choir and a fantastic pipe organ. Crowded beside vested acolytes and lay ministers, I chanted the ancient liturgy of the church.

But out above the heads of the worshipping congregation, through the haze of the candlelight shadows, I would invariably see and hear that little boy trudging across the barren and frozen field on a Christmas Eve of yesteryear, asking again the haunting and proverbial question: *Is this really what you wanted to become?*

Beyond that, the greater question — am I really the man that this boy wanted someday to be?

Chapter 2

My mother was very instrumental in bringing electricity to our ranching community. Mom investigated the possibility of organizing a Rural Electrification Association (REA) in Sheridan County and encountered opposition from the very beginning. Not because people were opposed to it, but because it "couldn't be done" — not by a woman, anyway. After all, the REA worked only down in Tennessee and in the more heavily populated rural areas of the United States, not in isolated Wyoming ranch country. I vividly remember her putting together all the documentation she could find and presenting her case to the Piney Creek Farm Bureau.

"No, that won't work for us, Mrs. Todd," came the reply. "There's no way in the world you're gonna work through all the governmental bureaucracy of Roosevelt's New Deal to get something like that going for us. That's years away."

But Mom persisted. She wrote letters to our congressional delegation and the governor of Wyoming, enlisting their support. She arranged appointments with REA officials whenever they were in Wyoming. She called organizational meetings with farmers and ranchers in other rural communities through which the power lines would pass if the REA could ever be persuaded to build them. To make a long story short, and without going into the corporate details, it happened. Not with the REA, however, but with Montana-Dakota Utilities out of Sheridan. They recognized this as an opportunity to sell more electricity and agreed to construct the line out of Sheridan through the community of Banner, up into Story, and then down Piney Creek to Ucross.

Sometime in the fall of 1941, when the electrical power finally came on late one evening, the Todd ranchstead lit up like a city. The chickens, who had already gone to roost in the chicken house, came stumbling out across the barnyard as if in a daze, disgruntled at the shortness of the night. The roosters began crowing as they do at daybreak.

Electricity brought the dawn of a new day for everyone living in the Piney Creek valley and truly revolutionized our life on the ranch. With the flip of a switch there was brilliant light and power everywhere. No longer did we have to carry kerosene lamps from room to room as we moved through the dark shadows of the house. Their flickering dim lamplights may seem romantic in our nostalgia about them, but they were messy and a constant fire danger. A refrigerator replaced the old ice box and did away with the need to put up ice every winter. An automatic pressurized water pump was installed in the basement. We no longer had to hand pump all the household water up three floors into a large holding tank stored in the attic. An electric stove replaced the old cooking range in the kitchen and home-baked pies and bread never tasted the same again, my father always maintained.

The purchase of these basic electric appliances was made possible because, for the first time since the flood and the bank crash of 1929, ranching was becoming profitable again. The Great Depression was beginning to subside. Instead of leasing his pasture, Dad restocked the range with his own cattle, and the investment was beginning to turn a profit. The economy was starting to improve, and agricultural products were in great demand, mainly because of the gathering storm of World War II. Dad even bought a new Pontiac.

Now the Todd family could listen to the radio without constantly worrying about conserving expensive batteries. The folks bought an upright radio console. It was about the size of an old-fashioned jukebox and was intended to be a handsome piece of wooden furniture in the living room. You switched it on and waited several minutes for its tubes to warm up; then you could tune in distant clear-channel radio stations from Des Moines, Chicago, Salt Lake, and Little Rock.

We gathered around the radio, like all families across America, and laughed at the antics of George Burns and Gracie Allen, Jack Benny, Fred Allen, Fiber McGee and Molly, and my favorites: Edgar Bergen and Charlie McCarthy. We heard contestants play carpenter saws and washtubs on *Major Bow's Original Amateur Hour*. On Saturday night we listened to the *National Barn Dance* out of Chicago starring Uncle Ezra, with Lulla Belle and Scotty on the banjo. It was terrific.

Every weekday night at nine o'clock, we listened to Bob Burlingame with the news from WHO in Des Moines. And the news wasn't good. With increasing alarm we listened to reports of a man named Hitler moving across the face of Europe with his deadly intent to conquer the world. Other dictators — Mussolini in Italy, Stalin in Russia — were extending their reach. The free world was falling apart. My folks lamented, "Something's gotta be done about it. But America has gotta stay out of it."

One Sunday afternoon we were listening to the Grand Opera on the radio. An announcer suddenly cut in with a news bulletin. I didn't know what it was about, and since I didn't particularly enjoy listening to opera anyway, I thought this would be a good excuse to scan the dial for something a bit more enjoyable. Mom came running into the living room from the kitchen and shouted at me to turn back to the news announcement. In the hysteria of the moment, I couldn't instantly relocate the station, and she began screaming at me,

"We are at war!
Pearl Harbor is being bombed by the Japanese!
We are at war!"

Mom's words became the screaming headlines of newspapers all across America the next day. The teacher at our Ucross school, Miss Crawford, brought a radio into our schoolroom, and we listened to President Roosevelt declare that a state of war existed between the United States against Germany and Japan. At first, as I remember, there was general hysteria that the Japanese were going to invade the United States with help from all the Japanese immigrants living in this country. It was all part of a massive conspiracy to destroy America from the inside. Even peaceful Japanese Americans who lived down in Clearmont, fourteen miles away, were suspect.

For the first time I learned the sinister meanings of such political concepts as fascism, communism, imperialism, and military dictatorship. All of us on Piney Creek were absolutely united in our opposition to the forces of darkness threatening to engulf the world. Even the many people of Russian-German descent who lived down along Clear Creek around Clearmont expressed their patriotic loyalty to the U.S. cause.

Although the war seemed far away from our peaceful ranching valley in northern Wyoming, the radio kept us well informed. The gigantic mobilization of our country for war began radically to affect the way we lived. Wage and price freezes, food shortages, and gas rationing became commonplace. The war was becoming more real and personal to us. But much more was to come. Material things we all took for granted became scarce, drastically crimping our lifestyle. Little things such as overshoes, machine parts, warm clothing, and cigarettes were in short supply. Big things such as tractors, automobiles, and electrical appliances became things of the past. People traded food stamps among themselves. Sugar was severely rationed. We'd have to put our names on a waiting list to buy a pair of Levi's and actually prove to the merchants we were ranchers and that the wearing of Levi's was *essential* to the war effort.

Agriculture was considered a vital industry, and because of that a few concessions were made. We were allotted more gasoline (intended for tractor fuel) than most Americans. As during the Depression, living on a ranch gave us a hedge that other Americans didn't have. Mom gardened and canned in a big way. We butchered our own meat and raised our own dairy animals and chickens, giving us a constant food supply. All these products were in serious demand, and now, suddenly, we were on the supply side.

As a teenager, I was vividly aware of all these things, but I didn't seem too bothered by the inconveniences of the war. However, the sudden appearance of uniformed soldiers and sailors on the streets of Sheridan caught my attention. Later I learned the difference between officers and enlisted men by the uniforms they wore and the way they exchanged their snappy salutes. Selective Service kicked in with all its organizational fury. Chartered buses filled with draftees left from the American Legion halls amid patriotic speeches, band music, and loud cheering.

Joe Byrtus, a neighbor kid who'd worked for Dad one summer, enlisted in the Army Air Corps and became a navigator. He would visit the folks when home on leave, wearing his distinguished officer's uniform. I was sick with envy. There I was, this skinny ranch kid dressed in clothes I'd long outgrown, with scuffed shoes and patched jackets. And there he stood in the kitchen with all the spiff and polish of an army officer.

I wished I'd been born five years earlier. Then I would have been old enough to enlist in the Army Air Corps, to have become a pilot and fight for my country. I lamented that the war might be over before I had a chance to fight in it. My mother wasn't very supportive — she said that wars were terrible and that many men who fought them either were killed or maimed for life. "Besides," she said, being very practical, as mothers often are, "you're prone for motion sickness and would probably get a sick headache and throw up in an airplane or on a ship." Somehow I hadn't thought of that revolting possibility.

The war radically affected my first two years in high school at Clearmont, Wyoming. The draft, military enlistments, and massive employment in the defense industries dried up the pool of qualified teachers. High school enrollment at Clearmont was pitifully small in the first place — less than thirty students. Under any standard, you can't offer much of a balanced curriculum to a student body that tiny. But the absence of trained teachers made things worse. As I recall, we had only two full-time teachers, and one of them was the superintendent, who shouldn't have been allowed within fifty feet of a student.

Her name was Mrs. McClintock. She was an older woman, hired out of retirement, not out of a mental hospital, as was rumored. Actually, she was a good algebra teacher, and I learned something in that class — which is a wonder, given my total lack of math aptitude. But her school administration was a disaster. She freely handed out corporal punishment, not after an established policy of school discipline but because of her own temper. She stormed into our English class one time in a rage at some boys who dillydallied too long around the drinking fountain between classes. Her tirade escalated until she ran completely amok. Bryant Ellis and I were seated in the front row, and we got the giggles. She landed into us with kicks and shrieks and nearly yanked the hair out of our heads. Our books were scattered across the floor. After she stormed from the room, the horrified substitute teacher loaned us her comb, and we raked out clumps of loosened hair.

Once she locked Lavern Sayles, Morris Kimble, Harry Huson, and me in a little storage closet during the lunch hour because of some minor infraction of the rules. I don't deny that there was an infraction, but I can't remember now what it was. The closet was pitch black, we were cramped in like sardines — and if this wasn't punishment enough, we were also going to miss lunch. We decided to sing a song. This must have been Lavern's idea, because he was the only one who could sing. So he took the lead, and we sang backup, as we bellowed out a popular tune called "Pistol-Pack'n Momma." Mrs. McClintock yanked open the door and tore into us with her fists and feet, shattering Morris's glasses right on his face.

Another time she left Dale Connally and me alone in the school all day while she accompanied the students and faculty to a basketball tournament in Gillette. Dale and I were the only boys in school who were not members of the basketball team, and all the girls were members of the cheering club. So Dale and I were disqualified from the trip, although the bus was not filled, and the two of us stayed behind while the entire school, students and teachers, took off for an all-day athletic outing.

Since we had an empty school building all to ourselves, we decided to explore the science lab. We scrounged up a miniature steam engine among the

My high school education during World War II was so marginalized because of the war, it's a miracle I ever made it to college. Only twenty-seven students in all four grades at Clearmont, Wyoming.

pile of junk on the dusty shelves and decided to fire it up and watch it puff away. We filled the little tank with water, located a Bunsen burner, lit the thing, and waited for the steam pressure to build up. It did. The minor explosion blew the engine off into a corner of the room and knocked the burner over, spewing its alcohol across the table, with the whole thing afire. Luckily, we were able to douse the flames with buckets of water from the sink. Otherwise the whole school could have burned to the ground. And, since there was no fire department in Clearmont, the blaze would probably have taken the town with it.

Those first two years were a total loss. I didn't get anything resembling a high school education. The all-consuming war effort was directly responsible. The school recruited community volunteers as substitute teachers, but Clearmont was bereft of anyone who had even been to college. They did the best they could with what they had, but it was dreadful.

The only reason I endured it as gracefully as I did was that, finally, I got into radio broadcasting, with a weekly program all of my own.

It happened in September 1943, when I was fifteen years old and in my freshman year in high school. I boldly walked into the manager's office of KWYO and offered to buy half an hour of broadcast time every Saturday afternoon for a radio program called *The Clearmont Roundup*. I spoke with Jim Carroll, station owner Bob Carroll's brother. I would pay for the time at the regular commercial rate, but I would sell advertisements to Clearmont merchants, which I would intersperse with the playing of country music — and whatever I cleared would be my profit. I would write my own scripts and produce my own show.

Not only was such a plan absolutely crazy for a fifteen-year-old kid to be proposing to an established radio station, it also, I later learned, violated FCC rules. But Jim Carroll accepted my business offer. By this time he had become accustomed to seeing this country kid hanging around the KWYO studios. However, he would never have considered the harebrained idea had he known that I hadn't even consulted my parents about it. His only stipulation was that I must pay him in cash every month.

All the way through high school, every Saturday morning, I would hitchhike into Sheridan to broadcast *The Clearmont Roundup*. During the week I regularly contacted the few merchants in Clearmont for their radio advertisements. The grocery store, the locker plant, the grain and feed elevator, the barber shop, several gas stations, the auto garage, and occasionally a bar or two bought commercials. At first, Mom helped me write them, but later I learned to do it myself. I publicized country dances. I talked about local basketball games. I described the spring floods. I talked about planting and harvesting and I described the threshing crews.

Between all these little ads and newsy commentaries I played country music. It wasn't called *country* then, though; it was called *hillbilly music*. It wasn't very popular because this was the era of the big band sound. The big bands moved across the country, and everyone liked them. Only hill-billies, it was believed, listened to songs by Eddy Arnold, Roy Acuff, and Hank Williams — but I played them all. Sometimes local entertainers would ask to appear on my show. They were probably worse than Rambling Bob, but people enjoyed listening because these were live broadcasts. KWYO even expanded my air time from thirty to forty-five minutes and eventually to sixty minutes.

Although it was corny, there was something authentic about it. Many years later I attended a cocktail party at a broadcaster's convention in Denver and told the banquet speaker, a university professor of media communications, of my first venture into radio.

He asked, "How much did KWYO pay you for these broadcasts?"

"Nothing — I paid them," I answered, "And I paid full commercial broadcast rate. That was the deal."

"My god," he said, "a program like that was worth a million dollars in PR to any radio station who knew what they had on their hands. Original, authentic, country broadcasting from a ranching community — pure country corn. At that time, in the late 1940s everyone had country roots, and there was a nostalgia about the rural life. Your program was authentic grassroots Americana. The fact that you were too naive to recognize this fact probably gave your program a distinctive character all of its own — and made it something people wanted to hear. You must have sounded like Garrison Keillor talking about Lake Woebegone — except his town was fictional and yours was real."

An exaggeration to be sure, in order for the professor to underscore his point. But maybe Jim Carroll of KWYO did appreciate the PR value of my little country radio program, because when he expanded the time slot from thirty to forty-five and later to sixty minutes, there was little or no rate increase. I'm grateful to this man.

And I'm even more grateful that I remained unaware of any link between country music and the national psyche. Had I made this sociological connection and anticipated that country music would soon take America by storm, I'm afraid I would have been tempted to pander to it — just as many country comedians of later years deliberately flaunted their country accent and southern humor in a condescending sort of way.

I do know that my little weekly radio program provided all my spending money through high school — for country dances, hamburgers, ice cream, and Cokes at the soda fountain, movies, even an extra pair of tight-fitting Levi's for my school wardrobe.

Infinitely more valuable to me than the spending money, however, was the deep satisfaction of doing something creative that I dearly loved. The knowledge that my voice could be heard throughout the countryside, thanks to the miraculous radio connection between sky and earth, was a pure delight.

✧

World War II raged on, along with the civilian sacrifices necessary to sustain that war. Many young men from Piney Creek were serving in the armed forces, and some had been killed. The folks attended funerals for these soldier boys from our valley, who were buried with solemn military rites as American heroes. I remember Mom sitting in front of the large living room window, looking out onto Piney Creek, quietly weeping for the Byrtus and Belus families, who lost their sons in the war.

In May 1945 the Nazis surrendered, and the stories broke about the Nazi atrocities, the terrible concentration camps, the gas ovens where millions of Jews had been put to death. Then I realized, in spite of all my patriotic fervor, that war wasn't such a fun thing for anyone. Still, I was obsessed with the hope that maybe someday I could become a pilot in the Army Air Corps, wear the uniform of an officer, and serve my country.

In the meantime, I had to finish high school.

I must say again, the quality of education in Clearmont wasn't very good. In grade school at Ucross I had been challenged to excel. Not so in Clearmont. I thought of transferring to high school in Sheridan. There was a possibility I might not meet college entrance requirements. As a sophomore in high school, this thought terrified me.

Again I sought refuge among my little islands in the river or in the towering hills on the ranch, where I could be alone with my thoughts. But these moments of self-reflection were becoming fewer and farther between. I was now seventeen years old and was called upon to do much of the hard manual labor every working ranch required. The war effort eliminated unemployment. Hired ranch hands were a thing of the past. We had to do it all ourselves: plowing in spring, seeding the grain crops, cutting and stacking hay, mending fences, harvesting and threshing, feeding cattle, and the thousand other things always waiting to get done.

I became pretty good at irrigating the beet fields. You'd tap into the ditch for a head of water and then carefully channel little streams down each of the long rows of sugar beets. You'd have to walk along to make certain the water reached the far end of the field. You'd wait an hour or so for it to soak

A nasty springtime chore on any cattle ranch. Branding, castration, and inoculation all in one operation. I'm the one standing, having delivered the vaccination syringe to Dad. Later I was trained to administer the shots.

A painful and bloody ordeal with horns sheared from skull of cattle. It left them dazed and crazed with excruciating pain, and with most of us sprayed with blood. This brutal operation deeply troubled me as a young teenager.

in, then move on to another set of rows. I enjoyed this process. During the waiting times, listening to the trickle of the water in the background, I would pull out a book and read biographies of great men such as Gen. Dwight Eisenhower, Gen. Douglas MacArthur, President Harry S. Truman, Governor Thomas E. Dewey, and British Prime Minister Winston Churchill — all men who, in spite of humble backgrounds or trying circumstances, made something of their lives.

Winter work was the most difficult. What I remember most is the bitter cold. Although we wore long-handled underwear, the truth is, I was always cold. This was before the day of insulated clothing which became common after the war. (In this book I have included a photo taken of me at this time which I find extremely revealing. Not only am I wearing a skimpy jacket, but one that I've so outgrown that its sleeves extend only halfway down my arms below the elbows. Yet the

Dressed for winter ranch chores. This photo is quite revealing in that it shows me ill clad for bitter cold weather. No wonder I was freezing most of the time.

Todd family's innate denial of physical discomfort is so deeply ingrained in me that I would never have asked the folks for a heavyweight overcoat.) All winter long I would be shivering, and my feet would be numb before we even left the barnyard to drive a horse-drawn hayrack several miles into the upper fields for a load of hay.

I vividly remember one cold winter afternoon when Dad and I were on horseback, delivering a mare to someone living back through the hills near a little railroad town called Ulm. Time got away from us, and it began turning dark when the wind whipped up a snow squall. I thought I was literally freezing to death. We headed back toward home with eight miles yet to go, and then all the chores to do after we got there. We trotted along the Burlington railroad tracks for a short distance, when out of the darkness approached a passenger train, slowly puffing along a steady incline, moving no faster than 5 mph up the steep grade. As the train crept through a narrow cut, I could look directly into the windows of the passenger cars, no farther than fifteen feet away as I sat on my horse atop the embankment.

Dad and me heading out to pasture for a frigid winter's ride.

The coaches were packed with passengers, mostly soldiers and sailors, crowding the aisles and standing to the rear of each coach. Then came the dining cars, slowly moving along, and I looked in on people sitting at tables covered with white linens, eating their dinner and drinking coffee from china cups that glistened from the overhead chandeliers. Stewards wearing white jackets and bow ties scurried up and down the aisle carrying large serving trays and pouring tea from silver teapots. Bringing up the rear of the train was the club car, filled with men who looked like military officers and fat government contractors, sitting comfortably on overstuffed chairs, all smoking what surely would have been Cuban cigars while sipping cocktails from the adjoining bar. It seemed as if I could hear the tinkling of the ice in their crystal glasses.

Inside the brightly lit railroad passenger cars were people from all walks of life, all enjoying warmth and comfort, gourmet food and elegant dining, relaxation and good wine — and all going somewhere. Then the train disappeared into the swirling snow, its red taillight blinking until it faded out of sight. It was like a passing vision of city elegance, so close I could almost reach out and touch it before it vanished into the darkness of the night.

There I sat on my horse in dead stillness, surrounded by the empty sagebrush-covered hills, the dark cold and spitting snow, with eight miles yet to ride — and already chilled to the bone. I said to myself, *Someday I'll get the hell out of here and catch an enchanted train that goes somewhere. Anywhere but here — in this frozen Siberia.*

✧

In the summer of 1945 I took an emergency job in the Kansas wheat harvest. My sister Edna worked for the Missouri Pacific Railroad as a night depot agent in a small Kansas town, preserving the seniority for her husband, Walter Fay, who was still in Europe with the wrap-up of World War II. There were public appeals for anyone who might be willing and able to exercise their patriotic duty by working a few weeks in the Kansas wheat harvest. Otherwise the whole crop might be wasted, and this would be a terrible loss to the war effort.

The folks consented for me to go. They must have decided I needed exposure to the outside world. I got to take my first train ride. A happy pagan must have been the engineer; at least, he did not disappear with the rapture of Christ's Second Coming. I rode to Denver, where the railroad depot was packed with thousands of troops and military personnel. The trains ran late, and they, too, were packed to capacity. People sat on luggage on the outside platforms between cars and slept in the aisles.

Mom warned me about the dangers of lone young men like myself taking their first train ride. Pickpockets everywhere and smooth-talking men and women operating their scams in the shadows of every building. She sewed extra money inside my undershirt. I heeded her warnings and made it to Ness City, Kansas, safe and sound.

When word got out that a potential harvester was in town, over a dozen wheat farmers descended on Edna's apartment. I took a job at one dollar per hour, with board and room provided, driving a truck from the field combine to the nearest silo in town. We worked twelve to sixteen hours a day, seven days a week, whenever sufficient grain cars were available at the railroad silo. Otherwise I had to shovel the wheat out the back door of the truck bed into large storage piles on the ground, which we covered with tarps for later removal and shipment. With no personal expenses and earnings of up to sixteen dollars a day, I was fast becoming a rich man.

The harvest was over in only a few weeks, but that didn't matter. I could get a job anywhere. There was no unemployment; everyone needed workers. I got a temporary job working for an insulation roofing company. The stifling Kansas heat in August was unbearable during the daytime, so we worked only early mornings, wearing suffocating masks over our faces to protect us from inhaling the dangerous insulation (probably pure asbestos). Workers sometimes passed out in the heat.

While on the roof of a new home being built, I listened with a group of workers to the startling news announcements that an atomic bomb had exploded over Hiroshima. We were astonished to learn that this new weapon, which they said was no bigger than a suitcase, could level an entire city and kill a million people. Eight days later, everyone stopped work and came downtown to stand around on the street corners listening to the stilted voice of President Harry Truman declaring that Japan had surrendered. World War II was over.

I returned to Wyoming on a train even more crowded than the one I had taken to Kansas, with hordes of jubilant soldiers and sailors drinking from open flasks of liquor freely provided by civilian celebrants. At every mail stop, the passengers would pour out onto the brick patios of the depot for dancing and celebration. The party would be continued at the depot platform of the next station.

It's hard to imagine today the euphoria everyone felt right after the war. The forces of right had prevailed over the power of darkness. Fascism, Nazism, and political-military tyranny had been defeated. The world was safe once again for democracy and peace. The United Nations would guarantee that another world war could never happen.

Euphoria was not limited to the political affairs of the world, however. Economic prosperity reigned. People remembered all too well the agony of the Great Depression only a few years earlier. Now there was zero unemployment. Rationing and price controls were lifted, and everyone predicted that personal incomes would soar. There was great excitement about the possibility of things to come.

But the war's presence lingered, even in my little Wyoming ranch community. In the fall of 1945 a German prisoner-of-war camp was built right outside Clearmont in response to emergency requests from sugar beet farmers for field laborers. It was imperative that field hands be recruited from somewhere, or the whole crop would rot in the ground. The temporary camp consisted of a few temporary frame buildings for administration and a series of tentlike barracks for the prisoners.

Most of these German POWs had been captured in Hitler's failed North African campaign and were being detained in the United States since the social-military situation in Germany was still in shambles. They were generally young, in their midtwenties, and most were attending makeshift English classes in camp. Some were quite proficient in our language; others spoke very haltingly, but they enjoyed trying to converse with anyone who would take the time to speak with them. One Sunday afternoon I watched several hundred of these German prisoners, wearing ragtag uniforms, marching in close formation down through the little town of Clearmont. In their deep voices, in cadence with their tramping, they sang the marching songs of Hitler's now defeated army. They would sometimes go out to a cow pasture on the other side of town and play soccer with violent aggression. The townspeople would gather around and cheer them on.

While the war was still raging, the POWs worked in the beet fields under heavy armed guard. Military police with loaded rifles kept moving around the parameters of the working area. After the war ended, however, these precautions were gradually relaxed. Eventually the guards were allowed to leave their guns behind and hire themselves out as farm hands to earn a little extra cash. The POWs could be assigned to work as individuals for anyone who requested their services. They had a trained medic among them, and he soon became the "doctor on call" for anyone in Clearmont who had emergency medical needs.

Some of these POWs worked for us on the ranch. Dad would invite them to lay aside their meager little sack lunches and eat with us at the family dinner table. He always maintained that you got better work out of field hands if they were well fed. How those guys loved eating home-cooked food and being within a family setting once again. One of them enjoyed milking cows and would always come out into the cow barn and help me with the chores.

Once, during a breakdown on a threshing crew, a couple of the younger POWs joined me in the shade under a bundle wagon and shared their worries about their families in Germany. They had received no mail. In broken English, they wondered if their loved ones were alive or dead — and, if alive, how were they faring amid the destruction and starvation that was commonplace among the civilian survivors of war-torn Germany.

I mustered the courage to ask if they had heard the news about Hitler's concentration camps and the systematic execution of millions of Jewish civilians. They nodded that they had heard the news and realized that it was apparently true but denied any personal knowledge of the atrocities. Pensively, they shook their heads in sullen disbelief — but didn't say more. Then they changed the subject, telling me how much they liked my father and mother and that the Americans had been good to them.

The POW camp brought the war home to me on a personal level. The Germans were no longer just enemy soldiers we read about in the papers or watched on newsreels. They were real people. Honest-to-goodness human beings. Aunt Rose once told one of the POWs that Americans didn't have very good feelings toward the German military regime. He replied, "But you mustn't feel that way toward these young soldiers, who were involuntarily drafted into the German army just like your young men were drafted."

One would assume that our isolated Wyoming ranching valley was far removed from anything approaching enemy contact in World War II. But how many stateside Americans had seasoned German soldiers sitting at their dinner table eating roast beef and apple cobbler? Or milking cows with them in the barn? Or calmly talking with them, while stretched out in the shade of a horse-drawn bundle wagon, about their families' fates amid the devastation that Germany had brought upon itself in the terrible war it inflicted upon the rest of the world?

✧

Anthropologists tell us that every society has its rites of passage, and one of the most important ones is passage from childhood into adulthood. The rite of initiation for a young boy into manhood along Piney Creek was to drive a bundle wagon on a threshing crew. You had to know how to handle a team of horses and have enough physical stamina to load and unload bundled grain sheaves all day long — and this you did under the observation of peers and older men who worked alongside you. A kid would do a variety of odd jobs on a threshing crew, such as being a water boy, before he graduated to the bundle wagon.

During the harvest of 1945, I was sent out to the various ranches and farms along our valley as part of a threshing crew handling a bundle wagon. It was hard manual labor. You'd drive your wagon out across the field of shocked grain, and pitchers would toss the bundles up into the wagon bed. You had to arrange your bundle load with the butts out and heads in so that loose grain would fall inside your wagon and not drop off onto the ground. You'd stack your load as high as you could, then head toward the threshing machine, swaying and rocking along, and then wait in line for your turn to pull up beside the roaring monstrosity of spinning wheels and flapping belts. The deafening blare of noise made it impossible to talk to anyone, so everyone yelled at each other from the top of their lungs.

Work horses were terrified of the monstrous commotion and shied away from the thresher, whose cutting knives yanked bundles of grain inside its gigantic throat and whacked them into tiny bits of stalks before beating the loose grain kernels out of the straw. It's a wonder that more men atop careening bundle wagons, propelled by frightened runaway horses, weren't accidentally hurled into the slashing knives and shredded into meatsauce. It was dangerous and hard work, and you were always under the watchful and critical observation of all the seasoned elders in the valley. This made your rite of passage into adult manhood a precarious experience indeed.

After you got your horses calmed down beside the threshing machine, you started tossing your bundles into the loader and watched the rotating cutting knives gobble them up. You had to coordinate your unloading with the driver on the opposite side of the loader. Several things could cause a threshing machine to choke down: grain that was too damp and heavy, or a load of grain that was too big. It required real cooperation with your partner on the opposite wagon to keep it moving steadily, not too fast or too slow. Other things might cause a threshing machine to ball up — mechaical things beyond your control. Whenever this happened, somebody had to open up the belly of the thresher and literally pull out, by hand, a ton or more of the compacted garbage that was balled up inside the guts of the machine.

Our neighbor, Cline Fowler, who originally hailed from Arkansas, owned the thresher and was responsible for its operation. When it balled up, for whatever reason, Cline would let loose with a temper tantrum. This would traumatize anyone the first time they saw it — and thereafter provided steady entertainment. His kin, Ross Fowler, said one time, in his deadpan Arkansas drawl, "Cline had nine fits this mornin' — and two of 'em was real bad."

It was more coincidence than anything else which enabled two of us young bucks to be unloading into the thresher at the same time. But when the right opportunity presented itself, particularly if it was late in a long afternoon when we were both dead tired, it took only a wink as a special signal for the drama to begin. We would begin overloading the thresher with our bundles. You had to do this carefully so as not to be detected. Instead of tossing in one bundle at a time, we accelerated our pace and deliberately forked in two. When you heard the giant threshing machine start to choke down, right before it had one more chance to clear itself and regain its proper operating speed, then we'd each fork in three bundles or more — and then there was a gigantic WHOMMPH!

Everything stopped. Even the tractor powering the belt-driven contraption would choke down before the automatic governing device could give it more gas.

Silence exploded across the harvest landscape.

Then we teenage initiates would plop our weary bodies down on the edge of the bundle wagon, take a sip of cold water, chaff a little wheat in the palms of our hands, which we chewed like gum, and watch the most spectacular display of adult infantilism the world has ever known.

First Cline would stomp his feet and begin cussing. Then he'd throw his hat to the ground and start stomping on it. Then he'd start bawling, with tears streaming down his face and out of his nose. His repetitive cussing quickly accelerated into the staccato chant of an auctioneer, until all the words slurred into one long unintelligible tirade. Cline was a large sloppily dressed man, which made the tantrums all the more surreal. He'd throw himself to the ground and pound the earth with his fists and start kicking with his feet.

The grown men of the threshing crew, the tribal elders for our *Rite of Passage* into adulthood, would gather around in solemn assembly and, leaning on their pitchforks, watch the pitiful spectacle with curious compassion. The only thing they would openly say was, "Step back, boys, and give 'im plenty of air." Doc Fowler, another distant kin of Cline from Arkansas, would vary the routine by slightly posturing his body to make it appear as if he was looking away, then pull his hat down over his face. You could see his shoulders lunging uncontrollably in what was either hysterical laughing or hysterical sobbing.

In the meantime, we young initiates into the full rite of adult manhood would sit on our bundle wagons with hangdog expressions of grave concern, ritually chewing our cud. When Cline's convulsions took him out of our range of sight, we'd throw ourselves backward into the center of the wagon, pull our hats over our faces, kick up our heels, and howl with laughter. The show was more hilarious than any Hollywood comedy. And it made such an indelible impression on me that I can distinctly remember every detail as if it were only yesterday.

In fairness to Cline Fowler, Dad considered him the best neighbor a man could ever have on Piney Creek. When Cline first migrated from Arkansas to Wyoming as a young man, he worked for my father. A large number of "Arkansaw'yers" — and this is the slang name they applied to themselves — followed Cline to Wyoming, and most of them also worked for Dad at one time or another. Many of them remained in Wyoming, and their descendants schedule an annual Arkansaw'yer picnic on Piney Creek.

Many years later I was invited by Governor Mike Sullivan of Wyoming to have prayers at a statewide meeting of Democratic county leaders from throughout the state. A terrible snowstorm in Cheyenne kept attendance low.

A young governor from Arkansas was to address the small group about the League of Democratic Action, an effort to reorganize the national Democratic Party. Since I was sitting at the head table I told the Arkansas governor that there was an Arkansas connection in Wyoming. He wanted to know what it was. I explained the invasion of Arkansaw'yers into our ranching valley of northern Wyoming and then told him this story about Cline Fowler's temper tantrums on the threshing crew.

He leaned back in his chair, slapped his forehead and got a big belly laugh out of it, then corrected me, saying that people from Arkansas prefer to be called "Arkansans."

His name was Governor Bill Clinton.

Who would have ever guessed that this little vignette from our Piney Creek ranching valley would someday make its way to the president of the United States? Or that this kid who threw himself backward into the bundle wagon while kicking up his heels and guffawing at the farcical burlesque would be the one telling him the story?

✧

Now that I had experienced the rite of passage into adult maturity, something else happened that would profoundly affect my life. I discovered girls.

It couldn't have come at a better time. The war was over, gas rationing was lifted, and I had learned how to drive a car. Now my friends and I could go wherever we wanted to for entertainment and fun. Mostly, we went to dances.

Fortunately for my sister Sadie and me, Mom taught us how to dance. She said it's no fun to get out on the dance floor if you can't dance to the beat of the music. Across the slick kitchen linoleum she taught us how to waltz — the only slow dance she really knew — and showed us a host of country folk dances, like the polka and the schottische. The one called "Put Your Little Foot Down" was always a lot of fun. Our older sister, Edna, taught us to dance the fox-trot, and some girls I knew showed me the jitterbug. Sadie and I became pretty good dancers, and we often danced together.

My sister Sadie and me as teenagers when we attended country dances together. Mom taught us to dance all the traditional country steps and we danced well together.

It seems to me that we danced everywhere we went. There were juke-boxes in every bar and honky tonk for the adults, and in every hamburger joint and ice cream parlor for us teenagers. There was always a small dance floor where we could jitterbug.

A large dance pavilion in Story, Wyoming, called the Lodore was a favorite spot to go to hear the big bands that toured the nation right after the war. Orchestras with as many as thirty musicians filled a huge dance floor with dancers jitterbugging to such hit tunes as "In the Mood" and the "Muskrat Ramble." Large wooden panels along the outside walls were opened to let the pine-scented mountain breeze cool the place down.

We favored old-fashioned country dances at such familiar places as Piney Hall, Clearmont, Ucross, Ulm, Arvada, Banner, Kearney, Buffalo, and Kaycee. We always dated in groups, with bunches of us attending these dances. At the country dances, you would dance with anyone and everyone. Square dancing was especially fun, with the spirited music. These country dances were wholesome fun for the entire community. Never did we dream that they would quickly become things of the past.

Country dances in those days always lasted until two o'clock in the morning, and often the hat was passed for dancing until four. There was a supper waltz at midnight, and you scurried to find the right gal for your dancing partner because she was the one with whom you ate supper. The supper was always the same: chicken or ham salad sandwiches, dill pickles for relish, chocolate cake for dessert, and coffee. Adults ate inside the dance hall at tables folded down from the walls. Teenagers ate outside in our cars because, we claimed, there was no room for us in the hall. Actually, it was an excuse for our extracurricular social activities.

The only adults who came outside were men nipping at the bottle, and quite a few did because liquor was never allowed inside the dance hall. It was during this time that Jeff Bolinger and I decided to get drunk. The adults seemed to enjoy it, so why shouldn't we give it an honest try? Since it was a cooperative effort, we each contributed one dollar to buy a pint flask of cheap whiskey in town and brought it out to Piney Hall. We both realized we'd have to do more than sip the bitter-tasting stuff and spit it out as if it were mouth rinse. We'd have to actually swallow it. So we took big breaths, held our noses, and chugged down several big gulps. It burned our throats and caused us to shake and shudder all over. Then we hid the flask behind a fencepost and went back inside to the dance.

We both got to feeling better, much better — no doubt about it. Jeff even danced the polka for the first time in his life and did so with incredible footwork. I tried jitterbugging the polka and discovered that it could be done.

In fact, our dancing was so good we decided that we needed refortification to do it even better, so we went out to our fence post. But the flask was gone; someone had stolen it. I've always suspected Jeff of swindling his partner and to this day believe he owes me half a pint of whiskey — with interest.

We went back into Piney Hall empty-handed and unrefortified, but maybe that was for the best. The dance floor became unstable and began swaying. I was getting dizzy, and in direct proportion to my dizziness came a feeling of putrid nausea. I decided right then that if getting drunk meant getting sick, I wanted no more of it. That was a lesson I learned early in life, and it has stayed with me ever since. It was worth the dollar bill I paid to learn it. I call it my famous "one-dollar lesson."

Sex was another matter, however. The only sex education I had on the ranch was from the hired men, who told me that it was very much the way horses did it, only more so. But if they knew so much about it, I wondered, how come they were still bachelors sleeping alone, or with one another, in our bunkhouse? I concluded that I was badly misinformed in this area.

Around this time, an elementary schoolteacher in Clearmont took Jeff and me to a hotel bed and taught us how to do it. He was a junior in high school, and I was a senior. We didn't actually do it, but she taught us how to do it. There is a dramatic difference between the two. I learned a valuable lesson from this experience — namely, that the hired men were all wrong.

I decided right after that episode that I would never mention the incident to anyone as long as I lived. In the first place, no one would ever believe it — it would be immediately dismissed as nothing more than the fanciful imagination of a teenage braggart. Although it remained a positive experience in my memory, I stuck to my original commitment and never mentioned it to anyone. Until 1991. That's when I saw my old friend Jeff Bolinger for the first time in forty years. He looked much the same as I remembered him, although now with graying hair. We had a cup of coffee in a Sheridan restaurant and reminisced about old times. He fidgeted his coffee cup with a hand that was missing several fingers — fingers frozen off during a drinking binge when he wrecked his car one night, when it was forty degrees below zero. (Jeff didn't learn the one-dollar lesson I had learned at Piney Hall while we were both teenagers.)

Finally, Jeff, with a twinkle in his eyes, hesitatingly asked, "Gene, do you remember that time when Miss —— took us to bed in her hotel room?"

I said, "Jeff, I'm glad that you haven't forgotten because I decided never to tell that story because no one would ever believe it. But now that you say you specifically remember it, I feel affirmed in my memory of it."

We both laughed, and I added, "I guess we'll have to admit that our high school curriculum at Clearmont was more modern than what we thought — it included a course in sex education!"

Many years later I would help establish a program of sex education in our public schools in cooperation with a Supreme Court justice and a prestigious physician, but I can assure the reader that both its intent and content were far removed from what Jeff and I experienced in Clearmont.

Before I graduated from high school, I won an all-expenses-paid trip to the National 4-H Convention in Chicago as a representative of Wyoming. I had been active in our Piney Creek 4-H Club ever since I was ten years old. Our project was the raising and fattening of baby beef. My sister Sadie and younger brother, Lewis, also were 4-Hers. The trip to Chicago was a series of firsts: my first visit to a large city; my first stay in an elegant hotel; my first visit to a museum of natural history and an art gallery; my first attendance at a live symphony concert. For this Wyoming country kid who had never been exposed to the cultural wonders of a large city, it was an overwhelming trip.

My champion 4-H steer which I exhibited at the Denver Livestock Show in 1946. My 4-H activities won me an exciting trip to the Chicago 4-H Convention in the same year.

I had to come back to Clearmont and finish out my senior year before graduating from high school in the spring of 1947. The last two years of high school had been much better than the first two. A new school superintendent, Mr. A. P. Anderson, arrived in 1945 and made all kinds of improvements. He was the first person to ask me seriously what I wanted to do with my life and what kind of a career I might choose for myself. He seemed to enjoy analyzing the professions — law, medicine, teaching, dentistry, radio broadcasting, engineering — and why people chose them. He had interesting insights as to what kind of personalities fit best within the various professional modes.

"Dentists," he would say, "primarily are mechanical craftsmen; doctors primarily are faith healers; preachers primarily are demagogues; and lawyers primarily are ambulance chasers. But you've got to go to college and graduate school to professionally disguise these personality traits."

Puffing his pipe, he would continue, "The point is, Eugene, I urge you to choose a college real soon. You may not get in, because they are so crowded with veterans on the GI Bill right now."

I followed his excellent advice and began writing for catalogues from colleges all over the nation. I spent hours browsing through them trying to decide which would offer me the best course of studies in preparation for a profession I had yet to choose. My interests seemed to revolve around law and radio management, and I wanted to attend a university that offered a four-year program in the military Reserve Office Training Corps (ROTC). Early on I decided that I didn't want to attend the University of Wyoming. I found myself returning again and again to the programs offered by the University of Denver. I applied for admission and was accepted. Classes were to start in the fall of 1947.

In the meantime, however, I took my first radio job away from home, as an announcer in a new station just going on the air in Deadwood, South Dakota. The station wouldn't be ready to start broadcasting until the first of July, so I took a temporary job working for a family friend, Carl Sneed, an electrical contractor in Clearmont. Also working for Carl that summer were my good friend Don Dexter, who later would marry my sister Sadie, and my older brother George, who was learning the electrical trade. We wired houses and barns in preparation for an extension of the REA power line into these ranching communities.

Carl's first love was not electrical contracting, however, but law enforcement. He got himself elected town marshal of Clearmont and also got himself appointed deputy sheriff. Neither of these two roles was very important to anyone except Carl. He took his job very seriously. The only reason I digress to this subject at all is that I became his sidekick, his unofficial assistant law enforcement officer.

That summer a serious law-and-order crisis invaded our peaceful little town: the sudden influx of over 200 gandy dancers into Clearmont. Gandy dancers were temporary railway construction workers who were usually hired to upgrade railroad beds and tracks. They would eat and sleep in special railroad bunk cars and remain out on the job site for days and weeks on end. Most of them were winos and chronic alcoholics hired right off the skid rows of Chicago and Kansas City. It took several days, if not weeks, to sober them up before they could work at all. But far removed from all temptations of the big city, along isolated stretches of rural railroads and only being paid once every two weeks, these "dry drunks" provided fairly steady service between paydays. But when payday came, look out! They would hop aboard empty freight cars and ride into Clearmont in droves. They would run straight to the bars like sheep who'd gone a week without water, and all hell would break loose.

This is where town marshal and deputy sheriff Carl Sneed and his sidekick (me) come into the sorry picture. This invading army of winos more than doubled the population of poor little Clearmont, with its 200 peaceful souls. It was worse than the invasion of the Mormon crickets. They were literally everywhere, drinking, drunk, and passed out. They were sprawled along the streets and alleys, in the gutters, in the crawl spaces under people's houses, between buildings and inside abandoned cars. When the supply of bottled liquor gave out, they would drink shaving lotion or anything containing alcohol, and when this gave out, it was rumored, they would drink gasoline. Local bar patrons fled from town as if the black plague had descended upon them.

As the evening rampage worsened, Carl Sneed secured a copy of the train schedule from the depot agent so that we could clear the tracks for an approaching train. Most of the gandies, by this time, were in such a stage of advanced intoxication that they were literally unable to be responsible for their own safety. They would stretch out between rails, using one rail as a sleeping pillow. It's a wonder that those men we may have missed were not mangled to death.

At first I helped Carl load them into the Clearmont City Jail, but the jail held only about half a dozen men. The pitiful little open-air jail was filled to overflowing, and there were still over a hundred gandy dancers on a drunken prowl throughout the town. The situation was becoming desperate.

As part of their employment contract, the Burlington Railroad promised free passage back to Chicago for gandies who chose to leave their job. Knowing this, many of the gandies would purchase their booze and take the bottle to the depot. There they would tie shipping tags around their ankles with written instructions: "Load me on the first eastbound passenger train to Chicago." They would then consume their bottle, stretch out on the depot lawn, and pass into alcoholic oblivion.

When the late evening passenger train pulled into Clearmont, it was a sight to behold. First the conductor, with brakemen and porters standing directly behind him, blocked a horde of about forty gandies who tried to push him aside and board the train.

"You're all drunk and I'm not letting you on this train. Back off, every one of you," he ordered, swinging his railroad lantern back and forth in front of him as if it were a billy club.

Things began to get out of hand, and Carl approached the conductor. "These are railroad employees and they've overrun this town," he pleaded. "I need help here from the railroad special agents. You can't just dump a gang of 200 drunks like this on such a little town and expect us to manage."

The conductor countered, "Then talk to the railroad authorities. You're the town marshal, that's your job. My job is to run this train, and these drunks aren't boarding it."

Carl countered, "Then how about taking them over there. They sure as hell aren't going to cause you any trouble" — pointing with his thumb, over his shoulder, toward the gandies stretched out like corpses on the depot lawn with shipping tags tied to their ankles.

The conductor flashed a look of contemptuous disgust at Carl for his idiotic suggestion.

"Look, damn it," Carl snapped, "The railroad has got some responsibility here."

"Then load them in the baggage car," the conductor shrugged, intending to be absurd.

Carl motioned for me to follow him as we gathered up the first inebriated stiff and swung it up through the open doorway of the baggage car. Then a second and a third. The railway mail clerk (also called baggage handler) appeared from the darkened interior of the train and suddenly realized with horror what was happening right in front of his eyes and began a torrent of loud protests.

"Conductor's orders," Carl shouted as we swung several more inside the baggage car like cordwood.

The baggage handler jumped from the railroad car to the depot platform and raced toward the conductor screaming violation of company rules. In the meantime, Carl and I heaved the last unconscious gandy aboard.

The conductor, without saying a word, highballed his red lantern toward the engineer, signaling for the train to move. The air brakes released, the whistle blew, and the train slowly began chugging out of the station. The distraught mail clerk raced back to his baggage car and barely scrambled aboard, while the conductor disappeared up the steps of the passenger coach. The train was puffing down the tracks with the mail clerk standing in the doorway and shaking his fists and cussing at Carl, until the whole commotion passed from view, down the tracks.

Left behind on the platform was the same mob of drunken gandies, still attacking one another with accusations as to who was the *drunkest* and who was the most guilty for the sorry mess which caused them to lose their free railroad passage back to the skid rows of Chicago.

"Let's push them all away from the tracks and head them back toward town," Carl said.

So we herded them like squawking geese across the highway into Clearmont where they gradually dispersed between the darkened storefronts into the secluded alleys behind. The Ranger Bar had conveniently shut down — early.

The next morning several large livestock trucks pulled into town, compliments of the railroad, and loaded up the rest of the gandies like cattle and drove them away. Clearmont returned to peace and quiet. Carl handed me a bushel basket and told me to gather up the liquor bottles that littered the town. There were literally hundreds of them. Most were empty, but a few contained an inch or two of whiskey that some poor fellow didn't quite finish off before he passed out.

As I moved along the alley, gathering up my bottles, I spotted a lone gandy curled up under a bush with a flimsy jacket pulled over him like a blanket and a hat across his face. I squatted beside him and lifted the hat. He looked up at me and said, "I'm awful sick."

"Do you need a doctor?" I asked.

"No. I need a drink."

Remembering my famous one-dollar lesson I naively asked, "Why do you want a drink if it makes you sick?"

"It's the other way around, my friend. I need a drink because it keeps me from being sick." He pushed himself up into a sitting position and held out his trembling hands, "See these hands? Only a drink will cause these terrible tremors to subside." He spoke with perfect diction, clearly pronouncing every syllable.

I sat down beside him and, being the Good Samaritan, rifled through the bottles in the bushel basket and came up with a little leftover whiskey. He downed it with only a few noisy swallows and leaned back against the bushes as if already experiencing medicinal relief.

"Are you the marshal's deputy? I saw you with him last night."

"Naw," I answered, "I'm only helping out. I'm going off to college this fall. The University of Denver."

"The University of Denver, eh? That's a great university. It's a sister university to the one I graduated from — the University of Chicago. Both liberal institutions of higher learning with great graduate schools attached."

"If you graduated from there, what happened?" I asked.

"I took a graduate course under Professor John Barleycorn. I haven't quite completed my internship yet," he said, cracking a smile at his own cleverness. I was dumbfounded. Much later in my life would I come to a better understanding about the disease of addiction and chronic alcoholism.

I stood up and pulled him to his feet. He shook himself off, straightened his clothes, rearranged a floppy hat on his head, and lit up a cigarette.

He glanced my way several times but avoided direct eye contact. I suddenly felt some sense of emotional rapport with this pathetic wino, this graduate of the University of Chicago, whom I had found along the back alley of Clearmont. I noticed that he actually would be a good-looking man if his flushed cheeks and bloodshot eyes were normal. Instead, they revealed the ravages of alcohol abuse, which was surely destroying him.

"Well, guess I'll be going," he said. He turned and started to slowly walk away.

"Where you going?" I called after him, "You've missed your transportation out of town — the trucks left about an hour ago with everyone aboard. You're the only one left behind."

He faced me, with his hat cocked slightly to one side, exposing a lock of blond hair down across his forehead, his jacket casually tossed over his arm, looking both puzzled and surprised at my question.

"Goin' nowhere," he answered pensively, carefully choosing his words, "Goin' nowhere. Been goin' there a long — long time."

He walked a short distance and paused, then turned to me once more and said, "Besides, this would be a good day to get hit by a train."

I watched him as he slowly made his way with an unsteady gait across the highway and drifted off toward the coal chute in the railroad yards. I felt a sudden impulse to grab him by the arm and say, "Come on fella, let's turn around and go back to *somewhere* with your life . . . anywhere but *nowhere*."

But I didn't. Soon he was gone. But his words hung heavy in the air and have forever become a haunting refrain in my life and the lives of many people I've known: *Goin' nowhere . . . Been goin' there a long — long time.*

It never occurred to me to check the next morning's newspaper to see if there had been a casualty along the railroad tracks leading out of Clearmont.

✧

On the evening of July 1, 1947, my nineteenth birthday, I crawled up on the roof of Ray Yates' Garage and rigged up a long copper aerial wire so I could listen to the trial broadcast of the new radio station in Deadwood. If all went well with the trial transmissions, I was scheduled to leave the next day for Deadwood and become the first announcer for station KDSJ.

Carl Sneed called me down from the roof, saying he needed my help with an electrical problem at Helen's Quick Lunch restaurant, which was plunged into darkness. When we stepped inside, the lights flipped on — for my surprise birthday party. Many Piney Creek ranching neighbors, school classmates, and 4-H friends gathered around for hamburgers, ice cream and cake. Of course, the evening wouldn't have been complete without dancing to the jukebox.

That party is significant to me not only because of its personal affirmation but also because it became my going-away celebration. My departure for Deadwood would be a permanent leave-taking. I never returned home to the ranch again except for limited vacations.

The next morning I left by bus for the Black Hills, which I loved at first sight. The historic little gold mining town of Deadwood, quaint and rustic in its narrow canyon setting, appeared as a Hollywood backdrop for a western movie. Its winding streets were teeming with tourists. You simply climbed wooden stairways from one street to the next up the canyon wall.

During the war Deadwood was declared off-limits to military personnel because it was an "open city." Gambling halls and rampant prostitution prevailed. State authorities closed down the gambling halls, but open prostitution remained and was vigorously defended by the city fathers and businessmen, who convinced themselves that both their economy and the preservation of law and order depended on it. Their reasoning was that regulated prostitution would protect the morals of young people by shielding them from promiscuous sexual behavior, safeguard women from "rapists" roaming the streets, and keep venereal disease under strict health control. (Such flawed reasoning wasn't very complimentary of themselves or their community, I didn't think.) Besides, they argued, prostitution fits the image of the Wild West. After all, Calamity Jane, who's buried beside her beloved Bill Hickock up on cemetery hill, plied her trade here in Deadwood.

No wonder I had the feeling of being transported backward into the nostalgia of the Old West. To make it even more enchanting, the broadcast studios of KDSJ were located on the third floor of the charming Franklin Hotel. In those days it was common for radio stations to locate their studios in the most prominent hotel of the city.

The big thrill for me, however, was signing radio station KDSJ on the air for its very first broadcast in the summer of 1947. I can't remember if it was the day before or the day after the Fourth of July. Finally, after all my many years of being obsessed with radio broadcasting, I was at the control board of an authentic radio station. "You are in tune to the voice of the Black Hills, KDSJ, with studios located in the beautiful Franklin Hotel, downtown Deadwood, South Dakota." That was my station identification lingo, read every thirty minutes as required by the FCC. It sounded quite impressive at first, but the hotel, which was quaint and interesting but not necessarily so beautiful, was soon identified as the "historic" Franklin Hotel.

Radio broadcasting still had a romantic and curious charm in that era just prior to the advent of television. Listeners would hear the voices of radio personalities and fantasize about what the people really looked like. It was nothing unusual at all during this first summer of broadcasting for KDSJ to have as many as a dozen people standing outside the large plate windows of the broadcast booth. Someone posted a little sign: "Please don't toss peanuts to the announcers."

Every evening I hosted a request program, a type of show common to most radio stations back in the 1940s and 1950s. People would write cards and letters requesting a certain song to be played for a sweetheart or special friend. In 1947 a raunchy little ditty entitled "Cigarettes and Whiskey and Wild Wild Women" hit the charts. It was silly but still kind of fun to listen to, particularly with its musical refrain:

Cigarettes and whiskey and wild wild women
They'll drive you crazy, they'll drive you insane . . .

I began getting daily requests for this particular song, always dedicated to an individual by the name of Clark. The station soon learned that a Mr. Clark was a prominent property owner in Lead, South Dakota, who had strong objections to the use of tobacco and alcohol — and had sufficient political clout to shut KDSJ down if it didn't cease ridiculing him with these phony requests. It was my job to explain to the radio audience that we no longer would accept requests for that particular song. This resulted in a howl of telephone protests from rebellious listeners who objected to "anyone telling the rest of us what songs we can't listen to."

The station manager, Truman Walrod, decided to appease our listeners by allowing them to select, by actual votes, which tune would become the theme song for the popular request program. The listening audience chose all right, sending hundreds of cards and letters for — you guessed it — "Cigarettes and Whiskey and Wild Wild Women." It was the most ridiculous theme song imaginable. "But we had to honor the democratic vote of our many listeners even for a short while," the manager said. I learned a lesson from his mistake — don't let the listeners do your radio programming for you unless you're willing to abide by the whims of their illogical decisions.

While in Deadwood, I visited my first brothel.

It was common in those days of radio to do live broadcasts from popular nightclubs. Deadwood's population included an exceedingly large number of musicians from the big bands which were touring America at that time.

Bands like Sammy Kaye, Tommy Dorsey, and Eddy Howard. These men had reached the midpoint in their lives and wanted to settle down in a community to raise their families, and they chose the scenic Black Hills.

There was a hot and jazzy piano player at the Bodega restaurant in downtown Deadwood, and it was decided that the Bodega would sponsor thirty minutes of his popular dinner-hour entertainment. However, in order do this, it was necessary for the radio station to drop a telephone line from the third floor of the Bodega down to the ground level, then through a window onto the little stage where the musicians performed.

The restaurant owner, his bartender, and the station manager handed me a roll of telephone cable and asked, "Since you're the youngest and most spry, won't you race up those three flights of stairs to the people living on the top floor and ask them to let you tie into the inside telephone junction box, then drop the loose end down here to us in the alley courtyard?"

I did as they asked, sprinted up the back stairway, and knocked on the door. The moment the door opened I knew exactly what I had gotten myself into. The red-haired madam was wearing a black miniskirt with an attractive matching blouse. Having already been alerted to the prank, she told me to follow her down a short, dimly lit hallway into an open room, where the radio hookup was to be made. The room contained six or eight skimpily dressed women, all wearing excessive makeup, all smoking cigarettes, drinking Cokes, and engaged in animated conversation. (Later I was to learn that this was the afternoon shift just coming on duty for the busy night ahead.)

The madam introduced me as the man from the radio station who needed to make a connection — a play on words not missed by the girls, who all broke out in hilarious laughter. I went about my duties, fastening the two wires into the terminal box, while the madam assisted me in draping it around a corner cabinet, then stringing it behind the sofa and along the hallway leading back to the entrance.

"So you're the young voice we all listen to on the radio, huh?" one of the girls asked. "You don't look at all like I imagined you would."

"No, he's better looking than his voice sounds," quipped the dark-complexioned one, trying to be funny.

I couldn't think of one word to say in response, so I just got extra busy with my cable duties. Obviously, they could see my acute embarrassment and enjoyed it.

"Who's dumb idea was it to let people vote for that dumb song as your theme song for that request program you have every evening?" another asked.

"The station manager," I answered honestly.

"Well, that's the dumbest song I've ever heard for a theme song. 'Cigarettes, and Whiskey and Wild Wild Women' may be okay by itself. But not as a theme song for a radio program. It just doesn't fit."

I nodded — I couldn't agree more.

The peroxide blonde turned to the others and mockingly teased, "What does a young fellow like him know about those kind of songs anyway?" I heard them giggling in the background and felt my face blushing crimson.

Then directly to me, Blondie said, "Honey, you're so wet behind the ears that one good cigarette, and one good shot of whiskey, and one good wild woman — all in one night — would kill you."

"But, oh, what a death it would be!" squealed another.

Blondie came back, "Handsome, if this is your first time here, how about one on the house?"

Peals of laughter erupted as they all looked my way, relishing every moment of the misery they were inflicting upon me. The room was heavy with cigarette smoke and incense, mixed with the fragrance of their lush perfume. I had entered into a sensual realm of sin and feminine mystique that I knew nothing about.

As I strung the cable through the hallway and out the window, where it dropped to the alley below, the madam said, "They're just teasing you. Pay 'em no mind."

All the way down the outside stairway I could hear and see the men below — bellowing in hysterical laughter, holding their stomachs, slapping each other across the shoulder, and staggering back and forth, then howling some more. I could appreciate the comedy of it. This naive country kid, having absolutely no idea what he was getting into, with a roll of telephone wire looped over his shoulder, innocently bounding up the back stairway into a whorehouse. That's classic comedy.

Not so funny was my gullibility to the prank. After all, I had just turned nineteen and should have had enough worldly sense to know what the comedians were up to.

Obviously, the education and edification of Gene Todd had a long way yet to go. In another month, my formal education would take a giant step forward when I entered the University of Denver.

Chapter 3

In September 1947 I walked up to Highway 14, which wound its way down through our ranch with pastureland on both sides, and flagged down a Burlington bus. I carried only a small soft suitcase and an overcoat. The overnight trip wound through Gillette, Newcastle, Lusk, Torrington, and Cheyenne before arriving midmorning in Denver.

At the Union Station in downtown Denver, I asked directions to the University of Denver and was told to take streetcar No. 6. The only problem was, I didn't know how to get on a streetcar. I stood around watching people using tokens and paper passes and wondered where you got them. I finally got up the nerve to ask at a nearby drugstore and was told you buy them from the conductor.

I climbed aboard the wooden streetcar, which rocked and swayed down the rails in the middle of the streets, with electric sparks flying off the overhead power lines like exploding firecrackers. We rolled through neighborhood business districts, residential areas, and industrial centers, past schools and city parks, winding back and forth, and then began looping back toward downtown Denver. No University of Denver was in sight. It was obvious to me that I must have missed it — so I hopped off the streetcar.

I stood around on a quiet street corner in a lovely residential area of green lawns and beautiful flowers, still clinging to my bag and overcoat, until a little old lady asked where I was going. I told her my story and she said, "Get back on streetcar No. 6 and stay on it until you get there. This is a big city, young man, and it will take you a long time to get there." She instructed the conductor to clearly let this Wyoming greenhorn know when I'd reached my destination.

The University of Denver was much larger that I had ever imagined, and it was overrun in 1947 with thousands of veterans returning to college on the G.I. Bill. I finally found the housing office and joined a line that must have contained 2000 people. There I stood, with suitcase and overcoat still in hand, all afternoon. At five o'clock they slammed the window shut. There I was, a homeless person, on my first day in the big city, with no idea where to go.

Having not eaten all day, I was hungry, so I ambled across Evans and University to a corner drugstore for a hamburger and waited until dusk. Then I took my few precious belongings and crawled into some campus bushes, bunched up some autumn leaves, and bedded down for the night, using my soft suitcase as a pillow and my overcoat as a blanket. It never occurred to me that there was anything unusual or illegal about this behavior. The words of my high school graduation speaker rang in my ears: "Making it through college ultimately has nothing to do with money or family connections but commitment — the commitment to do whatever you need to do to make it through."

I was simply doing what I *needed* to do, under these immediate circumstances. I'm sure the campus police wouldn't have agreed with that interpretation of my commitment had they discovered me there, but I was well concealed in my hideaway sleeping nest.

Next morning, I was first in line at the housing office, where I was handed a list of more than 5000 Denver homes that might have rooms for rent. There were no dormitory spaces at all. How I managed from this point on is only a blur in my memory now, but you can well imagine how it probably went.

My first couple of days in college never appeared unusual to me until many years later, when I became chaplain at the University of South Dakota. There I observed how it was supposed to be done. I would watch anxious parents arrive in a van, their freshmen well in hand, pulling a U-Haul trailer loaded with wardrobe, phonographs, record collections, typewriters, personal bedding, golf clubs, and tennis rackets. The parents would camp out at the nearest Holiday Inn for several days, until Johnny or Susie was all moved into a high-rise dormitory and registered for classes, and they wouldn't depart for home until they attended the required orientation sessions for parents and students.

My Wyoming ranching parents never knew that this was the way to get their kid off to college. No one ever told them. Consequently, I never knew any better myself. I had only the *commitment* to do whatever I needed to do to make it through.

In 1965, when I was being interviewed for the position as rector of St. Mark's Episcopal Church, the historic pioneer church of Wyoming, I was asked by a member of the vestry if I believed in miracles. I answered by telling the story of my arrival in Denver, then commenting, "The fact that this Wyoming kid not only survived his first year at a big-city university but remained on campus through two graduate degrees after that is a greater miracle than all the biblical miracles rolled up in one."

They all laughed, but I was dead serious.

My first Denver home was a boardinghouse located in an old home on Franklin Street, close to East Colfax Avenue. This had once been a proud neighborhood of stately old homes but now was in decline. The owner-operator was the cranky and austere Mrs. Brown. There were probably around twenty boarders, all male, crowded onto the second and third floor of the old mansion. Most were DU students. However, my roommate was not. He was a middle-aged man who drove a delivery truck for Denver's prestigious Davis & Shaw Furniture Company. This burly brute of a man had such massive arms and shoulders that he probably could have heaved an upright piano across the Platte River.

His name was Elmer Hicks.

Unfortunately, his intelligence matched his Neanderthal build and looks. This born loser's income barely covered his room and board — plus his Saturday-night drinking binge at a local pub. He had a girlfriend, Tillie, an alcoholic barmaid at the pub. He had no car, and the only place they could find for privacy was our attic bedroom. Therefore, it was necessary for him to give me advance notice of her conjugal visitations. He'd give me a dollar so I could buy myself a late-evening snack at an all-night eatery on East Colfax. One night I came home and found Tillie asleep on my bed.

"Elmer, I don't think this arrangement is working for either of us."

"I know," he said, "but right now, it's the only arrangement I've got."

I made up my mind to take it in stride. This was just another adjustment that a young man needed to make if he had the commitment to make it through college. Besides, I was the newcomer who intruded into Elmer's attic kingdom.

The commitment I had!

The first program I signed up for during university registration was the Reserve Officer Training Corps, simply called ROTC. This was voluntary on my part; the University of Denver was a private college and not required to offer military training. The program was in its first year of operation at DU, and I was the first registrant. I was still enchanted with the idea of someday becoming a military officer. It was thrilling to wear my newly issued uniform. Whatever college major I eventually declared (pre-law and radio management being the leading candidates), I fully expected to honor my two-year postgraduate obligation to serve my country as a young army officer — and possibly to make a career of the military.

In my college courses, for the first time I was intellectually challenged by new ideas, stimulating classroom discussion, and interesting reading assignments. For my government class, I would entrench myself for hours in the mahogany-paneled reading room of the International Studies Library, browsing through the Federalist papers of Alexander Hamilton, James Madison, and John Jay, as well as the writings of Thomas Jefferson and John Stuart Mill and Charles Beard's *Economic Interpretation of the Constitution of the United States.* When my vision became blurred I would push myself away from the large reading desk and gaze out the Gothic window of the Mary Reed Library and say to myself, *If grasping all of this brilliant scholarship is necessary to graduate from college, I don't see how I'll ever make it. But how fortunate I am to be here in such an invigorating environment.* I would then return to my books and try again to understand these theories in a general sense before bogging down in the details. Sometimes, I would cheat and go to the reference library for condensations, then return to the voluminous works and try again. I later learned that this methodology was not cheating, but an acceptable scholarly way to study the works of these intellectual giants.

However, I was haunted with the realization that I was living in two different worlds. Each day I would thrive in the intellectual environment of a great university. Each evening I would return to the dreary atmosphere of my cheap boardinghouse and the desperate shenanigans of Elmer and Tillie.

Every night, after our boardinghouse dinner, Elmer would come up to our room and yank off his white Davis & Shaw coveralls, flop himself down on the bed stark nude, pop open a can of warm beer he had concealed in his closet and proceed to lecture me on the philosophy and morals of the common man. First Elmer would ask me what I was studying, and when I attempted an explanation he would invariably interrupt me with a running diatribe that all this book learning was pure bullshit, a waste of the taxpayer's money, and not at all useful to a real common man like himself.

I noticed, with interest, that his thinking didn't match John Locke's theory of the common man, which I had been earnestly reading. But then, John Locke was a seventeenth-century English writer. Perhaps I needed Elmer's updated 1947 version of the common man's views.

After he wore himself down with his daily lectures, he'd pop open another can of warm beer and picture-gaze himself to sleep with a selection from his private collection of pornographic magazines. This was my first exposure to them.

In many ways this Neanderthal roommate was just the opposite of what a greenhorn college freshman needed. Having a roommate such as Elmer had its advantages, however. First, everyone avoided our room like the plague. After he fell asleep, I had the peace and quiet of the room to myself. Second, in a roundabout way he helped me focus on my work. When my readings were particularly laborious and difficult for me to understand, I would get fed up with intellectual pursuits. But when I heard these same sentiments articulated from the lips of Elmer, then I knew such thoughts must be dead wrong, and I attacked my studies with renewed vigor.

I didn't realize how much college would cost, and I terribly underestimated it. When I was ten years old, Dad deeded me a registered Hereford heifer. I soon accumulated a small prodigy herd, which Dad refused to sell except for the bull calves. I even had my own brand: *Lazy Heart S Bar*. The idea was that by the time I got to college, with postwar prices still relatively high in the livestock market, the income from these cattle would largely pay for my tuition, books, and living expenses. It did cover the basic tuition and books but not room and board. This I had to earn on my own. I had to get a job.

In 1947 Denver's East Colfax Avenue was a chic place for upscale boutique shopping, medical clinics, restaurants, and nightclubs. I soon learned that restaurants and nightclubs always needed part-time help during their busy evening hours, particularly on weekends. I landed myself a Friday and Saturday evening job at the Beacon Supper Club. In those days, supper clubs were particularly attractive. You could eat, drink, dance, and enjoy a lively floor show, all in one place.

Lo and behold, I discovered that the two men who owned and operated the Beacon Supper Club, Jerry Bakke and Willie Hartsell, were the musicians who originally recorded the hit song "Cigarettes and Whiskey and Wild Wild Women." They performed it every night as the grand finale to their stage show. Their wives were also gifted musicians and provided backup support on the electric organ and piano. All four of them performed, with the men rotating through a variety of instruments: guitars, banjo, saxophones, and horns. But the crowd waited for their unique rendition of "Cigarettes and Whiskey and Wild Wild Women." Jerry decked himself out in a horrendous red wig, a ridiculous wraparound sarong, and excessive makeup as he sallied among the tables, smearing his lipstick kisses on the bald-headed men while doing his high-pitched falsetto obbligato aria on the last chorus of the song.

It brought the house down every time. The nightclub patrons would jump to their feet in a standing ovation and cheer for an encore. It was hilarious, I must admit. I never had the nerve to tell them that their famous rendition was chosen as the theme song for my radio program at KDSJ in Deadwood. I felt they would have considered it a put-down.

I washed cocktail glasses and tidied up behind the bar, a unique vantage point from which to observe the strange, pseudo-sophisticated behavior of the customers. The gentlemen all wore pencil-thin mustaches like Clark Gable, and the ladies were decked out like Mae West, striking up glamorous poses for one another. I particularly noticed the affected Hollywood mannerisms of those sitting at the crowded bar, flashing flirtatious "come hither" signals back and forth. The coded body language fascinated me — how they ordered and held their drinks, lit their cigarettes, avoided and then re-established eye contact before finally moving in beside one another for more intimate conversation. I determined that without the use of the cigarette, this courtship ritual would be infinitely more complicated.

I wrote the folks about my new weekend job and Mom responded with warnings of dire consequences for working in such a sinful environment. I think she thought that since the University of Denver had nominal Methodist ties in its early days, that all current professors were retired Methodist ministers — who would be horrified if they saw me there during their night of sinning out on the town. I had been at DU just long enough to know that ministers they were not. I decided it was time to conceal from my parents how I earned my board and keep while attending college. This was another mature step in my grand *commitment* to do whatever I *needed* to do to make it through.

After several weeks as bar boy, I got promoted to salad maker. This was quite a step forward, everyone said. My new job consisted of peeling over 100 pounds of potatoes for the usual nightly rate of consumption. Then I had to cut open and wash dozens of heads of lettuce and prepare the fresh vegetables that went into every salad: green onions, radishes, cucumbers, and sliced tomatoes. It took several hours before I had all the ingredients in place for my night of professional salad making. The chef told me to dump all my trimmings into a neat pile just outside the back door, where later they would be scooped up into a large garbage bin.

I quickly learned how special privilege and payola merge with money and prestige. When a very important person was seated at a table, and the message of his arrival reached my ears from none other than either Jerry or Willie, I was to use a larger bowl and put together an extra-scrumptious salad — a VIP salad. And we had many VIPs, all wanting to hear and see the "Cigarettes and Whiskey and Wild Wild Women" grand finale.

One evening Jerry came bursting through the swinging double doors with the excited announcement that a general at Fitzsimons Army Hospital and his wife had just entered the Beacon Supper Club and were being seated at a table directly in front of the show stage. Two VIP salads were ordered.

I carefully followed the recipe: a large bed of crisp, hand-torn lettuce hearts; extra slices of thick tomatoes; sliced and curled cucumbers; olives and green onions artistically arranged with scallion brushes. On top of the whole concoction sat my greatest work of decorative art: a large *crudit'e radish* feathered into the design of a rose. I was taught the use of a special *crudit'e tool* for this exquisite ornament. Over it all I poured a pungent dressing made from wine taken from the bar. Jerry personally and proudly delivered both VIP salads to the VIP table, ceremoniously serving the general and his wife with all the aplomb appropriate for a U.S. president.

"If we make a great impression on this high-ranking general, just think of all the subordinate officers who'll feel obligated to start coming here," he explained.

Later he appeared in the kitchen and personally supervised the chef's handling of the steaks to make certain they were extra large, extra thick and juicy, cooked slowly to medium-rare perfection. Everything was to be *extra*. The bartender was even instructed to give a boost to the drinks, using only the finest liquor (which was stored in a secret compartment under the bar). It was turning out to be a VIP evening for Jerry and Willie.

As the show commenced, many salads later, Jerry popped through the kitchen doors with the terse announcement that the general's wife had drunk too much and had taken ill. A cab had been called and instructed to drive around to the back kitchen door so as to avoid embarrassing the distinguished guests of honor. The general and his wife were to be escorted through the kitchen and out the back door.

A minute later the entourage appeared, Jerry and Willie on each side of her, gallantly assisting her. She moved unsteadily, her head wobbling back and forth, as they walked her along. Jerry gave me a *come-along* motion to follow them. They sat her outside on a straight-backed wooden chair, assuring the general that soon a cab would discreetly arrive and all would be well.

"Now you watch her," Jerry ordered, speaking to me as he made a hasty retreat back to the stage show that was in full progress.

As I stood there — watching her — I noticed that she was a very attractive middle-aged woman, probably in her forties, just a little bit on the matronly plump side. Her heavy makeup and dangling jewelry seemed a little extravagant. She was of Italian or Hispanic (perhaps Cuban) descent. Her coal black hair, beautifully coiffured earlier in the evening, was now slightly awry. She kept her eyes closed as she sat limply holding herself upright with one arm braced stiffly against the rim of the chair. She was wearing seamed black knit stockings, and her shoes were gilded silver.

Yes, again I must say, a very attractive woman for me to watch. If only she weren't so drunk and so miserably sick.

The general, in the meantime, was angrily pacing back and forth, his wife's expensive fur coat draped across his arm. "This is beginning to happen every time we go out. You know that, don't you?" he griped. "You're not handling your booze very well anymore. You know that, don't you? If word gets out that the general's wife can't handle her booze, and I can't keep it covered up — just think what's gonna happen to my career. You know that, don't you?"

He leaned over to peer into her sullen face, then mumbled, "Yes you do know it, don't you? That's just the son-of-a-bitchin' problem, you don't know that you know it. Goddamn it."

By this time the general was talking pure nonsense. He was as drunk as she but apparently not as sick. Jerry's boosted VIP drinks had hit their mark!

He continued his tirade, but she totally ignored him. She never lifted her head nor opened her eyes nor attempted to make any verbal response. She just sat there, swaying slightly, barely holding herself upright in the chair on her stiffened arm. Suddenly her arm buckled, and she tumbled off the chair right into my garbage pile of potato peelings and vegetable trimmings, which actually cushioned her fall. Her chair crashed to the pavement. I leaped to where she was lying, lifted her to her feet, and started to brush the coffee grounds and scrap lettuce from her beautiful dress. But she couldn't stand upright and collapsed on top of me. There was nothing I could do now but pull her back up to her feet, grab her with both arms around her waist, and hold her tightly as she slumped up against me.

For the first time, she opened her eyes to get a better look at this kid who was holding her, flickered her false eye lashes, and with slurred speech flirtatiously drooled words intended only for her husband's infuriation, "You're kinda cute, you'se know it? . . . I juzzh think I'll just take you'se home wisch me. How would you like that? We'd have a great time. Juzzh you and me . . . forget the ol' bashtard over there. He can juzzh wasch us make love on the floor if he wants to. The ol' bashtard."

She kissed me on the mouth with a drunken slobber that reeked of bourbon. When I tried to turn my face away to ask her husband to please upright the chair — no, to *order* the general to pick up the damn chair so I could put her body back down on it — she grabbed both my ears and twisted them so painfully that I couldn't free myself.

Meanwhile, the general roughly ran his hand through her hair as if examining her scalp and said, "I think maybe she's had a concussion, maybe even a fractured skull." Letting go of her hair and feeling her leg he said, "Maybe she's suffered a broken femur. She broke her ribs during a bad fall at the officer's club one time. Perhaps a broken shoulder bone," he went on.

I could tell by the way she was kissing that she wasn't in any pain. She kept up her act, sensually moaning and groaning for her husband's infuriation, and I knew I had best get myself disengaged or the general would be whopping me across the head with something far more lethal than potato peelings.

About that time the cab pulled up, and the general jumped into the front seat with the driver and began discussing the weather, leaving me to maneuver his wife toward the rear door. I had to drag, pull, and eventually tug her into the back seat — all by myself.

When I finally extracted myself from the back seat and out onto the pavement, slamming the rear door shut as the cab pulled away, there stood Jerry, dressed in full regalia for his grand finale, looking like a Parisian drag queen, flaming red wig and all. He stood with his mouth wide open, aghast.

"I thought I told you to watch her!" he shouted.

My answer surely qualified me as the simpleton of the twentieth century. "You told me to watch her, which I did," I said. "But you didn't tell me to hold onto her in the chair while I watched her."

The incredible stupidity of this remark knocked the wind out of Jerry as surely as if I'd hit him across the chest with a sledgehammer. He staggered a few steps backward, gasped for air, and then turned, holding his wigged head in utter disbelief, and disappeared inside the nightclub.

I went to the kitchen sink to wash up. As I washed coffee grounds and radish toppings out of my hair, while in front of the mirror, I discovered that my lip was bleeding. *I had been wounded. She bit me. The general's wife had bitten my lip. Damn it! Since I was in the ROTC didn't this qualify me for the Purple Heart? After all, this was a military encounter.*

As I went back to my salad making, I heard Jerry's falsetto voice belting out again his famous "Cigarettes and Whiskey and Wild Wild Women," but I had the sinking feeling he could never sing that song quite the same way again.

And I also had the sinking feeling that my life would never be quite the same again either. My worshipful adoration of military officers had just suffered a mortal blow. Maybe, just maybe, it wasn't all that I had cracked it up to be.

I lost my job at the famous Beacon Supper Club, but other jobs like it were easy to find at restaurants and hamburger joints up and down East Colfax Avenue. These jobs were the best for me because I could work weekends, usually evenings, and usually I could snitch a free meal — which was important for this guy, who was always hungry.

✧

In the fall of 1947, I was introduced to the most extraordinary pulpit preacher in Denver. The orator's name was Dr. Kelly O'Neil, and he was the senior pastor of Central Christian Church (Disciples of Christ) in downtown Denver. Every Sunday morning, regardless of how late I had worked the night before, I would roll out of bed, dress up in the only suit of clothes I had, dash up to Colfax, and catch a streetcar to Central Christian Church.

I preferred sitting in the balcony so I could view the pulpit master at work. Everything in the service was either a prelude or a postlude to the sermon. When the hymns, prayers, and choir anthems were finished, it was as if the curtains went up on center stage for the grand act. Everyone settled back into a comfortable position, the chandeliers would dim, and a hushed silence descended across the congregation for the beginning of the great performance.

His bald head shone brightly as he stepped up to the pulpit, adjusted his eyeglasses and with a slow cadence began his sermon. Instead of opening the Bible, he would simply quote the scripture from memory — not just an isolated verse here or there, but many verses all strung together. This man gave the impression that he had committed the entire Bible to memory. His sermon always dealt with some practical issue vitally related to living. Invariably he crowned the sermon with a long poem, beautifully enunciated — and all from memory.

I was enthralled with this kind of captivating pulpit oratory. I always walked out of Central Christian Church on an emotional high of some kind, perhaps a spiritual high, although I hesitated to call it that. I felt I had been lifted up and touched by a power greater than myself and that I was a better person than when I had entered the church. Then I'd find my streetcar and head back to the grim boardinghouse for our Sunday dinner — the only meal served on weekends.

Every Sunday I would do this. And every Sunday Elmer would spend his entire day "recovering," as he described it. I would go back up to my room after dinner and begin reading my college assignments, and he would snore away until evening, when he would rally just enough to settle in for a long night's sleep before returning to work on Monday morning.

One Sunday, as I entered the boardinghouse after church and before dinner, Mrs. Brown met me at the door with the angry demand that I accompany her to her apartment for a private little talk. Sitting opposite me in a matching wing chair, she bluntly asked, "I want to know if it's true or not that Elmer and you are harboring a paramour in your third-floor bedroom."

In Wyoming we'd never heard of such foreign things as *harbors* or *paramours*. The nearest word to a paramour that I've known was parakeet, but I knew that this was not the object of her ire.

"I honestly don't know what you're talking about, Mrs. Brown. What's a paramour?"

Raising her voice, she answered, "A woman of ill repute!"

"Would it make a difference to you if she were a woman of good-repute?" I admit it was a dumb question, but I was stalling for time, because only now did I have an inkling as to where the inquisition was leading.

Indignantly she stiffened herself, then marched me out into the common hallway of the old mansion and pointed to the rules posted on the wall. "Now these are the rules — and they strictly forbid any women beyond the front parlor. Now, to answer your question. No, it wouldn't make a bit of difference to me whether she was a woman of ill repute or good repute. No women of either repute are allowed upstairs — period!"

Looking squarely at me, she said in a high-pitched shriek, "Now don't play dumb with me. The police reported that Tillie is a prostitute who works the taverns along East Colfax, and they followed her here last night. She can work the streets of Denver all she wants, but she's not working out of my house here. I'll have you to know that I operate a first-class boardinghouse here, and I'm not having Elmer and you turn it into a first-class whorehouse!"

The ludicrous insinuation that Tillie was the common property of Elmer and me would have catapulted me into the perpetual sanctuary of a Trappist monastery — had I known there was such an easy way out. Instead, I was mortified, and I could feel the mortification turning my skin purple from the toes up. I had been duped into a Deadwood brothel as a joke. Now here I was, only several months later, being openly accused of operating a whorehouse in Denver — and I was still a pristine virgin!

Before I could conjure up a coherent response to the accusation, a group of fellow boarders, reading the Sunday papers in the front parlor before dinner, poured out into the hallway and leaped to my defense. Leading the pack was a DU law student. "Mrs. Brown you've got the wrong man here," he said. "The man you need to be talking to is conked out in the upstairs attic bedroom where he always sleeps it off every Sunday. He's the one you need to be talking to, not the Wyoming kid here."

Mrs. Brown tried one more time. "But Elmer couldn't have Tillie up there if it wasn't without the complicity of the Wyoming kid. And in my opinion, that's make them both equally guilty."

Me at Mary Reed Library as a DU freshman in 1947. This photo was taken about the time when the general's wife bit me.

The budding lawyer rose to the challenge. "But the Wyoming kid here knows nothing about that. Gene here isn't on the G.I. Bill, like the rest of us. He doesn't get his college expenses paid for by the government like we do. He's having to work his way through college by working nights at the hamburger joints along Colfax Avenue. And while he's out working his tail end off to pay tuition at DU and your exorbitant rates here at the boardinghouse, Elmer slips his concubine up the backstairs into their attic bedroom. The kid here isn't playing dumb about that because he honestly doesn't know anything about Tillie and Elmer."

Which, of course, wasn't exactly true. But since when does a lawyer have to tell the whole truth when defending a client in deep trouble?

I also resented their referring to me as "the Wyoming kid" but wisely decided to leave well enough alone. Now my public defender was waxing eloquent: "The kid here has just returned from church. As far as I can tell, he's the only one among the boarders here, including you, Mrs. Brown, who's been to church this morning. A fine, upstanding, young moral Christian young man like this" — pointing to me, as if to remind everyone that I was the saint whose virtues he was exaggerating before proceeding to the heart of his legal defense, "He doesn't need to come home from worshipping the Lord to the accusation that he's running a whorehouse. The sins of Elmer Hicks are not on the soul of Gene Todd to be rooted out by you, Mrs. Brown! You owe this kid a public apology."

I'll give Mrs. Brown credit, the poor woman knew when she was whipped. Surrounded now by a dozen of her jury-boarders, all mumbling their amens of moral agreement with the public defender, she apologized profusely and then stormed upstairs where we could hear her pounding on Elmer's door. Within the hour, Elmer Hicks was gone. I never saw him again.

The next morning, back at the DU library, I pushed my books aside and gazed out the windows upon the campus quadrangle, so beautifully landscaped and aglow with autumn colors. I didn't know which accusation was more offensive — that of operating a first-class whorehouse or being a Christian. This was the first time in my life that I had ever been called a Christian. True, I enjoyed hearing the powerful sermons of a pulpit orator, but this hardly made me a Christian. The Baptist lay preachers back at Ucross certainly wouldn't have defined me as a saved, born-again Christian, and frankly, I was relieved to be spared the definition.

That I had a religious inclination or a private spiritual bent I would freely admit — as evidenced by my solitary sojourns in the hill country of our family ranch and in my personal journals, which I had always destroyed. But I had never put a religious label upon it, and I resented being called a Christian at this point in my life. I wasn't sure I liked it. It conjured up too many negative images for me.

Having been defended as a Christian among my fellow boarders meant that I also had been *indicted* as one. Hence, I needed to look for a more wholesome place to live.

Fortunately for me, a new friend came into my life. His name was Pete Tomte. He was a former pilot with the Army Air Corps, a young first lieutenant, attending DU as an architectural student on the GI Bill. His military background naturally impressed me. Additionally, he had a car, which meant easy transportation in the big city.

We rented a basement room in a stately old home located at the corner of Lafayette and Seventh Avenue in Denver's Capitol Hill area. The apartment was spacious but had no cooking facilities. It contained a large circular oak dining room table, which was perfect for a couple of students. I could spread out all my books and papers on my half without disturbing him. However, he spent most of his time bent over a drawing board, working on architectural designs. Our landlords, Mr. and Mrs. Johnson, were an elderly couple who continually reminded us that they had been people of considerable means before losing their fortune in the bank crash of 1929. I think this was probably true, because elegant and beautiful furnishings graced the top floors of the old house.

One evening, upon returning from my DU classes, I noticed an antique electric car being driven repeatedly around the block. The driver, a middle-aged, ruddy-faced gentleman, beamed from ear to ear and waved at me while honking the strange-sounding horn. I sat down on the front steps and waved back as he continued encircling the block.

Mrs. Johnson came out onto the porch and asked, "Do you know who that gentleman is that's driving that little electric car and who keeps waving at you?"

"No, I've never seen him before," I answered.

"Well you may not have seen him before in person, but you know all about him. That is General Dwight Eisenhower!"

I gasped, and she continued, "Mrs. Dowd, Mamie Eisenhower's mother, lives in the next block up Lafayette Street there — the house with the old-fashioned hitching post out in front of it. Whenever the Eisenhowers visit Mrs. Dowd, which is often, the general enjoys driving her antique electric car around and around the block. And that's him you see out there."

Here was a five-star army general, the supreme allied commander of the liberation forces of Europe and a future president of the United States, wheeling his little vehicle around the block, tooting its horn and waving at me like a kid with a newfound toy.

This second brief encounter with a military general was much more pleasant than the first.

The basement room at Lafayette and Seventh Avenue was considerably cheaper than my boardinghouse quarters. It was cheaper because Pete and I didn't eat. No cooking was allowed, but it was too expensive to eat out. We had to compromise by shopping every day at a little market on Sixth Avenue for a few slices of cheese and bologna, which we used to make sandwiches back in our room. There was no refrigeration, so we couldn't keep any perishables on hand. Eventually we sneaked a little hot plate behind the furnace, where we'd warm up a can of soup and slurp it right out of the can. Pete's sister loaned him a small electric percolator for making coffee or brewing hot tea. Our eating arrangement was not very good. But, echoing Elmer, we had to say, "Right now, it's the only arrangement I've got!"

Our biggest problem was that we were broke most of the time. My weekend jobs helped out a little. An African American classmate named Leon recruited us for a temporary job as special banquet waiters at the Brown Palace Hotel. When we got there we discovered that we were the only Caucasians among the thirty or forty blacks assembled to serve a large Republican fund-raising dinner in honor of U.S. Senator Robert Taft, a presidential aspirant. We donned white jackets and black bow ties for the auspicious occasion. When the bell rang, we special waiters were to gather up our huge trays and make a grand fanfare entry into the ballroom with serving trays high aloft. Neither Pete nor I could maneuver the trays to our shoulders and tote them out on balanced hand. That takes practice. So we brought up the end of the line tugging one tray between us. Poor Leon had to load us up in the kitchen and download us at the tables.

It didn't take long for the maitre d' to conclude that we were washouts as banquet waiters. He fired us between the main course and dessert. The hotel couldn't risk scalding a presidential candidate with our carefree style of slinging hot coffee. Even I would concede that we were as dangerously inept as special banquet waiters as any of them would have been driving a horse-drawn bundle wagon on a Wyoming threshing crew.

Once in a while we would visit a downtown pub for a beer, and I would try out my new courting skills with the single women. I had even taken up cigarette smoking specifically for that purpose. Not much luck befell either of us. Pete went along with my suggestion that we try a country music dance hall because country people were more fun. We found one called 20th Street Corral just off Larimer Street, which at that time was Denver's skidrow area.

There I learned a powerful sociological lesson: City people's perception of country folk didn't match the reality I knew. No one at a Wyoming country dance would have been caught dead in the outlandish Roy Rogers outfits these city dudes were wearing. Men were dressed like rhinestone cowboys and danced with their hats on. Women wore fringe leather jackets and short skirts exposing their multicolored cowboy boots, with lavish hairdos and makeup that would have shamed the harlots of Deadwood.

But the girls who knew the country steps that I knew were good on the dance floor. Pete remained at our table, glum and dejected, because he didn't know the dances. I told him, "They're good dancers, but I wouldn't want to take them home to meet my mother."

"Believe me, Gene," he mumbled, "that's not where they want you to take them."

When a booth of country burlesque queens invited us to their table for drinks and to their apartment for a "little party" afterward, Pete wisely warned me that although we were desperate, neither of us could afford the luxury of such debauchery.

So much for country dancing in the big city!

Later we started attending Friday night dances at Colorado Women's College. These were great. We met beautiful and cultured young women. I was even invited to escort one the night she was crowned beauty queen. But Pete and I were so broke we couldn't afford anything more on a date than a casual walk in the park. Our finances were getting desperate, indeed — and we were getting hungry.

The decision was made that we would move again, this time to a basement apartment with cooking facilities only ten walking blocks from the DU campus. I would live at this address on South Downing Street for the remainder of my college career.

✧

In the summer of 1948 I returned to KDSJ in Deadwood for another three-month fling at radio announcing. It's a summer I shall never forget. Tourists thronged the brick streets and mobbed the restaurants, bars, and nightclubs. The fake gun battle re-enacted regularly on Main Street for the "Trial of Jack McCall," who murdered Wild Bill Hickock in 1876, was a real attention-getter. I rented a room on Third Street — that is, three flights of stairs up from Main Street — looking down on the roofs of the buildings directly below. Pine scented the early morning air as I made my way to the radio studio in the Franklin Hotel for my daily six o'clock program.

That summer I witnessed firsthand an encounter between Christian fundamentalists and the entrenched political power structure of Deadwood. Two evangelical preachers connived a novel scheme to force the gospel upon an unwilling city. (As I have said, Deadwood is located in a narrow mountain gulch where gold was discovered in the 1870s by General Custer.) They mounted large public address speakers on top of their cars, parked high atop Cemetery Ridge directly above the town, turned up the volume and blasted everyone into smithereens with their condemnation of the wickedness that was openly practiced in Deadwood's den of inequity — prostitution, gambling, drinking, and everything else.

The preaching reverberated off the canyon walls, bouncing back and forth on everyone's nerves until a chorus of complainants demanded action from the city fathers. The police tried to shut them down on grounds that their excessive noise was disturbing the peace. The preachers countered that loud speakers used in connection with the fake gun battle of Jack McCall on Main Street were equally offensive and constituted a public nuisance. The battle lines were drawn between the forces of darkness and sin on the one hand and the forces of light and goodness on the other.

I got caught in the middle because the preachers bought time at KDSJ every morning to defend their position. Truman Walrod, the station manager, always found an excuse to be out of town during their broadcasts. He gave me strict orders to keep my hands on the control board and cut them off the air every time they became too aggressive and obnoxious in their self-defense.

A restraining order was issued until the matter could be resolved in court. Knowing the power structure of Deadwood as I did, the preachers didn't have a chance. And I'm glad they didn't. To have won the right to offend the public with their version of the Gospel would have been a hallow victory, indeed. But I learned something from the fray. Although I respected the spiritual fervor of the preachers and their good intentions, I didn't respect their means of attaining it. It trivialized and scandalized the Christian faith, making it that much easier for cynics to seriously dismiss religion as an object of mockery.

But the main reason the summer of 1948 was one I shall never forget is that for the first time in my life I fell in love.

She was to me the most beautiful girl in all the Black Hills. And, miracle of miracles, she fell in love with me. Her name was Norma Jean. She worked as a hostess in the Bodega restaurant. (Remember, it was on the third floor of the Bodega that I visited my first brothel the summer before. I want to make it plain, however, that the Bodega restaurant on the ground floor had no connections with the activities that flourished on third floor.)

I had matured beyond group dates. I didn't want to share a date with another couple, not even if they had a car. I would rather walk than share a ride with someone else just so I could be alone with my date. As a dining room hostess, Norma would often work past midnight. But that made no difference. I would hop out of bed and walk her home, then sit out on the front porch until the sun rose, when I'd dash back to the KDSJ studios for the six o'clock show.

Occasionally, we did things with other couples. We'd take midnight swims in the cold mountain lakes of the Black Hills or dance to the music of the big touring bands at the large open-air pavilion in Lead. But we preferred being alone. The people who owned the home in which I rented a bedroom took a long vacation to California and left me in charge. This proved wonderfully convenient.

In early September Norma even accompanied me on my first commercial flight, from Rapid City to Sheridan. I took her to the Todd ranch. We rode horseback in the daytime and hiked alone into the hills at night. We husked sweet corn in the field across the creek, shelled newly picked peas from the garden, and dug fresh potatoes for Mom's dinner table at night. Norma tried milking a cow for the first and only time in her life. Even the most mundane chores on the ranch were buoyed with the passion that only comes when one is young and in love for the first time. It was pure ecstasy.

I was to learn, however, that you can't have the ecstasy of love without its agony. Returning to the grinding loneliness of the University of Denver was the last thing in the world I wanted to do. At the same time, I knew that I must. Though I was insane with love, a few strands of practical wisdom plunged me back into reality. The image of that little boy trudging through crusted snow in the beet field on a cold Christmas Eve would come floating back to haunt me. Only I could exercise the choices, and make the sacrifices, to become what I ultimately wanted to become.

Another image terrified me — the one of the alcoholic gandy in Clearmont, before walking off into oblivion, mumbling, *Goin' nowhere . . . Been goin' there a long time.*

There was no way I could get married and finish college at the same time. Marriage would have to wait.

So back to Deadwood went Norma. Back to the University of Denver went I, returning to the basement apartment on Downing Street. Pete and I shared the space with two other men, both from Livingston, Montana: Jim Shadoan and Herb Brawner. In our lives we meet many people and develop both casual acquaintances and permanent friendships. These people are important and, when woven together, form a pattern of great meaning. Meeting Jim and Herb became a pivotal event in my life. They helped trigger a series of events that permanently shaped the future direction of my life.

Jim and Herb were several years older than I. Both were bachelors. Jim attended DU in the same sophomore class as I. Herb was already a graduate engineer beginning a new job at Gates Rubber Company.

The two-bedroom basement apartment, shared by the four of us, was perilous, with heat provided by dangerous little gas burners (nonventilated) in each room. Our kitchen was our landlord's basement utility room. A lot of living took place in this one multipurpose room: cooking, showering, shaving, and eating — even the toilet was located here. The dual laundry tubs were excellent places to do our own laundry, wash our dishes, and shave. We'd put a board across it to serve as a counter when preparing meals. The whole arrangement was pretty primitive and unworkable, but somehow we made it work. I find it hard to believe that I lived there for the rest of my college days at the University of Denver.

All four of us chipped in a certain amount each week for food, and we took turns grocery shopping, cooking, and doing the dishes. Eventually, I became the primary cook because I preferred this chore over trying to eat the concoctions others attempted to make. I would do the daily shopping at a little corner grocery store (we had no refrigerator, only an ice box). Everyone else was only too glad to do the dishes and tidy up the kitchen afterward. Occasionally I might be invited out for a meal with a Denver family or with other students in their apartment. Rarely after moving to South Downing did I ever eat in a restaurant.

I settled in for my second year of college. I would walk to campus, about a mile away, for my morning classes, walk back for lunch and return for afternoon classes. Usually there was an evening class as well. These three round trips amounted to six miles of walking a day, but it was good exercise and I thought nothing of it, except when it was bitterly cold.

Jim invited me to attend services at First Baptist Church with him. I wasn't much interested. I remembered too well the well-intentioned Baptist lay preachers back at my country school at Ucross, Wyoming, who tried to terrorize me into a conversion. I also remembered the fundamentalist preachers at Deadwood who mounted loudspeakers on their car and blasted the little gold mining town below. I wanted no more of that. Besides, I was now passionately in love and didn't want religion interfering with my love life.

But Jim was persistent, "Gene, it really isn't what you think it is. This is an American Baptist, not a fundamentalist-type Baptist church that you've bitterly experienced before. This is quite different, believe me. Come give it a try."

Only because a friend kept inviting me did I eventually decide I would give it a try. First Baptist Church of Denver is located directly across the street from the Colorado State Capitol. It was a stately colonial edifice, just as lovely and dignified on the inside as on the outside. There were no little campfire ditties being sung with a song leader flapping his arm while directing the congregational singing. A thunderous pipe organ brought forth the compositions of Bach, Mozart, and Beethoven, and the choir performed glorious anthems.

A vested choir marched up the aisle, followed by the pastor, Dr. Erdmann Smith, attired in a formal cutaway frock coat and striped gray trousers. He had a powerful baritone speaking voice that carried to every corner of the large auditorium. His first sermon, I remember clearly, was an appeal to the liberal American Baptists to reject the anti-intellectualism of the fundamentalist Christians, including too many Baptists, who eschewed scholarly biblical studies.

He preached, "Anytime a Christian must close his mind to the latest scientific facts of the universe, or shut down his thinking to the most current scholarship, or close off his heart from the great art and music of the world, he is then rejecting the image of God in which he was created."

I was impressed.

That evening Jim invited me to join him in attending a young adult fellowship, which consisted mostly of college students and young working adults of Denver. They were friendly. But I was noncommittal.

In the meantime Norma Jean and I maintained a heavy exchange of love letters. It was decided that I would come to Deadwood for part of my Christmas vacation before heading back to the Todd ranch. Jim Shadoan decided to visit his sister, who lived just outside of Deadwood, so we both took the train up through the Black Hills.

It was a memorable trip as the train slowly wound its way through the wintry mountain passes of deep snow and ranching meadows, and because of the continuous curving railroad roadbed the puffing steam locomotive was almost always in full view out our coach window, first to the left and then to the right. There was no diner on the train, but a steward brought us a tray of sandwiches and a large two-gallon pot of coffee. Since there were so few passengers aboard, he joined Jim and me in our seats while we chatted the afternoon away.

The train chugged into Deadwood at dusk, and thus began a weeklong vacation I will never forget. Deadwood was even more charming in the winter, with banks of snow along the narrow streets and the lovely pines clinging to the canyon walls. The holiday decorations made it look like a picturesque Christmas card. I returned home for Christmas, but Norma came up to Sheridan for a fantastic New Year's Eve dance in Buffalo. It was the last country dance I would ever attend in Wyoming. The townspeople and ranching folk, young and old, melted together in a single celebration. The dance floor was packed when the midnight whistle blew at the fire station announcing that the new year of 1949 was upon us, and merry pandemonium erupted. I wondered what the new year would bring to Norma and me.

I soon found out.

First, the infamous blizzard of 1949. I drove Norma, my sister Sadie, and her boyfriend up to the highway to catch the bus to their various destinations. The cold was so bitter that the radiator of Dad's car froze — even with the motor running. After the bus picked them up, Jim Shadoan and I had to thaw out the car before driving down to Clearmont to catch the train to Denver. The train never came.

Fortunately, we had a place to stay in Clearmont. We tried the next day and the day after that — still no train. The blizzard was so severe that roads and railroad tracks were completely shut down. We finally got word that Norma, Sadie, and Don were holed up in Newcastle, where, fortunately, they found a home in which to stay. Then we heard startling reports that the Union Pacific passenger trains were stalled in southern Wyoming, with emergency relief crews trying to reach the stranded victims.

The notorious blizzard of 1949 stands as one of the most talked-about natural disasters of the century in the Rocky Mountain West. Steam locomotives and homes were completely buried in the drifts, and highway crews worked weeks opening up the roads for travel again.

A week later, Jim and I managed a frigid ride on the Salt Creek Bus Line from Buffalo to Casper. Out of Casper we took the train to Cheyenne and learned that the Burlington Railroad rented the Union Pacific tracks into Denver.

The exterior of the train was so heavily coated with ice that the brakeman couldn't secure the doors until they used axes to chisel them free. The steam lines froze which plunged our passenger cars into frigid ice boxes. As the train slowly made its way down across the plains of northern Colorado we were told to observe the livestock out in the fields, strung out along the fences and bunched up into the corners — standing erect and frozen stiff!

Ferocious winds would blow the snow all over the place, and the roads would shut as quickly as snowplows opened them up. It was a frightful experience for everyone who lived through it.

Even more devastating to me, however, was the cooling of my romance. The more I moved along through college, the more Norma and I drifted apart socially and psychologically. But not emotionally — at least, not for me. That was the problem, I couldn't let go emotionally, even when she informed me in October 1949 that she had given up on waiting for me to finish college and had fallen in love with another man. It was one of the worst devastations I have ever had to survive.

Winter feeding of cattle during monthlong Christmas vacation of 1949-1950 when I had to manage the ranch alone with the help of a hired man. Using a horse-drawn hayrack wagon we could buck the deep snowdrifts.

The Christmas vacation of 1949-1950 came just in time. Dad had taken a bad fall at the ranch and was confined to the house with a shoulder cast. Lewis was away, and so was my older brother Roger, who normally lived on the place. I found myself completely responsible for the operation of the ranch during that Christmas vacation. The folks sent me to Sheridan to hire a man to help. It turned out to be bitterly cold that winter, with snowdrifts so deep that we could barely bust through them with a team of horses pulling a hayrack stacked with hay to feed the cattle.

The astonishing thing was, I was in charge!

While running the ranch, I'd roll out of the sack at six in the morning to milk the cows, do the chores, harness the horses, feed the cattle, chop water holes through the ice in the creek, haul extra feed and straw into the hayloft, clean out the barns, and do the evening chores. If there was an hour to spare, we did a little rough carpentry in the cow barn. Dad was nearby in the house if I needed advice, but if something was physically to get done, I had to get it done.

It was a miserable Christmas, in sharp contrast to the unforgettable holiday only one year earlier. But the responsibility for running the ranch during this Christmas vacation probably preserved my sanity. There was simply too much hard work to be done to think about my broken romance. Somewhere in my collection of papers I have a wonderful letter from Mom thanking me for taking charge of the ranch. She wrote, "I know that you wanted to go to Deadwood to be with Norma this Christmas. Instead, you came home to help us out, and we are very grateful. Both your Dad and I are proud of the way you managed the place, which proves you've come a long way."

That was the nearest they could come to expressing shock that I had matured at all. College must be doing me some good, after all. My parents certainly would never have entrusted me with the ranch before. What I find remarkable about Mom's letter, however, is that I hadn't even revealed to her that my romance with Norma was over. I was so secretive about my broken love affair that even my folks didn't know that something was terribly wrong.

I generally kept my emotions to myself, even when I returned to Denver. Pete dropped out of the architectural school at DU and returned to the University of Arizona. Jim Shadoan moved to a private apartment closer to the downtown campus of the University of Denver. Herb Brawner moved in with me. This was fortunate, because Herb was exactly the kind of a roommate I needed. He was about six years older than I, born and raised on a Montana cattle ranch, with a background very similar to my own. He was a devout Baptist but not a fanatic about it. He had a car and insisted that I accompany him to services at First Baptist in spite of my reluctance to do so.

The only person I really talked to about my broken love affair was a fellow DU student by the name of Bryan, with whom I worked at Montgomery Ward. I worked late every Friday evening until around ten o'clock and then all day Saturday until closing time at five. Usually I clerked in the shoe or hardware departments. I really didn't enjoy retail salesmanship, but it was a steady job.

I could discuss my personal pain with Bryan because I felt less vulnerable with someone I didn't intimately know. He was a good listener and soon began sharing some of his experiences with me. His problems seemed even worse than mine. We usually talked during lunch breaks or late Friday nights in a nearby coffeehouse after closing time. When I returned to selling shoes at Montgomery Ward after Christmas vacation in January 1950, Bryan did not return to work. When I investigated, I discovered that he had committed suicide during the holidays.

Again, Herb Brawner was my rock of Gibraltar. He was a man of Christian faith who never resorted to sanctimonious judgment of others. He had a dry and subtle sense of humor. He was hotblooded enough to go looking for a girlfriend and he took me along. His luck was better than mine, however, for he soon found the sweetheart of his life, a very attractive Southern Baptist nurse we met at church who loved to smoke and dance. Her name was Nina. Whenever we picked up Nina, Herb would automatically hand me the car keys and say, "You take over." And I chauffeured them all over Denver for the next two years. It was a wonderful trade-off for me, because I learned more about the city of Denver and its night spots than I could have otherwise. After Herb and Nina were married, I often accompanied them to church and social events because their car provided the transportation I so desperately needed.

I earned enough at Montgomery Ward that I could afford Saturday night dates, but I didn't have enough money to buy a secondhand car. With another full year of college still ahead of me — and many more if I went to law school — anything more than casual dating was completely out of the question.

To supplement my income a little bit, Jim Shadoan and I took to washing dishes on Wednesday nights at the First Baptist Church for several dollars and a free meal. These church dinners normally served from 100 to 200 people. I also took a part-time job in the afternoons delivering groceries out of a little neighborhood store located just around the corner off South Downing. The car was so decrepit that it had no flooring on the driver's side and was missing a window on the passenger side. But the grocer gave me permission to use the car sparingly for my own social purposes as long as I kept it filled with gas. When it rained my pant legs would get soaked from the wet pavement. However, if it was a warm dry evening and my date didn't mind the abundance of fresh air, the thing worked fine.

✧

I spent the summer of 1950 as a full-time soldier at Fort Lewis, Washington. During my three years of college at DU — I had faithfully attended ROTC classes and participated in close-order drills on the campus greens.

Upon completion of my first two years, I was issued my officer's uniform and began drawing a monthly military paycheck of $27.50. This may not seem like much today, but back in 1950 my share of the apartment rent was $25 a month.

My ROTC summer camp at Fort Lewis was much as I expected — rain, early morning calisthenics, endless hours of close-order drills, many classes, more rain, parade marches, twenty-mile hikes in combat boots, more rain, overnight camps in pup tents awash with rainwater, barrack inspections, KP duty, target practice on the rifle range, mess hall grub, and all-night guard duty. But the less pleasant assignments were punctuated with wonderful dances in the officers' club with coeds recruited from nearby cities and bused in for the occasion. It gave us a glimpse of what being a commissioned officer might be like, and this, of course, was exactly their intention.

While on maneuvers one afternoon, we were all assembled in an open field. Our ROTC commanding officer, a colonel, announced that President Truman had just ordered U.S. military involvement in the Korean conflict. Depending on how that war developed, he said, there was a very good chance that we would all be called to active duty as second lieutenants.

ROTC summer cadet at Fort Washington in 1950.

I must admit I felt a glimmer of exhilaration with the news. Ever since my boyhood days during World War II, I had been obsessed with serving my country as a military officer. I still found the idea compelling. However, I also experienced a profound sense of disillusionment with the peacetime army at Fort Lewis. We ROTC cadets observed outright lying and cover-ups of people's foibles. Particularly galling to me was the pervasive military attitude: "As I take the guff from above, so I dish it out below."

There were moments of professional class among the officers, however. A group of top-ranking generals came to participate in retirement ceremonies for the commanding general of Fort Lewis. Among them were generals of World War II distinction, such as General Mark Clark. This entourage was chauffeured around the sprawling military complex in special limousines, each bearing on its fender a little blue flag containing the number of stars the highest-ranking general carried on his shoulder. It was quite impressive.

While out on maneuvers one day as a member of the quartermaster corps, I was assigned to a hillside perch to observe a group of artillery cadets taking target practice with the big guns. The exercise wore on with not much excitement until a young artillery officer misinterpreted his orders and fired away. The monstrous gun roared, making the earth shake and blasting a hole in the valley floor, shooting up a cloud of sand and dust so thick the target was totally obscured from view.

We focused our binoculars on the target area and waited patiently for the dust to clear. When it did, we saw to our horror that directly in the middle of ground zero was a shiny military limousine with a blue flag on each fender filled with many white stars!

There was no sign of life whatsoever.

The major in command quickly pulled us together into a little huddle and, with incredible emotional restraint, began an unforgettable speech.

"It has been a good career," he said, deliberately calming his quivering voice. "I started out to be a lawyer, you know, but before I graduated from college World War II came along and I enlisted as a private. I was later recruited for OCS and worked my up through the ranks until I am now a major hoping to serve out my time until retirement, not really knowing what my wife and I might want to do after that. We have been real ambivalent about that."

He cleared his throat while regaining his composure. "Gentlemen, I want to thank you for removing all this ambivalence out of my life. I will not have to worry about that anymore. After what has just happened here today — killing more high-ranking American generals in one blast than died in all of World War II — I will surely be court-martialed and spend the rest of my life inside a military prison. No more ambivalence for me. I will now bid you farewell and go down to the scene of mayhem to see how many generals we've blown to kingdom come."

Glancing down into the dust cloud once more, he could see the command car, its blue flag of white stars still gently fluttering in the breeze as if in meek surrender. And still no sign of life. The major shuddered, and his face turned ashen white. He started down the slope, then paused and turned back toward us with his final orders, gesturing as he spoke, "Whatever you do, don't shoot. Unless you see me standing off by myself, waving both arms above my head. That means the situation is far worse than what I expected. In that case, gentlemen, train your sights on me and fire away — and goddamn it, don't you miss!"

Not many people could be so professionally cool under such enormous pressure. Without one word of condemnation nor accusation, he had reprimanded us so severely that we could scarcely talk.

Fortunately, there were no generals in the limousine. The terrified driver, running late after visiting a pub, took what he thought was a short-cut through the artillery range and almost got himself killed. Both the major and driver were only too happy to agree that neither would report on the errancy of the other.

I returned to the Todd ranch in northern Wyoming in the finest state of physical and emotional health that I have ever known. I had gained a few pounds at Fort Lewis. I was suntanned, rainlogged, and feeling wonderfully alive. I even enjoyed working on the ranch for the few weeks of summer that remained before I began my senior year at the University of Denver. The folks had a hired ranch hand by the name of Bower Whittington. We were about the same age. We would work side by side each day out in the hay fields, but on weekends we would head for the night spots in Sheridan and Buffalo. A new supper club opened up just east of Buffalo, and a great little band played there every Saturday night. Dressed up in our western shirts, tight Levi's, and shiny boots, we'd dance the night away with any woman we could find at the bar. Then we'd order a steak sandwich in a basket of french fries with a bottle of beer before heading back to the ranch.

In September 1950 I ushered at my sister Sadie's wedding to Don Dexter at the First Baptist Church in Buffalo. Then I returned to my senior year of studies at Denver University. My younger brother, Lewis, enrolled as a freshman at the University of Denver and began training to become an airline pilot. But he soon found college not to his liking and dropped out.

For some reason, my senior courses that fall proved to be particularly difficult. I had to hit the books and study especially hard. I was also student teaching, a requirement toward getting a teaching certificate in the event I had to support myself by teaching a few years before I entered law school. I was not properly focused on choosing a life profession, and I felt myself floundering in confusion. I knew I would soon have to make a career choice.

Somewhere, in the midst of all this confusion, my life took a religious turn. No longer was the church simply an object of curiosity; it was now an instrument of faith. I went forward one Sunday morning at First Baptist and made a public profession of faith in Jesus Christ as my Lord and Savior. I had no idea, of course, where this profession might lead me. Had I known, I probably wouldn't have done it.

Even though I made a public profession of faith in Christ, my commitment was to the Lord, not necessarily to the Baptist denomination. I liked the First Baptist Church of Denver. I liked the formality of the worship services, the great choral music with its classical bent and the absence of religious fanaticism. Even more important, I liked the people who worshiped there and the young adults I came to know. Their religious devotion superseded the frenzied extremism so often associated with the Baptists I had previously known. Most of all, I appreciated the scholarly preaching of Dr. Erdmann Smith. He was a liberal theologian who scorned fundamentalism.

I reflected on the two styles of preaching in Denver that had profoundly influenced me. First there was Dr. Kelly O'Neil at Central Christian Church, whose biblical preaching was poetic and spellbinding — something like listening to a great symphony. Then there was Dr. Erdmann Smith, whose biblical preaching was scholarly and intellectual — something like listening to a great lecture. When I put the two together, they touched both my heart and my head, and I was converted to the Christian faith.

One crisp autumn evening I invited a friend to accompany me to the DU observatory to watch an eclipse of the moon. Bill and I walked to the observatory and listened to an astronomer's lecture, then peered up through the giant telescope and saw the magnified lunar surface for the first time. It was explained that the eclipse was a special opportunity to see the craters of the moon because we could watch the earth's shadow creep through their crevices much like the sun moves across the Grand Canyon. It was truly spectacular. I found the heavens awesome and inspirational.

Walking through the residential neighborhood where the observatory was located, we came upon a little Gothic church and decided to peek inside. A sanctuary lamp flickered shadows across the white stone walls, and a pungent scent of incense permeated the interior, replacing the musty smell of most empty churches I had known. We walked down toward the front, where I picked up the fragrance of fresh flowers on the altar, reminding me of the Wyoming hills in the springtime, when the whiff of sage mingled with blossoms of the wild plum trees.

"What kind of a church do you suppose this is?" Bill asked.

"I have no idea," I answered, "but it sure seems like a holy place doesn't it?" He nodded.

At that moment, an elderly priest entered the church from a side door carrying a lighted candle, which illuminated a face of deep wrinkles and a head of white hair. We startled him but quickly assured him we were only students who had been to the observatory and had simply dropped in to visit the church.

"What denomination is this anyway?" we asked.

"Episcopal," he answered. "I invite you into my study in the adjoining room to have a cup of tea with me and we'll talk about it." We followed behind as he led us into what actually was a small living room filled with antique furniture and a baby grand piano. The walls were lined with books, which gave it the appearance of a library. He introduced himself as Father Layman and tried to explain that this little church, called St. Mary's, represented the high church tradition, the Anglo-Catholic liturgical practice, within the larger Episcopal Church of America. I tried to follow his explanation but lacked a clear understanding of what he was trying to tell us.

Instead of tea, he poured us some sherry, sat at the piano, and began playing a classical piece. It sounded lovely and enchanting. As he played away I thought to myself: *This is wonderful. Truly wonderful. Sitting here in this room filled with antique furniture and books, listening to classical piano played by an old saintly priest at the keyboard while sipping a glass of sherry wine — this is the closest I've come to anything resembling what I've always been searching for within a religious context. Music, books, faith, fresh flowers, and good wine — all mingled with the love of God and grounded in the goodness of His creation! Yes, this is what I've been yearning for in a church.*

This was my first experience of the Episcopal Church.

I wanted more of a good thing. The following Sunday I made my first appearance at Father Layman's St. Mary's Anglo-Catholic Church. The liturgy was beyond my understanding and comprehension. Parishioners tried to help me find my way through the prayer book but to no avail.

Over the next few months, I would slip out of First Baptist after the service began and sneak over to St. John's Episcopal Cathedral at Twelfth and Washington. I detected a slight liturgical resemblance to St. Mary's — both used the same prayer book, for example. But, oh, how magnificent the pageantry, grandeur, and power of the larger cathedral service.

I took venison steaks from Wyoming over to Father Layman and discovered he had a new assistant, a young curate just graduated from seminary. His name was Jim Mote, and I later attended his ordination to the priesthood. I talked with him about my religious quest, my rich friendship in the Baptist Church, my recent profession of faith, the two great

Denver preachers I was admiring, and most of all my favorable impression of the wonderful services at St. John's Episcopal Cathedral.

I was shocked to learn from him that almost everything I admired about the cathedral services was dead wrong. His dogmatic objections could be summarized as follows: *If they claim to be Protestant Episcopal, as they say, then let them become Protestants and quit calling themselves Episcopal.* Then he told me exactly what I would be *required* to believe if I intended to become an Episcopalian. It sounded far too Catholic and radical for me to accept. His views had the same rigid judgmentalism that I detested in Protestant fundamentalism. He displayed a religious fanaticism that disturbed me. I was severely disappointed and went back to First Baptist to hear the great scholarly preaching of Dr. Erdmann Smith.

I came later to know Father Mote much better, and I now realize that what he said was sincere from a narrow theological point of view. The problem was, he didn't tell me that this doctrinal point of view, the Anglo-Catholic liturgical tradition, was not necessarily shared by all Episcopalians. Had he done so, I'm convinced that I would have attended confirmation classes at the cathedral and probably would have become an Episcopalian right then.

But it didn't happen that way. Unfortunately, later in life, Jim Mote's theological rigidity made it impossible for him to remain within the fold of the Episcopal Church, and he was martialed out. He claimed to the bitter end, like all religious fanatics, that it was he who was right and all others who were wrong — that it was the rest of Anglicanism that was out of step with the Lord, and not he.

✧

I finished all my required courses at DU a quarter early. At spring break, around Easter, I was already a college graduate. I had applied and been admitted to the University of Denver School of Law. During spring break I stayed in Denver to tidy up my affairs with the university. One day I did some work in the yard and, still wearing wet Levi's with holes in the knees, I decided to drop off my certificate of completion to the ROTC headquarters.

The major looked over my files and said, "I think you're all done with your requirements. According to regulations we have some leeway with students who graduate early. I'll call the colonel right now and have him come over for your commissioning."

"But, as you can see, sir," I said, "I'm not in dress uniform. I'm not prepared nor appropriately dressed for the commissioning ceremony."

"Don't need to be," was the curt answer.

The colonel burst into the room from a golf game, invited the other officers to come in as witnesses, and proceeded to commission me as an officer in the U.S. Army. Without a military uniform, there was no way they could pin the bars of a second lieutenant on me, so they simply handed them to me.

The major also handed me an officers' ID card, which gave me access to any officer's club in the United States. Standing at attention in my tight-fitting jeans, still wet, I saluted. They applauded and congratulated me for being the first ROTC cadet commissioned at the University of Denver after completion of the four-year program. (Veterans were excused the first two years, so some of them were commissioned before I was. But mine was the first commission of the full four-year ROTC program.) A college newspaper reporter was sent in to write up a story.

An hour later I traipsed back to my empty apartment. My pant legs were still damp, my scuffled loafers a sloppy mess. And I thought to myself, *Is this all there is to it?* Ever since my teenage days during World War II I'd dreamed of the day I would become an army officer. Finally it had happened — and how anticlimactic it was.

I hoped my wedding night wouldn't turn out to be as disappointing as this.

I celebrated by making myself a hot dog sandwich with extra mustard and pickles and made a date with an attractive coed. We went to the officers' club at Buckley Air Force Base and danced. I donned my dress uniform, the enviable olive green jacket with the officer pink trousers and shiny buckled shoes. Pinned on my shoulders were the golden bars of a second lieutenant. An MP at the gate flashed a snappy salute as he waved me onto the base. For that one night I was attired as an officer and gentlemen of the United States Army.

Sadly, it proved to be the only time I ever wore the dress uniform of a second lieutenant.

Finally a 2nd Lieutenant! An "officer and gentlemen" of the U.S. Army—but not for long. I resigned my commission when the "ministerial quota" would not permit my admission into the Army Chaplain's Corps.

✧

Long after the death of my parents, I came into possession of a packet of letters stored away in Mom's trunk. The packet consisted of every letter I had written since leaving home for college. I had no idea that each letter had been carefully saved. As I thumbed through the bundle I found a letter written to the folks at the time of my college graduation, giving them careful instructions as to how they were to find their way through the terrifying maze of Denver to the University of Denver.

It contained a hand-drawn map in which I directed that they take Colorado Boulevard as the bypass around the city of Denver, on the eastern side, and proceed to follow it down through a series of cornfields until they turned west on Evans Road to the DU campus. Hard to believe that the heavy concentration of towering banks, massive shopping centers, elegant hotels, office buildings, and condominiums concentrated along Colorado Boulevard today were nothing more than open fields when I graduated from the University of Denver in June 1951.

Student at Denver University. Exposure to a great university in a large city (1947-1951), although ominous at first, greatly expanded my intellectual horizon.

Following the graduation exercises, I drove the folks to Missouri and Iowa for them to visit once more their places of birth and childhood homes. They both knew, as well as I, that this would be their last visit to the Pleasant Hill farm at Passaic, Missouri — where Mom was born and raised — and to Elliot, Iowa, where the Todd farms were located.

In Passaic we visited the little Methodist country church Mom had attended as a child. It was just as she remembered it from sixty years earlier. She had me sit in a pew beside a window and look up the gradual slope toward her family's graceful Victorian home standing on top of the hill (hence the name Pleasant Hill Farm). As a child in Sunday school, she could sit in that same pew and watch her father in his rocking chair on the front porch. She wanted to be left alone in the little church for a while, so Dad and I wandered about outside. When she finally came out I could tell that she had been weeping. She died nine years later.

When we returned to Wyoming, I plunged myself into summer jobs to earn money for law school that fall.

For several weeks I worked on an REA crew installing power lines into an isolated ranching area of southern Montana, northeast of Sheridan, Wyoming. We were more than seventy-five miles from the nearest settlement amidst rolling pasturelands covered sparsely with spruce and cedar trees and hay meadows ringed by distant bluffs. Occasionally we'd come across a secluded cattle ranch, and it was our job to dig the post holes for the drop lines into these places. It was hard digging, usually in locations that were inaccessible to power machinery or where the rock formations were so solid that they had to be dynamited.

Two incidents from my REA experience left a lasting impression on me.

One time I was dropped off at a little homestead cabin to dig a hole for a transformer pole. The crew foreman was showing me where to begin the digging when out of the log cabin came a quaint little woman wearing a home-stitched cotton dress with a shawl over her shoulders and an old-fashioned sun bonnet. She approached the foreman and gently said, "I don't want you bringing your electricity into my house here."

"Lady, your son wants you to have it, and he's made all the arrangements to string this line in here to you," he said, chomping on his cigar. "You'll like it once you get it. Just think, you can have electric lights, a refrigerator, a new electric range and hot water heater — and a motorized pump at your water well. It'll bring modern civilization right inside your house, ma'am." He roared away in the truck, leaving me to begin the digging.

As I encircled the stake with the first round of shoveling, she took me by the arm and said, "I beg you. Please, please don't do this to me. My husband and I homesteaded this land over sixty years, and this is our little homestead house made out of cottonwood trees. We raised our family here, and we've done very well without electricity. In the first place, I'm afraid of it. But even if I wasn't afraid of it, I don't need all those electric gadgets at this point in my life."

"I'm sure you'll find it very safe," I tried to reassure her. "And you'll come to like the electric lights even if you don't use any of the appliances."

"Please," she implored. "Please don't force something into my life which I really don't want. I'm eighty-six years old and I don't want those electric lights you're talking about. I've used my oil lamps to raise my babies by and cook my meals — and to nurse my sick husband 'til he died. These little lamps bring back special memories to me, and I shouldn't be forced to give them up."

I noticed tears streaming down her cheeks and I could tell from her eyes that she was pleading with me from the very depth of her heart, "I won't live much longer out here, and no one will want to live in this little log cabin after I'm gone. It isn't much, but it's all I have and it's the only thing left that's all mine. People say a man's house is his castle. This is my little castle, and it's alive with all my memories. This is still a free country, and this is my decision, isn't it? Please, don't force something into the privacy of my home and life that I don't want or need. You're a young man who seems to be reasonable. Please try to understand."

She tightened her grip on my arm.

She was right. I put the shovel over my shoulder and hiked several miles over the ridge back to the crew and told the foreman, "I can't and I won't do something that's just plain wrong. For the best of intentions her son wants her to have electricity, and he's probably right in thinking so. But at this stage in her life, she shouldn't be forced to let others intrude her home and life with something she doesn't want — even if everyone thinks she needs it."

"What are we gonna do now?" he growled.

"Tell the REA officials to talk it over with both her and the son. And tell them to be compassionate and kind. In the meantime, respect her as if she were your own grandmother."

I've often wondered what the final outcome was.

The second incident occurred one evening when I was driving the equipment truck down a dirt a trail to pick up some crews. I drove over a little swell and came upon a natural spring seeping out of the sandstone bank, surrounded by trees. Encamped there were thirty or forty Crow Indian men, women, and children who had just unloaded their supplies from less than a dozen horse-drawn wagons. The harnesses were strung out over the side of the wagon boxes, and the ponies were grazing nearby. Off to one side were several tepees and tents grouped around a campfire, over which they were cooking their evening meal. It was a scene right out of the picture books of the Old West — something from the last century.

I stopped for a moment and struck up a conversation with them. They told me they were on their way home from the big rodeo in Sheridan. It took them several weeks to return to the Crow Indian Reservation in southern Montana. These gentle people had reverted to their traditional way of travel. I can now honestly say to my grandchildren: *Once upon a time, long ago, I came upon a small encampment of Crow Indians in the isolated hills of southern Montana, far away from white man's civilization. Their tepees encircled a campfire in a secluded little hideaway near a spring of water. I rode into their camp and talked awhile with them. They were a very peaceful people, and I liked them.*

After the REA construction project was phased out, I took a second summer job on a seismograph crew working out of Buffalo and Gillette. Seismograph crews contracted with oil exploration companies to help find geological faults deep in the bowels of the earth that might contain pockets of oil. It was a dangerous job; I carried countless sticks of live dynamite on my truck, bouncing around amid the loose load of drilling stems and tools. But the job paid very well in overtime. We worked fourteen hours a day, six days a week.

We discovered a major oil field outside Gillette. Those dryland farmers, trying to scratch out a living in those barren, forsaken hills, needed a little prosperity in their lives. They found it once the oil royalties began pouring in. At the time we were out there, it was rough going for these isolated families, most of whom seemed poverty-stricken.

I remember driving my tank truck near a little basin in the land that had collected a few inches of water immediately after a brief rain shower. Three kids were skinny-dipping in the bog hole. They were having the time of their lives, splashing in the shallow sludge, belly crawling and riling up the mud from the bottom. The more they splashed and wallowed in it, the muddier they became, until they were caked from head to toe.

In another fifteen years these same children would be young adults, enjoying their families' newfound oil riches. But I doubt they enjoyed swimming in their private swimming pools nearly as much as they enjoyed wallowing in that miserable bog hole.

I once told this story to a women's group which I felt was riling up more muck and mire than was necessary over some insignificant church issue. The irate ladies reminded me that two inches of murky water was shallow, indeed — but still sufficient to drown a nosy rector.

✧

That summer I began dating the young woman who later would become my wife. Shirley Mae Hall was the daughter of the Reverend and Mrs. Willard Hall. He pastored a small but vital congregation of good people known as the First Baptist Church of Buffalo.

Shirley was a good musician, a trait she inherited from both her parents. Willard could play a variety of musical instruments, and his wife, Gladys, was an accomplished pianist and church organist. She could play anything — and did, much to the consternation of her husband. She could play a solemn hymn for congregational singing with all the power and versatility of dual pianists; I'll never know how she could move her hands so rapidly across the keyboard. Or she could belt out the "Twelfth Street Rag" with enough pizzazz to shame the top recording stars of the day.

Shirley was not as gifted at the piano as her mother, but she could play it very well. She was better at the violin, on which she had taken lessons ever since childhood.

I met Shirley at my sister's wedding in September 1950, although she doesn't remember the occasion. In the summer of 1951 we began dating. Because her father was a conservative Baptist preacher, we weren't permitted to do many things for social recreation. Dancing, movies, card playing, smoking, and drinking were strictly forbidden. But we could go on mountain picnics and accompany her folks on fishing trips. As time wore on we attended a few movies, but only with the intervention of Shirley's mother. We always knew it was an occasion for a bitter exchange of angry words between her parents the moment we left the house.

It seems incongruous to me now that I would begin dating the daughter of a fundamentalist Baptist preacher when fundamentalist Baptist preachers were anathema to me. But I was beginning to feel myself falling into love — and as the old adage goes, *love is blind which overcometh everything*. However, I had three years of law school still ahead, so I was in no position to be making a long-range commitment. And Shirley was entering nurse training on a scholarship at the Michael Reese Hospital in Chicago. It was obvious that we wouldn't be seeing much of one another in the immediate future. This discouraging reality had become a fact of life for me during the past four years of college — and now it stretched interminably into the future as well.

Having earned plenty of cash that summer, I felt flush and bought a secondhand Buick.

My first car as a DU graduate, a secondhand Buick Roadmaster. This purchase alone greatly enhanced my courtin' and spooonin' opportunities as I prepared to enter law school.

Driving my own car, I headed back to Denver the third week in September to enter law school.

Chapter 4

As a freshman law student at the University of Denver, I gathered up my armload of law books, walked across campus, and attended my first class — on the Old Testament.

People have often asked me why I did that. I can no more answer that question intelligently today than I could back in 1951. Maybe it was an instinctive avoidance of something I truly didn't want to do — becoming a lawyer. Or perhaps it was the hand of God that led me to that seminary class at the Iliff School of Theology. However, since I am hesitant to assign irrationality to God, I feel more comfortable in accepting the responsibility myself.

I don't mean to imply there wasn't any thought given to the matter at hand, because there was. I talked with several people whose judgment I trusted. Dr. Erdmann Smith said the call of God into the ordained ministry was not necessarily a dramatic Damascus road experience such as the Apostle Paul's, in which he was struck by lightning and personally encountered the Lord Jesus Christ.

"The calling usually comes," Smith said, "when a person feels he has the talent to meet a specific need."

My dear friend Herb Brawner said the religious calling is probably no different from any other — you feel a nudging in a certain direction and can't shake it.

It was of some consternation to me that I was drawn toward a religious vocation when, for most of my life, I had resisted both the messenger and the message of the gospel I heard preached as a boy. Biblical fundamentalism repulsed me as much then as it does today. However, I had found a religious liberation with the poetic preaching of Dr. Kelly O'Neil and the scholarly sermons of Dr. Erdmann Smith. Somewhere in the mix was the mystical sacramentalism of Father Layman and the grandeur of worship at St. John's Episcopal Cathedral. What a tangle of influences. It would take me years to straighten out the religious impulse I so keenly felt.

95

Indeed, in entering the Iliff School perhaps I was seeking to resolve my own religious confusion. Maybe I would study theology and philosophy for a little while, then return to the study of law. Perhaps I could fulfill my military aspirations by becoming an army chaplain for a tour of active duty before returning to the study of law. But I have to say, in all honesty, that I really don't know why I headed out for law school that morning and ended up in a class on the Old Testament.

I do know, however, it wasn't very smart to enter a graduate school of theology when I had never taken a single course in religious studies during my entire four years of college. I never had to study as hard in my life as I did that first year at Iliff. I lacked the basic skills of religious language and couldn't even discuss the subject intelligently. If ever someone had an excuse to bow out of an impulsive decision, it would have been me. Needless to say, my first year of seminary studies was a grueling academic ordeal.

The Iliff School of Theology is located on the southern edge of the University of Denver campus. It was then, and still is today, one of the most liberal Protestant theological seminaries in the nation, with a heavy emphasis on academic scholarship and intellectual pursuit. This stretched me out and pounded me hard. But it also saved me. Open inquiry to every theological question sustained my interest and kept me going.

Also, I recognized that I needed to be among other seminarians if I was ever to succeed in my religious studies. After living for nearly four years in my basement apartment on South Downing, I moved to a sprawling old house owned by the Iliff School of Theology and used as a dormitory for single seminarians. It was the historic former home of John Evans, who established Northwestern University in Illinois before moving west, where he not only founded the University of Denver but also became the first territorial governor of Colorado.

The stately old house was typical of those built in the 1890s. I was assigned to a large room on the first floor, off the former dining room, which was the original Evans library. It was a spacious old room with high ceilings and a fireplace that actually worked. As much as I loved it, the house had seen better days and was now into a state of steady decline.

The place was known as Gray Gables, but the fifteen occupants affectionately renamed it Gay Stables. This was long before the word *gay* had come to be associated with homosexuality. If it had had such connotations back in those days, we never would have used the term. But we were all bachelors, and within that context the word *stables* seemed particularly appropriate. We cooked our meals cooperatively, organizing ourselves into teams for cooking and kitchen duties. We all contributed cash to the common grocery fund. Strangely, the system worked. I would live here for the next three years of my seminary life.

Living at Gay Stables was a theological education in itself. Almost all of the seminarians were Methodists, but there were always a few pagans like me in the mix. We took our studies seriously in order to survive. Enough students failed or dropped out each semester to catch our attention and sober us up. We also learned, however, that a fellow could study himself blue in the face and still fail if he remained in social isolation from fellow seminarians. Bull sessions were constant, and they kept us in touch with one another and in contact with academic reality.

We occasionally played highly organized pranks to keep each other spiritually humble and emotionally agitated. I tried once to grow a mustache and was quite successful until a gang of hoodlums pounced upon me in the middle of the night, held me down in bed and shaved half of it away. I must admit, however, that I did more than my share in the hazing of others. The pranks broke the monotony and relieved the pressure of constant graduate study. Scholarship, not spirituality, was the basis of our survival. Prayer didn't seem to help very much anyway. At least, no one would admit to using prayer in lieu of hitting the books.

One of my seminarian buddies, a Methodist by the name of Jack Richards, has become a most intimate and devoted friend ever since we first met at Iliff back in 1951. In later years, Jack told me that the other classmates always looked upon seminarian Jim Kirk and me as the intellectuals, the real academicians in seminary. For Jim Kirk this would be true; he later acquired a Ph.D. and distinguished himself as a college professor and religious author. But including me in his category was incredibly absurd. I had to struggle hard to get passing grades. I can only assume that I gave the appearance of being intellectual because of maintaining an open mind to all theological issues. (Sometimes they said my mind was so open that everything passed right through it.) At this point in my education I was searching for the meaning of life more than direct answers to biblical questions. And since I had not been nurtured in a lifetime of Sunday school and church attendance, I had no religious preconceptions to overcome.

I refused to accept pat answers to theological questions. I disdained anyone who quoted scripture as proof during an intellectual discussion. If I were in law school instead of seminary, it would be acceptable to quote the law to win an argument. That's what lawyers are supposed to do. But the Bible was never intended to be used this way. Anytime you have to hit someone across the head with the Bible to prove the logic of a religious point of view, you've already lost the argument.

In the fall of 1951 my parents made a momentous decision to sell the ranch. They had lived there for over forty years. All seven of us kids were born and raised there. Every hill, ravine, and nook was hallowed by special memories. And the Piney Creek ranching valley was a community of friends and neighbors that had nurtured our life together. This was now to change. Dad was sixty-eight years old, and the time had come to retire. The ranch lands were sold to the family of Mr. and Mrs. Jack Cooksley. A large public auction in November dispensed with most of the livestock and all of the machinery.

The folks moved temporarily to a lovely stone house sitting vacant on the upper ranch of our neighbor, Cline Fowler. I spent Christmas vacation with them in their temporary home on the hill and took advantage of the opportunity to resume my romance with Shirley Hall in Buffalo. It briefly blossomed into a full-blown love affair but had to be put into cold storage when we returned to school in January. And there were very good reasons to cool things down.

The first reason was that Shirley had lived all her life in the parsonage goldfish bowl, where her every movement had been under the critical scrutiny of a moralistic and judgmental church congregation. If she so much as smoked a cigarette, the local Baptist congregation would have heaped condemnation both upon her and her father, the Reverend Willard Hall. Never mind the double standard — most Baptists used tobacco themselves. Shirley had good reason at this point in her life not to pursue a romantic relationship with a young seminarian studying for the ministry.

I had reasons to cool the romance, too. After all, marrying the daughter of a fundamentalist preacher did not seem like a match made in heaven for me. So the romance cooled for a while, and reason prevailed.

I plowed my energies back into my theological studies and did not date another woman again for two years. This concerned my good friend Herb Brawner, who drew me aside one morning after worship services at First Baptist Church and said, "Gene, your interest in God shouldn't detract from your normal interest in women. That's not healthy."

"Herb, my pursuit of one doesn't diminish my pursuit of the other. It's just that I don't seem to have time right now for both."

He gave me a little talk about setting priorities and doing those things that are really important to us. Good old Herb — a Christian who was always so practical. When Christ talked about Christians being the salt of the earth, he was referring to Herb Brawner.

Herb and Nina did more than just talk, however. They lined up for me a dinner engagement with a redheaded United Airlines stewardess. She was beautiful. After dinner she drove me to her apartment for tea and conversation, but I was so preoccupied with an upcoming examination on theology that I couldn't concentrate either on her or the conversation. Herb was right — my graduate studies were pushing me out of character.

One course at the Iliff School of Theology, titled "Philosophy of Religion," made an everlasting impression on me. The professor's name was Dr. William Bernhardt. He said, in a nutshell, that religion primarily functions in those areas of life over which people feel a loss of control. In other words, we pray to bring about results we otherwise cannot achieve by ourselves. Although he never used this example, I interpreted his theory to mean that ancient cavemen probably prayed earnestly for lightning when they were totally dependent upon it to provide fire. As they developed their fire-making technology, however, they no longer had to pray for lightning. They could simply build a fire whenever they needed one.

There are always areas of our lives that transcend our control: issues of health and prosperity, the problems of temptation and evil, personal failure and sin, the meaning of life and death — and what happens to us after we die. It is these uncertainties that motivate people to reach beyond themselves for divine assistance and understanding.

The truth is, a lot of things about my life at that time were beyond my immediate control. I had many questions for which I could not find answers. Consequently, I would say to my seminarian classmates, *Don't ask me to believe something, or do anything in the name of religion, if it doesn't make good sense. God created us with the ability to reason and think, and we reflect the image of God. When we renounce our thinking, even in the name of religion, we are renouncing our imagery in God.*

Iliff abounded in intellectual stimulation, with a heavy bent toward training potential Ph.D. candidates for college teaching. The spiritual and pastoral emphasis left something to be desired. Although the lovely Iliff chapel on the second floor of the old building was, indeed, a quiet and wonderful place for private mediation, attendance at weekly chapel services was not good. Generally speaking, many of us gathered at the DU Student Union for coffee and doughnuts at chapel time. Occasionally, however, a well-known preacher or prominent lay speaker would make an appearance, and usually we attended these special chapel sessions.

One such service proved to be a pivotal moment in my life.

A contralto soloist of African American descent, while visiting the Denver area, was invited to sing in the chapel. I'm terribly sorry that I don't remember her name. This beautiful black woman, slender and well groomed, carried herself with great dignity and performed magnificently, graciously acknowledging the generous applause from her seminary audience.

She introduced her final selection as a Finnish folk hymn composed by Austris A. Wihtol. She walked with her accompanist to the back of the airy chapel, where the organ console was mounted on the south wall, near the large Gothic doorway leading out into the second-floor vestibule. While the organist played her prelude, the soloist looked up to the beautiful stained-glass windows, which were bathing the whole chapel area in lovely soft shades of color. Then, closing her eyes in a meditative stance, she tipped back her head and began singing, with enormous warmth and powerful feeling, the most beautiful words of song I had ever heard:

My God and I
Go in the field together
We walk and talk as good friends should and do
We clasp our hands
Our voices ring with laughter
My God and I
Walk thru the meadow's hue

He tells me of the years that went before me
When heavenly plans were made for me to be
When all was but a dream of dim conception
To come to life, earth's verdant glory see

My God and I will go for aye together
We'll walk and talk as good friends should and do
This earth will pass
And with it common trifles
But God and I
Will go unendingly.

When she finished her solo, there was no applause. The chapel quickly emptied out; someone closed the door, and I was left alone. I felt so profoundly moved that I wept.

The song's imagery and haunting melody struck a responsive chord deep within my soul. For the first time ever in my lifetime — my spiritual quest had been put into words and music.

My God and I / Go in the field together . . . and up into the Wyoming sagebrush hills in the springtime, when the draws are resplendent with the fragrant blossoms of the wild chokecherry and plum bushes; where the newly born calves wobble up to their mothers for their first drink of warm milk; and, down among the little islands in Piney Creek, where the ducks and geese have built their nests, and the mink and beaver have dug their underground homes and padded corridor paths.

We walk and talk / As good friends should and do . . . not haranguing or condemning or terrifying someone into a religious conversion. Good friends don't do this to each other. We don't use religion to intimidate and hurt someone, and we don't ask God to do it either.

We clasp our hands / Our voices ring with laughter . . . yes, genuine laughter and heartfelt joy. Not dour bitterness, sanctimonious hypocrisy, or, worst of all, self-imposed religious martyrdom. People can worship the Lord in the beauty of holiness and celebrate life by enjoying the laughter of a child at play or drinking tasty wine with good friends or dancing the polka.

He tells me of the years that went before me / When heavenly plans were made for me to be / When all was but a dream of dim concep-

Seminarian at Iliff School of Theology in Denver (1951-1954). My seminary study, although rigorous, had a powerful, liberating religious impact on me.

tion . . . Mine was a lonely childhood in many respects, a world of private thoughts and ideas. I kept journals to try to make some sense of it all, always wondering if there was some master plan. Walking behind the milk cows across the snow-crusted beet field on a Christmas Eve, all was but a dream of dim conception beginning to dawn on my consciousness — that ultimately I could make those decisions which shape the destiny of my life. Would I ever become the man that this boy inside had hoped to be?

This earth will pass / And with it common trifles / But God and I / Will go unendingly. The hymn is not good theology, because it basically ignores the social dimension of a one's personal existence. Religious beliefs are not just a private affair with God — but something shared within the larger body of the local congregation and society as a whole. However, it is true that each of us has an individual spiritual journey that is known to God alone which transcends the passage of this earth and all its common trifles — and will go unendingly with Him.

This Finnish hymn, "My God and I," would follow me the rest of my life. It would be sung as a choral anthem at my ordination into the Baptist ministry, again at my ordination into the priesthood of the Episcopal Church, and again at my retirement from the pastoral ministry nearly forty years later. And I have requested that it be sung at my burial. It's a very personal thing for me and might not make much sense to others. This is the one hymn that somehow, mysteriously, brought it all together for me.

✧

I believe that there is a special place in heaven for all the little churches who take on young ministers-in-training year after year — to love and support them, to nurture and sustain them, to raise them up if they fall, and to create within them a pastoral ministry that administers the grace of God to all. By the same token, there is a special place in hell for all the big churches who grind up their ministers like hamburger and destroy them.

The good people of Community Baptist Church of Padroni, Colorado, will always have a special place in heaven. On October 19, 1952, they had the courage and grace to take on Gene Todd as their seminarian minister.

I was granted a preaching license through the First Baptist Church of Denver. This document, nothing more than a beginner's license, allowed someone attending a seminary to assume limited responsibility for a small country church, with permission to preach and bury the dead but not much else. And the bearer had to operate under the watchful supervision of the American Baptist denominational leadership of Colorado.

Padroni is located in the northeast corner of Colorado, near Sterling, about 125 miles from Denver, very close to the Nebraska and Wyoming state boundaries. It was (and still is) primarily a farming community, with thousands of acres under irrigation along the lower elevations of prairie land. Sugar beets were the dominant crop. The majority of these farmers were sharecroppers, most of Russian-German descent. Although there were a few successful privately owned farming and ranching operations, by far the majority of the people around Padroni were not very prosperous.

Generally, the terrain was flat and expansive. Beyond the irrigated fields were successive benchlands, ascending like stairsteps toward the distant bluffs, whose higher elevation made them exceptionally good for dryland wheat farming.

The town of Padroni wasn't much. It was approached along a dirt road about fifteen miles out from Sterling. With everyone at home and in bed, the population was seventy-five, counting the dogs. There were no public utilities and no telephone service. Under one roof there was a general store, barbershop, locker plant, and post office, all operated by Dee Johnson. Also, there were a blacksmith-machine shop, something resembling a filling station and a small tavern that sold only beer. That was Padroni's business district.

A country school sat upon a gentle rise just outside of town, only a five-minute walk from the post office and general store. The school was the social center of the community. Most of the teachers, however, lived in Sterling and drove out to their jobs every day.

Oh yes, and there was the Community Baptist Church. It had endured bad luck almost from the day of its construction back in the 1920s, when a Baptist chapel car was switched off the Burlington Railroad siding there and a small congregation was organized. Hundreds of small rural churches like this were doomed from the beginning, but particularly in the 1920s, with the increasing urbanization of the United States and the abandonment of agrarian communities. Little towns like Padroni clung to their existence for dear life, but the incessant prairie winds and dust storms blew many of them away.

So Padroni wasn't much of a town, and Community Baptist wasn't much of a church. But I wasn't much of a preacher or a minister either, so we were all on common ground. There was no way the town, the church, or I could possibly fail, because there was little hope or promise of success in the first place.

Pitiful as the little church may have seemed to others, who didn't know rural churches, the people of Padroni and I had two things in common. First was the Lordship of Christ. Their personal walk with Jesus had been much longer than mine. Second, the people of Padroni and I were pure country. Country living was the only thing these beautiful people had ever known. Even though I had been in a big city attending the University of Denver for close to six years now, there wasn't an urban bone in my body. These country people were as natural to me as the family and neighbors I had left behind along the Piney Creek ranching valley in northern Wyoming.

So a little group of hearty souls gathered in the Community Baptist Church the third week of October 1952 for my first Sunday worship service. We sang a few hymns and we said a few prayers and I preached a few words — and we all went home. Except I had no home to go to. Construction of a tiny parsonage next door had just begun, with walls made from ammunition boxes abandoned by an army quartermaster dump near Sydney, Nebraska. It was roofed over and the shell was enclosed, but there was no flooring and no interior walls. This work had been done by the previous pastor, a saintly old man by the name of Reverend Hargis, who didn't have much formal training in the ministry but was a real Christian soul who worked the Padroni field part-time for a few years ahead of me.

Since no funds were available for finishing the parsonage, I was assigned to board temporarily at the farm home of Mr. and Mrs. Ray Reike, about two miles out of Padroni. I would live weekends with them for the next year. Padroni was classified as a "seminarian charge," meaning that I would leave Denver after Iliff classes on Friday afternoon and not return to seminary until Monday afternoon. Theological studies at Iliff were tailored to accommodate students who spread out across the Rocky Mountain region every weekend to take "pastoral charge" of these small rural churches that could not afford a full-time minister.

I occupied a guest room at the Reike home and usually ate my Friday suppers there, but it was commonly assumed that I would eat all my other meals with parishioners — uninvited. At mealtime, I was simply to drop in at someone's home and pull up a chair at the dinner table. It took me awhile to feel comfortable doing this, but if I didn't do it I went hungry. There was no restaurant around. Since there was no parsonage either, this social convention was considered part of my salary package. You soon learn to do what you need to do to keep body and soul together.

Since this was the way it worked, I cultivated my cafeteria of homes, refining the selection process to a very sophisticated art. Eventually I learned where I most likely would get the juiciest meat loaf on a Saturday night, where the best fried chicken dinner was served every Sunday after church, where homemade soup was always extra smooth and tasty, and where delicious leftovers were abundant for a snack at any time.

When I stopped at a farmhouse for supper, I would almost always go out into the barn and help with the milking and the evening chores. It was relaxing for me to milk a cow again. One never forgets. The farmers would appreciate the gesture, and I would have a wonderful opportunity to visit with him one on one.

Likewise, after every meal, I always made it a practice to wash the dishes, even over the protests of the woman of the house. I learned that dishwashing time was when everyone pulled a vanishing act and stayed away from the kitchen if they could. Now I could visit privately with the wife and mother of the family with no interference or interruptions. This was my way of letting her know that, in addition to my gratitude for the wonderful meal, I valued her friendship in my life and her membership in our little country church.

I don't mean to imply that I panhandled all my victuals from door to door because occasionally I received invitations for special suppers with families of my congregation. One of my earlier invitations came from a family who lived in a railroad boxcar right there in Padroni. The father had a temporary job on the Burlington section crew, and the company provided housing in a freight car that had been lifted off its wheels and set on the ground between the main line and the side track. The home had no water and no electricity. The outhouse was located across from the side track, which was all right under normal circumstances. But if by chance some freight cars were switched off there, which wasn't often, the family had to crawl under the string of railroad cars to get to the toilet. Their home couldn't have been more than twenty feet from the main railroad line, which meant that the thundering roar of the passing trains would surely have rocked them out of their beds at night.

But this man and his large family were deeply grateful to have the beginning of a permanent railroad job, which someday would enable them to live in a better home in a larger community. The wife with five children, ranging from a teenager to a toddler still in diapers, graciously made the most of their living accommodations. A kitchen with a coal-burning cook stove stood at one end. This stove had to be stoked all night during winter, providing the only heat the boxcar had. Three or four beds, bunched at the opposite end of the freight car, served as a living room. I sat on a bed as if it were a sofa and visited with the father and children while his wife busily completed preparations for supper.

Our meal consisted of fresh homemade bread with bowls of ham and beans. It was absolutely delicious. I meant it when I told them that ham and beans had always been one of my favorite country dishes. They all ate it just like it should be eaten, slurped up in a spoon with the bread crust dipped in the tasty soup. The mother and her thirteen-year-old daughter quickly cleared away the dishes and wiped the table clean, and the family gathered around for their Bible lesson and prayer. The mother told me that they had only recently become converted to Christianity and that my predecessor, Reverend Hargis, always led them in a family Bible study. She relayed further how very good God had been to them by giving her husband a job on the railroad section crew.

The light from the dimly lit kerosene lamp in the center of the table was hardly sufficient for me to read the fine print of the King James Bible they handed me. The flickering flame of the little lamp illuminated the faces of the children, whose arms or chins rested on the table, looking up at me with eyes filled with expectation and awe, as if I were the Christ. The rest of the boxcar room around them was plunged into dark shadows. Poverty was very evident here, but abundant Christian hope prevailed. They were all babes in Christ, and so was I. The whole scene became transfigured before me as a visual image, as if it were an actual photograph, of what the pastoral ministry was all about. I thought to myself, *I'm not sure I can measure up to this.*

I remembered seeing a folded quilt on the bed where I sat before supper. Nothing fancy at all, just many colored squares of material, probably heavy clothing donated to the Salvation Army and passed on to the mother, who pieced the blocks together into a warm and colorful quilt. I walked back to the bed, gathered the quilt up in my arms, and rolled it out in front of me on the table. "See this beautiful quilt of many colors which your mother has made for you?" I said. "I want to tell you a Bible story about a little boy whose father made him a coat of many colors. His name was Joseph."

I told them about the jealous brothers who threw little Joseph into a pit so deep that he would surely die from the desert heat and lack of water. But then the brothers decided instead to sell him as a slave and knew they would never ever see him again. They took his beautiful coat of many colors and dipped it in the blood of a slaughtered sheep to make the father believe his little boy was killed by a hungry wolf. But they knew that Joseph was alive, except he now could be nothing more than a slave to destitution and hardship for the rest of his life.

I paused. They sat there with their eyes fixed upon me. "What happened to him, Rev'ner?" they asked.

I told them how the brothers traveled to Egypt many years later and met the handsome governor of the nation, who rode in a golden chariot pulled by the fastest horses with a special driver. The powerful, rich man asked the men to bring their old father. And when they did, the governor put his arms around the old man and said, "I am your little boy Joseph." They all wept. Then Joseph forgave his mean brothers, who had taken away his little coat of many colors and sold him into slavery.

But now he could wear a beautiful new coat as governor of Egypt, "a coat as beautiful as this quilt of many colors," I said, draping the mother's quilt over the shoulders of the children at the table. "These many colors mean that you are loved and very special to your father and mother, to God, and to our little church." They hugged the quilt and stroked it as a thing of exquisite beauty, which it really was, made by their mother's hands. She beamed with pride in her handiwork and her family.

As I left their humble boxcar home, I wasn't at all convinced that I had taught them anything about the Bible that they didn't already know. But I knew they had given me a spiritual gift, which I hadn't gleaned from the seminary professors. Their simple faith and quiet dignity touched me deeply.

"Blessed are the poor, for theirs is the kingdom of God" (Matt. 5:3).

That poor family had more of the kingdom of God in their railroad box-car home than the Queen of England in Buckingham Palace.

✧

In Padroni, I developed a method of sermon preparation which would remain with me for the rest of my ministry. The main idea of the sermon, suggested by the scriptural readings scheduled for that Sunday, would begin as a seminal germ of thought no later than Wednesday. I would pray for God's guidance as I began jotting down random ideas which popped into my head — *brainstorming* I called it. I would check through a large file of clippings which I was always collecting to see if there was anything here which might be relevant. By Friday, I would begin forming a general outline of the sermon. On Saturday, I would sit down at my typewriter and peck out the entire sermon with special emphasis on the introduction and the conclusion.

I would then go back through the manuscript and mark in red ink those coined phrases and special quotations which would seem most important to the final delivery of the sermon. Then I would outline the sermon one more time, either in the margins of the original manuscript, or separately on a fresh sheet of paper, and this I would carry into the pulpit. Thus, I never read a sermon from the pulpit — neither my own and certainly never one written by someone else. Reading a sermon from a manuscript, for me, would have been anathema because it would have become a barrier between the spontaneous interaction of the congregation and myself.

Beginning in Padroni I also began recording my Sunday morning sermons. First on a wire recorder, then later on a reel-to-reel tape recorder and cassettes. I would compel myself to listen to that wretched sermon sometime during the following week. This was real penance for me. As painful as it was, I usually learned something, if nothing more than saying, *Promise yourself — never preach another sermon like that one again.*

In addition to the formative influences of Dr. Kelly O'Neil and Dr. Erdmann Smith in Denver, my own mother was very influential when it

Although it was a small country church in rural Colorado, after interior renovation of the building, I wore a pulpit robe when conducting worship services in the attractive, newly decorated sanctuary.

came to sermon preparations. Out on the ranch, as she listened to the radio broadcasts of Sunday morning worship services, I remember her speaking out loud and asking herself, "So what?"

She would further lament, "Preachers so often just argue with themselves about triviality in the Bible. Or they belabor some obscure point that has little or no direct application to the common struggle of everyday people who are trying to live a better life with meaning and purpose. Why don't preachers ask themselves 'So What?' before the delivery of every sermon? Will this sermon help people to know God and serve Him better? Will it help people to love a neighbor who is irritating the hell out of them? Will it help bring peace to a family conflict that's tearing them all apart? Will it help people keep going, when they just want to quit?"

Consequently, I have had the words **SO WHAT?** gold stamped on the inside cover of every Bible I use in sermon preparations. The first question I ask myself is: *Does this sermon have the potential of making a positive difference in the lives of people who must listen to it? If it doesn't, then forget it.* People simply are too busy for irrelevant nonsense anymore.

I'm forever grateful to my mother for her provocative **SO WHAT?** in my sermon preparations. And it all began in Padroni.

✧

Back to the little church. Early on I recognized that I had a problem with the interior of the place. It looked dingy, neglected, and not very edifying as a place of worship. When I read the psalmist's call to worship — "Come, let us worship the Lord in the beauty of holiness" — I would look around without seeing much beauty. "It's not what we've got, it's how we take care of what we've got that makes it beautiful," I told the

congregation. I suggested that we move the pews down into the basement and worship there until such time as we redecorated the upstairs
to make it look like a church is supposed to look.

It didn't take long.

With volunteer help we patched the broken plaster, installed new ceiling fixtures, sanded and refinished the floors, and completely painted the
interior. The women made curtains to drape the barren windows. We
moved the pulpit off to one side so that our focus of worship would center on a little altar we constructed — instead of focusing on the preacher
and the sermon. We mounted indirect lights along the front wall so that
we could turn off the overhead fixtures for soft candlelight services. We
refinished the pews.

We had no money when we started the project and none when it was
finished. But we had a beautifully redecorated little church. Only the
volunteers who steadily
worked on it saw the
transformation, how-
ever, because it was
decided that the finished
product would be
revealed to the congre-
gation only on the night
of its dedication.

Following a Saturday
night pot-luck dinner, we
all removed our shoes —
the third coat of varnish
was not yet completely
dry — and proceeded
upstairs to see our newly
redecorated sanctuary.

*Community Baptist Church at Padroni in 1952 (near
Sterling in northeastern Colorado) right after completion of small parsonage and before steeple was
erected on church.*

The candles were lit, the lights slightly subdued, while Bernice Herzog
softly played the piano, and everyone stood in hushed silence while I read
the traditional Call to Worship.

"Surely the Lord is in this place. Let us worship the Lord in the beauty
of holiness."

"Thanks be to God," came the joyful response.

When the dedication was over and we were recovering our shoes back
down in the basement, someone said, "Now I know why God told Moses:
'Remove thy shoes, thou art standing on holy ground.'"

The truth is, we were more proud of our newly transformed cathedral out on the windswept prairies of northeastern Colorado than was the massive crowd, many years later, which dedicated the National Cathedral of Washington, D.C. — after nearly seventy years of construction at a cost of half a billion dollars.

Our next project was the completion and furnishing of the little parsonage next door. Work crews were organized, and within a month's time it was finished. There was no water on the premises, not even a well, so it was necessary for me to carry my water by pail from the McCulley well some 500 yards away. Fortunately, Leonard and Alice Green had a modern bathroom in their home only five miles from town, and I was invited to drive out there for a hot bath at any time.

After moving into my new parsonage, it was easier for me to move about within the Padroni community. When a country square dance was scheduled in the school gym, I walked up the hill to attend. Half my congregation was there dancing away, and I joined them. We danced square dances, the polka, the schottische, and even the Bunny Hop. After the supper waltz toward midnight, I had a sandwich and a cup of coffee with a group of non-parishioners I was getting to know, then walked back down the hill to the parsonage and went to bed.

I expected a little consternation from my Baptist congregation. But not a word was said.

"You may not have heard the consternation," a friend named Stanley Fluharty told me thirty years later, "but there was plenty of it. This was the first time in anyone's memory that a Baptist minister went to the local dance not to condemn it — but to dance it. Believe me, the telephone lines burned for a week."

If the Padroni congregation had created an uproar over my attending these country dances, I most likely would have concluded right then and there that the ordained ministry wasn't for me and gotten out of it. It would have been that simple. Not that I was right and they were wrong. Not that attending country dances was essential to the Christian ministry. I simply would have known early on that my personality was not appropriate for the pastorate. The earlier you learn that a square peg doesn't fit in a round hole, the better off you are.

✧

The redecorated interior of the church was now very worshipful. But the outside still didn't look much like a church. There was nothing about the building that would have distinguished it from an abandoned schoolhouse or a lodge meeting hall. We decided that a bell steeple with a cross mounted high on top, would make it look more like a church. I scoured the countryside and purchased a bell from an abandoned rural schoolhouse, then designed and helped build a steeple. A parishioner offered to hoist the steeple onto the roof with his tractor's hydraulic forklift, but the roof would have to be replaced first, since past tornado winds had literally torn away most of the splintered shingles. Replacing a roof was no simple matter. We couldn't afford to have it done professionally, and during the busy summer months we couldn't recruit enough volunteers to get the job done. Eventually I buttonholed some folks at a country dance and told them that once the steeple was in place we would toll that bell every time

Volunteer farmers from many faiths who installed a new roof on the church all in one day. Hydraulic farm tractor forklifts elevated workers and materials to the roof, and then the race was on as to which side finished first. The women volunteers cooked us a country fried chicken dinner complete with apple cobbler dessert.

Partially finished bell steeple is lifted up to its place by forklift tractors. I'm second from left, nearest camera, helping to steady its wobble while soaring high above peak of church.

someone died in our community, regardless of who they were or what faith they proclaimed. We would do it because everyone was important to the overall good of the whole community, and if anyone died they would be sorely missed by all the rest of us.

The appeal worked, and we got the number of volunteers we needed. We did the job without scaffolding or a single ladder. Farmers, using their hydraulic forklifts, elevated workers and bales of shingles right up to the roof level. The workers were evenly divided between both sides of the roof, and the race was on to see which side finished first.

The women served a fabulous fried chicken dinner at noon, complete with an assortment of homemade pies. In the middle of the afternoon, when the roof was hottest from the sun, I carried around a pail of iced tea and paper cups for an afternoon refreshment break.

At five o'clock the forklifts lowered all the workers to the ground, and we all stepped back to admire a country community church with a brand-new roof and a gleaming new steeple, lifting high the cross of Christ for all to admire. Inside the steeple was the old rural school bell. Right then, it was decided, we should ring the bell for the first time to celebrate that Christians of all faiths could work side by side under the cross that unites us all.

We were very proud of the finished project. I promised to ring the bell every time someone died in the community, regardless of faith, because everyone was important to the communal welfare of all.

The little church continued to fill up on Sunday mornings with a worshipping congregation much larger than the official population of Padroni. During the worship services on a beautiful summer morning I'd look out upon this gathering of country people, all dressed in their Sunday best — men with faces sun-browned up to the brow line of their straw hats, their complexions seeming all the darker in contrast to their white shirts and ties; women wearing their hats, as was the custom then; children crowded in beside their parents — all singing their hymns and praying their prayers with heartfelt feeling and emotional power.

I had eaten at the family table of every home, washed their supper dishes, milked their cows, and slopped their hogs. I had stood with them beside the open graves of their loved ones, officiated at weddings, and blessed the babies of proud parents. I had wept with them. I had laughed with them. And danced the square dance with most of them.

As I looked out upon these beautiful people, I thought to myself: *How fortunate I am. No young seminarian could begin his ministry among a greater people than these. How very good God has been by giving me a congregation like this as my first pastorate. How blessed they are to me.*

How greatly I loved them.

✧

But I was still in seminary, attending theological classes during the week and driving out to Padroni for my weekend ministry. Both consumed all my energies. I had another year at the Iliff School of Theology before I would complete my studies for a Master of Theology degree, and I had to maintain a satisfactory grade average, at the graduate level, if I hoped to gain entrance into the Chaplains Corps of the U.S. Army. This kept my nose to the grindstone.

However, I did allow myself one illegitimate pleasure, a forbidden sin, considered not appropriate for a young licensed Baptist minister. It wasn't the consumption of alcoholic beverages because I set that minor indulgence aside the moment I was licensed. It certainly wasn't sex, because my life was barren of all romance. My life had become as stark and austere as a Catholic priest who had taken the perpetual vows of poverty and chastity. The only problem was, I wasn't a priest who had taken the perpetual vows. Consequently, my poverty and chastity were not a vocational choice. It was simply my inevitable misfortune.

But the one forbidden pleasure I allowed myself — was smoking a pipe!

Baptists honored strict obedience to the biblical Ten Commandments. The sins of murder, idolatry, adultery, and thieving were *mentionable* sins. Sins that were mentioned in the Bible could be forgiven. But the sin of smoking was too *unmentionable* to be contained in the Bible and, therefore, was unforgivable. At least, that seemed to be the contorted logic.

So I smoked a pipe. But always in seclusion. It was my secret sin. And what a delicious sin it was. I'd take a thermos of hot tea with me for a drive out along a lonely country road leading to the highest-stepped bluffs along the Great Plains of northeastern Colorado, where I had a panoramic view of the surrounding countryside — so far that you could see a car approaching five miles in either direction. Then I would shut the motor off, reach for my pipe and pouch of damp, smooth-tasting *Rum & Maple* pipe tobacco, conveniently stashed away under the front seat. Ceremonially, I would tamp the sweet aromatic mixture into my pipe, then climb out on the fender of my Buick, pour myself a cup of hot tea, and light up.

How sensual it was.

In quiet stillness, I would watch a glorious sunset casting its golden shafts of light out across the vast expanse of the wide-open prairie land. The intoxicating rum and maple taste, so mellow and rich, washed down with sweetened hot tea, touched the core of my physical being with euphoric contentment. The smoke would rise up toward the heavens like swirling incense. Its honeyed aroma, drifting off across the prairies, would actually attract pheasants out of the sky who would land nearby in the pasture, and out of curiosity would gradually edge their way to within a few yards of my car. Magnificent creatures they were, with feathered coats of exquisite colors. If I sat perfectly still, they would venture even closer until I could see the expression of their eyes, as if imploring me to toss out a handful of the golden nuggets that I surely must be eating. Then they would fly back to where they started, as if shocked by their own lack of caution, and then begin creeping closer again.

The reader may question my embellishment of this secret forbidden sin. But you must remember that this was the only self-indulgent personal pleasure I was allowing myself to enjoy at this particular time in my life. The fact that it was forbidden made it all the more rapturous — hence, the words I have used in trying to describe it.

✧

Because my experience at Padroni's Community Baptist Church had proven to be personally and spiritually fulfilling, I felt called to proceed with full ordination before I entered my last year of study at the Iliff School of Theology. This required my writing a doctrinal paper to be read and defended at a meeting of Baptist clergy at a regional association level. I worked hard at it, wanting not to make it too academic, to keep it simple enough that it flowed theologically with conviction and understanding.

The association clergy gathered at Padroni and among them, of all people, was Dr. Erdmann Smith, pastor of the large and impressive First Baptist Church of Denver. I read my doctrinal paper with fear and trepidation and was pleased that the initial reaction appeared favorable. However, at length someone asked if I agreed with the biblical interpretations of historic Christian beliefs or the theological interpretations of these beliefs.

I took a deep breath to steady my nerves and achieve some semblance of inner calm, then proceeded to make the worst answer I could have made. "How can you separate biblical interpretations from theological interpretations? They go hand in hand. Which biblical and theological interpretation are you talking about? There are many, you know. Mine may not completely agree with yours." I went on to describe the various biblical interpretations we had recently studied at seminary.

My interrogators were confused and then stunned when they discovered that there wasn't complete agreement even among themselves on these classical doctrinal questions. A debate erupted as the fundamentalists began challenging the orthodoxy of one another.

Dr. Smith came to my rescue, jumping into the fray and saying, "It's obvious to me that even though you gentlemen may know your Bible, you haven't done your theological homework." He then lectured them on the original scholarly contributions of the theologians I had previously mentioned. He argued that clergy, like college professors, should be professionally trained scholars, that each minister should be a theologian-in-residence to the local congregation.

By this time everyone was so intimidated by the great man's presence, standing there in his pinstriped suit, that no one dared to further complicate the evening. Someone timidly proposed a motion that I be recommended for ordination into the ministry of the American Baptist denomination. It passed.

Although I had been approved for full ordination, however, I knew that I had blown it.

While everyone hastened out the door, Dr. Smith gently took me by the arm and suggested that we go for a little walk. We shuffled along the darkened country lane, silently for awhile, me with my head down and hands in my pocket like an errant school kid, and he clutching my elbow and leaning toward me in this intimate fatherly talk.

"Gene," he said, "when they asked you if you agreed with the biblical interpretation of the classic Christian doctrines, you should have answered simply 'Yes' and let it go."

"Please explain."

"You see, Gene, fundamentalists know that there may be several interpretations of classical Christian doctrines. But they have the security of believing that there is only one *biblical* interpretation — and they have it. Had you simply answered 'Yes' to their question, they would have assumed that you were agreeing with them and they would have questioned you no further. Your mistake was in volunteering to tell them there might be several equally valid biblical interpretations."

I obviously had failed to measure up even to the minimum standard of theological discretion required of a new Baptist clergyman.

Nevertheless, a few weeks later, on June 29, 1953, I was ordained. The Padroni parishioners went out of their way to make it the best occasion ever. The exterior of the little white church was freshly painted. Work crews redecorated the basement of the church and practically installed a new church kitchen. Beautiful flowers were cut from their gardens and artistically arranged all over the church. A scrumptious fried chicken dinner was served to the visiting guests of honor before the ceremony was to begin. Another group arranged a lavish reception afterwards. My parents and both sisters, Edna and Sadie, were present, and it pleased me greatly. The Padroni choir sang my favorite anthem, "My God And I."

The words were more meaningful to me than when I first heard them sung by the contralto soloist at the Iliff Chapel.

Dr. Harvey Potthoff, the esteemed professor of Theology at Iliff was the preacher. He was then, and still is today, my mentor. His brilliant mystical intellectualism and the many books he's authored have always been an inspiration to me. I am convinced that he tossed aside the esoteric sermon originally prepared and, instead, delivered an entertaining and powerful message — perfectly tailored to the rural folk who packed the little church. They loved it!

It was a memorable evening. As the Denver delegation climbed in their cars, Dr. Smith drew me aside and said, "I can't ever remember an ordination that was as beautiful and touching and enjoyable as this one. I shall never forget it. And, Gene, I want you to come to Denver at your earliest convenience because I want to talk to you. Please call for an appointment."

I was ordained into the American Baptist ministry in 1954 and loved the people — but couldn't tolerate the prevailing religious fundamentalism which surrounded me.

A week later his secretary called. "Dr. Smith wants me to make an appointment for you to come and see him. When can that be?"

"Well," I answered, "I'm not sure. I'm leaving soon on vacation."

"Good," she said. "Stop by on your way through Denver. When will that be? He says it's urgent."

The truth is, I wasn't passing through Denver. I was on my way to Chicago to see my old flame, Shirley Hall, at the Michael Reese Hospital School of Nursing. We had resumed our correspondence. But since Dr. Smith said it was urgent, I drove out of my way to Denver first.

✧

I arrived at First Baptist Church in Denver a little early for my appointment, so I wandered about the great old church for awhile. Its colonial architecture was always most impressive. I was amazed to rediscover how large and beautiful it was. The sanctuary alone was large enough to hold twenty Padroni churches with pews to spare. I stopped and listened to the massive Skinner organ as the full-time organist and director of music swayed back and forth at the console to the rapid movement of his hands gliding across the tiered keyboards — and flying feet on the base pedals.

I paused in the lovely reception room, newly redecorated and furnished, and remembered the formal reception lines there with the clergy attired in their cutaway frock coats and gray-striped trousers. I visited the formal board-room with its long conference walnut table and matching leather-covered burgundy chairs.

Being at Padroni, I had forgotten how prestigious a large city church could really be.

Dr. Smith motioned me into his office and invited me to pull my chair up beside him, behind his massive desk. I had steeled myself for the reprimand that surely was to follow regarding my disastrous doctrinal pre-sentation and had already decided that I would not become defensive. I would simply listen carefully to his words of wisdom, reflect on them for awhile, and at a later day discuss it with him when I had a more balanced perspective. Never would I debate him.

"Eugene," he began, "it's obvious to me that you deeply love your little Baptist congregation at Padroni, and these people reciprocate that love. How I envy you. You may never again experience that much love and affection from a congregation you serve. It's a rare thing when it happens like that. Cherish every moment of it. Most experienced clergymen know, regard-less of their strengths and talents, that there will always be a contentious group who's out to get rid of them. You don't have that at Padroni. Not yet, at least. Cherish your days there, because you probably will never have it so good again. Don't let it spoil you forever."

I nodded, not knowing what else to do.

He continued, "Unfortunately, you can't stay there much longer. In another year you'll have your advanced graduate theological degree, and you must move on in the furtherance of your career. Those wonderful people will accept another seminarian as their pastor and their rural church life will go on as always before. You must prepare yourself for this real-ity, and you must help them prepare for it, too. The good Lord, in His infinite wisdom, will take care of you all."

He removed his glasses, swirled his large leather chair to glance out the window of his study, then turned it back, leaned forward and faced me directly. I thought to myself, *Here it comes, brace yourself.*

"Eugene, this is very confidential. In another year I want you to become the assistant pastor of First Baptist Church of Denver, Colorado. My current director of education aspires to this position, but I'm letting him go before the year is out, although he doesn't know that yet. You can't run a church any more than you can run a corporation if your executive staff is not absolutely loyal. He's not."

I tensed, wondering what he was leading up to.

"So I'm creating a new position just for you when you finish seminary one year from now. I want you to become the assistant pastor, next in line to me. I insist, however, that you begin your Ph.D. program immediately upon your graduation from Iliff. It usually takes a couple of years to wrap up the required coursework before you begin writing your doctoral dissertation. And that can take a year or two, depending, of course, on the nature of the research you'll be doing in your chosen field."

I gulped.

"I'll insist that you take time from your duties here to attend the required doctoral courses during the day. But you'll have to do the studying on your own time at night. I suggest you rent a high-class bachelor's apartment right here in the Capitol Hill area of Denver, within walking distance of the church — and there are many good ones located near here. By the way, are there any plans for marriage in the near future?"

"No."

"Well, that's good right now. But not forever, you understand? Rent yourself a two-bedroom apartment and you can use the second bedroom for your study. We'll provide you a housing allowance to cover these rental costs. Without a wife or family you can devote yourself wholeheartedly to your doctoral program and probably have your Ph.D. completed in about three years. Are you following me?"

I nodded.

"If you don't want to pursue your Ph.D. at Iliff in theology, then the University of Denver would be great for a host of other doctoral fields. I did my graduate work at the University of Chicago, and it's a sister university to the University of Denver, you know."

Yes, I thought to myself, *I've heard that expression before somewhere, using almost identically the same words, but where was it?. . . Ah, yes, the gandy dancer in Clearmont. The one who said, "Goin' nowhere . . . Been goin' there a long — long time," just before he went out to get himself hit by a train. And to think, that gandy was a fellow alumnus of Dr. Smith!*

My mind had wondered. I refocused on the serious conversation at hand.

Reaching out and placing his hand on my arm, Dr. Smith leaned forward and said, "You see, Gene, I'm personally grooming you to take my place here at First Baptist. You'll attend all the board meetings as my first assistant. I'll see to it that you become personally acquainted with the corporate executives on our Board of Trustees and socialize with their families, and they will come to know you personally. I'll see to it that you have plenty of congregational exposure through pulpit preaching and pastoral administration.

"In about four years, I plan to retire. By that time you'll have your doctorate, and depending on how well you do in your maturity of scholarship, in your preaching, in your personal relationships with the congregation, in your pastoral work much like it is in Padroni, you'll be in an excellent position to be considered as my successor. I can't guarantee anything, of course. But I do know that after my retirement here, they will be wanting a much younger pastor. By that time, you should be well groomed and ready to take it on, providing, of course, you've done all your homework and mended all your fences."

Sitting back, pleased with his proposition, beaming from ear to ear, he crossed his arms and asked, "Now, tell me, what's your initial reaction to my proposal?"

At first, I was speechless. When I recovered my balance just a little bit, I told him that I had an obligation to serve several years in the Army Chaplains Corps following my graduation from seminary. He told me that would make it too late for his master plan to work, because he would almost be ready for retirement by that time.

"I urge you to reconsider that commitment," he said, "because I'm offering you the career opportunity of a lifetime. Please think it over carefully and prayerfully, and let me know."

The interview was over.

I dashed to a telephone and called my good friend Herb Brawner, an engineer at Gates Rubber Company, and insisted that we meet for lunch. I told him what had just transpired and he said, "That doesn't surprise me one bit. Although Nina and I are attending a Baptist church in Littleton, closer to where we now live, I did see Dr. Smith the other day and he was telling me all about attending your wonderful ordination. Then he told me that he was dedicating himself to the advancement of your career. He's very fond of you."

"Herb, it scares the hell out of me." I said. "After seven years of college and graduate school, I'm not ready to jump into a Ph.D. program right now. I wanna take a little time off. But he's got it all planned out for me, even to where I'll live and the kind of apartment I'll be renting. Not that the plan is necessarily so bad, but it's so all-encompassing. It's Erdmann Smith's plan for my life, not Gene Todd's plan.

Herb reaffirmed my point of view. "Gene, being the prodigy of Dr. Erdmann Smith may be more of a millstone around your neck than a lifesaver, simply because self-appointed successors are always suspect."

Then, smiling, as if he suddenly caught an inspiration directly from God, he looked at me and said, "Besides, even though I love that man, you don't have the girth to take his place at First Baptist yet. My friend, you've got a lot of gut work yet to do."

Herb was right, as usual. Especially his clever and humorous double-entendre reference to the enormous physical girth of Dr. Smith in comparison to my trim thirty-two inch waist. Obviously, he knew I had a long way to go to match the intellectual likeness of a Dr. Erdmann Smith. He hit the nail squarely on the head. Herb was always my lifesaver when I needed to talk.

Dr. Erdmann Smith wanted to groom me to replace him as senior pastor of First Baptist Church in Denver. I appreciated the honor but didn't feel myself ready for the heady assignment.

As I drove out across Nebraska, then up through Iowa, heading for Chicago, I carefully phrased the letter I would write Dr. Erdmann Smith. I would let him know how honored and flattered I was with his magnanimous offer. I would try to tell him, in great detail, the remarkable influence that he had indelibly made on my life and faith. Since his stature was so great, it would be all the more difficult for me to separate myself from his shadow and create an identity of my own. But I must do it. Also, I needed to honor the military commitment I had made to my country and myself to serve in the Army Chaplains Corps. And I needed the experience of a medium-sized parish church before I aspired for something as magnificent and challenging as the First Baptist Church of Denver.

Not often does a person have the personal satisfaction of knowing that an intangible thing called "emotional maturity" has subconsciously broken through, that one has made the right decision for all the right reasons despite being sorely tempted to do otherwise for all the wrong reasons. Such was the case when I declined Dr. Erdmann Smith's gracious offer.

At the same time, however, I recognize that maybe I missed a great opportunity. Many celebrated people, from all walks of life, attribute their notable success to one great break that came their way. There's no question that Dr. Smith's offer could have represented a turning point in my life. But it also could have been a disaster.

I find it incongruous, however, to remember that only six years earlier there was this Wyoming country kid who didn't know how to ride a streetcar, who slept out in the bushes his first night on the DU campus, who watched a general's drunken wife fall off her chair into a garbage heap — and who put up with Elmore and Tillie in his attic bedroom. Who sat in a church pew, wearing his blue jeans, intimidated by the prestigious congregation which swallowed him up, listening spellbound to the scholarly sermons of Dr. Erdmann Smith. It's preposterous to think that only a few years later, this same country greenhorn would be considered a possible replacement for the pulpit master himself, and that he would be invited to accept the master's grooming to assume one of the largest pastorates in Denver. Unbelievable!

The powerful lesson I've learned from this experience is that one must never underestimate the potential of opportunities that come one's way, regardless of the adverse or humble circumstances in which one may be engulfed. In my opinion many dreams are never fulfilled because too many people never allow themselves to believe the dreams were possible in the first place.

Although I have often wondered how different my life might had been had I accepted and followed through on the offer of Dr. Erdmann Smith, I still believe I made the right decision to go my own way, and I have never regretted it.

Chapter 5

The trip to Chicago was the first vacation I'd taken all by myself. En route I stopped in Springfield, Illinois, to visit the home country of Abraham Lincoln. All my life I have been enchanted with the story of Lincoln. I began collecting Lincoln books while in high school, everything from biographies and speeches to the definitive multivolume work of Carl Sandburg.

As I drove into the older part of downtown Springfield I was stirred with the fantasy that every old building I saw would have been seen and known by Abraham Lincoln during his many years there as a resident country lawyer. Somehow I got myself lost while searching for the street address of the Lincoln family home. Since it was late in the afternoon, with the Illinois heat and humidity becoming unbearable, this in a day before air-conditioning, I decided to stop at a local diner for a chilled glass of iced tea and more specific instructions.

My waitress at the counter was wearing a flamboyant blonde wig and had the most frightening black eye I had ever seen, either from being pounded on by her man or getting hit by a freight train. When I asked for directions to the Lincoln home she said, "He never lived here. I don't know why tourists like you seem to think that since Illinois is Lincoln country he lived everywhere here. He ain't ever lived in Springfield."

"Lady, I beg your pardon," I protested in stunned disbelief. "Abraham Lincoln and his wife, Mary Todd, owned a home here in Springfield where he practiced law before he was elected our U.S. president. That's a historical fact."

"It's history, huh? Well, let me tell you something, mister, history ain't always got its facts straight." Then she shouted over her shoulder to the cook in the kitchen, "Hey, Dixie, did Abraham Lincoln ever live here in Springfield?"

"Hell, no," came back the answer. "He lived in Chicago. Any damn fool knows that."

"See? You got it all wrong. Tourists are all alike," she smirked, "They just don't listen to us natives."

The bimbo noisily gathered up some empty beer glasses from the counter, then turned to me and said, "Honey, if you're new around here, I can recommend a little hotel nearby for a cheap room tonight."

I don't know why I allowed myself to feel so devastated. I was incensed to think that I had driven a thousand miles to visit this historical site only to be confronted with such abysmal ignorance of a local resident. I slithered off my stool and stumbled outside. Heat from the hot sidewalk hit me like a blast furnace. A policeman, leaning up against a building and wiping his sweaty face with a handkerchief, told me, "Why, the Lincoln home is just around the corner here. If you're already parked, it would be closer to walk."

Sure enough, there it was, quaint but supremely dignified. The shuttered windows gave it a distinguished charm. Surrounded by a wrought-iron fence, it looked exactly as it did in a photograph I vividly remembered of Lincoln standing out in the front yard with his younger son. As I stepped up to the door, a woman said, "Sorry, we close at five o'clock. But we'll be open at nine in the morning. Please come back."

I really didn't mind. I could have just stood there on the stoop all night. Spotting some people sitting on the porch of the neighboring house, fanning themselves, I walked over and brazenly asked, "Do you have a bedroom I could rent that faces out toward the Lincoln home?"

"Yes, but you wouldn't want it," the woman said. "The heat is unbearable up there."

"I'll take it, anyway." I said and paid her cash before I even went up to look at the room. "I'll be back," I told her, "when the evening cools down a little."

That night I learned that in Illinois, unlike Wyoming and Colorado, the evening doesn't cool down. Never in my life have I tried to spend a night in such smothering heat. I tried sprinkling the sheets with cold water, which produced only an initial coolness but quickly gave way to a sweltering humidity that almost suffocated me. There was no cross-ventilation, but if I sat in front of the wide-open window and *imagined* air moving against my perspiration-drenched body, at least, I had a *perception* of coolness.

There I sat all night, looking out upon the actual home of Abraham Lincoln no more than forty feet away from my window. Not one moment did I sleep in that bed. But that was all right with me. I watched the caretaker in the Lincoln home, now a national historic site, as he moved from room to room throughout the night, making his periodic security rounds with a flashlight before returning to the second-floor library to read a book, the lamp casting his shadow upon the drawn shade.

The haunting words of a poem came drifting back to me, a poem I had once memorized and recited but had long-ago forgotten. Snatches of the lines began reshuffling themselves into orderly verses in my mind:

It is portentous, and a thing of state
That here at midnight, in our little town
A mourning figure walks, and will not rest,
Near the old court-house pacing up and down.
Or his homestead, or in shadowed yards
He lingers where his children used to play,
Or through the market, on the well-worn stones
He stalks until the dawn-stars burn away.
He cannot sleep upon his hillside now.
He is among us — as in times before.
And we who toss and lie awake for long
Breathe deep, and start, to see him pass the door.

In the stillness of the night and early dawn I meditated on the awesome role this man played in the abolition of human slavery in the United States and the horrendous price that was paid by so many during the Civil War. I did not know at that time that my own grandfather fought with the Union Army in the Civil War — not my *great*-grandfather, as one might expect, but my mother's father, Richard Wilcox. That startling revelation would come to me many years later when my family examined his personal documents and found among them his discharge papers.

I can honestly say that the night spent looking out upon the family home of Abraham Lincoln from the sweltering second-floor bedroom of the neighboring house was one of the most inspirational of my life.

I made it to Chicago the next evening and went to a YMCA hotel, securing a tiny interior room on an upper floor with no air-conditioning and no windows. The next morning I found the Michael Reese Hospital nurses' residence and waited in the lounge for Shirley to return from floor duty. She looked very professional and lovely in her student nurse uniform — and our romance picked up exactly where it had left off two years earlier.

(Selected verses of "Abraham Lincoln Walks At Midnight" by Vachel Lindsay in his volume of *Collected Poems* edited by Mark Harris. Published by Macmillan Company, New York, N.Y. Used by permission of Simon & Schuster.)

We did the usual things that sweethearts do in the city of Chicago. We toured the shoreline by boat, walked the ritzy streets in the boutique shopping areas, and dined in quiet inexpensive restaurants. We made our plans. We would be married during Christmas vacation at the First Baptist Church in Buffalo, Wyoming, where her father once served as pastor. (Her parents had since moved to a new pastorate in Riverton.) Naturally, her father would officiate at our wedding. These short-range details were simple.

The long-range plans were a bit more complicated. We would set up housekeeping at the little parsonage in Padroni. When I graduated from seminary the following June, I would join the Army Chaplains Corps, and while I was away for the first year, completing the basic chaplain training program, Shirley would return to Chicago and finish up her nursing instruction. Then we would be reunited and request overseas military duty. As a nurse, she would surely find employment at the same military hospital complex at which I was stationed. This would enable us to get out of the continental United States and travel the world before settling down to start a family.

It was a great plan, and it made perfectly good sense any way you looked at it. After all, I was twenty-five years old and ready to settle down to married bliss — and also see the world. But I had a long five-month wait before Christmas and the wedding.

Fortunately, I had many things to do. Padroni had a chapter of the largest youth group among any of the Baptist churches in northeastern Colorado, the Baptist Youth Fellowship (BYF). I enjoyed working and playing with these delightful country kids (junior high and high school age). We met every Sunday evening for study or a program, always followed by games and refreshments, usually in one of their homes. I spent a lot of time with the young people during the summer months, when I was in Padroni full-time. Including skinny-dipping with the boys in the irrigation canals. Attendance at group meetings steadily held up because the kids were earning points to take a BYF vacation trip to the Black Hills Passion Play in August. I expected only one carload to qualify for the trip; instead, we had *five* carloads.

It was a great trip up through the beautiful Black Hills, past Mount Rushmore, overnight in Deadwood, evening performance at the famous passion play, then on to Devil's Tower in northeastern Wyoming and finally back to Padroni. The young people had a fantastic experience, and it was a memorable trip for me as well.

Then it was back to classes for my final year of studies at Iliff that September — and finally on to Sheridan for Christmas vacation and our wedding on December 29, 1953, at the First Baptist Church in Buffalo. Groomsmen included two dear friends from the basement apartment at 2328 South Downing Street in Denver, Herb Brawner and Jim Shadoan, and two seminarian friends, Jack Richards and Jim Kirk.

An hour before the ceremony was scheduled to begin, my groomsmen and I had to isolate ourselves in a little room off the front of the church. The room had no exit except out into the sanctuary in full view of the gathering congregation. Unfortunately, the nervous groom had to visit the bathroom, and this triggered the same urgent need with the others. In desperation, we lowered one another out through an open window and dropped a few feet to a snowdrift below. Some startled wedding guests on the outside thought the groom had lost his nerve and was staging a grand getaway. Then we had to hike each other back up through the window, with the able assistance of a rancher friend who told me, "You must have forgotten that in a Wyoming wedding it's customary to have a getaway horse waiting just outside the back door for such emergencies as this."

We got back inside without injury, and the ceremony came off without a hitch. (Or using Wyoming terminology, should I say it came off with a *good hitch?*) Shirley looked radiant in her lovely wedding dress as we took out places beneath a decorated archway fashioned by her mother. Shirley's father officiated and sang the Lord's Prayer in his beautiful tenor voice.

We honeymooned at the historic Sheridan Inn, made famous by its former owner, Buffalo Bill Cody. My own father and mother honeymooned there in 1906. Then we drove to Denver and spent a week as houseguests of Herb and Nina Brawner in Littleton. It was so great that I called Pa Reike back in Padroni and asked, "Can't I just stay another week before coming out for Sunday services? It's so beautiful here in Denver."

His classic answer to a groom on his honeymoon: "Come on back to Padroni. It's beautiful wherever you are."

But it couldn't have been all that beautiful there for Shirley. We had no kitchen in the parsonage and no water. We had to run over to the church basement to use the electric stove and refrigerator, but there was no water there either. We had to carry two pails of water every night from the McCulley home. This situation was intolerable. And to make matters much worse, I returned to my classes at Iliff during the week, and Shirley had to remain continuously at Padroni. Fortunately, she immediately got a job at the hospital in Sterling, relying on others for daily transportation. On weekends, unfortunately, when I was in Padroni, she often was assigned the midnight shift.

Shirley and me outside church shortly after our marriage. I attended classes at Iliff Seminary in Denver during the week, leaving Shirley alone in the parsonage with a nursing job in Sterling. It was a "weekend marriage" that first year. I served here from 1952 to 1955.

This deplorable situation was more than any modern bride in the 1950s could possibly have bargained for, although Shirley never complained. We'd vowed to love each other "for better or for worse," but things were turning out to be far worse than better for either of us. But we looked forward to the long-range plan we had agreed to back in Chicago — that when I graduated in June I would enter the Army Chaplains Corps and she could return to Michael Reese Hospital to complete her nurse's training. This would be only a few months away.

In the meantime, the congregation at the Padroni Community Church continued to grow steadily. Shirley was a tremendous helpmate. She had a good role model in her mother as to what was expected of a Baptist minister's wife. This role model, however, places a heavy burden of expectation upon the wife and family of a Protestant minister. Today most clergy spouses make it clearly understood that they are not the assistant minister who comes cheap, with no salary. But this is not the way it was in the 1950s. So Shirley sang in the choir, performed violin solos as part of the anthems, occasionally played the piano for congregational singing if Bernice was away, taught Sunday school, worked with the BYF, and helped me with Vacation Bible School. It was a bit too much.

But we were very much in love as newlyweds, and I was too young to acknowledge a deficiency within myself — the inability to say "no" when too much was too much. We seemingly had inexhaustible energy to do whatever was asked of us.

✧

Something which Shirley nor I had ever contended with was a real, honest-to-goodness dust storm!

Yes, this part of Colorado was in the historic dust bowl area of our nation which figured so disastrously in the first years of the Great Depression.

I thought a dust storm was what happened when the wind blew hard, drying out the soil and eventually blowing it away. There was plenty of that. But there was also something else about a dust storm I never knew.

One summer afternoon when I was returning from Sydney, Nebraska, to Padroni, after a funeral, I noticed the horses and cattle galloping over a knoll. The horses were racing full speed and the cattle were running with tails above their backs which indicated real fright. I also noticed that the birds were flocking about as if they had been chased from their nests of young ones.

Then I saw it. A huge billowing mushroom of something, hundreds of feet high, that was slowly rolling and tumbling across the prairie. Never before in my life had I seen such a phenomenon. I stopped my car and sat on the right fender to watch it. As I recall, the air was perfectly calm where I was. But I could hear a low thunderous rumble and could see lightning flashing within the apparition.

Then it hit and totally enveloped the car and me. Dust and silt, finer than sifted flour, turned the afternoon so dark that the visibility was reduced to zero. I leaped in the car, rolled up the windows as tightly as I could to wait it out. But the dust filtered inside the sealed car and clogged my nostrils and sinuses so badly that I could scarcely breathe.

Two hours later it blew over. The landscape looked like the surface of the moon. Everything was one color of dirty gray: the hills, sagebrush, grasslands, trees, fence posts, highway — and, yes my car. I wiped off my windshield and started to drive down the paved highway only to notice that a cloud of dust was kicked up behind me as if I were driving down a country dirt road. I knew now what it was when the old-timers around there talked about the dust bowl days, when a blizzard of dust drifted as high against the fences and buildings as a howling snow storm in the winter. I learned a healthy respect for the deadly ravages it could bring.

But Shirley didn't know. She had never experienced such a dust storm either. One Friday morning she went to work in Sterling and left her windows open to catch the fresh spring air. Early that afternoon a dust storm moved through. Our neighbor remembered seeing the windows open earlier that day and raced over to our parsonage to close them. But it was too late. When I returned from Denver for my weekend in Padroni, I stopped first in Sterling and picked Shirley up and headed out for the country. What we found was much worse than expected. Literally, there was a half inch of the shifted silt everywhere in the house. The only way we could clean it up was to sweep the stuff into heaps in the middle of the floor and then use a scoop shovel to pitch it out into the yard.

Every dish in the cupboards, all our clothing in the closet, and the bedding was shrouded in layers of dust. It was weeks before we finally got it cleaned up. It was miserable. And to this day I can still taste the grit in my mouth, when I think about it, and remember trying to sleep with sand in the bed, and suffering nosebleeds when my nostrils and sinuses were caked to capacity. Temporary relief came from Dr. Palmer, the eye-ear-nose specialist for whom Shirley later worked, when he packed my nose with gunk which shrunk the swollen tissue, and prescribed some medication for the sinus headaches which followed.

✧

In the 1950s, to qualify for a Master of Theology degree instead of a Bachelor of Divinity it was necessary not only to successfully complete a three-year course of study but also to be re-examined on every course before graduation. These re-examinations were called *comprehensives.* They were formidable, indeed. But the graduating seniors at Gay Stables invented a clever procedure to prepare ourselves for the ordeal. We assigned each person to become an expert in one particular area of study and to lecture and tutor the rest of us. We would all gather up on third-floor attic room of Gay Stables and go at it. This program of study became our daily routine. It was rough.

The grueling comprehensives consisted of eight-hour shifts of continuous examinations for three consecutive days. Some candidates simply quit and walked out of the room because the stress became unbearable. We had to wait a week for the final grading results. It was a long, long week. But when the results came in I learned I had passed easily.

My sister Sadie and Shirley's parents attended my graduation in June 1954 and saw the crimson hood of a Master of Theology degree slipped over my head and draped across my shoulders. The first thing I did upon graduation was carry my certificate to the Colorado Military District so I could apply for active duty in the Army Chaplains Corps. This was the personal commitment I had made when I entered seminary three years earlier, and it was the long-range plan which Shirley and I had agreed upon when we were married.

I laid the certificate in front of the silver-haired colonel, with whom I had met several times over the past three years, and said, "Finally, sir, I'm ready to enter the Chaplains Corps. I can go within a week, even today if I must, but I would prefer a month delay if that's acceptable to you."

He carefully examined my certificate, congratulated me, cleared his throat and hesitantly said, "Lieutenant Todd, it would take an act of Congress to get you into the Chaplains Corps right now. The quota for Baptist chaplains is so top-heavy with men who want to make a career of it that we're having to phase out majors and colonels. Truly, it would take a special act of Congress to change that."

I said, "Sir, you've got to be kidding me. I have been talking with you for three years about this enlistment, and never before have you said the quotas for Baptist chaplains were all filled up."

"That's because I never knew, lieutenant. I talked with you only in a vague, general sort of way about the Chaplains Corps. But when you made the appointment last week to meet with me, I immediately contacted the chaplain general's office for specific information and was told that your chances of getting into the Chaplains Corps right now would be about as good as a snowball rolling through hell."

Immediately, I arranged lunch with Herb Brawner for consolation and guidance. Poor Herb. But he was my friend, and this is what friends are for.

With him, I ran through the long-range plans that Shirley and I had made when we married — and now all to no avail. I pined away about losing what might have been a successful ministerial military career. It was too late now to ask Dr. Erdmann Smith to renew his offer. I knew I needed a break before embarking on a Ph.D. program.

I also knew that since I wasn't in school any more that I had an obligation to pay off a $3000 student loan from the Whitney Scholarship Foundation at Sheridan, Wyoming. My salary at the Padroni Community Baptist Church was $190 a month. Any way you looked at it, I was in deep trouble.

Herb was a good listener, silently gulping away at his sandwich. At length he shoved aside his empty plate and said, "Gene, you haven't eaten one bite of your lunch. Now you listen to me while you eat."

He said, "Gene, you've been on this military track for such a long time that you seem to think it's the only track you have. But a bridge up ahead has washed out. Take a detour. There are hundreds of other possibilities. Maybe find yourself a church here in Denver, or one not far away, while Shirley completes her nurse's training at St. Luke's Hospital. And then go from there."

That suggestion made perfect sense to me — except I didn't want a city church in Denver. I said, "Herb, it's obvious to me that even the best-made plans can go up in smoke. Since my plan hasn't worked out, maybe I need to rely a little more on God's will for our lives right now. The problem is, how does one really know the will of God?"

"About like getting kicked by a horse. When it happens, you'll know it," Herb answered as we pushed ourselves away from the table. He dashed back to work at the Gates Rubber Company, and I started out on the long road back to Padroni.

The truth is, I was far more distressed about the immediate future than I dared to admit to Shirley. The next morning she had no more than left the house for the Sterling hospital when the Padroni school principal walked up to my house and said, "I'm needing a high school history teacher this coming fall, and I'll be needing him to drive a school bus as well. Would you be interested? The pay is $3000."

Talk about getting kicked by a horse!

Herb was right, you'll know it's God's will when it happens. I endorsed every school paycheck directly over to the Whitney Scholarship Foundation. Thus, in one year, I repaid the entire $3000 that had been loaned me. (I was much distressed to learn later in life that many professional people, doctors and lawyers, who benefited from the scholarship fund never made an attempt to repay their loans.)

I enjoyed school teaching. The students hated history, just as I had at their age when the coaches taught it in high school. They were up front with their expressions of intense dislike and kept reminding me that history had nothing whatever to do with their lives in the here and now.

I reminded them that at the school dances I saw them dancing a funny little dance, something like a polka — a little hop and a skip, a few fast steps, and then the same thing all over again. I asked them where that little dance came from, because never before had I seen it danced by young people elsewhere. They said their parents had taught it to them.

I gave them a homework assignment: They were to ask their parents about the origin of that little dance. The students reported back that it was the variation of a folk dance their German ancestors had learned during their exile in Russia beginning in the 1700s, when Catherine the Great encouraged German agricultural settlement of the Russian steppes. When Catherine's promises were no longer honored by the Russian government in the early 1900s, these German-Russians immigrated in large numbers to Colorado, Nebraska, Wyoming, Montana, and the Dakotas.

Here were these high school kids dancing a Russian peasant dance called the Dutch Hop while steadfastly maintaining that history had no immediate impact on their lives. From this beginning, they all gathered information and wrote reports on what it was like for their ancestors to live in Russia and then immigrate to America. German was the second language in most of their homes, and for some of their grandparents it was the only language. They interviewed their families, collected photos, and brought ancestral mementos to class for their animated oral reports. Personal tales like these made the learning of history more interesting and fun for all of us.

✧

With my acceptance of the teaching position, Shirley and I were committed to staying in Padroni for another year. But something had to happen in the parsonage. First of all, we needed a kitchen. And we needed water. Both would take a lot of money, which the little church didn't have.

The kitchen was the easier of the two problems to fix. Bill Bunning and I, with a group of volunteers, quickly built a wall across one end of the living room and furnished the new space with a donated refrigerator and two-burner electric stove. The old refrigerator leaked freon gas so badly that twice service men from Sterling had to drive out and don gas masks to attempt their repairs. They gave up on it, and another one was donated. The stove never worked. So we finally replaced it with a little hot plate. Shirley continued using the oven over in the church basement and had to run the hot food back and forth through rain, wind, and snow.

Installing running water was something else. This required drilling a well, digging an underground pump room where the pump wouldn't freeze, digging a cistern and a sewage draining system, and installing the necessary plumbing. The basic equipment and supplies alone would cost a lot of money, even with all the labor volunteered. But if it was God's will that we stay in Padroni one more year, it must be His will that we install the water system — because surely no other rural pastor would consider coming to Padroni without these basic modern conveniences. But it would be a hard sell, because the majority of the dryland farmers and sharecroppers didn't have modern plumbing in their modest homes, either.

Nevertheless, we gave it a try. It was obvious to me that we needed a special rallying event to kick it off, something that might attract the whole community. While driving out of Sterling one day, I saw a herd of buffalo grazing in a pasture owned by the large Sherwin Livestock Company. The Sherwin ranch was one of those pioneer cattle ranches dating back to the historic beginnings of the cattle barons out on the open range of northeastern Colorado and southern Wyoming. The thought occurred to me, *Why not have a buffalo barbecue?*

The church leaders were lukewarm to my proposal but agreed to accompany me on a personal call on Mrs. Sherwin to inquire about the possibility of purchasing one-quarter of a buffalo carcass. Mrs. Sherwin, whom I had never met, was an elderly widow, the matriarch of the vast family ranching estate and the epitome of what you would expect of such a grand lady of the Old West. She parted the purple velvet curtains and made her regal entrance into the stately Victorian drawing room of the spacious ranch home.

It had been agreed that after the preliminary social pleasantries, I was to do the talking and make the proposal. "She probably wouldn't want to refuse your request," my companions said," since you are a young man of God who is awfully good with words." This line of reasoning is often used with the clergy, but terribly flawed. Lay people carry far more influence than ministers when it comes to the presentation of a bold project or a new idea. Since people expect ministers to be good with words, they therefore tend automatically to discount whatever a minister may propose with his or her use of good words.

Mrs. Sherwin quietly listened to my proposal, occasionally smiling at me during my presentation as if the idea sounded trifling and ridiculous. She made no other response to any part of my presentation, either by gesture or word. Finally, like a courtroom lawyer building his case to its logical conclusion before the judge, I popped the final question as to whether we could purchase from her a quarter of a buffalo for the barbecue.

"NO," she answered, carefully emphasizing the single word with the circular formation of her lips, otherwise not stirring a muscle or blinking an eye, her arms folded against her chest.

Her answer hung in the air like a death sentence to a cattle thief. I could feel an emotional freeze grip my partners in crime, as if they were saying, *Now, preacher, how do we get ourselves out of this one? Why don't we just slip outside and let you handle this? After all, remember, you're so good with words . . .* But I couldn't think of an appropriate response and shrunk back, almost in terror. She continued staring at me as if I had threatened to invade her cattle kingdom with 10,000 head of sheep.

Finally, she broke the awkward silence with words firmly spoken, "I will not sell one pound of meat. But I will **give** you a whole buffalo, because you'll surely need it — if your plans and goals are as ambitious as you say they are."

She was absolutely right.

At first, the ticket sales were listless. I had a weekly program on the radio station in Sterling and began using the broadcast time to talk about the buffalo barbecue. Soon the newspapers took it up. Then I mounted loudspeakers on my car and drove around the countryside telling people this was something they wouldn't want to miss.

Shirley and another young woman in the church agreed to handle the dinner preparations. Volunteers made baked potatoes, vegetables, and homemade pies. At first, when we exceeded 100 tickets, we had to move the whole event from our church basement to the high school gymnasium so that we could use the school kitchens. When the sales reached 200, then

500, Shirley and Lillian had to arrange to use all the home economics kitchens on the second floor as well. Finally, we had to limit ticket sales to less than 1000. Think of it — 1000 people scheduled to hit the little town of Padroni in one night, a town whose total population was only seventy-five. To this day, people in Padroni will say that the buffalo barbecue was the largest single assemblage of people in the history of the little town.

Other local volunteers presided over the serving tables, and the youth group organized a liquid refreshment cadre to keep all water and coffee cups replenished. Needless to say, the gym was mobbed. Patrons who had eaten surrendered their places at the table and moved to the side bleachers to wait for a "Women's Fashion Show" presented by the men of the parish.

I recruited the society editor of the Sterling newspapers to take the microphone and describe the attire of each beautiful "model," invoking all the superfluous flair of a New York fashion show. These men, all seasoned ranchers and farmers, decked themselves out in the most lavish women's outfits imaginable, modeling everything from bikini swimwear and formal gowns to a wedding dress. All wore cosmetic makeup and extravagant wigs. Each would individually sashay back and forth on the stage, stopping and striking theatrical poses for the cameras, while the society editor continued her deadpan descriptive monologue.

The place roared and howled with laughter, not only because of the outlandish outfits but more because of the unbelievable footwork and hilarious poses of these men.

In fact, the thunderous roar became so intense that the social editor couldn't make herself heard over the public address system and had to keep repeating herself. As I write these words, forty years later, I bend over my keyboard with laughter remembering the exotic Marlene Dietrich poses these hardscrabble ranchers would strike, their outstretched arms, gloved hands, maudlin faces, and flamboyant plumed hats. I don't know how we ever persuaded them to lay aside their macho self-image and let themselves go with such a theatrical performance. It brought out the country ham in every one of them.

For a month afterward, I avoided direct eye contact with any of these men in church while preaching for fear of breaking up. I could not even look at their faces without getting a flashback of their nellie queen performances. The Marlboro men of my congregation had become transformed into a congregation of ravishing transvestites!

The buffalo barbecue paid for the water system — that is, for all the equipment and plumbing supplies. The work still had to be done by hand. Shovels and tools were left in place, and anyone who had an hour or two to spare could drop by the church and dig for awhile, or crawl under the parsonage and install piping, or pour a little cement. On and on it went, by volunteer work crews, until Easter of 1955. At last Shirley and I had hot and cold water and could bathe inside the parsonage. We felt like royalty.

✧

In the fall of 1954 the *Denver Post* sent out a staff writer and photographer to do a feature story on the Padroni church for its Sunday *Empire* magazine. Bill Hosokawa, who later became the *Post's* chief editorial editor, was assigned to write the story, and he and the photographer followed Shirley and me around for several days. They took photos of the church, of me conducting Sunday morning worship services, teaching high school and driving the school bus; of Shirley administering vaccine shots to people in Padroni under a physician's care, of me milking cows on Vern Johnson's farm, and of Shirley and me dancing at one of our country dances.

The lengthy story was entitled "Pastor From Padroni" and contained many photos. Bill Hosokawa did an excellent job, I think, but some of the people in Padroni couldn't help but take offense at the way he described the barren little town, its dusty dirt streets, and the incessant wind blowing across the rolling plains of northeastern Colorado. The truth is, Hosokawa saw Padroni very much as any outsider would have seen a little rural town. It takes a heap of living in such a place before one can describe the human relationships that make the community so precious to the people who live there.

Because the huge circulation of the *Denver Post* covered the entire Rocky Mountain region, hundreds of letters poured in with additional donations to the water system fund. These extra contributions made it possible to bring water into the church basement and improve the kitchen there. There was still no new cooking stove for the parsonage, however. Had I honestly confronted the congregation with the impossibility of the old stove, I'm certain a new secondhand stove would have been acquired. But I couldn't bring myself to do it because so many people in my congregation had no inside plumbing in their own homes. Not that they begrudged it for Shirley and me, but they couldn't help but regret that such conveniences were beyond their economic means. These proud, dignified, and generous people were not poor in spirit, but many of them knew they were slipping deeper into the poverty of rural America.

I kept telling them that the water system was not for Gene Todd. It would stay behind when I left, and it was necessary if they hoped to secure a full-time or even part-time pastor in the future for their country church. Actually, the water system was their gift of love, a luxury they themselves could not afford and never had, which made it all the more precious for them to give and all the more difficult for me to graciously accept.

As a result of the *Denver Post* story and my radio broadcasting, I began getting many invitations to speak in northeastern Colorado. Sterling was a bustling city at that time, the center of a prosperous agricultural and livestock region. A successful oil boom bolstered the county's economy, and the discovery of richer oil fields was very much the promise of things to come. The square in the middle of town, surrounding the Logan County Courthouse, was a busy place.

Since it was the commercial and medical center of northeastern Colorado, Sterling hosted many conventions of oil exploration developers, farm equipment dealers, and agricultural organizations. They would often invite me to attend their banquets and give a little talk — not a sermon, heaven forbid, nor a speech about their business, about which I knew nothing. What they wanted was a little story of one kind or another. Storytelling is a real art, and I don't pretend to excel at it. But I think most rural people have a gift for it. I grew up among storytellers on a Wyoming ranch, and I had lived for three years among country storytellers at Padroni.

I loved to drop by the farm home of Slim Bunning on Sunday afternoons. There were always a bunch of people there from Padroni and Peetz and another little place called Iliff, named after the same cattle king whose wealth made possible the Iliff School of Theology. The women would gather in the living room, the men in the kitchen. Slim, wearing his bib overalls and rolling his own Bull Durham cigarettes, would spin yarns with the other men.

His farm was located in an area of southern Wyoming and northeastern Colorado known as the "hail belt." These poor dryland farmers would seed a grain crop and watch it mature, only to have the inevitable rip-roaring hailstorm thunder through, shearing limbs off the trees, shattering windows, and denting roofs already knocked barren of shingles — and pounding the wheat crop six inches into the ground. This common occurrence made good harvests few and far between The truth is, this high prairie land should never have been plowed in the first place — and even the farmers knew it.

I would sit among these farmers and hear their grim stories of adversity, always told with grievous humor. Slim, talking about the last hail storm, would say, "The hail thundered down but there wasn't one drop of rain or moisture. The hailstones were the size of golf balls and every time one of them hit the ground it would kick up a puff of dust. Pretty soon it was the *gol-darnest* dust storm you've ever seen, right in the middle of a hailstorm."

Slim's neighbor, whom I'll call Claude, was constitutionally unable to admit his good fortune. In the same hailstorm, Claude's farm was spared. (Sometimes a devastating hailstorm would seem to follow a fence line; at least, there were lots of stories about this sort of thing among these farmers.) "His wheat crop stood tall and bowing in the wind when everyone else's was nothing but mud," Slim would joke. "Everyone knew it was a bumper crop, more bushels per acre than ever before on that dryland farm. When he came to get his mail at the post office, someone asked him, 'Isn't it great, Claude, that your farm was spared?' And he answers, 'No, it really isn't. A bumper crop like that sure beats hell out of the soil.'"

Or like poor Orville, another destitute dryland farmer who struck it rich with thirty-six oil wells on his pitiful place netting him a monthly royalty check equivalent to $350,000 in today's (1996) currency, but who, like Claude, was constitutionally unable to admit his extraordinary good luck. Instead, he grumbled about the oil trucks knocking down his mailbox. "But, Orville," his neighbors exclaimed, "the oil company moved your mailbox down the road only ten feet so those tanker trucks could make the sharp turn into your driveway, but you bein' the ornery cuss you are moved it back."

"It's the principle of the thing," Orville groused.

Slim bellowed, "Even the king of England would gladly walk an extra ten feet once a day if the principle of the thing was worth four million bucks a year! But not ol' dust bowl Orville — he needed to suffer and bitch."

And then there was Arney who back in his pioneer homestead days, boasted of walking twelve miles to the nearest spring, twice a week, to tote home two five-gallon buckets of water for his thirsty family and chickens. But forty years later his feat was totally debunked as myth by a cantankerous neighbor who actually paced it out on his car's odometer and proved it was only 10.9 miles down to the spring. Poor Arney went to his grave in disgrace.

"Wouldn't you think," Slim reasoned, while everyone chuckled, "that ol' sorefoot Arney couldn't have been given the benefit of one 1.1 mile grace when the return trip was all uphill with a full load?"

I would listen to these remarkable stories all afternoon, and they stayed with me because they were so authentically country. They weren't jokes. I can't tell jokes because I can never remember the punch line. These stories were different because they emerged from the actual life experiences of these wonderful rural people. For that reason, they were classics to me and I retained them sufficiently to begin passing them on to others.

I was frequently called upon to tell these country tales at public gatherings in Sterling and surrounding towns. Some were funny, some were sad, but all hopefully carried a moral message for the listeners. I was introduced at first simply as the "Pastor from Padroni," but later Colorado's legendary U.S. Senator, "Big Ed" Johnson, whenever we spoke at the same occasion, referred to me as the "Country Parson." I liked that tagged description better.

✧

At our Easter service that spring, twenty-eight people came forward to unite with the church, the largest single contingent of converts at any one time in my pastoral career. The parsonage was modernized with modern indoor plumbing and a new water system. We had the rudiments of a kitchen, and things were looking good for the long-range plan of the church.

After a feature Denver Post *article entitled "Minister From Padroni" — I was frequently invited to be a "parson storyteller" at major farm conventions and oil equipment association meeting in northeastern Colorado, and to share the speakers platform with the famous U. S. Senator, "Big Ed Johnson." He tagged me the "Country Parson."*

But the long-range plans of the Todds, formulated at the time of our marriage, had hit another snag. We learned that we were pregnant!

This development radically altered the course we had long-ago charted, whereby Shirley would complete her final year of nurse's training while I pursued the possibility of a pastorate somewhere in the Denver area. I sensed sheer panic as I arranged an appointment with Dr. McDonald, the executive secretary of the Colorado Baptist Convention of Churches, to discuss alternatives. He was both helpful and discouraging.

He was helpful in that he advised me not to remain in a small rural church, where I had to supplement my meager salary of $190 a month by teaching school and driving a school bus, while getting ready to begin a family. "Pastoral opportunities will pass you by and in a few years you'll be history," he said. "You need to make the break from Padroni and do it immediately." I found this advice hard to accept but probably true and, therefore, helpful.

His additional comments, however, were quite discouraging.

"Gene you need to get back into the conservative mainstream of the Baptist tradition. You graduated from a seminary that basically trains not pastors but academicians aspiring for college professorships. You've done a splendid job out at Padroni, but that little rural congregation is so desperate for pastoral attention that they're willing to put up with anyone — even a minister who goes to their barn dances and has a picture of it splashed all over the *Denver Post*. No other Baptist church in Colorado would tolerate such moral indiscretion."

I strongly disagreed with his interpretation of the Iliff School of Theology. The seminary did have a heavy emphasis on theological scholarship and intellectual integrity, and many of its graduates did pursue doctoral degrees afterward, but it had also done a great job in training pastors. And I resented the put-down of Padroni and the snide implication that my success there was due only to the congregation's desperation.

"I recommend you set aside all those theological books I see on the shelves of your library and concentrate on the Bible," he continued. "Instead of focusing on those Ivory Tower theologians, why don't you make Billy Graham your role model?"

I burned.

You should never tell a denominational executive what you're really thinking, because somehow the job gives them a mystic sense of infallibility. Since I didn't know any better at that time, I mumbled, "You mean the old revivalist routine? *With every head bowed, and every eye closed, will you simply raise your hand if you want Gene Todd to pray for you? . . . And now that I've got you hooked . . . will all of you who raised your hands, simply slip out of the pew now and come forward . . . because this may your last chance for eternal salvation before you burn forever in the fire and brimstone of hell.* All while the choir is singing 'Just As I Am' to give it a real emotional punch before they might change their minds. Is that what you mean?"

Trying to ignore my inappropriate sarcasm Dr. McDonald said, "What I mean is that you should toss in a few current event comments to make it sound relevant, then preach an evangelistic sermon that's simple and noncontroversial. Don't express an opinion on anything unless the Bible says it."

He could tell that I was bristling and sought to comfort me. "Don't make it so hard on yourself, Gene. Believe me, it's a lot easier to preach only evangelistic sermons Sunday after Sunday. A sermon intended for only one thing — conversion."

"But, Dr. McDonald, I believe very strongly that Christian preaching should try to help people apply Christianity to the daily living of their lives." I remembered the *So What?* of my mother's persuasion.

"Gene, as a Baptist minister you are to pastor people, yes. But your mission is to win souls and dollars for Christ. Just like Billy Graham does."

"You mean, 'Give your hearts to Jesus and send your money to me?' If we all did that, Dr. McDonald, you wouldn't have a job because the local churches wouldn't have any money left to send you. They would have sent it all to Billy Graham."

It was obvious to Dr. McDonald that he was going to get nowhere with this young non–Billy Graham Baptist liberal. He tried to wrap up the conversation with one more piece of Godly advice.

"Gene, I say again, make it easy on yourself. Preach only for conversions. You don't need to worry about the practical applications of Christianity. Leave that up to the converts to figure out for themselves. That's the way Billy Graham does it. But since you're not impressed with his success, I'm telling you that's the way we Baptists do it here in the midwestern part of the United States. If you want to get yourself involved in all these other social and theological issues, you'll need to move to the East Coast. All the American Baptist ministers out there are flaming liberals."

That did it!

I was so distressed when I left McDonald's office that I immediately phoned for an appointment with Bishop Phillips, Methodist bishop of a multistate area of the Rocky Mountain region. When I arrived in his office, he told me that he had already checked my seminary credentials and had read the "Pastor From Padroni" story in the *Denver Post*. He most graciously extended an invitation to become a Methodist minister but wisely cautioned that he wanted me to think it over all summer, and pray about it.

"If by fall nothing opens up for you in the Baptist Church then, rest assured, I will have a place for you in the Methodist church somewhere in Colorado, Wyoming, or Montana."

Before leaving town, by religious impulse, I stopped by St. John's Episcopal Cathedral. As I walked down a long stone corridor leading to the humongous nave, I passed two priests who were smoking their pipes and casually chatting. The aroma of the Anglican pipe tobacco smoke reminded me that my Baptist pipe was secretly stashed under the front seat of my car. I stopped by the bulletin board, where I saw an announcement that the wife of an Episcopal rector in Denver was presenting a program on the need for Christians to support a Planned Parenthood Clinic for the city. There was to be a conference on prayer, followed by Evensong in the Martin Chapel, and on Saturday night there was to be a square dance in the parish hall with live music.

I dropped to my knees in the nave and earnestly prayed, "Oh Lord, this is where I think I belong. Right now I seem to be a minister without a denomination, and I don't like this state of limbo in my life right now. For three years I expected to graduate from seminary and become a military chaplain. That door has been slammed shut. Your Baptist denominational leader has just told me that I must become another Billy Graham, which I resent and refuse. Your Methodist bishop tells me he'll make a place for me somewhere in Montana. Yet here I am in an Episcopal cathedral feeling that this is where I truly belong. But I'll never be Catholic enough to become Episcopalian. Back in Padroni I have a young wife who is preparing to have our first baby. I can't dilly-dally around this issue much longer. Lord, I'm needing some direction here."

When I returned to Padroni, I was most eager for Herb and Nina Brawer's forthcoming visit with their newly adopted baby daughter, Donna Kay. I needed desperately to talk. I poured it all out on poor Herb and confessed that I wasn't handling the situation very well. I wanted to be more supportive of Shirley in her first pregnancy, but I was in inner turmoil because our master plan, which sounded so logical and reasonable at the time we were married, had totally fallen apart. I didn't trust my own judgment very much anymore, and I seriously wondered what the Lord had in store for us.

"Something much better than those silly old plans you've made for yourselves," he quipped.

He lifted little Donna Kay out of her bassinet and said, "Just look at this, Gene. Isn't she most beautiful child you have ever seen? Look at her face, her eyes, and lips. She's absolutely perfect, isn't she? Just think, you're gonna have a baby like this next November and she'll be your own flesh and blood. Having a baby of your own biological inheritance is far greater than anything you've ever dreamed about before."

He was right, of course. Herb was always right. I just hadn't thought of it as positively and beautifully as he expressed it. Of course, I needed to do a little extra planning to keep my family economically afloat, but Herb provided that little extra push which prompted me into action. I agreed with both Dr. McDonald and Bishop Phillips that I needed to get out of Padroni and move on with our life. I made an application to take summer employment manning a fire lookout in the Big Horn National Forest up out of Sheridan, Wyoming, and was immediately offered the job beginning June 1, 1955.

Then I wrote my letter of resignation as the "Pastor From Padroni."

A community-wide farewell potluck dinner was staged in the school gymnasium and we all said our tearful goodbyes. Shirley and I loaded everything we owned into the trunk and back seat of my Buick and left town. As I drove away, I wouldn't look back, because I already knew that what Dr. Erdmann Smith told me about Padroni would always be true: "You may never again experience that much love and affection from the congregation you serve. It's a rare thing when it happens. Cherish it forever."

Believe me, I have.

✧

Nearly forty years later, I was invited to officiate at the burial service of Gloy Bratton in Sterling, the first person I ever baptized into the Christian faith there at Padroni. Following the service, I drove out to Padroni just to see what it looked like in 1991. The old dirt road out of Sterling now is paved, and that's a great improvement. But the little town is far less now than it was in the early 1950s. Dee Johnson's general store, barber shop, and locker plant are gone. There is, however, a small post office in a new adjoining building. The school is closed and boarded up. District consolidation, they say. The town population has drastically shrunk from the number of seventy-five that it was when I was there.

The Community Baptist Church of Padroni is closed. Part-time lay preachers tried to keep it going for a number of years, but to no avail. Time has run out on hundreds of little rural towns like Padroni. The parsonage next door was rented out, and it was the rental that primarily funded the church. The water system still worked.

The church itself sat vacant, but not empty of the pews and improvements that were made when I was there. It seemed so incredibly small in comparison to the way I remembered it. I wondered how it could have held 100 people back then when it was packed full. No wonder it seemed crowded. Now it was silent — except for a strange tinkling sound that occasionally caught my ear. I couldn't tell where the sound was coming from. When I dismissed it as only my imagination, then I would hear it again. I walked around the exterior of the little building thinking maybe something was loose and flapping in the wind, maybe the rain gutter.

Nothing.

Standing out in front, as I was about to climb into my car, I heard it again, only this time it was louder, a muffled gong. I looked up toward the steeple, and there I saw the church bell slightly moving from the force of the wind. This time it gonged again, as if begging, "Come ring me one more time."

As I pulled down on the rope I remembered that this bell formerly rang in a one-room country schoolhouse, calling the children to classes. Then we moved it into a steeple specially designed just for it, where its ringing called people to worship. And then I remembered the promise I made to all those Lutherans and Catholics who helped us hoist the steeple up to its place on the roof: "We will toll the bell whenever someone in our community dies because everyone is important to the welfare of all."

So I tolled the bell, allowing the hammer to clap against only one side, for Gloy Bratton. I tolled for a community and a lifestyle I once knew and loved. I tolled the bell for the people and children who once worshiped here, sang their hymns, and said their prayers, whose voices rang with laughter. I tolled the bell for the little church that once seemed so full of life and promise but since had died.

Then I rang the bell, fully striking the clapper from one side to the other, for whatever the future will be.

I drove away — again, not looking back at the little parsonage where I began my married life, nor at the country church where I began my pastoral ministry. The place that Dr. Smith said I would cherish forever.

I had trouble enough looking straight ahead, because my eyes were blurred with tears.

Chapter 6

T he Black Mountain Lookout is located atop the highest point of the northern slope of the Big Horn National Forest. You take Highway 14 out of Sheridan to Dayton, then begin your spectacular ascent along hairpin curves up into the Big Horn Mountains, rising higher and higher through palisaded cathedral canyons until you reach the summit-plateau of the majestic mountain range. Then the highway drops down to the basin towns of Lovell and Greybull on the western side. Black Mountain stands more than 9600 feet high and is clearly visible even from Sheridan, more than forty miles away.

Shirley was about four months pregnant when the U.S. Forest rangers with pack horses first hauled our belongings up the spiraling two-mile trail from the base of Black Mountain to its lookout summit. It was a steep and laborious climb, even for the pack animals. You can imagine how difficult it was for Shirley as we slowly trudged along, frequently stopping to catch our breath, then plodding upward again. By the time we finally reached the lofty summit, the rangers had already unloaded the first round of packs and were heading back down the trail for a second load. Groceries, bedding, dishes, and a three-gallon tank of water were left for our use the first night we were there.

One of the first things I noticed when we finally reached the lookout summit was huge copper cables running up the

U.S. Forest Service lookout located on Black Mountain overlooking Big Horn Mountains near Sheridan, Wyoming. Three sides extended over a dropoff of several hundred feet. Notice lightning rods high above roof with telephone pole to the left. There was no electricity except that generated by horrendous lightning storms.

144

four corners of the enclosure and converging up on top into a lightning rod which extended fifteen feet above the highest point of the roof.

The ranger noticed my apprehension and said, "This is the highest point of the northern slope of the Big Horn Mountains and it will attract every bolt of lightning that's coming along this whole range. Sometimes the weather up here can be ferocious. The wind can blow so hard you may think the building will move from its perch. Believe me, it won't. It is well anchored, although sometimes the glass panels have blown out. Sometimes it will rain so hard up here that you'll think you're in a flood, but you aren't — because the torrents of water will be gushing away from you, far below on the rocks. Sometimes the heat will be unbearable and the only shade you have is under the hot roof. On the other hand, at this altitude, expect sleet and snow anytime in July!"

He shrugged, "You'll quickly adjust to these mountain storms, however."

Then becoming dead serious, "But lightning is something else. Each thunderstorm is dangerous and life-threatening. It will be the worst ordeal you'll have to face up here. Lightning will strike continuously and absolutely terrify you. But if you remain inside the lookout, these large copper cables will ground the electrical charges and you'll remain perfectly safe. Don't ever try to use the radio equipment or the telephone whenever an electrical storm is anywhere near in the area, which is often, because it can zap you real bad. In fact, there have been deaths when lookout attendants became careless about these precautions I'm giving you."

To be perfectly honest, I had never given these dangers a thought when I made application for the job with the U.S. Forest Service.

The ranger went on, "For God's sakes don't ever step outside during an electrical storm because then you'll become the magnet to draw the lightning and it'll slice you right down the middle and fry both sides of you like strips of crisp bacon. During a lightning storm, don't even think about running to the outside john located down the pathway at the first level of open rock, about 300 feet away, regardless of how long you're cooped up here."

Anticipating our next question, he pointed to the lower door of the little cabinet below the window sill and said, "In there is your chamber pot. Use it in here — or outside along the catwalk because that area is protected too. Grounding cables encircle that entire overhang and you're safe."

He could tell that I was almost quaking in my boots.

"Now," he concluded, "I'm not trying to scare you. I'm just advising you not to ignore these warnings. But if you take seriously what I'm telling you, and exercise extreme caution, you'll probably be safer up here than anywhere else in the Big Horn Mountains."

Then he was gone. We unpacked, made up the bed, cleaned the place a little with a tiny bit of our precious water (which hereafter would have to be packed up daily), and cooked our first meal. Evening descended before we finished the dishes.

The rising sun flashed directly in our faces the next morning — much too early. Since the lookout was perched 9600 feet high, it was one of the first points to catch the rising sun. The looming mountains and rolling prairies, stretching 100 miles to the east of us, were still bathed in the twilight shadows of the early dawn. Gradually the skies lightened, the mountains below us were illuminated, and the sun fanned out across the whole northeast corner of northern Wyoming known as Powder River country. Off to the east, as far as our eyes could see, there was a hazy smudge on the horizon which, the rangers maintained, was the Black Hills of South Dakota.

This was to be our home for the next three months. The lookout consisted of a twenty-by-twenty-foot enclosure with glass windows on all four sides,

Shirley cooking supper on woodburning stove. Everything was below window level to provide unobstructed lookout view of mountain range for outbreak of forest fires. Constant fire alert.

Supper on the narrow catwalk during spectacular sunsets while watching the movement of wild game grazing out into the shadowed mountain meadows far below.

built atop a narrow pinnacle of granite. The building actually extended out over the rocky ledge, which towered several hundred feet above the jagged boulders straight below. A three-foot catwalk with wooden railings completely surrounded the lookout. I was absolutely terrified when I first tried walking along this catwalk. I could do it only by dragging myself sideways along the wall while looking straight out across the mountain vista beyond. Looking down would paralyze me with sickening fright. But soon I would learn to sit out there on a little stool with my feet propped up on the railing to enjoy the scenery, and eventually I conditioned myself to lean over the railing while looking down on the perilous rocks below. But this conditioning required considerable willpower.

I had to make a daily backpack supply run to base of mountain for food and several gallons of water. It was a vigorous one-mile climb back to the lofty lookout perch.

When the weather was nice the panoramic view of northeastern Wyoming was glorious. But the lightning storms were horrific.

The four corners of the 400-square-foot log enclosure were conveniently organized into areas of essential activity. One corner held shortwave radio equipment for basic communication with the U.S. Forest Service. Another corner contained a bed mounted on top of a wooden base, which meant that even when we were in bed we could look out upon the forest for the possibility of fire. A third corner had a small wood-burning stove, an enclosed cupboard below the window sill, and a wooden table. Nothing obscured the view in any direction. The center of the lookout was taken up with a sextant, firmly mounted, so that we could accurately pinpoint the location of a fire we sighted.

We soon established a living routine within our new home on the lofty peak. I learned to shave with one inch of hot water in the small washbasin we had. We heated our water either on the wood cook stove or sparingly on a portable butane burner. I learned why mountain men grew beards.

But I was an open candidate for a pastoral call to either a Baptist or Methodist church in the fall, and beards were not fashionable at that time.

Every day I would make my pilgrimage down off the mountain to the base camp, where our car was parked. There I would pick up the day's nonperishable grocery supplies and fill the three-gallon water tank from a nearby spring. Usually I would take a quick bone-chilling splash in the icy spring waters, thereby conserving water I carried in my backpack so that Shirley could take a warm sponge bath up in the lookout. Then I'd begin my invigorating two-mile ascent back up the steep mountain, winding back and forth on a trail laid out many years earlier by the Civilian Conservation Corps, more commonly known as the CCC. In the afternoons I would scout out the mountainside for an armload of dry wood to burn in our small cook stove. This was quite a task because much of the mountain timber was too green or damp to make a good fire. Often I had to chop down a dead tree with an ax, then trim off the wet bark before I reached dry wood on the inside. I enjoyed the daily routine, and it was a good physical workout.

The scenery was beautiful and peaceful. But there wasn't much audible peace because the shortwave radios were in continuous use between all ranger stations and the head office of the U.S. Forest Service in Sheridan. These radio units were in constant contact with Black Mountain but not necessarily with each other. The electric static was usually so terribly noisy that their communications were impossible unless we intercepted and translated their official messages back and forth from Lovell, Greybull, and Sheridan and all the ranger stations in between. This was my first close-hand exposure to the intricate workings of the federal bureaucracy. Endless official reports, purchase orders and invoices, personnel problems and policy violations were the order of the day. Usually, however, this fervor of communications calmed down in late afternoon and there was a semblance of peace and quiet in the lookout. Also, the human brain protectively conditions itself to tune out superfluous noises, like the harsh irritating sound of radio static.

And then we had our first lightning storm!

We saw the thunder clouds gathering as they often do in the mountains in the early afternoon and gradually billowing our way. We threw the switches to the phone and radios, thereby disconnecting any possibility of an electrical charge finding its way into the interior of the lookout. We didn't have long to wait before a terrifying crack of lightning struck the lookout simultaneously followed by a deafening roar of thunder.

Then the full fury of the storm struck.

The lightning strikes came like a furious bombardment of artillery assaults on the lookout itself — again and again they struck. We could breathe pure ozone in the air. Static electricity caused our hair to stand on end and crackle. Then Black Mountain struck back as if open warfare had erupted between the mountain peak and the gigantic thunderhead above. This was my first astonishing scientific discovery that lightning strikes both ways. You could quickly tell the difference between a downward strike from the sky and the answering salvo shot upward from the lookout. The downward strike produced no warning whatever. But a flicker of blue light, like a sphere or a floating ball, would hover and sizzle just above the network of copper grounding cables before the mountain peak fired back with a blinding bolt, bursting upward into a deafening explosion of flashing light and thunder. You could hear the sound waves reverberate away from you, echoing upward for miles through canyons of the sky.

The thunderous exchange of lightning fire power was bombastic. The intensity of the explosive sound pressure caused the glass paneling to pop and vibrate so severely that we could feel the pulsations of air whip against our faces. We both threw ourselves down upon the bed and pulled a blanket over our faces for protection from the flying shards of glass if the shattering panels exploded inwardly upon us. There we waited out the storm as sheets of driving rain drenched the lookout exterior making it appear as if we were submerged in a sea of water. It was truly awesome.

Then the storm passed and the clouds lifted, exposing the setting sun. The warfare between the earth and sky was over. A truce had been called. The fury of the thunderhead slithered down off the mountaintop in defeat and dissipated itself out across the plains far below. Black Mountain lookout stood victorious, like an immutable fortress.

As the shadows lengthened we looked through our binoculars and watched a herd of elk and deer emerge from the dripping forests out into the sun-drenched meadows. The calves and fawns frolicked around the grazing mothers, leaping into the air and chasing one another at top speed. They reminded me of my very special friend Tinker Bell, the bum lamb I raised when I was about twelve years old.

One of the things that astonished us was the almost complete absence of man-made sounds at the lookout. The only exception was the buzz of airplanes above. But numerous natural sounds reached our ears. We could hear many cries of the wild, although most animal calls were unidentifiable to us. Hawks and eagles would encircle the lookout almost as if to say, *You are inhabiting our natural nesting places high on your rocky perch.* Since the speed of sound is faster than the travel of wind, we could hear it swishing through a trillion trees before reaching us at the lookout. And if it was more than a breeze, like a squall, we could hear its approach cascading through mountain ravines and whistling along the ridges, giving us sufficient time to pick up our stools and be safely locked inside before its fury hit Black Mountain. I will always remember the elegant sunsets we watched as we ate our evening meals.

Although we spotted many small smoke spirals from time to time, only one major fire occurred while we were at the fire lookout. Shirley spotted it and promptly reported her sighting to the forest officials while I was on my morning water run. It turned out to be a major conflagration involving scores of imported fire fighters, aerial drops of chemical fire retardants, and constant surveillance of national forest officials. Shirley and I were paid overtime for monitoring and translating radio communications all day and half the night. Within a week the blaze was brought under control. Then it was back to our normal quiet routine at the Black Mountain Fire Lookout.

We relayed fire danger information not only to the Big Horn National Forest offices in Sheridan but also to radio station KWYO. The fire danger index was calculated from a formula based on three factors: temperature, humidity, and wind velocity. Each day we measured the conditions atop the mountain, calculated the fire danger, and radioed the results into Sheridan.

After making these boring statistical reports to KWYO for about a week, I started livening things up with colorful reports about our life up in the lookout. The radio station asked permission from the Forest Service to record these daily reports and play them back several times a day. They would run something like this:

Good morning. Top of the world to you from the Black Mountain Lookout, 9600 feet atop the Big Horn Mountains. What a view we have today. It's as clear as a bell. We can look down on the valley floor, where all you people live in the sweltering heat around Sheridan, and tell you that up here today it is a balmy 72 degrees. It's so still and quiet up here that the lookout's pet chipmunk running along the catwalk sounds like Tonto's getaway horse. . . .

On and on I would go with little vignettes about lightning storms, visitors to the lookout, suppers out on the catwalk, and herds of elk below. Sometimes we admitted our loneliness; for example, while Sheridan celebrated its annual rodeo, culminating with a huge country dance, the only excitement we had was flipping peanuts to the scrambling chipmunks. After I'd told my tale for the day, Shirley would usually give the fire danger report to provide a change of voices.

These little blurbs soon became so popular that KWYO wanted to run them on a regional radio network and incorporate the fire danger readings from a series of forest lookout stations. There wasn't sufficient time remaining that summer to get the idea implemented. The director of the Big Horn National Forest called and asked, "Where are you getting these fascinating little stories?"

"I'm simply telling what's going on up here."

"We would like for you to send us this material, written in a radio-script format," he said, "because we think this is a novel idea for the Forest Service to use in educating the general public about fire danger."

Although I already had loads of radio experience, I never dreamed I'd end up doing daily live broadcasts from an isolated lookout tower high in the Big Horn Mountains. But it worked very well and it was a lot of fun.

✧

As the summer wore on, so did my increasing anxiety over what would happen to us that fall, when our job ended at the lookout. Spending days and nights in the lookout seemed to isolate us from reality. But I trusted in the Lord and simply waited, refusing to become anxious. Never again would I be quite that relaxed about what the future held for me.

I soon found out.

Out of the blue came a formal invitation for me to become pastor of the University Baptist Church at Vermillion, South Dakota. I was not only to pastor the Pioneer Church of the Dakotas but also to serve as student chaplain at the University of South Dakota. The congregation consisted almost entirely of faculty and their families. They wanted to hear good biblical preaching that didn't insult the intelligence of the professors, and they wanted a chaplain who could relate to Baptist students at both the collegiate and graduate level. I considered it a calling tailored exactly for me, and I hastily accepted.

For the first time in our brief marriage, Shirley and I were to have a modern dwelling, a four-bedroom parsonage with two full baths. The only problem was, we didn't have one stick of furniture. Everything we owned, including all our clothing and wedding presents, could be stuffed into the back seat and trunk of the car. It was time to begin the basic furnishings of a home and our final preparations for the birth of a baby, now only four months away.

The time had come to liquidate the tiny herd of cattle my father had helped me acquire to cover my college expenses. After the folks sold the ranch, I paid pasture rental for nine head of cows on my brother's ranch. Roger bought them from me at market value, which provided Shirley and me with the cash necessary for our first acquisition of furniture. It was decided that Shirley would come down off the mountain and accompany her mother to Omaha to buy the furniture and have it shipped 130 miles up the Missouri River to Vermillion.

I was alone at the lookout for over a week. Up in my lofty mountain perch, in total isolation from other humans, I discovered how lonely the monastic life of a hermit can be. I knew then I was never destined for the contemplative vocation of a Trappist monk.

During this time a radio technician brought up to the lookout an experimental FM transmitter. Shortwave radio generally worked in the national forests, except, as I've already mentioned, the roaring static was so severe that often you couldn't decipher the communications. The FM transmission signal uses a different frequency altogether and is absolutely quiet, even in the midst of a horrible lightning storm. The problem with FM radio, however, was its line-of-sight transmission, although the signal would tend to bounce back and forth against the mountainsides.

The technician gave me instructions for an experiment. Forest Service officials wanted to know how successfully the FM signal could transmit at night to a receiving station at Terry Peak, more than 200 miles away in the Black Hills of South Dakota. At ten o'clock on Saturday evening, I was to carry the portable battery-operated unit out onto a rocky ledge, away from the lightning rods of the lookout (which might interfere with the signal), and try to establish communications with Terry Peak. I was to continue trying until midnight, and if there was no response I could shut it off and go to bed.

I did exactly as I was instructed. The night was pitch black, but using a flashlight I found a flat place on a rock pinnacle, apart from the lookout, and set up my equipment for the experimental broadcast. I felt conspicuously foolish, talking to myself on a lonely mountain peak in the middle of the night, my voice the only sound breaking the total stillness of the mountains.

"From Black Mountain Lookout in the Big Horn Mountains of Wyoming to Terry Peak in the Black Hills of South Dakota — can you read me? Over."

Silence.

I tried again and again at five-minute intervals. No response — not even the crackling sound of static from distant lightning strikes, maybe sixty miles away. What a great invention FM radio was — if only it worked in situations like this.

After a half hour of repeated calls and no response from Terry Peak, it was obvious to me that the FM signal wasn't reaching its proper destination. But I had been instructed to keep trying until midnight. To relieve my own boredom, I decided to sing a few songs. I didn't know many and never could sing, but I'd always thought it would be great to become a radio singer if you had the voice for it. And since no one was listening, it didn't matter that I didn't have the voice for it.

So I started in on my repertoire of popular songs. The only one whose lyrics I had completely memorized was, "Mares eat oats and does eat oats and little lambs eat ivy. A kid'll eat ivy too, wouldn't you?" What a classic. (We seniors shouldn't scorn the silly lyrics of rock songs when we sang such intelligent songs as these back in the 1950s.)

First I crooned it like Frank Sinatra. Then I sang it with the honky-tonk nasal sound of the legendary Hank Williams, who'd died just two years earlier. Then I did my operatic Italiano rendition of it. With a lot of vibrato.

Look, if you're all by yourself at night, on the highest peak of the Big Horn Mountains, and you're on the radio and no one is listening to the sound of your voice except a million cattle across 200 miles of hills, you might as well make the best of it. And I did.

After I exhausted my repertoire of popular songs, I decided to preach a sermon. Radio preachers are the only ones who make any money, so I preached a sermon inviting everyone to send their donations to the radio preacher, who at 9600 feet atop Black Mountain was standing closer to God in the starry heavens than anyone for hundreds of miles around.

I soon wearied of the radio ministry.

Then I decided to be Bob Hope and tell a few jokes, but I had to quit because I couldn't remember the punch lines. Besides, by this time, it was approaching midnight and time to end this foolish nonsense.

I tried one more time: "From Black Mountain Lookout in the Big Horn Mountains of Wyoming to Terry Peak in the Black Hills of South Dakota. Do you read me?" No response whatever. Not even a muffled FM squelch.

So I spoke into the microphone, "Well, I've been trying to reach you since ten o'clock and here it is midnight and I'm quitting. I'm unplugging this mike and going to bed."

The instant I yanked out the microphone plug, a booming voice blasted through on the receiver: "Finally you turn off that goddamn microphone! We've been listening to your bullshit for a solid two hours up here. Your preaching is better than your singing, but we're not sending you any money. We were supposed to go into Deadwood for a party tonight. But, instead, we've been stuck out here on this godforsaken mountain peak listening to your chatter."

I sat there, stunned speechless, and the voice said: *"Don't you know, stupid, you can't receive — when you're in a transmitting mode?"*

(Later I learned that the push-button microphone switch was defective, causing the unit to remain in a constant transmitting mode as long as the mike cable was plugged in.)

I've told that story many times since when I've talked about the efficacy of prayer. So many of us think that praying is a one-way monologue with God, when so often our soliloquy becomes chattering nonsense — and we never listen to the still, quiet voice of God in return.

Don't you know, stupid, you can't receive — when you're in a transmitting mode?

Never since then have I sung that great American classic, "Mares Eat Oats and Does Eat Oats." Deep chagrin engulfs me whenever I think of it and I simply choke down. Someone might still be listening.

Chapter 7

I f ever there was a perfect church for my first full-time pastorate, it was the University Baptist Church of Vermillion, South Dakota. Vermillion was a charming little university town located along the bluffs of the Missouri River. Though South Dakota is usually considered a Western state, its eastern edge is Midwestern corn country. The Iowa border was only a few miles away, and Sioux City, Iowa, was the shopping center for all of southeastern South Dakota.

This was my first exposure to Midwest America.

Thousands of acres of cornfields flanked both sides of the highway. Stores were open late Saturday evening for corn farmers from the surrounding countryside who swarmed into town for shopping and socializing. The men all dressed alike, attired in clean bib overalls over which they wore suit jackets. While the women shopped, the menfolk would sit on their car bumpers and street curbs to gossip and discuss hard times. There were no Western cattle or sheep ranchers in this crowd.

Summer days and nights in Vermillion were so hot and sultry that the furniture drawers would swell shut, and winters were bone-chilling cold from the damp humidity. Sprawling oak and walnut trees graced all the residential areas, their branches arching over the streets. Squirrels freely scurried from one side of the shaded street to the other and never had to leap from limb to limb. Stately old homes, mostly two stories high, were set back from the street with shuttered windows and inviting porches.

Within a month after arriving there, I would view with wonder the magnificent fall colors of the Midwest. It looked as if God had taken a giant paintbrush and splashed shades of vermillion, orange, burgundy red, and brilliant gold upon the foliage along the Missouri River bottomland and up along the bluffs where the town was located. The maple, oak, and walnut trees along our street literally were aglow with such an amazing display of colors that they appeared to be aflame. No wonder the little university town was named Vermillion.

This small town of fewer than 5000 people was totally dependent upon the University of South Dakota for its economic, social, and cultural survival. The Baptist parsonage was on Yale Street, only a few blocks off campus. It was even closer to downtown Vermillion, where the University Baptist Church was located. Unless I needed the car for pastoral or hospital calling, I preferred walking to work. Our four-bedroom home was the largest Shirley and I had ever enjoyed. Now we had a full-size living room, a formal dining room, a breakfast nook off the kitchen, and two large bedrooms on the first floor. Our brand-new furniture arrived from Omaha, the limed oak style that was very popular in 1950s and soon to be forever dated as a passing fad. But we were proud of our new furnishings and made good use of them.

The University Baptist Church was very impressive to this former "Pastor from Padroni." It was a descendant of the Pioneer Church of the Dakotas, which had been organized in 1868, when that vast Dakota Territory included what later would become the states of North and South Dakota, Wyoming, and Montana. Vermillion was originally located along the banks of the slow-flowing Missouri River, on which flat-bottomed steamships plied their trade. But in 1881 a massive flood washed the old town away, and a new one was created on top of the bluffs. A state historical sign marked the place where the original church had stood. The new church, an impressive stone edifice, stood right along Main Street downtown. Later, in 1925, they enlarged the structure. The facility was considerably more than adequate for the congregation of University Baptist Church in 1955.

On the third Sunday of September I conducted my first worship service. I will never forget how impressed I was with the beautiful classical music that morning. A chamber ensemble consisting of faculty from the University of South Dakota music department, led by Professor Usher Able and his talented wife, Barnes, played the prelude.

University Baptist Church of Vermillion, South Dakota — "The Pioneer Church of the Dakotas" — established in 1868. Most of the membership was faculty at the University of South Dakota where I served as student chaplain.

The mechanical-action tracker organ was mounted high above the choir, directly behind the pulpit, and elevated just enough that I had to look up to see the robed choir. The organist, Theo Rayburn, was a brilliant student of music at the university who later studied at the Julliard School of Music in New York. The choir director, Martin Bush, had a master's degree in music of the Reformation and managed the university public radio station. (For me, another fortunate entry into broadcasting). Many in the choir were faculty members. You can imagine the magnificent music we had that Sunday morning and every Sunday thereafter at the University Baptist Church.

Following the service a formal reception was held in the church social hall. Coming through the reception line was a new assistant professor of history. His name was Dr. Monroe Billington. He had just completed his Ph.D., and this was his first university teaching assignment. His wife and my wife were both six months pregnant. He introduced himself and his wife, Mary Elizabeth. "We are both Southern Baptists," he said, "and we would like very much to discuss theology with you some time very soon."

I nudged Shirley and said, "Just like a dammed Southern Baptist. He wants to argue religion the first thing."

From this inauspicious beginning, Monroe was destined to become my closest lifelong friend. Since he was Southern Baptist and I was American (Northern) Baptist, we were poles apart theologically. But our friendship over the years has so transcended those trivial differences that we both look back upon those early years with great amusement. Monroe doesn't remember that introductory comment when we first met and would prefer to deny that he ever said it, but I will never forget my negative reaction to it.

Monroe and I were the same age, twenty-seven, and other ironic similarities bound us together. He started out for the Baptist ministry but switched from seminary to graduate school, where he completed his doctorate to teach history. Much later in my ministry I would take early retirement so that I could teach college history, too. We were both married at about the same time, and our wives became good friends. Our first and second babies were born only a few weeks apart. We each fathered three children, two girls and a boy. We both encountered midlife crises at about the same time, with much the same results. And through it all we became intimate confidants for each other — that one single person on the face of this earth with whom we could share every personal secret. We became soul brothers. Every person needs and deserves at least one lifelong friendship like this, but most are never so lucky to find it.

People actually thought we were biological brothers. Forty years later, at a car wash in Denver, a woman came up to the two of us standing nearby while an attendant finished buffing the car and said, "You're identical twins, aren't you?"

Monroe Billington and me in Breckenridge, Colorado in 1989. We share the same age, same physical build, and same mental outlook on life — and a common heritage in our love of history. We are closer than brothers. Every human deserves one friendship in life like this.

"No, we're not."

"Well, if you're not twins I can sure tell you're brothers."

She found it impossible to believe that we weren't even related. Neither of us ever thought that we physically resembled each other that much, but we both knew that we shared a common bond emotionally, psychologically, intellectually, and spiritually. We have remained in constant contact with one another throughout the nearly forty years that have passed since our first encounter in that church reception line in 1955.

At that time I also was in touch with my good friend Herb Brawner in Denver. After Shirley and I got ourselves settled into the parsonage, I phoned Herb and told him about the beautiful university town and the prestigious church edifice. I raved about the wonderful people in my congregation. I told him that our parsonage was big enough now that Nina and he could visit with their little girl, Donna Kay, and they could use both bedrooms with adjoining bath upstairs as their private suite. But I wanted them to hold their visitation until after Shirley's delivery so that they could become acquainted with our newborn baby. Herb seemed delighted with my excitement and found it amusing.

"You're like a kid with a whole bunch of new toys," he said.

He was right. I'd dash off to work in the morning so excited with the possibility of things waiting to be done that I could hardly contain myself. Having a church secretary was a new experience for me. I had a new title, Chaplain to Baptist Students, and was invited to numerous university functions. Instead of being selective, I tried to attend them all. I was gone almost every night at church or a university committee meeting. I'm not sure how supportive I was to Shirley as she went into the final months of preparation for the birth of our first baby.

One day I stopped to buy gas at the Standard station up the block from the church. The attendant noticed my license plate and said, "I see you're from Wyoming. Your state is very much in the news right now."

"How's that?"

"Haven't you heard? There's been a plane crash up near Laramie. They're flashing it on the radio news right this minute. Special bulletins every ten minutes or so." He proceeded to tell me that a big United Airlines plane had crashed into the sheer vertical wall of Medicine Bow Peak and exploded upon impact, strewing charred bodies all over the canyon floor hundreds of feet below. The four-motored airliner, en route from Denver to Salt Lake City, had to fly north over southern Wyoming because it was too heavily loaded to clear the Rocky Mountains. There were no survivors at all.

I drove away, in a hurry to get back to my exciting new job. But as I approached campus, I thought to myself how casual our conversation had been about the tragedy but how devastating it must be to the families and loved ones of the passengers aboard that ill-fated airliner.

I got home late, and Shirley was holding dinner. The phone rang.

"Reverend Todd, this is United Airlines of Denver calling. You probably have heard the news of the crash in Wyoming of our flight to Salt Lake City. You probably don't know that aboard that flight was your dear friend Herb Brawner."

A shock ripped through my body. The voice on the phone trailed on, saying something like, "Herb's widow, Nina Brawner, has asked that you conduct the services for her deceased husband. . . ."

I took the train out of Sioux City to Denver. I'm certain United Airlines would have preferred that I fly. In retrospect, I'm glad I took the train, because it gave me time to reflect. I sat alone in my compartment and watched the Nebraska landscape slip by through the shadows of the night. I don't recall sleeping at all. This was my first confrontation with death on such a personal and emotional level. There was no way I could make sense of it. Neither could I convince myself that somehow this was the will of God. In fact, I knew it was *not* the will of God, and therefore, I would not try to comfort Nina with the mindless suggestion that somehow it was. No, the crash was caused by pilot error, or a mechanical failure, or severe turbulence, all of which we could more easily accept if we were honest in admitting it. There was no need to blame God.

However, I wished I hadn't agreed to conduct the funeral service for Herb. Herb was too close a personal friend, and I was still too new in the ministry to handle such a grim task. I could simply have sat with Nina and the Brawners as one of the grieving family and everyone would have understood. But it was too late. I had already accepted the invitation to officiate at the burial of Herb Brawner.

Nina was doing her grief work very well. She would openly weep and wail, then feel better for having done so. The service was scheduled at two

o'clock in the funeral home, and just before lunch Nina drew me aside and showed me their collection of photo albums. Many of the pictures were those I had taken with their camera. Too many showed me posing with Herb and Nina in front of church, at restaurant tables, up in the mountains, and inside their apartment. All happy times.

"Now," she said, "I will put together one more album of his death and burial. All the newspaper clippings. All the photos. All the mementos. Your sermon notes. Everything. Perhaps this will help me to close the book on my beautiful and wonderful life with Herb Brawner."

One of the few photos showing Herb Brawner and me together.

We both wept.

I didn't eat lunch, only nibbling at some vegetables forced upon my plate. While everyone scurried about dressing for the funeral, I sat on the back steps while sipping a glass of iced tea. The funeral car arrived — it was time to go. We waited for Nina. She didn't come. The funeral director told us the chapel was already filled to capacity, and we would be late. Nina was called again but didn't appear.

Herb's mother, sitting in the back seat, said, "Poor Nina. Bless her heart. It's her last, desperate hope. Maybe if she doesn't come to the funeral there won't be a funeral. If there isn't a funeral, maybe Herb didn't die after all. Gene, you're the only one at this point who can persuade her that she must come and face reality."

I found her standing in front of the dresser mirror, wearing her black dress and veil, fidgeting with her earrings. I walked up beside her, put my arm around her shoulder, and, speaking to her into the mirror, said, "Nina, I know you don't want to go through with this. Neither do I. But we must. The time has come for us to bury Herb. The funeral home is packed with all your friends. We mustn't keep them waiting any longer. We're already late. The limousine is waiting."

Nina, looked up at me, through the mirror, and asked, "Gene, tell me, is it a Cadillac?"

"Why yes, as a matter of fact it is, why do you ask?" I was startled at her question.

She tipped her head back with hysterical laughter. "I asked Herb one time, when we passed by a funeral at Olinger Mortuary, 'Honey, why do they always have those big long black limousines at funerals?' And he said, 'Nina, dear, that's so everyone gets a chance to ride in a Cadillac before they're buried.'"

Herb may have been about to be buried, but his subtle sense of humor still prevailed.

Indeed, the funeral home was packed to capacity. The breeze of a cooling fan was deflected up under the American flag stretched over Herb's sealed bronze casket (he was a veteran of World War II), causing it to billow upward. I had to leave my sermon notes at the lectern to steady the flag with my hands. The moment I touched his casket, it seemed as if I had touched Herb himself in some mysterious way — and I became very calm. I proceeded simply to speak from my heart instead of "preaching" a traditional funeral sermon. I have no memory of what I said, but a Denver newspaper reporter printed my words as follows:

Those of us who live in the West near the majestic Rockies always find ourselves looking up to the snowcapped mountain peaks for our daily inspiration. Always they are beautiful. But now that we know it was a mountain peak which took the life of Herb Brawner — we may be inclined to feel that we never want to look upon these mountains as an object of beauty again.

But we must remember that Herb was born and raised on his parents' cattle ranch along the banks of the Yellowstone River in southern Montana, with spectacular mountain ranges flanking both sides of the Paradise Valley where he lived. He grew up among these beautiful mountains. He went to college in full view of these mountains. He came to Denver where he married, built his first home, and worked in the shadows of these mountains. It was among these mountains that he died. These mountains gave him life, they nurtured his life, and they took his life. And he will be buried among these mountains.

Even though these mountains look icy cold and foreboding today — even deathly and frightening, as they prepare themselves for a long harsh winter ahead, we must remind ourselves that spring will return and they will become beautiful and inviting to us again. As God does not abandon these mountains to a perpetual winter, so He will not abandon us. As He brings the annual visitation of a springtime to these mountains, so He will visit us with the springtime of His eternal hope.

The day will come when we will lift up our eyes unto these eternal mountains again and say, How beautiful they are. They remind us of Herb Brawner. Thank God for Herb's presence among them.

So Herb who always had an obsession with cars, got his final ride in a Cadillac. I watched the black hearse carry his coffin away to Montana for burial. The whole Brawner family traveled together by auto. After the funeral cortege had left, I felt alone and isolated in Denver. While waiting for my evening departure on the train, I walked the streets of Denver. I had a spaghetti dinner in Herb and Nina's favorite Italian restaurant, located in the historic Navarro Building, right across from the Brown Palace Hotel. I even waited for their favorite booth, behind drawn velvet curtains, to which they would invite me to dine with them during their courting days.

My thoughts turned toward Vermillion and the new home and aspirations that awaited me there. I went into a jewelry store and purchased a tiny gold baby ring for our new baby, which would be arriving before long.

We didn't have long to wait.

On November 29, 1955, Shirley gave birth to a beautiful baby daughter. We named her Lorilee. Mothers were confined to the hospital almost a week following childbirth in those days, so it was the first week in December before Shirley was ready for dismissal. In preparation for the momentous arrival of our new baby, I decorated the house for Christmas. When we entered the parsonage I immediately placed the bassinet under the Christmas tree, and little Lori became our Christmas baby. Both Shirley and I shed tears of joy.

I was more than just a man and a husband now. I was a father — and would be forever more. I was absolutely thrilled with this new dimension to my life. We converted the study of the parsonage into a nursery. We used the bookshelves to stack diapers and baby clothes, and I built an expanded padded top to the chest of drawers to serve as a changing table, complete with plastic pockets mounted on the side for extra baby things.

I resumed my pastoral duties at the University Baptist Church with renewed gusto. There was much to be done. Not only did I have all the regular responsibilities of pastoring a congregation, but I also had special obligations as a college chaplain to the university students. This was no small task. When I look back on it now, I wonder how I did it all. I met with various student groups throughout the week and several times on Sunday. But I was only twenty-seven years old, full of energy, and honestly believed there were no limitations to what might be done.

(I later learned that when I was under consideration for employment at University Baptist, Dr. Mark Delzell, the dean of education, had said, "My only problem with the credentials of Gene Todd is that he's only twenty-seven years old." Claude Huetson, an old farmer on the board, replied, "Well I could do a lot of things when I was twenty-seven that I can't do now that I'm eighty-two." That quip cinched it — I was offered the job.)

One of my more enjoyable duties was to lead a group of students on an annual trip to a student legislative seminar in Washington, D.C, and to the United Nations in New York. I had never been to the East Coast, and here I was transporting and conducting student tours to these exciting "foreign cities." Every year I outdid the students, rushing to every historic site and witnessing every governmental function in our nation's capital: sessions of Congress, Supreme Court trials, congressional hearings, and so forth. Each night in our hotel conference rooms we gathered with American Baptist students from all over the country to share our experiences and hear lectures from prominent politicians and governmental leaders.

During these trips I witnessed the social unrest and political despair building up in our nation's capital. Civil rights for "Negroes" (as African Americans were then known) was becoming a national issue, and it was recommended that we invite an infamous U.S. senator from Mississippi to address our student assembly. Our purpose was not to challenge his position on civil rights but to attempt to better understand it. The senator's formal reply to our invitation was read to our student assembly as follows: "I will speak on the condition that no niggers, Jews, or Catholics be allowed in the room." We were a Baptist delegation, so there were no Catholics or Jews among us, but there were a number of African American students enrolled in the seminar; and, in any case, the senator's statement was blatantly offensive — something right out of the Ku Klux Klan. We immediately and unanimously withdrew the invitation.

That particular senator was one of the most notorious segregationists in Congress, so his bigotry, though offensive, was not entirely unexpected. But we were dismayed to watch southern senators who otherwise were among the leading liberals in the Senate lead a filibuster blocking an early voting - rights bill. The obstructionists included Lyndon B. Johnson and J. William Fulbright of Arkansas. Here was a scholar, a former state university president and founder of the Fulbright educational and cultural exchange program, filibustering on the Senate floor to block the right of all Americans to vote.

While attending these annual seminars with my students, I learned the harsh demands of political reality. The political reality for Fulbright in the late 1950s was that unless he opposed civil rights legislation, he wouldn't remain in the U.S. Senate to pursue his otherwise liberal legislative agenda. He was foremost a southern politician who sought re-election, necessitating this unconscionable compromise. If things were ever to change, the Christian Church would have to become involved. I realized then that I could never become a professional politician.

One year Shirley accompanied me on my trip east. We hailed a cab one Sunday morning in Washington and asked for a ride to a particular Presbyterian church for services. The cabby made a mistake and took us to the wrong church. A lot of police and security personnel had gathered there; no parking was allowed in front of the building, and we had to stand in a long line to enter. I thought all this a bit excessive for a simple Sunday morning service. Then a phalanx of motorcycle policemen pulled up in front followed by a large black limousine with American flags waving from both front fenders. Out stepped President and Mrs. Dwight Eisenhower. They were escorted along the walkway and entered the church. Both looked radiantly handsome. We all applauded them.

As they passed by, I remembered sitting on the steps of my rooming house at Seventh and Lafayette in Denver a few years earlier and watching General Eisenhower as he circled the block driving his mother-in-law's antique electric car, honking the horn and waving at me. Shirley and I were thrilled that, because of the cabby's mistake, we ended up viewing a U.S. president from only fifteen feet away during her first visit to our nation's capital.

The annual student legislative seminars made an indelible impression on me. A Christian social conscience was slowly taking shape deep within. I could not separate my personal faith in Jesus Christ from the world around me. If God was love and all people were the children of God, then I could not in good conscience exclude that love from others on the basis of race, creed, gender, or nationality. (Much later in my life and ministry I would learn to include another category: sexual orientation.) If Christianity doesn't speak to the larger world of which I am a part, I decided, then it doesn't have much to say to me in the particular. Later this conviction would become a painful one for me.

This new Christian social awareness became all the more intense now that I was a father to a beautiful little baby girl. When I held Lori in my arms, I would say to myself: *No father should have to tell his little daughter that she will never be able to go to a certain school, or play in a certain park, or enter the university of her choice, or eat in any restaurant she wants, or even drink from a particular public water fountain — and that if she attempted any of these simple acts, things assured to any American citizen, she might be lynched.* To me it was an abomination that any Christian nation would compel some of its citizens to say this to their children.

I felt a Christian obligation to become involved in social and political action. I chose the Democratic Party as my vehicle, not because I thought it had a corner on public morality but because I thought it offered a better platform for social reform. I must admit, however, that it was also the political party of the Todd family in Wyoming and this probably had a lot of influence on me. Moreover, South Dakota was solidly Republican, and I believed the two-party political system needed to be restored there — much as I believed that the best thing that could happen to the American South would be a restoration of the Republican Party there. Unless the multiparty system is alive and functioning, the party with a monopoly on power, whichever it is, inevitably loses sight of the people's welfare.

Power corrupts.

I was naive enough to tell my church board that Christians had a solemn obligation to become politically active and that I had no right to ask this of my laymen if I was not willing to set the example by doing so myself. I honestly believed Christians could work in either the Republican or Democratic Party. Indeed, we needed to do so; and then we could and should all worship together on Sunday morning as brothers and sisters in Christ. I told them of my intentions to work in the Democratic Party but encouraged them to work just as hard in the Republican Party if that was their political persuasion.

Why did a mostly Republican church congregation in a solidly Republican state put up with such foolhardiness on the part of its young pastor? For two reasons, I think. One, my congregation at the University Baptist Church consisted largely of college professors. Even though they were mostly Republican, they were liberal Republicans, intellectual scholars who recognized that the two-party system simply was not working in South Dakota. Also, they knew my ideas were suicidally naive and that I would miserably fail. There's something seductive about watching a Greek tragedy unfold and play itself out in front of your eyes. Particularly when you're not the tragically flawed figure on stage.

To show just how ignorant I was about political reality in South Dakota, there wasn't even a functioning Democratic Party in our county at the time I announced my bold commitment. I had to organize one. By default I became the Democratic chairman of Clay County. Elsewhere the title might seem impressive, but in Vermillion it was more like a handicap. It has been said that our initial gatherings were like secret meetings of a communist cell group and that we met in basement rooms with curtains pulled across the windows. It wasn't quite that bad, but almost. We must remember that the late 1950s was a time of anticommunist hysteria, the era of McCarthyism. Senator Karl Mundt from South Dakota was very much involved in the early stages of this insanity.

Some college professors were willing to attend these formative sessions on the condition that their attendance was never made public, lest they jeapordize their tenured faculty positions. They were good men, scholarly and far better informed on political issues than I was; and they were willing to advise and work behind the scenes. But I had to be the guy up front, the guy who took all the heat.

I was idealistic and naive enough to do it.

It was at this time in my life that I was fortunate to meet a young history professor in South Dakota by the name of George McGovern. He taught American history at Dakota Wesleyan College in Mitchell and had taken a leave of absence to accept a temporary position as executive secretary of the state Democratic Party. He was most helpful to me in my efforts to revive the party in Clay County.

He also tried to persuade me to run for election to the state legislature. He presented facts and poll figures indicating that voters were prepared to vote for candidates other than those hand-picked by Republican leaders. I hadn't been around Clay County long enough to become controversial, he argued, and since I had some experience as a public speaker I would make a good candidate. His arguments were most persuasive, but this was more political involvement than I had originally proposed to my church leadership. Running for political office might be not only divisive in my church but ruinous to my pastoral career.

However, I agreed to recruit some active candidates who would make a serious run at election to the assembly. Not a single professional person, not even a budding young lawyer, would touch it with a ten-foot pole. I finally recruited a young farmer who had never worked in the party and had never delivered a public address. And he got elected. George McGovern was right: the time had come for a resurgence of the two-party political system in South Dakota.

At about this time I decided to begin working toward a Ph.D. in history and maybe become a college professor in the event that things didn't work out for me in the Baptist ministry. First I had to complete requirements for a master's degree in history. I began my course work, one class per semester, so as not to interfere with my pastoral duties and with the promise that I would take no days off from the church. That was a mistake. I worked my fanny off. But I loved the academic study of history on the graduate level.

George McGovern kept dropping in on me at Vermillion, encouraging me to accompany him on speaking engagements on campus. When I told him of my ambitions to acquire a Ph.D. in history he said, "Gene, I'm not satisfied as a teacher of history, and I don't think you will be satisfied with it either. I want to be a maker of history, not a teacher of history. I ask you again, why don't we both run for political office and become makers of history?"

George McGovern became my personal friend and frequently overnighted in our home while pursuing his political career which eventually led him to the U.S. Senate and Democratic nomination for president of the United States. Here he is holding our first baby, Lori, born in 1955.

Shortly thereafter he announced himself a Democratic candidate for South Dakota's lone seat in the U.S. House of Representatives. He invited me to attend the small rally with him. Later we ate a pathetic chicken and noodle supper in a shabby little eatery. George began his campaigning then and there, walking through the dingy place to introduce himself to patrons. Not a single soul recognized who he was. I realized again that I had neither the heart nor stomach for running for political office.

Two years later he holds our newly born son, Barry, in 1957. We've lost the photo of him holding our second daughter, Sheridan, born in 1960.

Later that fall, while on the campaign trail, George stayed overnight several times in our Vermillion parsonage. Late one evening, around eleven-thirty, he called and asked if he could spend the night because the home in which he was supposed to have stayed didn't pan out and he couldn't afford a motel. I offered him a midnight snack, which he gladly accepted, and then I discovered to my horror I had nothing to serve him except cheese and crackers. Shirley was already in bed, so I made some hot tea while we ate and talked.

Never did I dream that this man, sitting at my table and munching on cheese and crackers, some day would become the Democratic candidate for president of the United States. On the hot summer evening of his nomination in 1972 I told my children that I had photos of McGovern holding each of them in his arms when they were only babies, taken on various occasions when he stayed overnight in our Vermillion home. They didn't believe me until I retrieved the photos from an attic trunk.

Miracle of miracles, George McGovern won election to his congressional seat in the U.S. House of Representatives. Later he would become U.S. senator from South Dakota — and history tells the rest of the story. He meant it when he said that he wanted to make history — not just teach it. In that same election we were shocked to learn that South Dakota had also elected a Democratic governor. There was just enough agricultural unrest in the heartland of America, particularly with Ezra Taft Benson, Eisenhower's secretary of agriculture, that voting Democratic became a protest vote.

The morning after the election, I drove my car down toward the church and saw Helen Wilson, my secretary, pacing up and down out on the sidewalk wringing her handkerchief. She was beside herself. The moment she saw me, she came running up to my car and in a panic-stricken voice said, "Gene, the parish hall is filled with a whole bunch of men all looking for you. They're real burly looking, and they told me they wouldn't leave until you came in, even if it took all day. What have you done to them?"

I started to open the parish hall door when Helen rushed up to me, crying, "Don't go in there, Gene. They may do you harm. Please, call the police first."

I was completely confused but entered the reception hall anyway and saw twenty or thirty men sitting in a semicircle, most of them wearing hard hats. All rose to their feet, and one stepped forward as a preappointed spokesman. Nervously twisting his hard hat in hand, he said, "Reverend Todd, we're all state employees working here in Clay County, mostly doing highway maintenance work and things like that. After the election last night of a new Democratic governor for South Dakota, our jobs all depend on you, the Democratic County chairman."

I was stunned. It had never occurred to me, and no one had ever told me, that this was how political patronage worked on the county level. The poor spokesman continued, "We've had Republican governors almost forever, and we all got our jobs through the local Republican County chairman. Please understand, we're all just honest, hard working men. Most of us aren't even involved in politics at all. As a matter of fact, many of us vote Democratic, but we have to declare ourselves Republican in order to keep our jobs."

That last assertion was probably an overstatement, if not an outright lie. I wasn't aware that *anyone* voted Democratic in Clay County. He asked me to exercise Christian leniency and allow them all to remain at their jobs to support their families.

Crass political patronage! So this is how county chairmen build a political power base for themselves at the grassroots level, I thought angrily. Years later, in Wyoming, I discovered that the same system applied to temporary employees who worked while the state legislature was in session. Only people, mostly women, who belonged to the majority party need apply. I still say it's wrong.

The system of political patronage has changed in recent years, I've been told, and I'm glad. Fitness and skills for the job should be the only criteria for public service jobs, which have nothing whatever to do with partisan politics. Appointments should be politicized only where partisan policy is to be decided upon and carried out. It shouldn't affect the hard working laboring people who grade the county roads. It would have been cruel to have replaced these men and women who had worked twenty years for the state. Besides, a Republican governor would probably be elected two years later anyhow, when the agricultural protest vote had played itself out.

In the spring of 1960 Ted Kennedy came to South Dakota to drum up support for his brother, John F. Kennedy, a candidate for the Democratic nomination for president. The central committee of our Clay County Democratic Party met with him in a large farmhouse outside Vermillion. He seemed very young and intense and insisted on talking to each of us individually. I was amazed at how much personal information he had acquired about me before we even began our private conversation, and I thought to myself, *If the Kennedys are this intensely organized I bet his brother Jack has a good crack at the presidency.*

✧

I've spent so much time talking about my political activity in Vermillion that one might conclude I did nothing else.

Such was not the case. In fact, I did political work only in my spare time. I spent twelve to sixteen hours a day doing all the things an average minister does: making home and hospital visitations, meeting regularly with church deacons and trustees, recruiting and training Sunday school teachers, teaching Bible classes, and doing pastoral counseling and church administration. In addition, I had a heavy assignment as university chaplain to Baptist students.

Radio broadcasting remained a hobby. I was grateful for the opportunity to do religious broadcasts with others ministers from Vermillion over the 5000-watt university public radio station, KUSD. My colleagues were generally disinterested in broadcasting, so I did most of these weekly fifteen-minute broadcasts by myself. Religious newscasting was not my favorite format, and it required a lot of preparation because no religious news was available on the wire, but I did it faithfully because of my love of radio.

I continued the regimen of sermon preparation in Vermillion I had begun in Padroni — taking it even more seriously. You can't preach slouchy sermons to a congregation of university faculty and get away

Teaching a Sunday morning college class in Lewis Hall. I truly enjoyed my ministry as a student chaplain and my daily association with the university faculty.

with it. College professors don't want to be insulted with dull ideas or factual misinformation. I became extra conscientious about my use of historical facts and would often check them out with my parishioners before using them in a sermon.

I would like to believe that the increased effort I put into these sermons began to show. Attendance regularly increased at morning services. Fraternities and sororities began attending worship services as a group and sometimes filled a whole central section of pews reserved for them. After this first visit, many of these students would return individually to worship at University Baptist. It frequently became necessary for us to tidy up the balcony to accommodate latecomers. For the first time in my life I had to establish eye contact with the people sitting in the balcony. I didn't want them to feel excluded.

Monroe called it "preaching to the balcony."

University students often commented on how naturally preaching seemed for me. Nothing could have been farther from the truth. I often had to rewrite a sermon several times. Words and thoughts did not come easily to me. In fact, I was often terribly discouraged that I had to work so hard to make a sermon fly when other preachers could do it by the seat of their pants. It was not unusual for me to completely rewrite a sermon late Saturday night. Preaching was not easy for me at all — and this realization greatly disturbed me.

The thing I enjoyed the most was having contact with interesting people from all walks of life. I soon developed a regular routine to maximize this part of my job. Every weekday morning I joined a coffee klatch in the downtown drugstore consisting of a Lutheran optometrist, two Catholic lawyers, a Congregational funeral director who operated a furniture store directly across the street, the Catholic druggist himself, and two ministers: one a Lutheran and the other a Congregationalist. Not one of these men was a parishioner of mine, and I considered that a good thing. This little coffee group kept me vitally plugged into the pulse of the community. (The Lutheran pastor, David Preus, later became national president and bishop of the American Lutheran Church, or ALC.)

In the afternoons I had coffee at a different location every day. On Tuesdays I attended the faculty coffee hour at the university, always a most pleasant experience. On Wednesday I usually had coffee with the Clay County Republican chairman in the back of his men's clothing store. He was slightly younger than I, a recent graduate of the university school of business, and we shared a mutual disdain for "politics as usual." Most of our social goals were almost identical; we differed only on how to achieve them. He found racial segregation as abhorrent as I, and we spent a lot of time discussing what might be done about it. We both agreed that our candidates for county office would never verbally attack the personal character or integrity of opposing candidates. It worked.

On Thursday afternoons I would take coffee with Raymond Collar, the county judge and a member of my church. Judge Collar was about seventy years old and suffered from severe curvature of the spine. His wife was equally handicapped with arthritis, which had literally frozen her body and confined her to a wheelchair. Even her fingers were frozen stiff. But she was a marvelous cook. She would propel her wheelchair with one foot and do all the food preparation and cooking while pressing her two hands together like wooden stumps. She often invited me to dinner whenever Shirley and the family were away. Her homemade bread and pies were a wonder. I don't know how in the world she did it.

The Collars were devout Baptists and staunch Republicans, and I dearly loved them both. Later I drove the judge regularly to a hospital in Sioux City for his cancer radiation treatments, and I literally cradled him in my arms while he died. Mrs. Collar gave me the beautiful ivory gavel he used in his county court chamber, where we regularly drank our afternoon coffee; to this day I cherish it as a most precious gift.

I wanted to believe that my family came first and career second, but I'm afraid that actually my career came first in many ways. However, I enjoyed my family life immensely. My little daughter, Lori, was growing into a delightful child of joy and wonder. When I was home in the evening, which sometimes wasn't all that often, I insisted on giving her a bedtime bath and tucking her in bed. Right after dressing her in her pajamas I would roll her up in a heavy comforter my mother quilted especially for her and carry her out into the darkness of the cold night to view the majesty of the heavens. The first words she ever spoke were "moon" and "stars." Holding her in my arms out under God's evening sky as she snuggled down in her comforter and peered out from under its covering became a hallowed joy.

When she grew a little older, around two years of age, I would phone Shirley and let her know that I was heading home afoot from the church. It was only a few blocks. Shirley would stand outside and release her at the right moment to walk a block to meet me at the corner of Yale and Main. As I approached the corner I could see Lori hopping and skipping down the sidewalk, under the shade of the towering walnut and maple trees, her ponytail bouncing in the breeze. I can remember saying to myself, *There's nothing in this world more beautiful than the image of an excited little girl dancing down the street to meet her daddy — when that daddy was you.*

On September 5, 1957, I was called away from a Women's Guild Luncheon to come to the hospital, where I had taken Shirley earlier that morning. Before the women adjourned their meeting that afternoon, I had returned to announce that we were the parents of a baby boy named Barry Eugene. I could scarcely contain my joy. If being the father of one beautiful child was the greatest gift of God, then having two caused our cup of blessings to overflow.

Barry was a sweet little boy who later would hold up his arms to me when I came home and utter his first sentence: "See you, Daddy! See you!" When I gathered him up in my arms he would vigorously hug me and then affectionately stroke my face and shoulders for a long time afterward. What a joy it was to be a father!

During the night, whenever a severe lightning and thunderstorm shook the ground and drenched the house, Barry always crawled into bed beside me for protection, snuggling down under the covers and pressing tightly up against me with the explanation, " 'Nunder, Dad . . . rain and 'nunder." Holding your little child through the terrors of a storm is what parenthood is all about. Life could never have been better than it was right then for this dad.

✧

In my pastoral calls I tried to visit people in their place of work in addition to seeing them in their homes. I'd call on Daryl Jorgenson as he worked the milk bottle line in the dairy, Dr. Mark Delzell in his office as dean of education, Professor Ed Hadd at the School of Law, and Dr. Monroe Billington in the history department. I'd also visit folks like Ole Anderson, a semiretired stone mason and an artistic wood-carver. He once carved an image of me, attired in my black pulpit gown. I still prize that wood carving.

I also called on John Barstow, a lab technician in the School of Medicine. His job was to prepare and preserve specimens — including human bodies — used in anatomy classes. Sometimes bodies were willed to the medical school, but most cadavers were unclaimed bodies of patients who died in the state mental hospital, located only twenty miles away in Yankton.

Sometimes in the evening I would accompany him on his rounds. Four or five medical students would cluster around each cadaver, and often the body was totally shredded into muscles, nerves, blood vessels, and bones. They quietly went about their dissections with the dignity of true scientists. When they were finished with a cadaver, John would place it in a body bag, and I often accompanied him to the cemetery, where I conducted a short committal service.

Many times I visited John while he was "hard-embalming" a body, and it never bothered me. But one time I made the mistake of asking what he did with embalmed cadavers that were awaiting a new anatomy class. Without batting an eye, he lifted up a heavy wooden door in the floor, and I found myself gazing into a tank of formaldehyde, in which were floating six or seven human bodies. The sudden stench of the formaldehyde and the grisly sight of naked human bodies floating one on top of the other, the women's hair rising to the surface, was so overwhelming that I nearly slumped into the tank myself. John caught me by the arm and steadied me momentarily, asking, "Are you all right? . . . Are you *sure* you're all right?"

I was all right, shocked more than anything else. I had never expected to see such a horrific sight so suddenly. But I had asked a question, and John had simply provided the answer. I assured him that I found his laboratory work fascinating and said I would love to watch an autopsy sometime.

I got my wish one Christmas vacation while the medical students were away for the holidays. Dr. Michael, the medical pathologist, invited me to accompany John Barstow and him to the state mental hospital for an autopsy. He clothed me in a surgical gown and rubber gloves, almost as if I were his assistant, and the work began. The only part that really bothered me came at the very beginning, when John surgically peeled back the dead man's scalp and began using a small rotary saw to cut away the top of the skull. The blade got hot and smoked, and there was an unpleasant stench of burning bone. When the skull wouldn't easily detach, they pried it loose with a screwdriver, and suddenly it popped loose and clattered across the cement floor, wobbling to a stop with the hollow sound of an inverted cereal bowl.

Dr. Michael was a reserved and quiet-spoken man, a real scientist at work. He spoke affectionately, if not reverently, to the deceased, calling him "fella." He would say, "Aw, fella, you had a ruptured appendix in your younger days. How come that was allowed to happen to you? Didn't anyone pay attention to your complaints of pain? I'm sorry about that, fella, I really am."

I was amazed at the crudeness of the tools he used to open the chest cavity, sawing through the sternum and folding back the rib cage. I stood off to one side during the autopsy, but Dr. Michael occasionally peeked around at me to say, "Eugene, if you have any questions, don't hesitate to ask." But I didn't ask — I simply watched in rapt attention.

Soon he turned to the intern at his side and said, "Aha, I think we found it. But before I tell you what I know it is, you take a look and tell me what you think."

The intern probed with his stainless steel instruments and muttered something that was complete medical gibberish to me. Dr. Michael nodded his agreement, then turned to me and said, "The cause of death was a heart attack. This is what we suspected from the symptoms of his sudden death, but the purpose of an autopsy is to determine the exact cause of death clinically rather than rely on our educated hunches."

Turning to me again, "Eugene, are you sure you have no questions? The body is now fully open, and I'm perfectly willing to show you anything you'd like to see."

For the next couple of hours I enjoyed one of the most incredible learning experiences of my life. First Dr. Michael showed me how the heart and lungs were interrelated, then severed the separate organs and dissected them, all the while explaining in great detail the function of each nerve and muscle. He was a born teacher who loved to impart knowledge at whatever level of understanding his student was capable of handling — which in my case wasn't much. But this didn't diminish his enthusiasm one bit. It was contagious. I found myself asking questions — sometimes rather profound ones, according to him — which I would never have thought of asking before. We explored the extraordinary human body as if it were a magnificent work of art.

But it was more than that, and I finally blurted out, "Dr. Michael, how could anyone look at something as intricate and beautiful as the human body and question the creativity of God?"

He looked at me with a studied expression on his face and said, "That's what I wonder, too."

He sat down on a stool and lit himself a cigarette while we discussed the theology of evolution: how God built into His master plan the ingenious seeds of internal evolution. How something simple could mutate, adapt, and evolve into something infinitely more complex; and how this evolutionary creativity is miraculously and mysteriously coded naturally into the basic substance of all growing things on the earth and probably in the whole universe.

He suddenly stood up and said, "Well, we've got to reassemble this poor fella for a proper burial. While we're doing that, and since all theologians should be social scientists, Eugene, maybe you'd like to examine this fella's chart and see what brought him here to the state mental hospital in the first place."

He tossed it to me and I sat down and began reading it. The patient was ten years older than I. He'd been born and raised in an isolated South Dakota farming area. No developmental problems were apparent to his parents on the farm, and he was fairly competent in school until social problems appeared in junior high. His interpersonal relationships with other students began rapidly to deteriorate in high school. His fellow students began picking on him, inflicting emotional and physical abuse. On one occasion the teachers found him hiding under a bench in shop class to avoid their terrorizing. He rapidly became more hostile and antisocial.

At home he became terribly withdrawn from reality and centered all his attention on a pet lamb he was raising named Rex. They became practically inseparable. He returned home from school one day and discovered that his parents had slaughtered and butchered Rex, leaving the bloody pelt out on the yard fence. The boy went into a convulsive rage so threatening that his family had to physically restrain him and call the sheriff. He was held in jail for several days. A hearing was scheduled, and he was diagnosed as "mentally insane" and committed.

As I read through the committal papers, I noticed teardrops dropping on the pages — and they were coming from me. Memories of Tinker Bell, my pet lamb, came flooding back — my finding her dead in the cow barn, burying my face in her fleece and weeping, then burying her in a snowdrift to make certain no hired man would skin her for the pelt. Although I didn't experience the social alienation that obviously overwhelmed this young man, I could sense how he'd extended his affection toward the only thing in life that seemed to love him in return, unconditionally — and then had that object of his affection brutally slaughtered and butchered. He was forever punished for loving the only thing he was capable of loving at that time in his tortured life.

Did a social worker ever question the parents as to why they slaughtered their boy's pet lamb and hung the pelt out on the fence as if it were a bloody red flag of their offense — when they knew Rex meant everything in the world to him? Wasn't their outrageous parental insensitivity nothing short of cruel emotional abuse? What about the teachers? Were any of his fellow students ever chastised for their bullying, which became so intense that he had to hide under a bench?

Maybe so. Perhaps everyone tried to do everything they could and nothing worked because there were no professionals in rural South Dakota to diagnose his mental or emotional condition and treat him. Maybe they all did the best they could do with what limited resources they had. But maybe not. How do you define mental illness anyway? Parental emotional neglect? Human abuse?

Dr. Michael, busily putting organs back into the body as if packing apples, bananas, and oranges into a fruit basket, noticed my emotional distress and said, "Now you see why I can't read things like that. Unless we physicians remain emotionally detached we can't do our job. I mustn't let my emotions interfere with the scientific job that has to be done."

Darkness descended early, as it always does in late December during Christmas vacation, while we drove back to Vermillion. I recalled from the medical chart that the patient died on the day after Christmas, and I wondered if any of his family came to see him during the holiday? Did they send him a gift? Was he ever invited back home again? What kind of a Christmas Day did he have in the state mental hospital?

I shared these thoughts with Dr. Michael, who mused, "You're probably right, Eugene. From a medical point of view his cause of death was heart failure. But from a human point of view, on the day after Christmas — maybe he died from a broken heart. Who knows?"

Who knows?

This experience sparked my interest in mental health. Back in the late 1950s a new public awareness of mental health was just beginning to emerge. There were no psychiatrists and few professional counselors in the smaller towns and rural communities of America. Pastoral counseling was often the only form of counseling available to vast numbers of people. Consequently, seminaries began offering courses in pastoral counseling, and we were required to do clinical training in psychiatric hospitals. While attending Iliff School of Theology I did my training at Colorado General Hospital, now called University Hospital. But these attempts barely scratched the surface of what needed to be done in the broader field of mental health.

I felt inspired to ask the chaplain at the state mental hospital in Yankton, only twenty miles away, what we might do as a church in Vermillion, to be helpful in his ministry there. He had a good suggestion. In those days most mental patients were committed to state hospitals for life and lost all normal contact with their church of the outside world. He recommended that University Baptist periodically hold some of its women's guild meetings in the hospital and allow the Baptist female patients to freely mingle among our own parishioners and participate.

My women's guild, consisting largely of faculty wives, immediately bought the idea, and we began a series of guild meetings in the state hospital. The plan worked beautifully. The women all came together, both from our church and from the hospital. Psychiatric counselors carefully screened the patients they felt were most able to comprehend and participate in a meaningful way. Like any typical women's guild meeting, first there were brief devotions, then some kind of program, and finally refreshments. Some of the hospital patients usually made coffee and graciously assisted with serving.

One afternoon, during refreshments, I noticed a table of women, all of whom happened to be patients, engaged in animated conversations and laughing with delight. I thought to myself, *This is exactly what we wanted to accomplish with this outreach experimental ministry.* Here we had a group of women, all psychiatric patients in a state mental hospital, thoroughly enjoying our guild meeting and socializing with one another. So I joined them.

To my utter dismay, I discovered that although they were engaged in animated conversations and laughing with delight — they were not relating to one another at all. Not a single woman was listening to what the another was saying. Each women was speaking only to herself, hallucinating. They were totally disengaged from one another. It was pure gibberish.

I shared my distress with the Lutheran hospital chaplain who pulled me aside and said, "Pastor, look at it this way: They are only one step removed from the reality of what goes on in any women's guild meeting in any Christian church anywhere in the world — at any given time."

The women of my church and I laughed about that astute commentary all the way back home to Vermillion. And, I might add, the chaplain's observation applies equally to such things as men's groups and brain-numbing clergy meetings.

Chapter 8

I was pastor of the University Baptist Church from 1955 to 1960, and this period is among the happiest of my life. I loved my church, I loved the congregation — and I loved being a college chaplain.

However, it was a rough time financially. My salary was $3600 a year, and with a growing family we barely got by. We paid cash for everything because we had no other choice. Once I went to the banker, who was a member of my church, to inquire about a loan to buy an electric clothes dryer. With two babies at home and everything freezing stiff on the outside clothes lines during South Dakota's long, frigid winter, I thought Shirley needed help.

The banker, dressed in his double-breasted gray flannel suit, callously told me, "We're not into installment loans. Besides, Reverend Todd, an electric clothes dryer is not considered a good financial investment."

The sad thing is, I bought into that stuffed-shirt, male-macho contention. That is to say, I didn't exercise the courage to stand up and argue against such flawed chauvinistic reasoning.

So Shirley continued drying diapers by draping them over the steam radiators, and they dried stiff as a board. We tried everything to soften their coarseness so that they wouldn't further irritate the diaper rashes the babies already had. We finally resorted to heat lamps on the babies' bare bottoms while they slept.

We bought only bare essentials and literally counted our pennies on the dresser before buying groceries. I remember walking to our morning coffee group at the drug store with the Congregational minister and telling him I didn't have enough cash to buy a loaf of bread.

He asked, "Do your lay people know about that?"

"Thank God they don't," I answered.

"Well, I'm gonna tell them because they haven't given you a salary increase in four years. Gene, unless you ask for a raise, no church will give you one. The universal attitude of laity toward clergy salaries is, 'Lord, you keep him humble, and we'll keep him poor.' Remember that."

179

"For God's sake, Van, please don't tell anyone," I pleaded. "I don't want any of them to think that we aren't managing our money any better than we are."

The serious money squeeze we faced was no worse than that of most other young couples, whether they be teachers, lawyers, or ministers. We agonized and sacrificed just like everyone else in order to get by with a growing family on a very limited income. We never ate in a restaurant, with the single exception of a rather elegant cafeteria in Sioux City that charged two dollars per person. We'd eat there once a year — on our wedding anniversary. Nor did we ever take a vacation, other than an overnight trip every August to stay with my folks in Sheridan. This was before the days of auto air-conditioning, so we drove all night to avoid the excessive heat of the day. I'd build up the back seat so that it was level clear across to the front seat, and the two children would bed down for the night. By dawn we'd have entered Wyoming. I'd stop the car and ceremonially step across the state line. There I'd stand out in the cool morning air, free from the suffocating humidity back along the Missouri River, and breathe deeply the fresh air scented with the fragrance of sagebrush. It was wonderful to be back in Wyoming again.

These were cheap vacations, because once we arrived in Sheridan we were guests of my parents. Mom still cooked her fabulous meals, and in August she borrowed heavily from Dad's vegetable garden. I enjoyed taking Lori and Barry with me to help Dad pick green beans and vine-ripened tomatoes, then dig up mounds of new potatoes, fresh green onions, and bunches of radishes. Dad and I would sit out on the shaded back porch steps of their little retirement home and prepare all the vegetables for the noon dinner. At the last minute I'd run out and break off a few ears of corn to be husked just before dropping them in the kettle of boiling water. Mealtime was always so special.

In the evenings Mom would retire early out on the front porch while I took the kids down to the Burlington Railroad yards, only two blocks away. There we'd sit and watch the switch engines move back and forth, banging cars together while forming a huge freight train, which left Sheridan every evening, going east. We did this so regularly that the engineers began inviting me to lift the children up into the diesel cabs, where they showed us all the gadgets. They even allowed us to pull the whistle announcing that the train was ready to pull out of the station and head east.

These vacations were the only ones we could afford, but they were wonderfully simple and easygoing. This was the only time of year that the folks could be with Lori and Barry. Even more important for me, however, it was the only time I could enjoy being with my parents. Time was running out for Mom, as I would later learn.

(Shirley's parents, however, had moved to Fontana, North Carolina, and provided funds for an annual visit of her and the children there. I could never afford the time or money for the trip.)

✧

As a Baptist college chaplain I automatically became a member of the American Baptist Higher Education Association. This professional group consisted of college and seminary presidents, faculty deans, college administrators, and university chaplains. These individuals were often considered the denomination's intellectual elite. I was tremendously impressed with the high quality of their scholarship and educational leadership.

Every September, over the Labor Day weekend, a Baptist student conference was scheduled at the American Baptist Conference Center in Green Lake, Wisconsin. It was and still is unquestionably the most impressive denominational conference center in the United States. Each Labor Day weekend the American Baptist Higher Education Association met at Green Lake in conjunction with the annual conference of Baptist college students. The conference lasted about five days, extending through the weekend. It was always a fantastic experience. Most of the college and seminary administrators were from either the East or West Coast, and almost all of the college chaplains were from Eastern universities. They were brilliant fellows — all with doctoral degrees. They were articulate and very liberal theologically. The intellectual stimulation of rubbing elbows and matching wits with these guys was always the high point of the year for me.

On one occasion, only one student was free to accompany me to the annual Green Lake conference. He was a sophomore at the University of South Dakota, and his legs were partially paralyzed from polio, which required that he walk with crutches. Denny, an African American, had an angelic voice and sang in our church choir. But his free-form solos drove my organists up the wall. He was constantly volunteering to sing solos, and everyone loved his singing; but, coming out of the black church tradition, he would break out with his own improvisations whenever the spirit moved him. He would tip his head back, close his eyes, and ad-lib his way through verse after verse while the poor organists had no idea where he was, where he was going, or where and when he was ending it.

These organists would come to me in tears. "Gene, I simply can't handle accompanying Denny on his solos. I'm a nervous wreck just thinking about it, and I'm wrung out like a limp dishrag by the time we finally wind it up. You've got to persuade him to stick to the music or I quit."

I couldn't persuade him, so I spent a lot of time rehiring and pampering the organists.

Denny and I started out for Green Lake for a most remarkable trip. He was a delightful travel companion. Whenever we got out of range of a radio station I would ask him to sing, and he freely obliged. There was a music rage in the late 1950s known as "cha-cha." It had something of a Latin beat, as I recall, with an accompanying rhythmic dance step. Denny delighted in singing old Baptist hymns and adding the cha-cha beat whenever he could, just to watch my irritation:

> *On a hill far away,*
> *Stood an ol' rugged cross . . . cha-cha-cha*
> *The emblem of suffering and shame*
> *cha-cha-cha and cha-cha-cha*

It became a very long trip — not because of his cha-chas, as irritating as they were, but because of a social tragedy I had never encountered before. When we'd stop for lunch in a roadside diner (this was before the days of interstate highways and fast-food restaurants), we couldn't get waited on. The proprietors would tell us first that they were all filled up when it was obvious to me that booths remained empty. Waitresses would completely ignore us until the place had nearly emptied, then finally approach our table and slop some food our way. I couldn't figure what was wrong. Denny was slender, neat, a handsome lad and always meticulously dressed. Never before have I ever been so poorly served in a restaurant. Denny became more sullen as we approached mealtime.

After a breakfast and lunch with this routine, Denny offered to remain in the car and suggested that I go in and eat, then bring out a sandwich for him. It then occurred to me what was happening — racism, pure and simple. Not in Mississippi or Alabama, but in Iowa, Minnesota, and Wisconsin. My blood boiled.

For supper that evening I entered a restaurant, was immediately seated, and ordered two meals, explaining, "My buddy will show up any minute." When the plates were served, I went out and accompanied Denny back to our booth, where we both ate our meal. I was angry and defiant. But he was frightened and intimidated and scarcely ate at all. It never occurred to me what my private protest was doing to him personally.

Later, I stopped at a motel and ordered a room for two so as not to arouse suspicion, but Denny wouldn't get out of the car until it was dark. I awakened in the morning to find him gone. He'd been sitting out in the car waiting for me since early dawn. I was beside myself with rage. He sensed my turmoil.

"Reverend Todd, please don't make me do something that could endanger your life or mine," he kept repeating. "I know what's happening. I'm used to it. I've grown up with it. Obviously you haven't."

For the first time, while driving across Wisconsin, I discussed racial segregation with an actual victim of it. He told me that people of African American descent hardly ever took vacation trips, even if they could afford one. Service stations wouldn't allow you to use the rest rooms even if you filled up your gas tank; there were no motel rooms to rent, no restaurants in which to eat, no public parks where you were allowed to eat a picnic lunch — and always the shadow of lurking danger.

"It might be easier if you live in the South," he explained, "because there you learn where colored people can get accommodations, usually in the colored section of town. But in the northern states you never really know where accommodations might be available, and many towns have no colored sections. That makes it even more dangerous. My dad's cousin was murdered when he demanded a room that he had already paid for."

When tears welled up in my eyes, he reached over and touched my arm, saying, "It's all right Reverend Todd. I've lived a lifetime with this. There's no use for you to grieve yourself over something that neither of us invented or neither of us can change right now. We both just have to live with it, that's all."

Why should Denny be comforting me when American citizens of my own race had perpetuated this injustice upon him and his people? No, we shouldn't just live with it. It had to be changed.

Ironically, at Green Lake, our Baptist student conference was to close with a special address by a young Negro reformer whose name only recently had become known in association with the Montgomery bus boycott of 1956: Martin Luther King Jr. I first saw him in a small side room immediately outside the conference center where he was to speak. There were only about twenty of us in this room, all from the higher education association, and it was only an accident that I happened to be there. Into the room he walked where we all introduced ourselves and shook hands. He was much younger than I anticipated, actually my age, slender, well groomed, very polished and debonair in his manners. A few minutes later he began his speech in the larger conference room, packed to capacity. I'd heard much about black preachers' oratorical gifts. I soon heard them for myself.

Dr. King wasted no time with preliminary niceties and moved right into his theme of passive nonviolence. He spoke without notes. The topic was obviously well rehearsed, but it was fresh to all of us gathered in that room. The cadence of his voice lent itself to the eloquence of his speech, which escalated in power and emotion until it became impossible to sit quietly and listen passively. I was spellbound. Here was a man articulating a movement of human freedom and civil rights that would soon generate the momentum of a powerful steam engine and roll across America.

His thoughts are well known to Americans now, but at that time they seemed brand new: *We love you too much to allow you to demean yourselves with the perpetuation of your racial segregation any longer. We will march in the streets for what is right. You can club us, you can jail us, you can even kill us — but you cannot destroy the movement we have begun. The chains of racial injustice must break. The walls of separation must come tumbling down. We will wear you down with our love.*

It was truly a remarkable experience for me. This marked for me the beginning of the end of the abominable institution of racial segregation, which was so vicious and evil, so dehumanizing, that it could not be endured any longer.

✧

Working with students occupied a great deal of my time. But I loved it. Each spring I would take several carloads of students out to visit a Hutterite colony located along the banks of the Missouri River, about sixty miles from Vermillion. The Hutterites are part of the pietistic Anabaptist movement, which began in Germany following the Protestant Reformation of the fourteenth century. The Amish, Amana, and Mennonites are all a part of this larger religious group that immigrated to this country to escape increasing German persecution.

The Hutterities, however, are rather unique because they believe in communal ownership of all physical and material properties, including land. Consequently, in the late 1950s they were accused of being Communists when McCarthyism and the Red scare were still very much alive in South Dakota. As a matter of fact, a bill was introduced in the state legislature prohibiting the future sale of land to Hutterities. They also suffered chronic prejudicial harassment because of their religious belief in pacifism, their strange dress and manners and, most of all, their separation from the modern world. All the men dressed in black — married men wore beards, single men were clean-shaven — and the women wore long German peasant dresses. Work was communally shared, and all chores were rotated so that no individual got stuck or bored in any one area of activity. They had trade specialists, too: furniture makers, honeybee tenders, blacksmiths, teachers, and preachers.

They were a simple people whose religious lifestyle and theological outlook were so profoundly different from everything else in America that I thought my college students could benefit from meeting and talking with them. Even though I made prior arrangements with the headmaster to drive out on a Sunday afternoon, they made no effort to welcome us when we arrived. We'd find a group of men resting in the shade of the barn, and they'd direct us to the headmaster's unit in a long row of apartments. Each apartment had a few bedrooms and a very small living room, sparsely furnished.

The headmaster was very shy and spoke English with a strong German accent. But he graciously answered our questions and then invited us to walk through the colony and visit any part of it we liked. Several giggling children, attired as miniature adults, would lead us to the kitchen, dining rooms large enough to accommodate more than 150 people, laundry and sewing rooms, and so forth.

Out under large cottonwood trees along the banks of the Missouri River we would see groups of men and women, with children running around and about, sitting on long benches, resting in the shade, quietly visiting. Some sat by themselves and simply watched the river flow by. They practiced a strict observance of the holy Sabbath — rest and absolutely no work except minimal chores. It was a peaceful and restful scene, reminiscent of a bygone pastoral day.

When the students and I returned to the church for our evening snack and discussion groups, I would ask, "Out of everything we saw and observed, what was the single thing that impressed you the most?"

I thought surely they would have a strong reaction to the Hutterites' communal lifestyle and the frequent charge that they were Communists. Their simple religious faith of separatism and doctrine of pacifism, including their refusal to serve in military service, also seemed likely to get a reaction.

Instead, the students invariably responded to "their queer observance of the Sabbath. Where did they get that weird notion that the Sabbath was to be kept holy with no work and all rest? How could any group of people just sit out there on benches all day and watch the Missouri River roll by?"

This generation of college young people, all Bible-believing Christians, had absolutely no concept of the scriptural commandment regarding the Sabbath. They were flabbergasted when I opened the Old Testament and read:

But the seventh day is the Sabbath of the Lord thy God: in it thou shalt not do any work, thou, nor thy son, nor thy daughter, nor thy manservant, nor thy maidservant, nor thine ox, nor thine ass, nor any of thy cattle, nor thy stranger that is within thy gates; that thy manservant and thy maidservant may rest as well as thou. (Deut. 5:14 KJV).

The idea of keeping the Sabbath as a holy day of rest was beyond their comprehension. "You mean no shopping? No catching up on all the things that you didn't get done during the week? Not even taking your boat out to the lake for waterskiing? You mean just doing nothing? Sitting around all day and resting? And you call that holy?"

Needless to say, something had been lost in the rural-to-urban transition of modern America. Although the Todd family never observed the Sabbath as strictly as the Hutterites, and Sunday was frequently looked upon as a day to catch up on the fun things we might otherwise not get to do, I did know that the Sabbath was supposed to be a holy day of rest. But these university students seemed to have had no earthly concept of this at all.

In my later years there were many times when I yearned for a Hutterite Sabbath, where I could just sit under the shade of a towering cottonwood tree and watch the river roll by all day. I would gladly have welcomed that kind of holiness.

Though I loved my college students, in the late 1950s they were maddeningly withdrawn from the social issues of the day. Once, when I participated in the university baccalaureate service, I made this comment to the graduating class: "In other countries of the world university students are out on the cutting edge of change and revolution of their society. But here in America it seems that our college generation is caught up in the social image of the gray flannel business suit. Our activism consists of swallowing goldfish and discovering how many people can we stuff into a telephone booth."

I remember the frustration I once experienced while trying to lead a discussion about world hunger. At that time the United States was dumping surplus grain on the ground and burning it. The typical reaction I got from the students was, "But not dumping that wheat on the world market would upset the balance of trade." It was, indeed, the era of the gray flannel business suit.

A few years later, however, the word to college students was, "Cool it!"

✧

While I was in Vermillion, about half of my funerals were held in the church. The other half were held in the Elmore-Wagner Funeral Home, located only half a block from the parsonage. For some reason, it seems, I had many funerals. But there is one I remember with particular embarrassment.

Every town has that section "south of the railroad tracks," that part of town where the poorer people live. In Vermillion, that part was down at the bottom of the bluff, where the town was located before the great flood of 1881.

Living there in a tar paper shack were two old men, Clem and Zeke, who were notoriously known as the town drunks. They weren't mean-spirited or anything like that — in fact, they seemed to be happy drunks. They didn't like to work any more than they had to, but they would do little odd jobs for people, earning just enough money to get plastered again. Everyone knew them as the town characters. You couldn't help but like them. Something like the Otis character in the *Andy Griffith* television series, the police would rather drive Clem and Zeke down the hill to their shack after another of their many binges than put them in the jail for the umpteenth time and feed them the next morning.

One morning, after a drinking binge the night before, Zeke awakened to discover that Clem was dead. The Methodist minister and I were to share in conducting Clem's funeral service. I can't remember how it came about that the town drunk warranted two clergymen for his burial when neither he nor his friend ever attended church. Probably one had been raised Baptist and the other Methodist and Zeke had forgotten which way it was. Or perhaps it was Zeke's thinking that it would take the prayers of two ministers to get ol' Clem through the portals of heaven.

The Reverend Walter Forred was the Methodist minister and a good friend of mine. Walter was no more than five feet tall and weighed less than about 120 pounds. Even friends who loved him the most acknowledged that he had a "small man complex," which sometimes afflicts those who must physically look up while talking to others, while they're looking down on you. Walter would drop his voice a few octaves lower than normal and speak extra loud in order to boost physical presence among people with whom he was conversing.

He had a magnificent gift for preaching. He never used a note when he delivered a sermon or public address. Either he committed it all to memory or simply spoke extemporaneously, which made him the envy of all the other clergy. When we were discussing some issue that needed resolution at one of our interminable clergy meetings, Walter would just sit passively, looking down his nose to the floor, eyes almost closed, eyebrows arched as if he was bored to death or deep in thought. After about an hour of our ecclesiastical wrangling, Walter would suddenly lift his arm and shake his hand as if quieting the group (even if the room was already perfectly quiet) and proceed to beautifully summarize everything we had said. And then he would come forth with a brilliant conclusion to our problem. He was awfully good at this.

The only problem was, after we went home and got to thinking about it, his summary conclusions weren't very profound at all. In fact, they didn't even make much sense. Still, they seemed profound at the time and we were grateful to Walter for this extraordinary gift. Without it our insufferable meetings would have ground on and on until we were all brain dead.

Back to the funeral. The mortuary was packed because the townspeople loved these two old characters, Clem and Zeke. Since Clem had no relatives — at least, none who would admit it — it fell upon Zeke, his surviving drinking buddy, to make all funeral arrangements. It was decided that I would conduct the opening prayers, scriptural readings, and benediction. Walter, naturally, would deliver the spontaneous sermon. I completed my part of the service, and Walter slowly walked up to the pulpit, stood there for a long moment to make certain everyone's attention was riveted on him, and then, dropping his voice a few octaves, began his extemporaneous funeral oration. You could tell it was going to be *awfully* good. It always was.

The problem was, it's not easy for a Methodist minister to eulogize the deceased at a funeral whose only claim to fame was being the established town drunk. There just wasn't much he could say that was complimentary. So Walter shifted his approach and began sermonizing on the fact that, according to St. Paul, our bodies are to be the temple of the Lord. Therefore, he continued, it was of extreme importance that we pay attention to what we do with our bodies. His words conveyed a subliminal message apparent to all, he thought — except for poor Zeke, the surviving drunk, for whom it was specifically intended.

Walter was just beginning to wax eloquent on the subject, rocking back and forth on his heels to lend emphasis to the profundity of his words (which preachers are prone to do when waxing eloquent) when, to our horror, Zeke stood up, hat in hand, reeking and reeling, with eyes bloodshot from partaking of too many spirits not normally associated with the Methodist Church, and drawled in a distinctive southern accent, "Now, now, Rev'ner, let's don't *gillygag* on all that ol' spiel right now. Why don't we just let that ol' sleepin' hound dog lie and get on with the business at hand — what do ya' say?"

Then the toothless old fellow plopped his rumpled hat on his head and sat back down in the front seat, in full view of a packed funeral home. The bored onlookers, who up until this moment were simply tolerating the temperance lecture, sat there aghast, every mouth dropped open and eyes agog. Everyone wondered what the Reverend Walter Forred was going to say now to get himself out of this one.

Walter sputtered like air released from a deflating balloon as it hisses toward the ceiling before fizzling to the floor. He tried to recover by saying something profound, but it was terribly garbled. He choked and tried again, but it was even worse. Only guttural sounds emerged from his throat. Walter Forred had been struck mute, as surely as if he had suffered a stroke.

The surrealistic scene before me seemed like something from Mars. This was a spectacle none of the assembled mourners had ever expected to see: a minister of the Gospel openly confronted in the midst of a funeral oration by the deceased's closest surviving friend with a request he get it *over with* quickly. The silver-tongued orator, master of the art of extemporaneous grandiloquence, was not recovering from this indignity but simply croaking in full view of the whole world. Every clergyman's worst nightmare was unfolding right in front of us.

I buried my face in both hands, about to explode with laughter. Then I slapped a handkerchief over my face, fled from the front of the parlor, and ducked behind a bank of gigantic funeral ferns. When I got there I bumped into Wagner, the funeral director, who had escaped there for the same purpose. He was bent over, convulsing with both hands over his mouth, tears running down his cheeks.

I've tried convincing myself that no one in the funeral parlor suspected I was concealing my laughter when I covered my face and fled from the room. Instead, I would like to believe, they simply wondered why the Baptist minister was mourning so excessively for the deceased he didn't even know.

Walter's arm went up dramatically. That famous gesture meant that he had regained his composure and was about to come forth now with something very profound, a beautiful summary of what he earlier had intended to say, a brilliant conclusion — something *awfully* good. And we'd all go home satisfied.

Instead, it was pure gobbledygook. Walter not only didn't have anything to say, he had lost the basic skill of human language, which anthropologists say took a million years for mankind to acquire.

Behind the ferns, I discovered that if I held my mouth wide open and breathed deeply, I could avoid laughing so loudly that everyone would hear me.

Finally, Walter did the only thing he could do under the circumstances. He simply sat down, slumping into his chair with the look of a whipped dog.

Then he discovered that I wasn't in my chair for the final benediction, which we had earlier agreed that I would do. I knew better than to go back out there. Every clergyman has the benediction committed to memory, and I knew these words would automatically return to Walter without his even having to think about them. After all, he was so *awfully* good at this. Therefore, he could redeem himself from what otherwise had become a grave personal calamity.

He rose up to this one last chance to recover his lost dignity. But the traditional benediction, familiar to everyone — "The *peace* that *passeth* understanding" — instead came out as, "The *pass* that *peaceth* understanding."

This was the crowning defeat of Walter Forred.

After the funeral home emptied of all mourners, Walter stomped back to where Wagner and I were still hiding behind the funeral ferns, still covering our faces, still convulsing. He was absolutely livid. Who wouldn't have been? He stiffened himself in a stance of outright defiance and then, collecting his wits about him, dropped his voice a few octaves.

"Gentlemen, if a fella is piloting a B-51 bomber over the Himalayas, and he loses all four engines, he needs to feel he has just a little bit of support," he said, holding up his hand with his thumb and forefinger about a millimeter apart.

In carefully measured words, he continued, "But when he looks around and sees that both his co-pilot and flight engineer have bailed out, leaving him to bring the B-51 down into a safe landing onto the icy peaks all by himself — he then realizes that the others in his flight crew can just go to hell." (Only Walter could fantasize such a singular feat.)

The funeral director desperately tried explaining to him that the best way we could show our support was by getting ourselves the hell out of there and letting him handle the situation all by himself, which he was always capable of doing so beautifully.

But Walter didn't buy that rationalization. The poor guy knew he had bombed. The trouble was, the whole town knew it, too. He wouldn't speak to us for a week.

By this time, the story had become legend in all Vermillion. Every morning coffee klatch was bantering the famous expression back and forth whenever the topic of conversation became too close for comfort: "Now, now, Rev'ner, let's don't *gillygag* on that ol' spiel right now. Why don't we just let that ol' sleepin' hound dog lie and get on with the business at hand — what do ya' say?"

Much to Walter's credit, he later realized that the best thing he could do to cover his losses was to reverse the tables and tell the story on himself. Which he did, with great aplomb. Listeners howled as he embellished it into classic folklore. Instead of laughing at him they were now laughing with him. He became the star performer in his own comic opera.

Walter recovered his lost honor.

I'm the one who hasn't done okay with it. To this day, when I recall the story, I collapse into hysterics. At the same time, however, I'm filled with remorse to think that I couldn't muster enough emotional maturity to remain somber, as normal people are at funerals. Hiding behind a bank of potted ferns and giggling myself silly at a funeral, particularly when I was a participating officiant of that burial service, is not one of my proudest moments.

Ironically, the quaint expression of the old geezer has never left me. When I sat in the U.S. Senate gallery viewing the southern filibuster to block a voting rights bill — and later when I became chaplain to the Wyoming State Legislature — I often wished someone had the nerve to stand up and say, "Now, now, Senator, let's don't *gillygag* on all that ol' spiel right now. Why don't we just let that ol' sleepin' hound dog lie and get on with the business at hand. What do ya' say?"

✧

I remember another death much differently. I became acquainted with a young professor of physics who was a member of no church in town and proudly had no intention of becoming one. But what a neat guy he was. I have never known anyone who was all cerebral in everything he said and did. Harold and his wife, Christy, lived in a modest home he had renovated mostly by himself. He had inherited the skills of a master carpenter from his late father.

He converted the basement of his home into a rustic office and study. Wall paneling and wide floorboards gave the place a special charm, especially when lined with elegant bookcases filled with a large library of books. He was the first person to introduce me to high fidelity sound with built-in speakers through which he could play his voluminous collection of classical recordings.

At a farm auction he purchased a quaint old woodburning cook stove, a small one with an oven which was perfect for baking crusty loaves of homemade bread. It provided the only source of heat for the room. An ornamental stainless steel grill graced its exterior parameters. It was his priceless antique and he was most proud of it. A few comfortable chairs were grouped around it.

He was an obsessive perfectionist. Everything in his mind and on his desk, or in his room, was neatly organized and always in place. He was immaculate in his personal dress and behavior. Besides his love for books, he shared a secret passion with me — a love of pipe smoking tobacco. Every Friday afternoon I'd be invited over for English tea and a round of good pipe smoking.

These sessions were like a ceremonial religious ritual with Harold the officiating high priest. He would place a tea kettle on his antique stove, all fired up with crackling wood, and then we would fill our pipes from an array of sealed glass jars all containing different types of tobacco. When the sealed jar was popped open, a pungent fragrance would fill the air. When the water came to a boil he would slowly steep the tea the way he learned to do as a Rhodes scholar at Oxford and pour me a generous serving in a china cup. Then we'd light up our pipes, and smoke would fill the room like incense at high mass.

Our discussions were seldom light or casual, always intense and profoundly intellectual. He was the first true environmentalist I had ever met, long before this movement became fashionable in American society. He was passionately concerned about air pollution, poisoning of our river systems and water supplies, erosion of our topsoil, and loss of our natural resources.

He considered himself an intellectual agnostic — not an atheist, who arrogantly rebels against God, but an agnostic who saw no vital reason for believing in a deity. Choosing his words carefully and speaking slowly, he would respectfully remind me that the existence of God can be nothing more than a *God-hypothesis*. He would say that from an empirical point of view, something remains a hypothesis until incontrovertible proof emerges. Since God cannot be proven either to exist or not to exist, then he must remain nothing more than a hypothesis, albeit an attractive one.

"You see, Gene, I don't need your *God-hypothesis* to explain the glory of what I see through a telescope or a microscope," he would say. "The beauty and wonder of the universe is inherent unto itself, whose meaning and purpose I can accept for what it is without having to drag in your *God-hypothesis* to explain it."

I continued, however, speaking of God as the rational intelligence of the universe who had proven His existence to me, a God in whom I lived, moved, and had my being. A God with whom I had a personal relationship through His Son, Jesus Christ, my Lord. He would always correct me with, "You mean, of course, your *God-hypothesis*."

Our academic exchanges never abated all through our tea and smoking sessions, but I began to feel that I was no match for his intellectual brilliance. He must be getting bored with my insistence on the existence of God without proof of my hypothesis. When I missed several Fridays, he called me: "Gene, where have you been? I've missed you. I've got a fresh batch of some maple-sweetened pipe tobacco we must try. Its aroma and taste is terrific."

Back I went. His sense of humor was extremely dry, but he seldom laughed. He did, however, when I told him that I almost left the ministry in Colorado because my denominational executive advised me to become like Billy Graham.

"You become like Billy Graham?" he laughed out loud. "How absolutely ludicrous. Why would anyone ask someone to become like someone else in order to become someone? I wouldn't want to drink tea and smoke my pipe with the likes of Billy Graham and lose the companionship of you and your wonderful *God-hypothesis*. I've grown rather fond of you both."

One beautiful spring morning, Harold and Christy went hiking in the dank woods along the Missouri River. Shortly afterward Christy became ill with symptoms of the flu, but she didn't improve. After a dangerously long delay she finally was diagnosed with Rocky Mountain tick fever, and a tragic allergic reaction to experimental medications resulted in Christy's sudden death.

Harold was devastated with the loss. Our Friday afternoon tea and pipe smoking sessions became much more somber, but they continued. One Friday when I clumped down the steps from the outside entrance to his basement study, he met me at the door with the words, "Gene, I don't want to talk to anyone today. Please understand, I don't want any conversation."

"I respect that, Harold, and I understand. I shall return at another time."

"Didn't say that, Gene. I simply said I don't feel like talking today," as he held open the door and motioned me in.

In silence he poured the boiling water from his kettle into the teapot and let it steep. Together we filled our pipes with a pinch of this and a pinch of that. He served the steaming hot tea in a china cup and we lit up our pipes. The fragrant tobacco smoke swirled upward toward the ceiling, filling the whole room. The late afternoon sun streamed across the barren wooden floors, polished to a glistening shine. I refilled my cup and filled his, too. Not once did he look at me while we sipped and puffed away. The silence became as heavy as the dense smoke that settled down upon us.

As I put on my jacket and started up the stairs to leave, he pulled open the door and called after me, "Gene, you'll never know how much this has meant to me. Your sitting here in dead silence with me. Your total acceptance of me in my vulnerable state. I'm very fragile right now and I need to protect myself." I saw tears trickling down his cheek.

The next week, he was pensive but talkative.

"How ludicrous it is," he mused. "A beautiful young woman like Christy, an artist, a creative soul, with a heart as big as the whole universe, a natural-born teacher, a genius with a master's degree for teaching art to children — all destroyed by a tiny microbe in a miserable crawling tick. Christy struck down by a tick with a brain no larger than the head of a pin. How absolutely grotesque. It doesn't make sense. Absolutely no sense at all. Senseless!"

After a long pause, with no comment from me, he went on. "For the first time in my life, Gene, despite two doctoral degrees, nothing in this universe makes sense to me anymore. Nothing!"

A week later he picked up where he left off the Friday before.

"I've always said, Gene, I didn't need the *God-hypothesis* to bring eternity to the human situation. All humans find our eternity through the genes we pass on to succeeding generations and by the collective memory we leave behind.

"But neither Christy nor I could have children. There are no genes to pass on to the collective pool of humanity which successively follows each generation. There's no biological eternity here for her — or for me. What's left is the memory of the love we intimately shared which still abides in me. But when I die, the memory of that love will die with me and vanish as a puff of dust in the universe. Then there will be nothing eternal anymore about the love which once we shared."

In silence he poured more tea, restoked his pipe with a few more pinches of tobacco and lit it up again, carefully disposing of the match by lifting the stove lid. Settling down in his chair, he propped his feet up on the ornamental stove railing and said, "The only way that memory could become eternal would be for it to be remembered by God."

This was the first time he referred to God, personally, rather than to the *God-hypothesis.*

"Only when our love is remembered by God will Christy and I have anything that is eternal. For the first time, the existence of God is beginning to make sense to me."

I said, "Harold most people arrive at that intellectual deduction from the basis of a religious faith. But you move toward a religious faith from the basis of an intellectual deduction. It doesn't much matter how we get there, from one direction or the other, as long as we get there and find God waiting for us."

As I headed up the stairwell, again he opened the door behind me and asked, "Gene, what time are your chapel services this Sunday? I think maybe I need to come."

❖

My work on my master's degree in history steadily progressed. I finished all the required courses of study and came to the writing of my thesis. Theoretically, a research thesis at the graduate school level should represent an original contribution to that particular field of knowledge — in other words, it should yield information not commonly known in history before.

After much frustration, I decided to write my thesis on the reaction of professional American historians to the ten-volume *A Study of History*, written by the British scholar Arnold J. Toynbee. It was Toynbee's contention that the proper unit of historical study must be the broad sweep of human civilizations rather than the nation-state.

I have always been fascinated with the haunting question of why the great civilizations of the past rose to such colossal heights of power and brilliance and then crumbled into decay and oblivion. What caused the ancient Egyptian, Persian, Babylonian, Greek, and Roman empires to fall until even the ruins of their past glory became an enigma to us? Or the Chinese dynasties? Or the Mayans and Aztecs in South America?

Tonybee was not content to become a conventional ancient historian. His mind was geared toward a "philosophy of history," a common theme in the study of history itself that might link the various human civilizations of the world. If one undertook a panoramic study of these great civilizations, their rise and fall, would a pattern emerge that might be predictive to those of us now living in what Toynbee calls Western civilization? Toynbee maintained there is such a pattern — and implied that Western civilization is already sliding into a steady decline.

Dr. Cedric Cummins, professor of history at the University of South Dakota, was my faculty advisor. He was not only an excellent professor but also became a trusted friend. He advised me to obtain the ten volumes of *A Study of History* through interlibrary loan and read them through, cover to cover. But after seeing how massive they were, he compromised a bit and said that I should just skim through them and be generally familiar with Toynbee's historical approach and philosophical conclusions. I was to thoroughly read a scholarly condensation of the volumes, however.

I plowed into the project with enthusiasm. It practically became an obsession with me. Every night, after putting the kids to bed or returning late from a church meeting, I would race upstairs to a guest bedroom that I had converted into a working study, bury myself in the enormous leather-bound tomes, and read away. I would spread out the books and papers on a large oak dining table that someone had given the parsonage.

The research demands of this project were great. I had to check back through all the book reviews written by American professional historians after each Toynbee volume hit the bookstores. This was some undertaking. Most often I didn't shut off the lights and head for bed until long past midnight.

My greatest moment of success came during one of my annual treks to the Baptist Student Seminar in Washington, D.C., and New York. The Library of Congress was most helpful, and I spent two wonderful days at the magnificent Public Library of New York. As my research notes began accumulating, I couldn't get myself started on writing the thesis. After lengthy exposure to the eloquent prose of Arnold Toynbee, I couldn't think of an opening sentence or phrase that was profound enough to honor the man about whom I was writing. My good friend Monroe Billington broke the logjam and told me just to start writing somewhere, anywhere, in the middle, and leave the opening and closing remarks for a later time.

I did exactly that.

I wrote my first drafts in longhand, then corrected and rewrote them. Then I would laboriously type my handwritten notes into a readable form for Ced Cummins. He ordered me to cut everything I had written in half. Eventually the thesis began to take shape and came into being. My oral defense of it before a committee of faculty members from the College of Arts and Sciences was easy, and it was a fantastic joy to graduate with a master of arts degree in history.

Often I would see in the history department a young history major named Tom Brokaw, later NBC's evening news anchor. Monroe Billington was his faculty advisor.

When I became discouraged, Monroe told me that writing a master's thesis is much like having a baby. First there is the ecstasy of conception, the seminal beginning of the original idea. Then there is a gradual evolution, a slow assembly of all the parts, a translation into pages of words and thoughts. Eventually the whole thing begins to heavily burden you down. Then the pain of final completion on deadline and the oral examinations which follow. At last the baby is born, and the pain of delivery is forgotten in the joy of a new creation. And it usually takes about nine months.

The analogy was most appropriate, because at that very time Shirley and I were preparing ourselves for the birth of our third baby. She was born on February 21, 1960, and we named her Sheridan Jen. Although she looked like her maternal grandmother, called "Mommie Pops" by our other two children, her dark hair and brown complexion took after me. We have a wonderful 8mm movie of her trip home from the hospital while her older sister and brother, Lori and Barry, gaze into her dimpled face for the first time with awe and wonder.

With Sheri's birth, I took new stock of my family life and professional career. Vermillion was a perfect little mid-western town in which to raise a young family. With a major state university only a few blocks down the street, my children would be able to acquire college educations at minimal expense. If they aspired to postgraduate study, this would be affordable. Shirley and I discussed the possibility of our committing to a long-term ministry in Vermillion and purchasing our own home to avail ourselves of the IRS clergy tax break. I even began talking to some of my laymen about the idea.

Priceless photo of my showing newly born baby, Sheridan, for the first time to her older sister and brother. Lori is truly fascinated with the little bundle "with a face" — but big brother Barry is not.

✧

My ministry at University Baptist Church took on more maturity, I would like to believe. I loved the people and had a wonderful relationship with them. I enjoyed the intellectual stimulation of being a college chaplain and interacting with students and faculty.

The church's physical plant was extensive and adequate for future use but needed serious repairs and major modifications. The church, originally organized in

Sheri, Barry, and Lori as small children in Vermillion. It was an overwhelming joy to be a father and I played with them continuously, whenever time permitted — especially preparing them for bed.

1868, would be celebrating its 100th anniversary less than ten years away. It was at this time that I founded and brought into being something we called the **Centennial Trust Fund**. Its corporate purpose was to receive and generate funds, hopefully large bequests, for extensive long-range renovations of the historic church property. We engaged the services of an architectural firm in Sioux Falls who sent a crew of structural and mechanical engineers swarming over the property, and we drew up a series of long-range goals, some of which were scheduled for completion by 1968 in time for the church's centennial celebration. I felt very good about this achievement. (Particularly so in 1968 when I was invited back to a centennial celebration of its successful completion, paid for mostly by the accumulated trust fund.)

✧

But behind the sunshine of our lives lurked a cloud that was increasing the shadows of my discontent. It had nothing to do with the local church in Vermillion, nor with the national leadership of the American Baptist Convention. Quite the contrary, I highly respected these denominational leaders and to this day consider them the finest church administrators I've known. The Green Lake conferences I attended, which featured many of these people as speakers, consistently proved to be inspirational and educational.

Then what was the problem?

Biblical fundamentalism, pure and simple. Although not prevalent among the Baptist churches back east, it seemed rampant here in the midwestern United States. Whenever I attended clergy meetings sponsored by the South Dakota Baptist Convention, I would return home depressed and dispirited. These Baptist ministers sincerely loved the Lord, but their anti-intellectualism and biblical fundamentalism assaulted my intelligence and patience.

Once I happened to be presiding over a morning worship service at Sioux Falls College, and the guest speaker was an associate evangelist of Billy Graham. In my presence, the dean of students told the speaker, a TV personality from Ohio, to please refrain from glorifying his past sins in order to demonstrate his radical conversion at a Billy Graham Crusade. "The students are getting sick of hearing this sort of thing," he warned the evangelist.

The speaker agreed. Then he stepped to the pulpit and proceeded to do the very thing he had just agreed *not* to do. He raved on and on about how he boozed and womanized, even though he was already a born-again Christian, but then attended a Billy Graham meeting and was born again *a second time* — and had now become an evangelist himself.

When I asked him why he did something which the college specifically asked him not to do, he answered truthfully: "Because this is the only way

I can validate my conversion to give credibility to my preaching!" After hearing him preach I could understand why he needed credibility.

Ever since then, I have deplored Christians who validate their Christianity by glamorizing the dramatics of their conversion. I realize, of course, that evangelistic crusades encourage this sort of thing. But spiritual exhibitionism and voyeurism is not my cup of tea. I strongly believe that Christians who quietly make personal commitments to Christ or who don't even remember their original conversions are no less Christian than those who withhold their conversions until the theatrics of the next revival comes to town.

Furthermore, if the witness of a Christian life doesn't have much validity without the dramatics of the conversion, then glamorizing the conversion won't make much of an impression. That would be like asking a married couple the secret of their successful marriage and getting only the romantic story of their passionate courtship, glamorous wedding, and fantastic honeymoon. Don't get me wrong, I rejoice that people can have dramatic conversions, the same as I rejoice that people can have glamorous honeymoons. But neither have much to do with the permanency of the long-term relationship. The decision to accept Christ as one's personal Savior, like the decision of a man and woman to commit themselves to a lifelong marriage, must be followed by hundreds and thousands of nitty-gritty decisions to carry the commitment through. And here is where the emphasis is conspicuously absent in most evangelistic crusades.

I remember listening to a lecture delivered by a guest professor of the Old Testament from Southern Baptist Seminary in Louisville who, in trying to make his point, made incidental references to the "Creation myth" and the "Noah and Jonah myths" within the Bible. The majority of the Baptist ministers in the room went berserk over his terminology. The poor man tried to explain that the word *myth* was another ontological word for a story or legend that reveals a profound religious truth far beyond the technicalities of the story itself. "The point of the *Creation myth*," he tried to say, "is to show that in the beginning of all creation . . . it was God who created."

He got nowhere. According to his attackers, the earth was created a little over 5000 years ago and the Bible provided a literal description of how it happened. He tried again to explain the powerful religious message revealed through the legend of Noah's ark and was shouted down. He tried once more to explain that the ontological message of Jonah really had nothing to do with whether a man could survive three days in the belly of the whale. He was drowned out.

At dinner that evening, I asked one of the Baptist ministers that if the world was created only 5000 years ago, what about the dinosaurs, which became extinct 60 million years earlier?

He answered, "Ah, Satan sprinkled those dinosaur bones around just to confuse the scientists to make them think they can prove the Bible wrong."

I gasped in disbelief!

This kind of religious fundamentalism was foreign to all the seminary training I had received and all the theological thinking that defined my Christian faith. Their anti-intellectualism was appalling to me. Although I personally liked many of these men and respected their spiritual sincerity, their religious mind-set was becoming increasingly intolerable to me. Christ said, "Know the truth and the truth shall set you free." If one must deny or distort the truth in order to bolster one's religious belief, then one is harking down the wrong path.

These conservative ministers had as much religious right to their biblical fundamentalism as I do to my theological liberalism, but the two were inherently incompatible. I was out of step with the Baptist fundamentalism so prevalent at the grassroots level of midwestern America. I was the one who needed to change or jump ship.

I shared my inner turmoil with Father Bob Crawford, vicar of St. Paul's Episcopal Church of Vermillion, already in semi-retirement after a long ministry among two of the highest Anglo-Catholic parishes in the nation — one at St. Barnabas in Omaha, Nebraska, and the second in Fond du Lac, Wisconsin. As an Anglo-Catholic priest, he was high on ceremony and low on marriage. He was a confirmed celibate. He was also highly opinionated. Few people could tolerate what they considered to be his aloof snobbery.

He was a most unlikely candidate to become my trusted friend and religious confidante. But he was one of the funniest human beings I've ever known. His sense of humor and cutting cynicism about everything sacred, including himself, was most refreshing. He was also the most honest human being I've ever known. He would tell it exactly as it was with the most elaborate vocabulary imaginable. When I told him about Satan's sprinkling dinosaur bones to confuse the scientists, he roared with laughter and pounded the armchair, saying, "What delightful bullshit!"

After honking into his handkerchief he howled, "Who needs New York theater when you have live comedy like that? Gene, why don't you remember all those one-liners and write them up into a Broadway comedy someday? You have great potential to become a playwright with original material like that."

He loosened me up until I quit taking myself so seriously. When I got around to talking about my secret love affair with the Episcopal Church, dating from college days, he pounded me hard. "Stay the hell out of it, Gene, if you possibly can. If anyone can possibly talk you out of it, then you will know you shouldn't embrace such insanity."

At the same time, he gave me a beautiful leather-bound Episcopal prayerbook and explained how I could use it for reading the daily offices (morning and evening prayers) and for the first time, explained the meaning of liturgical worship.

"The central act of worship for Episcopalians," he said, "is the prayer book liturgy of the people — of which good preaching is a part, of which good music is a part — but the center stage is reserved for the sacramental presence of Jesus Christ."

I persisted with my questions, and he persisted with his discouragements. But he was honest enough to tell me two things which I greatly appreciated:

1). Although he held the high Anglo-Catholic persuasion of faith, which emphasized the rich Catholic heritage, he admitted there was also a low church persuasion that emphasized the rich Protestant heritage. I could become Episcopalian without necessarily having to embrace the high Anglo-Catholic persuasion.

2). If I was serious in pursuing the Episcopal Church, he contended that I should make an appointment with the Rt. Reverend J. Wilson Hunter, the low church Bishop of Wyoming — and not pursue the religious vocation of the Episcopal priesthood in South Dakota, which might hurt the feelings of the Vermillion Baptists. "You love them too much, and they you, for that ever to happen." I appreciated his sensitivity and good advice.

During our August vacation to Wyoming in 1959, Shirley and I drove to Laramie and met with Bishop Hunter. I have never met a more gregarious extrovert. When he invited Shirley and me to the Diamond Horseshoe restaurant for lunch, just a few miles out of Laramie, everyone in the place came rushing to our table for an exchange of hilarious greetings. If there was anyone in the restaurant he didn't know, he went to their table to introduce himself and soon was loudly bantering with them as if they were long-forgotten acquaintances.

His store of jokes was inexhaustible, and his enthusiasm for telling them soon wore us out. I couldn't decide if, indeed, he was honestly the most congenial extrovert the world has ever known or if he was driven by a pathological need constantly to be the center of attention.

Bishop Hunter did leave this counsel of sound advice with me: "Eugene and Shirley, I ask that you both take a year to think this over. Don't act on sudden impulse. I ask you to pray about it. Remember, whether you remain a Baptist minister or become an Episcopal priest, either way you are a servant of the Lord. My hunch is that a triggering event will push you to decide one way or the other. Until that happens, wait upon the Lord."

After Shirley and I returned to Sheridan, I revealed my inner turmoil with my mother. I think it greatly distressed her at first because she knew little about the Episcopal Church except that it seemed awfully Catholic. However, she acknowledged that a lot of her good friends, people she greatly admired, were Episcopalians.

She reasoned, I think, that Episcopal ministers — wearing clerical collars, smoking their pipes, and being reverently addressed as "Father" — were really nothing more than Catholic priests who flunked *Latin* and *celibacy*.

She thought it over for several days before inviting me to sit with her on the front porch during the coolness of the early evening, as was her habit. "You know," she said, "I've come to the conclusion after living seventy-five years on this earth that it doesn't make much difference if you're Baptist, Catholic, Episcopalian, or Lutheran. Excluding the fanatical fringe, the religious zealots of every religion that you must ignore, no one denomination has a monopoly on Christian morality and good works. When you live in a ranching valley as long as your father and I have, you soon separate the good Samaritans from the phonies. Denominationalism doesn't seem to have much to do with it one way or the other."

Then she concluded, "Gene, if you'd feel happier in the Episcopal Church, if it makes you more comfortable with yourself, then do it. I'm convinced that ultimately it's not a theological decision — even though you might like to convince yourself that it is — as much as it is an emotional search for meaning and fulfillment, a spiritual calling from deep within your soul."

My mother's words of wisdom have remained with me all my life. The older I have become, the more experiences I've tucked under my belt as a clergyman, the more convinced I am that she was right. We are driven more by our emotional religious needs than we would care to admit — and we justify them with our abstract theological rationalizations.

I returned to Vermillion with the realization that I had reached a vocational crossroads. Either I would pursue the Ph.D. program to prepare myself for the academic world of university teaching and writing, or I would remain within the American Baptist Convention as a Baptist minister, which would necessitate my gravitating toward larger city pastorates east of the Mississippi River — or finally, I would enter the priesthood of the Episcopal Church and remain in the West.

Bishop Hunter was right: I needed a triggering event to get me off dead center. I also knew that it wasn't a decision I could make all by myself and that I needed to seek and find the will of God for my life. Devotional prayer was something I had long practiced. There was a charming little unused room in the Vermillion church. One corner of it curved with a small Gothic stained-glass window in front. I set up a simple little altar there and pulled in a few folding chairs.

I called it my meditation chapel. Regularly I would sit there in quiet prayer. I always remembered the words of the park ranger from Terry Peak in South Dakota when I was at the Black Mountain lookout in the Big Horns of Wyoming, testing the FM transmitter: "Don't you know, stupid, you can't receive when you're in a transmitting mode?"

My prayers consisted more of listening than transmitting. I discovered, however, that quietly reading morning prayer from the Episcopal Prayer Book was a marvelous way to get me centered on the Lord so that I could spiritually receive.

✧

In early spring of 1960 my mother wrote me several disturbing letters. She had experienced a series of "mini strokes" and wanted me to come home for a visit. I wavered. Then she wrote a longer letter, telling me she was deeply worried about her health and feared a major stroke. I could tell from her handwriting and the way her sentences meandered across the page that indeed her forebodings were warranted.

She begged me to come home immediately. "We have appointed you to be the executor of our estate. I'm afraid your father and I have made loans to your older brothers which we may never collect. I'm worried sick about our financial affairs. We're needing help. I don't want conflict over the family inheritance. I'm fearful that our older daughters-in-law will destroy the family peace if we don't get things settled right away. Won't you please come home immediately?"

I wrote her that I couldn't come immediately, as she requested. But I was invited to deliver the commencement address at the Padroni, Colorado, high school graduation in May, and I assured her that I would then drive up to Sheridan from there and spend a week with them.

"Mom," I wrote, "please don't worry about your financial affairs. It really doesn't make that much difference in the long scheme of things. When I get there, I will help you establish a family trust with the bank so that everyone will be treated fairly. I promise."

A week later, I received word that Mom had suffered a massive stroke while visiting my sister in her home at Casper. I was to come at once. When

I walked into her hospital room my family told me to talk to her; they had reason to believe she could understand what was being said, although she was too comatose to respond. I put my arms around her shoulder and told her I loved her. I told her that I was the father of a new little baby girl, named Sheridan Jen, who had dark hair and brown eyes and a big dimple in her cheek. I could say nothing more — words failed me.

Perhaps she heard me, but probably not. She died the next morning. The family asked me to conduct her funeral service back in Sheridan. I didn't know if I could handle it, so I asked an old family friend, Dr. E. K. Morrow

A priceless heirloom family photo showing my father, Fred J. Todd, meeting the stagecoach which ran between Buffalo and Clearmont, Wyoming, in the early 1900s. The stage was pulled by a fast-trotting four-horse team which has just made its "stop" at the mail pouch pole on lower Piney Creek. Dad has an extra horse for his "bride-to-be" onboard, Gladys Wilcox, arriving from Missouri to teach school — later to become my mother.

— a former Methodist minister who once had been a neighboring rancher to the folks on Piney Creek and who had recently retired as president of Kansas Wesleyan University in Salina — to stand by in the event I failed. But by this time I had been in the ministry long enough to steel myself emotionally for almost anything. Ministers can't break down and cry at funerals, because if they do the funeral can't proceed, and everything collapses into a maudlin spectacle. The minister must be strong, even though he's weeping on the inside. Besides, as a child I had learned to always cry alone — up in the hills, when there was no one else around.

As I stood by her casket in the crowded funeral home, as friends and neighbors filed by, I reflected that her lifetime bridged the gap between the old frontier of the American West and its modern age. She came to the Piney Creek ranching valley in a horse-drawn stagecoach, a beautiful and slender school-teacher. I have a photograph of my handsome dad standing behind that stagecoach holding the reins to a second saddle horse. "School marm meets cowboy" — the familiar theme of western romance novels. The creek at Double Crossing was flooding, so the horses leaped into the swollen waters and swam across with the coach floating behind. The current was

Fred and Gladys Todd. "School marm marries cowboy" — their wedding picture in 1906.

swift, washing them several hundred feet downstream before the horses secured footing to pull the stage up onto the bank. Mom was terrified.

It was from the flooding waters of the same creek, twenty-five years later, that she rescued me from what otherwise would surely have been my drowning. As a young clergyman officiating at her burial in 1960, I was only beginning to comprehend the incredible influence she quietly had upon my life. I subtly learned from her that religion, whatever its doctrinal form, should be a broadening expansion of the human spirit and mind, never a narrowing restriction of it. That faith is an openness to all truth in God's universe, however revealed, and never a fanaticism about one single strand of that revelation. That unless Christianity makes you a better person and neighbor in a very practical sense to this good earth and all its creature inhabitants — then God doesn't have much relevance, and it's a waste of people's time to preach otherwise.

Furthermore, I realized and appreciated as never before, the interfer-ence she must have run in my behalf to placate my macho-rancher father, allowing me to pursue a destiny different from ranching. Her encourage-ment helped me to continue writing newspaper columns when I was just

Gladys Wilcox Todd (1885-1960) — Mom

a seventh-grader, to enter radio broadcasting when I was only fifteen years old and to hike off to college and graduate school when no one else in the family had much interest in doing so.

In the fall of 1951, while I was briefly home on the ranch for a week long vacation before returning for graduate study, she convinced my father that she needed me in the kitchen for garden canning more than he needed another hand in the hay field. Both my sisters were married and away, and she desperately needed help — there was simply too much hard work to be done by herself alone. After all, she was sixty-six years old. Fresh garden vegetables: peas, green beans, corn, and tomatoes had to be picked daily in wooden bushel baskets and prepared for canning. Cucumbers were pickled in large crocks. Apples were peeled, then mashed and cooked for the making of jam.

Much later in life I realized she had an ulterior motive. This was her only chance to get this college graduate son of hers, someone she wasn't seeing too much of anymore, completely to herself — not only for help with the strenuous garden drudgery but for conversation about the future direction of his life. We sat out on the back porch, husking corn, shelling peas, snapping beans, and talking.

In addition to canning well over 100 jars of garden produce daily, she organized a typically sumptuous ranch supper for Dad and the weary hired hands that evening. As she pulled a pot roast out of the oven, complete with all the trimmings, she flipped a linen cloth upon the table and asked me to take the scissors out to the garden to clip a fresh bouquet of flowers for a centerpiece.

I protested. This was a superfluous cultural refinement that no one expected or appreciated. Particularly a haying crew.

I will never forget her response: "Only when you do the extra things to bring goodness and beauty into the lives of people you love, over and beyond what they would normally expect, does your life make a significant difference in this world."

Her life made an immeasurable difference, because she did all the extra things no one ordinarily expected in order to bring bouquets of goodness and beauty into the lives of the people she loved.

✧

Returning to Vermillion, I remembered my last conversation with her about joining the Episcopal Church while relaxing on the shady porch of their Sheridan home. Her words hung in the air: "I'm convinced that ultimately it's not a theological decision . . . as much as it is an emotional search for meaning and fulfillment in your life, a calling from deep within your soul."

But I still needed a triggering event to make that ultimate decision.

Out of the blue I received an invitation to interview for the pastorate of a very large Baptist church adjacent to the enormous campus of the University of Minnesota, where more than 30,000 students attended classes. The student enrollment alone was five times the entire population of Vermillion including the university. This was my first trip to Minneapolis, and I found the city traffic overwhelming. At their request, Shirley accompanied me, holding in her arms our three-month-old baby, Sheridan Jen. Typical of many city parishes, its once huge congregation had largely dissipated because of the urban sprawl and now consisted mostly of faculty and students from the adjoining university. The church plant was excessively large for the dwindling congregation but magnificently constructed and laid out.

The search committee was most gracious, consisting entirely of university faculty. The professors asked all the right questions, and I felt I had all the right answers. It was apparent they didn't want a fundamentalist and were pleased that I wasn't one. They were also pleased that I had written my master's thesis on Arnold Toynbee and might pursue my Ph.D. at their university. While walking through the church, we entered the large sanctuary, and I observed that the church's Gothic architecture made it appear more Anglican than Baptist. Suddenly, in the center aisle I stopped, turned to the committee and said, "May I ask you a question now?" They nodded.

"Why would you want me to become your pastor?"

Pointing to the balcony behind us, they said, "See that empty gallery up there? We want it filled with students every Sunday morning listening to your sermons. We understand that's what happening at Vermillion."

With all the naive confidence of a thirty-two-year-old, I brazenly said, "I can do that."

I knew it was a challenge that I could meet. I would work harder on my sermons than ever before. With the help of God and with bold determination, I would become an eloquent preacher. I would pray harder than ever before.

But on my way home to Vermillion I kept thinking, *But that's not what the worship of God is all about.* The words of Bob Crawford began haunting me, "The central act of worship," he said, "is the prayer book liturgy of the people — of which good preaching is a part, of which good music is a part — but the center stage is reserved for the sacramental presence of Jesus Christ."

My mind was made up.

I sat down and wrote two letters. In one I resigned as pastor of the University Baptist Church of Vermillion and announced my intention to pursue further graduate study at the Episcopal Virginia Theological Seminary. In the other, to Bishop Hunter of Wyoming, I asked to become a postulant to study for holy orders in the Episcopal Church.

Saying our goodbyes to all the great people of Vermillion was not easy, but we managed our way through the final worship service, followed by a magnificent potluck dinner.

It so happened that a Sunday evening wedding was actually my last official act as a Baptist minister. After officiating at the wedding and signing the marriage license, I slipped out of the church into the beautiful evening air of a warm summer night and sat down on the curb just across from the church. I watched the bridal couple and wedding guests flitter in and out of the reception hall, doors flung wide open, amid much spontaneous laughter and celebration.

Suddenly it hit me. *Gene, why have you done this to yourself? You love this church. You love this small university town and its rich cultural environment. You have intellectually thrived here. Your three children were born here. They could all be college educated here by simply walking a few blocks to campus. You could pursue additional graduate study here at the university for as long as you live. An ordained clergyman switching denominational loyalties is a momentous thing to do. You may have made an enormous mistake.*

I had sought God's will through this tumultuous decision and felt I was leaving its guidance up to Him to lead me through — but now I snatched it back unto myself and was panic-stricken. My eyes brimmed over, and I trembled with deep remorse and foreboding fear.

I walked home and bathed Lori and Barry, ages four and two, and tumbled with them on the floor before tucking them into bed with stories and prayers while Shirley attended to little Sheri. Later that evening I made love to my wife, then went to sleep in perfect peace that God's will was unfolding before me.

He tells me of the years that went before me
When heavenly plans were made for me to be
When all was but a dream of dim conception
To come to life, earth's verdant glory see
. . . This earth will pass
And with it common trifles
But God and I
Will go unendingly.

Never again was I to regret the decision I had made.

Chapter 9

There were two very important reasons why we needed to return to Sheridan after leaving Vermillion in August 1960. In the first place, it was important to us to visit Dad, who was now living alone following Mom's death in April. Although her passing had occurred only a few months earlier, I could tell from his correspondence that he was not grieving well. In fact, true to the Todd family heritage, he was denying his grief all together. We needed to see him.

In the second place, now that I had made the decision to become an Episcopal minister, it was necessary that I first become an Episcopalian. This required that I be confirmed by an Episcopal bishop into the Anglican communion of faith. Prior arrangements had been made that Fr. Ray Clark, rector of St. Peter's Episcopal Church of Sheridan, would provide Shirley and me with abbreviated confirmation instruction so that we technically would qualify for the bishop's official "laying-on-hands" ceremony.

Ray and Mary Clark were destined to become my dearest friends in the Episcopal Church. Ray's tenure at St. Peter's stretched into thirty-nine years (he retired in 1988), and he was affectionately loved by everyone in Sheridan. Including Dad.

This affection didn't come naturally with Dad. He didn't know what to think when Ray, attired in a clerical collar, came to the house every day to give Shirley and me an hour or two of pre-confirmation instruction. Dad knew Ray wasn't Catholic, but he was surely something very close to it. When Ray came to the door, Dad would simply disappear, leaving his pipe still smoldering in the ashtray. But one time he was caught off guard and found himself accidentally greeting Ray at the door. He was entrapped for the next half hour, just long enough for both to light up their pipes and visit awhile. That did it.

"He's not so bad after all," Dad would say. "Hell, he sat here and made perfect good sense all the time he was visiting with me. He knew as much about all the old-time ranchers around here as I did. Didn't put on any religious airs at all."

That statement said more about Dad, I'm afraid, than it did about Ray Clark.

Bishop Hunter came flying into Sheridan like a whirlwind from Jericho to officiate at the initiatory rites of the entire Todd family into the Episcopal Church. This meant the rite of holy confirmation for Shirley and me and the rite of holy baptism for our three children. As I mentioned in the previous chapter, Bishop Hunter was the most gregarious extrovert I've ever known. The words attributed to Alice Roosevelt Longworth, in describing her father, Teddy Roosevelt, would equally apply to Bishop Hunter: "He wanted to be the center of attention of every public gathering he attended. If he went to a meeting, he wanted to be the speaker. If he went to a wedding, he wanted to be the groom. If he went to a funeral, he wanted to be the corpse."

When a Sheridan physician just happened into the chapel during our private initiatory rites into the Episcopal Church, the Bishop greeted him with a joke: "Did you hear about the doctor who called on the Episcopal minister suffering from a fever? When he got to the rectory he discovered he didn't have a thermometer in his doctor's bag, so he borrowed one from the minister's wife, who mistakenly handed him the barometer instead. After leaving it under the priest's tongue for five minutes he pulled it out and said, 'Just as I suspected — dry and windy!'"

Then he howled with laughter at his own joke. Poor Barry, three years old, watched the hilarity as if it were a spectacle from another planet — this man in the flowing white robes and colorful stoles, bantering as loudly and rapidly as an auctioneer at a livestock sale, then cackling like a chicken. When Barry saw the bishop pouring water in the baptismal font and laying out the white napkins, as if preparing to perform major surgery, he whispered to me, "Dad, why don't we just leave?"

"We can't, Barry. The bishop is going to baptize you with water just like we explained to you before we came here. We can't leave. See, the chapel door is closed."

Barry momentarily disappeared from sight, only to return, whispering to me, "Dad, I found a door through the kitchen into the alley. Let's run for it."

We didn't run. We stayed, and within a few minutes we were no longer Baptists but Episcopalians.

Then Bishop Hunter drew me aside for a moment of privacy. Now in a serious mood, he informed me that the arrangements had been completed for me to enter the Episcopal Theological Seminary at Alexandria, Virginia, for a one-year program of Anglican studies before returning to Wyoming for ordination into the Episcopal priesthood.

Back at the house, Dad seemed pensive as he went about his old routine, gardening and hauling in armloads of fresh vegetables for dinner and supper as if Mom were still cooking for threshers. We'd sit out on the back porch, as in summers before, while we husked corn, peeled cucumbers, sliced tomatoes, and topped onions and radishes. But Mom's painful absence was never mentioned. I knew all too well how the Todds handle anything emotional: *Don't talk about it and you won't have to think about it. Above all, at all costs, don't allow yourself to feel anything.*

It was too painful for me to play the game of denial, as if Mom had never existed. I knew better than to ask Dad directly how he was coping with her loss. Even to hint at it would cause him to look away and go silent — with tears welling in his eyes. So instead of talking about Mom's loss, I began asking Dad about the things they had done together in the past. This he would talk about.

"Our first baby was born during a blizzard while I was out feeding cattle. A young doctor and his wife were staying at the house, but Mom's labor came on real fast. When I came home for the noon dinner, she motioned me into the bedroom and lifted up the blanket and I saw the baby for the first time. But the baby died. So I built a little wooden casket and lined it with baby blankets, and we buried it ourselves in the apple orchard.

"When our third baby (Roger) came along, I had to drive Mom in a horse-drawn sleigh seven miles back through the hills to Ulm to catch a train into Sheridan. It was twenty below zero and the snowdrifts were so high I had to ride the ridges because the horses would break belly-deep into the snow. We put her on the caboose of a freight train, and there were several other pregnant women riding that caboose, all for the same reason. The conductor moved up to the engine, refusing to ride back there in case his caboose became a railroad maternity ward."

"Dad, why don't you write these remarkable stories down for the rest of us in the family to read and remember?"

"I can't write, you know that. Mom did all the letter writing. She was good when it came to penmanship and spelling. I can't spell worth a damn. I had only an eighth-grade education, you know, and it wasn't very good at that. No, I'll never try writing anything down because I don't know how to string the words together like you do."

Suddenly a spark of inspiration struck me. "Dad," I said, "I'll loan you a tape recorder. I'll show you how easy it is to operate. You send those tapes to me and I'll copy down your stories and write them up. What do you say? But you'll have to promise me that every day you'll sit down and talk."

He thought it over for several days. Then, one morning, he said to me, "Show me how to run that tape recorder."

Two years later those stories would be published in a book entitled *The Recollections of a Piney Creek Rancher*. But I'm getting ahead of my story a little bit. First Shirley and I, with the three children, had to get from Wyoming to Alexandria, Virginia.

✧

The 2000-mile journey was the first big trip our little family had ever taken together. We were leaving the security of the Rocky Mountain West and the familiarity of the Midwest and moving to a very large city on the eastern seaboard: Washington, D.C. It was scary.

But we had a good trip. Again, I built up the back seat so that it functioned as a playpen and sleeping crib for Lori and Barry. Little Sheri, only seven months old, had a most delightful trip. We placed her bassinet lengthwise up along the passenger window of the front seat. Shirley sat in the middle with one arm resting on Sheri who loved the close proximity and constant attention of her mother. She took long naps, then would sit up in the bassinet to eat and play while she watched the scenery flow by just outside the window, then drift back into a drowsy sleep. Sometimes she was content just to lie in the bassinet, while her mother sang and her older sister and brother entertained her. After three days on the highway, we commented that Sheri not once cried or whimpered. No wonder Indian mothers carried their babies constantly on their back so that they never fussed for attention.

I had a cousin, Doris Sampson Walter, living in Silver Springs, Maryland, a suburb of Washington. Her husband, Rudy, took the weekend to help me find my way through the major thoroughfares of the confusing city to our apartment complex nestled at the intersection of the bustling Shirley Highway and Seminary Road — not far from the Pentagon. Rudy and Doris and their young family proved to be lifesavers for us during our year in Alexandria.

We learned that Alexandria, the hometown of George Washington, is actually much older than the city of Washington. In fact, we regularly worshipped at historic Christ's Church in Alexandria, the family parish church of the first president of the United States. When we first attended services at the beautiful old colonial building, Shirley and I opened the little door into the empty pew box and discovered, according to the historical plaque mounted there, that we were actually worshipping in the private family box rented and reserved for George Washington.

The Virigina Theological Seminary (VTS) campus spread over several hundred acres of beautiful rolling countryside. Out across these gentle hills were perched the gracious homes of the seminary faculty. Every home was of Georgian architectural design, with huge shuttered windows reaching nearly to the floor of each room. Each included a spacious library-study where the professor would meet with students for private consultation or group discussions. There was much more formality at VTS than at Iliff, where students often wore blue jeans and open sport shirts to classes. Not at VTS. Here dress jackets and ties were the normal attire, and far more southern reserve typified their interpersonal relationships than at Iliff.

At VTS the professors and students would smoke during formal classes and meet for beer after school at nearby pubs. This was definitely an Episcopalian way of doing things. We had chapel services every morning, and a small group of us held a daily prayer service late in the afternoon — before "reflection and restoration" (R & R) in the pub.

Students and faculty were required to share the noon meal together at a large refectory (dining hall). We each had to take our turns as waiters, setting the tables and serving the food. The meals were simple but wholesome and always included soup. We waiters, one assigned to each table, would ladle the soup out of large stainless steel containers into the individual bowls, then slice homemade bread and cheese on wooden cutting boards. The open availability of professors to the students was most welcome, and table conversations were warm, stimulating, and inviting. I loved the gracious southern way of doing things.

My courses were carefully selected for me by my advisor, Dr. Albert Mollegan, whom the seminarians affectionately called Molly. "You're not here to repeat the basic theological and biblical core of studies you had at Iliff," he told me. "You're here to learn only those things that will teach you how to become an Episcopalian — courses like Anglican theology, Anglican liturgics, Anglican history, Anglican spirituality, and Anglican canon law."

Then he leaned back in his chair, lit up another cigarette, and in a cultivated southern drawl said, "But I'm afraid we'll never teach you the essential *ethos* of Anglicanism through the formal course work I'm assigning you. I'm convinced you'll only learn that from your total immersion into the Anglican community of faith here on campus: our worship services, classroom discussions, coffee sessions, and informal luncheon conversations around the table in the refectory. Gradually you'll metamorphose from a Baptist into an Episcopalian, without your even being aware of the change."

I loved the heavy course work at VTS. Every day I rode off to VTS in a carpool of married seminarians who lived within our apartment complex. When I had an hour's break I'd dash off to the library trying to absorb everything Anglican I could find.

I needed a part-time job somewhere and found one at the University of Maryland, about forty miles away. Once a week I drove there to serve as an interim lay chaplain to Episcopal students until such time as a full-time Episcopal priest could be found for the vacant position. I was a natural for the job because of my five years' experience as chaplain at the University of South Dakota.

High-powered speakers were already lined up to meet with the Canterbury Club, the name commonly used for campus associations of Episcopal students. They included the Rt. Reverend Angus Dunn, the scholarly bishop of the diocese of Washington (who had already distinguished himself as an author of several books on Anglican theology), and the Rt. Reverend Wm. F. Creighton, bishop co-adjutor of the diocese. I enjoyed greeting and hosting these esteemed bishops, although I felt myself in awe of them and somewhat intimidated.

Another personage of considerable renown was the Very Reverend Francis B. Sayre, dean of the great National Cathedral of Washington, D.C. Dean Sayre's claim to fame was the fact that he was born in the White House while his grandfather, Woodrow Wilson, was president of the United States. In fact, Sayre's physical profile perfectly matched that of his famous grandfather. (President Wilson's tomb lies within the National Cathedral.) Dean Sayre claimed to be a "Wyoming cowboy," which caught my interest. Although I had never heard of the Sayres in Wyoming, it was conceivable that his father was a Wyoming rancher about whom I just hadn't heard. So I asked Dean Sayre what his Wyoming connection was.

"I spent six weeks one summer on a ranch at Jackson," he answered. When he mentioned the name of the place I knew instantly it was a dude ranch. *Bullshit*, I said to myself. *When I take a Caribbean cruise someday I'll remember thereafter to call myself a sailor.*

I enjoyed my part-time job at the University of Maryland and needed the extra cash it provided. Our finances were tight enough that Shirley and I couldn't afford even the simplest of the luxuries an international city like Washington offered. One day the wife of a former governor of South Dakota, whose mother I had buried back in Vermillion, invited Shirley for lunch at one of the great hotels. Her husband was now serving on the Board of Governors of the Federal Reserve System. After lunch she took Shirley to one of the richest upscale department stores of downtown Washington, where they spent the afternoon trying on furs. The cost of each garment exceeded the accumulated salaries I earned during my five years in Vermillion.

The fall of 1960 was an exciting time to be in Washington, with a presidential election in full steam. Shirley decided to take the three children to visit her parents, now living in Fontana, North Carolina. I drove them to the railroad station in Alexandria to catch the evening streamliner and found the depot packed to capacity on one side and completely empty on the other. Without thinking, I carried the luggage and kids into the empty side and settled down to wait until the train was called. A black soldier in full military uniform sat down in a bench near us. Nothing was said, but I observed the strange looks coming our way from passengers crowded in the other section. Then I noticed a sign posted on the wall: COLORED SECTION.

I glanced toward the drinking fountains and saw two — one clearly marked WHITES ONLY and the other COLORED.

I was outraged. I glanced at the black soldier, sitting close to us, and thought, *How can you possibly fight in the army of a nation that denies you even the most basic rights of citizenship? How can you lay down your life to defend a system of government that denigrates you and your people?*

This was my first confrontation with the dreadful racist symbol of the southern drinking fountain. But I didn't know what to do. Would I be offending the black soldier by remaining in the "colored" section? I didn't have enough familiarity with the expectations of southern apartheid to know how the system worked. I took a chance — and it may have been dead wrong — and decided to remain defiantly in the "colored" section just to show the whites, crowded on the other side of the depot, that I wasn't on their side of racial bigotry. In fact, I deliberately walked over and drank from the "colored" water fountain and spit the rinsing into the "whites only" fountain. Probably no one noticed my personal act of civil protest. But I knew that I could not passively accept a bitter racist symbol that, to me, violated the very spirit and integrity of both my country and my religious faith.

While Shirley and the kids were visiting in North Carolina, I joined other seminarians and listened to the election returns until past midnight. Later the next afternoon we learned that John F. Kennedy would be the new president of the United States.

I was genuinely pleased that Americans could elect a Catholic to the White House, that we had a youthful president for the first time in my memory, and that he appeared to be an intellectual with considerable charisma, leadership, and inspiration. I was deeply distressed, however, with the dynastic family patriarchal ambitions of Joseph Kennedy Sr. There was no question in my mind that the old man was fully prepared to invest his enormous fortune to assure that all three Kennedy brothers, his sons, made it into the White House.

I'm afraid my suspicions of the old man's intentions have been largely confirmed by subsequent revelations.

For Thanksgiving I drove down to North Carolina to spend the holiday with Shirley's parents in Fontana Village, near the site of the large Fontana Dam. This was my first exposure to the Appalachia of the South.

While there I drove a fellow seminarian to his little country church in Virginia. His wife and children lived in a charming old colonial house. We cooked our breakfast over burning coals in the gigantic fireplace of the kitchen, where the windows looked out over the picturesque forested hills of Virginia. He told me he was a Republican, and I remember telling him that if I lived there I probably would join his ranks to help restore the two-party political system to the South.

It was only a few hundred miles from there to Fontana Village, so I assured Shirley by phone that I most certainly would be arriving there in late afternoon. However, I had not accounted for the Appalachian Mountain roads, which were so narrow and winding that I couldn't exceed twenty-five miles an hour. I drove through barnyards where geese and goats slowly ambled out of my way. On both sides of the forested country lane there stood small weather-beaten shacks with hill people sitting out on the porches, waving at me as if I were their long-lost kin. Many were strolling barefoot along the road and reluctantly made way for the passage of my car, then turned around and stared after me, pointing to the bucking horse on my Wyoming license plates.

The sun went down, the evening shadows lengthened, darkness descended, and I wasn't anywhere near Fontana Village. It seemed I was lost and swallowed up in the smoky haze of the Appalachians. Finally, about nine o'clock that evening, I called Shirley and told her I probably wouldn't make it there before midnight. Shirley's dad came on the phone. I told him that I really didn't know where I was and that I was feeling nervous with the stares of the mountain people.

He said, "Don't worry. You're in moonshine country. They've had their shotgun sights trained on you all the way. Stay moving on the road, and if you must stop, stop where people are gathering round and about. They're gentle people and will do you no harm. But don't wander off into the trees to relieve yourself or anything like that. They might think you're investigating a still and blow your hat off."

I didn't think the situation was quite that bad, but his dire warning sobered my thinking and traumatized my bladder.

✧

Living in the West I had learned to cope quite well with a blizzard. But I had not learned how to cope with a blizzard that others didn't know how to cope with. On January 19, 1961, the night before John F. Kennedy's inauguration, a blinding snowstorm stopped the capital in its tracks. Traffic jams stretched for miles along the Shirley Highway leading away from the Pentagon; cars and public transportation buses were stalled for hours along the freeways. I rejoiced that I was home with my family where it was warm and safe, and I planned to watch the inauguration on television the next morning.

Then a seminarian invited me to accompany him to the inauguration in person — using his wife's ticket. "This will be in a special elevated section of seats," he explained, "because my father-in-law is the contractor who built the whole temporary inaugural complex. But my wife, who is seven months pregnant, wouldn't dare risk her health by braving the severe weather."

I didn't relish the idea of weathering the storm myself, especially to watch something I could see much better on television. I hesitated to give him an immediate refusal, stammering for excuses. Then Shirley interceded, almost shouting, "Gene Todd, you go! This probably will be the only presidential inauguration that you'll ever see in your lifetime. You'll see history being made."

Yes, but at what price? After departing the bus, we had to tramp down Pennsylvania Avenue about five miles in the bitter cold. The blizzard had passed over, but the cold humidity penetrated my sheepskin overcoat from South Dakota. My feet were numb. Our seats were located directly behind the diplomatic corps, so we watched ambassadors in formal frock coats and stovepipe hats slosh through snowdrifts several feet high to reach their chairs. Once there, they dispensed with the formalities, replacing top hats with fur-lined headgear and sticking their gloved hands into large ugly mittens.

I needn't recount the inaugural ceremony itself. But several lasting impressions of the occasion have personally ingrained themselves into my memory. One was the notable contrast between the elderly Dwight Eisenhower and the youthful John Kennedy; truly, a new generation of Americans had risen to leadership. Another was the horrid agony I felt when Robert Frost, the esteemed American poet laureate, couldn't read his lines, even when Vice President Lyndon Johnson shaded the page with his hat. We all realized that it wasn't just the brightness of the sun but a stroke of senility that was blinding him. I remember, too, the intolerable length of the prayers by all the participating clergy; there were five, I think. Sitting there in the bitter cold and listening to them drone on, the whole audience muttered an audible groan whenever the next cleric was introduced.

But the most indelible impression of all, of course, was the shortness and sharpness of Kennedy's presidential address and the cadence of his well-written, and now famous, inaugural lines.

Let every nation know, whether it wishes us well or ill, that we will pay any price, bear any burden, meet any hardship, support any friend, oppose any foe, in order to assure the survival and success of liberty. . . Let us never negotiate out of fear. But let us never fear to negotiate. . . And so, my fellow Americans, ask not what your country can do for you. Ask what you can do for your country.

After trudging back up Pennsylvania Avenue, we had walked nearly ten miles that day. We were both exhausted. Then, while driving home, my car slid off into a bar pit so deep that the trunk was buried in snow. It took me four hours to shovel myself out and mount chains on the wheels. It was dark when I finally stumbled into our apartment famished, nearly frozen, physically exhausted, and emotionally frazzled. That national historic day remains one of the most miserable and memorable days of my life. Even though we had words about it at the time, I am eternally grateful to Shirley for having pushed me into it.

✧

Dad's taped memoirs began to arrive from Wyoming. At first his stories were discombobulated and didn't flow from the beginning to a natural conclusion. He'd get sidetracked, couldn't remember what he had said, then repeat himself. After transcribing each tape I would erase it and then record a tape back to him with questions, comments, and suggestions. His storytelling improved over time as he became more relaxed with the microphone in hand, and eventually he became so oblivious to it that he would laugh uncontrollably at a funny tale he was telling, or choke up when the story turned sad, without remembering to hit the pause button on the recorder. Erasing his tapes was a terrible mistake. I should have kept them just as he recorded them.

At the end of each tape he would invariably say, "Well, there ain't much more for me to talk about. I've just about said it all. I can't think of a bloomin' thing more to say. This will probably be my last tape." I'd answer right back with more questions and encouragements because I wanted to keep the momentum going. I was honestly afraid that if we delayed the project very long he would lose interest and give up. He never saw the manuscript until Easter vacation 1961, when I persuaded him to take his first airplane ride and fly to Washington to pay us a visit. It took a lot of persuasion, and I had to bribe him with the promise that his younger sister, Della Todd Sampson, from Boise, would accompany him on the trip.

Dad got off the large United aircraft with the startling observation that "the wings weren't hooked on very well. They kept bouncing and wobbling all the way from Denver. Them pilots better tighten the bolts up on them there wings or they might just flop off that crate the next time they fly it."

He got an even bigger shock when he sat down and looked at the transcribed manuscript I was working on. His own words stared back at him from many typewritten pages — poorly typed to be sure, with corrections marked in red ink, sections cut out and pasted elsewhere, comments and questions penciled everywhere.

"Do you mean to tell me you're having to go to all this work just to copy down what I've been saying?" he said. "Hell, you don't need to do that. It ain't worth it. I would never have started this project if I thought you and Shirley were having to do all this work on it. It ain't that important."

But he could see an improvement from the original draft to the final version. "Yeah, this reads better than the first draft did. It reads more natural this way than the way I told it. You're doing a dandy job on it, Son."

Son! He called me "Son" for the first time in my life!

It was never his habit to call any of his five boys "son," so it wasn't unusual that he never addressed me that way. But all my life I felt I had been a disappointment to him. I was the one son who never aspired to become a rancher, to break horses, stack hay, work cattle, build fences, and plow fields. Maybe it's an overstatement to say that I was a disappointment to this rancher father of mine. It might be closer to the mark to say that he never understood this one boy of his who read books, wrote stories, and talked on the radio, who went off to college and then blew it all by going to seminary for another three years and finally ended up an ordained minister in a church that was a total mystery to him.

What's the good of all that? I'm convinced that was the constant refrain whenever he tried to figure me out. Each of his other four sons projected a bold image that was acceptable and pleasing — an acceptable image of himself. This he understood.

Finally, when I was thirty-three years old, he suddenly discovered that maybe, just maybe, this *prodigal son* of his didn't have to be a rancher to make a success of himself. Perhaps the written and spoken word could also make a worthwhile contribution to the world. In this instance, at least, writing provided another way that an acceptable image of himself could be projected — this time onto the printed page. His lifetime could be shared with family and friends long after he was gone from the face of the earth.

Finally, as adult to adult, father and son reached a common acceptance, a new understanding of the uniqueness we both could bring to one another, a new level of communication — a bond of trust and mutual respect that would enrich both our lives. From that moment on, Dad became a great friend whose adult companionship I deeply cherished. I also discovered that he had a terrific sense of humor.

✧

My yearlong transition from a Baptist into an Episcopalian was moving slowly on track.

One wouldn't think so, however, because traditionally the two denominations would seem diametrically opposed. What they share in common, of course, is faith in the Lordship of Jesus Christ. Episcopalians have no more faith than Baptists, or vise versa. My mother was correct in her observation that no one Christian denomination has an inherent monopoly on morality, ethics, or the grace of God.

Having said that, however, I must now say that there are some major differences between the Baptist and Episcopal faiths. The first major difference involves the doctrine of authority. For Anglicans the world over, the three bases of authority are vested in: (1) holy scripture, (2) church tradition, and (3) human reason. I think it interesting that even if scripture and tradition are in agreement, reason takes priority over both. Those subject to epileptic seizures, for example, no longer are considered "demon possessed" as labeled in the Bible, because modern science has shown that they suffer from a medically diagnosed physical ailment

This basic doctrine of authority translates itself into church government. The Episcopal system theoretically is governed from the top down to the local congregation through a hierarchy of bishops, priests, and laity. Technically, the word *Episcopal* is defined as a governing order of bishops. The authority of the bishops, however, is not absolute. In fact, it is so diffused by canon law, through tradition and practice, that clergy and laity also have authoritative rights that even a bishop dare not violate.

The Baptist system theoretically is exactly the opposite; the church is governed from the bottom up. The local congregation represents the ultimate authority. If tyranny must prevail, as often it does in any religious order, then among Baptists you have the tyranny of the local congregation. Among Episcopalians you have the tyranny of the bishop in the hiring and firing of priests, if he should be so foolish in trying to get away with it.

In actual practice, both systems of church government moderate toward the center. But you can't become an Episcopalian without recognizing the authoritative and pastoral role of the diocesan bishop as the "Apostolic Episcopal Presence" in our midst. Authority by consent.

The second major difference involves worship. Since the ultimate authority for Baptists rests with the local congregation, it follows that the local congregation determines its own mode of worship, which means that each individual Baptist minister actually devises his own service. Two Baptist churches located across the street from one another can have worship services so different that you wouldn't believe they were of the same denomination. Central to both services, however, would be preaching and singing of hymns. If the minister is on a spiritual high, everything soars. If he's hit a dry spell, the whole congregation suffers. Consequently, you never know how many Baptist churches you have in any larger community — it all depends on how well the sermon went last Sunday. If the preaching was sour, any group can easily organize a new Baptist church, ordain someone as the new minister, and they're off and running.

Episcopalians, by contrast, follow the order of worship directed by a *Book of Common Prayer*. This book prescribes a liturgical form of worship rooted in the historic Catholic tradition of the early Christian Church. The same practice is followed by all Episcopal churches everywhere — whether in New York City or Lusk, Wyoming. They may use variations of music and ceremony, but they follow the same basic order of worship. Consequently, the central act of eucharistic worship is the prayer book liturgy focused on Holy Communion, or the Mass, not preaching and singing. In fact, many Episcopal liturgies consist of no preaching and singing at all. Good preaching and good singing are highly desirable, but they are not absolutely essential to Anglican worship.

These outward liturgical differences between the Baptists and Episcopalians are obvious to any casual observer. But there is a more transcendent and subtle difference between the Protestant and Catholic historic traditions. And this is the theology and practice of sacramentalism.

Episcopalians are sacramentalists, which means that we believe that God uses material reality to convey spiritual grace. Bread and wine on the altar, for example, with the sacramental action of God upon them, becomes something more than bread and wine — they become the mystical presence of Christ. Episcopalians believe this happens as naturally as wheat, with heat and leavening, becomes bread. As naturally as grape juice, when allowed to ferment, becomes wine. They become transformed into something infinitely more than what they previously were.

Sacramental theology affirms that God makes use of His physical creation to convey the spiritual reality of Himself. The universe, our solar system, our planet Earth and the physical existence of life are all revelations of God's omnipotent power and glory. The biological birth, life, death, and resurrection of Christ are all physical manifestations of His sacramental love toward all mankind. Spirituality does not exist in some kind of ethereal vacuum, neutered and separated from physical reality. The physical magnificence of a sunset reveals the spiritual glory of God, as does the beauty of the sage-scented Wyoming hills, whose ravines are filled with wild plum trees, in whose shade the deer and cattle and sheep rest during the heat of the day. As does the rippling waters of Piney Creek winding back and forth in our ranching valley, where, along its banks as a kid, I watched beaver and mink swim and play.

All of these natural wonders reveal the nature of God. This was a vivid realization I keenly felt as a child, slowly maturing while growing up on our Wyoming ranch — that something material (physical reality) can convey something holy (spiritual reality). I learned at VTS that these are the outward and visible signs of an inward and invisible sign of God's grace. Technically speaking, this is the Anglican theological definition of a sacrament.

Sacramentalism doesn't ask us to deny all earthly pleasures as sins of the flesh. Rather, it asks us to affirm the joys of sex and the washing of slippery little children in the bathtub, serving soup to the sick, protesting civil injustice, cooking wholesome meals, drinking fine wine, celebrating life with delightful friends who laugh and tell great stories — and dancing the polka to the beat of a good polka band. In a broad sense of the word, these can all be sacraments.

What I learned at Virginia Theological Seminary was that I had always been a sacramentalist but didn't have the words to describe it or a philosophical theology to explain and define its meaning. VTS provided that for me — and much more, of course. I realized that even as a Baptist I had always been a "high church Baptist," in that I preferred a ceremonial sense of liturgical order in the services of worship I conducted. There should be beauty inside the church to reflect the beauty of God's holiness. Hence the renovation and redecoration of the church interiors at both Padroni and Vermillion. That's why I wore a pulpit robe, even when preaching at rural Padroni, so that there would be a sense of quiet dignity when worshipping God.

I was reaffirmed in my belief that original sin is not our sexuality but putting ourselves at the center of the universe instead of God and expecting the world to revolve our around needs and desires. When that happens in sex, it's sinful. When that happens among nations of the world, it's sinful. What that happens among races and cultures of people, it's sinful. When that happens among religions, it's sinful. When it separates the rich from the poor, it's sinful.

Furthermore, for me, it's sinful for preachers to condemn sinners to hell rather than the sin they commit. It's sinful to terrify people with the wrath of God in order to convert them — instead of winning them over with the love of God. It's sinful to bore people with irrelevant preaching.

In short, my one year of Anglican studies at VTS reaffirmed something my mother had told me during the last conversation I had with her, sitting out on the shaded front porch in Sheridan, only a few months before her death: "If you'd feel happier in the Episcopal Church, if it makes you more comfortable with yourself, then do it. I'm convinced that ultimately it's not a theological decision — even though you might like to convince yourself that it is — as much as it is an emotional search for meaning and fulfillment, a spiritual calling from deep within your soul."

Mom was right. Emotionally I had always been an Episcopalian. I had always felt a spiritual calling from deep within my soul.

✧

Spring comes early in Virginia. By early April the hardwood trees were fully leafed out, green lawns were being mowed, and the flower beds were ablaze with color. By May summer had come into full maturity. My year of Anglican studies at the Virginia Theological Seminary was over and it was time now to return to Wyoming.

Chapter 10

T he ideal Episcopal church for a former Baptist minister beginning his career as an Episcopal priest was St. John's Episcopal Church of Green River, Wyoming. But it didn't seem that way at first.

Bishop Hunter had told me all along that I would be going to All Saints Church in Wheatland. I was excited about the possibility of this assignment because I had driven through Wheatland, midway between Denver and Sheridan, many times during my college days. I liked Wheatland. Its fertile, irrigated farmland was especially great for growing grain — hence the name Wheatland. Its proximity to the Medicine Bow Mountains would make it an attractive place for a young family to live. Besides, it was only a four-hour drive from Dad in Sheridan.

At the last minute, however, while we were visiting in Sheridan upon our return from Alexandria, the bishop called. "Well, it's not Wheatland but Green River."

"Where in the hell is Green River?" Dad asked when I put the phone down.

We got out the map and found it, about fifteen miles west of Rock Springs, in the southwestern part of Wyoming.

"Rock Springs?" Dad shouted. "Christ almighty, I've never been there but everyone tells me it's the worst place in all of Wyoming. Nothing there but coal mines and foreigners. Not a blade of grass nowhere. Just dirty old barren hills blown clean by the wind that never stops. And the town straddles the Union Pacific tracks with black soot caked on everything. Anyone who's ever left there ain't ever gone back."

"Yes, I've heard that too," I muttered. "But that's Rock Springs. Green River is fifteen miles farther west, along the banks of a river by the same name, so there must be irrigation and green fields and lots of trees there." I was trying to convince myself that the bishop hadn't pulled a cruel joke on me.

I was wrong.

Shirley, I, and our children drove first to Rawlins, which was the farthest west I had ever been in the southern part of Wyoming, and then headed along Highway 30 toward Rock Springs. If the scenery at Rawlins is bleak and dreary, it worsens progressively from that point westward. Everything turned silent inside the car as we crossed the expanse of vast emptiness — nothing but distant buttes and empty space.

"Where have all the people gone?" Lori, five years old, asked.

A jackrabbit dashed across the highway and Barry said, "Don't hit him, Dad. He's the only thing alive out here, huh?"

"Except us," I said, vainly trying to restore hope.

"I'm not even sure about that," Shirley said. "This is worse than anything I could possibly have imagined."

Rock Springs was worse than the way Dad described it. Only a week earlier we were living in Virginia, where the biggest problem was how to keep trees from taking over your lawn if you didn't mow every week. Between Rock Springs and Green River there wasn't one tree in sight, just towering bluffs and sun-bleached rimrocks.

We rounded a curve and saw a lofty rock formation. Between it and the wide sweep of the river below was the semblance of a little town climbing up its lower slope. The extensive Union Pacific Railroad yards hugged the stream. This was Green River.

I phoned the senior warden, Dee Peverley, and told him we were in town. He said, "Stay right where you are. I'll be right there with good news."

"We don't have a place for you to live," he exclaimed. "We rented out the rectory because the church is broke and we needed the rent money to help pay our debts. There's nothing in town to rent. We've looked everywhere. But Dr. Sudman and his family are away on a two-week vacation, and the good news is they said you could live in their home until they get back. I don't know what you'll do after that. Follow me, I'll drive you there."

"If announcements like that are supposed to be good news," I muttered to Shirley, "I pray to God we never have any bad news here in Green River."

The Sudman home was large and spacious. We fed the kids and put them to bed. Neither Shirley or I ate because she was crying and I had a sick headache.

We had finally arrived into the ministry of the Episcopal Church!

The next morning was bright and clear. I took Lori and Barry with me as we climbed up to the base of the legendary Castle Rock formation itself and looked down upon the scene below. Green River was a grimy-looking place of about 5000 souls, but I noticed neatly trimmed patches of lawn around the houses. The streets all sloped downward off Castle Rock toward the Union Pacific depot and the sizable railroad yards. Green River was the UP divisional point, so all trains stopped and changed crews here. There were probably a dozen trains in the yards at that very moment.

The business district of Green River wasn't much. Everything seemed to be in pairs: two grocery stores, two bars, two drugstores — and not much of anything else.

I pointed to the river and told the kids that this was the beginning of the Grand Canyon formation, which Lori partially understood because she had a colorful National Park children's picture book. It was in the town of Green River that Major John Wesley Powell pushed his boats into the water to begin his historic explorations of the Colorado River system back in 1869 and again in 1871. You could see the river already cutting its way through towering bluffs as it raced on toward the distant buttes.

Although I had never experienced the desert before, I knew it had an expansive majesty and beauty of its own, which someday I might come to appreciate if I was open to it — if (and this was a big if) I didn't compare it to northern Wyoming, central Colorado, southeastern South Dakota, or lush Virginia.

Once I got this new perspective planted in my mind, sitting up there at the base of Castle Rock with Lori and Barry, I began to see that the town actually had a picturesque western setting. Surrounded on all sides by soaring geographical formations of barren sandstone, it seemed to nestle in a crevice of the canyon floor, carved out by thousands of years of relentless river action. The slopes of the lofty buttes were clearly marked with the descending shorelines of a primeval lake, which millions of years earlier had formed a great inland ocean, of which the Great Salt Lake is the final remnant.

Below us was the spire of St. John's Episcopal Church, located directly across the street from the courthouse. The three of us gradually slid our way down the steep slopes of Castle Rock to the church itself, perched on top of a barren embankment of ash-colored dirt. The whitewashed exterior looked much like the little church in Padroni, except it had Gothic windows. Inside, however, it looked Anglican — a dozen pews, counting both sides of the aisle, and the divided chancel with several tiny choir stalls facing one another, and directly beyond, in the sanctuary, the simple altar with a large brass cross on it. Very Episcopal.

The three of us stood there in silence for a moment and then I invited the children to kneel with me at the altar rail while I prayed out loud: "O Lord, help us now to make this little place our church home for the next few years of our life. May it be a holy place for all who come here. Help me, O Lord, to be the man that I need to become, to best serve you here as a dedicated husband, father, and Episcopal minister. May it be a blessed time for us all. Amen."

Sketch by Angie Bennett of St. John's Episcopal Church in Green River, Wyoming, showing proximity to the prominent Castle Rock formation. It towered above the church, town, and busy Union Pacific divisional point railroad yards — all sloping down to banks of the river. My tiny study-sacristy is to the back with separate stairway.

Every petition of that prayer was answered more fully than I could ever have imagined or wanted and certainly more than I deserved.

The pleasant childhood memories of all three of my children center mostly around our early years in Green River. Lori was five and would enter kindergarten that fall. A gentle child she was, precocious and ever the little mother to her younger brother and sister. Barry was three, and Little Sheri was less than two years old, dark-complexioned like me.

The most exciting thing for us to do at first in Green River was to go down to the Union Pacific depot and watch the trains pull into town, four or five at one time, going both directions — eastbound departures in the morning, westbound departures in late afternoon. They were glamorously named *City of St. Louis, City of Los Angeles, City of San Francisco, Portland Rose, Challenger,* and so on. They would sit along the siding tracks for as much as a half hour while fresh crews and supplies came aboard and passengers milled around inside the old depot. A lanky stationmaster by the name of Carlson, his railroad cap always tilted to one side of his head, called the trains inside the depot. I will never forget his drawl coming over the loud speakers: *N-o-w l-e-a-v-i-n-g on track n-u-m-b-e-r t-h-r-e-e — the beau-ti-ful C-i-t-y of L-o-s A-n-gel-es — p-a-s-s-i-n-g through Ogden — Las Veg-as — L-o-s A-n-gel-es — and on to the m-i-g-h-t-y P-a-c-i-f-i-c O-c-e-a-n.*

Every time I heard that train call I chuckled to think of that beautiful train plunging full speed into the Pacific Ocean.

✧

Spiritually, St. John's Church was in shambles. I don't exactly know why. Early on I made up my mind not to dwell on the negative past. This was particularly true after the bishop called me the second day I was there and said, "Eugene, something went terribly wrong with your immediate predecessor's relationship with that little congregation. Things just didn't mesh for either him or the people. The bottom dropped out financially, I know. They're busted. But at least they do have a rectory rented for you, and if they don't make the first month's salary, I'll want to know about it."

I didn't have the courage to tell him that, in fact, they didn't have a rectory rented and that we were living temporarily in Dr. Sudman's home. Nor did I have the courage to tell the bishop that there was no money whatever in the treasury and hence no way they would have the means to pay me.

"Don't overwhelm the parishioners with all the things they must do to become a functioning parish again," the bishop continued. "They're too discouraged for that right now. Just love them for what they are and can become."

They were easy to love.

But first I needed to find a place for my family to live. I finally got a lead on a vacant home located only one block from the church. It was owned by a family temporarily living in an oil camp more than a hundred miles south of Rock Springs. The man's daughter was living with her grandparents in Green River, attending high school, and I persuaded her to ride with me to provide directions to the oil camp. We headed out into some of the most desolate desert country on the face of the earth. The dusty country road, sometimes no more than a desert trail, was the only visible sign that mankind had ever passed this way. Towering buttes, canyons, cliffs, and distant rimrocks overwhelmed my car, as if we were being swallowed up into the bowels of the earth. It was frightening.

Antelope and deer would scatter as my car approached, along with the biggest jackrabbits I've ever seen. We saw herds of wild horses racing at top speed until they reached the summit of the buttes, where they would stop, whirl around, and look down upon us, heads held high and ears pitched forward. Occasionally one of the stallions would gallop our way with ears flattened back and barren teeth exposed, as if prepared to attack in defense of its harem. I was glad we were inside the car.

Something else caught my eye. Strange creatures would dart back and forth behind the huge boulders, flashing into sight and then disappearing from view, their grayish-tan coats perfectly camouflaging them against the rough sagebrush terrain. At first only one at a time would pop into view, but soon I would see a dozen or more loping off into a cloud of dust.

"What in the world are those things?" I asked the girl.

"They're wild burros," she answered. "People say they were originally used by the gold prospectors in Colorado a hundred years ago, but they were turned loose or got away and have returned to the wild."

I could see the creatures' resemblance to the floppy-eared beasts of burden with the strange tails. But out here in the vast desolation of this desert wasteland, racing full speed ahead with ears folded back and tails extended, they looked more like animals from another planet.

We were able to rent the house temporarily. Since it was only one block from the church we all walked to Sunday services. I was licensed by the diocese to read morning prayer from the Episcopal Prayer Book and preach my own sermons. The pump organ was a far cry from the beautiful baroque pipe organ at Vermillion, but the organist, Ann Brown, played wonderfully.

I did all my own office work with the messiest mimeo machine I've ever seen. In spite of its misery, I wondered how salvation was possible before invention of the mimeograph.

Dr. Sudman offered to pay for Sunday bulletins, but we had no funds for secretarial help, which meant that I personally had to type them and run them off on the messiest mimeograph I've ever known. My study was one-tenth the size of the one I had in Vermillion. In fact, I had no study; I simply cramped myself into the crowded little sacristy, where I shared space with the altar guild. St. John's-on-the-ash-heap, as it sometimes was called, was minimalist in every respect. Still, I was beginning to love the place.

But the housing situation was critical. We had only until Christmas to find ourselves a permanent home and nothing was available. This grim reality was actually good news in disguise because the reason for the acute housing shortage was due to an economic boom associated with the bulging trona industry just outside town. Trona is the purest form of soda ash that's commercially needed for the manufacture of glass and detergents. Big corporations were sinking mining shafts 1200 to 1500 feet below the surface into the silt bedrock of the ancient lake for the precious stuff. This meant a tidal wave of construction workers, miners, and chemical engineers. This sudden impact of people also meant future church growth.

My appeals for any kind of housing leads somehow reached the ears of an irate bishop, who called me, shouting into the phone, "Do you mean to tell me, Eugene, that St. John's Church has never had a rectory for you and your family? If this is true, then I'm pulling you out of there immediately. I won't allow any church in this diocese to do this to one of my clergymen."

"Please don't be upset, Bishop, because we have a place in mind," I begged. I had gotten to know the people in Green River well enough by now that I wanted very much to stay. So I didn't tell the good bishop that the "place" we had in mind was a vacant storefront building, a former dry-cleaning establishment, owned by Dr. Sudman — with no kitchen, a toilet with no bath, and one big concrete room in which we could group our furniture behind bedsheets suspended from wires. The bishop would have suffered a stroke had he been told the truth.

Fortunately, he never had to learn the truth, because a devoted layman within the parish, Gus Genz, purchased a rental home as investment property and rented it to the Todds.

The only problem was, the church had to pay the monthly rent — and the church treasury was bone empty. I called on Dick Waggener, the treasurer, to see what we could do. Dick and his attractive wife, Eleanor, lived in a modest home across the river, where their two little rambunctious boys tore around the place like monkeys. He invited me into a bedroom, sat down at a beautifully restored rolltop desk, and opened the church books to reveal our dire financial condition. I noticed, however, that he kept grinning all the time he was telling me that we were dead broke. He wouldn't quit grinning. I thought, *How can a man keep grinning while telling his new minister that the church is dead broke? What's with this guy?*

"We don't have enough money to buy crumbs for the church mice," he said sunnily. "And you know there's nothing poorer than church mice. We can't afford to rent a rectory anywhere in town, unless you find an old moonshine dugout up in some dry gulch somewhere left over from the days of prohibition. Providing, of course, you can tolerate the rattlesnakes."

My heart sank, my throat went dry, I needed a drink of water but feared I would only choke if I tried swallowing. And he just kept grinning at me.

Finally I mustered the courage to ask, "Dick, how can you keep grinning when you tell me grim things like this?" His silly little grin was beginning to irritate me.

"Because I have faith," he answered. "Faith enough to move mountains. If we waited until we had the money before we did anything here in our church, Gene, hell would freeze over first. I can tell that St. John's is ready to move into fiscal responsibility under your leadership. When faith moves, the money will follow. Go ahead and rent that house from Gus Genz. Don't worry about the money. The Lord will provide."

Here was Dick, a cradle Episcopalian, talking like a Baptist fundamentalist. I didn't know whether to grin or weep. As I walked out the door, I told myself, *Gene, you've made your bed in the Episcopal Church — now lie in it. Even if it means making peace with the rattlesnakes up in an old moonshine dugout.*

The thought quickly crystallized into a fierce determination. Driving across the bridge over Green River back into town, I pounded the steering wheel and shouted, "Come hell or high water, this church is going to pay its own way."

"And with a little help from Almighty God," I added, in a more reflective mood, because I've always believed that the Lord helps those who first help themselves.

No one, not even I, could possibly have dreamed that exactly one year from that day, St. John's Church would be building a brand new rectory — a two-story colonial home with full basement and separate furnaces for each floor. It would become one of the most beautiful rectories within the Diocese of Wyoming.

✧

Church canons are very specific as to what has to be done before one becomes an ordained priest. First, of course, were the formal educational requirements I had completed at the University of Denver, Iliff School of Theology and Virginia Episcopal Theological Seminary. In spite of all this formal theological training, I still needed to pass something called the "canonicals," which every aspirant to the Episcopal priesthood dreads. It's comparable to the state bar exam for budding young lawyers or board certification for aspiring physicians. My canonicals were held in Laramie, a three-day ordeal. I passed and was ordained an Episcopal deacon on July 25, 1961, at St. Matthew's Cathedral in Laramie, with Bishop Wilson J. Hunter officiating.

The impressive ordination was attended by my father and two sisters, Edna and Sadie, along with their husbands. For the first time this former Baptist minister could now wear a clerical collar. During the luncheon which followed, a priest watched Shirley light up a cigarette and asked, "Mrs. Todd, you don't look like a Baptist minister's wife."

"I'm not," she quipped. "He's now an Episcopal minister."

Back in Green River I proceeded to do all the things any minister does in a new congregational setting. I made pastoral calls on every parish family, helped get the Sunday school started in September, then worked feverishly on organizing an intensive Every Member Canvas (EMC) to secure sufficient pledges to get the church operating on some kind of a predictable budget. Fortunately, my excellent EMC training in the American Baptist denomination made my task easier, and it was a tremendous success. No longer was the church dead broke.

Around this time the vestry of St. John's debated, for only thirty minutes, a motion to build a brand new rectory at a cost of twice our annual operating budget — and borrow the money to pay for it. (Many years later, at St. Mark's Episcopal Church in Cheyenne, the vestry debated for six hours the merits of some new program costing less than one percent of our total church budget — when funds already were available.)

Never before had I done architectural drawings, but I sketched out the basic design of the new rectory, which contained a formal pastor's study on the main floor, because there was no room for a study in the little church. The beginning of construction was delayed until spring.

Late at night, I would lay aside church duties and began final revisions of Dad's book. Shirley was a better typist than I, and she would incorporate all the changes and corrections I had made. It was tedious work, and I'm forever grateful for her contribution. Finally I sent off a final manuscript to a publisher in Sheridan, and a month later he showed me the galley proofs of the new book on Dad's life as a cowboy and rancher on Piney Creek in northern Wyoming.

The first shipment of the books arrived in Green River in the fall of 1961, and we invited Dad to come visit us. It took some persuasion to convince him that southwestern Wyoming wasn't as bad as he had been led to believe. But when he arrived, he discovered the desert country far worse than he could possibly have imagined.

"My God," he would gasp as I drove him around, "this is wide-open country . . . so big there's nothing to break the wind as it blew everything away a million years ago."

Dad didn't know yet that the first copies of his book were already in our possession. We waited until after supper, while he was drinking coffee and smoking his pipe, when I presented him with the first copy of *Recollections of a Piney Creek Rancher*. He was totally surprised and absolutely speechless. He put on his dime-store glasses and fondled the book in his hands for awhile, too afraid or excited to open it up. Then he plunged into it, after the rest of us had gone to bed, reading it nonstop all the way through. The next morning he was first out of bed, skimming it through a second time, asking that we bring him only coffee because he wanted to skip breakfast

— something a rancher would seldom do, so accustomed was he to his regular oatmeal, bacon and eggs, and always fried potatoes.

At midmorning he suddenly appeared in my tiny study, still crowded into the tiny sacristy, and said, his voice choked with emotion, "That book is a dandy. I never expected to see anything like it in my lifetime. Thank you — my son!"

He turned and disappeared down the steps.

Although the book was originally intended only as a private publication for family and friends, it eventually underwent four printings, selling over 4000 copies.

✧

A deacon can conduct morning services, preach, and do the three things most often done in any church — *hatch'n* and *match'n* and *dispatch'n* (baptisms-weddings-burials) — but he can't celebrate the liturgy Holy Communion (also called the Mass or Eucharist). Nor can he pronounce the priestly absolution of sins or deliver the priestly blessing. These full ministerial functions are reserved for the priesthood.

Six months later, again according to canon law, on February 6, 1962, I was ordained to the Holy Order of Priesthood at St. Peter's Episcopal Church in Sheridan. The beautiful old church was packed to standing room only. Its rector, Ray Clark, and his wonderful wife, Mary, did a magnificent job with all the detailed arrangements. Mr. Oliver Wallop, of aristocratic English descent and father of a future U.S. senator from Wyoming, was the chief usher.

Before the service began, I quietly visited Mom's grave for only a moment and personally thanked her for the gift of herself, which had brought me to this pivotal point in my life. I remembered again her final words to me: *If you'd feel happier in the Episcopal Church, if it makes you more comfortable with yourself and the world, then do it. I'm convinced that ultimately it's not a theological decision . . . as much as it is an emotional search for meaning and fulfillment in your life, a spiritual calling from deep within your soul.*

It was a momentous occasion as I knelt in front of Bishop Hunter, with all the other Episcopal clergy in attendance gathering around and placing their hands upon my head, as I heard intoned the ancient prayer book words, *Therefore, Father, through Jesus Christ your Son, give your Holy Spirit to Eugene Fredrick Todd; fill him with grace and power, and make him a priest in your Church.*

Again, for the second time at an ordination service for me, once in the Community Baptist Church of Padroni and now at St. Peter's Episcopal

Church in Sheridan, the choir stood and sang the anthem that had such hallowed meaning for me: "My God and I."

During the formal reception that followed the ordination liturgy, several people were called upon by Bishop Hunter to offer brief remarks, including Dr. Sudman from Green River. But I panicked when the bishop said, "And now I want us all to gather around for just a moment while we hear a few words from Eugene's father, Mr. Fred J. Todd — the Piney Creek Rancher himself." (His book at that time was a best-seller in Sheridan.)

Never had Dad been called upon to speak in public. Never had he been the center of a public gathering. But with everyone applauding him, he walked out into the center of the crowd, acknowledging their recognition as if he had delivered impromptu speeches all his life, and said, "I'm much obliged to you all for coming here tonight. I'm just as proud as I can be of my boy here, and his wife, Shirley, and their three little ones. Thank you for coming and sharing this night with us. Please drive extra careful on your way home tonight because its awful cold and stormy out there. But I want you to know that inside this holy place you've made it warm and very special for me and all of us in the Todd family. Again I thank you from the bottom of my heart."

What more could the king of England have said that would have been as appropriate?

In the morning Shirley and I headed back to Green River for a very special event and reception scheduled the next Sunday evening at St. John's Episcopal Church: my first priestly celebration of the Holy Eucharist. Unbeknownst to us, *three* of us were making our way back home, not just the two who had originally come to Sheridan a few days earlier. It would be a pregnancy of ominous consequences.

Every newly ordained priest looks forward with keen anticipation to the first time he can stand at the altar of the

I found my true niche when ordained into the Episcopal priesthood in 1962. My first communicant was a "Mary Magdalene."

church and take the bread and chalice in his hands to celebrate Mass — the Holy Sacrament of the Lord's supper — and then administer the sacred elements, first the body and then the blood of Christ, to the faithful as they kneel, one by one, at the communion rail to receive His mystical presence into the daily living of their lives. Some priests fantasize the occasion as taking place in a mighty Anglican cathedral with a magnificent choir, while huge Canterbury carillons ring out the chimes of an immortal hymn of the church. I must admit that something like this was in my mind when, the afternoon before the momentous evening service, I received a call from a woman I had heard about but had never met.

"Father Todd," she said in a weakened voice quite strained as she spoke, "My name is Margaretta. I've been ill for quite some time with congestive heart failure. Dr. Sudman tells me there's nothing more he can do for me. Against his orders I checked myself out of the hospital and decided that if I'm to die, then I'll die in the comfort of my little home with my little dog, Poodie, right by my side."

"Yes, Margaretta," I said. "What can I do for you?"

"I would like for you to bring me Holy Communion this afternoon. Believe me, I'm very sick and I know that I'm dying. I'm alone here in my little house with my little dog right beside me, and it's all right for me to die here. That's the way I want it. I made that very clear to Dr. Sudman. But I do want to receive Holy Communion. Will you please bring me Holy Communion right away?"

"But I can't, Margaretta," I quickly responded. "You see, I haven't as yet celebrated my first Holy Communion in the church, which is scheduled for tonight. Now tomorrow I could bring you the Blessed Sacrament."

I was talking like a deacon, which is what I had been for the past six months.

"But you are now a priest," she argued, her voice reduced to only a whisper, "I read about your ordination in today's paper. And I may not make it through the night."

She was right. I was now an ordained Episcopal priest. And it wasn't true that I had to wait until after my first official eucharistic celebration in the church before I could celebrate it for this woman on her deathbed. But at the same time, her request sounded a little histrionic to me. I better check this out.

I called Dr. Sudman, a devout parishioner at St. John's and an excellent physician, and asked about this strange telephone call. Much to my surprise, he confirmed everything Margaretta had said. "She checked herself out of the hospital over my strenuous objections," he stated, "But deep in my heart, I don't blame her for wanting to die at home, even though she's all alone up there on that barren hillside."

Then he continued, "Gene, it's an open secret that she was a madam in San Francisco before she came here and became a recluse up there in that little tar paper shack she's living in now. I think she was probably a prostitute before operating her own hotel business. But they closed her down and she went broke. She always pays her bills but lives on mostly nothing. She's a courageous old lady, I'll say that for her. But make no mistake about it, she is dying. It may not be tonight, as she's leading you to believe, but certainly within the week."

I was disappointed. My long-awaited festive eucharistic celebration in St. John's actually wasn't going to be my first celebration after all. I was going to handle my first communion in a home, on a deathbed, something like a young physician making his first emergency house call.

I fully vested in my new priestly robes. Then over my shoulders for the first time I pulled on my brand-new black Anglican cape with a velvet collar, like the naval cloak President Roosevelt wore draped over his shoulders at Yalta. I packed into a little bag the essentials I would need for the private service of Holy Communion: a silver chalice, a small cruet of wine, some bread, two candles, a small cross, and a couple of napkins for purificators.

Dr. Sudman warned me that I could drive my car only part way up the hill and would have to walk up a very steep incline to the shack. The Wyoming wind was blowing as I scrambled my way up the slippery embankment, wondering how in the world this sick woman managed to climb it all by herself. (I learned later that she was carried there by the ambulance crew.) Poor soul, had she glanced out the window and saw me coming, attired solidly in black all the way from the bieretta on my head to the long cape reaching to my feet, I would surely have looked like the angel of death itself — if not Count Dracula.

It's a wonder she admitted me into her humble abode attired the way I was, but she did, calling out to me from within. Once inside I couldn't believe what I saw. I was standing in a small kitchen, sparsely furnished with only the essentials: a wood cook stove, a storage cupboard, a rough handmade wooden table and a few chairs. The walls were papered with newspapers, yellowed with age, but the place was tidy and neat. She motioned me into the second room, a combination bedroom-living room, where I got my first good look at Margaretta herself, sitting in a lounge chair stretched out full length. She looked to be in her late seventies or early eighties, a squatty old woman.

The room was warm from an oil heater in her bedroom, but there was a sufficient draft of air from the howling wind outside to keep a plastic wind chime tinkling overhead. Looking down upon the room were half a dozen framed portraits of Margaretta in her younger days — seductive poses in tight-fitting full-length evening gowns. Other old-fashioned photos, popular in the 1920s, showed her draped in white fur stoles, sometimes smoking a cigarette, flashing her use of long elegant cigarette holders. Overlooking the exaggerated lipstick markings of her lips, again fashionable forty years earlier, you could tell that she had once been a very handsome woman.

Sprawled in her lounge chair, she was wearing what once had been a lavish silk bathrobe. A purple turban was wrapped about her dyed hair, and her face was fully made up — the whole bit, complete with eye shadow, penciled eyebrows, rouge, and bright red lipstick, slightly smeared. True to the lifestyle to which she had been accustomed, she had dressed as best she could to receive a male caller. In her lap was a miniature white poodle wrapped in a baby blanket, peeking out its head.

But it was obvious to me that Margaretta was a very sick woman and in much physical distress. I learned that she had a sister in town who brought her a simple meal each day and attended to a few household chores. This was all she needed. She preferred to be left alone with the companionship of her sweet little Poodie.

I then inquired about her spiritual well-being and especially her ties to the Episcopal Church. Between spells of painful coughing and laborious breathing I learned that her father was a pioneer cattle rancher in Montana, where an Episcopal missionary priest established a small country church in their ranching valley. Her sister and she were confirmed in this little mission church prior to their mother's sudden death, at which time their "wealthy" father sent both girls to an "expensive boarding school" in California. But this didn't last long because hard times hit the Montana ranching business when their father went bankrupt shortly before he died, "leaving both of us penniless."

She continued, "I then worked at odd jobs to keep body and soul together, but times were rough until I finally managed a very successful little hotel business in San Francisco."

This admission was as close as she could come to a confession of the real "business" she operated within the hotel, which, according to Dr. Sudman, was finally closed down by the law. I had no need to push for more information.

When I opened my prayer book, she produced one of her own, and together we read the general confession of sin and I pronounced my first priestly assurance of God's forgiveness, marking the sign of the cross on her forehead. I paraphrased the "comfortable words" from the service of Holy Communion, telling her, "God loves you so much, Margaretta, that he gave his only begotten son to the end that you should not perish because of your sins, but as a child of God have everlasting life."

She softly began to weep, the mascara running down her cheeks, and little Poodie quickly raised up from his blanket on her lap and, sensing her distress, sympathetically licked the tears away. She pressed him to her breast as she reached out and touched my forehead, as if conveying to me her blessing in return.

I laid out my communion setup on her night stand and knelt on the floor beside her chair and celebrated my first Mass — for Mary Magdalene!

As I went out the door, I knew that I would never forget this day, that it would forever emblazon itself on my memory. The fantasy of a young priest's first Mass had been replenished by a reality of God's own choosing. No longer did I cherish the setting of some great Anglican cathedral, the ringing of glorious carillons in a church tower or the gathering of dignitaries for my first service of Holy Communion. The tar paper shack replaced the cathedral just fine. The tingling of the plastic wind chime replaced the carillons just fine. Having a madam and her little dog as my first communicants was just fine.

And *both* were my first communicants.

When I served her the consecrated wafer of bread, Christ's body, she broke it in half and quick as a flash served one piece to Poodie and popped the other half into her mouth. Under the circumstances, the spontaneous sharing of Holy Communion with her only creature companion didn't seem all that inappropriate to me.

I buried Margaretta a few days later.

✧

Every morning at nine o'clock I would sit in the chancel of St. John's Episcopal Church and read the prayer book service of Morning Prayer. Clergy call this "reading their daily office." I would do it out loud, however, because I remember it being done this way by old Father Layman at St. Mary's Church, the high Anglo-Catholic parish of Denver. Like Father Layman, I would invite anyone who happened to come along to join me. On rare occasions this happened, but mostly it was a private devotional time for myself, and I cherished it.

One morning, while reading the lessons and praying, I looked around the interior of the little Gothic church and noticed just how tacky it had become. The barren floors were badly scarred, and the pews were scratched and grimy — the place just didn't reflect the beauty of God's holiness. Don't get me wrong — it was a holy place, all right, because many holy things happened there. But there wasn't much outward display of it.

I stood before the congregation the next Sunday and said that I thought every church should reflect the beauty of God's holiness. Using sacramental language clearly understood by Episcopalians, I explained that God uses the material things of this earth to convey His spiritual reality. Just as bread and wine reveal the mystical presence of Christ to all recipients of His grace, so the church edifice should impart the reverence of God's holy place.

Without a single word about how broke we were, I invited volunteers to join me for a work party every night that week. We unscrewed the pews from the wooden floor and carted them downstairs to begin scrubbing them down. Next the communion rail, then all the chancel furniture, and finally the altar itself. We discovered that the pews required much more than cleaning; they needed a complete refinishing. That was a lot more work than what any of us had anticipated. So we assigned each pew to one crew of volunteers and instructed them to go at it.

Then we realized the refinished pews wouldn't match the old window casings, so they had to be redone. In the course of that job we noticed just how badly the walls needed painting. We tried sanding the floors, but they were gouged in so many places that we decided it best to install a brand-new wall-to-wall carpet. A parishioner sent me to ZCMI at Salt Lake City, the huge department store owned by the Mormon Church, to select the finest carpet available and charge it to him personally.

What started out just to be a general week long housecleaning became a major renovation that required us to hold services for three months in the local mortuary. When the church

St. John's was a charming little Gothic church located directly across from the court house square. The steep incline up to Castle Rock enabled the basement parish hall to open directly out onto the front sidewalk.

was completely gutted out, we redesigned the chancel-sanctuary area, moving out the altar toward the nave and greatly extending the communion rail. This gave us a free standing altar, a liturgical concept ten years ahead of its time. We then installed additional spot lamps to flood the altar with a soft new glow of indirect lighting. This required the installation of new electrical circuits.

The interior of the little church was gloriously transformed into a place of fresh soft colors, refinished furniture, and quiet plush carpeting — with a new aura of indirect lighting accenting the architectural space of worship and reverence.

Much like my Padroni parishioners after redecorating their little church, the congregation of St. John's at Green River marched into the newly renovated church behind the choir. The procession paused long enough for me to read the familiar biblical words: "Come, let us worship the Lord in the beauty of holiness."

"Thanks be to God," was the congregational response.

Before we proceeded with worship, however, I read a list of the renovation expenses, which were considerably higher than any of us expected but infinitely lower than normal because we had done all the work ourselves. Then Dick Waggener, the church treasurer, read a statement that all the congregation's bills were paid in full, with a surplus sufficient to paint the exterior steeple and install a spotlight to illuminate the elevated cross at night.

Everyone at St. John's had much to celebrate. The work project had miraculously pulled the congregation together. It was a joyful bunch.

And I had much to celebrate personally. It was a joy to be an Episcopal priest. I loved the 1928 Prayer Book and the elegance of the King James English it contained; its cadence and eloquence of language captivated my soul and sent my spirit soaring like a dove. It was beautiful. The liturgical expression of worship was equally captivating to my body: standing to *praise*, sitting to *listen,* and kneeling to *pray*. It was great to feel my body, as well as my spirit and heart, totally involved in worship. I loved chanting the poetic canticles of praise, most of them psalms from the Old Testament; hearing the biblical lessons read from the prescribed prayer book lectionary — and, most of all, celebrating the Eucharist every Sunday morning and receiving the mystical body of Christ into my life and being.

I realized that the dignity of prayer book worship was exactly what I had always wanted and needed all my life, and now I had it in the Episcopal Church. Finally I had found my long-awaited spiritual home. I was at peace with myself and with my Lord. And so it was with Shirley and the children.

But not for long.

The conception of another child on the night of my ordination into the priesthood would bring a pregnancy of many complications and much heartache. Shirley experienced bleeding almost from the beginning, yet Dr. Sudman's prenatal examinations showed that the baby was healthy and growing normally. After the first trimester the complications seemed to subside. We had time to reflect on this unplanned pregnancy and the meaning of another child, our fourth. However, I was preoccupied with the activities and excitement of our growing parish. Worship attendance had dramatically increased now that the church had been so beautiful renovated. We needed extra space for our expanding Sunday school. We canceled the lease on the old rectory, located directly across the street from the church, and converted it into a nursery and Christian school. We were already in the process of building an attractive new rectory, which would be finished in September 1962.

I had so many things occupying my attention that I was not particularly sensitive to Shirley's emotional and physical needs when complications resumed in a pregnancy that wasn't going well. In trying to put the best face on it all, I continued bathing the other three children every night and putting them to bed with stories and prayers, while Shirley minimized the foreboding apprehensiveness she could no longer openly share with me.

In the seventh month of our pregnancy, Shirley was driven to the Rock Springs hospital by Dr. Sudman on a Sunday morning while I took the children with me to church. Before worship services were over, the doctor called to say that Shirley had delivered a one pound, twelve ounce baby boy. The baby was perfectly formed and healthy for its size and was in the incubator for premature births, but saving a preemie that small would be difficult.

The little boy, my second son, closely resembled Barry. I watched him breathing on his own, thrashing his arms and legs about and crying, and I desperately wanted this child to live, to overcome all the difficulties of his premature birth, to grow and thrive. Now I understood more clearly the desperation that had consumed Shirley and felt profound guilt that I had not insisted that she confine herself to complete bed rest for the duration of the pregnancy, which the doctor had ordered.

The nurses allowed me to baptize him as baby Jonathan Todd. I reached inside the incubator as I poured droplets of warm water over his feverish forehead. He was struggling with every breath to keep himself alive.

Shirley's mother flew up from North Carolina to be with us, but all was to no avail. Five days later little Jonathan died. Shirley asked permission to hold him in death for only a few minutes, but the hospital would not allow it. We both wept together — but I wept more profusely when in the car alone, driving back to Green River. Just like a Todd, I would not allow myself to express my emotions overtly — a family trait that is a curse.

I made all the funeral arrangements and carried his little white casket to the church for a requiem Mass, celebrated by Father Frank Price from the Episcopal church in Rock Springs and attended by the supportive and caring parishioners of St. John's. We buried him in the picturesque desert cemetery of Green River. The outpouring of love from everyone was deeply appreciated, but nothing could assuage the pangs of deep personal guilt that I have carried to this day.

The most comforting thought of all, however, came from my older sister, Edna, who wrote, "I don't know how things work themselves out in heaven because no one has ever been there to report it back to us. But my imagination tells me that Mom is cradling him in her arms and all is well."

I believe that, too. But I also believe that we could have all held Jonathan in our own arms as we incorporated him into our family life, nurturing him through childhood into adulthood, had I only been more attentive to his mother's need for complete bed rest, thus enabling her to carry him to full term.

Within a few weeks of Jonathan's death, we moved into the newly completed rectory of St. John's — following a widely publicized open house celebration. It was located in a wonderful residential area within half a block of the local school (K-12), and from our back porch we had a spectacular view of Castle Rock towering above. The children could hike and play to their heart's content in a magnificent natural playground of huge rimrocks. (Later they would watch with great interest as Interstate 80 would be constructed right through this area, tunneling under Castle Rock itself.)

Beautiful new rectory built at Green River. Its interior design accommodated four bedrooms, study, formal dining room, and family den. Just above the roofline, are the high sandstone rimrocks, beyond our backyard, where the children loved to play.

It was a joy for me to continue supervising the evening baths for the kids, tumbling with them on the padded carpet, and tucking them into bed. But I now had help. We acquired an affectionate female dachshund named Taffy who loved the children as much as I. Each evening when I tucked the kids into bed, she was right there as my assistant. She would become quiet when the kids and I would say our bedtime prayer together:

Jesus tender shepherd hear me
Bless thy little lamb tonight
Through darkness be thou near me
Keep me safe 'til morning light

We would exchange our blessings — "May the Lord bless and keep you" — and as soon as I kissed Lori and Sheri goodnight, Taffy would jump up on their twin beds and give them a slobbering kiss as well. Then she'd waddle ahead of me down the hallway into Barry's room, where she'd jump into bed and snuggle up beside him with her head on his pillow so that she could get prayed over and blessed along with him. She made certain the evening ritual included her involvement every night, both as participant and recipient, and if she happened to miss the routine, she would dash back and forth from room to room upstairs, as if hoping to get it restaged again.

A rancher visited our home one evening who was intrigued with this dachshund and commented that this breed was "most certainly the strangest canine deformity ever perpetuated upon the animal kingdom." He turned to Barry, then five years old, and asked, "What in the world is a dog like this good for?"

Without batting an eye, Barry answered, "Lovin's and barkin's."

His answer was remarkably accurate. Taffy was a most affectionate little creature. She was also most irritating with her barking jags outside the house. She would bark at the moon if there was nothing else around to bark at.

✧

My Sunday evening services at the construction site of the Flaming Gorge Dam constitute one of the greatest experiences of my life. Engineers from the U.S. Bureau of Reclamation were supervising construction of the 500-foot-high dam, which would provide flood control on the turbulent Green River and create a new lake extending nearly 100 miles up into Wyoming. The 375-mile shoreline would become a large recreational park (the Flaming Gorge Recreation Area).

The massive engineering project took place on the isolated edge of the Uinta National Forest. The construction site was actually located just across the state boundary in Utah, near the little Mormon colony town of Vernal, which also has the distinction of being the headquarters of Dinosaur National Monument. Green River was the nearest rail center for supplies. But once the dam was built, access roads to Green River would be sealed off by the rising waters of the lake until modern highways were later built.

During the project, a brand-new construction town appeared on the map — Dutch John. A few permanent government homes were built for personnel who later would operate the huge water-driven turbines of the hydroelectric generators. But dozens of temporary homes were hastily built for the hundreds of construction workers and project engineers. The town included a school, medical clinic, mechanical shops, and a company-owned supermarket. There was also a very large dining facility to feed the laborers.

This temporary town was pitched high up on Antelope Flats, a bench of rugged mountainous terrain, and it was beautiful. Pine and cedar trees abounded. The place was a beehive, humming with people and activity. It was truly a throwback to the exciting frontier towns that flourished during the gold rush days in the Colorado Rockies a century earlier.

I drove out to this community on Sunday evenings to conduct evening worship service in the schoolhouse. I tried arriving early because I thoroughly enjoyed mingling and visiting with the captivating parishioners who lived there. The most interesting were the corporate engineers, many of whom had traveled the globe working on some of the largest projects in the world. Many were Episcopalian. People from all denominations were welcome to our services, however, and I immensely enjoyed them all.

Sometimes I would arrive in Dutch John early to accept an invitation to eat supper with the construction workers in the large company mess hall. These early afternoon Sunday meals were always like Thanksgiving, with a menu of roast turkey and all the trimmings. After church I was always invited to the homes of various families for coffee, refreshments, and delightful conversation. These social gatherings were the highlight of the week for many of these people, and I enjoyed them more than they.

In fact, I enjoyed myself so much in Dutch John that often I wouldn't get on the road back to Green River until midnight. It was nearly eighty miles of lonely highway, and I would seldom meet another car. It was almost frightening. Because of the isolation, I would turn up the radio for company. At that late hour I could regularly pick up clear-channel AM stations all the way from Los Angeles to Atlanta.

Once my car broke down during one of these midnight trips back to Green River. The electrical system completely shorted out, and the car went dead. It was bitterly cold, and the wind was buffeting the car so hard that I knew I must resort immediately to emergency mode. Stored in the trunk was my emergency kit, a large duffel bag stuffed with a sheepskin coat, woolen cap, overshoes, heavy mittens, and an old comforter. I settled in for a long wait in the middle of the bitterly cold night. My spirits rose when I finally saw the lights of an approaching car. For half an hour I watched the beam as it would disappear from view, then reappear momentarily, and then vanish from sight again.

Eventually, the car came within range and I flagged it down with the request that the driver phone my wife when he got to wherever he was going and ask her to send help. He said, "It will be nearly an hour before I reach a phone, and it will take at least another hour or two before someone can rescue you out here. This is a very stormy night, are you sure you're going to be all right out here all by yourself? It could be dangerous you know."

I assured him I would be all right. Out of my rear view mirror I watched his lights shrink into the darkness of the night until he disappeared from sight. Then remorse set in. What if he never calls at all? I should have asked permission to ride back toward Dutch John with him. What if it should begin snowing? The howling wind would whip it up into a raging blizzard in no time. Could I survive much of that?

The ferocious wind violently rocked my car. A herd of antelope crowded around and peeked in. They milled about for a short time, and it was both frightening and interesting to watch them close-up. Their presence assured me that, at least, no one else was around to do me harm.

Suddenly they bolted away, spooked by something far more ominous. Even though it was pitch dark, I saw the shadowy figures of men emerge from out of nowhere. They jumped on my rear bumper while leaning across the trunk and pounded on the back window. They began roughly rocking my car up and down. I could see their cupped faces pressed up against the window panes, only inches away. They tried opening the doors, which were firmly locked. As the car pitched and rolled, I heard their ghoulish voices and muffled laughter. Then I realized that these weren't men from a nearby hunting camp or auxiliary construction site but demons of the night — and I was under mortal attack. I was petrified with fear.

Then I saw a man's gloved hand in front of me tapping on the windshield, and over the roar of the wind I heard a voice shouting at me, "Are you all right in there? Open the door. Are you all right?"

My imagination had gotten the best of me. I moved toward the center of the front seat to make it more difficult for anyone to yank me out of the car. I reminded myself not to panic and flee into the desert because that would be instant death. Then came heavy banging on the windshield and door again, and this time a spotlight was flashed back and forth across the window. A voice shouted, "Open the door. Are you all right in there? Gene, open the door. This is Jack Wilson out here."

Jack Wilson was my senior warden at St. John's Church, a game warden whose official government vehicle was well equipped for highway emergencies like this. Inside his warm pickup, while he towed my car back into Green River, I never told him of the horrific nightmare I had just gone through. Obviously, I had fallen asleep because I never saw the approaching lights of Jack's truck.

After that terrifying experience, I would always phone Shirley before leaving Dutch John with instructions that if I didn't arrive in Green River within an allotted period of time she was to call a list of several men who volunteered to form a rescue party.

But my Sunday afternoon drives to Dutch John, in broad daylight, were something else. For the first time I began to savor the ever-changing beauty of the desert shadows and the constant ebb and flow of colors. The rays of the setting sun would reflect a cascading display of soft, and sometime brilliant, shafts of color that were never the same — hence the name Flaming Gorge.

Periodically, on Sunday afternoons, the engineers would lead me through the cavernous tunnels, myriad hallways, and hallowed chambers inside the uncompleted dam. Huge overhead buckets of wet cement, suspended from cables, were lowered into place by an operator who had

BLM engineers and me taking Bishop and Mrs. J. Wilson Hunter on tour of Flaming Gorge Dam construction site at bottom of canyon floor. The dam would rise 500 feet above where we are standing. I conducted Sunday evening services for construction workers and government employees. Nan Hunter and the Bishop are standing with me in front row.

no visual view of the construction site itself, receiving his instructions by walkie-talkies from the men below.

Perched high atop a jagged point of rock was a visitor lookout center. At their invitation I loaned them my best radio voice for tape recordings, which tourists activated by pushing a button, describing the construction process below and that when the dam was finished its three gigantic turbines (36,000 kw each) would produce electricity sufficient for 100,000 people. I embellished the written text with a little freelancing on my own about the Green River system, cutting its ways through layers of earth millions of years deep — thus creating spectacular flaming colored gorges.

I loved the frontier spirit that prevailed in Dutch John. The company-sponsored annual Christmas costume party was an event always to be remembered. The mess hall was decorated in bright colors for the gala occasion. A live country band kept the dance floor rocking in rhythmic beat while couples, all attired in outfits of the Gay Nineties, whooped it up. Many of the women decked themselves out as dance hall girls with their bearded husbands costumed as gold prospectors or frontier gamblers. All alcoholic beverages were free, and a fabulous midnight supper was served.

But the excitement of this temporary town was soon to pass into oblivion. When the humongous construction project was finished, Dutch John, with all its houses and people, would move away, leaving only a skeleton crew to operate the hydroelectric power plant.

The day of reckoning finally came. Tunnels that had diverted the flow of the Green River away from the construction site were finally plugged, and the water began backing up behind the nearly finished dam, forming the new Flaming Gorge Lake. The engineers could calculate far in advance when the rising waters would eventually cover the access highway to Dutch John, isolating it from further contact with the town of Green River and thereby concluding my ministry there.

Their predictions were so accurate that they informed me that when I made my last trip to Dutch John in May 1963, the waters would be lapping alongside the highway edge when I arrived on Sunday afternoon. During the worship service the rising waters would actually cross the highway, and it would be permanently shut down. But following the evening services, an engineer would pull aside the highway barriers long enough for me to drive through about two inches of water to reach the other side.

My final service at Dutch John was both a joyful celebration of all the good times we had shared together and a sad occasion at which we had to offer our final farewells. The Eucharist was especially meaningful, with a lot of extra music provided by the worshipping congregation. This was followed with a lovely reception of appreciation given in my honor. It was a beautiful evening, but the engineers cautioned me that we were under a time restriction as to when they could legally allow me to cross over a highway now sinking under the rising waters.

I drove out to the barricade, and when my lights flashed out across the black waters of the Flaming Gorge Lake my courage failed me. The engineer laughed and said, "I figured that would happen. That's why I brought along my fishing boots. You just follow me and I'll lead you across. Just stay right behind me and keep your car between the reflectors and you'll be all right."

Splashing ahead of me, brightly illumined by my headlights, I watched him literally *walk on water* across Flaming Gorge Lake, like a miracle right before my eyes, something Christ is reported to have done on the Sea of Galilee. But, miracle of all miracles, that night I literally drove my car across the surface of Flaming Gorge Lake from shore to shore.

Years later, boaters told me how eerie it was to look down through the murky waters of Flaming Gorge Lake and see traces of the old highway between Green River and Dutch John. Mine was the last automobile to travel on it.

I terribly missed Dutch John because I had become so emotionally attached to the fun-loving people I had met there. But I kept in contact. Several memories have stayed with me, one amusing and one sad.

One evening two rough and tough construction workers served as ushers, their eyes blurred and faces flushed from too much Sunday afternoon imbibing. Both were renegade Southern Baptists, or so they claimed. In their effort to cover their advanced state of inebriation from the worshippers, they became overly solicitous in their duties. I noticed them clicking their heels and bowing from the waist down to late arrivals as if greeting royalty. When it came time to take the collection, they passed the offering plates three times. And if that wasn't bad enough, the third time around they jiggled the plate in front of each worshipper, nudging for more contributions and patiently waiting until billfolds were opened and emptied. A number of twenty-dollar bills were deposited in addition to the perfunctory one-dollar bills that earlier had been contributed. Had they brandished a six-shooter, it would have been a Hollywood scene right out of the frontier west.

In the Episcopal liturgy the offering is taken while the priest is busy preparing the altar for Holy Communion, so I missed the commotion. It's a good thing I called the offering plates in when I did or I think the boys would have tried a fourth round on the traumatized congregation. The wonder is, no one got mad. In fact, just the opposite. These construction and engineering people had traveled the world enough to recognize a novel idea whenever it occurred and possessed the grace to see the humor of it. Of course, they didn't want it ever repeated again. Thereafter the ushers were instructed: _Only one offering per service._

Needless to say, it was the most bountiful freewill offering ever collected at Dutch John, and the people magnanimously designated it a "love gift" toward the purchase of a large walnut desk for my study in the lovely new rectory. I'm still the proud owner of this grand old desk, and as I write these words I can run my hands down along its smooth-grained finish and smile with warm and pleasant memories of time spent among these wonderful people.

Another memory will always remain with me of a melancholy event, which though sad contained a radiant thread of Christian hope.

I received a call from people in Dutch John telling me a young man who had gone out for a casual evening swim in the river had drowned. The mighty Green River was not safe for swimming, and everyone was warned about its swift currents and treacherous undertows. The drowning victim was a teenager from a large family that occasionally attended my services in Dutch John. The father was a construction worker on the Flaming Gorge Dam.

The family claimed membership in some southern fundamentalist Protestant sect who called themselves the "plain people" (not Amish). They believed only in using the most minimal of modern necessities. The girls wore old-fashioned cotton dresses and absolutely no makeup, with their long hair pulled into buns at the back of their heads. Their house was sparsely furnished with homemade furniture. But they were good people, and their kids excelled in school.

I followed directions to where they lived, an old abandoned ranch house far out in the desert wilderness, which they had rented for almost nothing. It sat on a high mesa looking down upon the broad sweep of the Green River desert valley. This was perfect for people who preferred to do without modern conveniences such as electricity and telephones. But they looked terribly isolated up there on that barren windswept bluff.

When I drove into the barnyard I saw the twenty-year-old sister, home for summer vacation from a Bible college, sitting by herself on a large boulder, gazing out across the desolate valley below. In the distance she could see Green River, shimmering beautifully in the morning sun, winding its way back and forth across the desert floor between towering buttes — a stark contrast to the dark terror the river had been to her brother only hours before.

The parents invited me inside with the explanation that the daughter had sat out there alone all night and did not wish to be disturbed. The old ranch house, mostly in ruins, seemed even more barren than it had been described to me on the phone. The place took on the dilapidated appearance of something out of the 1870s, when pioneers first settled that lonely desert country. The mother put a large coffeepot on the woodburning stove, pulled a hot loaf of bread from the oven, placed it in the center of the table, and sliced big chunks for us all to eat with honey.

I sat with them, father and mother and two teenagers, as they discussed the details of the funeral arrangements, then moved to the essentials of faith that sustained them now. The mother would share those emotions that surely would torment any parent who had to live through the drowning of a child.

"I wonder when Jamie first realized he was in desperate trouble?" she agonized. "In my heart of hearts I know there came that awful moment when he knew he was dying."

The father came quickly to her side. "Mama, we had no lifetime guarantee on Jamie when he was born to us. We don't need to worry ourselves with thoughts like that now. You know none of us are getting out of this life alive." That was the first time I ever heard that poignant expression.

"Yes, I know," the woman said, "but there came that awful moment when he knew he was dying — all alone."

"But Mama, we all die alone," the father reasoned. "No matter how many loved ones we may have around our deathbed, even holding our hands, when our time comes to go, we all have to die alone. None of us can take anyone with us when we die. That's one time when we all will have to let go and leave everything behind and take that last journey all by ourselves."

"Still," she persisted, "there was that last natural desperate instinct to survive when he kept sinking deeper into the cold dark water while frantically grasping out for a rock or a tree limb to grab hold of. Or someone's hand to save him. Anyone's hand. But there was no hand there for our boy — nothing but the swift current, sweeping him away to his death. That had to have been his last conscious thought. I'm dying . . . I'm dying." Her voice trailed off into a whisper.

The father had no immediate answer. The silence was interrupted only by the slapping of a loose screen against a broken window pane. I heard the wind whistle past the kitchen corner. My tin cup had cooled just enough for me to pick it up by the handle and take my first sip of hot coffee. I swallowed too loudly.

And then, from out of the deep reservoir of faith, the man spoke slowly and confidently, "Mama, at the last moment there was a hand reaching for our boy. It was the hand of Jesus who reached down and pulled him up. And just imagine Jamie's surprise when he found out it wasn't one of us but Jesus who saved him after all."

The woman shook her head as if unconvinced. Her husband leaned over, tenderly grasped her arm, and with a look of radiant joy on his face said, "Just think, Mama, how exciting that would be to Jamie. Can't you just see the excitement in his eyes? Far greater than when we let him keep that old secondhand bicycle that Uncle Bill gave him. And we wouldn't let him keep it by his bed the first night he had it, remember? So he slept out on the porch just so he could reach out and touch it all night long. And the next morning we found him sound asleep under his covers, with his hand out on that broken-down old bike. That's the way it is now, with Jamie reaching out his hand — and when he wakes up, he'll be so excited to learn that Jesus is holding his hand."

We all interlocked our arms around the crude little table, littered now with bread crumbs from the hot bread we had just eaten, while we prayed and they wept.

I stepped out into the hot desert sun. The oldest daughter was still perched on the boulder outside, gazing off into the void of the vast barren wilderness, as if in a trance. Her face was drawn and taut, framed by the long brown hair pulled tightly into a bun at the back of her head. She never looked my way until I walked up beside her and touched her arm. Startled, she jerked her face my way, and in the painful agony of her eyes I saw the pleading question, *Can you make sense out of this, Mister? You're supposed to be a man of God — can you explain this to me?*

I could feel the desperation of her anger and anguish, but for the life of me I could think of nothing to say. Words failed me. In sudden impulse, I simply reached out and put my arms around her. She buried her face into my shoulder and wept so profusely that my clerical shirt was sopping wet from her tears. I loaned her my handkerchief and drove away without saying good-bye, leaving her there alone on the rock.

As my car wound its way down off the mesa, in a billowing cloud of dust, I thought to myself that this conversation between father and mother came from the simplest of faith and yet was as profound as anything I had ever heard. Phrases like: *We have no lifetime guarantee on our children when they are born to us. None of us are getting out of this life alive. Ultimately we all die alone, for anyone's personal journey of death is reserved only for the one who specifically is dying. And at death we discover that actually there is a hand reaching out to us after all, the hand of God. And just imagine our surprise when we discover that Jesus was there to save us.*

I was called to minister to them. Instead, they ministered to me.

I envied their gift of a simple faith. Mine is a struggling faith. I struggle intellectually and spiritually over every theological issue that confronts me. I take one step forward and two steps backward. But these people piously walked forward with the steady gait of a simple faith in Jesus.

At the same time, I felt overwhelmed with an awesome sense of my own inadequacy. A priest should bring strength to a pastoral situation where overwhelming grief and weakness prevails. I brought only my emptiness and left it with them. Why was I so spiritually impotent once the conversation turned from social pleasantries to this family's raw pain and throbbing grief? All words failed me. They consoled one another. I was powerless to say or do anything that seemed helpful or comforting.

The memory of this dreadful ministerial failure would haunt me for many years to come. A professor of pastoral theology could share the story with his seminary class as a classic example of what an ordained minister is *not* supposed to do on a death call. I could never forgive myself.

Years later I shared this story at an Iliff Seminary pastoral workshop in order to make the point that sometimes we ordained clergy find ourselves being ministered to by those we're supposed to be ministering to.

The professor of theology, a woman, said, "I don't see it that way at all. Whether you or they recognized it or not, the church came to that family isolated up there on that 'windswept bluff' — as you described it, and you, in your Episcopal collar, became a symbolical representation of the Christ figure in their midst. You were the instrument that enabled them to articulate their pain and their grief and their Christian hope. Around that crude common table you all broke bread together, prayed together, and wept together. What more would Christ have wanted you to do than share that kind of Holy Communion among these simple people of faith?"

This was somewhat consoling, but it wasn't enough to erase my pain of the memory.

✧

The sealing off of Dutch John by the rising waters of Flaming Gorge Lake didn't end my missionary outreach. It simply shifted to a tiny place called Manila, just over the Wyoming border into Utah. People on the north side of the new lake, who had begun attending church in Dutch John, asked me to continue conducting worship services for them. Manila contained fewer than 200 residents, mostly Mormon, and was the only county seat in the United States that didn't have running water or public sewage. Even though it was Mormon territory, a few ranchers in the area had quietly converted to the Episcopal faith in Dutch John. I felt morally obligated to help sustain them in their newly acquired Anglican faith.

The courthouse was no larger than a two-story home, and we held our Episcopal services in the courtroom, no larger than a typical living room. I used the judge's bench as my pulpit and altar. After services we would retire to the family home of Jim Bossi, forest ranger for the Ashley National Forest, for coffee and discussion.

I shall never forget a Christmas Eve celebration among these people.

I promised to conduct an early Christmas Eucharist in the ranching home of a young couple whom I will simply call George and Karen. They had just become parents to a baby boy, but Karen wanted to host this eucharistic celebration and holiday gathering. A few non-Mormon friends in the valley had been invited.

On my way up the valley, just before I reached the ranch, I noticed a band of sheep bedded down on the hillside. When I arrived at the home I was introduced to a Basque sheepherder who had graciously been invited to attend the service. He could barely speak English but was delighted to have been included in the Christmas Eve festivities rather than spending another lonely evening in his isolated sheep wagon. To express his appreciation he brought along two holiday gifts sent to him from his family, still living in a mountainous area between Spain and France.

One was a honey cake, something resembling baklava; it was sweet and delicious, and the children devoured it as if it were candy. The other gift was a thick liqueur, which he called a "flavored brandy." Its alcoholic content could have been no less than 200 proof. One sip would enflame first your throat and then every organ of the body until your toes throbbed before going numb.

The Basque sheepherder, from a culture and language far removed from ours, had probably never been invited to a social gathering in America like the one he was enjoying so immensely that night. He probably thought I was a Roman Catholic priest and would never have understood the difference had someone tried to explain — and probably wouldn't have cared anyway. The joy for him was the invitation to be included in a Christmas celebration in the family setting of a home — so far removed from his distant European roots.

These former Mormons were not supposed to know very much about drinking alcoholic beverages, and they loved both the taste and effect of the Basque brandy as much as the children loved the honey cakes. I had the feeling we had better get the show on the road or none of us would be in condition to celebrate Mass. We moved into the living room area, where Karen had lovingly prepared an altar in the bay window looking out into the barnyard.

As I was vesting, George suddenly remembered that he had forgotten to milk the cow. He grabbed the milk bucket and headed toward the door when Karen interceded. "Do you mean to tell me, George, when you've had nothing else to do all day with our getting ready for this service tonight, that only now do you remember to milk the darn cow?"

He brushed her aside. "Ah, I'll have that cow milked before you even stand for the Gospel." Although a former Mormon, George had learned enough in the confirmation class to know that Episcopalians stand for reading the Gospel. Out into the night he went with his milk bucket.

We lit the candles and began the service.

Sure enough, just before we read the Gospel, here came George tip-toeing between my little congregation and me, carrying a pail of warm milk, which he placed on the kitchen counter. Then, yanking off his winter coat and hat, he stepped into the living room and flipped off the light, plunging the room into darkness.

Out of one corner of the darkness we heard Karen's quivering voice: "Do you mind turning on the light, George, so the rest of us can read the Gospel?"

Out of the other corner of darkness came George's obstinate reply: "Why? It's supposed to be a candlelight service, isn't it, Karen?"

I could tell that the rest of us were caught in the crossfire of two tired people who in addition to caring for a newly born baby had worked very hard that day to prepare their home, in this Mormon ranching valley, for this Episcopal Christmas Eve worship service.

By that time my eyes had begun to adjust to the moonlit barnyard which we could see through the bay windows directly beyond the makeshift altar. I said, "No, please, let's leave the lights off."

I walked over to Karen and picked up the baby son from her arms and carried him back to the altar and said, "You know there are thousands of churches all over the world this Christmas Eve that have prepared cardboard crèches so that the worshippers could view the nativity tableau of a barnyard scene. We are fortunate to see a real one, just beyond our altar, through the window."

I pointed outside.

"Looking out through the window we can see the cow that has just been milked. Her warm milk is in a pail right beside me here on the kitchen counter." I reached over and touched it. "Out there also are a few horses munching on the hay and straw we see piled there. Off on the slope of the distant hill, in the moonlight, we see a band of sheep bedded down for the night. Nearby is the sheep wagon."

We could all see the sheep wagon with smoke from its stove pipe spiraling upward into the crisp evening sky.

"This, my friends, is the kind of world into which the Christ child was born — in a stable, because there was no room at the inn. A baby no more real than the little baby boy I'm holding in my arms right now. And if we look out at the barn we'll see the familiar manure pile that none of the cardboard crèches ever show. This reminds us that Jesus Christ was born into the world no more than thirty feet from a manure pile. How more earthy in the real world can we become?

"Here tonight we have a shepherd who has brought us his gifts of golden honey cakes and sweet-tasting brandy. He joins us as one who has left his flock of sheep and come to be among us so that he, too, can worship the newborn Christ child."

The woolly little sheepherder shifted in his chair and leaned forward.

"It was into this kind of a real world that the Christ child was born. Not in King Herod's palatial fortress atop Masada. Not in some royal castle of a reigning monarch of the world. Not in some splendid cathedral where thousands have come to worship him amid the glorious sound of great choirs and thunderous pipe organs.

"No, Jesus was born to a young father and mother like George and Karen in a place called Bethlehem, a place every bit as obscure as Manila, Utah. Fewer people gathered there at the stable to worship him than are gathered here tonight. He was born into a world of tired and anxious people, where little babies cry when they're wet or hungry and young mothers become weary in the night as they care for them."

The room was dark and strangely quiet.

"How fortunate we are tonight. All the other churches of the world have to make-believe what this night must have been like. We don't have to make-believe at all. We simply must open our eyes to see the real world outside our window — and realize that this is the kind of a world into which the Christ child was born. And we open our hearts to make ourselves believe that the miracle of new birth can become real in us again tonight . . . as we celebrate anew the miracle of God's Incarnation."

After coffee and delicious hors d'oeuvres I headed back to Green River, a sixty-mile drive through white-chalked hills strikingly familiar to what the Wise Men from Persia would surely have traveled en route to Palestine. As I drove through the darkness of the night, without meeting a single car, I had the feeling that the midnight Christmas Eucharist at St. John's in Green River would be anticlimactic — because I had already been to Bethlehem!

Chapter 11

I liked Green River and I enjoyed being an Episcopal priest. Every morning after my daily office (devotionals) in the church, I would go into downtown Green River to pick up my mail from the post office, then drop in for coffee with Gus Gasson, who managed the Green River Mercantile. It was truly an old-fashioned general store that sold everything, from groceries, dry goods, ranch supplies to hardware. He even showed me a couple of caskets in the back room left over from the days when the place was also the local mortuary.

Gus introduced me to exploring the historic Oregon Trail, which one hundred years earlier crossed through that part of Wyoming en route to Fort Bridger — and then toward Utah, Oregon, or California. He showed me where General Sidney Johnson's army supply wagons, headed toward Salt Lake City for the Mormon War of 1857–1858, were destroyed by Mormon "Indian" raiders. You could barely make out the little mounds of charred wagon remains. Ed Taliaferro, a sheep man, drove me back into the isolated Immigrant Springs country, where thousands of pioneers carved their names on the sandstone ledges and buried their dead nearby in crudely marked graves.

St. John's congregation was filled with interesting characters. There was Granddad Hutton, from England, who would arrive in church for Sunday school at nine o'clock and promptly fall asleep, only to be awakened by the noisy arrivals to the ten o'clock worship service, whereupon he would dutifully ring the church bell. He overslept one morning and woke up with a start at the beginning of my sermon, jumped to his feet, raced out into the narthex, and began ringing the bell to the snickers of everyone in the congregation. "Well, at least your sermon woke him up," they were saying.

There was old Tom Welch, in his nineties, who drove a stagecoach as a teenager and personally knew Butch Cassidy. In fact, he claimed to have had a beer with the infamous outlaw in Lander long after Cassidy was presumed dead in South America. The statement is often quoted as proof that Cassidy returned to the United States and lived out the remainder of his natural life under a pseudonym. Later, when I buried Tom, I couldn't help but reflect on how recently the West had been a wild frontier. Here I was, burying a man who had been a stage driver and buddied with the likes of Butch Cassidy.

My parish included Keith Smith, a graduate of Yale University with many family connections to the eastern establishment, who as a young man ventured out West and established a major ranching enterprise along the Black Fork River. His daughter, Susan Young, helped him write his autobiography and submitted the manuscript to me for editorial comments and suggestions. I never saw Keith Smith dressed in anything less than a shirt, tie, and dark business suit with vest and gold watch fob. He carried himself with all the dignity of an English aristocrat.

An Iliff professor stated back during my seminary days: "Just remember, the life of every parishioner would make a best-selling novel and full-length movie if a good writer were to write it up." I thrived on getting to know the personal stories of every parishioner in my congregation. I guess it was this interest in people that caused me to become involved in a large number of community organizations, among them the Chamber of Commerce, Sweetwater County Historical Society, the Sweetwater County Wyoming Jubilee Anniversary celebration committee (which I chaired), and Southwestern Wyoming Community College, to which I was chosen a trustee by county wide public election. It was all very invigorating to this young Episcopal minister in his mid thirties.

I might add, Green River clergy were automatically expected to serve as substitute teachers in the school system because of the chronic shortage of substitutes. I had a teaching certificate and was told by the school board that pressure would be brought upon my vestry if I wasn't willing to help out. I arranged a trade-off with the school, which generously loaned the church all the audio-visual equipment it needed in exchange for my services.

I also enjoyed the regular clergy meetings in Laramie with Bishop J. Wilson Hunter. I would use my Clergy Railroad Pass and take a free ride on the Union Pacific Railroad. I'd save up my money to enjoy a long, leisurely dinner in the dining car each way. Nothing was more elegant than enjoying deep-fried shrimp or char-broiled salmon steak and good wine while seated at a linen-covered table, watching the sagebrush flats of southern Wyoming rush by outside the window.

The clergy meetings were just as good. No biblical fundamentalists or pentecostalists were around to depress me. There were only seminary-trained Anglicans, wearing clerical suits, continually joshing one another with good-humored camaraderie. Bishop Hunter would reserve us hotel rooms. Breakfasts and lunches were served by the women's guild in the cathedral undercroft, and roast beef dinners were always graciously served by Nan Hunter in the sprawling and spacious bishop's residence.

We would take our coffee in a huge basement room, paneled in knotty pine, where the bishop would preside over his clergy meeting. We'd all light up our pipes and lay down a smoke screen so thick you could cut it with a knife. I will never forget my positive image of these meetings: my fellow clergy and I, all males, sitting in the presence of our bishop, each with a leather-bound 1928 Prayer Book in our suit pockets, smoking our pipes, while being motivated and inspired to get off our duffs and move out into the world for the cause of Christ and the Episcopal Church. None of us would have dreamed that in only a few years, almost all of those colloquial images would be shattered by social and theological forces already taking shape, forces that would permanently alter the future direction and clerical makeup of the Episcopal Church.

Bishop Hunter confirmed me into the Episcopal Church, baptized my children, and ordained me into holy orders. I dearly loved that man as my "Father in God" — an Episcopal term respectfully used in reference to bishops. Nonetheless, I once said something that caused him to storm out of his living room in protest.

A group of us clergymen, as guests in his home, were watching an evening news report about a civil rights march promoting voting rights for blacks in Mississippi. The bishop, a bred and born southerner, was lamenting the fact that these "northern outsiders" were agitating the situation, which eventually would resolve itself if everyone else just stayed away to let the good people of Mississippi handle it their own way.

I commented, "But, Bishop, I would like to believe that if I was denied the right to vote in Wyoming that a few citizens of Mississippi would be concerned enough to come up here and protest my loss of that basic American civil right."

He stomped out of the room in a rage. The other clergy in the room, all who loved that man dearly as I, simply shook their heads in dismay and didn't say a word. It was becoming obvious to us that the face of America was rapidly changing and that some of the old ways, including the attitudes of great old bishops, were going to lose out.

(Such attitudes were distressingly common in Wyoming. One night the Green River school board invited me to say a few words. Before I spoke, the superintendent amused the board with some derogatory remarks about a "Negro graduate student" who had applied for a teaching position. I said something to the effect that the school system *should* someday hire a black teacher. A local physician on the board took me to task for my integrationist views, and we got into a terrible verbal brawl, with him shouting and jabbing his finger into my chest. "I think racial integration in our school system has to happen naturally and not be structured," he howled. He failed to see that segregation was already structured by default.)

Whatever differences the clergy might have had with the bishop, and there were many, we knew that he would always support us 1000 percent. (I use that percentage because it was always beyond 100 percent.) He was like our coach and cheerleader, and it was an honor to be on his winning team. Whenever he received a complaint from a parishioner about the rector, Bishop Hunter would immediately call the priest on the phone, read the letter in its entirety, and then ask, "What's the history of this situation? What can I say and what can you do to rectify this problem? How can I support both you and your good layman in the resolution of this?" Never was there a feeling of adversarial intimidation or conspiratorial aloofness between Bishop Hunter and his clergy, nor between the bishop and his laypeople of the diocese. No wonder we all loved him so much.

✧

I wrote earlier in the previous chapter that things went smoother once I quit comparing the desert of southwestern Wyoming with the beautiful ranch country of northern Wyoming; and more particularly, not to compare it with the fertile farming land around Vermillion.

Although I disciplined myself not to make these comparisons — occasionally I would slip up. Such an occurrence was the comparison between celebrations of Memorial Day between Vermillion and Green River.

I was pleased when Otis "Gilly" Gilbaugh approached me about the need to establish a new community-wide observance of Memorial Day in Green River. Gilly's primary interest in life was fighting the corporate world. A hot headed union agitator, he was an expert at riling up working men against management, wherever he was. Consequently, he was always out of a job because no one would hire him. This gave him a lot of extra time to spend with his drinking buddies at the V.F.W. post. There he'd dream up new patriotic schemes in behalf of God and country.

Gilly came to me with the proposal that we initiate a new annual patriotic tradition in Green River, a Memorial Day service up in the cemetery. He assured me that he would enlist a platoon of veterans, under his command, to perform the military honors. He invited me to be the honorable speaker for the most auspicious event.

His invitation met a responsive chord with me. Vermillion always had a magnificent annual Memorial Day celebration out in the city park. The weather toward the end of May in southeastern South Dakota was always warm and beautiful. The trees were fully leaved, and the flowers were blooming profusely. Veterans groups planted row after row of white crosses, each decked with a miniature American flag, around the park's band shell. The city band always entertained us with a concert of stirring patriotic music before a short speech was delivered, followed by special ceremonies from the veterans groups, which always included the honor guard gun salute and taps. It was most impressive.

One year I was invited to deliver the speech. The basic theme of my address was: *Sometimes it is easier to die for our country than to live for it.* After all, most of the men and women who have died for our country probably had no choice in the matter. They were ordered to be in a certain place at the wrong time. But living for our country involves an exercise of personal commitment. My speech must have been well accepted in Vermillion, because I was invited back two more years and asked specifically to deliver the same address. It's most unusual for a clergyman to receive a request to repeat a sermon.

It was with this reservoir of pleasant civic memories that I accepted Gilly's invitation to help him initiate a patriotic tradition in Green River. In fact, I planned to deliver essentially the same speech that had worked so well in Vermillion.

But the weather in southwestern Wyoming late in May is not what it consistently was in Vermillion. The day was overcast, and the cold winds were gusting at about sixty miles per hour as I headed out for the cemetery, located on a picturesque bench of land high above Green River. When I arrived at the cemetery I was shocked to realize that only one person was there, a woman of Japanese descent by the name of Suki who had come from a most remarkable immigrant family. Just the two of us.

Where were Gilly and his company of carefully selected honor guards? We soon heard them coming.

In a cloud of dust, here came Gilly in his beat-up pickup, with six drinking cronies all standing in the back pounding on the cab, whooping and hollering. They obviously were roaring drunk. Gilly wheeled his pickup around a bend in the cemetery road and headed our way, then came to a screeching stop, slamming his troops up against the cab. Decked out in the military regalia of a Latin American generalissimo, complete with gold braiding, he marched around to the back of the truck, stepped backward about ten paces, and shouted his first command:

"Fall - out!"

They literally fell out of the pickup bed, tumbling on top of one another and picking each other up. What a sorry spectacle.

"Atten-tion!"

They attempted to line themselves up. It was hopeless. Some were even facing opposite directions.

"Forward - march!"

Off across the cemetery they marched, following General Gilly, stumbling across tombstones, knocking off each other's caps as they kept bumping into one another, with guns clattering. It was a pitiful sight.

"Parade - rest!"

Their rifle butts hit the ground. They were so drunk they shouldn't have been allowed out on the street, let alone armed to the teeth with rifles and live ammunition. There they stood, reeling in their boots.

"Chaplain, deliver your speech!"

It was a direct military order.

I tried my old time-proven address, but the wind was blowing so fiercely that it literally blew my words away. And when you can't hear your own words it becomes difficult to monitor your speech. But I tried concentrating on the main theme: *Sometimes it is easier to die for our country than to live for it.* It was obvious to me that this speech was getting nowhere — unless you credited the wind with blowing it, word by word, toward Rock Springs, fifteen miles away.

On the spur of the moment I mentioned something I had just learned about Wyoming: that it had one of the most severe miscegenation laws of any state in the union. It forbade marriage not only between people of different races but also applied to a host of nationalities as well. I said, "Do you realize that Suki here is not permitted by our state statutes to marry a man of her own choosing unless he be of Asian descent? It might be easier to die for our country, when we had little choice about that, than to change a law on the books which is racially motivated and morally wrong."

The only responses were dazed, blurry-eyed expressions from my swaying and reeling troops, who would imminently collapse if I didn't end my speech. I stopped and stepped back.

Gilly assumed his role as the commanding officer.

"Present - arms!"

The rifles were lifted.

"Ready! Aim! Fire!"

One blast roared out, then two more, then another and another. Five shots. I counted them one by one. Where was the sixth shot? I was soon to find out.

"Arms - rest!"

The rifle butts hit the ground — and out roared the sixth shot! A veteran dropped to the ground with a mournful thud.

"Good God Almighty!" I shouted.

I leaped across some gravestones to administer final rites to the last casualty of World War II, his head blasted clean off his shoulders, no doubt — blood splattered everywhere. Graphically proving my point: *Sometime it is easier to die for your country than to live for it!*

As I stooped over the crumbled form of the dying comrade, Gilly busted in, "Aw, he's all right. He's just passed out. Maybe a little too much beer. There's only blanks in the rifle chambers anyway."

Then self-righteously, Gilly added, "I told him not to drink that last beer when we headed up here."

Yeah, Gilly, you command a tight ship here, I thought to myself. *Your troops know exactly who their commandant is and act accordingly.*

Turning to the others, standing there dumbstruck, like petrified figures carved in stone, he barked out one last command, "Come on, fellas, pick him up and load him in the truck." One grabbed the poor fellow by the arms and another by the feet and they carted the limp body off across the cemetery and swung him up into the pickup bed like a sack of potatoes. They all piled in around him while Gilly cranked the truck and roared away in another cloud of dust. We could hear them pounding on the cab, yelping and shouting like wild renegades on the warpath, as the truck wound its way back and forth down off cemetery hill, until finally the howling wind blew away the last sounds of the obscenity all together.

Suki and I were emotionally shaken to our cores. I turned to her and said, "Suki, I always thought we won World War II. But we couldn't have won that war with an army like that."

I believe in self-hypnosis. If memory recall is possible through hypnosis, so it follows that one could induce amnesia through self-hypnosis. I stretched out on the sofa at home and deliberately began the hypnotic process of erasing all memory cells of my first Memorial Day celebration in Wyoming — cell by cell.

Early the next morning, our front doorbell rang incessantly. I put on my bathrobe and stumbled downstairs, only to find on my stoop the last person I ever wanted to see: Gilly. There he stood, unshaven and disheveled, obviously up all night drinking, with his veteran's cap slid down over his right eye, leaving only his left bloodshot eye blinking at me like a salamander.

"Chaplain, I need to talk with you."

"Good Lord, Gilly, it's five o'clock in the morning. You got me out of bed. Besides you're drunk."

"Yes, I know, Chaplain. But this is real serious. Spare me a few minutes of your time about something real important."

I motioned him into my study, which opened off from the foyer, and sat down with him. He lit up a Camel cigarette and took a couple of deep draughts, blowing smoke into my face, then leaned back in his chair, giving me that mischievous silly grin as if to say: *Well, Chaplain, now that you've got me here, what are you gonna do with me.*

I wasn't about to play that cat and mouse game with Gilly.

"Gilly," I said, my patience running thin. "What is it you need to see me about at five o'clock in the morning?

"Chaplain, you may not have thought I was listening to your speech yesterday morning up at the cemetery. But I was. Especially that line about how it might be easier to die for my country than to live for it. I guess I've always thought that since I fought for my country then my country owes me a living. I've never done much living for my country. You grabbed me on that one. You know what I mean?"

I made no response.

"I've been up all night thinking. Doing a little drinking, too, I might add." He thought he was being cute with his clever admission. "But mostly thinking. And I've come to the conclusion that I need to start doing a little living for my country. Something kinda' constructive like, you know what I mean?"

I made no response.

He continued, "You mentioned that according to Wyoming law Suki couldn't even marry the man she wanted to marry if he didn't happen to be Asian. That law needs to be changed. That's not justice and freedom of choice here in America. That's not what I fought and died for. You know what I mean?"

"Gilly, you may have fought for our country but you certainly have not died for it. At least, not yet. Let's get that straight."

"My point is, Chaplain, that law is wrong and needs to be changed. Now since you've brought it up and are makin' such a big thing out of it, why don't me and you change it, startin' right now?"

To make a long story short, we did.

I contacted Bill Jackson, a Rock Springs lawyer, who drafted a simple bill rescinding the state statute. Then I persuaded Adrian Reynolds, publisher of the *Green River Star* weekly newspaper and a member of the state legislature, to introduce it at the next legislative session in Cheyenne. It passed with little or no debate. This was no major legislative accomplishment; most people were not even aware of that old miscegenation law, passed during the heyday of the KKK popularity in the 1920s, and most people simply ignored its existence. Besides, everyone knew it would be declared unconstitutional if ever challenged in the courts. But the rescindment was a symbolic victory for Gilly. He had done something constructive for his country, and he felt good about it. I was pleased about that.

✧

Another local character was Mr. J. Warden Opie, who owned and operated the local mortuary.

Once the family of a recently deceased hospital patient asked me to call the mortuary in their behalf. Several days later I received a check for twenty-five dollars from Opie (as everyone called him). I phoned and asked him what the check was for, and he answered, "That's my gratuity to whoever first calls me about a death. I do that with all the doctors and nurses at the hospital. I've learned that a little payola like that goes a long way toward giving me a corner on the mortuary business here in Sweetwater County."

"Well, you're not bribing me," I told him, which didn't seem to faze him the least.

Opie fit the old stereotype of funeral directors. Crass and crude, he epitomized almost everything modern professional morticians would like to discard about their public image. He was tall and always smoked extra-long Panama cigars, and his brash behavior endeared him to many and antagonized others.

His mortuary was located downtown in Rock Springs, and when you stepped into the foyer he would appear from a back room through a door of swaged maroon velvet curtains. The moment he saw you he would always reach up above the doorway and hit a button to activate a music tape system. He took great pride in demonstrating to me that if the visitors were Catholic he'd hit button #1, and strains of "Ave Maria" would drift throughout the mortuary. If they were Mormons he'd hit button #2, and we would hear the great Zion hymn, "Come, Come, Ye Saints." For Protestants it was button #3, "The Old Rugged Cross" — piped even down in the casket display area.

His wife was a character in her own right. Her straight black hair reached almost down to her waist, and she always wore dark glasses, white makeup, and purple lipstick. She looked like a character right out of *Dick Tracy* or *The Addams Family*. It was a standing joke among Rock Springs people that whenever the Opies had a marital spat, she would threaten to jump off the bridge into Bitter Creek and drown herself — which would have been a notable feat, because there was no water in Bitter Creek.

The Opies had one son, Jerry, who was convicted of murdering his young wife in the living quarters of the mortuary and sentenced to life imprisonment at the state penitentiary in Rawlins. I attended the murder trial, and when the guilty verdict was announced, Mrs. Opie whirled around to me in the pew directly behind her and said, "Oomph. What a railroad job that was!"

Once Mr. Opie and I had a burial in Mountain View, Wyoming, which required me to ride about fifty miles with him in the hearse. I noticed a gigantic set of telescopic binoculars in the front seat of the hearse and asked what they were there for. Without the least hesitation he bluntly answered, "Oh, when my wife and I visit our son, Jerry, at the prison in Rawlins about a hundred miles away, she uses those binoculars to scan the highway forward and backward. If she sees no patrolmen in sight, I goose this hearse up to over a hundred miles per hour, which means we can make it there in less than an hour."

Taking a few more puffs on his cigar, he continued, "You know, the chassis of a hearse is longer and wider than any other auto vehicle, which means that its center of gravity is such that it hunkers down to the road at one hundred miles per hour like a little Chevy cruising at sixty miles an hour. A good spin like that every week burns all the carbon out of this big Cadillac engine."

I had visions of a hapless state patrolman maintaining his lonely vigil out on some barren hilltop near Rawlins, scanning the highway for speeders with his binoculars (this was before the days of sophisticated radar). Suddenly he picks up the image of a black hearse racing his way at a hundred miles per hour. He sharpens his focus and finds himself peering straight into the barrel of Mrs. Opie's telescopic lens and, behind the binoculars, the face of a character right out of _Dick Tracy_. It would be enough to cause the terror-stricken trooper to leap out of his patrol car and flee into the desert with the screaming meamies.

I told this story once at a gathering of the peace officers, and a highway patrolman came up to the head table after dinner and said, "You know, Father Todd, you perfectly described it. Once when I was stationed in Rawlins, I spotted that black hearse speeding down the highway at over a hundred miles an hour. And when I looked through my binoculars, I saw that dragon lady staring back at me through her high-powered binoculars, it was a binocular lock-in, exactly the way you described it. It was terrifying. Only I didn't leap out of my patrol car and go running off into the desert with the screaming meamies, like you suggested. That would have been an insult to my professional integrity as a respectable law enforcement officer. But I did get out of the car."

"What for?" I asked.

"I fell on my knees and gave my life to Jesus, right then and there."

He went on to explain that he had the feeling his life was slowly going to hell in a hand basket anyway, but when he saw that black hearse racing his way at the speed of sound — he suddenly realized the devil was closing in on him faster than what he previously thought. And he'd be rolled away in Opie's hearse.

Who would have ever thought that antics of the Opies would result in the conversion of souls for Jesus Christ?

✧

Green River did not have a radio station, but Rock Springs did. Not long after arriving in town I contacted KVRS to inquire about my doing a live broadcast from Green River.

I called it *Over the Coffee Cups*, and it was broadcast weekly from a downtown bakery and coffee shop where all the natives gathered every morning. Normally I would have an invited guest who had some civic cause to promote or was anxious to debate some controversial community issue. It was the only live talk show in Sweetwater County, and it quickly became more popular than I could ever have imagined.

Whatever the topic of conversation for the morning, I would always reserve time to move around the U-shaped counter with my portable microphone and ask people's opinions. The counter was always full of men and women, mostly working men, who were simply socializing during their morning coffee break. It was fascinating to hear the opinions of these people on the large range of topics we openly discussed.

Once I invited two politicians, both candidates for the legislature from Sweetwater County, to discuss why each should be elected over the other — and it escalated into a shouting debate. They were sitting opposite each other along the U-shaped counter, and I had to run back and forth between the two with conciliatory comments.

"He said you insulted him. You didn't intend to do that now, did you?"

"I don't need to insult him because he can only be insulted with the truth," came the hostile reply.

With theatre like this, the ratings soared. *Over the Coffee Cups* practically became an institution in Sweetwater County. And it was fun for me to do. Beyond my enjoyment of working with live radio, however, was the subtle message that the church was involved in many public and social issues that affected our entire community.

In the fall of 1965, sudden disaster threatened the Green River community. Upstream a serious leak sprung in the large earthen Fontenelle

Dam. Even a small leak is dangerous in an earthen dam, because at any moment the enormous water pressure can burst through the minor fracture, causing the whole dam to collapse. A wall of water would be released, destroying everything in its way. The town of Green River was in serious peril. Government engineers opened the gates to release as much of the stored water in the reservoir as possible, causing the river to rise to a dangerous level.

The U.S. Bureau of Reclamation chose *Over the Coffee Cups* as the forum through which to address the public on the critical situation. First they flew me in a government helicopter to the dam site so that I could personally view the scene of impending disaster. Then the regional manager of the Bureau of Reclamation accompanied me on a choppy flight back to Green River for the morning broadcast. When we landed, I was pea green from the bumpy flight, and he was terrified at the prospect of doing a live broadcast. Neither of us was in the best of shape to go on the air.

He read a statement from a carefully written script. Obviously, every word had been cautiously crafted. Upon completion of his official statement, the questions began — good questions, honest practical ones. How much warning would we have if the dam burst? How high would the initial tidal wave be? What elevations in Green River would most likely be affected? Who's going to pay for the damages?

The poor fellow panicked. He was in mortal fear of giving the wrong answer and kissing his federal career good-bye forever. Finally, I gave him opportunity to emotionally relate to the anxiety the people of Green River were feeling. He began speaking openly to them. A family man himself, he quickly came to realize that people under the threat of impending doom seek human reassurances more than specific answers to hypothetical questions. The dam held, the state of emergency subsided and disaster was averted. And *Over the Coffee Cups* became one of the most listened-to radio broadcasts of Sweetwater County.

Had the dam broke, it would have been the year's second disastrous flood. Earlier that summer, during the closing minutes of *Over the Coffee Cups*, I was making casual chit-chat with some of the coffee shop patrons. I saw a woman sitting by herself at the end of the counter, sopping wet and visibly shaken. Noticing her distress, I casually asked her — on the air — how she was doing.

"Terrible. Terrible," she said. "I've just survived the worst nightmare that any human being should have to endure in a lifetime. It was simply God-awful terrible."

I asked, "Lady, what are you talking about?"

"The flood in Sheep Creek Canyon. It was awful."

Sheep Creek Canyon in the Uinta Mountains, down toward Flaming Gorge, was our favorite family camping site. It was a narrow canyon, sometimes no more than a few hundred feet wide, with the walls towering hundreds of feet high on both sides. Geological markers along the narrow winding road running parallel to the mountain stream of Sheep Creek explained how ancient some of the rock formations were. They were hundreds of millions years old, formed long before the dinosaurs lived. All along the creek there were beautiful secluded little camping areas. It was delightful to picnic up there and let the kids play in the water, climb rocks, and enjoy themselves.

"What flood?" I anxiously asked.

"Haven't you heard? There was a cloudburst and a wall of water came roaring down Sheep Creek Canyon thirty or forty feet high. It took everything. My husband and I were lucky. We scrambled to a higher ledge and escaped the water. But then we had to watch the terrible flood. House trailers were flipping end over end. Cars were tossed around like corks. All the bridges washed out. We could hear the screams of people drowning. Hundreds of people have died."

She began hysterically sobbing, "It was terrible. Sheep Creek Canyon is no more. It's gone and all the people we saw earlier in the evening — families with children, men fishing in the creek — they're all gone. Dead! Dead!"

My God, I thought. What do we have here? A crackpot? Who is this woman, anyway? What is she telling me? What do I do now?

This is an inherent danger of live radio.

Fortunately, my time was up and I signed off the air. Immediately I called the radio station. "Our phone lines are jammed," I was told. "We don't know what to tell people."

"Have you had a report about a flood in Sheep Creek Canyon?" I asked.

"No, nothing on the wires."

"Call Salt Lake City or Denver," I said. "Someone has got to know."

I waited a few minutes. The baker served me a hot cup of coffee and another fresh pastry roll. The phone rang. KVRS had contacted authorities in Salt Lake, who said they had no report of a flood. However, all communications to that isolated area of Utah were down. The officials were alarmed by our tentative report, however, because this might explain why the regional communications were all dead.

Shortly thereafter, news services and a Salt Lake television station called the bakery wanting more information, but my informant had slipped away in the confusion.

Unfortunately, she was no crackpot. Purely by accident, my live radio talk show broke a major news story. There had indeed been a disastrous flood that killed about a dozen people and turned scenic Sheep Creek Canyon into an empty washout. I never did hear the final death toll.

✧

August 17, 1964, was a big day in Green River and all of southwestern Wyoming. Flaming Gorge Dam and the Flaming Gorge Recreational Area were to be formally dedicated by Lady Bird Johnson, wife of the president of the United States. It was to be a two-part ceremony. The dam would be dedicated in Utah, but the recreational park was to be dedicated on the courthouse lawn in Green River. I was invited by U.S. Senator Gale McGee to participate in the dedication services, which made me a part of the official entourage.

Advance Secret Service agents began security preparations in Green River a full week before the event. Since St. John's Episcopal Church sat directly across the street from the courthouse square, looking down on the open area where the ceremony was to be held, the agents contacted me about securing the church. The agent happened to be an Episcopalian, and we became well acquainted. He attended church on Sunday morning and even agreed to be a guest on my radio program. He supervised construction of the temporary wooden platform where VIPs and Mrs. Johnson were to be seated and from which she would deliver her speech.

Our dear friends from Vermillion, the Billingtons, were guests in our home. A huge crowd gathered on the shaded courthouse lawn. Off to one side was to be an elaborate buffalo barbecue, and one of the cooks happened to be one of *The Three Stooges* of movie and television fame. I talked with him several times and never knew of his Hollywood connection until afterward. There were a number of important dignitaries on the platform, including Interior Secretary Stewart Udall, Director of National Parks George Hartzog, U.S. Forester Edward Cliff, U.S. Commissioner of Reclamation Floyd Dominey, Senator Gale McGee, and a group of other western U.S. senators. I was to give the invocation and benediction.

I found Lady Bird Johnson a vibrant personality and most gracious. She told me she was Episcopalian, which I already knew. Little Sheri was only four years old, dark complexioned with big rolling eyes, and Lady Bird lifted her up onto her lap and cuddled her for a moment.

It was all very exciting.

After the ceremony was over and Air Force One made its departure from the Rock Springs airport, the Billingtons and Todds left on an overnight camping trip to Salt Lake City. The Billingtons were professional campers, having camped all over America and most of Europe. The four of us piled into their little Volkswagen with all their camping gear stacked neatly on top. (We left our children behind with babysitters.)

Toward evening, as we made our way down historic Echo Canyon, leading into Salt Lake City, Monroe suggested that we stop at a public campground near a reservoir and set up our pup tent, large enough to sleep four. He commented how fortunate we were to be the only ones there that weekday evening. We raised the tent on a secluded little grassy knoll down near the water's edge.

It was a lovely summer evening, and after such a terribly hectic day, with Secret Service agents and police swarming everywhere back in Green River, we decided to go skinny-dipping in the lake. The water was perfect. Afterward, pulling on our pajamas (which I normally never wear), we climbed into our sleeping bags inside our little pup tent. Shirley and Mary Elizabeth were beside each other, and Monroe and I were closest to the tent door.

We recalled the excitement of the day, and Monroe commented again how unusual it was that we had this campground completely to ourselves. Not another car or tent was around — only the camp manager, an old man who lived in a small trailer house on the other end of the park.

As we were laughing and talking away in the darkness of the night, suddenly we heard a man outside the tent say: "I want you all to come out now. Each one of you. There's gonna be a killing here and I want you to come out . . . one by one."

Monroe stupidly said, "But we don't want to come out."

The voice repeated itself, "I don't care if you don't want to or not. I'm telling you to come out. My buddy and I are here . . . and there's gonna be a killing. I'm telling you now, I want you to come out . . . one by one!"

We then noticed the shadow, from the bright moonlight reflecting across the tent, of a heavy-set man with a heavy club or tree limb over his shoulder. He was pacing back and forth and kept muttering incoherent sentences. A wave of pure terror swept my body. I realized we had a psychotic on our hands, maybe an escapee from a mental hospital, and we were in serious trouble in this isolated corner of the public campground with not another human being anywhere within hearing range.

Then he became more threatening, "Well I'll call my buddy over here and we'll get you out of there." Cupping his hands over his mouth, he shouted out as loudly as he could, "Hey, Bill. Where are you? I need you here!" His voice reverberated down Echo Canyon.

Monroe set him off again, saying, "Fella, there are two men in here and one of you out there. Now go away and leave us alone."

This only agitated him. He came running to the front of the tent and shouted, "Come on out you bastards, both of you. I can beat the hell out of both of you at one time. I ain't got nothing to lose. Come on out, you bastards."

He dropped to his knees and stuck his bald head up against the mosquito netting at the front of the tent and said, "If you've got a gun in there, then I'm giving you first chance to kill me. Go ahead and shoot me right in the head. See here," he said, pointing to his head. "Go ahead and kill me. You might as well kill me first before I have to kill you."

I whispered to Monroe, "Don't talk to him any more. You're agitating him and making him more hostile. Let me talk to him. I smell liquor on his breath, and I think he's having DTs. Let me try calming him down."

I noticed that he was barefoot. But I also noticed that although he wasn't tall, he had the shoulders and probably the strength of an ape.

Talking softly to him, I kept telling him that if he was troubled, he ought to go up toward the highway, where help would be available. He admitted that he desperately needed help. He called out to his friend again, picked up the tarp outside our tent, pulled it over his body, and moved off to one side.

All was silence.

Monroe and I decided that we must make our move and make it fast. First we would position ourselves to burst out of the tent together, allowing our wives to dash to the Volkswagen and head out to Coalville for immediate help. Monroe and I probably wouldn't subdue him (after all, we were both slender lightweights), but at least we could distract his attention from the women long enough for them to make the grand getaway. We quietly pulled on our shoes and grabbed flashlights — which could also be used as clubs, if necessary.

Monroe and I, girded to our gills for the fight of our life, made our mad rush out of the tent to begin our attack. Mary Elizabeth and Shirley, with ignition key positioned in hand, made it into the car. The motor started, the headlights flashed on, and the car surged forward. Monroe and I dashed one way and the next. The element of surprise was essential. The moment we saw him, we would rush and try to catch him off balance before he could come at us.

We couldn't find him. We flashed our lights back and forth. Nothing in sight. By this time, the Volkswagen was just making the bend in the road ahead of us. We raced to the car and jumped into the back seat. The car lunged forward again, and soon we were on the highway to Coalville.

Wearing nothing but our pajamas at the Coalville police station, we spilled out our story of terror to the officer on duty, urging him to hunt for the deranged wild man in the camping park. He interrupted us.

"I think we got your man right here. Come and see."

The officer led us into the next room. There he sat, our man, in the middle of the room, in handcuffs. His chin was resting on his massive chest.

"A trucker reported seeing a man wrapped in a tarp sitting in the middle of the highway. He almost hit him," the officer said. "We're trying to question him and can't get anything from him. Tell us what you know."

Monroe started talking. The moment the man in handcuffs heard Monroe's voice, he leaped from his chair and lunged toward him like a wild animal. The police immediately grabbed him.

The next morning we were awakened in our tent by a Utah highway patrolman. He reported that not far away a deputy sheriff had been shot and killed in his car by a man who claimed to have a buddy near by. Could this have been "Bill"? Or was it the man who terrorized us? They didn't know. We didn't know either — and we weren't going to wait around to find out.

The flip side of any horror story is light religious comedy.

As the patrolman questioned us about our night of terror, the camp manager suddenly showed up. He was a little old fellow in his late seventies, no doubt. As the officer listened to our story, he turned to the old man and asked, "Where in the hell were you when all this was going on here in your campground? You're supposed to be in charge here, don't you know?"

The poor fella stammered his feeble excuse, "All I did was sneak out of here for a cup of coffee at the restaurant just up the road. I know good Mormons aren't supposed to drink coffee, but you'd think just a little nightcap wouldn't cause all hell to break out down here. Jesus Christ, can't an old fella like me have a little fun now and then?"

From protection of the Secret Service swarming everywhere in Green River, the finest and tightest security in the world, to no protection whatever in an isolated campground where a madman was on the loose and threatening to kill us all.

All in a day's work.

I told Monroe I had lost all interest in outdoor camping.

✧

Things were moving smoothly along at St. John's Church. Church attendance had increased to the point that we began talking about the need either to expand the present building or build a new one. The former possibility was eliminated because the church lot was simply too restrictive for future growth. We then concentrated on selecting a new location for the church.

I had a site in mind after I first arrived in Green River. It was across the river on a flat bench of land gently sloping down from a towering rock formation called Man's Face. There had been no real estate development in that area at all. In fact, it hadn't even been surveyed within the city limits. The wardens offered to provide an engineering survey of the area in exchange for the right to select the site for the church. The city agreed.

Parishioners Dick Waggener and Harry Young were both civil engineers. The three of us went out to the area, and I trudged about half a mile through the sagebrush flat up to the spot I had recommended as a building site. The land sloped downward in all directions and tilted north toward the river and the old town of Green River.

When I arrived at the perfect location I hollered, "This is the place."

"Don't use those words," Dick Waggener shouted back to me as he lumbered along with his tripod and surveying instruments over his shoulder. "Those are the exact words Brigham Young used when he first saw the Salt Lake basin from the back of his covered wagon. An impressive "This Is the Place" monument stands on that spot now, marking the beginning of the Mormon migration into Utah. Since those were his words, you've got to say something different. Something more original."

"Okay," I hollered back. Sweeping my arm out across the expansive view of raw land directly in front of me, deliberately trying to make it as dramatic and theatrical as I could, I shouted, "Boys — this is it!"

We paid cash for that piece of land, and on it St. John's Episcopal Church now stands.

We made another dramatic change in the quality of our worship services at St. John's. We raised money to buy a new electric organ to replace the old-fashioned parlor pump organ the church had used since 1892. We organized an organ committee to make the selection. After reading through volumes of reports on electric organs, the committee decided to explore the possibility of purchasing a new Allen organ. It was more expensive than what we wanted, but it came closest to duplicating the actual sound of a pipe organ.

We made the purchase in Salt Lake City, and the Mormon who owned the music store tossed in a bribe we couldn't resist: a free organ recital in Green River by Dr. Frank Asper, the distinguished organist for the Mormon Tabernacle Choir.

We could hardly contain our excitement. Dr. Asper proved to be a very gracious gentlemen, slightly stooped in the shoulders from years and years of bending over the keyboard of the great Tabernacle organ. I was surprised when he asked me for a robe to wear during the recital. I told him it wasn't necessary that he wear one since this was a public recital and not a formal worship service. "But I insist on one," he said. "You see, when I studied organ back east as a young man, I had the privilege of playing for services in an Episcopal church. It was glorious and I loved that job. I always wore a robe, which contributed so much dignity to the role of the organist in worship."

I found him a robe and he proudly slipped it on. He turned to the Mormon businessman, who had sold us the Allen organ, and said, "You know Episcopalians do a much better job with their communion services than we do. They are always so beautiful and reverent. They use real wine, you know, which they drink from a silver chalice as a common cup."

"Oh, is that right?" the Allen dealer responded.

"Oh yes. In my humble opinion, our Mormon communion services leave a lot to be desired. Frankly, our use of water and cracker crumbs is for the birds."

I had enough sense to let that little interchange between two devout Mormons fly by itself without commentary from me.

We were as proud of the magnificent "pipe organ" sound of music from our new Allen electric organ at St. John's Church in Green River as any Mormon could rightly be of the famed Mormon Tabernacle organ in Salt Lake City. It tremendously enhanced the presence of God in the beauty of holiness. What a joy it was to worship the Lord with the accompaniment of a beautiful organ for the singing of our hymns and canticles.

Things couldn't have been better for the future of St. John's now that our little church had been beautifully renovated. We had a lovely new rectory, a wonderful new organ, — and plenty of land for future expansion.

Things couldn't have been better at home either. Lori was now in the third grade, Barry a first grader, and little Sheri getting ready for kindergarten. The kids had lots of friends up and down our block, and they were only one minute away from the school playground. Shirley had joined a bridge group and enjoyed the game. Occasionally, we would go dancing at Ted's Supper Club, which specialized in good steaks and always featured a lively dance band. It was fun. For the first time we didn't seem so financially strapped. We could even drive to Salt Lake City for our wedding anniversary and stay overnight in the elegant Hotel Utah across from Temple Square.

My church activities kept me well occupied. I enjoyed serving on the elected Board of Trustees of the Western Wyoming Community College. We went about buying land and selecting an architect to build a brand-new campus between Rock Springs and Green River. Since Dr. Gaensslen and I were the two college trustees from Green River, we kept insisting that the campus move toward Green River so as not to be monopolized by Rock Springs.

Green River was within the western deanery of Episcopal churches in Wyoming which meant we had many meetings of clergy and laity at places like Jackson, Dubois, and Pinedale. Those were fun places to visit, especially in summer. I was elected dean (clergy chairman) of the deanery, which gave me the new Episcopal title of Dean Todd. But I would jokingly sign all my correspondence as Deanery Dean Gene.

I had a unique experience in Green River that not many clergymen ever experience: I personally dressed a body for burial.

It so happens that Fr. Callahan, a retired Episcopal priest, lived in town. When he died, Mrs. Callahan asked that, according to church tradition, he be buried in his Episcopal vestments. Since the Mormon mortician, Dick Francom, had no idea how to do this, he requested my assistance. I completely dressed Fr. Callahan's body for burial, with clerical shirt and collar, cassock, surplice, and stole. I'm not saying it didn't bother me at all, because our mortal remains are cold and stiff when prepared for burial, but I was able to do it with an ease that surprised even myself.

In 1965 I had three funerals in Green River that I will always remember. Clergy always say that burials come in clusters of three; and this cluster of three bothered me because they were all young men. One was Ted Sudman, the only son of Dr. and Mrs. Bert Sudman. He was to enter medical school in only a few more weeks. He died suddenly in a car wreck near Jackson, Wyoming. What a tragic devastation this loss was to the Sudman family.

Equally difficult however, was the burial of a seventeen-year-old youth who left behind a fifteen-year-old pregnant wife. He was instantly killed when struck by a UP locomotive. And then a nineteen-year-old young man, despondent because of his unresolved rebellion and consequent estrangement from his parents, stepped out in front of a speeding eighteen-wheeler. Every bone in his body was broken. The mortician had me examine the body so that I could persuade the family not to encourage a public viewing.

None of these young men had even reached the prime of their life. All three died within weeks of each other.

People often ask me, "How can you conduct services for children and young people and keep yourself from breaking down?"

The only answer I can offer is: You must steel yourself emotionally with a lot of prayer. That doesn't mean the clergyperson can't openly grieve, because often I do, but they must always do it either before or after the burial service. It's best to do your grieving within a supportive group that can impart a caring ministry of strength and hope. Unfortunately for me, I grieved alone.

But there was something else I usually did that was restorative. When my children were small, I would usually go home immediately following burial rites at the cemetery and play games with them. Their infectious laughter and joy at being alive and having fun with their dad somehow enabled me to cross the bridge back to life again.

✧

One range animal could thrive in southwestern Wyoming: sheep. Somehow they could feed on the sparse grass and sagebrush and wring out a few drops of water from the snowbanks to quench their thirsts. One of the biggest livestock operations in that part of the state was the Taliaferro spread, which managed thousands of sheep with dozens of sheepherders and a large number of sheep wagons dotted all over the wide-open prairies. The Taliaferro family figured prominently in the political and financial power structure of the state. They were also actively involved in the Episcopal Church.

Many of their sheepherders were of Basque or Mexican origin and would spend many lonely months out with their herds. To maintain their sanity, it seemed, it was necessary for them to take a week off annually to hit the bars and brothels of Green River, where their binges would "break them so broke" they had to return to herding to break even again.

It was during one of these binges that I met a little dried up weasel of a man on the main street of Green River as I was headed toward Model Drug Store for my daily morning coffee break. He came reeling down the street with a bad hangover from the night before and was heading back to the bars for another day of high spending, heavy drinking, and common debauchery. He was dressed in the garb of a typical sheepherder: sheepskin coat, leather leggings up to his knees, and a woolen cap pulled down over his head to his eyebrows. The long locks of his matted hair flopped down over his forehead and mingled with his stringy beard so that all I could see of his face was his beady little bloodshot eyes and toothless grin. He looked like Gabby Hayes, the sidekick of Roy Rogers.

Noticing my clerical collar as I approached, he stopped in his tracks and made the sign of a cross with all the exaggerated mannerism of a French comic and held out his arms as if greeting a long-lost pal. I had never seen the man before. When I reached him, he threw his arms around me, planted a tobacco-stained kiss on both my cheeks, and said, "Padre, you may not know it, but we are soul brothers. Me and you have everything in common."

"How so?" I asked as I pulled myself away from his embrace.

"Whatever we do, we're both connected to God. When people think or talk about us — they always connect us to God. We can't get away from Him, me and you. We're soul brothers."

"What do we have in common?" I asked again, wondering what on earth he meant.

Tapping me on the chest, he said, "Well, you're God's blessed shepherd. Right?" Then, pointing to himself while shrugging his shoulders and gesturing with his arms, he continued, "And me? Well, I'm the _goddamned_ sheepherder. Either way, you see, we're both connected to God. We can't get away from Him."

"I see," I mused.

The little sheepherder went on, "Sheep are the same wherever they are, whether they be your flock or my flock. Sometimes ya gotta grab 'em by the wool and yank 'em where you want 'em to go. And sometimes ya gotta git behind 'em and kick 'em in the rump to make 'em follow up in the rear. But we never abandon our flock, do we? We always stay with 'em. Shepherdin' or sheepherdin' — it's all the same job. Let's me and you face it, Padre, it's one hell of a lonely job at times. But someone has gotta do it. Right?"

I've laughed about that chance encounter with this bedraggled sheepherder ever since. His is one of the better job descriptions of the pastoral ministry that I've ever heard. I'd like to have his words engraved on a bronze plaque and have it mounted in the chapel at the Iliff School of Theology or under the Good Shepherd window at Virginia Theological Seminary for all the young seminarians to read and ponder before they enter the shepherding ministry.

✧

At this stage of my pastoral ministry at Green River, into my fifth year, I knew the next big challenge would be building for the future. The horrendous job of raising funds and building a new church usually marks the end of one's ministry in a given place, because the stress simply becomes too much. I wasn't quite ready for it yet, but because of the overcrowding of both our worship services and Sunday school I knew the awesome day was fast approaching.

By this time, however, I had such an emotional attachment to our quaint and lovely little 1892 Gothic church building that I dreaded the thought of parting with it. So I began suggesting that when we built a new church on our new three-acre plot of land across the river, we should move the old 1892 building over and retain it as a historical edifice as well as a small chapel for weddings and small services. The idea was beginning to catch on with the people.

In the meantime, I had to follow through on a diocesan responsibility as chairman of the Department of Promotion. My job was to promote stewardship for missions within the Episcopal Church of Wyoming. Bishop

Hunter persuaded my department that we ought to focus on missionary work by inviting the popular Bishop Harry S. Kennedy of Hawaii to speak at a series of regional rallies throughout the state. Bishop Kennedy's jurisdiction included not only Hawaii but also many of the isolated islands of the South Pacific, where tremendous missionary work had been done by the Episcopal Church of America.

Bishop Kennedy was not willing to come to Wyoming during the winter months because he had been in the balmy South Pacific so long he had developed a serious aversion to snow and ice. Bishop Hunter persuaded his guest to visit Wyoming during the one month of the year most likely to be snow-free — September.

I organized about five regional dinner meetings throughout the state in large churches to accommodate bigger crowds. Both bishops and I were to travel from place to place together by car, and I was to preside over the dinner meetings and introduce the bishops. I soon learned that the extrovert Bishop Hunter had met his match in Bishop Kennedy. Both were cut from the same bolt of ecclesiastical cloth. They would warm up their audiences with an endless series of jokes, one after the other, until everyone was rolling in the aisles. Then Bishop Kennedy would describe the isolated Episcopal mission station at a leper colony on Molokai, for example, and the audience was visibly moved to tears.

It was a dog-and-pony show all right, but a darn good one.

The weather was beautiful as we moved about the state. As the master of ceremonies, I tried to preserve a semblance of order to each evening's festivities, which was hard to do because both bishops were in competition as stand-up comedians. The meeting in Laramie at St. Matthew's Cathedral was packed. We moved from there to a great meeting held in Lusk. When we woke up the next morning, we discovered that a howling blizzard had struck, and our car was totally drifted over.

Bishop Kennedy was in a state of mortal shock. How could Bishop Hunter have so miserably miscalculated the weather? Bishop Hunter was in a worse state, desperately trying to explain to his guest that a blizzard in Wyoming is as unpredictable as a typhoon in the South Pacific. Bishop Kennedy remained secluded in his room while Bishop Hunter sent out an urgent appeal to the Episcopalians of Lusk for an emergency donation of overshoes, caps, and mittens for the bishop of Hawaii.

After the goodwill wagon arrived, Bishop Kennedy sat in his room, bundled up from head to feet in borrowed woolens, looking like an Egyptian mummy. The radio reported thousands of stranded tourists all over Wyoming, mostly in the southern part of the state.

Meanwhile, John Tierney (the archdeacon of Wyoming, who arrived in a separate car to the missionary rally in Lusk) and I shoveled a path from the door of our motel rooms to the bishops' car, then dug it out from under a horrendous snowdrift. Bishop Hunter negotiated with the state highway maintenance crew that we be allowed to follow two snowplows into Gillette, where our final regional rally was scheduled for the next night.

It shouldn't have been a surprise for Bishop Hunter to discover in Gillette that there wasn't a single motel room available anywhere. Hundreds were sleeping in the hotel lobbies. By this time Bishop Kennedy was traumatized, his face bleached white. It was necessary for Bishop Hunter to roll out the "big guns," so he phoned his good friend, U.S. Senator Milward Simpson in Washington, D.C., to pull whatever political strings were necessary to secure us motel rooms in Gillette. It was a long chance — but it worked!

(I wondered at the time who got bumped into the storm. Even though I had been an Episcopal priest five years, I was still a novice as to how the power structure worked in Wyoming.)

Bishop Kennedy relaxed with several good scotch and sodas in the motel cocktail lounge. Although Bishop Hunter was a confirmed teetotaler and a rabid prohibitionist, he was at this point willing to provide whatever medicinal relief was necessary to tranquilize the bishop of Hawaii, who otherwise might go bonkers on him. It was without question a desperate situation.

After humongous slabs of prime rib beef for dinner, both bishops were becoming their congenial selves again. I decided to head for bed. Bishop Hunter instructed me to choose any one of the three reserved rooms, all listed under the Diocese of Wyoming. I climbed into bed after a very long and weary day. It has always been my idiosyncrasy to sleep nude — in the buff. Pajamas always wrap themselves too tightly around me.

I was just about asleep, when a key quietly opened the door to my motel room and in came the two bishops. I could hear Bishop Hunter muttering under his breath, "When I told Senator Simpson we needed a room for the three of us, at least, I thought he understood that each of us needed one room apiece. Not one room for all three of us together."

Horrors!

The bishops kicked off their shoes and draped their suit jackets over a chair, and both climbed into bed beside me, one on each side. All three of us in a queen-size bed. I had always heard it rumored that Episcopal bishops slept fully vested. I can personally vouch for the accuracy of that rumor.

It was the longest night of my life. As both bishops snored away on each side of me, I lay there fully awake, reflecting on the theological question:

At what one moment does one most fully become an Episcopalian? At bap-
tism? Confirmation? First communion? Ordination to to the priesthood?
 No, none of those things. For me, without question, I *most fully* became
an Episcopalian the night I slept naked between two fully clothed Episcopal
bishops, in a queen-size bed, in Gillette, Wyoming.
 I told this story once to a group of giddy bishops casually sipping
cocktails in a crowded hotel room while attending a Provincial Convocation
(regional gathering of midwestern Episcopal bishops, priests, and laity) in
Des Moines. They got a big bang out of it.
 During the hilarious laughter, one bishop blurted out, "Well tell the rest
of the story!"
 "What do you mean?" I asked. "That is the rest of the story."
 "It couldn't be," he countered. "Not with our bishop's ordained propen-
sity for the ceremonial laying-on-of-hands ritual!" — He got no further.
He was drowned out with a roar of guffaws from his fellow bishops.
 After this uproarious bashing, I vowed then and there never to tell that
story on myself again. But thirty years later I've rescinded — time
mellows with a humorous edge — so I'm telling it now for whatever its worth.
✧
A few weeks later, as we were getting ready for the ten o'clock worship
service at St. John's in Green River, three strangers showed up and sat conspicuously together in the back pew. They were at first surprised and then
a little uncomfortable as Green River people crowded into the pew beside
them. During the coffee hour in the undercroft, following the service, they
introduced themselves as members of St. Mark's Episcopal Church in
Cheyenne. They had attended a football game between the University of
Wyoming and the University of Utah the night before in Salt Lake City,
and they were on their way home. That's real religious devotion, I thought.
 The next evening I received a telephone call. "This is Frank Cordiner,
senior warden of St. Mark's Church in Cheyenne. I was among the three
who visited your services yesterday. Also, I was with our vestry that
attended the missionary rally in Laramie that you presided over, where
Bishop Hunter and Bishop Kennedy were speakers. You may not remember us there, although you introduced us."
 "Yes, I remember," I said.
 "Well, you may not know it, but Father Joe MacGinnis has just resigned
from our church to accept a call to a parish in New Jersey. And we are most
anxious for you to meet with us because you are under serious consideration
to become the new rector of St. Mark's Episcopal Church in Cheyenne."

Chapter 12

Had I listened carefully to the advice that immediately came my way upon announcement that I had been called as rector of St. Mark's Church in Cheyenne, I might have been prepared for what the future held in store.

My parishioner and dear friend in Green River, Dick Waggener, came to me with tears in his eyes and said, while grasping my shoulder, "Gene don't go there. I grew up in that church. I attended Sunday school there as a little kid and served as acolyte there until I went away to college. I know that church. Gene, they will cut you up into little pieces and throw you to the wind. You don't deserve what they will do to you. Gene, don't do it."

A more serious and shocking omen came from the bishop. "Eugene, there has always been a destructive and vindictive undercurrent in that church. You were not my first choice to go there, because they need someone in there who is going to knock some heads together until they shape up or else kick a bunch of the bastards out — excommunicate them, I mean. And I don't think you're tough enough to do it."

I had never heard the bishop use such strong language or speak with such vehemence. Later I would understand why he got so emotional whenever he talked about St. Mark's.

I should have paid closer attention to what they were all telling me.

Instead, brash thirty-seven-year-old clergyman that I was, I honestly thought I could prevail against all odds with hard work and good intentions. I had been well liked at Padroni and Vermillion and Green River and had every reason to assume the same would be true at Cheyenne — once they really got to know me. Such positive thinking was both naive and theologically unsound. The Bible never said that becoming a Christian would make one popular and respected. Jesus Christ, himself, didn't score very well in this department. Obviously, I had much to learn.

Fred Loomis, a devout Episcopalian and a highly respected lawyer in Cheyenne, wrote me a series of thoughtful letters upon my retirement from St. Mark's in 1992 in which he said that the church was "inherently schizophrenic." Because of this character defect, he said, "It would break the spirit of any rector who thought he could handle it." This would prove to be an understatement.

But I was too brash and naive back in 1965 to think there was any job I couldn't handle once I put my heart and soul into it. So it was in a spirit of exuberant confidence and reckless enthusiasm that I packed up the family in the old Chevrolet and headed out for my new appointment as rector of St. Mark's Episcopal Church in Cheyenne, Wyoming.

We arrived in Cheyenne at midnight with great excitement, watching the flickering lights of the approaching city as we drove over the summit between Laramie and Cheyenne. It was December 1, and the downtown area was decked out in a blaze of Christmas decorations. We drove past the state capitol, then circled the complex of state and federal governmental buildings, and stopped for a moment in front of the governor's mansion, with its huge pillars supporting the front porch.

Our oldest daughter, Lori, was ten; Barry was eight; and little Sheri was only five. To this day they still remember peeking over our shoulders while admiring the lights and sights of this large and beautiful new city that was now to become our home. We circled down around St. Mark's Episcopal Church at Nineteenth and Central Avenue. Its classic Gothic design, beautifully enhanced by its solid-stone construction, made it seem massive and impressive, silhouetted against the darkness of the midnight sky. An illuminated sign read: "The Pioneer Church of Wyoming, founded in 1868."

My first official service at St. Mark's was the Sunday before Christmas. The large church was packed with parishioners wondering what the new rector, Gene Todd, looked and sounded like. The enormous pipe organ roared like

The Todd family about the time we first arrived at St. Mark's in Cheyenne. Lorilee, Shirley, Sheridan, and Barry.

thunder. As the choir chanted the *Te Deum Laudamus*, a layman appeared in the doorway leading out of the chancel into the sacristy, frantically beckoning me to come his way. I did, and he whispered that my son, Barry, had accidentally locked himself inside the toilet just outside the chapel and was hysterically crying for his release.

When I arrived at the scene, another layman was desperately trying to unscrew the hinges of the old oak door while I tried in my most reassuring voice to calm Barry down. When the situation quieted just a bit, I distinctly heard the lay reader, out in the church leading the congregational prayers, faithfully bidding the Lord to bless the new rector and his family of St. Mark's Church: "By the might of thy Spirit lift them, we pray thee, in quiet and confidence to thy presence, where they may be still and know that thou art God."

If the congregation had only known how desperately I needed that particular prayer at that precise moment. Perhaps it was another omen of things to come.

✧

The rectory of St. Mark's didn't begin to compare to the lovely home we left behind in Green River. The vestry was aware of this discrepancy and in the official letter of calling contracted either to purchase a new home or to provide a housing allowance so we could acquire a home of our own. The real estate market was such that it proved a grievous mistake that we didn't exercise our option for the latter.

The rectory was located in a pleasant Eastridge residential neighborhood of Cheyenne with close access to an elementary school which the children began attending. We owned only one car, and I was nearly always away, which presented a serious problem for Shirley. She was essentially isolated at home. The purchase of a second car for my exclusive use helped alleviate her isolation, but she sorely missed the warm personal relationships she cherished and left behind in Green River. I was not as cognizant of her loneliness as I should have been because I was totally consumed with the demanding challenge of my new job. Hence, I committed the first of a series of mistakes in balancing the demands of both my profession and family.

Believing as I did that any obstacle could be overcome simply with hard work and good intentions, I threw myself into my ministry as rector of St. Mark's Church. I would leave the house at five-thirty in the morning, with Shirley and the three children still in bed, and dash down to the Frontier Hotel, directly across the street from the church, for a short stack of pancakes and a cup of coffee — which cost me the grand sum of thirty cents.

I was gone all day, home for supper, and gone every evening. When working six days a week didn't make things happen as quickly as I thought they should, I resorted to seven days a week. Hence, I set in motion an exhaustive routine that later would nearly break my health and ruin my life.

I wasn't at St. Mark's very long when I learned that the departure of my predecessor, the Rev. Joseph MacGinnis, to accept a rectorship in New Jersey, wasn't as pleasant as I had formerly assumed. Those who loved him most and were devoted to his style of leadership quickly pointed out that because his premature resignation had been hastened by a nudging from the vestry, they were in no mood to close ranks behind me. And although they didn't have anything personal against me, they had plenty to be personal about in their bitter dislike of Bishop J. Wilson Hunter.

Again, I naively believed that such attitudes would change once they got to know me. It was sad for me to learn that my assumption was dead wrong. I learned that, regrettably, some people need someone to be mad at. It seems to energize their souls. To remove their source of anger deflates their purpose in life and leaves them rudderless.

Worse, the bishop was just as bitter and unforgiving in his rancor toward the members of this group as they were toward him. Unfortunately, the bishop now considered me suspect because of my new association with a church that had brought him so much grief. Bishop Hunter was my "Father in God," the man who warmly welcomed me into the Episcopal Church and ordained me into the priesthood. Although I held him in high esteem and great affection, I could sense that he was transferring to me his stored-up bitterness about St. Mark's. But at that point I didn't know the source or substance of his bitterness.

Hoping to get to the bottom of the matter, I invited Judge Glenn Parker, chief justice of the Wyoming Supreme Court, a St. Mark's parishioner, and a dear friend of the Hunters, to accompany me on a personal visit to see if there was some way the bishop could be encouraged to vent his spleen about St. Mark's and allow the past to be forgotten.

"Bishop," the judge began, "we know that St. Mark's has been a burr under your saddle all these many years. But there is a new beginning there with Gene Todd and the vestry who support you and want to work with you . . ."

He got no further. The bishop interrupted him: "A burr under my saddle? Oh no, Judge, don't let them off that easy. It has been a thorn in my ass ever since I've been in this diocese. It began with Charlie Bennett who was rector there when I first came to Wyoming. I was deliberately snubbed every time I made my official visitation there. Was never introduced to the congregation or invited to preach. It was the wealthiest church in the Rocky Mountain West, but proudly refused to pay one dime of its assessments to the diocese and defied me to do anything about it. And then, when Joe MacGinnis succeeded Charlie Bennett, he tried, behind my back, to make a 'high Anglo-Catholic' parish out of it. He would stab me in the back every time I turned around."

The bishop began to weep.

Judge Parker gently placed his arm around the bishop's shoulder and said, "But Bishop, it's your prodigal son who has come back home to you and the Diocese of Wyoming. Now is the time to roast the fatted calf and celebrate. Gene Todd here loves you as his own father. You are my dearest friend. The majority of the people at St. Mark's greatly support you as our beloved bishop. Allow us now to move back into the full grace of your forgiveness."

But it never happened.

This guilt by association was a very personal loss to me. It was also double jeopardy. The dissidents at St. Mark's felt that since I was the bishop's "fair-haired boy," therefore I was suspect. And the bishop felt that I shouldn't have gone to St. Mark's because I wasn't tough enough to do the saber rattling and hatchet work which he himself could never do. But now that I was there, in association with a congregation that represented his greatest failure, I became suspect to him as well.

Judge Parker tried comforting me with the assurance that there was nothing he or I could do to bridge the chasm. But I wouldn't accept the obvious accuracy of that shrewd assessment.

I knew, of course, that I wasn't responsible for the impasse that had been brewing between the bishop and the congregation of St. Mark's long before I became an Episcopalian. But somehow I felt personally responsible for its resolution. I should simply have washed my hands of it all emotionally, sat in the shade, and watched the bishop and his "high church" opposition within St. Mark's hang each other out to dry on a barbed wire fence. I should also have laughed it off. But in retrospect, I'm sorry to say, I was losing the sense of humor that had always sustained me before.

I learned from this experience that one's perception of reality, even a bishop's, can be severely distorted. Perhaps Charlie Bennett's intellectual superiority was intimidating to Bishop Hunter. Similarly, the "high Anglo-Catholic churchmanship" of Joe MacGinnis was already becoming a liturgical norm of the Episcopal Church everywhere in America, and this surely intimidated the bishop as well. The only reason Anglo-Catholicism hadn't penetrated Wyoming was due to the bishop's militant "low church" opposition.

But there was no question about the bishop's deep emotional hurt from St. Mark's — whatever its source.

✧

The St. Mark's edifice was beautiful. The church was founded as the pioneer church of Wyoming back in 1867–1868, when the city of Cheyenne first came into existence as a winter camp during construction of the Union Pacific Railroad. The original wooden building was replaced in 1886 with a permanent stone structure financed by cattle barons of English wealth who had become kings of the western plains. It was patterned after the famous Stoke Poges Church of England immortalized by Thomas Gray's "Eulogy in a Country Church Yard."

This stone edifice remains essentially the same as it was in 1886, except electricity replaced its interior gas lamps, and a separate parish hall was added in 1915. Located at Nineteenth Street and Central Avenue, it had become a historical landmark for downtown Cheyenne. Its massive bell tower housed a set of eleven carillons, enormous in size and weight, whose peals of voluminous sound reverberated throughout the business section of the city and the neighboring residential areas.

Everything in this church edifice was of first-class quality. Its Gothic architectural design, stained-glass windows, antiqued woodwork, and marbled floors reflected striking beauty and expert craftsmanship. But the building was fast deteriorating. Worse yet, its lack of basic janitorial maintenance was evident everywhere, in spite of the fact that the church had a full-time sexton. Junior Warden Bob Read walked me through the building from top to bottom, visiting every nook and cranny. We observed Mr. Watchorn, the sexton, an elderly man of English descent and accent, slop his dirty mop across the floors, leaving a trail of mud wherever he worked. The poor old man was shocked when Bob told him, "Mr. Watchorn, this place is

Photo of St. Mark's when I first arrived there as rector in 1965 and before extensive outside renovation began in 1968.

a filthy mess. And after watching you here, I'm not convinced you're the man we need to clean it up."

When we finished our tour of the building and grounds, Senior Warden Frank Cordiner joined Bob and me to ponder our options. Bob said, "I remember seeing a photograph of Shirley Flynn's wedding where she is standing at the chancel steps and you can see her reflection in the marble floor as clearly as if it were a polished mirror. But now that marble finish is long gone, and its beauty probably can never be recovered."

Frank worked for the Wyoming Highway Department, where the janitorial crews managed to maintain a brilliant shine on the marble floors of the main office building. The same was true at the state capitol building. I contacted the maintenance superintendent of the highway building for consultation as to what we might do to rectify the serious maintenance problem we faced at St. Mark's.

The result was a massive cleanup.

Since most state janitorial employees worked the evening shift, they were available for extra income during the daylight hours. We had a five-man crew working almost continuously for several months. They were expertly trained in the use of chemicals and cleaning materials to strip away years of wax buildup on the grimy floors. Fortunately for us (and perhaps illegally), the state loaned us the use of its finest equipment as a training exercise for its in-service janitorial school.

Before long the beautiful rose-colored glow of the Italian marble began to emerge from the miry smudge. The heavy-duty buffers, gliding back and forth across the floor hour after hour, day after day, began to produce a polished mirror finish. Once again, as Bob Read remembered, you could stand on the chancel steps and see your reflection glistening in the tessellated marble floors.

This was just the beginning of a persistent program of general maintenance and capital improvement that would characterize the next twenty-seven years of my ministry at St. Mark's Episcopal Church.

There wasn't a day between 1965 and 1992 when I didn't meet for ten minutes to an hour with the church sexton to check a smudge on the marble floors, dust on the overhead beams, or grime on the stained-glass windows — or correct a heating problem in a Sunday school classroom, adjust the sound system, water the outside foliage in the summertime, or facilitate snow removal in the winter. These daily conferences with the sexton were important, because they conveyed to him that this church edifice was important to me. It was important to me because it was important to the congregation that sustained it. It was important to the congregation because it was in this holy place that we worshiped the Lord in the beauty of holiness. Its architectural space reflected what we thought about ourselves as Anglicans worshipping the risen Lord. Monitoring progress with the use of daily, weekly, and monthly maintenance checklists, with regular on-site inspections, I wanted each sexton to take special pride in this magnificent edifice we so dearly cherished.

The first major improvement was a renovation of the parish hall, which had been so beaten up by years of hard use that it hardly resembled its original appearance. The historical marker out front stated it had once hosted glittering social occasions and formal ballroom dances. But now the plaster had been knocked off the walls, the darkened floors had been gouged and badly scarred, and the wooden ceiling and massive overhead support beams were blackened from soot buildup.

It was so bad, in fact, that the vestry was considering installing a lowered ceiling to conceal the blackened overhead support beams, placing a tile floor over the damaged hardwood and mounting suspended fluorescent lighting — in other words, making it look like a renovated church basement. But it wasn't a church basement — it was a spacious first-story parish hall, a former ballroom, that had slipped into irreversible decline from years of neglect.

I challenged the vestry, arguing that instead of cheapening the appearance of the parish hall we should restore it to its former elegance and spacious beauty. But there was no money for such restoration. Fortunately, we had a marvelous resource person within the church who came to our rescue. Her name was Mrs. Willits Carey Brewster, more affectionately known as Biz.

Biz Brewster was the granddaughter of one of the most powerful figures of early Wyoming history. Joseph M. Carey not only had been Wyoming's first U.S. senator but also had distinguished himself as governor, territorial judge, banker, businessman, and pioneer cattle king. In addition to a family legacy of this magnitude, Biz also had impeccable taste when it came to historical restoration and interior decorating. She took complete charge of the renovation project, raised all the funding (with much of it coming from her own pocket, I'm certain), and personally supervised every minute detail, working hand in hand with all the skilled workers.

When finished, the gleaming new parish hall was a thing of exquisite beauty. We discovered that the hardwood ballroom floors, when sanded down, were solid maple. They were glazed to a mirror finish. The soot and grime of the overhead beams were scraped and scrubbed to reveal the warm wooden hues of oak, mahogany, and pine. The plastered walls were repaired and painted — three times, as a matter of fact — until the provincial gold perfectly contrasted with the antique-green window trimming. Storage rooms were built to hold extra tables and chairs. Draperies graced the windows. New chandeliers were suspended from the ceiling. Most striking of all, however, were the antique solid cherry doors, ten feet high, that had formerly been used in Senator Carey's mansion.

The room had been restored to an elegance that exceeded its former glory. Biz Brewster's artistic eye for architectural detail and interior decoration was evident everywhere. I marveled at her skill and ingenuity, and so did a grateful majority of the church. But a dissident minority griped simply because the project had been done, and largely paid for, by a member of the Carey family. I had yet to learn that, unlike my congregations at Padroni, Vermillion, and Green River, St. Mark's Church would always have a dissident and vociferous minority to loudly protest any project or program I initiated.

Simultaneous with the completion of the parish hall, another major capital improvement project was begun. The stone structures of the church and parish hall paralleled each other but were thirty feet apart, connected only with a sacristy at the east end of the two buildings. Consequently there was no way to walk from the parish hall to the church except by going down Central Avenue, then turning the corner and walking half a block down Nineteenth Street to the main entrance of the nave. All choir and bridal processions, for example, had to make this outside run through rain, sleet, and snow, which in Wyoming are always accompanied by hard-blowing winds.

It was obvious that we needed some kind of connection between the two buildings. I couldn't understand why St. Mark's, which had existed there for nearly a century, hadn't done anything about it before now.

The first proposal was that we simply build an enclosed ramp, maybe four feet wide, that people could pass through. But if we did that, we would close off the open space between the two buildings, which had become nothing more than a dump for trash and debris. I proposed that we enclose and roof the entire area between the two structures to accommodate not only a new passageway from the church to the parish hall but also additional space for rest rooms, offices, a new sacristy — and maybe a small chapel.

Again, there was no money for an addition of this magnitude. But I was convinced that the money would become available if the congregation could be challenged with a vision of how useful the improvements would be. I sketched out some ideas on a yellow legal pad and gave them to one of my parishioners, Paul Graves, an architect with Banner & Associates.

Paul returned with completely detailed blueprints. We had a serious problem: The two buildings were at different elevations. An inclined ramp between the two would have been too steep. Stairs seems out of the question because they would have butted them up against the stage of the parish hall. Because of these technical problems, I was strongly discouraged from pursuing the project. But I had Paul Graves on my side, and he was an architectural genius.

I honestly thought the vestry would suffer cardiac arrest when Paul first unveiled his blueprints. The original idea of a simple ramp between the two separate buildings had progressively evolved into a major addition to our church: brand new sacristy, new vesting rooms, curate's study, youth-choir room with small kitchenette, new rest rooms and, finally, a wide passageway with marble floors. But that wasn't all. The proposed passageway addition included a beautiful new outside walkway-entrance, with terraced bins for trees and flowers and street lamps along the brick walkway. Finally, Paul's blueprints called for a brand-new, expansive entrance off Nineteenth Street into the church — to match and blend with a lovely new lighted walkway to the west.

The vestry members were originally prepared to set aside $5000 for the original ramp project. Now we were talking about something that would cost $100,000 (nearly a half a million dollars today) — particularly with the use of stone from the same Castle Rock, Colorado, quarry (now abandoned) from which the original stone had been quarried back in 1886.

Pure pandemonium erupted within the vestry. It was apparent to them that Paul and I had gone wild with our imaginations. I finally persuaded them to set aside their hysteria and consider the merits of the overall plan, whether or not they agreed with its feasibility. They conceded that it was brilliant but insisted it was far too ambitious. They also lectured me that St. Mark's, although always flat broke, had never been in debt or borrowed any money and had no intention of doing so now.

The time had come for me to deliver my tried-and-true sermon — which first worked at Padroni, again at Vermillion, and then at Green River — that a church should reflect the glory of God. That whether it be a simple wooden building as in Padroni and Green River or a stately edifice like St. Mark's, a church should be a place in which the worshippers take personal pride. That the congregation should dedicate itself to the building's continual improvement to make it the most that it can become. And that when any major capital improvement project is finished, people should step back and say, "Let us worship the Lord in the beauty of holiness."

"But how do we pay for it?" the vestry demanded.

"It's simple how we pay for it," I answered. "When people see that there is a legitimate need; when we allow ourselves the gift of dreaming the dream as to what might be done to achieve that need; when we write the dream down as Paul has beautifully done in these blueprints; when people see that it's a dream that can come true with first-class quality workmanship and pride; that its completion will greatly enhance the church's usefulness for everyone in the congregation; and when we have done all of this to the best of our ability — then the project will be paid for. Because people pay for what they really want — when it's done right, for the glory of God!"

The vestry was sold.

However, most of the members felt we were pushing faith to a deadly limit. And I'm sure there were those who prayed for failure to prove me wrong. It did work, not because of me but because the membership of St. Mark's consisted of powerful people with strong financial connections. Quietly, behind the scenes, they extracted solid verbal assurances from local bankers that we would be loaned additional funds to complete the project once it began. But I'm pleased to say that the money came in, dribbling at first, then in larger batches, until construction was completed — entirely debt-free.

Construction went perfectly. Christiansen & Sons Construction Company was an established and trusted contractor. I would visit the construction site a dozen times a day and monitor the progress. Any problems or suggestions were listed on a yellow pad and shared with Paul Graves, who met daily with the contractors.

The priceless Tiffany stained-glass window, containing the authentic Tiffany signature of New York, was gingerly removed from the back wall by Mr. Christiansen himself to allow the passageway from the parish hall to connect into the vestibule area of the church. The window was then enclosed in a new wooden encasement within the passageway, with artificial lights enhancing its brilliance. The wood craftsmanship was so perfectly blended throughout the passageway that it beautifully matched the natural antiquity of the original structure.

Finally, the big day came for a dedication of our newly completed passageway and church addition. Once again it was with great excitement for me to shout from back of the church, during the dedicatory service, "Let us worship the Lord in the beauty of holiness."

"Thanks be to God!" came the joyful response from the congregation.

Now parishioners could walk on smooth polished marble floors from the church to the parish hall and never have to dash outside. And we acquired all the additional space for a fully equipped sacristy, curate's office, choir room,

Visitation of the presiding bishop of the U.S. Episcopal Church, the Most Reverend John C. Hines, to historic St. Mark's during our centennial celebration in 1968. I'm showing Mrs. Hines the woodwork restoration being done by craftsmen on high scaffolds while Wyoming Chief Justice Glen Parker chats with the presiding bishop.

kitchenette, modern rest rooms, and a handsome entrance from the terraced walkway outside. We had reason to be proud. I had the privilege of escorting the presiding bishop of the Episcopal Church of the United States, the Most Reverend John C. Hines, through the newly finished passageway when he made his historic visitation to St. Mark's Church on the occasion of our centennial celebration in 1968, commemorating our 100th anniversary as the pioneer church of Wyoming.

Unfortunately, Bishop Hunter was not present for much of the festivities because, as Judge Parker said, "He's still got that intolerable burr under his saddle when it comes to anything related to St. Mark's."

These two significant restoration and construction projects were only a portent of things to come. During my twenty-seven-year ministry at St. Mark's, every year would be occupied with either a minor or major project of restoration or construction.

A disgruntled treasurer once told the vestry that he could prove that over a million dollars had been spent on property acquisition and restoration during my rectorship at St. Mark's. Although his remarks were intended to be critical, I would have to agree with his figures. But almost every penny of that million dollars was generated outside the parish budget — and the church still has never been in debt.

Many people incorrectly think that benefactors simply walk into a church and hand the pastor a fat check for a new building program. It doesn't work that way. All significant bequests have to be carefully cultivated over a long period of time. People may initially offer $500 toward a project of one kind or another but might be willing to increase that amount to $5000 or $50,000 if they have the means to support it — and if they are challenged with the vision of a larger goal. But this

requires trust that the
project will be faithfully
carried out using skilled
workers and high-qual-
ity materials, that all
expenses will be prop-
erly accounted for, and
above all, that the fin-
ished project will greatly
enhance the overall
beauty of the church
building. Botch one job,
as I've known many
churches to do, and
benefactors are unwill-
ing to come forward for
future projects.

This sketch shows the exterior renovation to front steps and handsome addition of Kingham Walkway with new stone wall and tree bins leading to a newly created western entrance to church. Expansive parish hall is farther back. St. Mark's has always been an elegant and stately downtown church edifice.

During my tenure at St. Mark's, every square inch of that huge church edifice, inside and out-
side, was gone over and worked on as many as two or three times. These improvements would include two new roofs; pointing of the stone on the outside walls; hand treatment of the parish hall ceilings and interior woodwork with linseed oil; and restoration, renovation, and redecoration of all rooms. There was considerable replacement or upgrading of many invisible things as well: plumbing, electrical circuits, heating, and air-conditioning.

The installation of two new organs in the 1970s was a significant improve-
ment. First, the diapason organ was mounted on the wall of the chancel in memory of Ira Trotter. Second, the marvelous fanfare herald trumpet organ was added to the back wall in loving memory of the Reverend Charles Bennett. The main organ underwent a major renovation, gaining a new console in 1992 with funds accumulated during my tenure.

I offer no apology for doing whatever I could to stimulate the genera-
tion of memorial gifts or bequests to fund desperately needed capital improvements at St. Mark's. Obviously, I didn't do it alone, however, because I had a lot of help from a host of friends both within and outside the church. I thank God that I could be a part of whatever was accomplished.

But it was at a personal price. My health.

I was still going to work at about five-thirty in the morning. After check-ing in at the church, I would dash across the street for my thirty-cent breakfast at the Frontier Hotel. When things at the church didn't go as smoothly as I had hoped and wanted with hard work and good intentions, there was only one thing to do: *work harder* and *have better intentions.* It had not yet become apparent to me that I was burning my candle at both ends and blow-ing the smoke in God's face. When six days wouldn't suffice, then I would work seven days a week. My family began to suffer from my absence.

My health began to suffer as well. The migraine headaches that plagued me as a child returned with a vengeance. After an event of great stress, or a particularly trying day, when I allowed myself a moment to relax — then a migraine would strike. Almost as if to say, *Now that the crisis is over you've got time for a migraine.* My body was trying desperately to tell me something, but I ignored the signals. The severity of the headaches was such that there was only one thing I could do — lie perfectly still in a dark-ened room for several hours and wait for the pain to subside. Shirley or the kids would sometimes apply cold packs to my forehead, which seemed to help. When the attack would pass, my body felt wrung out, but my spirit energized to begin my duties anew. This, too, should have told me some-thing about the need for relaxation.

True to the family tradition of the Todds, I discounted the emotional and physical signals that something was wrong. Again like a Todd, I kept the migraines a secret; the congregation knew nothing of them. I was worried, however, that should one of these migraine attacks occur during a funeral, or a wedding, or a Sunday morning worship service, I would be incapaci-tated and let a lot of people down. That would have been unforgivable. I needed assurance that no bereaved family would ever feel abandoned at the funeral home, no hysterical bride feel stranded at the altar, because of my sickness. My physician provided me with my first prescription of Darvon, a mild pain sedative. It worked beautifully. When a migraine began its esca-lating attack, I headed it off with only one little capsule. The miracle of modern medicine.

I continued my early morning breakfasts at the Frontier Hotel, but I was not eating alone anymore. An elderly man began to join me at my table every morning. His wife and he were temporarily residing at the hotel while he recovered from a recent heart attack. His doctor had advised him not to climb stairs to his second-floor apartment during his convalescence, so they took up temporary residence at the hotel. His name was Robert J. Templeton.

"Temp," as he was affectionately called, reminded me a lot of my father. They would have been about the same age. He physically resembled my father in a way I couldn't quite describe. He talked like my father, with a simple homespun drawl. His sense of humor reflected a philosophical outlook typical of men born and raised in Wyoming ranch country. But he wasn't a rancher. He was a pensioned engineer from the Wyoming Highway Department living on a fixed retirement income.

I immediately liked him and enjoyed having his company at my table. Because he was a parishioner of St. Mark's who seldom attended, he became quite inquisitive about my hopes and dreams for the future of the church. I was only too enthusiastic to comply, ranting on and on with my vision of things to be. We were at that point very much involved in the early stages of restoration and construction at the church, so there were lots of things for me to be raving about.

Suddenly he died from a massive heart attack.

It was a personal loss for me because of the mutual affection we had developed. I officiated at his burial. His lawyer called to say that the church had been bequeathed approximately ten percent of Mr. Templeton's estate. I didn't even bother to inform the vestry of the pending bequest because it couldn't have been much. He had no income other than that of a highway engineer and had been living, as he told me, on his fixed retirement income. However, I do remember him telling me that an old college friend, who later became a Presbyterian minister, persuaded him to invest his small savings in a little upstart of a company known as Xerox.

I was shocked when Junior Warden Jimmy Wilson called me on the phone one evening and informed me that St. Mark's Church was due to receive one-tenth of the $1,480,000 estate of Mr. Robert J. Templeton. (A sum of $148,000 in 1969 would be comparable to nearly half a million dollars today.) When I spoke with Mrs. Templeton, she conveyed to me her appreciation of the many visits I'd had with her husband, including my vision of purchasing a new rectory and retaining the old one for the hiring of a curate (assistant rector) someday. Even though Temp's will was totally open-ended, she stated to me her personal preference that we acquire a new rectory, which would be named "Templeton House" in his loving memory.

It so happened that the lovely colonial home of Byron and Virginia Hirst came on the market at that precise moment. A beautiful three-story brick home located in a prestigious section of Cheyenne, it consisted of five bedrooms with four baths, a formal dining room, and a living room with a fireplace and study. It was graced outside with a formal terraced backyard surrounded by a stone wall and shaded with towering pines and white birch trees. Even though it was officially appraised at more than $90,000, the Hirsts were willing to sell it to the church for $48,000 — the exact sum

Front view (western end) of the beautiful Templeton House on West Sixth Avenue in Cheyenne. A most gracious and spacious colonial home — perfect for large formal entertaining as well as ideal family living.

the vestry designated for a rectory. The rectory committee, headed by Mrs. Edith Orrison, highly recommended that we not allow the bargain to slip from our hands. We didn't.

Benefactors who bequeath gifts for specific purposes are often vilified in a church. But an undesignated bequest often does more harm than good, because it gives people the opportunity to fight over something. Like family heirs, a church congregation may fight over an inheritance. St. Mark's chose to fight over the purchase of Templeton House and has fought over the Templeton Trust of $100,000 ever since. Perhaps it would have been better had we never received the gift in the first place.

✧

While the Todd family was moving into Templeton House just before Christmas of 1968, I received a telegram announcing the death of the Reverend Charles A. Bennett, whose tenure as rector of St. Mark's reached nearly forty years. It is an unwritten expectation in the Episcopal Church that the bishop presides at the burial of a diocesan clergyman. But the personal duel between Charlie Bennett and Wilson Hunter was carried even to the grave with a terse telegram: "The Bennett family specifically requests that only the rector of St. Mark's Church is to officiate at the service."

Charlie Bennett was making sure he had the last word.

I wouldn't have delivered that telegram to Bishop Hunter with it dangling from a fishing pole suspended over his back fence. So I took the wise and cowardly way out by having Judge Parker personally deliver it. Judge Parker returned from Laramie, came directly to our door at Templeton House, and told me the bishop perfectly understood that the intent of the telegram was to exclude his participation in the burial service and he would oblige.

"Don't you think, Judge," I asked, "that the bishop was relieved? After all, his participation in the funeral of Charlie Bennett would have been terribly awkward for everyone."

"Oh, no, quite the contrary," Judge Parker answered with a glint in his eye. "I think he was terribly disappointed that he won't be the one to bury Charlie Bennett."

Who started the original conflict between the Reverend Charlie Bennett and the Rt. Reverend Wilson Hunter, no one will ever know. I doubt if even they knew. But like all personal conflicts, this one was a tragic loss for both men. I never knew Charlie Bennett personally, but in the spring of 1968, while in Washington D.C., attending the College of Preachers, I had a lengthy phone conversation with him and found him charming and witty. Bishop Hunter was the same way. One would think they would have struck it off together in a great way, since both were blessed with the same amicable gifts. But I'm afraid that was exactly the problem: Neither could tolerate someone as charming and witty as himself.

As long as I remained at St. Mark's, I heard praise for the oratorical preaching skills of Charlie Bennett. His stimulating book reviews were in great demand. He once entertained at a luncheon for governors wives during a national governor's conference hosted in Wyoming by Governor and Mrs. Lester C. Hunt. With a public profile like that, who wouldn't have detractors? I think the Reverend Bennett had more than his fair share.

I instituted at St. Mark's the Anglican norm of having no mass display of flowers at a funeral. But I acquiesced to pressure brought upon me by Charlie Bennett's many friends to make an exception for a man who had faithfully served that church for nearly forty years as its rector. A pall of roses literally draped his casket, and I insisted that his body be lifted up into the chancel of the church, another Anglican tradition for the burial of a priest. The altar guild director resigned in protest because of my favoritism.

Three years later, in 1971, I buried Charlie Bennett's eighteen-year-old grandson beside the grave of his grandfather. John Clark was a freshman at Columbia University when the drug scene first struck many of our universities with a lethal fury. Young John was caught in its tragic grip. He returned to his home in California during a school break on the verge of an emotional breakdown, fearing he had permanently damaged his life. One evening, after all had gone to bed, he quietly closed his mother's bedroom door, moved the cat from her niche in the garage to the kitchen, returned to the garage and started up the motor.

At the funeral home, where I had final prayers with the family before burial services at St. Mark's, I stood beside the open casket while his beautiful mother, Gwinneth Ann, Charlie Bennett's only child, spoke to her dead son, who looked like a little boy in a grown man's suit. She placed her hands on the side of the casket's satin lining and said, "John, why did you do this to yourself and to us? We knew you were having troubles, and we told you it was all right not to return to Columbia for a semester until you got the help you needed. We even made an appointment for you to begin your counseling. We told you that we loved you and would support you through all of this. Your sisters told you that, too. We were prepared to stand behind you all the way, and you knew that."

Then, her voice trembling, she continued, "Now you've done this — and it is so terribly final. You were thinking only of yourself and not of us. John, my grief is beyond anything you could ever imagine because I loved you so much. But at the same time, John, I have to tell you as your mother, in the midst of this awful grieving — that I am very angry at you for what you've done to yourself and to us. I did not give you birth for this."

Her gut-wrenching confession and poignant honesty have lingered with me. I remember her words as if I heard them only yesterday. Her acknowledgment that her excruciating grief was painfully mingled with enormous anger toward her only son, who had destroyed himself rather than face problems he could have overcome, bears powerful testimony to the towering magnificence of a mother's love. Her courage in speaking these words of love, maturity, and open honesty from the depth of her heart and mind made an indelible impression on me.

Later that afternoon, as I officiated at the burial of this young man who had tragically ended his own life, I kept thinking, *John, what a terrible mistake you made to have cut yourself away from the strong influence of a mother like yours.*

In June 1988 I buried Vera Bennett, a brilliant church organist and wonderful composer, beside the graves of her beloved husband and grandson.

✧

Like all church congregations, St. Mark's consisted of a fascinating group of people. The church had elected to remain downtown rather than flee to the fast-growing suburbs of Cheyenne. Many parishioners were descendants of Cheyenne's earliest families, and many were well connected to the leading political figures of Wyoming since the state government was located in Cheyenne. Cheyenne was also the center of the region's federal and judicial offices, including the U.S. district courts. Above all, it was the location of the only major military installation in Wyoming, one of the largest and most significant in our nation's nuclear defense: Fort Francis E. Warren, a missile base surrounded with 200 missile-launching sites. Consequently, there were many historic military family connections in Cheyenne. All of this made for a fascinating combination of people.

One of my favorite old-timers was a distinguished country gentleman, a retired cattle rancher, by the name of Russell Thorpe. (He also figured prominently in the Wyoming Stockgrowers Association in its heyday.) He was already into his nineties when I first called on him in a quiet little retirement home not far from St. Mark's. He told me that his father owned and operated the famous Cheyenne-Blackhills Stage Express which ferried passengers and gold bullion between Deadwood and Cheyenne. Cheyenne was the nearest railroad terminal in 1876 when the fabulous gold strike hit Deadwood Gulch several hundred miles away. Russell told me that as a young teenager he actually drove the stagecoach for his father. There were always sharpshooters riding shotgun, and sometimes cavalrymen from Fort Laramie provided military escort, because outlaws could easily hide atop barren Rawhide Buttes to watch an approaching coach for many miles before swooping down for a holdup — hoping to find a shipment of bullion onboard. Often, however, they found nothing more than terrified passengers who traveled the notorious route, including troupes of well-heeled gamblers and *Shady Ladies* who were regularly shuttled back and forth between the two frontier hellholes: Cheyenne and Deadwood. This high drama scenario became the theme of countless Hollywood movies.

He joked that out along this weary desolate route, passengers would frequently ask the driver to stop the coach so that they could relieve themselves. Women would ask where was the nearest tree and he would offer them his stock reply, "Lady, about thirty miles due west of here. Catch tomorrow's stage on your way back!"

Curiously I asked, "Honestly, Mr. Thorpe, how would proper ladies of that Victorian age handle the situation if they needed an unscheduled rest stop out on those wide-open prairies?"

He answered, "Father Todd, the men would go out on one side of the coach with the women on the other. And if there was more than one woman aboard, and usually there were because women seldom traveled alone, they could provide *modesty curtains* for one another by holding out their long skirts around the woman squatting down behind." A very practical solution, wouldn't you say?

I marveled to think how close we are in Wyoming to the early history of the raw and wild American frontier. Here I was visiting once again with another honest-to-goodness stagecoach driver from the fabled, and not so romantic, Old American West. (The first one was old Tom Welch in

Green River.) A short time later, I officiated at Russell Thorpe's memorial service in Cheyenne before burial in Lusk, Wyoming.

I'm sorry now that I didn't ask him about the legendary characters of Deadwood Dick, Calamity Jane, and Wild Bill Hickock, because he would have known them all.

✧

A prestigious name in early Cheyenne history is that of the philanthropic Richardson family which consisted of three brothers and two sisters, all single, who lived in an ornate baronial home furnished to the hilt with the most massive pieces of furniture I have ever seen — imported from all over the world. No one could understand or explain their collective aversion to marriage.

Nor their propensity for making big money — on an international scale!

The remarkable brothers, Emile, Clarence, and Warren, amassed a considerable fortune from a variety of entrepreneurial sources: gold prospecting in Alaska, lumbering in Mexico, gas field production in Wyoming, oil freighting in the Atlantic (with their own ships) — to successful Eastern and European investments.

Incidentally, their Klondike gold rush was a disastrous failure (too much bitter cold and hard work) so they struck upon the fast-food idea of setting up a tent-restaurant high atop blizzard-swept Chilicoot Pass, serving hot coffee and doughnuts to the frozen and famished prospectors — and made a mint! Thus, proving that they were entrepreneurs to the core — never failing to turn a temporary misfortune into a bonanza of grandiloquence.

All the brothers and sisters regularly attended St. Mark's together as a group — including "paramours" of the bachelor brothers, I've been constantly told — with the entire entourage nobly processing up the center aisle toward the front "Richardson pew" as if they were English lords vacationing in Wyoming. Then back to the family home the assemblage would promptly go after church, in their limousines, to an elaborate Sunday dinner prepared by a permanent household staff fit for royalty. (Including a full-time gardener whose huge vegetable garden provided fresh produce for the family table.)

Although the bachelor brothers lived with their spinster sisters, Laura and Valaria, they were not reclusive. They enjoyed cavorting in high society and relished their privileged membership in exclusive men's clubs around the country. Emile was engaged for forty years to Ella, the family bookkeeper, but died before they could shuffle themselves to the altar. Like his brothers, his irresistibility to the feminine charm was exceeded only by his resistance to a hasty marriage.

With the use of a private railroad car, fully staffed, Clarence romantically courted the love of his life — an enormous fortune found in the development of the Casper and Lander oil fields in central Wyoming.

One of the brothers, handsome Warren, is credited with being the creative genius behind the founding of Cheyenne Frontier Days as a "rodeo show" and was its first organizational chairman back in 1897. He died in 1960 at the age of ninety-five, only five years before I came to Cheyenne, but legendary stories about him still abound. Like bragging about his physical fitness and slender build while nurturing pleasures of the flesh and all the bad habits, including heavy smoking and moderate drinking. He enjoyed his world travels and boasted of being a dashing bachelor with no intentions of marriage until he was 100 years old. But if he died prematurely before then, his ideal death wish was to be shot by a jealous husband.

Dr. Albert Pearce, a retired physician and longtime friend of Warren Richardson, told me about walking down the street one day with the ninety-four-year-old Warren when they met a very attractive young lady. As the shapely beauty clicked her high heels past the two elderly gentlemen on the sidewalk, Warren turned to Dr. Pearce and mused, "Oh, to be seventy again!"

From the legends I heard of his romantic exploits, he could just as easily bemoaned not being ninety again.

Florence Esmy Howar, widow of the popular Lt. General Rhodolph L. Esmy, both very active communicants of St. Mark's, reported that Warren once told them about his leading Teddy Roosevelt on a big game hunt in early Wyoming. Roosevelt was so pleased with Warren Richardson's hospitality that he asked what he might do to return the favor. Warren answered, "I would appreciate an introduction to a good harem."

It's my hunch that these are apocryphal stories which Warren enjoyed telling on himself to shock and amuse his listeners. He was always the delight of a party.

I buried the youngest sister, Valaria, in 1966. She was the last of the Richardson family to die. Earlier, when I called on the poor soul in the pretentious Richardson home on Capitol Avenue, she was so senile in her old age that her only response to anything I said, even my offer to say a prayer, was simply, "The hell you say!"

When she died, I met with a strange group of older women to plan her funeral. It was a bizarre sisterhood, I thought, and I never quite understood why these women were in charge of the Richardson household staff, catering to Valaria's childish whims, when none was directly related to the Richardson family.

"Paramours!" — again I was discreetly told by those who seemed to know. As I discussed funeral arrangements with this tightly knit sorority, my nose caught wisps of a strong chemical odor permeating the room. When I expressed alarm, in one chorus they all exclaimed, "Oh, they're embalming Valaria behind the screen right beside you!"

Apparently, in olden days it was a mortuary custom to embalm the body in the home of the deceased. And since it was done for all the other Richardsons, the cherished tradition was preserved for Valaria as well — although it was terribly outdated. She was "laid out" in silk linens in a special bedroom reserved for that purpose. Again, according to family tradition, after the body was finally placed in an open casket, we were all invited for cocktails and lunch prior to my conducting a private burial rite in the home parlor before a solemn gathering of distinguished guests — followed by a public service at St. Mark's.

Since the Richardsons were generous benefactors of St. Mark's — among other things, donation of the exquisite marble flooring (imported from Italy) and the expensive installation of massive carillons in the bell tower — I was invited by the family attorney to come by the twenty-room mansion during its dismantling. He told me on the aside that he was fearful of potential frivolous paternity suits against the estate by children of former domestic maids within the Richardson household — who might claim an inheritance from the dubious ancestry of the Richardson brothers.

"These indiscriminate romps in the hay have a way of catching up with you," he explained. Needless to say, since the Richardsons were all single, there were no descendants — "to speak of."

But the attorney's fears were unfounded. There were no paternity suits filed against the virile Richardson boys at all. Ironically, however, there was one against their father (an early Wyoming banker and civic leader who died in 1908) which the estate settled out of court. Despite their reputation for womanizing, it would appear that the Richardson sons were either more virtuous or precautious than was their pioneer father in these private domestic affairs.

In the attic we found numerous unopened cardboard boxes, all containing newly printed copies of a hardback novel written by a female psychic. I found its content weird and poorly written. I asked the lawyer why in the world Warren Richardson would finance the publishing of such a senseless book.

"Simple! The author was a paramour," came the stock answer — which, by this time, I should have known before asking.

What a remarkable and fascinating church family.

I would have enjoyed knowing the Richardsons, especially Warren, because these are the kinds of colorful and interesting people who keep the world turning. I could write a book about their adventurous money-making schemes, prominent civic leadership, and personal shenanigans. Indeed, their family legacy of humanitarian outreach is keenly felt in Cheyenne by many young people who are annual recipients of the Richardson Memorial Scholarship Fund.

✧

Another one of my early favorites was Gussie Bevans. Her name actually was Augusta. She was very august in some ways, but other parts of her personality made her deserving of the affectionate name of Gussie. She was an "old maid," a retired federal employee in her late seventies who had moved from her spacious apartment to a very small one within a block of the church. The only thing of luxury in her life was an expensive wardrobe of exotic clothing.

She made a striking appearance. Her coiffered hair was dyed a flaming red. She wore her makeup a little on the naughty side, with rouge a little too heavy, lipstick a little too bright, and fingernails a little too long and excessively colored. She loved wearing lavish dresses, complete with fur stoles and plumed hats. And she always said exactly what was on her mind. I loved her for this.

Still new at St. Mark's in 1966, I organized an inquirer's class for newcomers to the Episcopal faith. The weekly class was to meet in the guild room for a period of four months.

When I announced the formation of the class one Sunday morning in church, Gussie told me she would attend "because I never attended any confirmation classes when I was confirmed. When the bishop was here for confirmation, I simply walked up out of the congregation on a spur of the moment, knelt down in front of the bishop for his laying on of the hands ceremony, and was confirmed without ever taking one class of instruction."

I'm certain Charlie Bennett was too much a gentleman to publicly embarrass her in front of the bishop and the congregation.

"Now I think," she continued, "that maybe I better learn what I got myself into. I'll come to your classes and have you teach me what I missed. And if I don't like what I learn — tell me, is there a way I can get myself *unconfirmed?*"

My first class began with about thirty students, all young married adults. I've always taken these classes very seriously and have developed quite an extensive collection of curriculum materials. We all introduced ourselves, and I had everyone explain why they had come to the class. Some of the young husbands admitted they were there only to appease their wives.

I led a prayer and was just beginning my first lecture-discussion when the double doors popped open and Gussie burst into the room. Having made her grand entrance, she paused and looked us over. She was attired in a purple satin dress with a deep red sash. Over her shoulders was draped a beautiful mink stole. She was wearing white gloves that reached almost to her elbows, high heels with sparkling silver sequins, and a plumed hat. She was a sight from another century.

The room fell deathly silent.

All eyes were truly fixed upon her as she sashayed past me and down the corridor between the folding chairs, where she plumped herself down into an aisle seat, flipped one end of her mink stole over her shoulder, lit up a cigarette in a long gold cigarette holder, blew a smoke ring into the air above our heads, crossed her legs, and gave me a look that said *I dare you to teach me anything I don't already know.*

She outclassed us all. The rest of us in the room were a motley crew, and she was the prima donna. Even I felt so intimidated that I almost forgot what I had started out to say before her star shone in upon us.

Gathering my thoughts, I started out again. Since we were there to learn about the teaching of the faith, I said, why not begin with the Apostles Creed? I began reading it through:

> *I believe in God, the Father almighty*
> *maker of heaven and earth;*
> *And in Jesus Christ his only Son our Lord;*
> *who was conceived by the Holy Ghost,*
> *and born of the Virgin Mary . . .*

"Stop right there," shouted a young husband sitting in the back row who earlier had confessed that he was attending the class under protest. "What's this thing you Christians got against sex? That's all I ever hear from you preachers, the lusts of the body and the sins of the flesh."

Obviously, he was rebelling against the fundamentalist preachers of his own personal background which he had earlier admitted. Episcopalians just don't talk that way.

He continued with his tirade, "I simply don't understand this obsession that you Catholics have about being a pure virgin. Are we supposed to be proud of our virginity?"

Before I could stammer an answer, Gussie's gloved hand shot up, and turning in her aisle seat toward the young interrogator at the back of the class and quipped, "Hell no. Look at me."

They were looking at her all right, with eyes bulging and mouths agog, their attention fully rivited on this Grande dame from the nineteenth century.

"Look at me," she repeated, "I'm nearly eighty years old, I'm a virgin — and I'm not a damn bit proud of that deficiency!"

The whole class exploded with roaring laughter.

After that, Gussie became the crown jewel of the confirmation classes. Her irreverent quips kept us all in stitches. It seemed as if the class could not begin until Gussie made her grand entrance — always late.

One evening she didn't show. The class became worried fearing that something might have happened. I explained that an eighty-year-old woman who was already confirmed, was entitled to one night off from the classes if she preferred to do something else. That wouldn't suffice. Since she lived just across the street, less than a block away, two young men insisted on investigating (one of them being the fundamentalist previously mentioned). They returned fifteen minutes later with Gussie between them, arm in arm. She beamed sweetly and said, "Isn't it nice to be missed?"

Playing it to the hilt, she affectionately patted their arms, smiled at them flirtatiously while blinking her false eyelashes, and then added , "It's especially glorious for a damsel in distress to be rescued by two handsome young stallions like these."

Thank God, Gussie decided to remain a confirmed Episcopalian.

It was she who later decided that she wanted to establish a Rector's Gallery, which would contain portraits of all the past rectors of St. Mark's along the wall of the new passageway in the church. Using her skill as a retired executive secretary for the federal government, she zealously collected old photos with her usual aplomb. Photos of some simply were not available. Gussie insisted that each portrait should be adjusted in size by a professional studio so that all the images perfectly matched one another. She demanded that I pose for a photo session as well, for which she paid, so that my picture could be included. It was a proud day for Gussie when her Rector's Gallery was dedicated. It was a tribute not only to her perseverance for a job well done but also to her love of the Lord and her devotion to St. Mark's Church.

All through this project, I had an irresistible urge to draw her aside and ask, "Gussie, now look me straight in the eye and honestly tell me — you're really not a virgin are you? You just said that to pull our strings, didn't you?" But the opportune moment never came for such a personal question.

Before she died, she told me she hated funeral palls, particularly the purple one the church owned at that time. "If you put that purple thing over my casket," she told me, "I promise you that right in the middle of my funeral, in full view of everyone, I will sit up and kick it off."

That was her style: to do everything — with great flair — *in full view of everyone.*

I told her, "Gussie, if you do that, I promise that I will never ever use a pall again at any funeral for the rest of my life, so help me God."

When she died, I didn't put the pall on her casket. I instinctively knew that she would have relished another grand theatrical moment — *in full view of everyone.*

The world, and particularly the church, needs characters like Gussie Bevans. We need them to keep our rusty wheels oiled up and our sense of humor afloat. God bless her.

✧

When I wrote earlier that St. Mark's membership consisted of people historically well connected to the political and economic power establishment of Wyoming, I don't mean to imply they were the only members of the congregation. Far from it. The vast majority of the parishioners were common, ordinary Christian people of simple means who loved the Lord. They were loyal Episcopalians who were devoted to worshipping and serving Him at the beautiful old Gothic church at Nineteenth and Central.

They were people of many talents. The only problem was motivating them to offer their talents as a gift to God and to the world. St. Mark's was not alone with this problem. All churches face it one way or another. This task was never-ending. It seems I was continuously doing it with every sermon I preached, every pastoral call I made, every vestry meeting I attended, and every personal conversation I had at the coffee hours that followed Sunday morning worship services.

I would no sooner get a leadership base established in the choir, vestry, youth program, Sunday school, adult Christian school, women's guild, or financial committee when it would be begin to unravel again. The reason: the mobility of the American people, who move an average of every five years or so. This was particularly true in Cheyenne. Military personnel were seldom on base assignment longer than four years, and governmental employees at both the federal and state level were constantly in flux because their jobs were dependent on the political whims of the day.

The old idea that a minister should move every five years because the congregation gets tired of him may be true in Europe, but never in the United States. If a minister stays put, essentially he's got a new congregation every

Enjoying my study at Templeton House. This picture taken while teaching a "Religious Studies" class — which I was always doing.

five years or so. Consequently, recruitment and development of church leaders was an ongoing and time-consuming task.

Like all ministers, I worked hard at it. I organized a Rector's Teaching Seminar every January and February, a School of Moral Concerns teaching human sexuality from the Christian perspective for teenagers, a Lenten Study Series every spring, a Pairs and Spares young adult social fellowship, which met monthly in homes — the list goes on. These programs practically sustained themselves throughout my ministry at St. Mark's. Many other programs were more short-lived. Some were successful, others were not. The point is that without constant lay leadership development, churches would simply die on the vine.

Most of the times, the intellectual and spiritual stimulation of preparing and teaching these classes was most satisfying to me. But there were other times, I'm honest to admit, when they became an emotional drag.

Overall, it was evident to me that my ministry at St. Mark's Episcopal Church of Cheyenne, Wyoming, was going to be the challenge of a lifetime. Fortuitously for me at the time, I could never have imagined that it would totally consume twenty-seven years of my life!

Chapter 13

The excitement of family life was escalating for the Todds in Cheyenne. By 1970 Lori was fifteen, Barry thirteen, and Sheri eleven. They weren't little children any more. They all pedaled bicycles with friends from all over the Avenues, a residential area of Cheyenne. We enjoyed living in the lovely new rectory, Templeton House, located at 413 West Sixth Avenue. Its spacious backyard was often occupied with hamburger cookouts and teenage parties. It was fun watching the kids growing up and developing distinctive personalities of their own.

We still vacationed every year with my father, who lived alone in his little house on North Gould Street in Sheridan. He was now well into his eighties. Although he terribly missed Mom, who had died in 1960, he managed quite well by himself, doing all his own cooking and housekeeping. He kept a huge vegetable garden and canned hundreds of quart jars of peas, beans, tomatoes, and corn every summer. Then he would parcel his canned goods out to all his family.

Terraced backyard of Templeton House for quiet personal relaxation, frequent family reunion cookouts, and entertainment of large church groups. It was also a lovely place for formal wedding receptions.

It was fun and relaxing to visit him for a week or two every August. My kids helped him work his garden and husk corn, crack green beans, and pop peas for his old-fashioned home-cooked country meals. While they were relaxing, I would meet every afternoon with the trust officers of the Bank of Commerce, which handled the mineral trust Dad and Mom established after the sale of the Todd ranch on Piney Creek. From time to time oil and coal companies were interested in leasing large tracts of land for exploration purposes. No great fortune resulted from these leasing agreements, but the income had to be equally distributed to all the descendants of my parents. As co-trustee, it was my job to monitor the income and help the bank keep track of the family heirs.

Though he lived in town now, Dad never lost his love for horses. During his nearly sixty years of cowboying and ranching, horses were a necessity. Now, in his retirement, they had become his greatest pleasure and hobby. He rented a little land just outside Sheridan, and there he cared for about twenty horses. He would always have a "kid's pony" available for our annual visit. My kids knew nothing about horses, so the ponies had to be extra tame and gentle. I'd spend the mornings assisting them with their riding lessons, sitting in the shade of Dad's horse trailer as they trotted around the little alfalfa field. Some of the mares had young colts that frolicked along behind, and the kids became affectionately attached to them.

One morning while the kids were going through their usual routine, muffled banging came from within the horse trailer. The horses snorted and pulled away. Taffy, our family dachshund, put up a terrible fuss. I cautioned the kids to lead their horses away and stand back, fearful that a wild animal was trapped inside. The trailer was closed, and I didn't know what to do. But it was obvious to me that something had to be done.

Suddenly the back door of the trailer flopped open, and out came a barrage of beer cans and whiskey bottles, being swept out by a broom. The sweeper, a little old geezer of a man, said he lived in the trailer. "Today is my housecleaning day," he told us cheerfully.

He resembled the bedraggled sheepherder I mentioned in the Green River chapter, the man with the Gabby Hayes look. He didn't seem to be even slightly perturbed at our intrusion of his domestic tranquillity.

I loaded up the kids and raced back into Sheridan.

Dad was standing at the kitchen sink slicing tomatoes when I bounded in, blurting, "Dad, guess what? We found a cruddy old man living out there in your horse trailer. You'll have to do something about him."

"Oh, that's ol' Orly," Dad said calmly. "He winters here in town but vacations out there every summer. I know all about him."

"He lives in your horse trailer?"

"Yeah, that's his summer cottage. Once a month I drive him into town so he can cash his Social Security check and pick up a few groceries and a new case of liquor. He lives a very simple life. Goes fishin' every day in Big Goose River. He's a good fisherman. Always catches what he needs, then fries his catch right there on the beach. Then he lollygags around all afternoon in the shade and does his drinkin'. When it gets dark he returns to his house trailer and sleeps it off 'til noon the next day."

"Dad, it's not a house trailer. It's a *horse* trailer!" I shouted.

"If a horse is in it, it's a horse trailer," he replied. "When a man lives in it, it's a house trailer. What difference does it make? It's a good deal for Orly. He pay's me a dollar rent each month, includin' transportation into town. He likes it out there."

"But Dad, it's no wider than the width of a horse, and it just has a canvas flap pulled over the top. No human being should have to live in a contraption like that. I'm shocked you allow it."

"Gene," he said, laying down his knife, "your great-grandparents traveled by covered wagon from Pennsylvania to Iowa a hundred years ago. The floor of that covered wagon was no wider than the space Orly has in that horse trailer. And in that wagon they carried all their clothing, all their furniture, all their kids, and their first crop of seed. Orly has a lot more room than they ever dreamed of having."

"But, Dad, it's still just a horse trailer. And he's a pitiful old alcoholic recluse," I grumbled.

Dad set down his cup of coffee and looked me straight in the face, "Gene, you don't have to worry about Orly. If you want to worry about someone, you better worry about those uptown bankers you're meeting with every afternoon who wear those shiny boots and fancy western suits and big white hats. If you don't watch them, they'll take everything your mother and I worked a lifetime to accumulate. Everything. Those are the bastards you've got to look out for. Not Orly. Didn't they teach you any of this in college?"

As a matter of fact, they did. In pursuit of my master's degree in history I became acquainted with the "frontier hypothesis" of Fredrick Jackson Turner. In the late nineteenth century, Turner became the first historian to argue that the character of the American people was shaped not by eastern intelligentsia but rather by the pioneering people who pushed the frontier westward, inching their way across the continent. Here people learned self-reliance, fierce independence, and a basic distrust of European cultural institutions. The pioneers thought nothing of moving hundreds if not thousands of miles in ox-drawn wagons. New economic opportunities lay just over the hill and beyond.

Dad knew nothing about formal history; he had only an eighth-grade education and read very little. But in his defense of Orly, he perfectly articulated Turner's frontier hypothesis. Even his inherent suspicion of bankers.

Dad was right, of course.

It's true that Orly had more living space in that horse trailer than any of our ancestors who trekked in canvas-covered wagons during the great western American migration. And he probably had more creature comforts, too: fishing every day, swimming in the river, tanning in the sun, and lollygaging in the shade while he drank his booze. At some level of my being, there was something idyllic about this carefree and easy going lifestyle — if I allowed myself the freedom to ponder it for more than just a passing moment.

✧

Well, at least my college and seminary training had proved useful in the writing of Dad's book, _Recollections of a Piney Creek Rancher._ The book became far more successful than any of us could possibly have imagined. It went through four editions and sold more than 4000 copies. That's not much in terms of the best-seller list, but it's remarkable when you realize the book sold that many copies with no promotional gimmickry. It sold strictly by word of mouth.

Dad relished shipping his book off to people all over the United States and to distinguished libraries in major cities and universities — even in Canada. He enjoyed autograph parties at the bookstores in Sheridan, where friends would gather around to reminisce about the good ol' days. At home you'd find heaps of the books stacked on the living room floor awaiting his autograph. Newspaper reporters in Billings and Denver called to interview him.

He even got onto the radio. Both Sheridan radio stations invited him on for live interviews, and I marveled at how beautifully he handled it. I appeared with him on two such broadcasts and was far more nervous than he. He would simply sit there in front of the microphone and talk away, as naturally as if he were spinning yarns at the kitchen table. He would start answering a question and I'd wonder, _Now where is he gonna go with this?_ Without fail, he would drive home a punch line that caught everyone, including the interviewer and me, off guard.

Once a radio host, noticing that for an old man Dad was the picture of perfect health, inquired, "Mr. Todd, have you ever been bedridden?"

Dad took a heavy draw on his pipe and with a twinkle in his eye answered, "Oh yeah, many times — and, as the old-maid schoolteacher said, twice in a buggy."

The interviewer was so flabbergasted he could only sputter into the mike that it was time to take a commercial break.

Another time Dad was describing an early day frontier celebration in Sheridan where a stagecoach, filled with passengers, was to be attacked by marauding Indians. Crow Indians from Montana were to play the role of the hostile savages. Everyone was in on the prearranged act, of course, except the horses drawing the coach. Thus the Old West enactment took on more realism than what anyone had bargained for. When the horde of yelping Indians suddenly swept over the hill it frightened the horses who ran away with the stagecoach, pitching the passengers out onto the prairie, including the driver who suffered a broken leg — until the coach flipped over on its side, leaving wheels and other debris strewn along the way, as it bounced behind the stampeding horses.

Fred J. Todd (1883-1971) — Dad

Dad said the Indians whooped and hollered in laughter as they rolled on the ground, kicking up their heels and slapping each other on the back. Then they would throw themselves to the ground and do it all over again.

Then Dad added this line, "These Indians had never seen anything so funny since Custer's massacre."

Where did these one-liners come from? I never remembered him making spontaneous quips like this. But maybe I just wasn't listening for them. My wife, Shirley, coming from outside the Todd family, quickly picked up on these witticisms of Dad and was forever commenting on how the family seemed oblivious of them.

I never heard him tell an outright joke, but he was forever making social cracks or barbed comments that had a powerful ring of truth in them.

Describing Pat Nixon in the White House as he watched her on television one evening, he said, "Now there's a woman who looks colder than a cow's tit in the wintertime."

One reason these radio appearances came so easily for him was that there was absolutely no pretense of his being anything other than what he had always been. He was country through and through, a pioneer rancher on Piney Creek who lived out his life in a world of family, neighbors, and horses whom he knew and loved.

My children had an opportunity to catch a glimpse of this country world one summer afternoon when we were given permission by Jack and Peggy Cooksley, the people who purchased the Todd outfit from Dad, to climb "Lookout Mountain," located on our former ranch. This towering clinker hill consisted of molded red shale and rock deposited there millions of years ago from the gaseous fire and searing heat of underground coal beds. The whole countryside of northern Wyoming is littered with clinker hills like these.

But Lookout Mountain is unusual because on top of it are the stone fortifications of prehistoric people who once roamed and hunted in this part of the country. I wrote about these in Dad's book, which alerted the state archeological society to do an investigative study there. The agency confirmed that it was indeed a defensive fortification dating back 500 years before the advent of the horse on the North American plains — when Indian tribal units were smaller, probably no more than extended families. The men constructed circular stone walls on high pinnacles to protect their women and children from hostile attack. Defensive warriors had a tactical advantage here because the enemy had to scale the steep grade in order to make an offensive approach which made it easy for the defenders to pounce rocks down upon them.

Furthermore, the archeologists confirmed that, indeed, the peaked mountain was in a strategic location to function as an Indian lookout because the river valley below pivoted around it, providing an unobstructed view for many miles in all directions. The smaller circular enclosures of stone would have concealed no more than one or two men hiding up there scouting out the countryside for the movement of wild game and the distant approach of hostile forces. Hence, its name: Lookout Mountain.

As a child I played cowboys and Indians among these archeological ruins, and now I wanted my children to see them, too. It was a hot August afternoon as we began our climb. The kids were now adolescents and old enough to appreciate both the physical vigor of the climb and the historical significance of the site on top. We grabbed hold of the scrub brush as we pulled ourselves up along the steep slope. Shirley and I were amused as we watched the kids enjoying themselves, shouting back and forth to one another as they scaled the mountainside. Finally we reached the crest. The kids stood in awe at the summit, with the breeze blowing in their faces, looking down upon the world where I was born and raised, which had made its indelible mark upon my character and psyche.

For the first time they could see Piney Creek winding its way back and forth down through the narrow ranching valley. I pointed out the little river islands I had explored as a kid on homemade rafts, my island kingdom. I told them about my coming up into these hills when I was their age, concealing under my shirt a notebook and pencil with which to write down my secret thoughts and feelings. Far down below was the old family ranch house and bunkhouse, nestled in a bend of Piney Creek, surrounded by huge cottonwood trees, the barns and corrals nearly obscured from view. The swimming hole was still there. The irrigated fields and hay meadows were still there, worked now by expensive power machinery. No longer were there horses to be wrangled early in the morning, no milk cows to fetch on my little pony, Snake, who'd race as fast as his legs could run, his mane blowing in my face.

Up beyond the hills, off in the distance, rose the majestic snowcapped peaks of the Big Horn Mountains. The awesome beauty of it all took their breath away.

We explored the ancient Indian fortifications and wondered what must it have been like for prehistoric warriors to defend themselves, crouched down behind these stone walls for protection from an enemy who was out to kill or capture them all.

Before we began our descent, I remembered and shared with them my childhood dream that someday I would bring my own children up to this mountaintop, this secret place in my memory of memories, so that they could view with their own eyes the expansive countryside I had known as a child. That dream had come true on this day, and I rejoiced that they enjoyed it.

✧

Reunions had long been a tradition in our family. For some reason it became my job to organize them every ten years, and as the family expanded, so did the job of pulling everybody together.

The 1970 Todd reunion consisted of a buffet dinner in a Sheridan hotel, followed by a country dance. I asked Dad to prepare a few things to say to his family. He asked me to help him organize his thoughts. I didn't want to suggest the content of his remarks, but I showed him how to sketch some simple notes to remind him of what he wanted to say.

He sat at the head table with all seven of his offspring, seated in order of our birth into the family. His other descendants were scattered throughout the banquet room. I always served as master of ceremonies of these events, and after a few preliminary remarks I introduced Dad. Everyone in the room rose to their feet as he approached the podium. With great ease he leaned into the microphone and talked to us collectively as calmly as he would to any of us individually. His speech was full of wisdom. He said something briefly about each of his children and recalled the antics of our childhood. There was considerable humor and much laughter sprinkled throughout it all. He concluded by saying how proud he was of his family and pleased that we were all in good health. Somewhere I have a tape recording of the whole thing. It was marvelous.

We all gave him a standing ovation, which he acknowledged by shouting, "Let's dance."

Our little country band played old familiar dance tunes, and Dad danced with every female descendant in the family: daughters, daughters-in-law, granddaughters, great-granddaughters. He didn't miss a single one. If the youngsters were old enough to walk, they held onto his legs as he danced them around the room. If they were babies, he cradled them in his arms and waltzed them across the floor, bowing and whirling to the beat of the music. All the children, and there were many, loved the attention he gave them and cherished the fact that they all got to dance with the family patriarch.

It was his last Todd reunion.

That winter he fell on the ice and cracked his hip. It was only a hairline fracture, and the doctor advised that it would quickly mend if he simply stayed inside and walked with a cane. But he became impatient with this restriction and on a cold raw day in March took Queenie, his cream-colored German shepherd and inseparable companion, out to the horse pasture to visit his horses. He carried a sack of oats and sat down on a stump while the horses encircled him and took turns eating the feed from his hands. He had done this hundreds of times, and the ritual was well established.

A blizzard swept in. After stopping for coffee at my older brother Roger's ranch, he hastened out to the truck to get back to Sheridan before the storm worsened.

The next morning a snowplow operator was temporarily blinded by the blowing snow and decided to walk along a sharp curve in the highway to see exactly where he was. He spotted a truck down in a ravine, nearly obscured by the brush and drifting snow. He investigated and found them there. Queenie was alive and sheltering Dad's body.

I was asked to deliver the funeral oration. Thinking it inappropriate to eulogize my own father, I decided instead to honor all the pioneer people who settled the Piney Creek ranching valley. While Shirley and the kids slept, I sat up most of the night sketching out my thoughts on motel stationary.

The next day, March 20, 1971, in a packed funeral home, I read what I had written. I didn't say much in the funeral oration about Dad himself. I explained that I intended to pay tribute not to him in particular but rather to the whole generation of which he was a part, the pioneers who settled and worked the land, raised their families, and built communities like that affectionately known as Piney Creek.

Following the service, the funeral director asked permission to publish my "Tribute to the Pioneers" at his own expense on the condition that copies could be distributed to others and that one copy would remain on permanent display on a lectern at Champion's Funeral Home. Excerpts were later printed in the *Billings Gazette* and *Denver Post*. Red Fenwick, a famed columnist of the *Post*, wrote a wonderful article for the Sunday *Empire* magazine.

During a visit to Sheridan the following June, to settle Dad's estate, I drove out along the highway toward Piney Creek on a beautiful, warm afternoon and found the curve where the mishap occurred. The wild plum and chokecherry bushes were in full blossom, and the Wyoming hills were carpeted in shades of verdant green. I tramped down into the ravine. I could tell where the truck had slammed into the bank. The brush had been sheared away. Crushed bushes showed where the truck flipped over on its side after the final impact.

As I stood there, I was overwhelmed with a convulsing emotion, which later I identified as anger. Anger toward Dad. Why did he do this? The doctors had plainly told him the hairline crack of his hip was healing. All he needed to do was take it easy a little while longer. Had he followed their medical advice he surely would be alive, tending his garden as always before and hauling in armloads of fresh vegetables for supper that very evening.

Instead, on a miserable winter day, he decided to drive his battered old truck out to his horse pasture and risked everything. That decision cost him his life and took him from us. It was all so terribly unnecessary.

My older sister, Edna, reasoned with me that the last thing he would have remembered was feeding his horses as they gathered around him. All twenty of them. Handful by handful, they relished the oats he held out to them, licking his hands to savor the last slobbery taste. They would have followed him back to the truck, as they always did, where he would stroke their necks and talk gently to them before driving away.

"What final scene would you have chosen for him, if you were given the choice?" she asked.

"That one." I answered truthfully.

It was just that I missed him. Terribly. This dad I really didn't get to know as my father until after I had become an adult.

I am eternally grateful that in my last memory of him he is dancing with all his female descendants at the 1970 Todd reunion. That image will sustain me forever.

✧

There's a longstanding tradition among horse people that if a mare does not rise to her feet within a certain period of time following the birth of her colt, she'll never physically recover, or be "worth a damn," as the saying goes — and needs to be destroyed.

When I was growing up, such was the case with one of our horses, ol' Babe. (For some reason, we always addressed the draft horses on our ranch with the prefix *ol* in front of their names.) Ol' Babe was a sturdy Clydesdale who did all the heavy fieldwork on the Todd family ranch. Probably too old to be bearing another colt, she tried one more time, but her effort was in vain. The colt was stillborn high on the side of a hill, and Babe was so exhausted she couldn't move.

Dad tried to force the poor animal to her feet, but to no avail. He left her there and said if she didn't show some sign of physical recovery by the next evening, he would be compelled to put her out of her misery.

After supper the next day, Dad loaded a cream can of water and his rifle into the pickup and asked me to ride with him out into the Boxelder pasture to see how ol' Babe was doing.

I was about fourteen years old.

When we pulled up to the base of the precipitous hill, we could see that Babe hadn't moved at all. She remained stretched out, lying on her side.

"Well, she ain't gonna make it," Dad said regretfully. He lifted out the eight-gallon cream can of water and asked me to grab the other handle as we started tugging it up the steep incline. I carried an empty bucket in my right hand, he carried the rifle in his left hand, and the two of us carried the can of water, which was so heavy that we could barely climb the difficult grade.

"Poor thing. She's feverish and dying of thirst by now, lying up there in the hot sun all day," he said as we slipped and tugged at the can of water while struggling up the hill. "Too bad I have to finish her off like this. She's been a good ol' workhorse, and doesn't deserve to suffer."

I asked, "Why are we lugging this heavy can of water up to ol' Babe if you're gonna shoot her anyway?"

"Because she'll be expecting me to bring her some comfort. I don't want to disappoint her. She always did her best for me. Besides, I want her last memory to be my stroking and talking to her while she takes a cold drink of water."

When we finally reached her, she was more gone than Dad anticipated. But when Babe heard the water pouring from the cream can into the bucket, she raised her head and desperately let out with a low rumbling whinney.

"Yeah, Babe, we've got some water for you. You betcha' we have. You've been a good ol' girl, and here's a drink for you," he said compassionately. He sat down beside her and cradled her head up against his chest while she gulped water from the bucket pressed between his knees.

When she had her fill of water, nearly emptying the cream can, she laid her head back on the ground and closed her eyes while Dad gently stroked her neck and forehead and talked soothingly to her, trying to comfort the suffering mare. I looked away when the merciful shot rang out, echoing from the sandstone ridge down across the deep ravines below.

Silently we trudged back down the hillside.

"She was a good ol' workhorse," he said as we finally approached the pickup at the foot of the hill. "She put her shoulder to the load and pulled more than her share of the weight. Always gentle and dependable. Should have named her ol' Faithful."

He leaned against the pickup, "She was a good ol' mare who raised a dandy bunch of colts and was a good mother to 'em all — she really was. I'm gonna miss her."

The scent of the sagebrush seemed more pungent than ever in the darkened shadows of the cool evening air as he lit his pipe, the smoke swirling upward. Glancing back up the ridge to where her body lay, still and quiet, his voice cracked as he repeated, "Yep, ol' Babe was a good ol' friend. I'm gonna miss her."

This speech had the semblance of a eulogy. Dad praised ol' Babe progressively, first as a dependable worker, then as a good parent, and finally as a faithful friend he loved and would deeply miss. It was the closest thing to a spiritual experience that my father was capable of verbalizing at that time. Maybe it was his way of saying that we should offer gentle tenderness to all the injured and dying creatures of this earth. Maybe it was nothing more than a witnessing of my father's genuine grief and sadness, coupled with an expression of deep gratitude for all the horses that played such a prominent role in his life. Whatever it was, this memory would come back to sustain me when, many years later, as a clergyman, I often attended a dying person in a quiet, dimly lit hospital room.

"I want her last memory to be my stroking and talking to her while she takes a cold drink of water." Don't we all wish for a death as comforting and serene as this?

What Dad said of ol' Babe could be said of him and of his whole generation of pioneer ranching people. They put their shoulders to the load and pulled more than their share of the weight in creating and building a civilized community on the raw sagebrush hills.

Now that he was gone, I realized that he had been not only a good ol' dad to us all but also my beloved friend — and I would sorely miss him.

Chapter 14

T he spirit of the Old West comes alive every year in Cheyenne with the annual celebration of Cheyenne Frontier Days. The Frontier Days rodeo is billed as the "Daddy of 'em all," since it was in Cheyenne, in 1897, that the first cowboy rodeo was ever held. Sometimes I have referred to it as the annual disaster that rips through Cheyenne like an avenging tornado, leaving in its wake a city so exhausted that it takes us nearly a year to recover — just in time to get ready for the next one. It always take place the last full week in July, but it includes both weekends, which makes it a ten-day celebration.

As far as rodeos go, the professionals all agree that Frontier Days is the best of them all. But one rodeo, even the "Daddy of 'em all," does me well for a whole year. The four parades are marvelous, including, among other things, the largest collection of horse-drawn carriages in the world.

Being an amateur student of history, it didn't take me long to discover that St. Mark's Church, established in 1868, was in existence before the major Texan cattle drives came cross-country to the established railhead terminal in Cheyenne, beginning after 1869. The U.S. Cavalry, railroaders, and churchmen were there before the first cowboys ever swaggered down Main Street. Yet the myth would have us believe that the cowboys were there first and last and that everyone else was secondary.

Since St. Mark's is a national historical site, the "Pioneer Church of Wyoming," I decided we should become significantly involved in the Frontier Days celebration by staging an annual Frontier Days Worship Service.

Our first one was in 1966, my first summer in Cheyenne.

I thought it would be fun to dress in clothing commonly worn on the American frontier and sing some of the old hymns that everyone remembers and still loves to sing. Sioux Indians from South Dakota, who performed their traditional native dances during the rodeo performances, participated in our service — as many converted to the Episcopal faith during the missionary era. Even though the service would be held at St. Mark's Episcopal Church on the first Sunday of the ten-day rodeo event, it would be ecumenical

321

in nature. The natural antiquity of the old church, constructed in 1886, would lend itself perfectly as an appropriate setting for the first religious celebration within the context of the "Daddy of 'em all" blowout.

It immediately became a huge success.

The Frontier Days Worship Service evolved into a spectacular event containing many highly anticipated annual features: the visitation of Miss Frontier and her Lady-in-waiting; preaching by a Sioux Indian Episcopal priest; the governor of Wyoming as the guest lay reader; a guest performance of the "Wyomingaires," a vocal group consisting of more than thirty members from various Cheyenne barbershop quartets; choral singing of an old gospel hymn by an especially organized frontier choir; and guest appearances by rodeo clowns and performers.

It was a lot of fun — but it was always a lot of hard work.

Having a regular Sioux Indian guest preacher was quite a novelty. I became intimately acquainted with a number of the Sioux people. It was becoming increasingly difficult to contract skilled Sioux Indian dancers because those who held regular jobs on the reservation couldn't easily take a week's vacation to come to Cheyenne. Those who didn't work, the Indians said, often were not suitable because many of them couldn't perform the traditional native dances — or were in the grip of the acute alcoholism that plagues our Indian reservations.

One of the Indian chiefs was Norman Knox. His tribal Sioux name was Chief Iron Shell. He was a most likable fellow. I accompanied him one afternoon on a bus taking his Indian performers to exhibition dancing at the Veteran's Hospital in Cheyenne. The dancers were fully decked out in tribal regalia. They were to perform in the parking lot as hospital patients and personnel gathered in a semicircle to watch the performance.

A makeshift sound system had been arranged so Norman could announce and explain the dancing. I was standing beside him.

"First, we do Buffalo Dance," he said, stilting his English to make the most of his role as Indian commentator. "Watch the feet. They are like buffaloes stampeding across the sagebrush prairies."

The Indian singers cried "yi-yi-yi" as they pounded their traditional leather drums.

"Next we do Rain Dance," Norman announced. "Watch the feet. They are like the pitter-patter of rain across the sagebrush prairies."

"Yi-yi-yi" came the rhythmic sound of singers and drummer.

"Next we do War Dance. Watch the feet. They are like Indian warriors riding out to charge the cavalry." (Something, by the way, which Indians normally would not do. Their tactic was guerrilla warfare.)

Again, the "yi-yi-yi" as the dancers swirled in front of us.

Carefully watching their feet, as we were instructed to do, I turned to him standing directly beside me and said, "Norman, they're all dancing the same dance. The steps are identically the same."

Norman switched off his microphone, shrugged his shoulders and said, "Who cares? Makes good story for white man."

On the way back into town on the bus, I laughingly told Norman that even though history says that the Indians lost their war with the white man, the Indians probably won the battle of wits. Our collective guilt is so severe we're gullible for anything.

He laughed and said, "One of the best jokes we like to pull on a white man who comes into a gathering of Indians is to assign him an Indian name which is identifiable to us but unknown to the white man. Then we can spend hours laughing and talking about him, even gossiping about what we think his sex life might be like, and even get the white man to join in on the fun — without the white man ever guessing that we are talking about him."

We learned other things about Indian traditions.

For example, we learned about the extended family connections of all the Indian tribal people. Since the Sioux Indian priest and his family were invited to be guests in our home for the weekend of the Frontier Days Worship Service, we never knew how many would show up. The first count might be just the priest, his wife, and three children, let's say. We would make preparation to host the five of them. But when they knocked on the door there might well be twenty. As they drove across the reservation, heading out for Cheyenne, they would stop to visit relatives along the way. The uncles and aunts and cousins, on the spur of the moment, would decide to come along and join the party.

Sometimes Templeton House was filled to overflowing. Accommodating the Sioux didn't present itself as a problem for them, however, because they were perfectly willing to roll up in their Indian blankets and sleep on the floor, outside on the lawn, or anywhere. But it became a logistical problem for us.

Also, we learned that Indian parents are quite lax in their discipline of children and abhor the idea of corporal punishment. To watch a white missionary paddle his own children, for example, was blatantly offensive. Once we caught sight of two small Indian children crawling out the second-floor bedroom window of Templeton House and scaling the roof. A roof so steep that roofers used safety ropes. I was terrified because one slip and they could have fallen to their death on the brick patio below. I had to overrule the passivity of their parents and order them off the roof.

I don't intend to be critical of these our gracious Indian guests. I'm simply pointing out that a cultural difference still exists between us Americans of *native* and *immigrant* descent. On the other hand, I must say that there are many beautiful things about these Indian people which I highly respected. Once I complimented an Indian priest on the beautiful belt which he himself had so decoratively beaded. He immediately removed it and handed it to me as a gift. He seemed genuinely offended when I objected. I prize this gift but seldom wear it because I want it preserved within my family as a precious keepsake.

The night shows of the Frontier Days are big-time events. The most famous and highly paid country entertainers from Nashville are regular performers. Because of contractual agreements with the frontier committee, they are not allowed to make any other appearances while in the Cheyenne area. Nevertheless, I always invited them to our Frontier Days Worship Service. Many appeared incognito because they liked the idea of attending an old-fashioned frontier worship service in a historic church that was older than the rodeo itself.

One of the more interesting celebrity experiences I had was with Roy Rogers and Dale Evans. Their agent called on Sunday morning and asked if I would be willing to drive them to St. Mark's because they wanted to attend the frontier service and they needed transportation. My daughter Sheri sat on Roy's lap. Because of their public profession of faith in Jesus Christ, they both consented to say a few words as a personal witness during the standing-room-only service.

Later that afternoon, the agent called again and asked if I would be willing to make arrangements for Dale Evans to see a doctor because she had a foot injury that was giving her considerable discomfort. I arranged for our family physician and dear friend, Dr. Lundie Barlow, to make a personal call on her at Little America, a large motel complex on the outskirts of Cheyenne, where they were staying. He recommended that she consult an orthopedic specialist and made her an appointment. I drove her in my car and, for some reason, the specialist was late arriving at his office.

During this delay, Dale Evans told me about the death of their adopted son, Dusty. Apparently he volunteered for military service at a very young age and died after accepting the dare of his barrack pals to consume a whole bottle of hard liquor. He died from strangling on his own vomit. She described her agony at standing by his casket and seeing "this little boy in a soldier's uniform who more than anything else just wanted to be a grown-up man." Her grief was genuine. She was quite forceful in her theological interpretation of that tragic event.

"You can't tell me," she said, "that there is not a force of evil in this universe. Call it want you want: the 'given' of our human existence, or the evil one, or Satan; whatever, he's alive and well and in this universe — and you better believe it."

This from Dale Evans, the cowboy's sweetheart, who with her famous matinee-idol husband starred in more than eighty western movies.

That evening, we all had dinner at Little America.

The crowds got so large at our Frontier Days Worship Service that people began arriving an hour early just to get a seat. This meant that they simply sat in a hot sultry church with nothing to do but wait. I decided that we should provide good entertainment for them. We lucked out in scheduling the appearances of a country gospel singer in Denver by the name of Jerry Harrington. His Nashville background plus his conversion experience made him a delightful choice. So good was he that radio station KUUY extended the broadcast of our service to

In reception line following Frontier Worship can be seen toward the back in white hat Miss Frontier, Governor Ed Herschler, Harry Jumping Bull (grandson of Chief Sitting Bull), Father Broken Leg, and myself. Standing-room only crowds. Once featured in London Observer.

Introducing Father Noah Broken Leg as Indian preacher at our annual Frontier Days Worship Service. Beautiful Sioux Indian quilts on display. "Wyomingaires" male singing chorus directly behind me and "Frontier Choir" behind — neither very visible to camera. Sage and evergreen decorations on altar.

include his gospel concert as well. Now tourists crowded the church *another* hour earlier to find seating for his concert.

Each year attendance swelled and the whole thing became a little more unmanageable. Denver television stations would almost always include a visit to historic St. Mark's Church as part of their coverage of Frontier Days. Once it was written up in a London tabloid (*London Observer*) when two British journalists visited Cheyenne for the big rodeo. They wrote as much about our frontier service as they did about the rodeo itself, including a comment on me, the rector, trailing a microphone like a rock star.

One year the new young bishop of South Dakota, Craig Anderson, highly recommended an Indian priest I had never met. We made arrangements for his arrival in Cheyenne on Friday evening and invited him, as our honored guest, to attend the big Saturday morning parade, eat lunch with the Todds at Templeton House, and attend the afternoon rodeo. The rodeo grounds were within walking distance, only a few blocks from our home.

But he didn't show. I called him Saturday morning and he gave me assurances he would arrive by late afternoon. Still he didn't show. I phoned him again Saturday evening expressing deep concern, and he told me to quit worrying about him. He had been temporarily held up, he said, but would drive through the night and would surely be there in time to preach at the ten o'clock service.

"Please don't worry about me, Father Todd," he said. "I will be there with bells on my moccasins and a feather in my hair to fill your pulpit tomorrow morning. Trust me. Go to bed and sleep in peace."

The next morning, as usual, the church was absolutely packed. Jerry Harrington's country gospel concert was the best ever. Two radio stations were providing live broadcasts of the event, along with a Denver television crew. And — you guessed it — there was no guest Indian preacher in sight.

The only thing I could do was free-sail it. I introduced Harry Jumping Bull in the congregation, the great-grandson of Chief Sitting Bull, who shyly bowed to the crowd and sat down.

"Since Harry Jumping Bull has nothing to say," I said, "I am sorry to say that you'll have to listen to an impromptu sermon by me — Chief Talking Bull."

I tried to say something about the settling of the early West and how the Christian Church was here in Cheyenne, for example, before the coming of the cowboy. I briefly related the story of the rector of St. Mark's Church,

Dr. George C. Rafter, praying at the public hanging of the outlaw Tom Horn. I tried to convey that Hollywood's depiction of the Old West as dangerous and violent isn't entirely accurate, that many pioneer people of that era were busy raising their families and building wonderful communities with churches and schools.

My sermon was terrible, in spite of the fact that many said it was the best they had ever heard me preach — which, under the circumstances, wasn't much of a compliment.

My chagrin worsened during the week that followed when the radio personalities beat the absence of the Indian preacher into the ground with their usual diarrheic bantering, "By the way, if you see a lone Indian on his horse who seems to be lost, tell him he missed the Frontier Worship Service. Maybe we'll see him next year."

Listeners actually joined in the fun by calling up and reporting lost Indians here, there, and everywhere. One joker called the radio station and asked, "Has anyone thought to check the jail? There were a few cowboys and Indians rounded up by the sheriff last Saturday night, ya' know. Maybe he's been here all along and Fr. Todd just didn't know where to go looking for him."

I was embarrassed for the Indian people.

The Episcopal missionary priest at the Wind River Indian Reservation once told me that "Indian time" means "whenever they get there." He said, "The only thing that begins on time is an Indian Sun Dance — and that's when they all finally get there and they are ready to begin."

As the old saying goes, when something isn't fun any more, you better get out of it. The no-show of my Indian guest preacher by itself wasn't decisive. The cumulative hassle of putting on this extravaganza had simply worn me down. I announced that St. Mark's Church would no longer host the Frontier Days Worship Service.

In retrospect, the cancellation of this religious service, in conjunction with the largest rodeo in the world, was one of the worst mistakes I ever made as rector of St. Mark's. I should have enlisted the broader leadership base of the church, which would have eased the burden of responsibility falling directly upon me. There were critics within the church who complained it was too much of a dog-and-pony show, a public spectacle. But they were a minority. I should have listened instead to the vast majority who looked upon it as a marvelous way to reach out into the larger community with a public event that had religious and historic significance, a reminder that churches, too, can have fun — even within context of the biggest rodeo of the American West.

I share now the prayer I wrote and sincerely prayed at each celebration of our Frontier Days Worship Service. I find it quite revealing in terms of how I felt about the whole rodeo event.

O God, who reigns over work and play and our routine drudgeries
*   as well as our joyous celebrations*
We pray for the Festival of Cheyenne Frontier Days.
Help us to celebrate a fascinating sport
*   without cruelty to animals or people.*
Let not our applause be at the expense of pain or death to man or beast,
*   for surely our joy consists of something more than this.*
All creatures of the earth are thine, O Lord, and reverence for life
*   is our obligation of love to thee.*
Save us from violence on our streets,
*   from disorderly conduct which may damage life or property;*
*   from self-centered pleasure which hurts or harms another.*
Spare us from thinking "anything goes" in the name of pleasure
*   or profit.*
Help us to celebrate excitement with time to relax and enjoy
*   the companionship of family and friends;*
*   without being rude to strangers or gluttonous with ourselves.*
Hear our prayer, O Lord, over the din and confusion
*   of the teeming crowds.*
And may we listen for your still quiet voice of assurance
*   that even here, in a rodeo, you are always in our midst. Amen.*

✧

Tourists visit St. Mark's not just during Frontier Days but throughout the year because of its historic listing as the "Pioneer Church of Wyoming."

Cheyenne in the early winter of 1867 and 1868 was a typical frontier sprawl, a rip-roaring city of thousands of immigrant railroad workers, carpenters hastily building crude stores, livery stables, hotels, and homes. Originally a frontier "tent city," it came into existence along the banks of Crow Creek to serve as the winter quarters for construction crews of the Union Pacific Railroad.

Into this wild mix there came a newly ordained Episcopal priest from Philadelphia to begin his missionary work and build Wyoming's first permanent church structure. His name was the Reverend Joseph W. Cook. He arrived by train on January 14, 1868. He couldn't have picked a worse time, and it's a wonder he stayed, because Cheyenne had already established a national reputation as a den of iniquity.

Incredibly, in only eight months, he organized and built not only a church but also a school in Cheyenne. Thus, St. Mark's Episcopal Church became the first church edifice built in the future state of Wyoming.

Cook faithfully recorded his daily observations and activities in a personal diary. A published version had been around for sometime, but few paid serious attention to it. I found it fascinating, not only for its revelations of the spiritual temperament of a missionary priest in a frontier hellhole, but also for its descriptions of what the hellhole itself was like out on the American frontier. In 1981 I welcomed an invitation from the Wyoming State Museum to write a short stage play, a docudrama, featuring Joseph Cook as the only character on stage — telling his own story.

I decided early on that I would let the character speak with words lifted directly from the Cook diary. Nothing could have been more succinct and colorful than Cook's descriptive phrases: "This is a great center for all shades of roughs, and troops of lewd women, and bull-whackers. In the East, as a general thing, vice is obliged in some measure to keep somewhat in the dark, with a cloak of refinement thrown over it. But here all is open." Cook set out along the muddy streets on the heels of the devil to build a church and save sinners whether they liked it or not.

In his first entry he describes presenting a letter of introduction to a banker, who invites him to spend the night in his guest bedroom in back of the bank. After dinner, Cook discovers that six others had been invited to share the single bed — including the banker! (When the bank celebrated its centennial anniversary, I shared this little vignette at the banquet — to prove that frontier bankers had a unique way of cozying up to potential customers.)

Incidental to what he may have intended to record about his various ministerial activities was a first-person description of everyday life on the American frontier. He writes of burying the victims of gunslingers, as well as numerous young mothers and babies who died from the complications of childbirth. He attends the sick and the ravages of primitive frontier medicine. He writes of vigilante hangings — once three outlaws dangled from their ropes before his very eyes as he went to a church service. He describes life among the cavalrymen and officers at nearby Fort D.A. Russell (a military post established to provide protection for railroad workers from Indian attack) and their strained relationships with civic and railroad officials.

The reader learns that only the young and hearty lived on the raw American frontier; one old man, fifty-two years old, "simply died from old-age senility."

In spite of laboring faithfully in the vineyard of the Lord, with major accomplishments under terribly strenuous conditions, his most frequent comment was, "Alas, I'm doomed for disappointment." And when filled with despair, he wrote, "I feel like giving myself over to the Indians" — which is precisely what he did in 1870, leaving St. Mark's and spending the rest of his life as a missionary priest among the Sioux Indians near Yankton, South Dakota.

My original intention was to have only the character of Joseph Cook on stage for the one-act play. But I soon learned that the docudrama moved faster if I, as Cook's successor well over 100 years later at St. Mark's, remained on the side of the stage as a narrator to provide historical context and commentary on Cook's monologue.

I wrote it in such a way that Cook was oblivious to my presence on stage. When he sat down at a small table to write in his diary, I would then intervene with comments of my own. For example, after he notes that he was called to entertain some restless troops with a lecture on the honeybee, I quipped, "I really can't believe this. Really I can't. These are seasoned cavalry troopers, a thousand miles away from home, deprived of all feminine comforts and joys, demoralized and bored, and what does he do? He lectures them on the honeybee!"

Attired in a clergyman's outfit of the 1870s in front of state historical marker at St. Mark's Church, Cheyenne.

Cook, oblivious to my remarks, adjusts his gold-rimmed pincers and muses, "Of course, there will be those plebeians in any society whose lack of mental capacity and intellectual curiosity would dismiss a lecture on Natural History as an exercise in absurdity."

This line always brought the house down.

There wasn't much humor in what he wrote, at least, not intended. But at times I found it delightfully humorous. Like arriving late to a vestry meeting and discovering, to his horror, that his vestry was drunk. During his absence the vestry had produced a bottle of bourbon and were passing it round and round until they were all in a "maudlin" condition.

Although Cook's diary itself was an enormous help in capturing the essence of his thought and personality, writing the docudrama was more of a challenge than I had anticipated. I had tremendous help in the person of Patti Hunton Joder, who served as a volunteer theater advisor with the Wyoming State Museum, which sponsored the docudrama. Patti's sense of humor ran on the same weird track as mine. She assembled an auspicious crew of state historians and theater directors who critically reviewed every line that I had written. I was pleased that my historical interpretation of both Cook, the man, and the time frame in which he lived were considered accurate and well done.

While writing the play I worried about the poor actor who would have to memorize every word I had written. However, Dr. Richard Hart, an active member of the Wyoming State Art Gallery and the Wyoming State Historical Society, did a magnificent job in the lead role. He had Cook's character and cultural mannerisms down to perfection. Our premiere performance was at the governor's mansion to a packed house of legislators and their spouses — and from there we performed all over the state for the better part of a year.

✧

In addition to being recognized as a national historic site, St. Mark's has also become increasingly famous for its haunted bell tower.

It all started in the early 1970s, when Leslie Thomas, director of youth and Christian education, asked me to gather the church youth up in the bell tower during a Halloween party and tell them a ghost story. It sounded like a lot of fun. The bell tower was a perfect place for a ghost story. You entered from the basement level of the church and ascended a spiral staircase up to the first floor, which housed the pipe organ, then kept climbing higher and higher in the enclosed staircase until you finally stepped out into a pleasant room, completely finished with Gothic windows and hardwood flooring, high above the street below.

From this room, a wooden stairway with railing led directly above to the bell chamber, which held eleven enormous bells, known as the Richardson carillons, the largest of which weighs several tons. Actually, the carillons were mounted above a smaller interior cabin that housed the playing mechanism, with handles and levers corresponding to the scale of notes, which enabled a person to play the bells manually. Later, the bell clappers were electrified so that they could also be played from the organ inside the church.

All in all, it was a spooky and eerie place — especially on a dark Halloween night, when everyone was already predisposed to see ghoulish monsters at every turn.

"Make it extra good," Lesley told me, "so the kids will always remember it."

It didn't take much imagination to make it extra good.

Attired in my black cape and bieretta to help create an aura of spooky medievalism, I told them the historical legend about a Swedish stonemason who accidentally fell to his death during construction of the massive bell tower and whose body was buried in the thick stone walls by his partner, who feared arrest, perhaps for murder. I carefully explained how easy that feat would have been, because the walls were extra thick to support the enormous weight of the carillons above.

This was the legend. Nothing spectacular about that.

Then I told them the body most likely was laid on its side, to fit the natural curvature of the wall, and would therefore be no more than a few inches from the backs of the kids, who were sitting on the floor and leaning up against that very wall. "Of course, by now he's stoned, don't you think?" I cracked.

When you're in a darkened bell tower on Halloween, a story like that can send chills up your spine. Then I continued with the legend. The stonemasons who later completed construction of the tower were a superstitious lot who felt the bell tower was unquestionably haunted. So convinced were they of this, in fact, that they finished off the upper tower room to appease the ghost who dwelt there. Hence, to this day, it has always been called "the ghost's room." Perhaps this would explain why the big bells above occasionally would ring on their own — because the tower was haunted by a Swedish ghost. In fact, we were his welcomed — or unwelcomed?— guests simply because we were occupying the room specifically built for him.

By now even the bravest youngsters were clinging to one another as I invited them to ascend the final stairway up into the bell chamber itself to see if perhaps the tower ghost would make his presence known to us.

Most had never been up in that room in the daytime, let alone at night, which in itself would scare the socks off the bravest soul. Bats dart in and out above your head, and the massive bells hang there, suspended above like ships in the night. I flashed my spotlight around the premises and up toward the ceiling twenty feet above so they could see the motion of bats fluttering in and out of the belfry.

"If we're extra quiet," I said, "we may even hear voices of the night, which have been attributed to the ghost."

With a coded signal from my flashlight, some kid at the organ console far below would hit the key for the largest bell. Arc lightning would flash from the coil as it sucked the gigantic magnet down into itself, which in turn yanked the clapper up against the enormous C bell with an earth-shattering BONG that reverberated against your skull as if you'd been hit by a freight train. Everyone levitated twelve inches off the floor with blood-curdling screams of pure terror. Even those of us who were expecting it could not avoid the horrendous reflex action.

Another treasured annual tradition at St. Mark's was born.

Every Halloween I would tell the same story, to the same bunch of kids, in the same way — and every year more people began attending. Finally, I suggested to the youth group that since they were making it into a public event, they might as well charge admission.

And so they did. Touring the haunted bell tower of St. Mark's Church became a howling success. And it wasn't just for the young. Adults would host Vincent Price dinners in their homes and culminate the evening with a tour of the haunted tower. Men wearing tuxedos and women with long evening gowns made their quivering climb up the spiral staircase — now made all the more enchanting with the added feature of stereophonic sound. The sound of a rumbling pipe organ, played mostly on the foot pedals, added enough realism to the whole eerie experience that by the time the most adamant nonbeliever reached the ghost's private chamber, they were under the spell of the ghoulish host and susceptible to anything I might suggest. "By the time we reached the bell chamber," one observer confessed, "the brain-shattering clap of that bell was enough to make any mature adult choke on his Adam's apple and pee his britches."

Disney Studios could never have improved on the natural setup we had at St. Mark's for the annual tour of the haunted bell tower.

The kids had a ball with their biggest fund-raiser of the year. They didn't believe in the presence of ghosts any more than I did. But some of the adults in the church did — and they halted the annual event.

This was after the story had generated enough interest that it made the *National Enquirer* and all the regional papers. A local radio station hired a professional psychic from Denver, Lou Wright, to join up with a disc jockey for an all-night broadcast from the tower on Halloween night.

I considered it only a joke. But they didn't. After locking them into the tower for their night of broadcasting, I received an emergency call at home from the radio station to come rescue them. They reported that the big C bell above them rang spontaneously on its own and that a haunted voice cautioned them to leave. By the time I arrived at the church, a crowd of several hundred had gathered along with the police, because the whole thing was broadcast live.

Up in the ghost's room, I found Lou Wright and the radio announcer prostrate on the floor, visibly shaken with faces ashen gray. Both were overcome with their own self-induced hysteria. Lou described the appearance of an older gentleman who limped with a cane, with a white beard, who asked them kindly to leave. It was a perfect description of Dr. George C. Rafter, rector of the pioneer church in 1886 at the time it was built. But Lou would have known nothing about Dr. Rafter. Had she done some research on the church's past, then concocted the story to gain herself a little publicity? Or . . . ?

I learned from all of this.

I learned that people desperately need to believe in ghosts. Additionally, I learned that they desperately need to believe that all ghosts are evil and satanic. Therefore, if the bell tower was haunted, this meant it would require religious exorcism to remove the demons. But I'll admit that I added to the fervor with a spontaneous quip out on the street, during a live television interview: "I refuse to believe in ghosts. That's why I won't come down here at night and be spooked by something I don't believe in."

I thought the inherent contradiction was obvious. And I couldn't take it seriously when others took so seriously what I had said in jest.

And in a sense, I guess I do believe in ghosts. I believe in the Holy Ghost, which today we usually call the Holy Spirit. I believe there are friendly and evil spirits that profoundly influence our lives. There are many friendly spirits in St. Mark's from people who lived in the past. I feel surrounded by their presence all the time. In Episcopal circles, we call it Communion of the Saints.

Sometimes they can be unfriendly, too. In fact, I was warned about the unfriendly spirits that haunted St. Mark's back in 1965, when I was advised not to go there as its new rector. And I've let it be known that if anyone ever rips out the historic sanctuary and Chancel of St. Mark's Church in order to modernize it, thus destroying the original craftsmanship exhibited there, I personally will come back to haunt the devil out of the person who tries it.

To make a long story short, after demonstrating more maturity than many of the adults at St. Mark's, the youth finally won their right to once again conduct their Halloween tours of the haunted bell tower, as a fundraiser. The limit was 600 people per night. I refused to do it more than one evening per year, because with groups of thirty people at a time, which is all that the ghost's room could accommodate, I had to tell that complete fifteen-minute story twenty consecutive times. I would become too cold and hoarse to continue, in spite of their hoisting hot drinks up to me. In the meantime, the church youth entertained the waiting crowds in the parish hall by selling hot cider and doughnuts. It was a profitable evening for them.

Disney Studios never tried to duplicate it. But a national television program twice offered to pay my airfare to Los Angeles so that I could tell the story of St. Mark's haunted tower to a network audience. I told them I would, providing they allowed me to raise the question as to why people so desperately wanted to believe in ghosts.

They declined my offer.

✧

I once recruited memorial funds to have the carillons activated electronically from a player belt, like a player piano, to play the Westminster chimes from a computerized clock. Then, periodically during the day it would play a series of hymns — even old western classics during Frontier Days. They sounded beautiful.

The fund-raising occurred on a flight out of Denver when my seat-mate, a Standard Oil executive, told me he had Cheyenne connections. When our flight landed in Chicago he committed the necessary funding for refurbishing the Richardson carillons in memory of his parents Herbert and Celo Towle.

But we had a problem. The steady frequent use of the bells for the hour chimes and playing hymns began burning out the hand-wound DC coils, which were irreplaceable, and we had to discontinue their use.

We could have modernized the playing mechanism with new AC-driven coils but this would have cost nearly $10,000 which I felt was exorbitant when the church had more pressing needs — and I was unable to generate separate memorial funding.

However, hidden away up in that bell chamber is the first church bell that was ever used in the state of Wyoming. It was a gift from the home church of the Reverend Joseph W. Cook in Philadelphia. Cast right into the bell is the following inscription :

The Mountains and Hills shall break forth into singing.
From St. Mark's, Philadelphia, to St. Mark's,
Cheyenne, Wyoming Territory — 1872

It hangs up there in that bell chamber — silent and forgotten. It is not a part of the set of eleven carillons mounted beside it, which can be played from the organ console.

I was determined that this historic bell should be lifted out of its forlorn retirement, hidden from view and use in the bell chamber, and put on per-

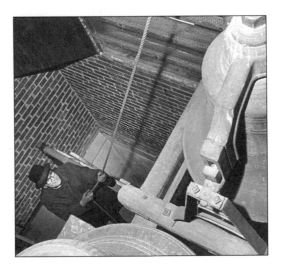

I'm in the famous "haunted bell tower," ringing the first church bell in the state of Wyoming. Inscription on bell says it was a gift of St. Mark's, Philadelphia, to St. Mark's of Wyoming territory in 1872. It now sits abandoned in belfry and is never rung. Beside it is the massive set of eleven carillons (corner is seen to the lower left) which can be beautifully played from the organ console.

manent historic display down in a newly created front courtyard of the church facing Nineteenth Street. But its joyful sound, intended to be rung out over the Wyoming mountains and hills, had been silenced for over a century of neglect and concealed abandonment.

Twice I had architectural drawings for this anticipated project and both times it had to be canceled for lack of funding.

A costly project like this can be achieved only with the cultivation and generation of special funding apart from the normal operating budget of the church. It would make a fantastic memorial. Had I delayed my early retirement from St. Mark's in 1992 — I'm convinced that I could have recruited the necessary funding to have financed it.

I still maintain that St. Mark's has a solemn obligation to someday put this historic first church bell in the state of Wyoming on public display so that it can be admired and its joyful sound heard once again.

✧

We must always remember that the church is rooted in Christ but lives in the world. Back in 1972, the whole social fabric of America was in convulsive turmoil with a series of "defining events." The civil rights movement had taken center stage of our political attention. The Vietnam War was tearing at the soul of America's conscience. The hippie movement was as revolting to the older generation as it was attractive to the college-age generation.

The churches of America could not escape involvement. The world around us was changing so rapidly that many of us were dazed and losing touch — not only with the outside world, but also with the core of our innermost being. So the social scientists were telling us.

Hence the appearance of a new phenomenon on the American scene: sensitivity training, sometimes called T-groups, or encounter groups.

We were told that we needed to become more sensitive to each other and to ourselves in a way we never had before. Clergy were probably not the most guilty of losing touch with reality, but we were guilty enough that we were encouraged to enroll immediately in sensitivity training.

A group of clergy met in a motel room stripped barren of all furniture. We had only pillows on the floor. First thing in the morning we did a music exercise, kicking off our shoes and slowly dancing, blindfolded, to the slow and rhythmic beat of the sensuous music. Next we had to roll around on the floor with our pillows, because you can't sit too long in the lotus position and still meditate. Then we had to confront one another by open expression of feelings we had never expressed before to another person. Only by doing these things, we were told, could we ever strip away the outer layers of our protective shells that separated us not only from one another but also from our innermost selves.

For three days and three nights, long into the early morning hours, we endured the ordeal of sensitivity training.

When we were finished, I didn't know if we had been sensitized, anesthetized, or brutalized. Some said we were brainwashed. But I couldn't be my old self again. The dignified reserve of an Anglican cleric, which I had tried so desperately to cultivate, was definitely stripped away. If I couldn't get in there and swing with my real thoughts and feelings — "let it all hang out," as the old saying went — I was forever a loser.

Somehow I retained my sanity through it all, I think. But there were some clergy who didn't. They went berserk, it seemed, dropped out of church and society or joined a hippie compound, never to be seen again.

In May 1972 Shirley and I attended a sensitivity training session for couples just outside Cody, Wyoming. It was facilitated by Bill and Beth Larson. Bill was rector of Christ Episcopal Church in Cody. Both were skilled facilitators, I might add.

The first thing we were to do was to pair off with someone other than our spouse, out in the woods, and share a secret about ourselves that we had never told anyone before. Most of us were cautious, admitting nothing more serious than something like, "A secret I've never told anyone before is that I don't like creamed broccoli." That evening we were to share with our spouses this newly revealed secret of our lives. And the next morning we were to report to the larger group how this exercise of self-revelation and self-discovery had gone.

All hell broke out!

One husband reported that his wife told him that she had gone into the woods and had sex with the man she was paired off with and had just met the previous morning. The husband blew his cork. The rest of us were caught in the worst social nightmare you could possibly imagine. We were witnessing a scene right out of *Who's Afraid of Virginia Woolf* — but instead of it being played out safely on stage or screen, this one was exploding for real, right in front of our faces.

The husband tore himself from the room, slamming the door twice, and then returned once more to scream to his wife that he was suing not only for divorce but also for custody of the kids — and that all of us in the room would be subpoenaed as witnesses to her public confession of promiscuous adultery.

I realized right then that this was more "sensitivity training" than I had originally bargained for and wanted immediately out. But I was not to be taken off the hook quite so easily.

After the irate husband stormed up the hillside to their cabin to pack his suitcase and leave the grounds, his wife began sobbing into her handkerchief and crying, "Is this what I get for being honest?"

Beth Larson, one of the most dignified and reserved clergyman's wives I've known, had the perfect answer: "It wasn't your honesty that's got you in trouble, Cindy. It was your fucking around in the woods!"

I hate that word. I have never used that word because it is so degrading to God's beautiful gift of human sexuality. But here was one time when I thought the word was used appropriately.

Bill and Beth Larson used their enormous facilitating skill to redeem the situation as best they could, not only for Cindy and her husband but also for the errant husband who was a willing partner in the sordid affair and his shaken wife. Obviously, there was much work that both couples needed to do to save their troubled marriages. The rest of us learned something about ourselves and our marriages, too.

But I wasn't convinced that I wanted any more sensitivity training.

I returned from that experience with something more than increased emotional sensitivity, however. My body had become physically sensitive to something I had never felt before. Within a week or ten days, what I thought were symptoms of the flu had become something much more intense. When one leg became highly inflamed with streaks of blue and red discoloration and stabbing throbs of pain. I finally consented to see my doctor.

He took only one glance to confirm his diagnosis. Behind my knee, invisible to my physical inspection, was the tell-tale purple circle, about the size of a silver dollar, of an embedded wood tick. I had Colorado tick fever! While at the sensitivity group in Cody we were warned about an infestation of ticks. But this one was behind the bend of the knee, and I missed it.

I became so ill that I was hospitalized for the first time in my life. After I went several days without eating or moving in my bed but simply lying perfectly still, the agony of a migraine attack compounding the dreadful tick infection, my doctor called in a neurologist. He undertook a complicated series of intensive examinations and concluded that the headaches were triggered by stress. It was time that I attempt to diminish the effects of stress. For the first time in my life, I was placed on a regular schedule of mixed medication: Valium three times a day, a sleeping sedative at night, and a mild anti depressant twice a day.

"The purpose of this regimen is to completely break the cycle of whatever it is that's triggering the migraines," the specialist advised.

I knew nothing about pharmaceutical drugs or their interaction with one another. Doctors, I've learned since, didn't know all that much about them at that time either. I hated the regimen but was determined, at least, to cooperate and see what would happen. After all, he was the doctor and I was the patient. I never exceeded the prescribed medications and began to feel better. But I didn't like the way I was feeling better.

Dr. Barlow, inquiring about my work schedule at the church, ordered me to take one day off a week. "Furthermore," he said, "I want you to announce in your church newsletter that you are taking Monday completely off."

It was good advice which I should have followed.

I did quit going to the church Monday in order to break the seven-day working cycle. But I didn't run his recommended announcement in the church newsletter because I felt it would be poorly received. And I allowed three meetings a month to remain scheduled on Monday evenings, including the vestry on the second Monday, which meant that I was only free to leave town, or completely get away, once a month.

I know now that I should have followed Dr. Barlow's advice to the letter. But clergy wellness was not something we knew anything about back then. I would soon suffer the consequences.

✧

In 1972 Shirley's folks were divorced. It didn't come as a surprise because we in the family knew the marriage was troubled. Pops, as he was affectionately known to my children, was a Baptist fundamentalist preacher of tremendous faith. No one could have had greater faith in the "precious blood of Jesus," a phrase he constantly used, than did he. But his was a faith that brought him no joy. Mommie Pops, the kids' pet name for Shirley's mother, wanted more spunk out of life than what the marriage could provide. Whatever the reason, they were divorced. Pops would die in 1989, a bitter and broken man. Mommie Pops would marry Jack Mariani, a man of considerable wealth in the San Jose area whose family prospered from successful walnut ranching and a multitude of other business interests.

The divorce was a source of considerable pain to Shirley. But to have insisted that her parents remain locked in an unhappy marriage would have been cruel to both of them.

That June our family took a once-in-a-lifetime vacation to Hawaii. We had been saving our money for such a trip for quite some time. With a little help from a small inheritance from Dad's estate, we were finally able to pull it off.

The timing couldn't have been more perfect for the kids. Lori was now seventeen, Barry fifteen, and Sheri twelve. They were handsome young people, full of life and laughter, who could spend hours swimming and playing in the warm ocean water along the sandy beaches of Hawaii. We were there for two weeks, which gave us plenty of time to take it all in, from island to island. It was a great family vacation.

The trip was extra special because we traveled to Hawaii on an ocean liner. It was our first and only experience on the open sea. None of us was seasick, though we fully expected to be. It was the usual routine on a cruise ship: lavish meals and scrumptious midnight snacks, hula lessons, dance contests, cocktail parties for the adults, teenage parties for the young, sunning and swimming in the pool during the day, shuffleboard on deck, movies in the theater, nightclub entertainment in the ballroom — and dancing all afternoon and every night. It was a good thing the voyage was only five days, because we needed to get ashore to rest up and thin down.

On board, we made the acquaintance of a handsome purser officer who cut quite a dashing figure in his white and gold uniform on the dance floor. Somehow he learned that I was an Episcopal priest and admitted to me that he had been an Anglican monk who fled the monastery in search of something more exciting. But he confessed that he wasn't finding what he wanted there either. He loved dancing with beautiful women too much to again take the vow of celibacy, yet wanted to serve the Lord in some significant way. He was thinking about becoming a postulant for holy orders and studying for the Episcopal priesthood. We had many long talks. When we arrived at our beach house in Honolulu, a beautiful display of flowers graced the coffee table with a note of thanks from him.

Everything on the ship was done with a Hawaiian theme. The decorations, the grass skirts of the ship hostesses, the Polynesian drinks and food, the dances, and the music. I would step outside onto the deck during the late evening hours by myself. Overhead were the brilliant stars of the Polynesian night. Dark shadows danced out across the black sea. The big ship would pitch and roll as the ocean waves pounded, splashed, and churned past its sides far below. While standing out there, all alone, I could hear the haunting strains of "Aloha" coming from the Hawaiian guitars inside. Sadness welled up within me, because I sensed this would be the last vacation my family would ever take together. The children were getting older now, and summer jobs would not make it possible to take extended vacations like this in the future. But this happens to every growing family. This was not the source of the sadness I felt.

The overwhelming sadness I identified deep within was the realization that my marriage was in deep trouble, that Shirley and I probably would never take another vacation together again. The Hawaiian farewell of "Aloha" meant farewell to twenty years of marriage. I couldn't articulate the foreboding feelings I had, but they were real, and waves of melancholy washed over me. I would return to the merriment inside the ship trying to shake the sadness I felt. It worked, temporarily — only to return when I was alone with my thoughts again.

It's fortunate that I had no inkling of the pain that was yet to come — or I would have jumped overboard.

✧

St. Mark's launched a tremendously successful summer camp program for the young people of our church. The diocese inherited an abandoned cow camp in the Medicine Bow Mountains between Wheatland and Douglas. With a lot of volunteer labor it was gradually expanded and improved into a church facility known as the HR Ranch Camp. It was located in a beautiful setting of rugged mountains, though the facilities were a little on the primitive side.

St. Mark's rented the whole facility for one full week in August. All the youth of our parish, from the second grade through high school, attended the camp together. (Normally denominational church camps are graded, with only certain age groups attending at any one time.) These integrated camps enabled the younger children to become well acquainted with the teenagers, whom they came to idolize, and the teenagers were specifically instructed to mingle and work with the smaller ones. The interaction worked beautifully, and the positive relationships continued throughout the rest of the year back in Cheyenne.

It was wonderful to watch the younger children mature through the years and gradually assume leadership roles. Contrary to common assumption, we discovered, for example, that the teenagers enjoyed taking the younger ones on climbing hikes along the rocky ridges because they remembered all too well how scary it was for them as children to take these same hikes.

Every morning we would all hike down along a narrow trail to a waterfall among huge granite boulders and there celebrate a free-form eucharist. The kids posted a sign on a tree beside the pool: "Don't walk on the water."

In the middle of the hot afternoon we'd go for a swim in the same pool just below the waterfall. I called it the "Death and Resurrection" pool because the only way you could enter the icy cold water was to dive into it. There was no way you could coax yourself into a gradual descent. When you plunged into its icy depth, rigor mortis would take immediate hold. When you reached the sandy beach on the other side, maybe thirty feet away, and discovered that you could still scramble your frozen self to your feet, it was a resurrection.

You measure any camping program not only on the merits of whether it generally benefits the group as a whole but also on whether it deeply influences any one child in particular. Such was the case with my son, Barry.

Barry, like many youngsters, struggled with his identity during his early teens. Like many others, he was having problems that could have become more serious. He once came under the influence of an older kid in our area of town who was seriously troubled, and Barry found himself in difficulty over an incident of vandalism. His being a "preacher's kid" probably didn't help either.

When he was sixteen, Barry finally found himself to be among the older teenagers at our church camp, which meant that he inherited responsibilities of leadership he had not known before. He discovered that earning the respect and adoration of the younger children brought tremendous personal pride and emotional satisfaction. He became an enthusiastic camp leader and role model among all the younger campers. Within one week I proudly witnessed the radical and beautiful transformation of a self-centered and somewhat rebellious kid into an outgoing, responsible young man.

Barry discovered, to his own surprise, how rewarding it was to carry the younger children on his shoulders up a steep and rocky mountain incline, to comfort a little girl who bruised her leg, to cheer up a homesick lad, or to fight off a swarm of wasps while others ran to safety.

One doesn't often have an opportunity to witness the transformation of a boy through the rite of passage into young manhood within only a week's period of time — but I did. I rejoiced that Barry was my son, and I've been proud of him ever since.

✧

Shirley and I were divorced in August 1973. We sought professional counseling, as all couples should when they find themselves in a troubled marriage. The counseling was revealing and helpful. But after a year of intensive individual, couples, and group therapy, which greatly improved our verbal communication and interpersonal relationship, it became increasingly apparent that the marriage was over.

Shirley was a wonderful person, a kind human being, a marvelous mother, and a talented musician who played violin with the Cheyenne Symphony. We celebrated many great times together. We shared much happiness and much sorrow. Together we laughed and cried and dreamed of a better tomorrow. Then what went wrong?

The older I become, the more convinced I am that I will never know.

The fact that she had lived all her life in the glare of a church parsonage probably had a lot to do with it. One of her earliest memories, when she was two years old, was being held up to a microphone while singing "Jesus Loves Me" in front of a thousand spectators at a huge evangelistic crusade. The first part of her life was spent in a Baptist parsonage, the second part in an Episcopal rectory. A lifetime in a fishbowl is not suitable for everyone.

In my own pastoral counseling I've always said to couples having marital difficulties that it does no good to focus on who is the most to blame. The odds are about even, and they switch back and forth every other day.

Valor would prompt me to shoulder the greater burden of blame for our failure if this would ease anyone's conscience. If only I had spent more quality time at home with my wife and family. If only I had been more patient, more communicative, more gentle, more sensitive, and more forgiving. If only I had been more mature and more Christian. If only I had been more of everything that I was not at that time — perhaps the marriage could have been saved. But I wasn't more of everything that I wasn't — and so the marriage failed.

Shirley moved out of Templeton House, the church-owned rectory, and I didn't do well managing a home and a family by myself. Although I remembered how to cook from my bachelor days, I couldn't cook now because I couldn't eat. And I couldn't eat because I had become so depressed that even the smell of a hamburger frying on the grill was nauseating to me. The kids managed as best they could and became fairly good cooks on their own. I would join them at the kitchen table while they ate their simple meals. But usually I ate nothing at all. Maybe I'd drink a Coke.

Obviously, this rite of starvation could not go on much longer.

I threw myself more diligently into my church work because this offered me the only relief I had from the incredible inner pain I was feeling. I was quickly losing weight. I went to the neurologist and protested that the medications he was prescribing might be impairing my judgment. He cautioned me that now, more than ever, I needed to stay on course with the long-range treatment plan he had originally devised.

When my weight loss became alarming even to me, I went to my personal physician and family friend, Dr. Lundie Barlow. He gave me a thorough examination and could find nothing physically wrong. Professional ethics among physcans required him to defer judgment on the medications prescribed by my neurologist.

"I can find nothing wrong with you, Gene, physically. But make no mistake about it, what's happening to you is serious. If we don't get this episode turned around, you'll die."

His stark prognosis startled even me. But how was I to turn the situation around?

Pastoral advice to people in deep trouble is to pray. I followed my own advice and prayed every morning at the altar of St. Mark's Church. While the staff went out to lunch, I would spend the noon hour praying. I would sit in the chancel of the darkened church in the evening and pray harder. At home that night, I would pray before I went to sleep. When I couldn't sleep, I would pray even more.

I prayed and prayed — and still I was dying.

One hot August afternoon I found myself back at the former Todd ranch on Piney Creek. Something had brought me to Sheridan, I don't even remember what. But I drove out to the old ranch and started climbing Lookout Mountain, familiar to my childhood. The heat was unbearable. I pulled off my shirt and tied it around my waist while I continued my ascent up the steep and slippery slope.

As I grabbed hold of the sagebrush above me to pull myself higher, I heard voices in the hot desert wind. I stopped and looked around. I was alone. Where were the voices coming from? I went back to my climbing and heard the voices again. It must be the cry of a bird or a wild animal off in the distance. I would ignore the sounds as I went back to climbing. But they persisted. Once more I stopped and really listened — and this time I recognized what they were.

They were the voices of Lori, Barry, and Sheri, carried by the wind from out of the past and reverberating against the side of the rocky peak — sounds of shouting and laughter from another hot August afternoon, a few years earlier, when they had climbed Lookout Mountain with me. There was no mistake about it. Call it a hallucination, call it a psychological flashback, call it what you will — I heard the voices of my children, as if reminding me that I was not alone.

But I was alone — and deep within me was a constant recurring theme, repeating itself over and over again: *You're gonna die. You're gonna die. You're gonna die.*

Then it occurred to me why I was there, out here on the ranch of my childhood. As a child, I learned how animals often would go off alone to some familiar and isolated place among these hills to die. That's why I was there.

When I finally approached the first in a series of clinker peaks near the summit, I walked over to the ancient archeological ruins but was stopped by the terrifying buzz of rattlesnakes hiding inside the stone fortification walls. I saw only two, coiled and ready to strike, but heard the rattle of many others. Chills raced up and down my spine. I slowly backed away and withdrew.

Then I climbed a little higher and ascended the grand summit, looking down on the panoramic sweep of Piney Creek valley, the rising foothills, and the looming majesty of the Big Horn Mountains beyond. It was as beautiful as ever.

While sitting on the highest pile of rocks I could find, I saw storm clouds gathering in the distance. It was interesting to watch their formation. Gradually a threatening thunderhead billowed ever higher into the sky and began moving my way. Soon it was directly overhead, enveloping the peak and obscuring my view of the valley below. The wind whipped up. Suddenly, a bolt of lightning struck only a few yards away, splattering the clinker shale as if a projectile had struck. Instantaneously, a deafening crack of thunder exploded upward into the heavens, its roar reverberating into the valley below. The lightning struck again, and again. There was no escaping its fury. I was sitting on the highest pinnacle, the spot most likely to draw the attack. I had no inclination to throw myself down upon the ground for protection. There was no place to hide. Besides, I really didn't want to hide — because I was there to die.

Then the heavens opened up, and it poured. There was nothing I could do but sit there, bare-chested, while the drenching downpour dumped itself down upon me. Sometimes the cascading sheets of water came on so furiously that I could scarcely catch my breath.

The storm passed.

I didn't move from my rock. I sat there motionless. The hot sun came out again and began drying the drenched clothes that clung to my body.

Strangely, I felt washed and cleansed—as if I had been baptized anew by God Himself.

An eagle appeared from out of nowhere, circling over my head, then swooped down into the valley below, then soared back up to my lofty perch, sweeping closer this time to get a better look at me, this intruder invading his private world of craggy heights. Then he rode the currents of still air and drifted downward over the hayfields and meadows.

I watched him and wondered what must it be like to be free and feel the wind beneath your wings as you sail through life.

Evening came. I watched the deer as they came out from their protective covering along the creek bed, their fawns frolicking beside them, as the shadows from the setting sun crept out across the field. Darkness descended. It was time for me to go.

But I had one final talk with the Lord.

"If you brought me here to die, then how come the lightning missed?"

There was no answer. But out of my biblical past came the ancient story of Elijah:

Go and stand on the mount before the Lord, for the Lord was passing by. A great and strong wind came rending mountains and shattering rocks before him. But the Lord was not in the wind. After the wind there was an earthquake. But the Lord was not in the earthquake. And after the earthquake a mighty fire. But the Lord was not in the fire. And after the fire . . . a low murmuring sound (I Kings 19:11-12).

As I made my way down off Lookout Mountain in the darkness of the evening, there was indeed a low murmuring sound. Earlier in the day, when I climbed the mountain, the low repetitive murmuring sound had been: *You're gonna die. You're gonna die. You're gonna die.*

But now there was a new murmuring sound — repetitive, and coming from deep within: *You're gonna live. You're gonna live. You're gonna live.*

✧

The first thing I did upon coming back from the old Todd ranch was flush down the toilet all the medications prescribed by the neurologist. I did this of my own volition, and not in consultation with either of my two doctors. This was a mistake. To attempt a sudden withdrawal from any kind of prolonged regimen of medication can be dangerous and potentially fatal.

To this day, I have never accepted a doctor's prescription for tranquilizers, sleeping pills, or anti depressants. Such miracle cures were commonly prescribed by the most competent physicians back in the 1960s and 1970s, and they proved helpful to millions of sufferers. But this was before the world knew about the side effects that often followed.

However, I retained my prescription for aspirin #3, a pain analgesic, to subdue the debilitating effect of migraine headaches.

A public health nurse and her three daughters moved into a new home directly behind Templeton House. She had recently divorced her husband, an Air Force doctor at Warren Air Force Base. Rosemary Adamson was also a devout Episcopalian who faithfully attended St. Mark's Church.

Rosemary often invited the kids and me to her house for dinner. They were hungry for good gourmet cooking, but I wasn't hungry for anything that tasted like food. She literally taught me how to eat and enjoy food again, almost as if I were a child. She would say, "Now this broiled chicken breast and baked tomato are good for you. Your body needs these nutrients. Now eat, at least, one half of each before you leave the table."

Gradually, my appetite returned. My depression subsided. I was beginning to feel healthy again. I had returned to the land of the living. Something else occurred which I thought would never happen.

I felt myself falling in love again.

Even though I had been divorced for over a year and was living the miserable existence of a single parent — still, I was in no position to pursue the insanity of another romance. A second marriage seemed completely out of the question.

I needed a little time to clear my confusion so that clarity of mind took precedence over the uncertainty of emotion — so that, maybe, the will of God would ultimately prevail.

Chapter 15

I never considered myself a social activist. Social activism requires personality traits that were never my own. I have never had the courage to be out on the cutting edge of public controversy, to march in the streets for a cause not cherished by the majority, to stand up in front of a hostile audience and shout my convictions. The fact that I was considered a social activist during my tenure at St. Mark's always came as a shock to me.

Before I retired from St. Mark's in 1992, I read an interesting article in a church publication. It stated that the period between 1965 and 1990 represented the most controversial years in the history of American Anglicanism — even more divisive than the bitter social upheavals surrounding the Revolutionary and Civil Wars. The 1960s, 1970s, and 1980s witnessed the civil rights movement, the Vietnam War, the battle over abortion, the rise of the drug culture, the environmental movement, and other highly charged issues. The Episcopal Church was undeniably caught up in these enormous social struggles. As if this external stress wasn't enough to play havoc in the lives of Episcopalians, the Episcopal Church grappled with numerous internal debates during the same time frame: liturgical renewal, prayer book and hymnal revision, issues of human sexuality and ordination of women.

Little wonder that droves of lay people in the 1960s and 1970s left the Episcopal Church, like most other major denominational bodies, simply because there were too many gut-wrenching changes with which to contend. People can tolerate only so much change before they go either into shocked paralysis or open rebellion.

The article went on to say that the only reason clergy were able to survive this frightful twenty-five-year time frame was that they generally would change parishes every five years or so. They never had to fight more than one battle in any one parish at a time. Woe to one who tried to survive more than one scathing battle in a parish.

Woe to me!

My service at St. Mark's stretched from 1965 to 1992. Every external and internal battle that would prove so divisive within the Episcopal Church arose at St. Mark's during my twenty-seven-year tenure. And we fought every battle. I would like to say that all these changes came and went without a ripple of discontent at St. Mark's. But such was not the case. The people of Cheyenne, the capital city of Wyoming, were too politically and socially involved in our America to have watched passively from the sidelines.

My first crisis at St. Mark's involved a conflict between the older and younger generation, and it occurred the first weekend after I had been installed as rector. On Saturday morning I had a telephone call from a frantic altar guild director telling me about a confrontation in the youth choir. She explained, "A certain young lady here refuses to wear the appropriate head covering which a female must wear in church, whether it be choir practice on Saturday or worship services on Sunday. We have given her the little lace beanie to wear, like we're all wearing, and she refuses to put it on. You are the new rector and you must come down here at once and resolve the situation, or your authority as the new rector will be forever compromised!"

Meaning, of course, that I was to resolve it her way, or I would be through as rector of St. Mark's.

I told the guild director that maybe it mattered more to the Lord what was **in** our head rather than on **top** of it, but that got nowhere. I shouldn't have said it. The grave situation was far too serious for an irreverent quip of logic like that. I must admit, it was traditional in 1965 for all females to wear head coverings in church. Any kind of a hat. If you didn't have a hat, you could wear a little lace beanie, which you kept folded up in your purse for that purpose. If you didn't have that, you could wear a single tissue of Kleenex. Anything would do as long as there was something on top of your head. This long-established tradition was traceable to scripture somewhere, but no one quite knew why this tradition was adhered to with such vehemence when many other similar traditions had long been abandoned.

Arriving at the church, I found the miscreant defiantly standing in the center of the chapel with her cello in hand, surrounded by a dozen altar guild members, almost as if she were holding them at bay. They knew by now that this was more than a rebel without a cause. Instead, they had a tiger by the tail. The other members of the youth choir had quietly disappeared for reasons of personal safety. She held onto the neck of that cello with the threatening defiance of a Kentucky moonshiner grasping the muzzle of a 12-gauge shotgun. One horizontal swipe of that weapon would have caused us all to hit the marbled deck.

"I'm not wearing something that makes me look stupid," young Audrey growled.

"But the Bible says all women are to wear head covering," countered one of the more brazen guild members. "It's a commandment of God!"

"Where in the Bible does it say I have to look stupid in order to be a Christian? Where does it say I have to wear a silly doily like this?" Audrey scoffed, flipping it to the floor.

The older women, of course, didn't know. That's when they turned to me. After all, I was the new rector and supposedly the biblical authority on female head coverings. But I knew better than get drawn into the fray on that level of contorted persuasion.

"Ladies," I said, turning toward them, "even though the Bible supposedly makes reference to women having their heads covered in church, it doesn't say what kind of head coverings we must have, does it?"

They all nodded that it didn't.

Then turning to Audrey, I said, "If that beanie makes you feel stupid, what kind of head covering in church would make you feel more comfortable?"

She plopped on her head the silliest looking big-rimmed hippie hat I had ever seen. From its floppy rim hung a dozen medallions and fish hooks. But I knew better than to allow my face to reveal even the hint of a smile because, in her foul mood, she would have bayoneted me to the marble floor with the metal spike at the bottom of the cello.

"Then it follows," I reasoned like a diplomat, "that the ladies certainly wouldn't object to your wearing a head covering of your own choosing. No two Episcopal women would ever be caught dead wearing identical hats to church on a Sunday morning."

It saved the day. The altar guild ladies were released from being held hostage by their own captive, the young lady they accused of church misconduct. They knew the club-swinging cellist was perfectly willing to use her cello not only as an instrument of beautiful music, but also as a weapon of mayhem against anyone who tried to impose upon her a worn out ol' church tradition which no longer made sense. Believe me, they were glad to let the tiger go.

And Audrey had won her point. Out into the choir stalls paraded the youth choir like a flock of submissive little chickens, all obediently wearing delicate lace beanies pinned to their heads. Among them, out into the chancel, stomped Audrey, scowling, dragging her cello behind her as if it were a horse saddle, her hippie hat flopping in the breeze like the wings of a giant vulture.

It was a win-win situation for both Audrey and the ladies. But what a hollow win it was for the older generation. Audrey was right: In only a few more years it no longer would be mandatory or fashionable for women to wear hats in church. To do so would only make them look stupid. Fashion overruled a time-honored tradition that, theoretically, was rigidly rooted in the Bible. Another cherished church tradition died a quiet death. Wyomingites would have more aptly described it as simply another Old World antiquity shot to hell on the frontier of western reality.

The whole incident was just another omen of the many changes which were to come to the Episcopal Church, changes none of us ever suspected back in 1965. Changes far more sweeping and convulsive than head coverings.

And to think — I would be privileged to be drawn into the fire of every frenzied battle for the next twenty-seven years. I just happened to be the officer on duty when all hell broke loose.

✧

Everyone knew that in Wyoming there was no racism. We believed this self-delusion only because there were not enough minority races within the state to make it a problem. There were no black communities anywhere in Wyoming, except in Cheyenne. Our schools were integrated, which fed into the belief that, therefore, there was no racism. That was our fantasy. Of course, subconscious racism was as rampant in Wyoming as in any other part of the country, although it had not been politically institutionalized as much as in the South.

In the latter part of the 1960s, during the height of the civil rights struggle in America, I decided that Cheyenne's churches should take leadership in promoting a new level of Christian understanding and goodwill between the black and white populations of our city. I approached clergy from other denominations with the suggestion that we make it an ecumenical affair. They gave me their wholehearted support "in spirit" but wouldn't touch it with a ten-foot pole in practice. I was on my own.

Only three blocks from St. Mark's downtown location was the Second Baptist Church, a black congregation. I approached the leadership about the possibility of our two churches entering into a companion relationship.

Initially, there was more resistance from them than from my own vestry. They looked askance at me. They had had offers like this before, which amounted to their black choir being invited over to a white church for a one-time concert of "Negro spirituals," followed by a chicken supper cooked by the black women. They became receptive once I assured them that this was exactly what we did *not* want.

Instead, our two churches would enter into a covenanted companion relationship at every level of our existence. Adult and youth groups, choir concerts, social fellowships, prayer and Bible study groups, pulpit exchanges, worship, and joint Holy Communion. Not every Sunday, of course, but often enough that the various groups could establish contact with each other and build a common base of mutual Christian friendship and trust.

We at St. Mark's learned more from the experiment than did they.

The people of Second Baptist were wise enough to know that the experiment wouldn't work very well, because they knew there was more latent racism at St. Mark's than what I imagined. The people of St. Mark's were wise enough to know that the experiment wouldn't work very well either, for much the same reason. Since their priest had become a social activist, which was an unpopular thing to be among the established mainline churches in the 1960s, I would eventually hang myself on rope happily provided by them. But both congregations were curious enough to give the venture an honest try.

I heard the usual objections that the church shouldn't become involved in the civil rights issue. The truth is, the Christian Church of America had always been heavily involved. The church preached on the issue from the pulpit, taught it from the Bible, and put it into practice every Sunday, week after week, for over 200 years — all on the wrong side. The segregationist scandal could be laid directly on the steps of the Christian Church, which in general not only encouraged it but also justified it theologically. No wonder the civil rights movement came out of the black church and found redress through the courts — the institutionalized white church offered little or no support. However, a growing number of white Christians, lay and clerical, individually rallied to the cause. The time had come for the church to take a new stand for a cause that was essentially Christian — justice and human dignity for all people regardless of race, color, or national origin.

I knew our social experiment to promote better relationships between the whites and blacks of Cheyenne could miserably fail. But it had to begin somewhere — why shouldn't it begin with the Christians of St. Mark's and the Second Baptist Church? No two churches could have been farther apart socially or liturgically. No two churches could have been closer in geographical proximity, located only three blocks apart.

One of the first things we did was move our annual Christmas concert from the edifice of St. Mark's to Second Baptist, with the performance done by the combined choirs. Our willingness to do this made an enormous impression on them. This was the first time that a white congregation had come over to worship and celebrate Christmas with them.

It was a tremendous success. People were packed to the rafters of the little frame church. The Baptist pastor, the Rev. Willie Lewis, graciously acknowledged all the leading participants in the Christmas concert. Then he proudly introduced himself, jokingly, as "captain of the ship" and me as "admiral of the fleet." I responded by telling the story of an Episcopal bishop drilling a young class of confirmands by asking pointed questions about the hierarchy of authority within the church.

"Who's captain of the ship?" he asked.

"The rector," the class shouted back in unison.

Then vainly, strutting back and forth in the chancel, the bishop asked, "Then who's admiral of the fleet?"

"Jesus Christ!" they shouted — completely bypassing the role of the bishop.

I went on to explain that the Reverend Mr. Lewis and I were both captains of our individual ships — the local churches we pastored. But the admiral of the fleet was, indeed, none other than Jesus Christ, who was the Lord of all Christians — Baptists, Episcopalians, and all other denominations the world over — regardless of race or color.

One of the things we learned about the black church was a startling revelation to us. Even though their worship services were informal and frenzied, especially the spontaneous congregational feedback during preaching of the sermon, they nevertheless maintained a very formal social relationship among themselves. Many members of St. Mark's affectionately knew these people in Second Baptist as domestic maids or hardworking manual laborers. They were known to us by their personal names — Tillie, Bessie, Benny, or Jimmy. But in church these people formally addressed one another, even in casual conversation, as Mrs. Jenkins, Mrs. Brown, Deacon Smith, or Mr. Higgins. Never a pet name.

I admired them for this. The various St. Mark's delegations that met with them were cautioned to respect this formal tradition. Even though we casually related to one another on a first-name basis among ourselves, there, in their church, we never addressed any of them on a first-name basis — even when they insisted that we do. It was good for us to know them formally for a change.

In church, the black worshippers assigned the full honor of human dignity to another. Men, women, and children were always dressed to the hilt in their finest Sunday clothes — men in white shirts, suits, and ties, women in high heels and fancy hats. Ushers wore white gloves. They may have worn the same outfit Sunday after Sunday, but it was always their Sunday best. It became obvious to us that their church was the center of their religious, cultural, and social life. It was here that they were most fully human. It was here that they assumed their full stature as men and women of God. They formally invested this spiritual respect and human dignity in one another and expected it in return.

It was fun to learn some of the idiosyncrasies we both had. For example, when they took a collection of the free-will offering, white-gloved ushers stood at the offering table while parishioners came forward with their contributions. I thought this custom strange in comparison to the white church idiosyncrasy of secrecy surrounding the offering plates. When I asked why their ushers carefully monitored the offering they simply said, "Sometimes our people have trouble making change!" The honest practicality of their answer suggested to me that maybe we should be checking the same thing in our white churches. No wonder white people shrouded the offering plate in secrecy.

In April 1968 Dr. Martin Luther King Jr. was assassinated in Memphis. I rushed over to Second Baptist and found myself to be the only white person there as they wailed over this shattering loss. The personal devastation they felt was beyond white people's comprehension. Because of this man and the civil rights movement he spawned, they, for the first time, could vote, take their children to a public amusement park, register for a motel room or order dinner in a nice restaurant without fearing rejection — or endangerment of their lives. Because of this one man, black Americans for the first time could become full citizens of the United States.

Their anguish over their personal loss made a monumental impression on me. The flip side of anguish is anger, and there was plenty of that. Some of it was directed personally toward me because I was the only white person in their midst to absorb it. Any explanation on my part that many white Americans shared their grief was beyond their willingness at that time to accept. My words fell on deaf ears.

I was shocked beyond belief the very next night when, during a women's board meeting at St. Mark's, a leader of the group announced, "What's all the fuss about the death of Martin Luther King? I don't think the blacks are upset about it. I asked Minnie, my cleaning lady, if she was a follower of Martin Luther King and she said she wasn't." Minnie, naturally, would have denied her support in order to retain her job as a cleaning lady. But the night before, Mrs. Jenkins, Minnie's formal name, was prostrate in grief and despair at the Second Baptist Church. I knew this firsthand, because I was there to personally witness it.

We had our fun times as well.

Our young adult fellowship of St. Mark's, known as Pairs 'n Spares, exchanged social visitations with the people from Second Baptist. On one such occasion they invited us to join them in a meal of chitlins 'n greens at their church. Before we ate, they briefly explained the history of chitlins among the black people of America.

"No one is gonna starve us out of existence. For a long time us black folk have learned to feast on whatever white folk threw away. The *massas* would butcher the hogs and after all the good meat had been cut away, they tossed us the leftovers. These leftovers became our chitlins, which we learned to cook into a rare delicacy for us black folk. And after we harvested the spinach for the *massa's* table we took the dandelion weeds and cooked 'em into greens for ourselves."

They deliberately slurred the word *master* into *massa* in order to make their solemn point. "No, nobody ain't gonna starve us black folk. We have a whole history of making do with what white folk throw away. We're survivors!"

It was a sobering lesson in sociology.

As I came along the buffet table, the people from Second Baptist told me they had already prepared my plate. I insisted on serving myself just like everyone else, but they would have none of it. It was obvious to me that both the men and women of Second Baptist had set aside a plate, covered with a towel, with a special serving of chitlins as a delicacy just for me to savor.

I accepted their gracious offer.

The chitlins had a unique taste which I wasn't sure I liked, eating it for the first time ever in my life. But I could see that, indeed, it could become a delicacy once you developed a taste for it. As I cleaned up my plate, I noticed the amusement was getting to be too much for our genial hosts. They couldn't contain themselves any longer. Finally, they told me that the tubular piece of tissue I had just eaten was not the pig's tail, as they had earlier led me to think.

Instead, it was something else!

Thereafter, whenever the Reverend Willie Lewis and I had a conference lunch in a Cheyenne restaurant, he would always lay down the menu, lean across the table, and whisper, "Gene, I don't think they serve your favorite piece of chitlin' here."

After many months of combined group meetings, Bible study, social fellowships and pulpit exchanges, the people of Second Baptist were invited to attend St. Mark's for a joint service of Holy Communion. A lot of preparation went into the organization of this unique and special event.

On the scheduled day, a few of the people from Second Baptist drove to church, but a large delegation preferred to march down Nineteenth Street to St. Mark's since the two churches were only three blocks apart. According to Anglican tradition, the Episcopalians were kneeling and quietly saying their private prayers before the service began. Suddenly they heard, in the distance, the choral refrain "We Shall Overcome" — growing in volume as the Baptist guests approached. Some of our young people, and a few adults, bolted out the church and down the street to join them for the last block to St. Mark's.

But I wasn't among them. Instead, I was confronted with another encounter which I hadn't expected and for which I wasn't prepared.

A small delegation of Episcopalians from St. Mark's, including a physician, came to me in the vesting room and said, "Father Todd, the experiment of an interracial communion service is distressing to us, but not because we are racists, you understand. It's strictly a public health problem with us. For this reason alone, we recommend that you kindly invite our black guests to receive communion after the rest of us have received our communions."

"That's like inviting them to sit in back of the bus in Montgomery, isn't it?" I asked.

"Well, then invite them to receive communion first, before the rest of us come forward," was their response.

"But reverse segregation is still segregation," I insisted.

"Well, we're just trying to make it easier on you and the rest of us," they said. "It's easier and more hygienic to serve the cup to one group at a time than to keep switching chalices back and forth between the blacks and the whites on an individual basis."

I knew what they were up to. I also knew that the moment of truth had come for me.

"There will not be two chalices," I firmly said. "There will be only one common cup from which God's children, black and white, are to receive their Holy Communion. Together, side by side, black and white, brother and sister, in our Lord Jesus Christ — we will drink from the common cup while we sing: 'Let us break bread together on our knees.'"

That particular service of Holy Communion with the black people of Second Baptist Church was one of the most memorable experiences of my entire ministry.

I had invited a black teenager to sing a solo, "Take My Hand Precious Lord," while we were receiving Holy Communion. She sang that solo at Second Baptist the Sunday of our pulpit exchange, when I preached in her church while the Reverend Willie Lewis preached at St. Mark's. Her rendition of that old country gospel hymn was beautifully done, and I wanted the people from St. Mark's to hear it.

But at St. Mark's, the Sunday of our joint service of Holy Communion, she got cold feet and asked to be excused as she glanced around at the beautiful and spacious Gothic interior of St. Mark's — and the large white congregation assembled for formal liturgical worship.

"I don't think it's gonna sound right here," she said.

"Vicki," I told her, "I want you to sing it your way. Exactly the way you sang it in your church. Don't ruin it by trying to sing it our way. Open up your heart and sing it with soul."

She did, reluctantly and hesitantly at first, as she stepped to the microphone and heard her amplified voice reverberate between the stone walls of St. Mark's. But then she tilted her head backward, closed her eyes and sang from the heart like an angel. I was moved to tears — and so was half the congregation.

It was one of the grandest moments of my life when I saw for the first time ever at St. Mark's the procession of black and white people coming forward to the altar rail, and there on bended knee, I served them Holy Communion from the common cup. My euphoria was tempered with the sad realization that those who earlier had come to me in protest would surely leave St. Mark's, regardless of what I said or tried to do to prevent it from happening. This is exactly what occurred. They were good people. I loved them and hated to see them go. In a sense, they were also victims of a segregationist mentality.

Their departure was a time of great sadness for me. I told my good friend, Dick Thomas, the United States Attorney for Wyoming, that I felt sorry for the church and I felt sorry for them. "Just think of their embarrassment," I said, "when they admit to others why they honestly left St. Mark's."

"Oh, Gene," Dick said, "they would never admit that this was their real reason. They are astute enough to know that their racial bigotry no longer is socially acceptable in mainstream America. They will come up with other reasons for their departure from St. Mark's. Like your sermons are too long, or the organ is too loud, or you're too much a social activist, or they're not being spiritually fed here."

Time would prove that Dick was absolutely right.

A week later I was invited for tea at one of the most prestigious homes of Cheyenne, whose family name still resonates in political circles of Wyoming. The domestic maid, Nellie, a member of another black congregation in Cheyenne, was busy pouring our tea and serving shortbread.

My hostess admonished, "This is an interesting social experiment you're conducting here at St. Mark's Church. Unlike others who refused, I want you to know that I did go up to the altar rail and receive Holy Communion alongside our black guests last Sunday. Nellie here agrees with me that we should maintain our separate ways. Even sheep know that black and white woolies don't mix on their own accord. But I suppose the church will next be advocating interracial marriages, won't it? And after that, I suppose, will come the ordination of black priests to preside over the communion tables of white congregations in our beloved Episcopal Church."

Nellie quietly replenished the tea, returning to her the cup and saucer.

"Mr. Todd, everyone is entitled to draw the line on what they will and will not socially accept. And I'm telling you right now," shaking her finger at me, "that I will never accept the cup from a black hand!"

"But you just did," I noted, nodding toward Nellie.

It was if I had never said it. Prejudice, by definition, is irrational. It's an emotional issue that must first be addressed on an emotional level.

Not for one moment do I wish to imply that hypocrisy was strictly the domain of the white church. The black church had it, too. In any church, the difference between what we publicly profess and what we privately practice can be worlds apart. Willie and I talked about it during one of our lunches. He said, "Racial hypocrisy on the part of the white man was conspicuously instituted into the American culture. Everyone saw it because it was so blatant. We blacks can be hypocritical, too. Perhaps our hypocrisy is more hidden."

When I asked him what he meant, he said, "Gene, since you're into learning about the black experience here in Cheyenne, I recommend that you go to one of the black 'after hours' dives here in our city. You'll probably see some of our church members there. What goes on there is a whole world removed from what goes on in our church. You need to see it. I can't go with you because they'd recognize me there. But you probably could get by undetected, especially if you camouflaged yourself just a little bit."

Arrangements were made for me to go. I wore casual clothing, which I seldom did in public, with a Greek fisherman's cap pulled over my head. My casual outfit disguise must have worked because no one recognized me.

The place was located in the basement of a large two-story structure at the corner of Eighteenth and Snyder, only a few blocks west from St. Mark's. My companions and I grabbed a table with a good view in the corner of the room at midnight, when the place was almost empty. It quickly filled up. By one o'clock in the morning it was packed. The atmosphere took on the surrealistic aura of a Chicago speakeasy from the days of Al Capone. The proprietor wore diamond earrings with diamond insets in his two front gold teeth.

The place had low ceilings and was dimly lit. A five-piece blues band took its place on the bandstand, and the action began. Everything there was illegal and for sale: the illicit operation itself, the food, the booze, the drugs, and the sex. I was the only white person there, secluded back in my corner, except for a hooker who actively worked the crowd out on the dance floor. She had a good night, according to my count of the johns who periodically slipped out the back door with her.

The band began playing soulful and mournful blues. People spontaneously took hold of the microphone to sing. I may have recognized the first verse of a currently popular song, but after that it became entirely improvisional, and extremely personal, with the soloist adding his or her rendition from the depth of emotional feeling. Sometimes it was a mixture of intimate expression which would escalate into the ranting caricature of a black preacher. And through it all was a rhythmic beat picked up by the drummer and accentuated on the base guitar, with repetitive chording on the synthesizer keyboard. It became hypnotic as the song went on and on . . . sometimes fifteen minutes before the soloist was emotionally wrung out.

As the music rambled on, I watched shadowy forms doing the most uninhibited and sensual dancing I have ever seen. The couples would slowly sway to and fro across the dimly lit dance floor, sometimes not touching at all, other times reaching out to follow the contour of their partner's bodies, dancing the blues in a sexual trance.

Yes, the Reverend Willie Lewis was right, I saw a few of his church members there. But only a few. So few, in fact, that Willie should have been proud.

One in particular caught my attention. She was an attractive black woman who had raised the loudest objection at a combined youth meeting between the teenagers of Second Baptist and St. Mark's when one of our Episcopalian boys impulsively suggested, of all things, an interracial dance. I had forgotten to forewarn my youth group that dancing was anathema to Baptists. When it happened, hushed embarrassment fell across the room as surely as if the Episcopalian youth had blurted out that they all have a sex orgy. The silence was broken with a castigating sermon on the evils of dancing — from the very woman who was now doing her sensual dance, in slow motion, out on the crowded floor, with a man who was not her husband.

Obviously, she knew whereof she spoke.

From the perspective of a white Episcopalian who loves dancing, who was I to judge this woman, dancing in the only public place in Cheyenne where blacks were allowed to dance in the late 1960s? The problem here, with me, was not her clandestine dancing in an "after hours" joint but her self-righteous judgmental hypocrisy at a church meeting in condemning the dancing of others. I was reminded of the old proverb, "Beware of one who protesteth too much." Such protests may be dangerously self-revealing.

Willie was right that hypocrisy is not only a monopoly of the white man. It's a sin of the human condition, whomever we are and whatever creed we profess. It's something we must always confess while seeking God's forgiveness.

I left the all-night dive at dawn and never went back. I'm grateful for what I learned from the experience.

After our joint service of Holy Communion, Willie and I were ready to move our companion relationship into a deeper level of interracial and interpersonal sharing between our two parishes, when the whole venture was abruptly terminated.

Willie got fired.

I never quite knew why the congregation voted for his termination. I heard the litany of reasons from both Willie and members of the congregation, but I resolved not to become involved. However, I found myself ministering to Willie through the hurt and pain of his rejection.

The vestry of St. Mark's stated that our companion relationship was with the congregation of Second Baptist and not necessarily with its minister, the Reverend Willie Lewis. Unfortunately, when Willie's successor, a retired interim pastor from Denver, told me that he was interested only in "doin' a little preachin' on Sundays and catchin' up on my reading during the week," I knew our interracial religious experiment was doomed.

It had been a unique and worthy experiment.

Instead of marching in the streets or staging protest rallies at the state capitol in behalf of civil rights, we tried promoting a new common ground of Christian understanding between the black and white people of Cheyenne. It was our intention that this nonconfrontational approach would help break down the racial stereotyping that leads to hostile interracial relationships, particularly if it was not done in a patronizing or condescending way. Instead of arguing about racism and civil rights, black Baptists and white Episcopalians could share traditions of our Christian faith on a personal level that would enhance our mutual appreciation of one another as brothers and sisters in Christ — children of one loving Heavenly Father.

One upswing of this endeavor was an invitation by the N.A.A.C.P. for me to serve on the board of directors for the establishment of a day care center for underprivileged children of working mothers — the first of its kind in Cheyenne. I gladly served for over two years.

In my judgment, our religious interracial experiment with Second Baptist church was a painful — but positive experience for us at St. Mark's. And you can imagine my special delight twenty-three years later, in 1992 when I retired from St. Mark's, that the church called an interim priest, Father

Jim Anderson, who was Afro-American. The congregation of St. Mark's dearly loved him and was oblivious to receiving the cup from a black hand. We have come a long way, wouldn't you say?

✧

But the Vietnam War was something else. This conflict nearly tore our country apart at the seams. At first I remained neutral. Like many other Americans, I thought it was our patriotic duty to fight any war that protected our shores and made the world safe for democracy. I also believed the United States would win any war we fought because we always had. So it was with disdain that I looked upon the student protest movements that first erupted on our nation's university campuses. It did seem a little far-fetched to argue that vital American interests were at stake in Vietnam. But our national leaders explained the "domino theory" as a justification for all-out war. After all, if Vietnam fell to the Communists, then it would be all of Asia, then the Philippines and Hawaii. Eventually, of course, it would include Alaska and California.

Our college students would surely understand the contorted logic of this — if it weren't for the hippie movement, which had severely distorted their thinking. I can remember it being said by politicians that the Vietnam War was justifiable if only to get the long-haired hippies off our campuses and into uniform to straighten them up, get their hair cut, and teach them a little military discipline.

By the late 1960s, open opposition to the Vietnam War was no longer confined to college campuses; it was spreading everywhere. Still I took no position. I was extremely busy at that time with the building project at St. Mark's, along with all the other normal duties of any clergyman: sermon preparation, preaching, rector's seminars, pastoral calling, weddings, funerals, and committee meetings almost every evening of the week. It was during this time that I invested much energy in the companion relationship with Second Baptist. I simply didn't have much time or energy for debate about the Vietnam War.

I never preached about it, nor mentioned it from the pulpit, except one time when I remember saying, "It seems that our country is dividing into hawks or doves when it comes to Vietnam. I'm neither. I guess that makes me a chicken."

Gussie Bevans came up to me afterward and said, "You described it right. I guess I'm a chicken, too."

As the conflict worsened, American church leaders shed their neutrality and began speaking out — mostly against the Vietnam War. The opposition intensified.

I believe now that this incredible involvement of Christian clergy and laity in their opposition to the Vietnam War was largely inspired by the horrendous guilt the civil rights movement had created. For over a century, the mainline denominational churches had become part of a silent conspiracy to allow, if not to openly encourage, the evils of racism and segregation to poison and undermine American society. Christianity's public standing had fallen to an all-time low. When was the church going to wake up and assume responsibility for social good? When was the church going to preach and teach redemption for society as a whole, as well as personal salvation for the individual souls within that society?

Enormous social pressure was brought to bear upon all clergy. Still I remained neutral.

With mixed emotions I accepted an invitation to attend a conference in Rapid City sponsored by Clergy and Laymen Concerned About the Vietnam War. The Reverend Roy Emery, a Presbyterian minister from Cheyenne, was also invited. Our airfare and all expenses were paid. This was my first exposure to an articulate and intelligent opposition to the Vietnam War. Gathered there were Catholic priests and nuns, clergy of all Protestant mainline denominational churches, along with lawyers, college professors, physicians, and business leaders. I was impressed with the depth of their commitment of moral opposition to the war and the passionate persuasion of their conviction.

The last morning of the conference was devoted to a presentation from a single representative from each state as to what their delegates would do once they returned to their home communities. I was stunned at what I heard. Here were men and women, clergy and laity, who were willing to risk everything to organize protest marches, deliver speeches, write newspaper editorials, stage nonviolent sit-ins and collect thousands of signatures for petitions mailed to politicians.

When Wyoming was called, Roy punched me and directed the conference leader to me. I stood up among these people whose courage and fortitude was beyond anything I could possibly imagine for myself and said, "I propose to stand on the steps of the Wyoming state capitol and begin reading the names of those who died in Vietnam. When I get to the tenth name — I'll run like hell, in zig-zag pattern, to dodge National Guard machine gun fire!"

"Get serious!" they shouted.

I *was* serious. To have done anything in Wyoming that smacked of public opposition to the war in Vietnam would have been pure suicidal.

I returned home not prepared to do anything. But now the opposition was becoming much more serious and universal. It had permeated every level of our American culture. There was a chorus of opposition from U.S. senators and congressmen, governors, former military generals, and state department officials. It had brought down the presidency of Lyndon B. Johnson. Richard Nixon's presidency was in serious trouble.

Still I remained neutral.

I never mentioned the Vietnam War in any of my sermons because I was convinced it would have been too divisive at St. Mark's, which had a long history of close association with the political and military establishment of Cheyenne. After all, St. Mark's Church was the glittering scene for the socialite wedding of U.S. Senator Francis E. Warren's daughter, Frances, to Captain John C. Pershing who later distinguished himself as General of the Armies during World War I. And it was here in 1915 that the same Mrs. John C. Pershing was buried with solemn military rites, alongside the three Pershing children, who lost their lives in a tragic fire at the Presidio in California. Military personnel from enlisted men to post commanders had always been devout members of the church from the frontier Indian Wars to modern times. In spite of this prominent military presence within the church, however, I was beginning to have serious doubts about our American involvement in the Vietnam War. But I kept it mostly to myself.

Finally, in 1970 a personal event changed me from a chicken to a dove.

Cheyenne's Francis E. Warren Air Force Base had now become a very large military installation with jurisdiction over missile sites spread over a 200-mile area. A missile officer named Lonnie attended St. Mark's where we joyfully celebrated his promotion to the rank of lieutenant colonel. He purchased a lovely home in Cheyenne and had the sweetest wife and family a man could ever want. He loved the Air Force and was intending to make a career of it. He was military through and through.

One afternoon, while sipping iced tea in the famous Mayflower Cafe, located in downtown Cheyenne, he told me of his fond admiration of Dwight Eisenhower. "He was the greatest American I have ever known," he said, "and the greatest president our nation has ever had."

I disagreed with him. I thought Eisenhower was truly a great American and a magnificent military general but I didn't think he was our greatest or strongest president. This difference of opinion between the two of us didn't matter because we were good friends.

He was also a devoted Episcopalian. I trained him to become a licensed lay reader in the church, and he assisted me in many Sunday morning services.

After winding up his four-year tour of duty at Warren Air Force Base, he was transferred to Vandenberg Air Force Base in California. His wife shared with me his beautiful love letters before she sold the home and joined him at Vandenberg. I heard later from fellow officers in Cheyenne that he had been assigned to active duty in Vietnam and was flying again as a navigator — something he loved.

Then I heard that Lonnie had been hospitalized, apparently from injuries sustained in the Vietnam War. We all became terribly concerned. From Japan he was transferred to a military hospital in the States. His wife didn't seem to have much more information than we but indicated that he seemed to have suffered a nervous breakdown. Our anxiety level heightened, partly because his medical situation seemed shrouded in secrecy.

One morning, out of the blue, Lonnie walked into my study at Templeton House. I hardly recognized him. He had lost a lot of weight, which made him appear haggard and much older. There was none of the joyful bounce that had always characterized him before. He looked and acted almost like a stranger to me.

"Lonnie, what on earth has happened to you?"

"You know, Gene," he replied, "according to everything you see on television and read in the papers, we're not supposed to cross certain boundaries into North Vietnam. Well, I've been a navigator on the reconnaissance flights we fly regularly up to North Vietnam. And, Gene, I was ordered to navigate our flights beyond these carefully prescribed boundaries and then to falsify my navigational records to make it appear that we hadn't crossed over."

His eyes brimmed with tears.

"I told them I wouldn't falsify my records. Furthermore, it was apparent to me that we were being deliberately ordered to fly north of these restricted boundaries so as to draw enemy fire to justify expanding the aerial bombardment farther into North Vietnam. In other words, our flight crew was supposed to be canon fodder so that America could expand the war."

He stood up and pounded his open hand with a clenched fist.

"Gene, the American people are being lied to by the generals and, consequently, by the president because he's relying on their telling him the truth. But they aren't telling him the truth! The information the American people is getting is false. We aren't winning that war. We're losing it!"

He plopped himself down into the chair, nervously shifting back and forth as he gazed out the window, and continued, "When I refused to falsify my records, they hospitalized me as a psychiatric case. Just like in Russia. Lying to the enemy is modern warfare. But lying to your own country is criminal betrayal. And lying to yourself is schizophrenic!"

Lonnie buried his face in his hands and began weeping.

"I would never betray my country," he sobbed. "But I feel my country has betrayed me. Gene, we've got to get out of there or it will destroy the soul of America."

Here was a lieutenant colonel, fresh from Vietnam, personally revealing to me the same kind of a tale that had been unfolding hundreds of times on national television. I couldn't dismiss him as simply another psychiatric breakdown. Nor could I question his patriotism. I knew Lonnie too well.

It had become obvious to me that something had gone terribly wrong. The war in Vietnam had gone amok. We had entered it with the best of intentions. Thousands of young people had suffered and sacrificed their lives in that war. They did so because they loved our country and wanted to serve it with honor and integrity. Those who favored the war did so because it seemed the American thing to do. Those who opposed that war did so because it, too, seemed the American thing to do. Lonnie was right, the conflict abroad and at home was destroying the soul of America.

On Christmas Eve 1972, I heard that there was to be a peace rally on the steps of the state capitol in Cheyenne. Maybe it was time for me to quit acting like a coward and stand up for my convictions. Clergy and laity of all faiths marched in the civil rights movement as their way of supporting human dignity and justice for all people, regardless of race. I didn't. Maybe the time had come for me to get off my duff and stand up for something I believed in.

I decided to attend.

Christmas Eve is never a convenient time for an Episcopal priest. I had delivered communions to shut-ins and hospital patients most of the day. Two big Christmas services awaited me that evening. I would not get home from the midnight service until two o'clock on Christmas morning. It would be an exhausting night. Still — I decided to attend.

I joined a crowd of several hundred people gathered on the capitol steps. The sun was shining, but a cold raw wind had set in. I dressed warmly, but I felt the wintry chill. The organizers announced that we were going to march out to the Warren Air Force Base. That was two miles away. When asked what we were going to do once we arrived there, the answer seemed vague and uncertain. This made me feel uncomfortable because I had nothing against my good friends stationed at the base. Then we would have to march two miles back. By then darkness would have descended. Also, I reasoned, it would be windier and colder. It was Christmas Eve. I wasn't too sure, at this point, if I hadn't lost my enthusiasm for the march all together.

On a sudden impulse of the moment, I stepped up to the microphone and invited everyone, instead, to walk only a few blocks down Central

Avenue into the warm interior of St. Mark's Episcopal Church. I told them that I would turn on the public address system so that anyone could say whatever they wanted to say about the Vietnam War. Everyone would be allowed the opportunity to express their feelings either for or against the war. Then we could say a prayer for peace and all go home for Christmas Eve with our families.

It never occurred to me at the time that I had taken the peace march out of the command of its organizers, who apparently had other plans. But most of the crowd obviously much preferred the shorter route to St. Mark's and a place of warmth to make their voices heard.

Down Central Avenue we marched, several hundred strong. Only then did I notice, for the first time, television cameras along the route. Most of the marchers were state and federal employees and working people from Cheyenne. A few were college students home for the holidays. I did not turn on any lights in the church, leaving the beautiful Christmas decorations subdued in dark shadows. Many people came to the microphone to speak. Most were opposed to the Vietnam War for a variety of moral and political reasons. But some spoke in defense of it, however. It lasted for about an hour.

After everyone had an opportunity to speak, I read a prayer for world peace from the 1928 Episcopal Prayer Book. Then we all went home. I didn't even mention it at either of the large Christmas Eve services that evening because I didn't think it was worth mentioning.

But on Christmas Day NBC showed national television coverage of a peace march ". . . in, of all places, none other than Cheyenne, Wyoming."

One parishioner came to a vestry meeting demanding that I be asked to resign. The vestry refused his request. But the incident was blown out of proportion with a series of newspapers headlines throughout the Rocky Mountain region and much of the nation, making it appear as if the church itself had asked for my resignation.

I was deluged with phone calls from everywhere. Most of them were supportive. Some were threatening. One of the calls came from the commanding officer of the Warren Air Force Base who thanked me for saving them from what surely would have been a major confrontation at the base. It was then I learned that federal marshals and FBI agents had infiltrated the crowd.

When I retired from St. Mark's in 1992, that peace march twenty years earlier was still being referred to as "Gene Todd's peace march." It was nothing of the sort.

Diehards would say to me, "I don't see any of those people from *your peace march* attending church here." Of course not, most of them were patriotic Catholic and Protestant Americans, good Christians who worshiped in their own churches. I had no intention of proselytizing them into the Episcopal Church, and they wouldn't have accepted such a brazen invitation. They were invited simply to address their heartfelt concerns about our country at war — and to pray for peace on Christmas Eve.

In 1975, when the Vietnam War finally ended, we scheduled a large commemorative service at St. Mark's for American Peace and Reconciliation. The Hon. John McIntyre, from the Wyoming Supreme Court and a Methodist, delivered the speech. We read the names and prayed for all the Wyoming men and women who died in Vietnam. A Vietnam veteran delivered a moving eulogy in their behalf. A representative from the Veterans Hospital read to us some grim statistics about the war: over 57,000 Americans had died, and over 305,000 were injured. Several Catholic priests and nuns attended. Few Protestant clergy did because they said the Vietnam War was still too divisive for them to participate. But they assured me that they were with me "in spirit."

I was sorry that most of the super-patriots at St. Mark's were not in attendance because this would have been a wonderful opportunity for them to have demonstrated that their patriotism was more than loud condemnation of anyone who disagreed with them about a divisive war. It was too bad that they couldn't have joined hands with us as we sang our national anthem and reaffirmed our faith in America within the context of honoring those who fought for our country in Vietnam.

The Vietnam War was finally behind us.

At least, this is what we thought at the moment. But time has proven otherwise. In 1995, former Secretary of Defense Robert S. McNamara reignited debate about the Vietnam War with his book *In Retrospect*. In this book, McNamara concluded that our national leaders, beginning with him, failed to grip reality with this war. Furthermore, he admits it was a terrible mistake. ". . . {We} were wrong, terribly wrong. We owe it to future generations to explain why."

Perhaps the simplest and most logical explanation is an old-fashioned theological term known as ORIGINAL SIN!

The final upshot of this tragic national saga was that Lonnie was vindicated. On the other hand, those brave people who served, sacrificed, and suffered the loss of loved ones in that awful war — believing in it because it was considered the patriotic thing to do — have reason to feel betrayed.

✧

There is one social action battle that I decided to stay out of — the fight over abortion.

I was asked once by a male social-activist to participate in an anti-abortion rally in Cheyenne. I replied that I personally opposed abortion for almost all the reasons that he had given me, but I strongly felt that the government should stay out of it.

"For heaven's sake, why?" he sputtered.

"Because," I answered, "for five thousand years men, meaning the male gender, have passed laws dictating what women can and cannot do with their bodies. From Orientals binding the feet and crippling their women; Mideasterners prescribing veils, dress, and custom; Africans sexually mutilating their little girls; India's sacrificing or abandoning female babies; and Western civilization imposing dual standards upon women regarding adultery, divorce, property ownership, human and civil rights, health care, career, and wages."

I went on, "In territorial Wyoming a woman's wages belonged to her husband. She was denied automatic inheritance of her husband's estate, but was declared responsible for his debts. Only male legislators would pass myopic laws like that. Down the list of idiotic abuses I could go."

He waited as I continued. "All these abominations against women were legislated by male-dominated societies, always maintaining that they were mandated by God — and 99.9 percent of these restrictions were dead wrong. It's time that men, who still maintain their majority in legislative assemblies and church hierarchies, get out of the arrogant business of controlling women regardless how morally right they may think they are on this one issue. Enough is enough!"

He gasped.

I added, "If women, collectively, tried to introduce legislation governing the reproductive capacity of the male anatomy or the consequences of our heterosexual behavior, you can rest assured that sucker would get tabled in ten seconds and hooted at for the next ten years."

That was it. He hung up.

I was never invited again to participate on either side of the abortion issue. I'm glad I stayed out of the fray, because I think males have totally lost all credibility on women's issues and it's time for women to take control of their own destiny — with men, for once, staying out of it.

How long have we waited for effective laws from male-dominated legislatures in dealing with deadbeat fathers? We're still waiting.

In order to be consistent with my theory of getting the government out of the abortion business, maybe someday a compromise will be necessary whereby abortions will neither be criminalized or publicly funded. Perhaps women will resolve the controversy not in a court of law but within the court of public opinion — through expanded sex education in our churches and schools, quality health care for women, and unlimited access to privately funded birth-control clinics for both men and women.

Looks to me like women are doing a fairly good job at trying to take control of their private lives — until another preacher-man comes shootin' his way into a women's clinic with both barrels blazing and then all hell breaks loose again.

Not this preacher!

✧

Would you believe that I was considered a social activist simply because I complied with the bishop's mandate to join Episcopalians throughout the United States in prayer book revision?

The decision was made in 1964 by the General Convention of the Episcopal Church, which required consensus of all bishops, clergy, and lay delegates that our church needed to participate in liturgical renewal, a movement that sprung out of the Vatican Council II for Roman Catholics.

I came into the Episcopal Church during the reign of the elegant 1928 Prayer Book. I loved the eloquence of the King James Bible, the Shakespearean cadence and wonderful simplicity of that old prayer book. I saw no need to change it. But then, I was new to the Episcopal Church. Understandably, old-timers in the church loved it even more than I.

Still, liturgical reformers, Catholic and Anglican, felt the compelling need for prayer book revision. We clergy were to introduce the new liturgy through a series of experimental prayer book study guides. I felt compelled to comply by my ordination vow, which clearly stated that I was reverently to obey my bishop who, according to the canons of the church, had jurisdiction over me.

Such obedience apparently was not binding upon my good friend and colleague in the Episcopal priesthood, the Reverend Stanley Guille, who was rector of St. Christopher's Episcopal Church in Cheyenne. He had many theological and liturgical objections to the proposed trial liturgies and chose not to conform with the bishop's admonition. Thus, a conflict was set in motion among the Episcopalians of Cheyenne — at my expense.

Here I was, doing the best I could to introduce the trial liturgies to the congregation of St. Mark's as mandated by my bishop. Here was Stan Guille implying that he was not required to do so. Consequently, many Episcopalians in Cheyenne concluded that use of the trial liturgies in Wyoming was optional and that I was deliberately imposing them upon my parishioners at St. Mark's. Furthermore, the perception invariably developed that prayer book revision was the sole invention of Gene Todd — even that I had personally written and edited the new liturgies.

It could never be said by the members of St. Mark's that a new liturgy was sprung on them on by surprise. Quite the contrary, every new trial liturgy was introduced during a week-day study-discussion session. Then, on the first Sunday morning of the new service, I would carefully introduce it to the congregation with a practice session, answering all questions and encouraging their comments.

One of the biggest sticklers was the innovation of passing the peace among worshippers. This was that part of the service where everyone exchanges the peace of Christ with one another with a handshake, embrace, or words of Christian greeting. The "frozen

Preaching the Word at St. Mark's was like broadcasting and writing the word. Persistent preoccupation with the written and spoken word began in my early childhood.

chosen" Episcopalians were not about to warm up to a Pentecostalism thaw like this. Opposition set in on the grounds that worship is a private matter between God and the individual, not to be interfered with by the friendly intrusion of a gushing stranger in the pew. I had to counter this erroneous opinion by teaching that public worship is, by definition, *public*. In fact, the Greek word "liturgy" literally means "public service" — a service rendered in public for the public good, like building roads and aqueducts in ancient Greece.

At first, I got nowhere with this new teaching. When it came time to exchange the peace, half the congregation would freeze like stone statues, staring straight ahead, their arms wrapped around themselves as if they were Egyptian mummies. Eventually, however, people began to realize that greeting someone in the name of Christ and exchanging His peace with them wasn't all that bad.

After a series of different trial studies, the national church settled on a finalized version in the "zebra book" (whose cover was marked with stripes). Copies were passed out for our first-time use on a Sunday morning. After a brief introduction, we began our long procession up the center aisle of the church while singing our majestic processional hymn. Typically, the priest brings up the rear in a church procession. I was only a few pews up into the aisle when I felt a jarring thump against my back. Startled, I whirled around to see a zebra book scooting across the marble floor. Some devout Episcopalian had become so frustrated with these trial liturgies of the church that he or she hurled the new prayer book at me — as if I were the sole source of all their religious frustration.

I scooped up the book and carried it with me into the chancel of the church and used it for the remainder of the service — with the explanation, "Some good Episcopalian within the congregation this morning has loaned me their personal copy of the new zebra prayer book, and I am most grateful."

I never asked who it was that threw their prayer book at me.

In retrospect, I can see I should have handled the prayer book controversy differently. I should have gone to the bishop and said, "Bishop, whether Stan Guille is in compliance with your orders is none of my business. But I think you have an obligation to make it abundantly clear to the parishioners of St. Mark's and to all Episcopalians in Cheyenne that it is your specific request that all clergymen in Wyoming are to comply with your mandate to introduce the new liturgies to our congregations. I should not have to bear the brunt of this opposition all alone here in Cheyenne — as if prayer book revision is only my harebrained idea."

But I didn't do that, so I became viewed as the social activist in prayer book reform.

The Reverend Stan Guille was a good friend of mine. He came from the conservative English-Canadian tradition of Anglicanism. He had served Episcopal churches for many years in Wyoming. He was an excellent priest and pastor. But the new prayer book and changes within the national Episcopal Church were becoming too much for him to accept. In fact, he later allowed himself to become deposed from the Episcopal priesthood over these controversial issues. This was most unfortunate, I thought, because he was already beyond the age of retirement. He could graciously have bowed out of the Episcopal ministry and no one would have criticized him. But Stan Guille was a priest of deep conviction and integrity. His principles were beyond compromise. Although I disagreed with him, I admired his courage and felt genuinely sorry that he was deposed from the priesthood.

A new Episcopal Prayer Book was finally ratified in 1976, and a new Hymnal was ratified in 1982. Our new prayer book restores the celebration of the Mass, or rite of Holy Communion, as the central act of worship, thus, making the Episcopal Church a Eucharist-centered church once again.

It also mandates more congregational participation in worship services and provides many options for liturgical variation and enrichment.

Many of the liturgical changes reflect a much older tradition of Catholic worship in the early church. Consequently, Roman Catholics and Anglicans now share liturgical traditions so similar that you can hardly tell one from the other.

I'm glad we switched to the new Prayer Book of 1976. However, I still cherish the old 1928 Prayer Book. I understand why Episcopalians get so emotional about prayer book worship. We become more attached to our prayer book than to anything else in life. It follows us through the vicissitudes of life, providing theological meaning and definition to all the pivotal events from birth to death: baptism, confirmation, marriage, childbirth, illness, and burial. We carry it on our person in every worship service and hold it in our folded hands in death. It's only natural that this has to be the one thing in life that never changes.

But this is only a comforting delusion. The only thing that never changes is the relentless steady pace of change itself. Alfred North Whitehead, the great philosopher and physicist, tremendously helped with my understanding of this phenomenon. All creation is in a constant state of dynamic flux, he maintained. Thus, God himself is dynamic — in movement with the dynamic universe He created. How futile for human beings to deceive ourselves into thinking that something precious to us, such as a prayer book, should never change. The Anglican Book of Common Prayer has been in constant revision since 1549. Failure to change it would eventually make it totally irrelevant.

Maybe its human nature that the older we get, the greater becomes our desire to slow down the pace of change, to create a semblance of manageable comfort. Having fought the 1976 Prayer Book revision battle, I'm in no mood to have yet a newer prayer book imposed on me. If any dutiful priest tries it — even if faithfully ordered to do so by his bishop — I'll throw the book at him. Hard!

I think I deserve that privilege.

✧

Another outreach into the Cheyenne community which further labeled me a social activist, but one I especially enjoyed, was the original institution of the annual Blessing of the Animals on St. Francis Sunday.

The ceremony was held in spacious Frontier Park and people of all faiths were invited to participate. I wanted it to be more meaningful than just another sentimental blessing of animals as it's usually done. So I wrote a set of solemn vows which I asked the owners to individually repeat after me when they came forward with their animals (dogs, cats, horses, ferets, goats, miniature housebroken pigs, and you name it) — for the blessing:

I promise warmth from the cold
Shelter from the storm
Healing from the hurt
Protection from attack
Freedom from fear
Food from hunger
Companionship from loneliness
Love and affection — always.

And then, putting my hand on theirs while touching the animal, I would pronounce them as, "One in God's love and affection." Coming out of my distant childhood rapport with the animal kingdom I knew on our family ranch, this simple service had powerful emotion for me as a literal reminder that when we take on any animal as a pet, we have a God-given obligation and moral responsibility to relate to that fellow creature of the earth as a loving friend and caring companion. I especially enjoyed holding the puppies during the blessing who were licking my face so fast I could hardly speak. Then I gave the owners an embossed *I'M BLESSED* certificate for framing, containing the vows they had spoken, along with the names of both the animal and its caretaker, as a visual remembrance of the promises made that day. It was important for me to believe that this little outdoor ceremony did something to reduce animal neglect and enhance a deeper spiritual relationship among all God's creatures. The Blessing of Animals has become an annual Cheyenne tradition.

✧

In spite of my general acceptance of those who will not take a public stand on anything controversial, there was one time when I lost my cool.

At a diocesan convention, I was leading a floor fight in behalf of establishing a minimum salary plan for all Episcopal clergy in the state of Wyoming. The plan clearly stipulated not only an adequate base salary but also provided for housing and travel allowances, insurance and pension premiums, and reimbursement of legitimate ministerial expenses.

I felt free to champion the cause with no conflict of interest because my personal salary package, as a senior rector of long tenure at a cardinal parish, far exceeded the minimal requirements for new or young clergy coming into the diocese.

I was willing to go to bat in their behalf.

During a coffee break from the floor debate, a clergyman motioned me out into the hallway and whispered, "I want you to know that I whole-heartedly support what you're trying to accomplish out there. I desperately need a salary package like you're advocating. But you know the bishop is temperamentally opposed to any kind of a decent minimal salary plan, even though he's got one that's automatically working very well for him, and will surely find ways to circumvent anything we vote on here today."

"So?" I asked.

"So it's best for me to remain quiet and very invisible during this convention floor debate. But I hope you keep the pressure up because our diocese is among the lowest in average clergy salaries in the whole country. I just want you to know that I'm with you in spirit."

Something snapped inside of me. For nearly forty years of my ministry, through all the tumultuous social issues that tore at the conscience of our church and nation — racism, war, social action, feminism, human sexuality, and so forth — I heard too many clergymen and laymen say: *I won't join ranks to champion the cause we commonly believe in, but I want you to know that I'm with you "in spirit" — if you do.*

On that particular afternoon, at the Episcopal Diocesan Convention of Wyoming, I was in no mood to once again hear that wimpish cop-out. I slammed my fist on the table and shouted, "If you can't get your ass out there in the heat of the action to voice and vote the strength of your convictions, then don't sneak up to me here in the hallway and offer me the timidity of your spirit. In the world of politics, whether it be secular or here in the church, hiding in the closet with your good intentions doesn't count!"

I apologized later, but I'm not sure that I should have.

But I understand why so many clergypersons take the easy way out. Our jobs and livelihood are highly dependent upon the voluntary goodwill of our congregations. That goodwill can evaporate quicker than a cup of cold water in a hot Judean desert if a minister champions an unpopular social cause. Our instinct for self-preservation dictates that we play it safe — usually, too safe.

And so we have cultivated a professional mask of sitting it out in the back row, with a plastic smile plastered on our ministerial faces, with the deceptive illusion that we are quietly working behind the scenes to usher in the kingdom of God. I'm proud to say, however, that there are many brave souls who have followed our Lord's example and are willing to move out to the front line of all reform, whatever it is, even it means getting themselves nailed to a tree.

Bless them!

Chapter 16

R osemary Fleming Adamson and I scheduled our wedding at St. Mark's Church for New Year's Eve of 1975. Our plans capped off nearly two years of courtship that began when she bought a home directly behind Templeton House. Like me, she was newly divorced with teenage children, and she began inviting my family over for evening meals.

We're all familiar with the old saying that the way to a man's heart is through his stomach. Perhaps that's true in some cases, but it wasn't in this one. At that particular time in my life I was simply too depressed to enjoy any kind of food that Rosemary brought to the table. Rosemary literally coached me to eat again, bite by bite, but I was becoming more smitten with the person who was doing the coaching than with the excellent cuisine and table wine she was serving.

She was born as Rosemary Fleming, on the Fleming farm along the banks of Fleming Creek, near the little town of Flemingsburg, in Fleming County, Kentucky. Obviously, the Flemings had played a prominent role in the local history. The family dated back to the original settlement of that frontier country prior to the Revolutionary War. She was a graduate in public health nursing from Vanderbilt University. There she married Dr. Douglas Adamson, a career military physician who later became hospital commander at Warren Air Force Base in Cheyenne. Their marriage ended in divorce the same year as mine. She and her daughters were active communicants at St. Mark's Episcopal Church.

Our friendship developed into a more serious romantic relationship, and in 1975 she invited me to visit her family home in Kentucky. This was my first sojourn into the American South, although Kentucky considers itself a border state. I loved it. It truly is the Bluegrass State, with the most brilliant color of green blanketing the rolling hills, always lush from the frequent showers. Dense forests of towering hardwood trees opened out into little fields of tobacco and corn, surrounded by pastures of white-fenced horse farms. It was beautiful.

One word best describes Kentucky: *gracious*. Gracious southern charm. Gracious southern hospitality in lovely old homes of Georgian architectural design. Gracious Southern lifestyle. Gracious lilting southern accents and colloquial expressions. Gracious little southern towns every mile or so along the winding country roads, where churches far outnumber taverns. (In this respect, the South was certainly different than the West.)

The Fleming family collectively owns a rustic cottage along the shores of Park Lake which is absolutely fantastic. It has since been modernized, but back in 1975 there was no water and plumbing. It was wonderful to sit out on the large screened porch in the cool early morning while drinking your coffee or eating lunch before swimming and canoeing again in the lake. Then that evening, while watching the evening shadows of the sunset reflect across the waters of the small lake, we could all enjoy a mellowing drink of genuine Kentucky bourbon before a supper of country fried chicken and fresh garden vegetables. (The famous *Ancient Age* distillery is located only a short distance away.)

We always ate every meal out on the screened porch, pulling up our chairs to an ol' fashioned dining table large enough to accommodate more than a dozen people, including all the children. Contrary to Wyoming, Kentucky gardens begin producing their bountiful supply of fresh vegetables in early June and keep accelerating throughout the summer. Consequently, our table was always crowded with dishes of creamed new potatoes and green beans, mounds of sliced tomatoes and cucumbers, and always heaps of roastin' ears snapped from the fields of sweet corn only hours before.

During the trip I became interested in the Shaker religion, which blossomed on the Kentucky frontier in the early 1800s. This utopian sect functioned primarily as a monastic order for both men and women. Strict celibacy was enforced through the use of separate doorways for the brothers and sisters into every room. Of course, celibacy was one of the reasons for the religion's inevitable decline; there are no Shakers today.

The Shakers conceived the idea that function determined design. Everything was made to the Lord's perfection of quality and functional simplicity. Their innovative architecture and farm machinery were good examples of this theological principle. In Shakertown, a marvelously restored village, you can admire the simple beauty of many unique architectural structures.

Their expert wood craftsmanship created a whole new concept of American furniture design, making it a favorite in the finest galleries of America. I collected a few reproductions of Shaker furniture, beautifully crafted from solid cherry, as accent pieces for Templeton House.

One of the Shakers' favorite hymns, "Simple Gifts," later became immortalized as the symphonic theme of Aaron Copland's orchestral suite "Appalachian Spring." The song reflected the quiet serenity of Shakertown — and all of Kentucky.

After my visit with the Fleming family of Kentucky and Rosemary's visit with the Todds of northern Wyoming, we were convinced that marriage was what we both wanted. We had many good reasons (including IRS considerations) for getting married no later than New Year's Eve 1975.

It was to be a simple wedding attended mostly by close relatives. I temporarily moved out of Templeton House in early December, living first with my sister Sadie in Cheyenne and then in a hotel, so that Rosemary could settle in with her family and furniture to make the place comfortable and presentable before the wedding.

We scheduled a wedding rehearsal on the evening of December 30 followed with dinner for all the Todds and Flemings at Little America and then went dancing at the famous Ole' Mayflower dance hall located in downtown Cheyenne. Since it was the night before New Year's Eve we had the whole place to ourselves. A five-piece country band belted out every old western we knew and the musicians joined us at our table for drinks.

But on the morning of December 31 a howling blizzard struck southern Wyoming. By afternoon the city of Cheyenne had shut down, and the wedding party was marooned in three separate locations. The Todds were totally closed in at my sister's home, the Flemings were cloistered at Templeton House with the bride, and I, the groom, was all alone in the Downtowner Hotel.

The storm's fury worsened by nightfall, and it soon become apparent to all that there was to be no New Year's Eve wedding for Rosemary and me. Then a ray of hope broke through the roaring storm. My church secretary, Sandy Jones, and her husband, Jerry, called to say that they had mounted chains on all four wheels of their Jeep, which had been modified to maneuver through deep snowdrifts.

That solved the transportation problem. But what about a minister? Bishop David Thornberry was stranded in Michigan because there were no flights into Wyoming. The Very Reverend Howie Wilson, dean of St. Matthew's Cathedral in Laramie, consented to fill in for the bishop, but the roads were closed out of Laramie. However, it so happened that the soloist who had agreed to sing at our wedding was more than an accomplished guitarist and musician; he was also an ordained minister of the Assembly of God faith. The Reverend Dave Vanley had become a good ministerial friend of mine. Fortunately, he lived in Cheyenne and consented to perform the ceremony provided that Jerry would pick him up; his own car was buried in six-foot drifts of snow.

Jerry and Sandy began their rounds of pickup and delivery, all in the name of marital bliss. To be honest, Jerry was anxious to see whether he could truly maneuver his newly outfitted Jeep under blizzard conditions. First they picked up preacher Dave, who lived nearest to their house, then me at the hotel, and finally the bride. Time was running out if we were to be married in 1975 rather than 1976. As the Jeep churned through the snow, Dave sang "Get Me to the Church on Time." We made it there at eleven forty-five.

By now, of course, we were fully aware of the severity of the raging storm. This was no ordinary Wyoming blizzard, the kind that ties up traffic along the interstate highways and strands thousands of motorists along the way. This one was so horrendous that even the Union Pacific trains stopped running. Nevertheless, we proceeded with the wedding.

It was some wedding party. All, including the bride and groom, were attired in heavy winter clothing with parkas pulled over our heads and boots on our feet. The wind was howling so ferociously that the overhead sanctuary lamp, suspended from the high ceiling, was literally swinging in a large circular motion. It seemed as if the brass angels ensconced on the bronze fixture were clinging for dear life as it rotated like a merry-go-round above our heads. The mammoth support beams above the nave were creaking and groaning from the frightful pressures exerted on the roof.

At eleven fifty-seven on New Year's Eve 1975, Dave Vanley pronounced Rosemary and me husband and wife. I dashed over to the organ console and played the twelve notes of midnight on the large carillon as a wedding bell — ringing in the new year of 1976 and the beginning of our new marriage. However, the thunderous sound of the carillons, like the old year of 1975, was blown away by the howling storm.

We all piled back into Jerry and Sandy's pumpkin-colored jeep, which by now had changed to the Cinderella color of a frosty white wedding cake, and began our treacherous journey out to the Hitching Post Inn where, many weeks earlier, I had made reservations for a wedding suite. The vehicle rocked along at the pace of a horse-drawn carriage. Jerry maneuvered that Jeep over and through snowdrifts six to eight feet high. I don't know how he did it, and several times I didn't think we would make it.

After treating everyone to a pancake breakfast at the Hitching Post Inn, our guests departed and safely made it home. I trotted down a long corridor to retrieve my small suitcase and noticed that the motel complex was swamped with stranded tourists who were sleeping on the floor, and thankful they were safely sheltered from the storm's fury. As I raced around a sharp corner, I somersaulted over a burly truck driver sprawled on the floor with his back to the wall. Somehow I ended up with my back to the same wall. He reeked of whiskey.

"That's all right buddy," he mumbled, "What else can us drunks do on a night like this except get bombed out of our senses?"

With my face only inches from his, I answered, "Get married!"

I thought he was going to hit me.

The newlyweds couldn't leave the premises for three days. Cheyenne's snow removal crews finally cleared enough streets that we could be rescued and taken to Templeton House.

That evening, we interrupted our honeymoon to attend our public wedding. All the Flemings and the Todds managed to congregate in the church for a beautiful ceremony, followed with a celebration of Holy Communion by the Fr. Stan Guille of St. Christopher's Episcopal Church in Cheyenne.

This time the church was reverently calm in its festive Christmas decorations; the chandeliers hung still, and the angels on the sanctuary lamp were serene, as if smiling in brassy quietude as they looked down upon us.

The bride was radiant in her full-length evening gown, and the soloist, the Reverend Dave Vanley, sang a song I had written myself. Ironically, it was a variation of the words to the song, "When the Snow Is on the Roses":

May God bless our wedding night
May He shine on us His Holy Light
WHEN THE SNOW IS ON THE ROSES
When the music fades away
May the tender vows we've spoken
Be the solemn words we'll pray

When I wrote that verse, what I had in mind was the roses being *dusted* with snow — not *buried* six feet under.

A lovely candlelight reception followed in Templeton House where the Todd family first experienced the elegant and graceful entertaining of the new Mrs. Rosemary Todd. The buffet table was spread out with an array of delicacies which included scalloped oysters, chicken crepes, and thinly sliced Kentucky country cured ham. The plum pudding was made from an old Wyoming recipe that my mother used on the ranch. I poured champagne and coffee from a tea cart.

Tragically, the Todd dance at the Ole' Mayflower on December 30, 1975, proved to be the last country swing ever held at the famous Cheyenne landmark. It burned to the ground under circumstances which also greatly affected our wedding plans for the next night. The horrendous blizzard on December 31 shut down the entire city of Cheyenne, and along with it, the Mayflower's New Year's celebration. When the help was let go early that afternoon — someone apparently left something turned on — and the whole establishment went up in flames leaving nothing but charred ruins. It was later rebuilt, but not with the charm of the original design and was never again Cheyenne's favorite gathering place and watering hole as it had been for many decades.

✧

With the wedding and snowbound honeymoon over, Rosemary and I began the formidable task of merging our two families into one. Between us, we now had six children — all daughters, with the exception of my son, Barry, and all teenagers.

Sometimes the merger seemed easy. At other times it was very difficult. Each separate personality has its own way of adapting to a new parental role model. Both Rosemary and I were put to the test. Their residual resentments over our former divorces would surface at unexpected times. Both our former spouses also remarried. Comparisons were made. One set of parents would be played off against the other. We thank God it all worked out as well as it did. Although sporadic tensions developed, no major conflagrations flared, and all six children moved into their maturity rather gracefully.

Rosemary and I were married at St. Mark's on New Year's Eve 1975 during a horrific blizzard. In addition to being a magnificent wife, nurturing mother, stepmother and Nana to twelve grandchildren, she was the ideal hostess for a busy Episcopal rectory.

Since then, frequent family celebrations and holidays have brought them all together under one roof. Fortunately, Templeton House was spacious enough to accommodate everyone. Rosemary has remained an entertainer par excellence, and the atmosphere is always pleasant and respectful.

We determined early on to make the merging of our families a spiritual endeavor. After mustering all the emotional maturity we could generate for the task at hand, Rosemary and I both realized that we needed to draw strength from a greater power. In a little alcove attic room, formerly a spare bedroom, we constructed a very simple meditation chapel. Every morning we celebrated a simple Eucharist, and every evening before bedtime we read Compline from the Episcopal Prayer Book.

Our love of God and one another sustained and nurtured us through the most difficult times in our pursuit of conjugal happiness and family tranquillity. We learned that peace of mind is not the absence of conflict but rather God's serenity in the midst of conflict.

✧

I officiated at the weddings of all six children in beautiful St. Mark's Church.

Lori Todd married Michael Gillgannon on December 28, 1973. They both continued as students at the University of Wyoming before moving to New York City, where Mike began a career with the federal Social Security Administration and where Lori graduated cum laude from New York University.

Barry Todd married Rose Kinsella on September 11, 1976. Barry was employed as a splicer at Mountain Bell and has since been associated with US West for over twenty years. He loves doing manual labor in all kinds of adverse weather conditions.

Mary Adamson married Tom Ingleby on July 12, 1980, and both returned to Salt Lake City so that she could complete her degree in interior design at the University of Utah while Tom worked as a survey engineer.

Kimberly Adamson married Jeff Neville on May 28, 1982, just before they moved to Nashville, where Kim began graduate study at Rosemary's alma mater, Vanderbilt University Hospital, to become a medical technologist. Jeff quickly became a construction superintendent.

Sheridan Todd married Tom Voycheske on December 27, 1982, and remained in Cheyenne, continuing her good job at Unicover Corporation. Tom became a licensed electrician.

Rebecca Adamson married Michael Kermode on August 15, 1984. Mike was a real estate broker in Denver, and Becky later graduated from the University of Colorado School of Engineering. They have since divorced.

After these six formal weddings, Rosemary and I finally had Templeton House all to ourselves — sort of. Now we had not only our own six children but six new in-laws as well. In our formal dining room at Templeton House we could accommodate all twelve descendants at one table for frequent family dinners and gatherings. But when twelve grandchildren later arrived on the scene, we had to resort to buffet dinners.

I'm proud to be the patronizing "Granddad" to all twelve children shown in these two separate family photos.

My descendant grandchildren. In front left to right (on lap), Riley Voycheske. Second row, Leah Gillgannon and Hailey Voycheske. Third row, Shaylyn Todd, Kristin Voycheske, and Daniel Gillgannon. Behind (tallest) Jonathan Todd.

Rosemary's descendant grandchildren. In front, Caitlin Ingleby and Spencer Neville. Back row, Christopher Neville, Aubrey Kermode, and Mathew Ingleby.

We also had buffet dinners for church groups, although they always required a lot of advance planning by Rosemary. Twice we served prime rib sit-down dinners to as many as seventy-five parishioners for our annual Christmas party. This was a bit much, however, and we had to move the affair to the parish hall. Through numerous parish functions we entertained over 500 people annually. Rosemary always handled her social responsibilities with great class and charm.

Her duties as rector's wife would have been easier to handle if Rosemary had been home all day at Templeton House. But she worked full-time as a nurse at the City-County Public Health Clinic in Cheyenne. She would leave the house at seven-thirty in the morning and not return until after six o'clock in the evening. Long days and hard work moved her up the ladder, and eventually she became nursing director.

Our two careers created emotional stress in our marriage. Rosemary was free on weekends to catch up on everything in our lives that needed attention. But my pastoral duties were the heaviest on weekends, so we never had time off together. We seldom could leave town for a day in Denver or a trip to the mountains. Such confinement was not good for the health and well-being of our marriage or for us personally. At the time, however, there seemed no alternative to the bind we were in.

One thing we did do every New Year's Eve, for a good many years, was enjoy a gala celebration of our wedding anniversary in Denver. Our insistence on getting married on New Year's Eve of 1975 was conditioned, in part, on the anticipation that this particular night would always be a party night, ideally suited for a wedding anniversary.

The Brown Palace Hotel was a perfect place. Built in the 1890s, it has always been the magnificent ol' historical landmark of downtown Denver.

As a lonely college kid at the University of Denver back in 1947, I could remember sitting in the grand lobby of the Brown Palace on a Saturday evening, wearing my tight-fitting Levi's, watching the gilded crowd of Colorado's most illustrious citizens flow in and out of the chandelier dining rooms. At that time, I distinctly remember thinking to myself that if this could ever happen to me, maybe after I finished college — this fact alone, would indicate to me that I had made a success of my life.

The grandeur of the old hotel had not diminished one bit thirty years later when wearing my tuxedo, I ushered Rosemary, aglow in a sweeping evening gown, into the Brown Palace Hotel for our wedding anniversary dinner. And then, the ecstasy to sashay across the elegant lobby to take an elevator to our suite on the top floor looking out upon the bright lights of the Denver skyline.

In addition to our annual anniversary trip to Denver, we did manage to get away for a three-week vacation every summer, which usually included a wonderful trip to Kentucky. I was pleased that our Kentucky trips were so pleasurable to Rosemary, because she was the one who was cut away from her roots. Living in Cheyenne was no personal sacrifice for me; I was within a five-hour drive of all five of my brothers and sisters living in the northern part of the state near Sheridan. And my younger sister, Sadie, lived within five minutes of Templeton House in Cheyenne. Although I didn't drive up to Sheridan but once a year, I knew I always could go more often if I wanted to. Rosemary didn't have that option.

Therefore, in fairness to her, we made plans to retire in Kentucky. We even purchased the small but beautiful old home of Rosemary's mother in Flemingsburg. By this time, however, all six of our children had married Westerners and lived (or planned to live) in the Rocky Mountain region. Retiring in Kentucky would actually mean moving away from the concentration of our children and grandchildren in Colorado and Wyoming. Rosemary and I preferred not moving ourselves too far away from this nexus of family. We enjoyed grandparenting too much.

✧

No church could provide a more perfect setting for a magnificent wedding than St. Mark's. The historic old Gothic edifice, with its towering overhead beams, its mixture of stone and wood, the play of light from its collection of lovely stained-glass windows, its marble floors polished like mirrors to reflect the bridal couple standing on the chancel steps, and the fanfare herald organ trumpets mounted on the rear wall of the nave, possessed a grandeur few places can match. As the bride stepped into the center aisle for her triumphant procession to the altar, the blaring of the fanfare herald trumpets always made my spine tingle.

A wedding reception in the beautifully restored parish hall could be just as exciting. The ladies guild became experts in doing decorative wedding receptions every bit as professionally as any hotel complex in Cheyenne.

Naturally, these advantages made St. Mark's Episcopal Church a very attractive and popular place for spectacular formal society weddings. It was also a lovely place for small simple weddings. I choose to mention three here because they were uniquely different from the norm that a minister usually encounters.

✧

One involved the marriage of a young Air Force captain named Lisa who was stationed at Warren Air Force Base. She explained that her beloved fiancee was an Air Force major stationed at Vandenberg Air Force Base in California.

In the Episcopal Church, premarital instruction must precede solemnization of the marriage ceremony. This presented itself as a problem to Lisa, who said her fiancee would not be able to come to Cheyenne until one day prior to the scheduled wedding. Such is often the case with military personnel. However, since she was leaving for TDY (temporary duty assignment) at Vandenberg for three months immediately prior to her wedding back at St. Mark's, I assured her that an Episcopal priest in California or a military chaplain could do the prenuptial counseling, provided that he send me a letter verifying that, indeed, the requirement had been fulfilled. In the meantime, Lisa could plan the entire wedding in advance so that when she and the major returned to Cheyenne, everything would be in place and ready to go.

As rector of St. Mark's, I instituted what I considered to be an ingenious wedding checklist system, which meant that a bride's family or a bridal couple would meet only with me instead of having to meet separately with the organist, sexton, altar guild, and reception committee. I would spend several hours with whoever was planning the wedding and check off all the options and special requests, together with the total costs involved. One check was written to the Rector's Discretionary Fund, and I was responsible then for making certain that proper payments were made to all the parties involved. The plan worked beautifully.

Lisa spent a lot of time with me selecting music and floral arrangements and finalizing special details. She felt very relieved that now she could leave for her TDY at Vandenburg, confident that the wedding was completely planned. All Lisa needed to do now was become reacquainted with her fiancee and complete the premarital counseling requirement in California.

Three months later, a radiant Lisa reappeared in my study, all ready for the long-awaited wedding. She produced a letter written by a military chaplain, an Episcopal priest no less, confirming that he had met with Lisa and her fiancee and successfully completed three lengthy sessions of premarital counseling. He felt confident that Lisa and Robert fully understood the seriousness of the religious vows they were making.

Lisa wanted to reaffirm all the previous wedding details we had worked out. Clipping the chaplain's letter to the folder, I opened the file and began itemizing with her all the previously made wedding plans.

Everything was perfectly in order, word for word, just as we had written it down three months earlier.

"I'm so pleased," she said, "that I worked all this out with you three months ago. Now I don't have to worry about a thing except Robert arriving here tomorrow in time for our wedding rehearsal."

She moved toward the door of my study to make her departure, but just before she closed the door she stepped back into the room and said, "The only thing that has changed . . . is the groom."

She was gone.

I ran after her. "Lisa, what do you mean, the only thing that's changed is the groom?"

"Well, previously I was to marry Major Robert Wells. But now I'm going to marry Colonel Robert Deming. This second Robert and I had previously gone together and then broke up. Then I took up with the first Robert and decided to get married. But during my TDY I accidentally came across the second Robert — who actually was the first Robert in my life — and we decided to get married instead."

I stood there flabbergasted.

"Don't worry, Father Todd. As far as the wedding goes, nothing has changed — just the groom."

Then, almost as if it were an aside, she said, "Besides this second Robert, who actually was the first Robert, outranks the other Robert. The Robert you're actually marrying me to, you see, is a colonel instead of just a major."

She turned and started down the stairs.

"Lisa," I called out after her, "please come back here. We need to talk."

✧

In every Episcopal wedding ceremony the priest reads the line, "If any of you can show just cause why these two persons may not lawfully be married, speak now, or forever hold your peace."

I've often wondered what I would do if someone stepped forward from the congregation with an honest-to-goodness objection. Would I try to clarify the objection and make a ruling then and there as to whether to proceed with the wedding? Would I ask the wedding party to retire into a separate room with the objector and seek to resolve the problem? Or would I announce to the whole congregation that the wedding was temporarily called off?

Thank God, it never happened. And then it did — although not from someone within the congregation.

Again, this was a situation where the premarital counseling was done elsewhere. I really didn't know the couple until they appeared at the church on the evening of the rehearsal.

I wasn't very impressed with the groom. He and his cronies isolated themselves off in one corner of the restaurant room in which we were having the rehearsal dinner. The bride had to practically pull him away to open a few wedding presents. I noticed that he never established direct eye contact with the bride or anyone else in the room and seemed to delight in making light of the gifts for the entertainment of his pals, always glancing their way to check out their responses to his wisecracks.

His antics were not funny to me or to others in the wedding party, only to his buddies, who howled in laughter at his inappropriate comments. I dismissed his behavior as extremely immature. But this wasn't the first time that I detected an attitudinal problem with the groom or the bride.

In the final minutes before the wedding the next afternoon, the bride's father drew me aside and said his daughter was extremely agitated after the rehearsal dinner. Apparently, according to him, the groom's buddies had staged a stag party in a hotel room, where they watched porno movies, romped with a striptease performer, and drank themselves into oblivion. "In fact," he said, "the groom and best man are both so sick from hangovers that they can barely function. And the whole bunch thinks it's all a lark. Frankly, I'm disgusted with them all. And I know that my daughter is terribly disappointed and upset. Almost in tears."

What else could we do at that late hour except proceed with the wedding?

As the wedding march began, the groom, groomsmen, and I made our entry into the church, as we had carefully rehearsed the night before. Down the aisle came the bridesmaids, the matron of honor, and finally the bride on the arm of her father. The bridal procession wasn't the usual pleasant scene one normally expects. An aura of considerable strain was evident to me, the glow was gone, although I could tell that the bride was struggling to put the best face on it all.

The wedding party assembled itself, and I began reading the opening address to the congregation. Shortly, I came to the proverbial charge: "If any of you can show just cause why these two persons may not lawfully be married, speak now, or forever hold your peace."

The usual silence prevailed from the congregation.

But there was a flutter of nervous movement from the bride, who hesitatingly spoke up and said, "I think — I think I object!"

There was an audible gasp from everywhere. The groom, swaying back and forth in his black patent shoes, suddenly awakened to reality. His bloodshot eyes popped open and his mouth flew ajar, as if this were only a glitch in his alcoholic haze, a sentence he hadn't heard correctly.

The bride mustered a bit more courage and said, "I've decided I don't want to go through with this wedding."

Then, leaning around her father, who was still standing between the bride and groom after escorting her down the aisle, she said directly to the groom in a loud clear voice, "Buford — you're such a pitiful jerk!"

Then she flew from the church, sobbing, followed by the bridesmaids like a flock of fluttering pigeons. The bride's mother and family made a hasty exit in pursuit of the fleeing bridal party, followed by the groom and groomsmen. Standing alone in the crossing was the mortified father of the bride.

When I finally reached the guild room, into which the bridal party had fled, I found the door blocked by the matron of honor, the bride's older sister, who had just been confronted by the groom as to what in the hell was going on. She minced no words. "Buford, not only are you a pitiful jerk, but you're a pitiful asshole as well!" Such graphic language made unnecessary any further comments from me.

Doors slammed, tires squealed out on the street, and the babble of confused voices faded off into the night. All turned quiet inside the church. Everyone was gone except the bride's family, the bridal party, and a few bewildered friends who had gathered around, wringing their hands as if at an Irish wake.

I returned to my study and lit up a cigarette, which was extraordinary for me because I had quit smoking long ago. Let's face it, there was too much stress in this situation for everyone, including me.

Soon the sequestered bride emerged from the guild room with mascara smudges all over her face. "Becky, I have to tell you," I said, "it took real courage to do what you have done. I also have to tell you that I have to admire you. Because if you had any doubts whatever — it's better late than forever."

I don't know where that line came from. It couldn't have been very consoling. But when you're in the midst of hysteria, how can anyone, even the priest, be expected to utter profound consolation?

Later we all toasted Becky with champagne intended for the reception. I asked her at what point she had come to the awesome conclusion that the marriage was off.

"Guess I've been in denial a long time," she answered tersely. "But during the long walk down the center aisle I suddenly realized that I've invited all these people here, my dearest friends and relatives, to watch me do something really stupid."

I only wish more of us could come to our senses during the long walk down the center aisle of the church.

I called the priest who did the premarital counseling and asked, "Weren't you aware that something was amiss?"

"Oh, yes," he answered, "but the bride's grandparents are pillars in my church and I wasn't about to rock the boat on that one."

WIMP!

✧

After forty years in the ministry I've come to the conclusion that weddings suffer a generational lag — if the mother of the bride (MOB) has anything to do with planning the wedding, that is. If the MOB is significantly involved it becomes the wedding she wished she could have had — had not her *own* mother become involved a generation earlier. Hence the generational lag.

It became obvious to me Sylvia was not in control of her own wedding at the time we went through the checklist of arrangements. She kept deferring all decisions to someone called Angela. Now Sylvia was a very attractive and intelligent college graduate who was marrying a handsome young officer who recently graduated from the Air Force Academy, and it was apparent to me that she was fully competent to make basic decisions for herself. But Sylvia kept saying, "Well, I'll leave that for Angela to decide."

In exasperation, I finally asked, "Who is this Angela you keep referring to?"

"Angela Francisco. She's my mother. I know it sounds strange, but she has always wanted me to simply call her Angela. She lives in Buenos Aires, Argentina."

"Really."

Sylvia explained that her father had died about ten years ago, and her mother, an Argentinian native, had been married and divorced three times since then. (The family inherited a silver mining fortune from the late grandfather.)

"Sylvia," I said, "we are here in Cheyenne, Wyoming, trying to plan your wedding, and you are deferring all decisions to your mother, who lives in Argentina. The distance is a little excessive, don't you think?"

"Not for Angela. Wait 'til you meet her. You'll see."

Her fiancee looked on as if he had heard this whole story several times before. "My mother is a very strong-headed woman," she continued, "and she's determined that since I'm her only child that this wedding must conform to her standards, not mine — even though this is my wedding. Don't get me wrong, she has impeccable tastes and does things well. But I know my mother well enough just to let her take charge. I'm okay with that."

A few days later I had a telephone call from a wedding consultant group in Denver telling me that a Mrs. Angela Francisco from Argentina had contracted with them, through a mutual friend in Aspen, to handle all preliminary wedding arrangements. They made an appointment with me to show them the church. It was as if I was escorting the Secret Service through the building. Every nook and cranny of St. Mark's was carefully checked out. Many questions were asked, and copious notes were taken.

"We can assure you, Father, that Mrs. Francisco will be most pleased with this church," I was told. "It's a beautiful church. More than that, however, it is in immaculate condition. It's obvious to us that it is beautifully cared for and lovingly maintained. The marble floors shine like mirrors. We can see that the antique pews have been hand rubbed with linseed oil. The stained-glass windows are exquisite. And those fanfare herald trumpets mounted on the back wall are truly astounding. We shall gladly report all of this to Mrs. Francisco."

The consultants explained to me that their firm would be responsible for every detail associated with the wedding, including a sit-down reception dinner served at Little America. They pulled a tape out of their briefcase and asked to measure me for my tuxedo.

"But I don't need a tuxedo," I protested.

"Father Todd, Mrs. Francisco wants this to be a very formal wedding and wants all participants in the ceremony to be formally attired."

"But a clerical suit and clerical collar are always socially acceptable for a priest at any formal occasion," I said.

"Mrs. Francisco is paying for your tuxedo, Father Todd. Maybe it's a little unusual for a priest to wear a tuxedo at a wedding reception, but that's only because this is a most unusual occasion for Mrs. Francisco. This is the wedding of her only daughter. Please, let's accommodate her wishes."

Finally, Angela Francisco swooped into town from Argentina, arriving in grand style in nothing less than a chauffeured white limousine from Denver. Attired in a very expensive businesswoman's suit, she cut quite a striking figure in burgundy red. The color only accentuated the loveliness of her face, her silvery black hair pulled into a coiffured configuration at the back of her head. Her dangling earrings and bracelets seemed a little excessive and ostentatious, especially for Cheyenne. I would guess she was about ten years older than I. She spoke English fluently but with just enough of a Spanish accent — intentional, I thought — to make her appear more aristocratic than she probably was. I must admit, however, that she was a very attractive woman.

I could also tell that she was a woman of strong will, a powerful force to be reckoned with, and I was glad that I was dealing more directly with the wedding consultants than with her.

The consultants conducted Mrs. Francisco on a church tour. Finally, the entourage met with me in my study. Our discussion of wedding plans was suddenly interrupted by Mrs. Francisco.

"My God," she stammered, looking straight at me, "You are the spitting image of my first boyfriend and lover. I wanted to marry him but, unfortunately, was forbidden to do so by my mother. I can't get over it. How could any two people, living on two separate continents, so perfectly resemble one another? You look just like him. You talk like him. You walk like him. How can this be?"

No one answered.

"Listening to my mother and not marrying him was the worst mistake I ever made in my entire life," she mused. "Later he died in a plane wreck. He was a pilot. You're his identical likeness."

I ignored her and went on with the wedding plans, but again she interrupted me, "It's haunting to sit here in this room and witness the physical reappearance of someone else you've intimately known who since has died. It's like a resurrection from the dead!"

Others in the room found this coincidence amusing and laughed nervously to relieve their obvious embarrassment. We resumed our conversation about the wedding. The consultants said, "Mrs. Todd and you are invited to both the rehearsal dinner and the formal reception dinner at Little America. We sincerely hope you are both planning to attend."

"There is no Mrs. Todd," I said. "We were recently divorced. I will be attending alone. Thank you for the invitation."

On the evening of the long-awaited wedding, I donned the tuxedo. The black patent leather shoes fit perfectly, as did the striped gray trousers and the swallowtail Prince Albert coat. I wore my black clergy shirt with clerical collar as I had insisted. I had to remove the jacket to vest in my white alb, stole, and chasuble to officiate the wedding nuptials.

The wedding went perfectly. The groom was attired in his formal air force uniform, flanked by fellow cadets in full military regalia from the academy. The bride was beautiful as she processed up the marble aisle of St. Mark's Episcopal Church, the fanfare herald trumpets resonating from the back wall with all the magnificent glory of a dozen trumpeters.

Following the vows, we moved into the second part of the wedding service, which consisted of Holy Eucharist. I served the blessed sacrament first to the bridal couple and their attendants. Then I announced that the families and congregation were now invited to come forward to kneel at the altar rail and receive Holy Communion.

In response to my open invitation, only Mrs. Angela Francisco — the MOB — rose majestically from her seat in the front pew. With great dignity she stepped out into center aisle, genuflected to her knees, then began her dramatic procession toward the altar. I motioned to other members of the families, on both sides of the aisle, to please accompany her, as we had carefully rehearsed the night before. Not a soul budged — instinctively knowing that if any of them dared to invade her space they would be struck dead by the Inca gods.

Mrs. Francisco made her grand procession across the open space between the congregation and chancel, stroked slowly and elegantly up the chancel steps, then through the chancel and up the altar steps. She bowed reverently to the altar, then knelt at the communion rail with all the regal dignity of the Queen of Spain. I served first the bread and then the chalice of wine, the Body and Blood of Christ, which she received with pious majesty. Then, crossing herself with an exaggerated motion, she rose to her feet and turned to face her adoring guests and with a look of grand nobility began her triumphant recessional, hands folded sanctimoniously in front of her chest as if she were the immortal Evita Peron herself. First across the chancel, then down the chancel steps with shoulders straight and head held high, she marched with her heels clicking behind her like little hammers on the marble floor and slid into the front pew.

No doubt about it, it was a first-class act. Every step had been carefully choreographed from the very beginning. It was Mrs. Angela Francisco's grand moment of glory, not to be shared with anyone else.

And there was no way the poor bride could compete with it.

While we were signing the parish register and wedding papers following the ceremony, one of the wedding consultants handed me a wrapped box and said, "Father, here is your studded shirt and tie so that you may be properly attired for the reception."

"For what?" I asked. "I don't need a shirt and black bow tie. I agreed to wear the striped gray trousers and cutaway frock coat, but I'm wearing my clergy shirt and clerical collar, just as I said I would. A clergyman doesn't need to wear anything more formal than that."

"Ah, Father, your religious duties are over and Mrs. Francisco wants you now to let go of your ministerial image, let down your hair, and deck yourself out for an evening of fun like everyone else."

I pulled off my shirt and clericals and they helped me into the stiffly pressed tuxedo shirt with a pleated front and high crimped wing-collar. They tied my black bow tie. I put on my swallowtail formal jacket and stepped in front of the full-length mirror. This was the first and only time in my life that I viewed myself in Prince Albert formal attire — as if I were attending the coronation of a king.

I felt conspicuously ridiculous and extremely self-conscious. A country Wyoming kid gone royal for a few hours of make-believe. Well, I might as well have fun playing the game.

At the elegant wedding dinner, my nameplate placed me at the head table beside Mrs. Francisco, who asked that we drop all formalities and resort to a first-name basis.

"Only my business associates address me as Mrs. Francisco. My family and friends call me Angela. My intimates call me Angie." Then, softening her voice she said, "Please call me Angie."

I didn't consider myself in that category of name calling. She in turn, would call me "Eu-shean," emphasizing her Argentinean accent. She had changed dresses. Instead of the lovely, flowing evening gown she had worn at the wedding, she was now wearing a long, tight-fitting outfit with a long slit up one leg, almost to her thigh. It looked more like something worn by a nightclub torch singer.

"Eu-shean," she said, "you say you're divorced. Look me straight in my eyes and tell me, is there another woman in your life?"

"No, not at all," I answered truthfully. This was before I began dating Rosemary.

"Tell me, Eu-shean, how's the divorced life treating you now that you're single and free?"

"Not good," I answered. I was only picking at the lavish presentation of food on my plate because I was still in such a depressive state of mind. "In fact, I'm not liking it at all."

"Oh, I know all about that, Eu-shean. You see, I've been married four times. My first husband died, but I divorced the last three within the past five years. It's not easy. Yes, I know all about it. When you're used to satisfying your man in bed and take great delight in doing so, and suddenly that's taken away from you, it takes a lot of emotional adjustment. Like you, I don't like it one bit."

That wasn't exactly what I had in mind when I answered her question.

The master of ceremonies announced the wedding dance. First the bridal couple was called to the open floor, while everyone ogled and applauded their close romantic dance. Then the attendants. Next the bridal parents.

Horrors!

Mrs. Francisco pulled me to the dance floor in full view of 200 wedding guests while the eight-piece orchestra played the anniversary waltz. She was a good dancer — except she did all the leading, which made me do the following. I dislike it when my female dancing partner insists on leading, because I'm not always certain I can follow. But with 200 wedding guests watching, all decked out like penguins at a presidential inaugural ball, what was I to do but put my best foot forward and follow?

Fortunately, other couples began crowding the dance floor.

"My God, I can't believe it!" she breathed in my ear, as we whirled, glided and dipped across the slippery floor dancing our *Ballroom Argentinio Grande* — with her still leading, grandstanding as the flamboyant dance mistress, and me her stooge, with every step feeling a greater fool.

"Believe what?" I asked.

"Not only do you look just like him — my first lover, I mean — but you walk like him. You talk like him. You laugh like him. Now you dance just like him too. Eu-shean, I bet you do everything just like him too, don't you?"

I ignored her question, dismissing it as only a frivolous comment. But then she repeated the same inquiry in such a way that I knew it was an open question. She was expecting an answer.

"Mrs. Francisco," I said. "Excuse me — I mean Angela."

"Please call me Angie."

"Angela, there's no way I can answer that question. There's no way I could really make that comparison, is there?"

"No, I guess not," she sighed. She snuggled up cheek to cheek for a closer dance, flirtatiously blew in my ear and whispered, "But I sure could!"

I knew right then I was in for an ecstatic evening I might never forget and would always regret. Also I knew that I must quickly decide, as a midlife bachelor, whether I wanted to become a one-night stand-in for the old flame of a mother of the bride.

A new job description for a single Episcopal rector!

This wedding wasn't for Angela's daughter; it was the wedding the MOB had hoped to have for herself twenty-five years earlier, had not her own mother intervened. And it was apparent to me that this was also to become her own wedding *night* — with the fantasy of the man she wanted to marry in the first place — her first love, now long dead — had not her mother interfered with that as well.

Poor Sylvia, the beautiful young bride. She must patiently wait for another generation, when her future daughter marries, before she can plan the wedding she should have had for herself at St. Mark's Episcopal Church back in 1974.

✧

Regarding this emotional depression, to which I have just referred in my little episode with Angela Francisco, and earlier in this book; a close psychiatrist friend of mine once told me that clinical depressions generally fall into two categories: *biological* and *situational*.

A biological depression, he explained, apparently is induced by physiological changes within the brain, which when treated with medication, often restores the delicate chemical balance that needs to be there.

On the other hand, situational depression generally results when someone experiences severe emotional stress or experiences a significant loss in their life.

My depression was situational.

Obviously I was feeling intense pressure from the emotional stress of my ministry at St. Mark's Church during America's turbulent 1960s and early 1970s. I discovered that I had become more of a Christian social activist than what I intended which exacted more of a toll on my emotional well-being than what I had realized and was willing to admit.

In addition to that, however, was the crushing defeat of my marriage and the overwhelming sense of failure that engulfed me. Experiencing firsthand a divorce prompts me to suggest that in many ways the breakup of a marriage is worse than the death of a spouse because you suffer not only the loss of a loved one — but bitter personal failure and rejection as well. With the death of a wife, for example, a grieving husband has the support and love of his community of faith. With divorce, too often, his grief is compounded with criticism and public scorn.

Treatment for situational depression, as I understand it, is not medication, which may be helpful in temporarily alleviating some of the symptoms — but passing through the valley of the shadows until you climb out into the sunshine on the mountain above it. It is growing and maturing through it.

Barbara Bush, our nation's former first lady for whom I have enormous respect, in her memoirs described a situational depression in her life, that nearly brought her down, triggered by the infant death of a child. She said afterward in a television interview, "I don't mean to be Pollyanna, but I'm glad now that I had that terrible depression back then. It matured me."

Four factors primarily contributed to my recovery from depression.

First among them was the awesome affirmation from God that I was going to survive it. That I would live — and not die — was a powerful message which I mystically experienced on the mountaintop back on my family's ranch, about which I wrote in a previous chapter. I am absolutely convinced that the Lord took me by the hand and led me through it, after I had reached out for Him.

Then there was the loving affection of my children and the emotional support of my closest friends. Most important was the mature understanding and nurturing love which came my way through my marriage to Rosemary. If the Lord held me by one hand, there's no question that she took me by the other hand — because I reached out to her as well.

A third factor was I worked hard at getting well. The more depressed I felt, the harder I worked at my job and ministry as rector of St. Mark's Church — because this preoccupation with human needs and concerns outside of myself distracted my attention and made me feel better. I would visit the sick in the hospital and say to myself, *Just think how much better off you are than that poor fellow with terminal cancer.*

Finally, I desperately tried never to lose my sense of humor. When I was caught in a crying jag, I would deliberately find something to laugh about. When you look around that's not hard to do. There are too many life situations or things about the world, yourself, and others which are hilarious if you allow yourself the healing grace of laughter. The old adage is true, "Laugh and the world laughs with you . . . cry and you cry alone."

The point is, the depression finally lifted like a hot-air balloon and slowly drifted up and away.

This is not to say that there hasn't been discouragements or times when I'm blue and in the dumps. In fact, many times. But these passing spells are intermittent and are nothing in comparison to the excruciating despair which painfully engulfed me during my personal "Great Depression" of 1973 and 1974.

My life was immeasurably enriched through the hell of it all. Like Barbara Bush, I can honestly fall on my knees and thank God for it! The president's wife, and all of us who have suffered depression, may take consolation in knowing we have noble company. The great Christian Carmelite mystic of the sixteenth century, St. John-of-the-Cross, wrote about the "dark night of the soul" when his vision of God faded into spiritual desolation. Abraham Lincoln frequently suffered such severe fits of melancholy that his friends feared for his life. Winston Churchill often talked about the "black dog" that continuously stalked him and would viciously attack when he least expected it.

It's important for me to say that God didn't abandon or punish me in my depression. He simply walked through the dark valley with me until we came out into the sun-drenched field on the other side.

My God and I
Go in the field together
We walk and talk as good friends should and do
We clasp our hands
Our voices ring with laughter
My God and I
Walk thru the meadow's hue
This earth will pass
And with it common trifles
But God and I
Will go unendingly.

Chapter 17

H arvey began attending services at St. Mark's very quietly. He would slip in and out of church without anyone getting to know who he was. He was about fifty years old and didn't seem acquainted with our Episcopal liturgical worship. He would sit by himself through the service while everyone else stood to sing a hymn and knelt to pray. He seemed lost in the liturgy yet kept coming back Sunday after Sunday.

Finally, at the end of one service I insisted that he accompany me over to the parish hall for the coffee hour. I learned that he worked for the Union Pacific in Cheyenne but owned a permanent residence in Denver, which he rented out. He was a bachelor who had never married. He was a member of the Church of God, but that denomination didn't have a church in Cheyenne, so he became attracted to St. Mark's Church for reasons he himself couldn't explain.

"Maybe it's your sermons," he said. "They always make me think."

I invited him to confirmation classes, which he attended, and for the first time he learned why Episcopalians do the strange things we do during liturgical worship. He began kneeling with the congregation for prayers and eventually came forward to receive Holy Communion at the altar rail. Yet he refused to be confirmed into the church, saying he wasn't ready for such a radical departure from his Church of God denominational background.

He attended Sunday services faithfully for another year and signed up for a second series of confirmation classes and was confirmed by the bishop. Even though he was now a full-fledged Episcopalian, he seemed hesitant and withdrawn from full participation in our community of faith. He seemed quite a loner, but occasionally pairs of male friends would accompany him to church.

This hesitancy bothered me, so one day I invited him into my study to discuss his ambivalence. In spite of his vagueness, I sensed that he was becoming quite fascinated with the Episcopal Church, particularly as he told about attending services at Grace Cathedral in San Francisco with a couple of friends he knew there. He explained that these men had accompanied him to church at St. Mark's one time when visiting here in Cheyenne.

On a sudden impulse of the moment, I blurted out the question, "Are they homosexual?"

"Yes, they are."

"Harvey, are you homosexual?"

"Yes, I am. Why do you ask?"

"I really don't know," I answered truthfully. There was no response from Harvey. Silence hung heavy in the room, and I realized I had no right to pry further into his privacy. So I resumed the conversation about liturgical worship in the Episcopal Church and was quite prepared to forget the interchange when I noticed that Harvey's eyes were brimming with tears. I went on with my liturgical explanation of things Episcopal and then saw tears streaming down his face. Suddenly Harvey burst into uncontrollable sobbing.

"Harvey, can I help you?" I said, as I moved toward his chair. "Did I offend you with that stupid question about something which is none of my damn business? I'm sorry if I did."

He buried his face into his hands, and his whole body shook from his weeping. Eventually he calmed down enough to finally say, "Father Todd, I always knew that someday a minister would discover that I am homosexual. And when that happened, I always knew that I would be publicly condemned to hell before the whole congregation and railroaded out of the church. It happens all the time to people like me."

He wiped his face with a handkerchief, "But when I made that confession to you just now, you didn't condemn me at all. You went on as if — as if it didn't make any difference to you. Almost as if I could stay in my new church home here if I wanted to do that. That I wouldn't be railroaded out. Is that what you're saying? If I'm reading you wrong, you won't need to publicly railroad me out of the congregation — because I'll just quietly slip away as if I had never been here in the first place."

I was absolutely stunned. I knew virtually nothing about homosexuality, but it had never occurred to me that a homosexual would not be treated like any other human being — a child of God seeking forgiveness and grace — to be warmly welcomed into the Christian Church.

Hence, began my odyssey of learning about homosexuality.

Several conversations later, Harvey invited me to join him in attending an evening service at a newly established church in Denver whose ministry was primarily focused toward the gay community. "What about this Sunday?" he asked.

"I can't this Sunday, Harvey. Maybe another time."

He persisted, and finally after five or six months of procrastination I realized I had better oblige the invitation or tell Harvey outright I simply was not interested. Fortified with prayer, I girded myself with all the courage I could muster and, for the first time, entered a church sanctuary completely filled with homosexuals. I expected to be either sexually assaulted or thrown into the alley.

Neither happened.

As a matter of fact, the service was the same as any other, perhaps a little on the evangelical side. There was enthusiastic hymn singing, a robed choir in procession, great preaching by a minister wearing a pulpit gown, and a service of Holy Communion to which everyone was invited. My naiveté was revealed when I whispered to Harvey, "Do you think the minister is gay? Or is he a heterosexual ministering to a gay community like a foreign missionary would minister to natives?"

"Of course he's gay," Harvey answered.

"Do you think the whole congregation here knows that?" I whispered. The question wasn't worth answering.

The Christian fellowship was called the Metropolitan Community Church (MCC). It was a new denomination organized by the Reverend Troy Perry of Los Angeles, who had just written a book on his life entitled, *The Lord Is My Shepherd and He Knows I'm Gay.*

I read that book. Then I read every book on homosexuality that I could find — scholarly books authored by psychiatrists and professional sexologists, as well as books of personal stories written by the parents and families of gay people. Although the practice of homosexuality was personally offensive to me, for reasons I didn't understand and couldn't articulate, I wanted to learn why it was that some people were gay and others were not; why one brother in a large family was gay while the others were not; why one sister was lesbian when no one else in the family was homosexual. They all shared the same family upbringing together, yet that one person seemed singled out, as if somehow destined to have a different sexual orientation.

I discovered that I had much to learn. Although most medical researchers believe the development of homosexual orientation is influenced by a constellation of environmental factors, they have reason to believe that that they have discovered a biological gene (or genes) which makes it difficult to regard homosexuality as solely a matter of personal choice. More recent medical research continues to confirm this contention that the basic root cause is more genetic than social. Whatever the basic root cause, however, sexual orientation seems to be permanently fixed by the time a child is four years old. I have talked to scores of homosexuals, and not one of them ever remembers making a conscious decision to become gay.

The same with straights. I've never heard a heterosexual confess that he made the decision to become straight, let's say, when he was seventeen years old while attending the high school senior prom. Obviously, his decision to become sexually active is enormously different from deciding his primary sexual orientation, which was well established long before he even thought about it — most certainly by the time he was four years old as well.

Psychiatrists and social scientists seem to agree that the only people who make a decision about their sexual orientation are bisexuals. Since they are attracted to both sexes, it follows that they must eventually make a decision as to which way they prefer to go. But this choice really isn't viable to bona fide homosexuals or heterosexuals, because we are born either to be one or the other. Our basic sexual orientation seems to be a genetic condition, a "given" in our lives, over which we exercise little or no choice. Hence, homosexuality is not a deliberately chosen psychological perversion that can be "cured" by fervent religious conversion.

My academic reading on homosexuality was an intellectual pursuit, a solitary venture conducted in the privacy of my home rather than in the real world of homosexuality itself. I soon discovered the human side of homosexuality.

I learned about it firsthand from many private conversations with the people I met at Metropolitan Community Church of Denver. Their personal stories were often tragic. Men and women whose heads had been bashed in during unauthorized police raids. Sons and daughters who had been rejected by their families and kicked out onto the streets. Church members who were publicly condemned in front of the whole congregation, literally pulled from their pew, and thrown down the front steps — as Harvey feared. Parents who lost custody of their children and were permanently denied all visiting rights. Workers who were indiscriminately fired from their jobs with no right of appeal. Tenants who were evicted from their apartments with no legal recourse. Homeowners who were ordered to abandon their premises or threatened with violent physical harm. Patients who were denied proper medical treatment. All these human beings had been forced to stay in the closet and lie about their sexuality — or be wiped out of existence.

Hearing these tales of horror directly from homosexuals made me wonder how anyone could be cruel enough to suggest that gays would deliberately choose a lifestyle which makes themselves the target of public scorn, personal ridicule, and group persecution? It became apparent to me that bigotry places homosexuals on the lowest rung of society, a step below the victims of racial prejudice. Even minorities, who have suffered severe discriminatory injustice, can be terribly prejudiced against gays and lesbians.

But the stories I heard from homosexuals weren't all tragic. I met men and women who were among the most creative artisans of Denver high society; doctors, lawyers, and professors; prosperous and successful businessmen and women; even carpenters and construction workers, people whose outward appearance or mannerisms would never hint at the lifestyle hidden from public view.

I also must admit that there were those within the MCC who would match the stereotypical image so often projected on our American consciousness, everything from burly muscled "dykes on bikes" to effeminate drag queens. The height of incongruity, it seemed to me, *is men dressing up like women to make themselves attractive to men — who are not attracted to women.* Tragically, these poor guys honestly believe they are women trapped in men's bodies. At first I was offended by the weird appearance and behavior of this conspicuous minority, then embarrassed for them. Later I came to accept them with a strange mixture of puzzlement and humor. But I never felt very comfortable in their presence, and consequently never mingled freely among them — generally avoiding them if I could. This says far more about me, however, than it does about them. But these extremes, however, were a small percentage of the gay and lesbian people I met.

It seems to me that the Christian Church has had an appalling 2000-year history of condemning any human condition which at first we don't understand, that appears threatening or unnatural. Lepers were treated as loathsome sinners. Epileptics were thought to be possessed by Satan and were burned alive at the stake. Those suffering from mental illness or retardation were chained and abused. The physically handicapped received similarly uncompassionate treatment. Alcoholics were condemned as sinners and excommunicated. Even the terminally ill were accused of lacking the necessary faith to effect a spiritual healing.

Once the medical cause was established for all these human ailments, then the church reversed itself and graciously offered a ministry of acceptance and compassionate healing to those afflicted. But deplorable harm had already been done to those who suffered not only from the disease itself but also from social ostracism, personal rejection, and spiritual condemnation.

It would seem to me that we could learn from this tragic church history. Christians today must have the courage and compassion to stand up and reverse our catastrophic pattern of judgmentally condemning a human condition which at first we don't understand. Particularly when all the scientific facts aren't yet available to us. And it's safe to say, the jury is still out on the ultimate root causes of homosexuality.

If redemption was Christ's mission, then why must we make condemnation the mission of the church? If the church must err when it comes to its dealing with homosexuality, why cannot it err on the side of mercy and compassion rather than on the side of judgment and condemnation?

The Metropolitan Community Church of Denver was reorganized into the MCC of the Rockies in May 1974, and I was invited to attend the chartering ceremony in a downtown Methodist church. Rosemary and I have graciously been invited back to each anniversary celebration since. Once I was invited to be the speaker. It's always a gala affair consisting of a large worship service late on a Sunday afternoon followed with wine and hors d'oeuvres in the parish hall. Then we sit down to a magnificent prime rib dinner.

Although I normally attend only the annual anniversary service, I have watched the church grow from a small struggling fellowship into a well-established congregation who purchased and beautifully renovated their own church building only a few blocks from St. John's Episcopal Cathedral. In this finely appointed edifice they offer an authentic and viable Christian ministry to the homosexual community of Denver. The place is in constant use, day and evening, for professional counseling, study groups, and therapeutic support meetings of every type and variety.

Its pastor, Dr. Charlie Arehart, has become a good friend of mine. Charlie acquired his doctorate at the Iliff School of Theology, my alma mater, and is competently trained and skilled as a preacher, counselor, and teacher. We have lunch together several times a year. Truly, Charlie is a "theologian in residence" to the gay community of Denver. His Christian sermons and lifestyle bring hope and inspiration to hundreds of homosexuals who otherwise would be condemned, rejected, and abandoned by the established religious communities of our day.

It was my privilege to spend some private time with Charlie when his life companion, Dan, a CPA and professional breeder and champion showman of Russian wolfhounds, was killed in a car wreck in 1993. Obviously, his grief was precisely the same as it would have been for any husband or wife suffering a similar loss. And I related to his grief exactly the same as well.

Charlie introduced me to Troy Perry, who founded the MCC fellowships throughout the world. Troy is a unique individual whose charismatic preaching makes him one of the most entertaining speakers I've ever met. Coming out of the Pentecostal movement of the deep South, he preaches like an evangelist at a Holy Roller camp meeting, but he's not fundamentalist anymore. Fundamentalism was pounded out of him long ago.

Several times I've been invited to Charlie Arehart's home for sherry and enlightened bull sessions with special out-of-town guests. One such special occasion was a delightful evening spent with Dr. Norman Pittenger, the famed Oxford don, Anglican theologian, and author of many books. He conversationally lectured us on the merits of process theology. Not one word was spoken about human sexuality, blunting the common heterosexual stereotype that sex is all that male homosexuals talk about among themselves.

My inability to relate emotionally to homosexuality was constantly brought to my attention. Once I complained about the practice of same-sex couples holding hands when they came forward to receive communion with the MCC congregation. "Why must they make such a public display of their affection in church?" I asked. "Heterosexuals don't do this in straight churches."

"Gene," I was told, "this is the only place in America where gay and lesbian couples can safely display their affection without the threat of public condemnation or physical violence. Heterosexuals can exercise this right anytime, anywhere. Don't you come in here and suggest that this safe haven be taken away from them!"

They were right and I was wrong.

Another mistake I made was to state that homosexuality was out of sync with the natural order of God's universe. Male and female genitalia are beautifully designed to perfectly fit each other in sexual intercourse, I maintained, so in that particular sense homosexuality is unnatural. I still believe this. But homosexuals were quick to point out that attraction to the opposite sex was not natural for them. And besides, they said, the glory of human sexuality is infinitely more than two bodies fitting perfectly together — but an emotional bond with mystical overtones which far exceeds the physical dimension of their intimate relationships. I believe that, too — especially when homosexual and heterosexual couples honor one another in a union of love and commitment.

I admit that I still have much to learn about homosexuality in general. But my ignorance gives me no right to condemn homosexuals in particular. I remain open to learning more about human sexuality, the same as I remain open to learning about everything else in life. God put us on this earth with the ability to study and learn about things we don't understand. That's what being created in the image of God is all about.

This personal experience with the MCC enabled me to take a public stand on the right of homosexuals to receive and enjoy the full ministry of St. Mark's Episcopal Church. This was at a time (the late 1960s and early 1970s) when homosexuality was first being openly acknowledged in America. Prior to this time it was a forbidden secret, never a topic of public discussion. Of course, homosexuality has existed in documented history since about 5000 BC.

For the first time in the Episcopal Church the question was raised: "Are we to allow homosexuals at our communion rails?"

Yes, the answer seemed to be, as long as we don't know about it — but not if their perversion becomes public knowledge. There was general agreement that all people are sinners, but their sin of homosexuality was somehow worse than ours. The topic became a subject of popular debate among Episcopalians.

Statistics indicate that roughly five percent of our population is homosexual. We had 200 families at St. Mark's, which translates to approximately 600 church members. That would mean we had around 30 members whose basic sexual orientation was homosexual. I personally felt that percentage was a little high. I knew of about a dozen people in St. Mark's who probably would consider themselves homosexual. They were active in our church, served on the altar guild, sang in the choir, and were elected to the vestry. Some were married, and some were divorced. Some were single and would never marry. And then there were parents whose homosexual sons and daughters were now adults who lived elsewhere. They too were active members of the parish.

We seldom talked about it. But I could see them wince when homosexuals were ridiculed or condemned at a parish meeting. I saw the expression of pain in their eyes when a fellow parishioner, a friend of theirs, ranted on and on about courting "undesirables" in our church. A mother told me, "My gay son faithfully served as an acolyte in our church many years before that man ever became an Episcopalian. The pure gall of that man to stand up there and pontificate as to whether a person like my son is worthy to receive communion in the Episcopal Church makes my blood boil."

In our weekly church newsletter, the *Messenger*, I reminded the parishioners of St. Mark's of Christ's command to those who were about to attack a woman who committed adultery, another sexual sin: "Let him without sin cast the first stone."

I then made it abundantly clear that those who considered themselves homosexual were welcome to the full ministry of St. Mark's Episcopal Church. Inappropriate sexual behavior by either homosexuals or heterosexuals would not be tolerated. Flaunting one's sexuality, whatever it was, was unacceptable. But basic sexual orientation, by itself, was not grounds for excommunication or deprivation of Christ's ministry to sinners. And when I said "sinners," I presumed that this included all of us.

Bishop Thornberry, who in 1969 succeeded J. Wilson Hunter as bishop of Wyoming, called me on the phone. "Gene," he said, "you are the first Episcopal clergyman in Wyoming that I know of who has publicly come out in defense of homosexuals' having a right to the full ministry of the church. I commend you for it. But I want to warn you, in case you don't already know it, that there will probably be those in your congregation who will accuse you of being homosexual simply because you've spoken out strongly on the subject. I hope you're prepared for that. I also want you to know that I'm prepared to back you up all the way."

"Yeah, I know, because it's already happened." I responded. "A man has already written to the vestry suggesting that if I wish to minister to homosexuals then I should leave the Episcopal Church and join a gay church. The same thing happened when I attended the Yale School of Alcoholic Studies — it was rumored that I was a secret alcoholic. When I delivered the invocation at a Republican breakfast rally for presidential hopeful Gov. Nelson Rockefeller, it was rumored that I secretly had become Republican. But when I had prayer for the Christian Cowboy Association no one even suggested the thought that maybe I had become a secret rodeo cowboy. Funny how people will believe whatever they want to believe."

The same layman who suggested I become a gay minister (who has since left the Episcopal Church, citing a multitude of objections to the liberality of our national denominational leadership) once said to me, "Gene, are you willing to prove to me you're not homosexual?"

"How, Frank?" I asked. "By finding you repulsive and your wife attractive?"

He didn't think my answer was funny — and it wasn't. Frankly, I thought his question offensive and inappropriate. No one has to prove their sexuality to anyone. And no one has the right to ask for such proof. Besides, my personal sexuality was none of his damn business. But it reminded me of a common complaint I've heard from gays and lesbians that once you're branded as homosexual, then your private sex life becomes fair game for inquiry and judgment by anyone.

An Episcopal priest in Colorado once said to me, "I'm willing to concede that the probable cause of homosexuality is genetic. It's in their genes. They're no more responsible for their sexual orientation than I'm at fault for my genetic makeup. But having said that, it seems to me then that the Christian thing for homosexuals is to take the vow of celibacy and abstain from all sexual activity."

On the surface this may seem reasonable. But none of us is genetically perfect. I was born with a genetic deficiency when it comes to music. I can't read music, play an instrument, or carry a tune. Choir directors have always begged me not to sing out loud because I was always off key. I was ordered never to sing on microphone during radio broadcasts from St. Mark's because it made an "abominable noise unto the Lord."

Yet should I deny myself the beautiful stereo systems I've installed in my home and study so that I could enjoy classical music night and day? Should I deny myself the pleasure of quietly singing hymns for my own private enjoyment? Or dancing the polka? Like most people, music greatly enhances my physical and spiritual well-being. Although I am not constitutionally gifted for music, I've made the most with what I had — and I've loved it. I have no intention of musical abstinence.

Perhaps the reader could say that the only thing wrong with my analogy is that an inherited deficiency in music is not considered a biblical sin whereas homosexuality is specifically mentioned as an abomination unto the Lord. But a homosexual could respond by asking, "If I was born this way, then why is it a sin to be what God genetically created me to be?"

I'll let those who presume to speak infallibly for God — answer that one.

There are those who score moral points by condemning homosexuality on the grounds that its anti-family — if everyone followed suite the traditional family would disappear. Presumably they would vehemently oppose monasticism for the same reason, or single people who prefer not to marry. But that dire homophobic prediction is absurd when only five percent of our population is inclined to be gay, in the first place, with no evidence that a primal heterosexual has ever been "talked into" becoming homosexual. Our inherent sexual orientation, one way or the other, is too deeply ingrained for such casual switching. I fail to see how the living relationship of a Susan and Joyce, for example, threatens any good straight marriage unless a scapegoat for failure is desperately needed.

Surely the moralistic proponents of the "anti-family" stance are not suggesting that all homosexuals enter into dysfunctional marriages in order to save the American family. Or worse yet, heaven forbid, implying that the fidelity and sanctity of straight marriages is dependent upon all gays and lesbians taking the vows of perpetual chastity!

The well-intended suggestion of the Colorado priest that homosexuals should simply practice abstinence because they're genetically flawed, is asking them to deny forever — and ever —the tender affection and physical joy of sexual intimacy which is a basic human need the rest of us simply take for granted. That suggestion, to me, is the height of arrogance.

Our human condition is flawed. No one can live out God's perfect intention in a fallen world. Since we're each born into this world with a flawed condition of one kind or another, let us not maneuver ourselves into a position where we say, "My flaw is acceptable to God — but yours is not."

If it were true that homosexuality is nothing more than a free-will choice and has nothing to do with genetics then, it follows, that there would be a simple solution to its eradification the world over: education. Beginning with kindergarten, we could simply teach heterosexuality to our kids and that would be the end of homosexuality. Such a step, of course, would fly in the face of the fundamentalists' vehement objection to anything resembling sex education in our public schools. But they probably would lift their objection if we turned sex education completely over to them.

But then, gay bashing is too lucrative a sport for filling the coffers of television evangelists. Most of them would not willingly surrender their easiest way to acquire a new gold-plated Cadillac.

As an irreversible heterosexual, I no longer am threatened by homosexuality. Therefore, I have no need to attack and condemn this human phenomenon, even though I don't fully understand it. I am reminded again of the old proverb, "Beware of he who protesteth too much." Homophobia is not only a deadly sin but also a dead giveaway of those who have not fully resolved their own sexuality.

At the same time, I personally affirm that, ideally human sexuality is God's gift to be joyfully shared between husband and wife within the bond and covenant of marriage, where they find a wholeness they cannot find separately, where it has the potential to connect us to our real selves.

One of my favorite quotations from the Episcopal Prayer Book is from the wedding ceremony:

The union of husband and wife in heart, body, and mind is intended by God for their mutual joy; for the help and comfort given one another in prosperity and adversity; and, when it is God's will, for the procreation of children and nurture in the knowledge and love of the Lord.

If we lived in a perfect world, perhaps, there would be no homosexuality. Neither would there be cancer, heart disease, and mental illness. Certainly not divorce. Nor would there be heterosexual hang-ups and aberrations. We would all be perfect.

But we don't live in a perfect world. We live in a fallen world, and we have all fallen short of the glory of God. St. Paul commends us to press on toward perfection of body and soul knowing full well we will never achieve it in our lifetime. Therefore, it seems to me that everyone, including heterosexuals and homosexuals, must accept our flawed human condition, whatever it is, and make the most with what we have and offer it as our gift to God. This requires moral choices — freely exercised and always motivated by love, accepting responsibility for our actions. Even here we shall fail over and over again. Nevertheless, we keep trying.

If God had it all to do over again, He might eliminate human sexuality altogether, since we seem to have allowed it to become the bane of our existence rather than the ecstatic gift of creation He intended it to be. God, in His infinite wisdom, could certainly dream up a less contentious and hedonistic way for humans to reproduce, if procreation is the only purpose of it all. Maybe new medical technology with DNA cloning could come to our rescue and scientifically get us off the hook.

But I'm not looking for a way to get off the hook.

I would rather deal kindly with all our sexual flaws, both heterosexual and homosexual, in this imperfect world than to live without sex in the perfect world. Christ once said that in heaven there is no marriage (Matthew 22). I've heard it preached that presumably this means there is no sexuality there either.

That's not my heavenly hope.

✧

My first contact with an AIDS patient occurred in 1985, when I purchased my first Macintosh computer from a Denver retailer. I was house-sitting a lovely mountain home up near Evergreen, which afforded me a perfect opportunity to get out the owner's manual and try to comprehend the awesome new machine. When I got myself into an impossible bind I would simply haul the computer back to the retailer for help, which he would usually provide immediately.

In the process of these computer training sessions, the people there got to know me quite well. One morning a clerk, who also had a home near Evergreen, looked up from the computer screen and said point-blank, "Father Todd, I'm not acquainted with your Episcopal church, but I would like to ask you what you think about an Episcopal church that ostracized one of its most valuable and talented members the moment the members found out he was gay."

"Sad. Very sad."

"Furthermore, what if I told you that this organist and choir director was discovered to be gay only when he became terminally ill with AIDS. He's my neighbor and has a beautiful A-frame home up in Evergreen. He has always been the best neighbor you'd ever want. But now he's dying. In fact, he's in the final stage of the disease and asked that he be allowed to die at home, in peace, by himself. He won't last much longer. He's not even forty years old. In fact, I expect to find him dead every night when my wife and I check in on him. My wife is a nurse and helps him with his medications."

He leaned back in his chair and pulled off his glasses. "You know what really pisses me off the most? Excuse the expression, Father, but that's how I feel. What really pisses me off is that his own priest refuses to call on him or even bring him Holy Ccommunion — which he desperately wants. What do you think about that?"

"Abominable!" I said, "absolutely abominable. That would constitute a grave violation of his priestly vow."

"Now then, let me ask you this. You're an Episcopal priest. As a personal favor for me in return for my helping you on your computering, would you be willing to take him communion?"

What could I say? To have excused myself on the technicality that I was outside the diocesan jurisdiction of Wyoming and was not licensed to practice my priesthood in Colorado would have been a heartless and dishonorable cop-out. Arrangements were made, and I followed directions up the winding mountain road to a lovely A-frame house. Beside my prayer book, I brought with me a miniloaf of freshly baked bread and a bottle of wine.

As I climbed out of my car and walked toward the A-frame home, I saw Craig for the first time. He came slowly shuffling along the deck as if he were an eighty-year-old man, stooped and haggard, leaning heavily on a cane. His clothes hung on him as if he were a scarecrow, and his face was badly blotched — at least, that part of his face which I could see, the part that wasn't hidden behind an enormous pair of dark glasses. I stepped out onto the deck and introduced myself as we shook hands.

His first words to me, almost inaudible because his voice was so weak, were: "Do you realize what you've just done?"

"No, I don't." I said, puzzled. "What did I just do?"

"You shook hands with me. You touched me!"

Frankly, I had momentarily forgotten what little I knew about the contagious nature of AIDS, and my shaking hands with him was more a spontaneous reaction than anything else. But I was stunned with the sudden reminder that, indeed, the victims of AIDS had become the new untouchables of American society. He led me toward the shaded front portion of the deck, holding onto my arm to steady his tottering gait.

"You do know that I have AIDS, don't you? And that I'm in the final stages of the disease and that I'm dying? I want to be very sure that you know that."

I nodded.

"Well, because of this terminal disease I couldn't even find a mortuary that's willing to cremate my body. Can you believe that?" He chuckled a gallows laugh, but it was neither funny to him or me. "That's why I marveled that you were willing to shake hands with me a moment ago. You touched me!"

He directed me to a patio chair and slumped into the other one. I placed my plastic bag containing the wine and bread on the little table between us. Stretching out below us were the foothills sloping down from the Rockies, and off in the distance we could see the haze of Denver.

"What a beautiful view," I said.

"It's always beautiful — winter, spring, summer, or fall. That's why I bought this A-frame a few years ago. I wanted a home in the mountains. And if you think it's beautiful in the daytime, you ought to see it at night. The flickering lights of the city are fantastic. I love it up here. That's why I checked myself out of the hospital, against medical advice, because if I'm to die at thirty-eight years of age I want it to be here and not in some sterile hospital room."

We talked for awhile as we watched the late afternoon shadows creep out across the mountain meadows below. He told me about his love for the Episcopal Church and its quiet steady faith. He especially loved the liturgical music, having played the organ and directed the choir of a small suburban parish.

"I loved that little church. I'm quite convinced that no one ever suspected that I was gay until I was diagnosed as having AIDS. With that diagnosis I was delivered a double whammy — the loss of my life and the loss of my church. And to be perfectly frank, Father Gene, I will never know if I contracted AIDS from unprotected sex or from a blood transfusion when I had surgery a few years back."

And then he added a rhetorical question revealing a strain of bitterness: "If I never knew how I contacted the virus, what makes others so damn sure that *they* know?"

I spread out a table napkin and placed upon it the small loaf of bread. Craig shuffled through the sliding doors and came back with two wine glasses. I opened the prayer book and celebrated Holy Communion. Into his trembling hands I placed the consecrated bread and guided the chalice to his lips with the immortal eucharistic words:

The Body of Christ, the bread of heaven.
The Blood of Christ, the cup of salvation.
Take them in remembrance that Christ died for you . . .

He made the sign of the cross, and I barely heard him utter a faint, Amen."
Silence prevailed. I was afraid to interrupt it with words, which would

have seemed like chatter in the presence of eternity. A slight breeze rattled the leaves in the nearby aspen grove. His dark glasses prevented me from seeing his eyes. Soon I saw tears streaming down his cheeks, but he sat there in stoic quietness, hunched over and alone. The rivulets pooled at his jaw before splattering into his lap, but he never moved. I reached out and stroked his arm, and ever so slowly, he took my hand and tightened his grip, as if I were the only friend he'd ever had. Still he didn't turn toward me or say anything. He just sat there in quiet solitude. Or was it broken rejection — like our Savior on the cross?

I knelt down in front of his chair and put my arms around his emaciated frame to exchange the peace of Christ. I could feel knobby lesions under his loose-fitting shirt.

"Craig, I am so sorry. Sorry for everything. Sorry that you're dying when you're only thirty-eight years old from this dreadful disease which no one knew was even lurking out there. Sorry that you feel abandoned by your church when you needed it the most. Believe me, that should never be."

He remained motionless.

"Craig, God loves you, and Christ died on that cross to redeem your life with grace and to prepare a place for you with Him in heaven. You are a child of God, and your gift of music has blessed the lives of many. You are a blessing to me here this afternoon. Please believe that."

He nodded slightly but said nothing.

For a long while I waited for some kind of verbal or physical response. Finally, I stood up and said, "Craig, as an Episcopalian, you know that priest and parishioners are supposed to consume all the consecrated bread and wine or pour it into the ground. But I have a whole bottle of wine left over. I need your help finishing it off."

He held out his glass and I filled it up. We divided the loaf of crusty bread between the two of us and began eating.

Before I left his mountain retreat I told Craig that I would find an Episcopal priest who would regularly bring him the church sacraments.

"Please don't," he said. "I'm okay. I've done all my grieving over the loss of my life and the loss of my church. But I've kept the faith. My grieving is over and I've accepted my fate with all the dignity and peace that the good Lord provides. Your time spent with me this afternoon was beautiful, and I'm eternally grateful. That was all I needed. Please believe me when I say that I don't want or need the hassle it would take to line up another priest. And it would be more of a hassle than what you think. I haven't the emotional strength to tolerate that now. Time has run out. I'm at peace with God and with myself."

Then, holding up his skeletal hand, as if dismissing me with a blessing, he said, "Go in peace to love and serve the Lord."

Coded words, they were — right out of the Episcopal Prayer Book, where at the conclusion of the Eucharist the priest calls out these words of dismissal for the worshipping congregation. Only this time, they came from the parched lips of a wounded child of God, broken and dying, who had been shunned and denied the very peace and love he was now calling out to me.

I hesitated. He must have sensed that welling up within me was a sudden compulsion to gather him up in my arms and weep with him — because he held up both hands as if to resist further leave-taking and softly said, "Go in peace."

But I didn't go in peace. In fact, it was pure torment as I drove under the shady pines along the winding mountain road to the neighboring house where I was staying. I couldn't help asking myself the haunting question, What if Craig had been my son?

The computer technician called me two weeks later and said Craig had died.

My ministry to Craig, such as it was, was purely coincidental. And the truth is, it wasn't Gene Todd that Craig needed. Where was his church choir? Why didn't the members bring up a potluck dinner and ask him to accompany them on his electronic organ, which I saw just inside the sliding glass doors, while they sang for him a few of the hymns he cherished so dearly? He needed their affirmation and love. At least, he needed to know they cared. Where was his parish priest? Why wasn't he up there with his communion for the sick and administration of last rites? Craig needed to hear the priestly reassurance of God's love and forgiveness. These were the people Craig knew and loved and so desperately needed in his final days as he lingered up there in his mountain home, isolated and alone — and dying.

In all fairness, I need to remind the reader that this was in 1985. AIDS had just exploded across the landscape of America. Hysteria was rampant as to how contagious this disease could be. Misinformation about how one contacted the HIV virus was such that undertakers, doctors, school principals and clergy isolated themselves from any physical contact with someone afflicted with AIDS. Indeed, the lunacy was becoming a national tragedy. Most certainly it could be said that I threw caution to the wind when I called on Craig at that particular time in our nation's history. In fact, what I did reflected more ignorance than courage.

I say this not to condone or condemn, but maybe help explain the tragic human and spiritual neglect of Craig by his church and priest. A neglect made easier, I'm afraid, when it was discovered that Craig was gay.

When the computer technician called me about Craig's death, he explained that Craig had used a Macintosh computer and that I was to receive that computer as a gift of his appreciation. That computer literally transformed the business office of St. Mark's Episcopal Church. I trained Bobbie Parrish, my office secretary and administrative assistant, how to operate it, and the computer was used for everything that went on in that office.

Craig made an immeasurable contribution to St. Mark's Episcopal Church in Cheyenne with his gift of this invaluable computer. He made a greater gift of himself to me, however, in opening my eyes to the human dimension of this tragic disease.

✧

Ellmore waddled into my study with a Bible tucked under his arm. I say "waddled" because that's the word we use to describe a well-fattened steer in a Wyoming feedlot.

But he was also well heeled. His coiffured hair style would match that of a rock star much younger than he. At his opposite end was a pair of the shiniest cowboy alligator boots I had ever seen. His expensive suit was set off with an open shirt exposing a flashy JESUS medallion dangling around his neck. Yes, I could tell that in addition to being well-fed, Ellmore was obviously well-heeled.

Furthermore, when anyone carries a Bible under his arm, except to attend a Bible class, you can rest assured he's intending to clobber someone across the head with his narrow interpretation of it.

Ellmore's visit proved itself to be no exception.

He attended services at St. Mark's the previous Sunday while visiting relatives in Cheyenne. His family told me earlier that although he was a confirmed Episcopalian, he had fallen away from the church since taking up residence in Colorado Springs where he joined a fundamentalist Presbyterian church — one which was no longer in fellowship with the national Presbyterian denomination.

The first thing Ellmore said to me, after making himself comfortable on the sofa and conspicuously laying the Bible across his lap, "Brother Gene, I want you to know that the Lord has blessed me real good."

I dislike that condescending colloquial expression, especially when spoken with a deliberate and artificial southern drawl. But I decided to overlook its conceit with my question, "How's that?"

"Well, after years of getting no where in my faith or in my career, and after two wrecked marriages and divorces, I finally gave my life to Jesus. That's right, brother, I was born again with an ol' fashioned religious conversion. I left the Episcopal faith because it was getting me nowhere and joined this church in Colorado Springs where the Bible is preached as the living word of God. I found me a good little woman to become my new bride and she's been baptized in the Holy Spirit, if you know what I mean? Boy, she can out-preach any man there is. She sure did last Sunday evening in our church. And after the mess I've made of my life, Jesus has blessed me real good — and now I'm well on my way toward becoming a millionaire."

"I'm glad you're doing well, Ellmore, really I am," I said. "But I'm uncomfortable with equating financial prosperity with spirituality. I don't know where that leaves poor people who have faithfully loved and served the Lord all their lives and still remain poor. The people about whom our Lord was speaking when he said, 'Blessed are the poor — for they shall inherit the earth.'"

A blank expression swept across Ellmore's face. I honestly don't think this thought had ever crossed his mind. It was obvious to me that this conversation wasn't going to go well. What he said next proved my point.

"Brother Gene, I've come here as a brother in Christ to confront you about the secular humanism which has swept the Episcopal Church off its feet and has taken you with it. My family here at St. Mark's thinks the world of you. You're a marvelous preacher. I wish other preachers could handle the English language the way you do. It's always so picturesque. You paint great pictures in the imagination of your listeners in the pew. But, brother, you're not preaching the word of God!"

He didn't know it, but excessive flattery was getting him nowhere.

He held up his Bible. "See here — between the covers of this one book is everything man needs to know about God and the precious salvation of Jesus Christ. Everything. It is the inspired word of God. Nothing more and nothing less. That's the way it's being preached to me in Colorado Springs and that's the way I believe it. Please don't take offense, brother, but you're not preaching it as the inspired word of God. You take what you want and leave out what you don't like. It's the literal word of God and you're pussyfooting with it."

The lines were drawn for a battle that I had no need to fight with this fundamentalist. So I asked, "Tell me, Ellmore, why are you here with this accusation? What's the emotional payoff for you?"

"I'm here, brother Gene, because we could make good use of preachers like you — if only you preached the truly inspired word of God. I'm actively involved with a group in Colorado Springs known as *Focus on the Family* under the direction of a man whose name is Dr. James Dobson. It's very successful. They've raised millions of dollars for their enterprise. We need people like you to help spread the good word."

"Ellmore, you don't want people like me with your *Focus on the Family* ministry because it's capable of doing all the good and harm it can do without me. I'm sorry, but I have little sympathy with these sleazy multi-million-dollar fundamentalist television and radio ministries who are out to plunder the Social Security pensions of retired little old ladies while they richly pad their own pockets."

"Brother Gene, you speak frankly. That's what I like about you. You've got fire if only it was directed toward preaching the divinely inspired word of God. Now my family here in Cheyenne showed me your church newsletter where you said queers and faggots were welcome to receive the full ministry of the church. That may be charitable on your part, brother Gene, but that's not what the Bible teaches."

Then opening the Bible, he turned to a verse heavily marked in pencil and proceeded, "It says here in Leviticus, chapter 20 and verse 13, that homosexuality is an abomination against the Lord. It says it very plainly here. If you claim to be a man of God, a priest of the Episcopal Church, then why aren't you honest enough to preach what the Bible plainly says? No more — no less. Word for word. The Bible is the only and final authority for Christians everywhere."

"No, it's not Ellwood," I countered. "For Anglicans, our authority is rooted in *Scripture, Tradition,* and *Reason* — and right now you are not being very resonable."

He ignored my correction with a direct challenge, "Are you familiar at all with Leviticus chapter 20 and verse 13?"

"I'm very familiar with it," I fumed as I reached for my own King James Bible, resenting his snide inference that no one else knew the Bible as well as he. "It says here that it is an abomination unto the Lord and furthermore it says they shall be put to death."

"There, you see?" — grinning like a cat playing with a mouse.

"I suppose this means that not only do you want homosexuals kicked out of the church, Ellmore, but also you want them all killed!"

"Well, I wouldn't go quite that far."

"Now wait just a minute, Ellmore. You just accused me of taking what I want out of the Bible and leaving out what I don't like. No more or no less, you said. But when I read back to you the identical verse out of Leviticus which you just quoted to me, you shrug your shoulders and say you wouldn't go quite that far. Now you're pussyfooting."

"Well, it's God's law — not mine. If you don't want them dead, then take it up with the Lord — not me."

"So you'd have them all killed?"

Ellmore shrugged his assent.

"Social scientists say that roughly five percent of the population is homosexual. That percentage may be a little high. But let's assume they're right, that means that out of 200 million Americans you'd have 10 million of them put to death. Machine-gunned into an open grave. Right? That rate of civilian human slaughter would exceed that of Hitler and Stalin. Some achievement you're proposing, isn't it — if you had your way?"

"Not my way, brother Gene. God's way!"

"I hate to think that this is God's way, Ellmore. That's not the God I know and worship. But let's read on. In this same chapter 20, verse 10, it says that if a man commits adultery — that also is an abomination unto the Lord — and he, too, is to be put to death. Statistics indicate that roughly half the American people have committed adultery. This would be another 100 million people put to death — including you, Ellmore, because you said you've been through two bitter divorces and now you're married to your third wife. That's the biblical equivalent of adultery."

"Not me, brother Gene," Ellmore loudly protested, "because those divorces were before I truly became a Christian. Back in the days when I was still Episcopalian — living in blasphemy. But now that I've been born again —"

"Ellmore," I interrupted, "Leviticus doesn't say one word about making that kind of an exception for you. And neither did Christ. Now you're being legalistic by creating your own loophole and once you've climbed through — you're slamming the gates shut on homosexuals, but not yourself."

"Let's don't get personal."

"I'm making it personal, Ellmore, because you have no hesitation in getting personal about the sin of homosexuality and soft pedaling your own sin of adultery. Read on here in Leviticus, and you'll see that it has many chapters on the holiness code of ancient Jewish tradition. Anyone who doesn't abide by these strict dietary laws, for example, is also to be put to death. Ellmore, soon there will be no one left to kill the last offenders because all 200 million Americans will be dead. Dead because of your literal interpretation of the Old Testament. Dead because this is what you preach as being the will of a loving God. Excuse me, Ellmore, I don't care for that kind of a religion. Who needs Satan when you've got a vindictive God like that?"

Ellmore's face flushed and for the first time he lost his composure, "That's exactly my point, brother Gene, you don't really believe and preach the wrath of God that's in the Bible. No, I wouldn't execute people because they sinned against God — because we're all sinners. God loves sinners. Out of my love for God, I would give faggots one last chance to repent of their ways and accept the salvation of Christ. And if they didn't repent, then they can just burn in hell."

"How generous of you, Ellmore," I interrupted again. "Something like a reprieve the Moslems in the eighth century were reported to have offered Jews and Christians before they whacked off their heads with the sword of Allah."

His smirk infuriated me as I leaned toward him and said, "Ellmore, I resent your dishonesty and hypocrisy of coming in here and singling out one little verse from the priestly holiness code of Leviticus and applying it specifically to homosexuals and then dismissing the rest of Leviticus as non-applicable to you and your sins. Your weaseling out of what you biblically demand of others is really getting under my skin. Your fundamentalist self-righteous judgmentalism is appalling to me."

"Well, skip Leviticus then," he said evasively, "The New Testament also condemns homosexuality, does it not?"

"Paul makes reference to it in his letter to the Romans," I conceded.

"You see, that's all the evidence you need," Ellmore countered. "Take the Bible for what it says. Nothing more and nothing less. Word for word."

"But Paul in First Corinthians doesn't seem to think well of marriage either, except as an institution of last resort for men who otherwise can't control their passions. That would include you and me. You must be really out of control by getting married three times. And in Paul's letter to the Ephesians he appears to condone slavery by warning slaves to be obedient and submissive to their masters as unto the Lord. Would you preach that to people in the bondage of slavery anywhere in the world today?"

He gestured resignation.

"And back again in Corinthians," I continued, "he tells women to keep their heads covered and their mouths shut in church. And I think I just heard you say that your wife was preaching last Sunday in your church."

"Now you're getting personal again," he snapped. "My wife preaches the word of God because the Lord has called her to do so. Those figurative statements of Saint Paul merely reflected the social conditions of his time, brother Gene, and were never intended to be taken literally. His condemnation of homosexuality, however, is to be taken literally."

"According to who, Ellmore? You and your narrow like-minded kin? Now who's selectively pussyfooting with the word of God?" I couldn't resist that.

Actually, what bothered me wasn't that Ellmore was being selective as to what he wanted to believe from the writings of Saint Paul. In spite of ourselves, we're all guilty of scriptural selectivity and we must exercise critical theological discernment as to the choices we make. What I found appalling was his blatant hypocrisy of doing the very thing he condemned others of doing. I was flabbergasted that Ellmore would dismiss part of Saint Paul's writings as socially irrelevant to the twentieth century but cling to Paul's pronouncement on homosexuality as sacrosanct — right after accusing me of not taking the *entire* Bible literally as the word of God — word for word. So it didn't surprise me when he seemed eager to shift the topic of conversation.

"Okay. Let's forget Saint Paul for the moment. Let's see what our Lord Jesus Christ has to say about homosexuality."

"Christ doesn't say one word about it in the entire New Testament. Not one word. Jesus had far more to say about divorce, but the church has modified that position so as to be more pastoral than judgmental toward those whose marriages have failed. And, Ellmore, both you and I have benefited from this moderation."

He stiffened his back and held up the limp Bible, waving it in the air Billy Graham style, then pointing his finger at me he continued, "That proves exactly my point, brother Gene. It's that very attitude that's bringing ruination to all the liberal-minded denominations. Your pussyfooting on the word of God and accommodating yourselves to every new fad that comes along. Your tolerating and associating with left-wing political radicals, secular humanists, abortionists, homosexuals, unwed couples cohabitating together before marriage, and the list goes on. You've weakened your witness to the holy laws of the Bible, my brother, really you have."

Still wagging his finger at me.

"Ellmore, are you aware that your accusations against the church are identical to those which were leveled against Jesus Christ by the Pharisees? His associations with publicans, tax collectors, harlots, women, and sinners? His violation of the Sabbath laws? His refusal to legalistically abide with the ancient holy laws of Judaism?"

He said nothing, as if his mind momentarily went blank.

I continued, "Our Lord said nothing about homosexuality — about which you are so rabid. He did make a rather strong statement about divorce — which you prefer to ignore. But consistently, all through the gospels in his preaching, he continuously abhorred the legalism and self-righteous judgmentalism of the religious right which you seem to wholeheartedly embrace."

"Brother Gene," Ellmore shouted, now becoming angry, "I'm proud to be a part of the growing religious right in America. I don't care what you think or say about us and our literal interpretation of the Bible. The point is you're losing and we're winning. The Episcopal Church and all other liberal churches of the apostasy are losing members and we're gaining. You're losing political elections and we're winning them. A good example is that we've sponsored passage of constitutional Amendment 2 in Colorado which states that it's unconstitutional to grant special rights to gays and lesbians."

"They weren't asking for special rights," I shouted, "and Ellmore, you all knew that. They only wanted the same civil rights protection that you and I enjoy — not to be unfairly discriminated against at work or in housing, without judicial right of appeal. Knowing that fact, you and your hate-mongering group there in Colorado Springs very skillfully crafted that amendment to make its wording appear to be the opposite of what you really intended, and that was to legalize discrimination against gays and lesbians. Surely the courts will never allow you to get away with that subterfuge."

"Subterfuge or not, it works," he screamed, "Anything is ethical if it works for the Lord — because the Lord is on our side! Of course, we don't want homosexuals having equal rights — because they have no rights in the first place. They are an abomination unto the Lord. They are already dead — dead unto the Lord. You read it for yourself — right out of Leviticus."

This exercise in futility had come full circle — right back to where we started from. Something froze within me. I simply glared at him. I was glad he gathered up his Bible and quickly waddled out of the room.

After his departure, I sat there alone in my study — outraged. Outraged with Ellmore but more with myself. Incensed that I allowed myself to be drawn into this impossible impasse with a rabid Bible-waving fundamentalist. I went to the sink in the outer office where I had a compulsive need to wash my hands of the whole sordid affair.

But it would take more than ceremonial washing to cleanse my conscience. Clobbering others with the Bible, although the stock-in-trade of evangelistic preachers, has always been personally odorous and repugnant to me. Even though he started it, I had no right to enter the fray at that low base of Bible-slinging rancor. I expected more spiritual dignity and professional integrity from myself and was disgusted for failing so miserably.

Dr. Erdmann Smith at First Baptist Church in Denver used to say that it wasn't the number of times you've been through the Bible that mattered, but how much of the Bible has been through you — in the broad sweep of its total message.

What is it about rampant fundamentalism which brings out the worst within me?

I wasn't raised in a fundamentalist home, so I have no residual rebellion here to be acted out in my adulthood. Fundamentalist laymen who preached their fire and brimstone sermons at our little country school were more a source of amusement to me as a kid than anything else.

The truth is, I have always had great respect for people who hold a very simple and quiet religious faith. I wish mine was more simple and less complicated. I envy the gentle spirit of those whose sincere biblical beliefs, although "fundamentalist" by definition, have been an inspiration to me. Many of the fundamentalists I know and love do not embrace a fire and brimstone mentality. Not all of their preachers are Elmer Gantrys. Indeed, it was my good friend, the Reverend Dave Vanley, a minister of the Assembly of God Church in Cheyenne, who officiated at the wedding of Rosemary and me. I cherish my fond admiration of the Hutterites in South Dakota, the Shakers in early Kentucky, and my attraction to the Amish lifestyle.

But my unfortunate encounter with Ellmore, and his religious militancy pulled me down to his level where I was as angry and judgmental as he. Perhaps it was his belligerency that God is only on his side.

Vanderbilt University in Nashville tells every new freshman class that the mark of a mature, educated person is that he has enough knowledge to know he's ignorant about most things — and has the intellectual courage to admit it.

I've come to the conclusion that the mark of a mature, educated Christian is that he has enough spirituality to know that nothing on this earth has a corner on the infinite wisdom and love of God — and has the intellectual and moral courage to admit it.

Not humankind. I've heard it said that God certainly loves a good joke or he wouldn't have made so many of us.

Not the church. If you concentrate on its colossal errors to the exclusion of its strengths — you would weep with shame.

Not the Bible. It was written by mortal men in both the Old and New Testament times. Inspired mortals, yes — but not infallible. The church came first, and out of its struggle to survive internal dissension and external Roman persecution during the first century of its existence — slowly evolved the New Testament. Fundamentalists want us to believe it's the other way around, as if God literally typed it out, word for word (on a heavenly Macintosh computer, of course) and handed it over as a how-to manual for the early church fathers. The truth is, the church had been around about 200 years before the New Testament, as we know it today, came into common usage.

When anyone claims something is absolutely infallible, whether it be the king, the pope, the church, the Bible, or a television evangelist — we're headed for big trouble. When anyone claims to speak for God, infallibly on all issues — look out, we're headed for unmitigated disaster.

It has been my historical observation that when militant religious fundamentalism links up with power politics — evil results. Whether it be politics of church or state. Fundamentalism, when politically empowered, becomes the firestorm of fanatic extremism which scorches the earth.

Allow the Reverend Jerry Falwell or the Reverend Pat Robertson, for example, to gain control of the American political process and you'll see exactly what I mean. Providing, of course, we survive it long enough to find out.

It goes without saying, of course, that religious fundamentalism has not only a solemn constitutional right to exist in America as do all religious beliefs, but also to thrive and flourish. Furthermore, its believers have the constitutional right and moral obligation to enter the democratic process and pursue their political agenda like everyone else. That's what our American democracy is all about.

Fundamentalists, for example, don't have to condone homosexuality. They can zealously preach and teach against it as much as they want. Some liberals and moderates, for different reasons, also deplore the homosexual lifestyle. In fact, as previously written in this chapter, being the irreversible heterosexual that I am, there's much about homosexuality that I find personally offensive and physically unnatural. Particularly, the kinky bizarre sexual orgies among gay men in the bathhouses, that I hear about, where dangerous promiscuity frequently abounds.

However, it's been my personal experience that aggressive fundamentalists are not content with the narrow persuasion of their moral convictions. A fanatic inner compulsion takes over, as if commandeered by God, to forcibly impose their rigidity against the will of those resisting its tyranny. So they enter the political arena, like was done in Colorado about which Ellmore was boasting, to legislatively stomp out homosexuality by legalizing a hostile cultural environment where gay discrimination and gay bashing once again becomes socially tolerable.

In my retirement years, I've come to the startling conclusion for myself that one's basic spirituality, apart from doctrinal sectarianism, is something like one's basic sexual orientation — it is acquired at a very early age. And we spend the rest of our lives trying to find a religious environment where it can be nurtured and empowered.

There's no question in my mind that as a Wyoming ranch kid, alone in the hills with my thoughts and notebooks, a certain kind of spirituality took root in my life. In the early chapters of this book I marveled as to where this might have come from. It was this seminal realization which prompted me to conclude that I was an Anglican in spirit long before I knew there was an Episcopal Church. Consequently, my own private spiritual journey became a search for a quiet place where the heart and mind could be nurtured and enhanced, in a special sort of way, by the love and wisdom of God. I found it in Anglicanism.

The spiritual search for others will lead them elsewhere, and that's fine.

Had I been reared in a Moslem society, I'm convinced that my private psycho-emotional spirituality is such that I would have been a liberal intellectually minded Mohammedan.

Conversely, Ellmore's basic psycho-emotional spirituality is such that he needed a highly structured fundamentalist religious environment to nurture his narrow-minded mentality. He found it in the fundamentalist hot bed of Colorado Springs. Had he also been reared in a Moslem society, he most certainly would have joined up with the militant Shiite right-wing faction. Jerry Falwell and Pat Robertson both would thrive in a theocracy like Iran where they could rule autocratically with the iron hand of God.

It has been said that people who don't know their history are doomed to repeat its tragic mistakes. Not so with the merger of religious fundamentalism and political extremism. Knowing their history compels them to repeat its violence. They call it their *divine destiny*. I call it history's *divine travesty*.

Indeed, there are historical scholars who maintain that militant religious fundamentalism has the inherent ear mark of a religion unto itself. Rightwing fundamentalists the world over, of all major world religions, have far more in common with each other than they do with members of their own mainstream religious faith.

Sometimes I think that these fanatic fundamentalists fulfill a unique function for God by doing all the mean-spirited, ugly, and bloody things which the good Lord, by definition, can't do for Himself and still be the *good* Lord. For example, Christ said that He came not to condemn the world but to save it. Unfortunately, since Christ won't condemn — then Christian extremists believe they must gallantly do it for Him.

Militant fundamentalists, the world over, seem particularly well equipped at doing this. Worst of all, they delight in doing it. As Ellmore said, there are no ethical concerns when something is done for God.

In other words, anything goes in the name of the Lord.

When I recall the heinous crimes committed against humanity down through the centuries, always rationalized as being done in the name of the Lord — I cringe.

Heaven protect us from the scorched earth this religious monstrosity perpetuates against life on our planet.

Therefore, I'm afraid that my theological encounter with Ellmore was futile and counter productive for both of us. We were trying to intellectually thrash out our differences of biblical interpretation, when actually it was a primeval conflict from the very beginning.

✧

A footnote: I realize that I would not make a good courtroom lawyer because I can't think fast enough on my feet — knockout punch lines come too late. After my unfortunate encounter with Ellwood, I later remembered that his family told me that they had all attended a Bronco football game on Saturday prior to his Sunday visit in church, and stopped over at a popular Denver barbecue restaurant for scrumptious pork spareribs before driving up to Cheyenne.

This errant behavior would have put Ellwood in serious trouble with the Lord on two counts since Leviticus 11 strictly forbids not only the eating of pork — but expresses shocking abhorrence at even touching the pigskin (football) of such an abominable animal. To my amusement, here he blithely violated both taboos in one afternoon of gluttonous reverie — and gloried in making a cheering sport of the latter.

Challenging the poor guy with another example of his selective illiteracy of the bible, while vehemently denying that right to homosexuals, might have given me a momentary glow of self-satisfaction — but would have gotten nowhere, so its just as well that I never brought it up.

Besides I knew that neither Ellwood or I had any intention of cleansing ourselves through the ancient rites of Jewish purification. Since we're both ritually impure, according to Leviticus, then it follows that neither of us can point fingers of condemnation at sinners less hypocritical or laughable than ourselves.

Eventually, the forward march of human liberation movements, seeking equal justice and basic human rights, will set us free in the civilizing discovery that all God's children live in a pluralistic society. That human diversity is not a social weakness — but our greatest cultural strength.

Chapter 18

S t. Mark's Episcopal Church of Cheyenne is not only known as the "Pioneer Church of Wyoming" — but is also often called the "Church of the Governors" because so many Wyoming governors have worshiped there — beginning with the legendary governorships of Francis E. Warren and Joseph M. Carey, and their many descendants.

During my twenty-six-year tenure at St. Mark's I buried three former Wyoming governors and five former first ladies. They were all fascinating people and a delight to know.

Wyoming is a large state with a very small population — fewer than 465,000 people. Consequently our elected state officials, from governors to U.S. senators, are commonly well known to all of us and work closely with the citizens of our state. We have easy access to them. They are not surrounded by an entourage of security guards and political hacks the way high-ranking political figures in other states are. Several times at the early morning Eucharist, I have discovered both U.S. senators in attendance. Once the governor and both U.S. senators, from different political parties, attended the same service. This was not considered unusual in Wyoming, whereas in most other states such a preponderance of prestigious public figures all worshipping in the same church would be considered highly extraordinary.

When I first came to St. Mark's in 1965, Governor and Mrs. Cliff Hansen regularly walked to church from the governor's mansion, located only a few blocks away. The Hansens hailed from Jackson, where they operated a cattle ranch, and they were two of the most gracious people I've ever known, the epitome of what the first couple of a state should be. Seeing them in church, at a political banquet, or on television always made me feel proud to be a Wyomingite. They were devout and loyal Episcopalians, and it was always delightful to visit with them during the coffee hour following morning worship.

Cliff Hansen won the office by defeating the incumbent Democratic governor of Wyoming, Jack Gage. Jack and Leona "Buddy" Gage were also devout members of St. Mark's Church. The Gages were marvelous

424

characters. Jack was an engaging storyteller and humorist who took to writing after he retired. His books, *Tensleep and No Rest* and *It's All a Pack of Lies*, were widely read not as accurate histories of Wyoming's frontier days but as one man's humorous interpretation of what that history was all about. For example, it was his contention that the traditional accounts of the infamous Johnson County Cattle War of 1892 were essentially untrue. *It's All a Pack of Lies* was deliberately written from two diametrically opposed point of views. You could read it from the front and learn the cattlemen's perspective or flip the book over and read it from the back and learn the homesteader perspective. History, he contended, is nothing more than a question of who can tell the better lie.

Once Jack Gage and I were invited for a wonderful horseback ride out on Ira Trotter's sprawling cattle ranch near Chugwater. Ira Trotter, a gentleman rancher, West Pointer, and law school graduate, thought Herbert Hoover was our best president and Franklin Delano Roosevelt the worst. Jack Gage thought exactly the opposite. The crusty ol' guys couldn't agree to disagree. So out across the hay meadows and grain fields, down along the creek, and up into the north forty, it was Hoover versus Roosevelt every step of the way. At one point, as we rode through the bull pasture, I tried changing the subject by asking Ira how many bulls he owned. But to no avail.

"Plenty of good bulls, and expensive ones, too, I might add," he answered. "But all the bullshit in modern cattle ranching comes from FDR's New Deal. We didn't have any bullshit in the cattle business from Hoover."

To which the governor retorted, "I agree with you on that score, Ira. That's because you ranchers were too flat-assed broke to own a good bull."

Finally I reined my horse down a long draw to escape their diarrhetic debate which was thirty years too late for political relevance. I figured it was best to let these two Great Depression scarred veterans have at it because it seemed to invigorate them both.

Jack Gage rented a little cubicle on the top floor of the Boyd building in downtown Cheyenne so that he could write uninterrupted by the telephone. He often invited me up to visit. It was a spartan room with nothing more than two straight-back chairs, a table and typewriter. There he would smoke and write. It was the smoking which eventually did him in.

One afternoon I met the governor on the street out front and casually asked him, "How are you Jack?"

"Not very good," he said, seriously. "I've just returned from the doctor who tells me that I'm gonna die."

"Aren't we all?" I quipped, thinking he was setting me up for one of his jokes.

"No, I'm serious, this is real. He says I have terminal lung cancer."

I stopped walking and realized from the look on his face that he was, indeed, being serious — but before I could say anything he shrugged his shoulders and said, "But that's just another one of these bugs that's kinda goin' around the neighborhood, ya know?"

During the final stages of this terrible illness, which he chose to deal with at home, he motioned Buddy out of the room and asked to speak to me alone. In his gravelly voice he whispered, "Gene, I've got to get this business of dying over with. It's wearing Buddy out trying to take care of me day and night. I don't want to die in a hospital, but neither do I want it dragged out any longer."

Again, I could tell, he was being dead serious.

"Gene, don't pray for my recovery, because that's just confusing the Lord and delaying everything. Pray that I will die tonight or even this afternoon. Can't you arrange this with the Lord? You're good with words; can't you put together a prudent and reasonable case before the Supreme Judge like a good country lawyer would plead a strong case to the county judge? I delegate to you the power of attorney. Work something out with Him and negotiate my hasty demise. You've got to do it for Buddy's sake!"

I assured him that long ago I had quit praying for his recovery and was praying, instead, for a peaceful death.

"How can it be peaceful for me when it's hell on her? You were born and raised on a Wyoming cattle ranch and know how to get things done. Promise me you'll work something out with the Lord, and do it fast!"

He died on March 14, 1970, during a snowstorm so bad that we had to postpone the funeral for a day so that I could catch a ride from Sheridan to Cheyenne to officiate. It would have been better had the Lord delayed his death just one more day for the storm to have abated, but my prayer was answered and Jack got his wish for immediacy. The governor's office asked me to plan some kind of public service in the rotunda of the state capitol before we took his body to St. Mark's Church.

Adjutant General Bob Outsen and I quickly put together a public ceremony involving the Wyoming National Guard, Wyoming Supreme Court, and elected officials, and all state employees in the capitol building were given permission to attend. It turned out quite well, considering the limited amount of time we had to plan it. I thought there was a good balance between the need for a public eulogy and civic recognition of a well-known political figure without infringing on the separation of church and state. So well was it received, in fact, that the public ceremony was formalized as a set procedure for future burials of governors and elected officials of the state of Wyoming. This format has been used ever since.

When Cliff Hansen was elected to the U.S. Senate in 1967, he was succeeded in the governor's office by another Episcopalian, Stan Hathaway, from Torrington. Stan and his wife, Bobbie, attended St. Christopher's Episcopal Church in Cheyenne because Stanley Guille, the rector there, had been their former pastor at Torrington. I frequently associated with the Hathaways, and they were always most cordial. He was elected to a second term with one of the highest plurality of votes in Wyoming history.

Hathaway was followed by another Episcopalian in the governor's mansion: Ed Herschler, who hailed from the small coal mining–railroad–ranching community of Kemmerer in Lincoln County. Ed Herschler prided himself on being "just a country lawyer" whose grandfather and father preceded him in the ranching business. His mother, however, was a staunch Republican who voted the straight party ticket all her life and who, according to "Gov Ed," as he liked to be called, didn't even vote for him, her own son, as the Democratic candidate for governor of Wyoming.

Ed Herschler distinguished himself as the only Wyoming governor elected to three successive terms, twelve years in all — and as a Democrat in a solidly Republican state. His raw-boned face resembled the rugged, wind blown landscape of a rough and tough Wyoming drought. His wife, Casey, was the most jovial person you would ever hope to meet, in spite of the fact that she was largely confined to a wheelchair because of debilitating multiple sclerosis, which crippled her body but never her mind.

Neither of them attended church, but I was constantly called upon to attend them in a multitude of social functions and political affairs. I led prayers to dedicate the new governor's mansion, first occupied by Ed and Casey Herschler. I did the same at the dedication of the new Herschler State Office Building, where I saw Ed's eyes brim with tears at the unveiling of a bronze bust of his rugged face. I was invited to participate in countless banquets and political gatherings at which Governor Hershler was the principal speaker.

On New Year's Eve of 1978 he phoned me and said, "Gene, you know I'm not much into public ceremony. When I was inaugurated for my first term, I just assumed that that inauguration would hold for as long as I served the people of Wyoming as governor. But according to state law I have to be reinaugurated for my second term. I hadn't planned on that."

He chuckled.

"I know this is short notice, but I'm wondering if I could persuade both you and Chief Justice John Raper to come up to my office tomorrow morning, on New Year's Day, and do the inaugurating? You do the prayin' and let John do the swearin'."

"That's all? Nothing more, not even a reception?" I asked.

"Naw," he laughed, "I asked the *girls* (meaning the three top elected officials of Wyoming, who that year all happened to be women) if they would be willing to bake a cake and serve some coffee, but they told me that office gals don't do that sort of thing anymore."

I'd wager that nowhere else in the United States would a re-elected incumbent state governor be that laid-back about his inauguration into a second term as was Governor Ed Herschler of Wyoming in 1979.

It is traditional for the governor to entertain all the legislators and spouses at the governor's mansion during the annual session of the state legislature. Rosemary and I were frequently invited. After we passed through the reception line, Casey Herschler had all the men draw names of women who were to be our dinner partners. One time, I drew the name of the wife of a Republican legislator whose husband happened to be an Episcopalian, elected to his first term in the House.

During dinner conversation my "date" for the evening made the announcement to all of us sitting at the table, "As a Republican I dearly love Casey but can't stand Ed Herschler. In fact, he makes me sick to my stomach."

I thought her caustic remark inappropriate and vitriolic on the occasion of a gracious bi-partisan dinner which prompted me to say, "But not so sick that you aren't willing to sit here at Ed Hershler's table as his honored dinner guest and eat his food and drink his wine, are you?"

Perhaps I shouldn't have said it. Our adversarial two-party political system is one of the best in the world, but it always bothers me when Democrats and Republicans can't be gracious and civil to one another in polite society. If this wife of a legislator felt that strongly in her animosity toward the elected governor of Wyoming, and couldn't keep her churlish comments to herself, I personally think she should have declined the invitation for dinner in the governor's mansion.

Ed Herschler would drive himself to the airport bar for a couple of drinks every evening on his way home from a long day's work in the governor's office. He would pull himself up onto a bar stool and begin conversation with whoever was beside him. Many, of course, knew who he was but paid no special attention to him. However, visitors to our state usually had no idea that this guy they were chatting with at the bar was the popular governor of Wyoming.

One time I had to meet some friends from Georgia at the Denver airport who were making their first visit ever to the western part of the United States. While waiting for them at the luggage carrousel I bumped into Ed Herschler who was returning from the Democratic National

Convention. We leaned up against the railing and chatted awhile. When my southern guests arrived I introduced them to the governor and continued our conversation until we picked up our luggage.

On our way to the car my guests turned to me and asked, "Who'd you say that was?"

"That was Ed Herschler, the governor of Wyoming."

They found it unbelievable that we in Wyoming would have such public access to the highest elected public official of our state, standing there alone without a single security guard. Also, they found it impossible to believe that this lanky old fella wearing Levi's, grubby boots, and a soiled cowboy hat and leaning up against the railing while smoking his cigarette and casually chatting could be anyone other than a ranch foreman picking up some dude.

After serving three terms as governor, the Herschlers tried retiring back at the family ranch in Kemmerer, but that didn't last long. They returned to Cheyenne, but then Ed was diagnosed with terminal lung cancer.

I called on him regularly both in the hospital and at their newly purchased townhouse. His health quickly deteriorated as death became imminent. One Sunday after church, I was visiting him in the kitchen of his home when he mixed for himself a bowl of instant oatmeal and then made one for me. While we ate our cereal, he asked me why it was that every time he attended a Jewish festival in a synagogue or a commemoration of the Holocaust in the state capitol — that I was always there as an honored guest as well.

This question led into a lengthy discussion about human and civil rights issues which had consumed the attention of mainline denominations and had been the source of considerable controversy during my ministry at St. Mark's Church.

"There's two things I can't stand about prejudice," he chuckled as he sat at the table with a bathrobe loosely hanging over his emaciated scarecrow frame, "I can't stand prejudiced people — and I can't stand Mormons!"

I never knew and I didn't ask what his negative experience with the Mormons was all about. Nor do I know whether he was being serious or trying to be clever in order to make his point about prejudice.

Governor Ed Herschler died shortly thereafter.

Father Carl Beavers, rector of St. Mary's Catholic Cathedral, graciously offered the larger seating capacity of his cathedral for the funeral. It may have seemed strange for Catholics to hear the Episcopal burial rite in their church but not if they had known Gov Ed.

Ed Herschler was so unimpressed with public ceremony that even his burial was laid-back. His body was cremated before state officials had the opportunity to finalize plans for the public rites in the capitol rotunda, which called for the use of a casket. There was a flurry of confusion as to what was to be done now. Finally, we inserted an urn containing his ashes inside a rented casket so that at least there was a proper coffin over which the American flag could be draped. I smiled at that, because it reminded me of his second inauguration. I could see him chuckling over the confusion of us all trying to get his funeral arranged when there was no body.

Following the funeral, a distressed Father Carl Beavers phoned me with the disturbing news that Casey Herschler didn't think the governor had ever been baptized.

I responded simply by saying, "I told you he was short on ceremony."

A year later I was at the bedside of Casey Herschler when she died from the inevitable complications of multiple sclerosis. Although the family requested that there be no public service in Cheyenne, there was such a demand for one that we had a memorial at St. Mary's Cathedral to accommodate the large crowd of people who knew and loved her.

✧

Former first lady Julia Carey died in 1971 at the age of eighty-eight, the widow of former governor and U.S. Senator Robert Carey. (Also, daughter-in-law of the elder "cattle king" governor and U.S. Senator Joseph M. Carey.) I became well acquainted with her during my frequent pastoral calls during her lengthy hospitalization and convalescence from a broken hip. She had a reputation as a "mean old lady" — a reputation she didn't completely disavow, telling me, "When I was the governor's wife, I'm afraid I misbehaved very badly."

She detested politics, and it has been estimated that during her husband's four-year term as governor, from 1919 to 1923, she resided only nine months in the governor's mansion in Cheyenne. She preferred capering at the huge and historic CY Ranch stretching almost from Douglas to Casper, all owned by the Carey family. There she would frolic away her time fishing, hunting, horseback riding, and cavorting with the hired hands.

She was a proud old woman who prided herself in letting you know she was a proud old woman. She might for this reason be called a snob. Her contentiousness would probably account for her lack of intimate friends during her final years, when she increasingly had to rely on her son's widow, Jena Carey, to handle most of her business affairs. She indignantly denied both her dependence on Jena and her need for God but passionately reached out to Jena and me for comfort from the terrible self-inflicted loneliness that finally engulfed her.

Frankly, I enjoyed her egocentric mannerisms and became quite fond of the elegant old lady. A woman who found it beneath her dignity to express affection for God would surely find it more so with me. However, if I missed one of our weekly visits she would regularly phone me on the pretense that she had something important to discuss with me. I vividly remember two tidbits about history from my many conversations with her.

One was the story of her father, Henry B. Freeman, who was stationed at Fort Phil Kearney in 1866, at the time when Captain (brevet Lieutenant Colonel) W. J. Fetterman flagrantly disobeyed orders and led eighty-one troops into a deadly ambush by the Indians. This fort was located only a few miles from the Todd ranch in northern Wyoming, and I remember visiting its historic ruins and battle sites many times when I was growing up.

Mrs. Carey told me that her father, who later became an army brigadier general, was only a young recruit at that time and was ordered to accompany another cavalry trooper to ride out to the battle scene in advance of a relief party. When the two riders came upon the scene of the gruesome carnage, "the sight and stench of blood and guts and bodily mutilation strewn across the snow was so repulsive that my father's horse reared over backwards — throwing my father to the ground, and then the horse broke loose and galloped full speed back to the fort. This panicked the rescue party into believing that the Indians were still on the attack. My father leaped behind the saddle of the other rider and rode back to announce that the Indians had already withdrawn from the battlefield."

As a student of western history, I have checked all accounts of the "Fetterman Massacre" and have found no record to substantiate this report. (American Indians are correct in reminding us that whenever the white soldiers won a military engagement with the Indians it was called a "battle," but when the Indians won it was called a "massacre.") However, her father's story sounds so logical we can only assume it must be true. Extreme caution, alone, most certainly would have compelled Captain Ten Eyck, who led the relief party, to order a couple of cavalry troopers to race ahead and peek over the ridge to see what danger awaited them on the other side — even though he may never have reported it.

The second tidbit of history Julia Carey related to me was more amusing. U.S. Senator Carey and she were often invited to the White House for Sunday evening dinners with President and Mrs. Herbert Hoover. The sumptuous affairs were an interesting experience in dining; the dinner plates were promptly removed from everyone as soon as President Hoover was done. When he finished his salad, for example, all the salad plates were cleared, even if some guests were still eating. "Consequently," she said, "we all had to carefully watch the president and keep pace with him or we would have our main course snatched away from us midcourse. So we all had to excel at speed-eating."

But the worst was yet to come. "Following dinner all the men would remain at the table for cigars, coffee, and enlivened political conversation while the ladies retired with Mrs. Hoover into a small drawing room for the most insipid and mindless conversation imaginable. We could hear our husbands debating national and world affairs in the other room, where I wanted to be — while we wives simply shriveled in the presence of Mrs. Hoover while sipping our tea. It was the most dreadfully boring evening you could possibly imagine. Whenever an invitation arrived from the White House, I would literally let out an audible moan so loud that it caused all the servants in the house to come running with alarm."

She laid down her knitting, looked at me mischievously, and smiled, "Now you see, Eugene, why I so badly misbehaved as a governor's, and senator's wife, don't you?"

Yes, I could see. No wonder it was reported that when she asked her husband what she could do to help him win re-election to the U.S. Senate, he tersely answered, "Stay home, Julia. Stay home."

Apparently she didn't stay home — he was defeated. The truth is it was not the political liability of his wife that brought him down, but the harsh reality of national politics. He was defeated by a Democratic landslide that swept our nation in 1936 on the coattails of a popular Franklin Delano Roosevelt.

In his campaign for a second term, President and Mrs. Roosevelt visited Cheyenne and worshiped at historic St. Mark's Episcopal Church. Although the American public knew that the president had been severely crippled by polio, it was never something fully perceived psychologically because photographs only showed him from the waist up. But the congregation of St. Mark's was shocked while it watched the highly esteemed commander in chief lumbering down the long aisle of the church on his withered legs, beaming from ear to ear, not really walking but "appearing to walk" on the arm of his eldest son, Jimmy. And then loosening the clamps on his clanking braces before pivoting himself into an end pew and, with his hands, lifting his spindly legs into place — one by one.

I saw to it that a brass plaque now marks the end pew where President Roosevelt sat when he worshiped at St. Mark's during his historic visit to St. Mark's in 1936.

❖

The legacy of the Carey and Warren dynasties made an indelible impression on every phase of early Wyoming history. Their considerable banking, ranching, and railroading empires were invariably intertwined with the political and power brokerages of the entire Rocky Mountain West. Obviously, they reigned supreme in Cheyenne's high society as well. Their elaborate Victorian mansions, lavishly furnished, became the glittering scene of royal entertaining and formal social functions. Since they were all former members of St. Mark's Episcopal Church, as the current rector I came into pastoral contact with the surviving descendants of these prominent old pioneer families. I think sometimes we expect too much of second and third generation descendants of famous and wealthy entrepreneurs. There's no way the younger Carey and Warren descendants could successfully compete with their forefathers who left such gigantic footprints across the broad Wyoming landscape.

In 1982 I buried Francis E. Warren Jr., the grandson and namesake of the legendary cattle king and popular territorial governor, Francis E. Warren Sr. The grandfather also served thirty-six years as the undefeatable U.S. Senator from Wyoming who often entertained his personal friend, President Teddy Roosevelt, at his huge ranching complex just outside of town. On top of this, he was the father-in-law of General John J. Pershing of World War I fame. How could young Francis Jr. compete with the towering stature of a granddad like that? Little wonder that his widow, Mary Adell, once confessed to me that Francis and she, as a last resort, competed with each other's illnesses. He seemed to live a reclusive life as a sad and lonely man in his palatial home located near Cheyenne on land formerly owned by the Warren Livestock Company.

Before young Francis died, however, he generously gave me a leather-bound set of the *Civil War Naval History*, which once belonged to U.S. Senator Francis E. Warren. The senator was a Civil War veteran who prided himself with this handsome multivolume collection. I proudly display this set in the library of my basement study — although I must confess, I've never read it.

✧

One former governor of Wyoming whom I buried was internationally known. She was Nellie Tayloe Ross, the first woman governor in the United States. Her husband, Wyoming's governor in 1923–1924, died suddenly in midterm. His wife was nominated to serve out his unexpired term and in 1924 won the statewide election in her own right. Miriam A. "Ma" Ferguson of Texas was elected governor of Texas that same year. But the lovely and gracious Nellie Tayloe Ross was inaugurated twenty days before her Texas counterpart, which distinguished her as the first woman governor in the United Sates.

She lived to be 101 and became a symbol of the feminist movement in our nation. I have in my possession several handwritten letters from her, which I highly cherish. I am sorry that I never had the privilege of personally meeting her. Although her casket remained closed during the service, in the Episcopal tradition, the funeral director did allow me to view her body in the mortuary. I couldn't believe that this woman was over a century old. She was beautiful even in death. She was buried on December 21, 1977.

During the centennial celebration of St. Mark's Church in 1968 I began a correspondence with Emily Nathelle Hunt, the wife of former governor and U.S. Senator Lester C. Hunt. The Hunts faithfully attended St. Mark's during his years as secretary of state and governor in the early 1940s before his easy election to the U.S. Senate. Although Dr. Lester C. Hunt, a dentist, was a vivacious and highly popular governor, things didn't go well for him in Washington , D.C., when in 1954, due to failing health and personal problems, he committed suicide and was buried from St. Mark's.

At her burial on October 19, 1990, I met her grandson, Douglas Chadwick, a former photographer and staff writer for *National Geographic*. Shortly thereafter he sent me his latest publication, *The Kingdom*, a large coffee-table book filled with exquisite photographs of wildlife in North America. Chadwick's eloquent and sensitive writing was inspirational. I read that book several times through.

On January 27, 1996, I buried the lovely Leona "Buddy" Gage, the widow of former governor Jack Gage. Once Governor Mike Sullivan said to me, "I understand that you have buried more governors and governors' wives than any other clergyman in the history of Wyoming."

"You may be right," I answered.

"Well, I hope you don't have me next on the waiting list — because I'm hoping to run for a second term!"

Mike and Jane Sullivan were another pair of gracious Wyoming people to occupy the governor's mansion. He was first elected in 1986 and handily won a second term. The Sullivans were Catholic, ending thirty-one years of Episcopalian governorship in Wyoming. I took part in many social, civic, and political events with them. Both attended my retirement dinner in 1992. The governor delivered a wonderful talk in which he humorously referred to the Episcopal Church as the "Republican party on its knees" and wondered aloud how I, a Democrat, could survive twenty-seven years in the hotbed of Republicanism that was St. Mark's Church.

I have news for the governor — this "hotbed of Republicanism" included not only devoted parishioners but also my closest friends. Though I had my private political loyalties, not once did partisan politics ever enter my mind when I prayed for the sick in a hospital, stood with a grieving family beside an open grave, or blessed the marriage of a couple in love at the altar. Not once.

When I was called upon to minister last rites to Estelle Stacy Carrier in 1993, I had to make several long trips to Douglas. This strong and courageous woman was secretary of the National Republican Central Committee at a time when George Bush was its chairman. Millions of Americans watched her call the roll of the states as the 1976 National Republican Convention nominated Gerald Ford for president. Yet, despite our political differences, she specifically requested that I become her priest and pastor during her final days on this earth and officiate at her burial.

For many years I had, and continue to have, regular monthly luncheons with U.S. District Judge Clarence "Bud" Brimmer. Bud was formerly chairman of the Wyoming Republican Party and once a candidate for governor. As a federal judge he is required to keep political and personal opinions strictly to himself, but he could confidentially bounce them off his priest and we shared many personal conversations while devouring prime rib sandwiches at Little America. It is always a rare privilege for a clergyman to have this kind of faithful layman as friend and confidant.

Some have probably accused me of being politically partisan in my ministry, but too many Republicans knew it wasn't so and were prepared to speak in my defense had these charges ever arisen. But they never did, mostly because of the pastoral relationships and intimate friendships that were mutually cherished.

Outsiders often wonder how Wyoming, primarily a Republican state, somehow manages to elect Democrats to our highest offices. It requires a lot of Republican votes for any Democrat to get elected governor or U.S. senator. A lot of tortured explanations have been offered, but I propose that the real answer is all too simple. In my opinion, it has less to do with political loyalties than with the Wyoming temperament. Voters in Wyoming, Democrats and Republicans alike, have an inherent distrust of entrenched political power. It is my theory that Republicans join up with Democrats to elect Democratic governors and senators to keep the Republican incumbents humble and honest. And it would be the same in reverse if Democrats ever became the majority in Wyoming.

Any elected public official in Wyoming, of either party, is politically doomed once the electorate gets the feeling that individual is getting too big for his or her britches. U.S. Senator Alan Simpson, a Republican, sizes up our native mindset very well when he says he always runs scared for re-election. The moment a political figure in our state thinks he or she has got it made, that person had better make definitive plans for early retirement. It has nothing to do with whether he or she is a good public servant or belongs to the right political party. It has everything to do with the rugged individualism of a fiercely independent electorate that won't abide concentrated political power.

✧

On the hot afternoon of July 16, 1979, a tornado ripped through Cheyenne destroying hundreds of homes and wreaking wholesale destruction and devastation. Among the homes blown completely away was the newly built house of my son, Barry, and his wife, Rose.

I attended an early meeting the next morning of civil emergency officials and church leaders to learn how a city goes about dealing with a disaster of such magnitude. I was pleased to see many ministers from nonmainline denominations volunteering to help out with the enormous task at hand. I returned to my office in a daze, completely overwhelmed with the chore confronting us.

Immediately following lunch, Church World Service leaders and a group of civil disaster officials from outside Wyoming called on me and said, "Gene what you saw this morning isn't going to work. We've been through all this many times before in other states. It's commendable that ministers from these nonmainline denominational churches are volunteering their services. We believe they are sincere. But it takes a lot more than sincerity to do the enormous ecumenical job at hand."

"Such as?" I asked.

"It will take money, lots of it. And this upfront funding will only come from the mainline denominational churches. Thousands of dollars will be required to pay the professionals who will train the volunteers to help the victims cope. We're sorry to tell you that not one dime will come from these conservative evangelical nondenominational churches. Furthermore, the inevitable bickering over whether nonfundamentalist Christians should be helped, followed by aggressive proselytizing among the victims, will turn the whole effort into a religious disaster of scandalous proportion. We've been through it too many times to risk it happening again."

"Why are you telling this to me?" I asked.

"Because you're the dean of the Cheyenne clergy; you've been around the longest. The power structure of this city knows who you are, and you know who they are. That's where we have to begin. We're asking you to pull this thing together for us."

"On one condition," I told them. "That it not be called an interdenominational disaster task force, because this implies that it's Christian. Instead, it must become an inter*faith* disaster task force to include the Catholic, Protestant, Greek Orthodox, and Jewish people of our community."

Permission was granted.

My first call was to Bishop Joseph Hart of the Catholic Diocese of Cheyenne, a man for whom I had the highest respect. The second call was to my dear personal friend Rabbi Myron Movsky of Mt. Sinai Synagogue. I explained my insistence to both of these esteemed religious leaders that we form an interfaith task force and that their participation was the sole condition of my assuming responsibility for organizing it. They both agreed, and the Cheyenne Interfaith Disaster Task Force came into being.

It proved itself a godsend to the tornado victims of Cheyenne. It functioned as an umbrella organization, coordinating all the relief resources of the community, both public and private, to provide direct assistance to those most desperately needing the help. It cut through the horrendous bureaucratic red tape of governmental agencies and demanded public accountability from insurance companies who stalled on technicalities. A personal file was maintained on every family affected by the disaster, and these people were constantly monitored as to how they were coping.

And I learned something about denominationalism.

The prediction of the Church World Service leaders and civil disaster officials turned out to be right on the money. Most of the fundamentalist and conservative evangelical churches, in spite of their early willingness to help, disappeared into the woodwork. They had no funds to contribute, and few were willing to work alongside people of other faiths — "liberal" Protestants, Catholics, Greek Orthodox, or Jews — even when it came to acts of charitable assistance. Most of the funding came from the mainline denominational sources: Catholics, American Baptists, Lutherans, Methodists, Presbyterians, Greek Orthodox, and Jews. The Presiding Bishop's World Relief Fund of the Episcopal Church was one of the earliest to respond, with an initial grant of nearly $10,000. What was true about funding from national religious entities was also true about the willingness of local lay people to serve on the governing board and take an active leadership role in administering it.

I developed a profound respect for the Mennonite people and the Reformed Christian Church, who sent crews of trained craftsmen from all over the midwestern part of the United States. These skilled volunteers would take on a job for a family that had no promise of relief assistance — reconstructing a demolished house, for example — and remain until the project was finished, at no charge whatever. All of this regardless of the victims' religious background. Edith Howard, our salaried director, told me, "We couldn't have managed that disaster recovery without these good people who did their noble work in such a quiet way."

One 100-year disaster is enough devastation for any community. But Cheyenne was struck again only six years later when, on August 1, 1985, a cloudburst dumped fourteen inches of water in less than an hour. My daughter Lori and her two children were visiting from New York. We had just pulled up our chairs to the dinner table when the storm began. It continued to worsen, and the roar of the downpour was deafening. We left the food on our plates and headed downstairs into the basement after being advised to do so by emergency broadcasts reporting a tornado threat.

The storm didn't let up, so I raced upstairs to peek out the window into our backyard and was horrified to discover that the entire area was awash in hailstones, several feet deep, with rainwater lapping against the sliding doors of the sunroom — and we were located on high ground. I screamed to Rosemary and Lori, still in the basement, to rush the children to the top floor of Templeton House. The lights went off. There on the third floor, in darkness, we waited out the deluge.

When it was over, it was perfectly calm. The stars came out as if there had been no storm at all. Within an hour the water had drained away from our house. Lori and I stepped outside and discovered that the evening had turned deathly quiet. But off in the distance we could hear the mournful wail of sirens. We got in my car and cautiously headed downtown. There were no streetlights. The homes were all dark. When we approached the downtown area we saw the damage: cars floating upside down in the city sunken parking lot; cars along the streets jammed together and piled on top of each other. The police building was flooded and abandoned. Everywhere it was dark, with no one moving about.

The next morning we learned the gravity of the damage. Hundreds of basements filled. Homes floated away. Bridges washed out. Businesses flooded. It was a full-scale disaster. Twelve people drowned, including a woman only one block away who was trapped in her basement when the window wells gave way, dumping in tons of ice water. She had retreated to her basement, with her little dog, as we all had been instructed to do. The window wells at Templeton House had held; otherwise we could have suffered the same fate.

In midmorning I was called by the mayor to come to the governor's office and asked to pull together another Interfaith Disaster Task Force. Fortunately, we had a successful model to follow. Better yet, we were blessed with Edith Howard, who agreed again to serve as the salaried executive director with the assurance that mainline denominations would immediately make funds available for disaster relief. We received a powerful shot in the arm when Neil Young, a famous rock star, performed a concert at the Frontier Day's outdoor grandstand, with all proceeds donated to the benefit of flood victims.

This time I asked that no clergy serve on the task force's board. The presence of clergy on a relief agency board creates the mistaken idea that somehow the whole disaster project is sectarian in nature. A disaster task force cannot be sectarian, even though considerable funding comes from religious sources. Its resources and voluntary assistance are intended for everyone.

Again, through the expert leadership of Edith Howard and her magnificent board, the Interfaith Disaster Task Force came through with flying colors. Everyone who needed assistance received it. Cheyenne recovered beautifully from another major disaster. Two 100-year disasters within six years of each other should spare us the agony of another one now for at least 200 years.

Both events demonstrated that church and state can work in harmony for the public good while remaining separate. Every community has a power structure, and clergy can discreetly work with it to get things done. But once you've done it, you best back away from it before resentment arises.

✧

Though I have taken time to write about the Wyoming governors and their families with whom I've had a nominal connection as rector of St. Mark's Church, I must say that these people alone are not the history of Wyoming. Far from it. Legislators probably have had more influence on our state than any governor could ever hope to have. I took my turn as house chaplain of the Wyoming legislature and became personally acquainted with many of them. As chaplain I had floor privileges, which meant I could freely move from desk to desk among the legislators before the morning session began. We have had hardworking legislators devoted to the task at hand, and we have had dim-witted ones who never quite knew, or cared to know, what the whole legislative process was all about. By and large, I must say, the voters of Wyoming have elected good men and women to the state legislature. The dim-witted ones can't help it that voters simply like 'em that way and vote 'em into office anyway.

But writing about the people who occupy high executive, legislative, and judicial offices doesn't tell the complete history of any state — certainly not Wyoming. The real history of human endeavor is written by the common people — in Wyoming's case, the people who homesteaded their farms and worked the land, railroaders and coal miners, cowboys and ranchers, business people, military personnel, and Indians — people who established thriving communities, raised their families, lived, and died in a vast and lonely wilderness frontier called Wyoming.

This was brought home to me one day when I visited a site in southeastern Wyoming known as the "Spanish Diggings." The name is a misnomer; the Spaniards never ventured this far north. In fact, these digging sites were ancient stones quarries of prehistoric North Americans, conceivably dating back 10,000 to 12,000 years, where Stone Age men had discovered a special quartz rock which could easily be chiseled into spear points and arrowheads.

My good friend Jena Carey, the daughter-in-law of Julia Carey, organized a trek to this remote landmark. Our party included Grant Wilson, a lay western historian and amateur archaeologist, and Virginia Cole Trenholm, the author of several authoritative books on Wyoming Indian history.

The four of us started out early on a beautiful June morning and headed northeast toward the wide-open desert country near Lusk. Our paved highway soon gave way to a gravel one, which became a graded dirt road and then a trail, and finally something even less. By this time we had been traveling for nearly three hours and realized that we were lost in the middle of a desolate area many miles from nowhere.

We got out of the car and stood around in total confusion. Our guide, Virginia Trenholm, had no idea where we were. In fact, we differed among ourselves as to how we would even retrace our route because we had encountered so many forks in the road and taken so many detours. Off in the distance were some towering rimrocks, at the base of which stood a cluster of large cottonwood trees. Virginia dimly recognized them as maybe being the isolated homestead of a Mr. Barnhill. "I'm not at all sure about that," she said. "But it kinda looks like the Barnhill place which once I saw long ago. He's an old-timer in this area and usually spends his summers out there, although he winters in California with his family. If he's still alive, he'd have to be in his nineties. He's a widower now. If he happens to be there, he could surely give us directions to the Spanish Diggings. I think some of them may even be located on his land."

We slowly bumped our way across the rough terrain, and the homestead house came into view. It was made of cottonwood trees, so thick in circumference that it took only three or four logs to build a single wall. An old man appeared behind the screen door of the kitchen, wearing his straw hat as if it were a security blanket inside his house. His hands were as gnarled as the twisted wood in his homemade cane.

Virginia introduced herself and explained that somehow we had lost the road to the Spanish Diggings.

"Of course, you have," he said. "There ain't no road from here to there. But I can tell you how to find 'em if you follow my directions."

He stepped outside onto the front porch and told us that if we proceeded up that large draw for about ten miles, skirting north of the big butte, we'd come across a trail that would eventually lead to them. "And these are the one's the public doesn't much see because they're too isolated for people to find 'em. But I know where they are and you'll find 'em without a road if you do as I've just told you."

We looked out across the barren landscape, which seemed like fifty miles of desolation, as the noonday heat was bearing down upon us. There wasn't a tree in sight.

"Mr. Barnhill," Virginia asked, "would you mind if we ate our picnic lunch here in the cool shade of your giant cottonwoods? We invite you to join us."

We could tell he was delighted to have company and slowly maneuvered his arthritic frame, short and stocky, down off the porch and out to a home-made chair of willow boughs. Jena and Virginia spread out a tablecloth, on which they placed a black kettle of fried chicken, a bowl each of chilled potato salad and baked beans, and a thermos jug of ice tea.

As they busied themselves with the final preparations for lunch, Mr. Barnhill began telling us about his life on that lonely Wyoming homestead. He told us that Hattie and he homesteaded there right after they were married. "In fact, we spent our honeymoon campin' out in a tent right where we're sittin' right now as I began buildin' our little homestead cabin. As you can see, I just chopped down a few cottonwoods that were growin' in the wild up here by the spring of water seepin' out of those rimrocks, and they was so big and round that it took only a few to build a whole cabin. We would eat our meals outside our tent, on the ground, just like we're doin' right now. Ah, that was good."

Mr. Barnhill repeated the philosophical refrain, "Ah, that was good," always with pleased satisfaction, as he continued his story.

"It took us most of the summer to build our little homestead cabin and we finished just in time before an early blizzard swept in upon us. But we weren't cooped up in our tent anymore. We were inside our new home where it was cozy and warm and we could just watch the storm blow itself out. Ah, that was good."

He lit up his pipe and took a few puffs as if pausing for reflection.

"Our first baby was born right here. I had to deliver it because we were too far away from a neighbor woman. I kinda knew what to do, 'cause I've delivered a lot of calves. It's basically the same thing, ya know. I must have done alright, 'cause he turned out to be a dandy little boy. More kids followed, and we began addin' rooms to our cottonwood cabin."

We were now content just to listen to our storyteller as we began eating our lunch.

"Ya know, that spring runs water all year-round. So I stuck a pipe into it and piped it right into the house. Now Hattie had runnin' water at a sink. And it never froze up because we kept it runnin' all the time. It would run through the house, then out into the yard and down over the rocks. Hattie had the best garden out here in this dryland country that you'd ever want. It was irrigated. Can you imagine that? We had runnin' water out here before a lot of you city folks did. Ah, that was good."

Now, really waxing up to the story he was telling us, he continued.

"Ya know what? With that springwater runnin' down over the rocks into the draw below us, I decided to do somethin' special with it for the kids. I took a team of horses and a slip and scooped out the dirt down to bedrock . . . just below us here," he said, pointing toward a little grove of willows a couple hundred yards away. "Then I diverted this flow of springwater down over the hot rocks and let it trickle into that hole I just scooped out, and my kids had a heated swimmin' pool. Can you imagine that? A thermal-heated swimmin' pool? I'll bet ya that my kids had the first private swimmin' pool in all Wyoming. And just think, we had that luxury way out here in this dried-up country where you'd least expect to find it."

He shifted his weight in the chair and moved his cane to the other side.

"During the peak of the homestead years, back in the early 1900s, these dryland homestead kids would ride in for miles around on a Sunday afternoon and have big swimmin' parties down there in my Willow Pond. That's what we began callin' it when the willows started growin' up round it. And while they splashed away in the water, I'd crank 'em up a freezer of ice cream with the ice I cut out of the pond in the wintertime and kept buried beneath sawdust in the ice shed. Them dryland kids never had so much fun. Ah, that was good."

He chewed a little on a leg of country fried chicken, smacking his lips.

"Then the kids grew up and left home, one by one. We lost one of 'em in the war, ya know. But then the grandkids would spend their summers out here with me and Hattie every year. They'd do the same thing their folks did. Help me put up a little hay, milk the cows, and do the chores. But mostly they'd ride their horses all over these hills pretendin' they were cowboys and Indians, and every night they'd go swimmin' in Willow Pond. Ah, that was so good."

He took a swig of iced tea and wiped his mouth on his sleeve, rather than using the napkin Jena handed him.

"Then these grandkids grew up and left home and got married. And would ya believe it, then my great-grandkids started comin' out here for the same kind of a summer vacation their parents and grandparents had before them. Gallop around the hills in the daytime and swim every night in Willow Pond."

He paused for a moment.

"Then Hattie died. They say I'm too old to live here year-round all by myself. I'm ninety-two, ya know. But I keep comin' out here every summer just so they'd all have a place to come back to. But now these great-grandkids have summer jobs and are goin' to school. My oldest great-grandson has just been admitted to the School of Medicine at the University of California. Who knows, maybe someday when I'm gone, his kids will come out here to Willow Pond just like he always did when he was a kid."

Then he sighed and said, "So this is the first summer that I've been all by myself out here — alone."

I was the first to speak. "Are you lonely, Mr. Barnhill?"

"Oh, during the day I am. I'm so gol' durned crippled up I can't do anything any more. I can't even walk out to the barn — don't even have a pony out there this summer. But I cook myself up a good breakfast every morning and a good dinner, and then I eat leftovers for supper."

I commented, "Normally when people find themselves living alone for the first time, it's the evening that seems the loneliest."

"Oh, not for me," he said, brightening up so much that you could see the animation on his face. "Not for me, 'cause you see, my whole family comes back up here into these hills every night. Every night they're here — all of 'em."

I hesitated, feeling that I had missed something from what he said only moments before about being totally alone this summer. "They do?" I mused — puzzled as to what he meant.

"Oh yes," he quickly responded. "Every night all my kids come back into their childhood here. Even the boy we lost in the war. They all come here every night. I sit out on the back porch and I hear 'em down in the Willow Pond splashin' in the water and laughin' and squealin' away. Just like an ol' mother cow can tell the sound of its calf bawlin' in a whole herd of cattle, I can identify which one it is I'm hearin' just by the sound of its voice. I sit out here on the back porch and enjoy myself — just listenin' to 'em. Ah, that's good."

Pointing toward an overgrown area of weeds encircled by a crumbling fence, he said, "And every night Hattie comes through the garden to see me. She gathers up vegetables in her apron as she passes through the garden, then she sits with me on the back porch. I talk with her and tell her everything that's goin' on in my life and heart. I read to her all the letters from the family. I told her about the boy that's studyin' to be a doctor. 'Ain't it great, Hattie,' I tell her, 'that we've got a boy who's gonna be a big surgeon some day, out there in California?' I talk to her like that every night out here and tell her everything.

"And every time, I'll recall some specific event which happened to us during the sixty-some years we was married. Maybe joyful or maybe sad. But I'll remember every detail about that event that I can possibly remember and then tell it to her again. Sometimes we laugh and sometimes we cry.

"And all the while, we hear our kids splashin' in the water down in Willow Pond. Ah, that's good.

"At night up here the stars come out so bright you can almost reach out and touch 'em — 'cause there ain't any pollution out here, ya know. Then when it gets late, Hattie goes back through the garden, and I go to bed."

The four of us sat there in silence, completely mesmerized by the haunting imagery of the old man's story.

He sat silently for a moment in his handmade willow chair, as if lost in thought and memory. When the silence seemed to hang heavy he suddenly pushed the brow of his straw hat up his forehead an inch or two with the tip of his thumb, leaned forward, and said, "Oh, I suppose you think I'm just a crazy ol' man livin' in the past. But that ain't the way I see it. The way I see it is this — if we live to remember, we'll remember to live."

The words rang heavy into my consciousness.

Later that afternoon, we found our way to the Spanish Diggings. We sifted through the flakes of chippings left over by prehistoric people, who had chiseled their spear points and tools out of the quartz rock. Grant Wilson proved to be a superb archaeological guide. As we ambled along the rocky bottom of a dry gulch, ever on the lookout for rattlesnakes, he would spot things never apparent to a casual observer like myself. In the washout of a ravine he spotted an ashy smudge in the high vertical bank, which he gently probed with his fingers. Out came loose flakes of quartz — stone that was completely foreign to the natural rocks surrounding it.

"Look here, Gene, this was an ancient fire pit. The people would have heated the rock and then chiseled a sharp spear point or cutting tool. These flakes are what they chiseled away. The depth of this fire pit from the top of bank would indicate that it's several thousand years old, long before the era of the modern American Indian; hundreds of years, if not thousands, before the advent of the horse in North America. If we actually found a broken spear point these people were crafting, we could more precisely determine the date of ancient man's occupation here."

The whole time we trudged along steep ravines and climbed in and out of the quarry pits, the words of Mr. Barnhill continued to reverberate in my mind.

If we live to remember — we'll remember to live.

It was the best definition of what memorial days are all about in the cultural history of mankind. When we live to remember religious saints, national heroes, distinguished benefactors, and special loved ones, past and present, whose lives have greatly enriched ours — it is then that we remember to live life more fully in the here and now of our human existence.

This ninety-two-year-old cowboy homesteader, living alone in his cottonwood cabin home in the isolation of that desolate butte country halfway between Wheatland and Lusk was nurtured and sustained by the living memory of his deceased wife and descendants long separated from him. He deliberately recalled the memories of these happy times and brought them forward into the living present — so vividly that he could sit on the back porch and listen to his children at play in their Willow Pond while he visited again with his beloved Hattie. This old man was not alone out on his homestead. He was surrounded by the living hosts of all his loved ones, who he invited back into the active memory of his life.

I have often wondered what might happen if I could find and revisit this old abandoned place up by the barren rimrocks, surrounded by cottonwoods watered from the spring. The old man is buried beside his beloved Hattie by the rosebushes. The homestead would surely be in ruins now, like so many old homesteads that litter the American West. If I were to sit on the back porch as the evening shadows crept across the sagebrush prairies, would I hear only the sound of the water welling up from the spring and trickling down over the rocks into Willow Pond? Or would I hear all the Barnhill children splashing in their Willow Pond swimming pool? Would I see Hattie and him coming through the garden? Would they come up on to the porch and sit there with me for awhile?

Probably not.

Even though I'm quite convinced these sights and sounds are lingering there, most likely I'll never have the eyes and ears to perceive them. These images belong to Mr. Barnhill, the man who lived among them and cherished them. They are the gifts of life to him. His gift was sharing them with us as we picnicked on his front lawn in the shade of his giant cottonwood trees.

But we all have our memories, too.

Maybe some day I can sit on the back porch of my life and live to remember the sights, sounds, relationships, and experiences that have given my life depth and meaning. I pray that I can call upon them, like Mr.

Barnhill did, and invoke their presence in such a way that they can sustain and enrich me for the time I have left on this earth. Enough so that I can look back upon them and always say with confidence and satisfaction, "Ah, that was good. It was so good."

If we live to remember — we'll remember to live.

Chapter 19

New York City in the early 1900s experienced an outbreak of typhoid fever after the spread of the disease had already been brought under control by Public Health. Investigation revealed that the source of the new outbreak was confined to certain restaurants throughout the city and therefore, it was quickly concluded, a "passive" carrier of the highly contagious disease was a transient kitchen worker. It didn't take long for the health officials to discover that it was a woman by the name of Mary Mallon, also known by various aliases. But when they tried to apprehend her, she came at them with a sharpened butcher knife and escaped.

She was quickly identified as "Typhoid Mary" and it became a question now for law enforcement as to how they could track her down. The police commissioner convinced health officers not to issue a public alert because this would only frighten her into moving to another city and thereby widening the outbreak into epidemic proportions. Rather, he advised that they all quietly await the next typhoid outbreak, centered around a particular restaurant, and then quickly move in for an apprehension.

They didn't have long to wait and this time the authorities were well prepared to successfully subdue her. She was apprehended in 1915 and detained for twenty-three years. Her case is well documented in the history of public health as the cause of ten major outbreaks of typhoid fever in New York City.

There was a *Typhoid Mary* at St. Mark's Church.

It took me a long time to identify who she was. But the scenario was much the same as it was for health authorities in New York City. There would be intermittent outbreaks of contagious discontent, vicious gossip. and outright dissension which would move from group to group. It would break out in the choir which required a lot of time and energy to resolve. Then it would break out in the women's guild. Then in the Sunday school. Then in the youth group. Then back in the choir again and next within the vestry.

It became apparent to us that these outbreaks of discontent were not spontaneous but were deliberately ignited. Like typhoid fever in New York, we

447

concluded that there was a common carrier who was infecting first one group and then another — and always with predictable results.

I would recruit a youth leader, for example, who was new to the parish structure and enthusiastic about specific goals we had mutually agreed upon. Once his success with the young people became apparent to the congregation as a whole, then something bizarre would happen which led us to believe that someone had contacted him with a laundry list of complaints and congregational unrest which predated his history within the parish. He simply wouldn't have known or cared about these past events unless someone had pumped them up.

But who was it? We became certain that it had to be a woman because men wouldn't have had access to the women's guilds. Furthermore, it had to be a person of long duration within the parish because the complaints often centered around my first few days on the job in the church. Therefore, we knew it was someone terribly unhappy that I had been called as rector of St. Mark's back in 1965, or was intimately acquainted with an early critic who was here when I first arrived. Although we began to strongly suspect one or two individuals, we could never be sure.

Finally, the big break came.

In 1975 I appointed a Mrs. Bea DeGarmo to teach a women's Bible study. She was new to St. Mark's and had volunteered her services as a teacher because of her past experience as a student in a class which followed a particular methodology in studying the scriptures. Formation of the class was announced in the church newsletter and prospective students were invited to call the church office.

One morning Bea came to my office, greatly distressed, asking to speak privately with me. (I have her permission to tell this story.)

"You've got a real troublemaker in your church," she began. "I received this phone call last night from a woman in this church I have never met or know anything about. But since she saw the announcement in the newsletter about this Bible class I'm organizing, she called and attacked my credentials for teaching it. The more I tried defending myself, the more she tried dissuading me.

"When she finally realized that I was more determined than ever to teach the class despite her opposition, then she changed her tactics and began attacking your credibility as rector with triviality that went back to the first day you arrived on the job here in Cheyenne. I told her outright that I had never worked with a more cooperative rector than you.

"When she realized that I was not buying into her paranoid opposition to you, then she began with vicious gossip about the church members as a whole. I suppose an average newcomer to the church, by this time, would have simply given up and withdrawn from the church rather than face that kind of mean-spirited hostility within the Body of Christ. But no one is going to separate me from loving my church and serving it with whatever talent I have."

I asked, "Will you please tell me who this person is?"

"I'll gladly tell you, Father Todd, because I think you definitely need to know. If she is calling me as a newcomer to this church — then she most certainly is calling all other newcomers to this church. Her name is *Mary*."

Mary was one of the women the wardens and I had suspected all along.

Now we knew, but what were we to do? The wardens and I discussed it at considerable length and it was our conclusion that we not openly confront her because, like the original Typhoid Mary, she simply would come at us with a sharpened knife. It might be wiser, we reasoned, to monitor her subversive behavior and counteract it with positive support for church leaders whose confidence she was deliberately trying to undermine. We called it our "containment policy" — patterned after President Truman's policy of containing the spread of communism worldwide.

There was no question, however, that we had correctly singled *Typhoid Mary* out. The next time I encountered another youth director, for example, who suddenly began demonstrating her infection I would carefully avoid asking who it was that had been in recent contact with him. Instead, I would casually introduce Mary's name into the conversation and before long, in the discussion that ensued, he suddenly discovered that he had already let the cat out of the bag.

What made the problem so difficult to manage was that on the surface she appeared as a loyal and faithful Episcopalian. She was a hard church worker. She regularly attended Sunday worship services. She sang in the choir and worked in the guild. She would be among the first to volunteer for a job that had to be done. But she was also very two-faced — pleasantly saying one thing to me during the day and saying exactly the opposite in her telephone networking that night. And then laughing it off to me again the next morning, as if no personal harm was intended — when I knew that it was.

One morning during the coffee hour after church, Richard Stacy (Wyoming's U.S. attorney) approached me and said that *Mary* had just come to him with caustic criticism of something I supposedly had done or said. "Watch her. You can see her moving from group to group here in the parish hall spreading dissension to everyone she meets. She needs to be stopped."

Immediately, I cornered the wardens and suggested that we invite her into my study and openly confront her. Maybe it was time we try a more direct approach — confrontation!

"Gene, everyone knows she's a cripple!" they said, "Observe the body language of the people with whom she's talking the moment she moves on to the next group. The roll of their eyes and the shrug of their shoulders and they way they shake their head and glance at one another. They know she's up to no good when it comes to anything concerning you or the general leadership of our church. She's doing herself far more harm right now in diminishing her creditibility than what we could ever do by openly confronting her."

Another lay person came to me once and said, "I think *Mary* needs friendship and I am willing to be her friend. But it has become apparent to me that a condition of her friendship is that you must become our common enemy. I am not willing to accept that condition."

By this time I wasn't convinced that our policy of containment was working. Twenty years of her subterfuge was beginning to wear me down. I arranged lunch with a psychotherapist within the congregation who knew her well and asked if the time had not come for us to openly pursue an intervention with her — much like what is done with the disruptive behavior of a chronic alcoholic.

"No, it wouldn't work Gene. Her neurotic opposition to you has become pathological. As long as she focuses on you and your flaws, then she doesn't have to confront the flaws or emptiness of her own personal life or marriage. It's obvious to her by now that she can't control the unhappy direction of her life. But if she can subversively change you by her compulsive opposition to everything you say and do, then this gives her a semblance of power in life which otherwise she doesn't have."

I didn't find his message very comforting or encouraging and openly questioned the wisdom of allowing *Mary* to destroy the church program in order to destroy me. I told him that once my Christian education director laughingly told me that Mary had been calling prospective members of a Lenten Bible class asking them not to attend — because their attendance would make me look good. But it's backfiring on her. More people are signing up than what we expected.

"That proves my point," the therapist said. "Believe me, the congregation knows her all too well."

And then he offered some profound advice. "It should be apparent to you by now, Gene, that you and your succession of wardens are not changing *Mary*. And you never will because her condition is pathological. But you can change yourself. You are giving her control by allowing her opposition to dominate your attention. Quit doing that, Gene. Don't let her nail you to the cross and when she tries — pray for her forgiveness the same as Christ did when he hung on the cross."

This was good pastoral counseling — coming from a lay professional to his priest.

The president of our women's guild came to me and said, "I'm very certain that if you said Jesus Christ was Lord — she would do everything she could to prove you wrong. We must all take to heart the commandment of our Lord who said, *'Blessed are you when they revile and persecute you, and say all manner of evil against you falsely for my sake . . . rejoice and be exceedingly glad, for great is your reward in heaven, for so they persecuted the prophets before you.'* Father Todd, this is the only Christian way I know in dealing with Mary."

This also was good spiritual direction — coming this time from a dedicated lay woman to her priest.

But it took me awhile to adopt these two recommendations. But eventually I did when the wardens and I shifted gears in developing a new strategy in dealing with *Mary* at St. Mark's. Instead of trying to prevent her from doing her damage, we simply predicted the inevitability that she would — and concentrated our energy in warning potential church leaders, in advance, on how to cope with that reality before it actually happened.

I would tell the new youth director, again using him as an example, "You need to be expecting a phone call or a personal contact sometime in the near future from a parishioner who I will not name at this time. She will try destroying confidence in yourself, in me, and in the general leadership of this church. At that point, you will need to decide whether you want to work for the vestry and me in your new leadership position in the church — or whether you want to work for her. If you choose to believe what she says and want to work for her, I will respect that choice. But I ask of you one thing in advance — that you will be honest with me and have the personal integrity to resign. Because you cannot work for both of us at the same time."

In only a few weeks they would meet me in the hallway with an all-telling smile or wink and say, "I got the call!"

The new strategy worked and I'm sorry I waited too long to put it into practice.

Although *Mary* perpetuated a climate of chronic discontent, threatening to undermine both the leadership and program of the church, I learned some valuable lessons from the painful encounter. For example, I learned that when dealing with people who become a severe problem to us, there's no need to seek revenge because they are bound to be a similar problem to others — and most of all, the greatest problem to themselves. They have suffered enough. This doesn't mean, however, that we must allow them to make us suffer. Nor, worst of all, allow their vindictive pettiness to make us petty in dealing with them.

One would like to believe that the activities of a *Typhoid Mary* would not happen inside the Christian Church, but it does at all levels of its organizational existence. I'm afraid that seminaries are not well equipped to help prospective clergy deal with grim realities such as this. But it would be helpful if, at least, they alerted seminarians that there surely will be a *Typhoid Mary* in the future of all ministers — and they better be prepared to cope with the challenge of its potential disaster when it happens.

Theological reflection tells me that even though the kingdom of God calls for perfection, we live in a fallen world. I am flawed. *Mary* is flawed. Indeed, we are all flawed because the human condition is flawed. Only when we concentrate on the potential merits of each other, rather than the flaws — do we discover that good usually exceeds the bad. That's when grace-in-community abounds. This spiritual exercise in humility finally enabled me, in my personal dealing with *Mary*, to muster forgiveness for her chicanery.

It has been said that most people who enter the ministry have a pathological need to be loved by everyone. But we soon learn, as did Abraham Lincoln, that you can only please part of the people part of the time in your servanthood for the Lord. So it becomes a primal shock in life to discover that not only are there people out there who don't love or even like you — but are religiously and pathologically committed to your early demise. I take consolation that once there was a Jewish carpenter-rabbi who learned that bitter lesson at a much younger age than I. And the funny thing is — he told us all along that this was the way it was gonna be.

I'm grateful for an abiding sense of humor which enables me to laugh at silly church antics like this, now that I'm retired — when at the time, this annoyance consumed so much emotional energy during the many years that I had to endure these periodic outbreaks of typhoid fever in my parish ministry at St. Mark's Church.

✧

As Episcopalians, we have always prided ourselves on being the "frozen chosen" people of God. Everything we do in worship is written word-for-word in our prayer book; we always know exactly what everyone is going to say and do, with no surprises. Although canon law allows freedom of expression at the pulpit, it is incumbent upon every parishioner to exercise considerable caution to make certain that the sermon doesn't vary too much from the Anglican norm.

The Anglican norm is not precisely defined, but often it is understood to be nothing emotional. We Episcopalians like to think we're broad-minded enough to tolerate almost anything that's said at the pulpit, providing it's done properly and in orderly fashion. If the sermon is preached with even a hint of emotion, Episcopalians quickly become emotional about restraining it.

So imagine the furor that arose in the late 1970s and early 1980s, when St. Mark's was hit with an invasion of the Holy Rollers, who had formerly been confined to Pentecostal churches out on the fringe of town. Generally speaking Episcopalians want no part of such bizarre manifestations of religious fanaticism and out-of-control emotionalism; consequently, we tend to exceed the speed limit when passing an Assembly of God church along the freeway.

When we were told that the Holy Spirit was causing some of our staid Episcopalians to lift their arms above their heads or sway their bodies while singing a campfire ditty not authorized by our hymnal, or start praying out loud a prayer not found in our prayer book, in a language that was pure gibberish — "speaking in tongues" — we Episcopalians suddenly become very emotional about stomping out such emotionalism in worship.

Hard as we tried, we couldn't stomp it out because we couldn't find a way in our canon law to control the Holy Spirit. Before we knew what hit us, we found ourselves in the midst of a Pentecostal revival within the Episcopal Church. Its adherents preferred to call it a "charismatic movement" to differentiate it from the religious frenzy found in Pentecostal churches. Later it was renamed a "renewal movement." Not only were we having to contend with individual parishioners who had become infected with religious lunacy, but also a few bishops had lost their Episcopal dignity and cool reserve and suddenly began dancing around the church chancel.

Whenever I confront something new and different in my life, intellectually oriented as I am, I undertake a serious study of it. I was determined to learn everything I could about charismatic Christianity. I soon learned that it was rooted in the New Testament experience of the early Christian Church, which is partly described in the book of Acts and to which the apostle Paul makes oblique references in his letters to congregations he was founding. Theologians refer to the phenomenon as *glossolalia* — which means speaking in tongues. The charismatic movement gets its name from the word "charisma," which refers to extraordinary power and gifts of the Holy Spirit for healing and empowerment.

From my initial study, this appeared to be something that had enough merit to commend itself to me personally. Although there is considerable emotion in my personal religious faith, I am not one to express it *emotionally* — my private religious experiences seem more intellectually oriented. But I have never believed that heart and mind are mutually exclusive when it comes to seeking and following the will of God. I recognized that maybe my personal faith had become slightly lopsided and I needed a little more heart.

I also believe that Anglicanism, historically, is broad enough to embrace many expressions of faith. The charismatic movement, I thought, had desirable qualities that would enhance the overall worship and practice of the Episcopal Church. Warmth and joy, willingness to share the faith, and openness to the guidance of the Holy Spirit were things our church needed.

Slowly and cautiously, I began opening up St. Mark's to the positive influences of the charismatic movement. We introduced guitar accompaniment to our congregational singing of inspirational hymns. We scheduled midweek "Prayer and Praise" services for those who wanted to engage in Bible study and sing "spirit-filled" songs. Our church sponsored and hosted a national Episcopal Renewal Conference, which brought to Cheyenne the top charismatic leaders of our nation as well as priests and lay people from all over the Rocky Mountain West. St. Mark's was becoming one of the leading churches of the charismatic movement in the diocese of Wyoming.

Needless to say, there was considerable resistance from traditional Episcopalians at St. Mark's. I spent a lot of time trying to convince parishioners that the charismatic influence would not dominate the church or its worship. I argued that the charismatic expression, in fact, might bring a warm and friendly presence to enhance our traditional liturgical worship. I strongly believed that our built-in Anglican restraint would prevent the excesses and abuses that were beginning to trouble other mainline denominational churches. I pointed out that the Roman Catholic Church seemed to be tolerating the charismatic influence very well. As a matter of fact, Catholics and Episcopalians enjoyed sharing Prayer and Praise services together and relished that here was a new area of ecumenical faith building.

A vestryman came to my office and said, very frankly, "Gene, in spite of all your persuasion about the charismatic movement, I am not convinced that it's going to become the wholesome thing that you predict. You're being too idealistic. If ever you cross them they will kick you in the ass so hard that you will never recover. And this church may never recover either. I have seen churches ripped apart at the seams over the charismatic rampage. I don't want that to happen to you or this wonderful old church."

Even though his language was graphic, he, like Isaiah, spoke with a prophetic ring of truth.

In fact, I was already becoming acquainted with some negatives about the charismatic movement. Its anti-intellectualism was troublesome. The conflict between heart and mind was coming down heavy on emotionalism to the exclusion of intellectualism. I have always known that many, if not most, people are initially drawn to God on a deeply personal level to meet emotional needs. Others, including myself, are initially attracted on a deeply personal intellectual level. Both viewpoints are equally valid. But to sustain a meaningful relationship with Christ requires that we exercise both the emotional and intellectual qualities God created within us. Practicing either expression of the faith to the exclusion of the other quickly leads to a religion out of balance with itself.

I remember attending an Episcopal Church women's annual convention in Wyoming. They always had a late-night healing service. I believe in healing, because I believe all healing comes from God whether it be through prayer or surgery or medication. Eleanor, a woman I have known in the diocese for many years, knelt for healing. All the women gathered around for the laying-on-of-hands and prayer. Eleanor began crying. I didn't even know that she had been sick.

They all began crying. It was obvious to me that Eleanor was far sicker than I thought.

Then they became hysterical, trying to hold each other up. It was obvious to me that Eleanor's sickness was terminal.

In spite of their effort to hold one another up, they began dropping to the floor with shrieks of wailing. It was apparent to me by then that Eleanor's condition not only was terminal but also that death was imminent. Maybe even that evening!

I was shocked that somehow I never heard about the seriousness of her condition.

Later I saw Eleanor sitting by herself, alone, emotionally wrung out. I went over to her and said, "Eleanor I am sorry that you have been so terribly ill. No one told me anything about it."

"Oh, there's nothing wrong with me," she shrugged. "A healing service like that makes me feel good emotionally. We all feel better emotionally. It gives us a real spiritual 'high' on Jesus. That's why we do it."

Her "high" became my "low" which greatly accelerated my gradual disillusionment with the charismatic movement. I can think of a hundred better ways to get my spiritual "high kicks" than engaging in these contrived crying jags. Emotionalism was getting the upper hand.

The historic triad of Anglican authority is *Tradition, Scripture,* and *Reason.* Emotion is not listed — not even highly charged emotionalism energized by the Holy Spirit. Maybe it should be added to the former three. But even if it were, it should never negate reason. Anglicans should always remind ourselves that Christ died to take away our sins — not our minds.

It is all right to have feelings and to express them emotionally in an appropriate way. The charismatics, however, were going beyond the bounds of what I considered appropriate.

Another feature of the charismatic movement that frightened me is its obsession with Satanism. This satanic obsession almost seemed demonic in itself. If I'm guilty for not taking it seriously enough, charismatics are guilty of taking it *too* seriously. It doesn't take long in the presence of charismatics to feel that Satan reigns as lord of the universe. They refer to Satan as often as they talk about our Lord Jesus Christ. They pit the two against one another in a battle for control of the world, taking literally the symbolic imagery of the Book of Revelation in the New Testament. They call it "spiritual warfare." Usually, it seems, Satan is winning out.

A charismatic once brought a cake to Templeton House with the instructions that it was intended only for Rosemary to eat for dinner that evening, and not me — because I was under the control of Satan. Obviously, I had done or said something which displeased her and, poor soul, this was her most logical explanation.

Most terrifying of all, however, is the natural affinity that exists between the charismatic movement and religious fundamentalism. Biblical fundamentalism, as a belief system, is theologically and intellectually unpalatable to me for all the reasons I listed in chapter 17 of this book. There's no reason for me to repeat or belabor my objections here. But everyone is entitled to believe whatever they wish and worship however they choose. As I have written previously, religious fundamentalists also have a right to pursue their political agenda the same as I. That's the strength of our democracy. What offends me is not their belief system, or their right to pursue it, but their inherent self-righteousness and galling judgmental condemnation of those who disagree with them. That God is only on their side. Or as Ellmore said, again in chapter 17, if I disagreed with his narrow interpretation of the Bible — then take it up with the Lord. Thus inferring that God was only in his corner. This smug belligerency brings out reverse judgmentalism within me — a character flaw I bitterly dislike about myself.

Gradually I came to realize that I could not deal kindly with the spectre of Christian fundamentalism slipping through the back door of St. Mark's disguised as the charismatic-renewal movement of the Episcopal Church.

I had fled the Baptist Church to the Anglican faith to forever escape the ravages of religious fundamentalism. Now my safe haven was invaded by the very thing that I desperately wanted to escape in the first place.

I came to the conclusion that charismatics and fundamentalists sleep in the same bed. Even though they deny having intercourse, once two people, passionately attracted to one another, shut the door and crawl under the covers, nature has a way of taking its course. I'm not interested in hearing what they didn't do.

It doesn't have to be this way. I believe that a warm and joyful charismatic expression of the faith can be practiced without regressing into fundamentalism. But you must constantly be on guard to keep them separated — or you come off like an ogre trying to keep two young lovers apart at a college beach house. Regardless of how hard you try, charismatics slip off in the cover of night to rendezvous with the fundamentalists, and by morning you've got a pregnant Bible-thumping charismatic-fundamentalist on your hands, condemning the world to hell in the name of Jesus. Self-righteous judgmentalism is the dominant genetic trait of such unholy offspring.

Although the joyful charismatic expression can be successfully integrated into Anglicanism, biblical fundamentalism cannot, in my humble opinion, because it is inherently incompatible with the open spirit of Anglicanism. The traditional and historical essence of Anglicanism is openness to all spiritual and intellectual truth, whereas religious fundamentalism by attitude and behavior is closed. The two are mutually contradictory.

Rosemary never shared my initial interest in the charismatic movement. In fact, she was disenchanted with it from the beginning, which deprived me of the benefit of her insight and counsel. I found myself becoming isolated in my inner turmoil about it. I should have sought out the services of a good spiritual director, who could have helped me sort through the theological confusion and mixed emotions that were burdening me. The problem was compounded by my own denial — I did not want to acknowledge the pain of personal abandonment many of the charismatics at St. Mark's must have felt toward me. My schism of the soul was beginning to tear me and the congregation apart.

In retrospect, I probably should have pulled the group together at St. Mark's Church and honestly confessed my disillusionment with the charismatic movement, explaining my specific misgivings about its magnetic attraction to fundamentalism. Most of all, I should have openly admitted my innate inability to provide the leadership they wanted and expected. Maybe we could have worked something out.

But maybe not. The rector of a large Episcopal church in Denver, a former Catholic priest who considered himself and his parish leaders of the charismatic-renewal movement, did exactly what I'm proposing I should have done — and for the same reasons. He bitterly said, "I got kicked in the ass so hard that I just about never recovered. In fact, we had to invite Bishop Frey into the parish to help resolve the volatile situation. It was a nightmare. Finally, the whole charismatic group pulled out, leaving the church broke and flat on its face. And we were considered one of the wealthiest Episcopal churches in Denver. Frankly, I don't know if we'll ever recover."

I thought it a strange coincidence that the priest made the same reference to the human posterior when talking about the charismatic rampage, just as my vestryman, Fred, had in his dire prediction of what would happen at St. Mark's. I have since learned that this expression is commonly used everywhere in description of what the charismatic movement can do to a local church because it seems so accurate.

I've always said you get more light from a slow-burning candle than from a flashing comet streaking through the sky. It seemed to me that charismatics were in constant competition even with one another as to which one was the flashier comet and which one had the greatest miracle to report. I remember attending a Prayer and Praise service one evening when the conversation turned to a discussion of long-time St. Mark's parishioners who were not filled with the Holy Spirit. It flipped my gizzard when someone mentioned Freddie Nelson as an example of such a person.

I said, "Freddie makes more hospital calls in a month than the rest of you do all year — combined. In addition to this, she faithfully delivers soup to those who are sick at home."

"Who needs soup when we have supermarkets, electric can openers, and microwave ovens?" they asked, almost in chorus.

"We may not need the soup," I retorted, "but we all need loving people like Freddie Nelson who care enough to bring it to us, people who love us and genuinely want us to get well. This brings us healing and makes us whole again."

Unfortunately, I didn't leave well enough alone and went on to say, "You people gather here every week to see what Jesus can do for you. Freddie goes out every week to see what she can do for Jesus, in her quiet and unassuming way. Don't you dare tell me that Freddie Nelson isn't a spirit-filled Christian!"

No longer could I "talk the talk" of the charismatic movement, because now I knew where "walking the walk" would invariably lead me — and I didn't want to go there.

✧

In 1986 there was a charge of lay sexual misconduct involving an adult with a sixteen-year-old minor who both were members of St. Mark's. Although the offense didn't happen on church property or within the context of a church program, it was reported to me. This was several years before stringent denominational guidelines had been established for dealing with sexual misconduct. But I'm pleased to say that I handled that case as professionally as the new guidelines would have required. There was no cover-up. It was reported to civil authorities, leading to a court conviction and sentence. Psychiatric referrals were promptly made for both parties in the offense. I made no attempt whatever to provide psychological counseling on my own. I left this to the professional outside experts, offering instead all the pastoral support I could muster to the individuals involved and their extended families.

But the offender did all the right things, too. He made a formal priestly confession and received formal absolution as prescribed by the Episcopal Prayer Book. He entered psychiatric treatment and paid for court-ordered psychiatric care for the minor. Although he vigorously disputed many of the allegations leveled against him, nevertheless he pleaded guilty and served his court-ordered sentence — which included temporary interruption of his professional career and subsequent loss of income.

Eventually, he suffered a divorce and became painfully separated from his children, whom he adored (and they him), when they moved to another state. To his credit, however, he faithfully maintained a close parental relationship with them and frequently visited them.

What more punishment is a repentant sinner to endure to atone for his sins? Throughout the darkest days of his bitter ordeal, according to what I observed, he exercised exemplary Christian behavior. Not once did he speak with malice toward those who viciously maligned him.

Needless to say, it was an excruciatingly painful time for everyone. I can think of nothing that I could have done differently to handle the difficult situation any better than I did.

I chose not to excommunicate the offender from the church. Had I done so, I probably would have generated considerable support for myself from within the congregation. However, I don't believe a repentant sinner should be shunned, crucified, or expected to commit suicide. Instead, I believe he should be restored, redeemed, and resurrected into the fullness of life we all share in fellowship with our risen Lord.

Two psychiatrists in separate medical practices wrote letters assuring me that it was their considered professional judgment that this individual had neither the sociobehavioral profile or psychosexual makeup of a sex offender and was absolutely not a threat to others or the congregation in any way — that this one episode was an aberration, which they would not expect to be repeated. I felt morally obligated to honor the clinical medical diagnosis of the highly competent psychiatrists, who actually treated him, over the lay opinion of others who knew nothing about the case.

Consequently, I urged the penitent to remain within the church so that we could continue to offer him the ministry Christ affords to all for-given sinners. I urged him to worship and come forward to receive Holy Communion every Sunday because he needed the grace of God, which the blessed sacrament brings to us all. I offered the same pas-toral advice to both families, who were devastated by the public revelation of the sexual offense.

I told the congregation, without mentioning specific names, that I hoped we would relate to any sinner in our midst the same as we would want the church to relate to us if the secret sins of our private lives were made pub-lic and flashed across the television screen on the evening news. Had I chosen the easy way out by advocating expulsion of a sinner in our midst or denying him access to the altar rail of our church for Holy Communion — then my ministry as a priest would have been over! That's how strongly I felt about it and I took a lot of guff for my decision. But I believed from the depth of my heart that if I waffled on this decision, then the redemp-tion of Christ's forgiving love would have lost all credibility for me.

My utmost conviction is that whenever the church — whether it be the worldwide institution of Christian believers or the local congregation — says that God forgives *my* sin, but not the sin of another whose transgression I judge to be worse than mine, then that church no longer has validity as the Body of Christ. Through such behavior, Christians, both in thought and practice, have booted God out and put themselves on the judgment throne, as if mankind were the center of the universe — and this is not only the ultimate lie but also the ultimate sin.

Although the parishioners of St. Mark's deplored the sin that was com-mitted, I had confidence that most would forgive the offender if he humbly sought their forgiveness. I did not ask him to stand up before the congre-gation with a public confession but rather, in our parish newsletter, make a statement that he recognized the pain his actions brought upon our church and offer a short apology. Or make a brief statement to the vestry as the elected representative body of the whole congregation.

He declined my invitation on the grounds that he had suffered enough. Who was I to judge his decision?

But I felt trapped. I asked but did not receive permission from either party to openly discuss the situation with the congregation even after it became publicly known. I also knew that the congregation needed an opportunity to deal with it. I sensed there was a deep reservoir of repressed anger and tangled emotions swelling up within the congregation. If you can't talk about something that's bothering you, then the anger will erupt in another form. And I knew only too well that it most certainly would become focused on me.

I told Rosemary that I had a foreboding sense of impending doom.

Aging into the priesthood during troubled times at St. Mark's Episcopal Church in Cheyenne, Wyoming (1965–1972).

I sensed dark storm clouds towering like a thunderhead and I could hear the rumble of distant thunder.

I didn't have long to wait.

✧

In June 1987 a Billy Graham Crusade came to Denver. A satellite rally was scheduled in Cheyenne. Elaborate preparations are necessary to make a Billy Graham Crusade the great success it always is. Sponsoring congregations must commit to packing the stadium with their own church members, preferably to a capacity of standing-room only, to create the emotional environment conducive for mass conversions. Local churches are expected not only to bolster attendance but also to generate the massive funding to keep afloat the expensive evangelistic enterprise.

I preferred not to be a part of it. A few parishioners from St. Mark's volunteered to sing in the mass choir and help with organizational matters which was fine with me. As a matter of fact, I encouraged them to participate however they wanted. They had the same right and freedom to sing the praises of Billy Graham as did I to do otherwise.

I was to learn that this naive assumption was dead wrong.

A young Billy Graham associate, a Bible school student in charge of the Cheyenne rally, personally called on me to enlist my support. I told him, as graciously as I knew how, that I preferred not to board ship. He told me that, as the pastor of one of the leading Cheyenne churches and minister with the longest tenure in the city, I had a higher calling to God and community to rise above my personal objections and support the Billy Graham Crusade. Again I told him that I cared not to participate and was beginning to resent his hard sell. He simply couldn't understand my disinterest in this once-in-a-lifetime opportunity to permanently change the religious landscape of Cheyenne and maybe all of Wyoming.

Finally, he shook hands with me and said, "May I ask right now, Reverend Todd, while we're still shaking hands, that you pray out loud, here in my presence, for the success of the Billy Graham Crusade here in Cheyenne — to demonstrate to skeptics like yourself that Billy Graham can convert more sinners to Christ in one hour than the rest of you ministers in Cheyenne, combined, can convert in a whole year?"

I considered this prayer request brazenly offensive. Not only was it an arrogant put-down of the ordained Cheyenne clergy, as if we were all incompetent, but also it was grossly inaccurate. (If the clergy and laity of Cheyenne were that inept and dependent on outside help, we best fold up our tents and steal away in the night.) The facts are that mass evangelism is responsible for less than one percent of new church growth.

Furthermore, his comment reflected the Billy Graham team's private disdain toward local churches, quite a departure from what they publicly proclaimed. Worst of all, his words indicated the crass obsession of TV evangelists with numbers: *thousands were turned away because of standing-room only . . . thousand-voice choirs . . . thousands converted . . . millions of television viewers . . .* and, of course, the chronic need for *millions of dollars to pay it all off.* I'm not diminishing the power of numbers, only suggesting that they are not the only measure of the success of any ministry.

I was now more convinced than ever that I wanted no part of the Billy Graham Crusade in Cheyenne.

A day before the Cheyenne rally, my interview with a local newspaper reporter, along with other clergy, accurately reported my reaction to Billy Graham's coming to town. With my usual candor, I said exactly what I thought about the Billy Graham Crusade. Among other things, I said that this was another dog-and-pony show, like the many tent revivals that rolled into small frontier towns to convert sinners with a lot of mass hysteria and emotion. And when the show is over, the revivalist jumps on his white horse and, like the Lone Ranger doing his "Hi ho Silver away" routine, gallops off into the sunset — leaving the wicked little town every bit as wicked as it was before the revivalist arrived.

Not bad imagery, but a little too picturesque for local consumption.

In a more serious vein, I said that crusades like this are not the effective tool of Christian evangelism that evangelists purport them to be. The vast majority of new converts are those who have been personally invited to attend church with a friend or relative. They may come "forward" with a public profession at a rally, thus inflating the success of crusade evangelism — but their introduction to the life and faith of the church was through the warm invitation and personal attraction of a friendly Christian. Since personal evangelism is the method that really works for church growth, I said, why didn't Billy Graham develop a national program to help local churches with personal evangelism rather than perpetuate the least effective methodology — crusade evangelism?

I also said that Billy Graham was among the more respectable of the radio and television evangelists and certainly one who had demonstrated his unwillingness to profit personally. I highly respected him for the fact that his financial affairs were entrusted to a committee of local citizens. But when all is said and done, and the chips are down, I predicted that one of his sons someday will be appointed to perpetuate the dynasty known as the Billy Graham Evangelistic Association. Thus raising the inevitable spectre again, sadly, about these independent high-media ministries, all centered on the charisma of its founding personality, as to whether their ultimate purpose is to serve the will of God or family nepotism.

If I had the interview to do over, I probably would dispense with the Lone Ranger imagery, although I still think it rather descriptive. But I would hold unequivocally to the main point I was trying to make, which statistical studies consistently verify — that crusade evangelism is not the main source of new church growth.

Unfortunately, I came off as opposing the appearance of Billy Graham as a religious celebrity. In reality, I had no objections to anyone's going out to the rodeo stadium as a fan of Billy Graham, including members of my own church. Whether they attended the rally or went fishing mattered little to me — both endeavors could make for a rewarding afternoon. Although quoted correctly by reporter Kirk Knox, my comments deserved nothing more than a lively one-hour coffee discussion after church. Instead, they created a firestorm when they wound up on the front page of the Cheyenne newspaper on the Sunday morning that Billy Graham galloped into town.

My detractors now had something to grab on to with all the furor of a wild horse race at a Cheyenne rodeo. A letter to the editor appeared with signatures from a small group of parishioners, including many who, like me, had not bothered to attend the Billy Graham Crusade. They stated that they did not share my lack of enthusiasm for Billy Graham. Furthermore, they contended that I had no right to make public my personal opinions about Billy Graham — or about TV evangelists such as Jim Bakker, Oral Roberts, and Jimmy Swaggart, about whom I had earlier made uncomplimentary statements. They implied that I was presuming to speak not for myself alone but for St. Mark's Church — indeed, for all of Anglicanism the world over.

This was my first inkling that anyone considered me a local spokesman for the Archbishop of Canterbury.

The fundamentalists in Cheyenne got their hackles up, as if their patron saint had been brutally attacked and mortally wounded. The truth is, nothing I could have said or done would have distracted one iota from the celebrity status of Billy Graham. Many, if not most, of the mainline denominational clergy, including the Catholic Sisters at DePaul Hospital in Cheyenne, phoned me their personal support indicating that they, too, had become disillusioned with the whole enterprise.

We were told by the Billy Graham executives that we must wait five years before the full impact of new religious conversions would be felt on the local level. One minister is reported to have said that not even a traveling medicine show would defer its claim for a "magic cure" quite that far into the future.

To those who wanted to argue the facts, I told them that although I had very little money, I probably could cash in on my insurance policy to scrounge up a $10,000 bet, to their $1000, that five years from now if you polled the churches in Cheyenne there would not even be a slightest bulge of new memberships directly attributable to the crusade. There were no takers.

An intensive study ten years following the famous Billy Graham Crusade in England revealed that the crusade made no significant impact on church growth. Episcopal Bishop Bill Wolfrum from Colorado said there were no increases in confirmations in his diocese following the Denver crusade and he expected none.

The Graham statistics reveal mass number of conversions. There's no denying that many are genuine, and I rejoice in this. Statistics, however, do not reveal those conversions that are not real. Their statisticians don't talk about the people who become "burned over" by the simplistic promise that once they've come forward at a crusade rally and promise to pray (and pay) that Jesus will somehow take care of all their problems from then on out. The Billy Graham associates are long gone from the scene when this inevitable fallout occurs.

Graham's evangelical insistence that one absolutely must have a dramatic born-again religious conversion experience before one can ever hope to attain the portals of heaven flies in the face of spiritual reality for those who were born and nurtured in the bosom of the church.

In all fairness, I must point out that Billy Graham does say that his own wife is one of those who cannot remember her conversion experience — it was gradual and undramatic. But, of course, his emphasis at his mass rallies is just the opposite.

We can all rejoice if someone has had a dramatic conversion. But it's not a necessity for everyone. Whether we remember our first decision for Christ matters little as long as we continue to make decisions for Christ every hour of every day, as long as we live the Christian faith. Episcopalians make an "altar call" every Sunday in church when they come forward, on public profession of faith, to accept Jesus Christ anew as their Lord and Savior — when they kneel at the communion rail and reach out to receive him afresh in the Holy Sacrament.

I must say again it mattered little to me whether any of my parishioners attended the Billy Graham Crusade in Cheyenne. I felt everyone had the right to attend or stay home. That was not the essential issue for me.

But there were those in St. Mark's for whom it was.

In fact, a small group of dissidents felt they had sufficient cause to stampede the congregation of St. Mark's into removing me as rector.

They organized it well.

First, they phoned every parishioner to persuade them to sign a no-confidence petition, which they wanted to submit to the vestry and bishop. Around seventeen families signed on. They called members of the congregation a second time, encouraging people to appear before the vestry with a laundry list of my mistakes reaching back twenty-two years, sins of omission and commission. The word was out that Gene Todd was doomed.

Maybe so. I had no way of really knowing. I had heard of things like this happening to other clergy, but never had it happened to me in my thirty-five years in the ministry. I needed professional assistance to cope with a parish insurrection of "vast proportions," as it was described to me by the dissidents.

Bishop Bob Jones of Wyoming recommended that I make an appointment with a Bishop David Richards of Miami, who headed up a special program on behalf of the national church to provide counseling for bishops and clergy struggling with unforeseen stresses.

Rosemary accompanied me to Miami.

In our consultations there, I revealed a health problem that had plagued me now for many years: headaches. I had controlled this affliction with a medication prescribed by my physician — upon which I had now become dependent. Bishop Richards advised that maybe the time had come for me to go to a specialized headache clinic to free myself from medication dependency and see if the doctors there could root out the basic physiological cause of the headaches.

I admitted myself into a treatment hospital in Atlanta.

I weaned myself from Tylenol #3, which contained a small dosage of codeine. Excruciating sick headaches now took over full force, and I had no relief. I was virtually incapacitated with pain and nausea. I was pleased to be free from medication, but the depressing truth was, I knew I couldn't function either as a normal human being or as a priest in the church. My life was totally consumed with a debilitating illness.

Counselors in the treatment center asked me to write down what I intended to do once my hospitalization was complete. With a blinding headache, I slowly wrote that the deterioration of my health left me no choice other than to resign as rector of St. Mark's Church. There was absolutely no way that I could preach, celebrate the Eucharist, or function at a burial or wedding with a nauseating headache. Following my resignation, I would move into a mobile home on the ten-acre plot of land along Piney Creek that I had purchased from my father shortly before his death. I would move there alone and try to recuperate from the headaches. If recuperation was not possible, then I would endure them in solitude so as not to inflict my suffering on anyone else.

The counselors went crazy. Where did I get this idea of going off by myself to suffer alone? Initially, I thought there was nothing unusual about such an idea. Wasn't this natural for everyone when they were sick? Don't animals go off by themselves to lick their wounds when injured or sick?

"No, it is highly unnatural," the doctor said. "Even a terminally ill patient wants and needs to be surrounded by his family and loved ones when he suffers. To withdraw from this primary human support system is not normal or natural. Now try to remember, where did this idea come from?"

I had no earthly notion. He relentlessly pursued it with me . . . and out of a dim recollection of my childhood experience, buried so deeply that I actually had no immediate recall of it, I gradually remembered being sick as a child on our Wyoming ranch, with headaches so severe that I would crawl up into a quiet hayloft and lie there, perfectly still, in the solitude of darkness, or lie down by the creek with my forehead dipped into the cold water, motionless, for hours on end.

Although I have described this childhood pattern of dealing with sick headaches in chapter 1 of this book — prior to 1987 I couldn't have written about it at all, so repressed were my painful memories of this time. Only because the Atlanta doctors pried this memory out of me am I able to write about it now and reflect on its possible significance.

The revelations were interesting and perhaps helpful. But the headaches continued. I began biofeedback, learning to listen to the rumbling roar of my body's tension and going through a series of deep relaxation exercises until the sound diminished to a soft murmur. From this I learned an important lesson about the integration of the physical and mental, how even a fleeting thought can cause your muscles to tense. Healing and wholeness of body, mind, and spirit are inseparable — the theory of holistic medicine.

The psychiatrist at the Atlanta headache clinic suggested that we try a series of experimental medicines that sometimes brought relief to headache sufferers. By a process of elimination, he thought, we might stumble across something that worked for me. I balked, telling him that twelve years earlier I had flushed away all medications except the painkiller to which I had become addicted. Now that I had finally been set free from that chemical dependency, I vowed never to take another pill. They convinced me that only by trying various medications could they determine what the root cause of the headaches might be. With their assurance that none of these drugs were mood-altering or habit-forming, I reluctantly agreed to give it a try.

They suggested a mild medication that had been around for years and that occasionally calmed chronic vascular spasms of the forehead and scalp. I swallowed the innocuous little pill and crawled into bed.

I woke up the next morning — and the headache was gone. Completely, absolutely gone. I sat up in my hospital bed in the quietness of the early morning hour and thought: *This is only a momentary calm. Maybe if I move my head very slowly and climb out of bed very carefully, with no rapid movements, I can take a quiet shower and shave before it comes cascading down upon me and knocks me flat. Maybe if I walk very slowly down the hallway to the cafeteria and eat something I might feel better before it strikes.*

Actually, I was starving. For nearly two weeks I had virtually not eaten; I couldn't keep food in my stomach. But that morning I filled my breakfast tray with fried eggs and bacon, even some fried hominy (which Georgians can't eat a single meal without). I poured a little maple syrup over the goop, drank two cups of coffee, and headed back to my room — very carefully and cautiously.

Still no headache.

My apprehension was mounting; I kept expecting something dreadful to happen. Maybe I should just bang my head against the wall and get it over with to relieve the anxiety of anticipation.

But the migraine headaches never returned. And they never have — to this day in 1995.

I voluntarily withdrew myself from that medication a year later.

Perhaps one reason for my remarkable recovery was a recognition that instead of immediately returning to Cheyenne I needed to remain in Atlanta and take therapy in stress management. Working harder and longer and faster to make things happen doesn't necessarily make things better. I was beginning to realize that I could never achieve my own high expectations. If stress was triggering the headaches, then I needed to manage stress more satisfactorily. Above all, I needed to avoid stress of my own making.

I was transferred to an out-patient residence in Atlanta which was completely across the city from where the hospital was located. Two weeks later the hospital called and asked me to pick up three postal sacks of accumulated mail. I retired to my room and began opening it. Many were simple get-well cards, which I greatly appreciated. Most, however, were handwritten letters from parishioners not only wishing me a speedy recovery but also urging my hasty return to St. Mark's. This was my first indication that the state of insurrection wasn't as widespread as I had been led to believe.

Many of these letters were especially valuable to me because the writers went into considerable detail, recalling special moments of my ministry among them. A time when I spent a long night beside a sickbed. A time when I stood with them beside the open grave of a loved one. A joyful time when I danced the polka with the bride at her wedding reception. A sermon that had particular meaning to someone.

Most precious was a little note from someone named Maggie, who had since moved away from Cheyenne but had heard of my difficulty and had written. She reminded me of the time she sheepishly made her first appearance at a Thursday morning eucharist. Now that she had reminded me of it, I remembered that Maggie continued to attend these midweek celebrations but always sat out in the shadowy nave of the church rather than coming up into the lighted chancel where most gathered for Holy Communion. I had remembered her from another context but couldn't identify where it was. She was not helpful in refreshing my memory when we had coffee afterward in the Frontier Hotel directly across the street from the church. I could tell by the heavy lines on her face that she had seen rough times. Beyond that, I knew little about her.

One morning, while reading the Gospel at the Thursday morning eucharist, I read a passage referring to Mary Magdalene — and suddenly, like a bolt out of heaven, I remembered where I had seen her. It was at the after-hour nightclub on Eighteenth Street, among the sea of black people, their bodies sensuously dancing with the slow rhythmic beat of the blues band (chapter 15). Through the dimly lit smoky interior I saw a white woman moving from one man to the next, working the crowd — as a hooker.

It was Maggie!

It took me a long time before I had the courage to share my remembrance of that night with Maggie. When I finally found the appropriate moment, she offered no pat denials nor complicated rationalizations. She was perfectly frank about it. She made basic living expenses during the week working out of other Cheyenne bars, with Fridays and Saturdays her nights for pure profit. We talked about this as casually as would any local businessmen have used the same explanation about making expenses throughout the year versus cash profits during Cheyenne Frontier Days.

Eventually she came to the Sunday morning worship services, sitting quietly by herself, never socializing with others, saying her prayers with her head bowed down behind the pew, and finally coming forward to receive Holy Communion. Then she slipped away, and I never saw her again.

Here was her note telling me she was alive and well in Kansas City, surviving yes, but barely — still going to church and struggling with life. A friend in Cheyenne had sent her a newspaper clipping of my trials and tribulations. She thanked me for our many coffee conversations and my acceptance of her as a friend when I invited her to receive Holy Communion at the altar of St. Mark's Church. She signed it *Mary Magdalene.*

I treasured it.

(By the way, not for one moment do I believe that Mary Magdalene was a prostitute despite the long hazy tradition that she was. Sometimes I'm inclined to agree with modern biblical scholars who wonder if the early Gospel revisionists, mostly male ascetics, trashed the reputation of Mary Magdalene and neutered Mary, the mother of Jesus, so as to elevate the holiness of Jesus as noncontaminated by womanhood and human sexuality. Biblical evidence supports the thesis that Mary Magdalene was among those devoted women included in the constant company of Christ's entourage. Perhaps she was the wife of a disciple. Some bold biblical historians have even suggested that maybe she was the wife of Jesus himself. I find this idea preposterous. Even if that contention were proven irrefutably true, I would still continue to worship him as the Christ, my Lord and my God! I have never equated celibacy with holiness of life or purity of spirit.)

While in Atlanta, I worshiped in an Episcopal church every Sunday because it was no more than a two-mile walk away. I read again Margaret Mitchell's *Gone With the Wind* and recruited a friend with a car to drive me out into the lovely Georgian countryside where the mythical Tara plantation would have been located between the little towns of Fayetteville and Jonesboro. Rosemary shipped me my camera so I could photograph old plantation ruins and private family cemeteries sinking out of sight under the overgrowth of dank neglected forests — forests littered with Civil War battle sites and steeped in history.

A tremendous boost of self-confidence came my way when my very dear friend, Dr. Monroe Billington, professor of history at New Mexico State University, sent me his rough manuscript for a book he was writing on the buffalo soldiers of the American Southwest. His historical research on the significant role African American soldiers played in subduing frontier Indian uprisings immediately following the Civil War distinguished him as a historian of considerable note. The fact that he called on me to critically review his manuscript and pencil in editorial suggestions for improvement of both its historical content and style of writing conveyed a powerful message: *Gene, not only are you my close friend, but also I value your professional ability as a student of history.*

Boy, did I need that personal affirmation at that particular moment of dark despair in my life. No one could have done it as indirectly and yet as magnificently as my soul brother of all these many years, Monroe Billington.

Finally it was time to return home to Cheyenne and face an uncertain future. My first service was the Sunday before Christmas, and the church was unusually crowded. At the conclusion of the service, Bethel Wilkins, the altar guild director, came forward, placed in my arms a large bunch of red roses and welcomed me over to the parish hall for a surprise return-home reception.

I was flabbergasted and overwhelmed.

Cutting a "Welcome Home" cake upon my return from Atlanta in 1987. The cake fed 250 and we ran out.

But not for long. I began receiving brazen telephone calls from members of the dissident group — calls that were carefully calculated intimidations. I was told that I should not interpret the display of goodwill at the reception as a sign that the congregation was welcoming me back as its rector. I was reminded that the dissidents were nominating a new set of wardens and vestry members who would easily be elected and call for my immediate resignation. It would be easier for everyone concerned, they said, if I tendered my resignation in advance to avoid an embarrassing showdown — but should it come to that, it would be quickly over, because the majority vote was clearly on their side.

Another one "graciously" offered me two months' reprieve in vacating Templeton House. Then I would have to step aside for a "spirit-filled" rector who would transform St. Mark's into a "charismatic citadel" for the whole state of Wyoming.

Typhoid Mary continued to work the Sunday morning coffee crowd after church as aggressively as *Maggie* had formerly worked her Saturday evening crowd at the *All-Nite-Brothel-Saloon*. The only difference was, *Maggie* was trying to reform her behavior.

My trusted friend Dick Thomas, a justice of the Wyoming Supreme Court and chancellor for the Diocese of Wyoming, had done a masterful job as senior warden holding the parish together during my absence, and he advised me not to react too hastily to their threats. He was quite convinced the dissidents had neither the votes nor the congregational support they claimed. "If they can achieve their purpose through blackmail, then they are spared the test of strength which they may not have," he said.

Jack Palma, a bright young lawyer and our newly appointed parish chancellor, said feverish telephone activity had been reported to him, which indicated the dissidents were not all that confident of their congregational strength. He begged me, "Don't empower a clamorous group like that by allowing yourself to become hostage to their threatening intimidations. It would be terrible to allow them to gain control of this church through such tactics. Especially now that they know the vestry is not on their side. Hence their strategy to pack the vestry with newly elected members of their own choosing."

The calls shifted from criticisms of my leadership style to accusations concerning my personal spirituality. They were attacking not only my spirituality but also that of most of the vestry members and over half the congregation. The dissidents conceded that "maybe" we were Christians but certainly not the kind of Christians that St. Mark's needed. Most of us, they contended, had been neither "born again" nor recently "baptized in the Holy Spirit" — and worst of all, certainly none of us demonstrated the greatest spiritual gift of all, "speaking in tongues."

Here again was the ugly specter of appalling self-righteous judgmentalism at its worst which spews from a charismatic-fundamentalist coalition once it gets a toehold. Imagine the galling arrogance of attacking the spirituality of fellow parishioners? In my view, not only was this unacceptable Christian behavior in any denomination, but also conduct which was anathema to the spirit of Anglicanism. It was apparent to me that nothing was spared to develop a negative momentum within the congregation of St. Mark's Church.

Strangely, I became remarkably calm in the midst of the storm. I was concerned about St. Mark's but not too worried about myself. My Atlanta exile had given me sufficient emotional and spiritual detachment to decide that the will of God would ultimately triumph, and its final determination was beyond my control. I was also buoyed with a tremendous sense of physical well-being now that my body was free from migraine headaches. Exterior stress would not get to me as it had in the past. I had at my disposal new tools of stress management and was confident that I would survive and thrive regardless of what happened.

The showdown finally came at the annual parish meeting on Super Bowl Sunday in January 1988. The dissidents, by secret ballot, could now demonstrate the groundswell of congregational strength they claimed they had. When the first vote tally came in, it was obvious that their cause would not prevail. They not only had failed in generating support within the larger congregation but also had lost votes from within their own small group.

Judge Glenn Parker, the distinguished retired chief justice of the Wyoming Supreme Court, cornered me the following Sunday after church and said, with tears in his eyes, "Gene I am so proud of our Episcopal church. We let that obstreperous group whip up their frenzied nonsense all they wanted, then the main body of this church came down here last Sunday and quietly voted our strength, then went home and watched the Super Bowl. They wanted a church fight, a brawl which would rip this church right down the middle, and we didn't give it to them. This kind of parish maturity is Anglicanism at its very best."

Common sense told me that significant parish support for me wasn't solely an indication that the majority of parishioners were enamored of me, nor that they were in agreement with everything I had said or done. Instead, they voted their strength, as Judge Parker phrased it, because they knew it would be a fatal mistake to turn the leadership of this church over to a vociferous minority.

And it was a minority that was experiencing considerable erosion within its own ranks. A few weeks after the annual parish meeting the dissidents gathered in one of their homes for a display of mutual support. The next morning I had a call from one of them, who stated outright, "Gene, I apologize for signing that petition of no confidence. Early on I realized what the ringleaders of that group were up to, and I lost all confidence in them. I want nothing more to do with those neurotic people in control who were projecting their unresolved emotional problems out onto the landscape of the church. Imagine the audacity of those women asking everyone, even us men, to come to the vestry with a laundry list of complaints reaching back twenty years. That must be how they fought with their husbands."

He went on to say, "And, Gene, I'm not alone. Three other families will be calling you shortly with the same message."

And they did.

A retired army colonel was another person who signed the original petition but became disillusioned with the dissident group's leadership. After I served him Holy Communion one Sunday afternoon in the Veteran's Hospital, where he was suffering from terminal cancer, he said, "When I first signed that petition I thought this was a legitimate way to address a few concerns and issues that the church needed to resolve. But it didn't take me long to see that the core leaders weren't interested in resolving anything. They wanted only a bloodbath — with your blood. Then I realized that the core leaders — not the group as a whole, but the core leaders — had gone amok with their neurotic behavior."

The colonel paused for a moment and then reflected, "You know I strongly suspect that one of the women was involved in an abusive marriage and her real fight was with her husband, and not with you."

This came as no surprise to me.

A member of the altar guild dropped into my office one morning and said, "After the dissidents lost their congregational vote, their insistence that you owed them an apology for all the divisiveness which they themselves had caused, was the height of absurdity. It was like a Laurel and Hardy comedy, 'Look what you made us do to ourselves.'"

My newly elected wardens were both women, Joan McConnaughey and Claire Davis. We immediately put into place a process of reconciliation patterned after chapter 18 in the Gospel of Matthew, where Jesus commands his followers to speak directly to the person with whom they had a disagreement, in the presence of a witness to avoid misinterpretation of what was said — and offer one another forgiveness.

The wardens and I offered to meet with anyone who had a grievance about me or anyone else in the church. We tried very hard to listen to the truth other people spoke, and we critiqued each other as to how we handled it. We constantly monitored one another. We learned that controversy can be averted if we carefully listen to those who have legitimate concerns and feel encouraged to express them. We also learned that "troublemakers" flourish secretly only because they do not have to deal openly with their half-truths, which are revealed for what they are in the light of day.

Teddy Roosevelt, one of our greatest American presidents, once wrote:

In the battle of life, it is not the critic who counts; not the person who points out how the strong person stumbled, or where the doer of a deed could have done it better. The credit belongs to the person who is actually in the arena; whose face is marred by dust and sweat and blood; who strives valiantly; who errs and comes short again and again because there is no effort without error and shortcoming; who does actually strive to do the deeds; who knows the great enthusiasms, the great devotions, spends herself in a worthy cause; who at the best knows in the end the triumph of high achievement; and who at the worst, if she fails, at least fails while daring greatly, so that her place shall never be with those cold and timid souls who have tasted neither victory nor defeat.

The only serious discussion of religion that I ever remember having with my father occurred on a bright Sunday morning when, as a teenager, we saddled our horses and rode out into the summer pasture to check on the cattle. We discovered that a young steer had fallen into a deep washout from which he couldn't escape. The poor thing was nearly dead from heat and exhaustion. His tongue was so swollen from dehydration and thirst that he was literally gasping for breath. With a rope we pulled him to safety and gently guided him to the nearest spring of cold water, then stretched him out in the shade and cooled him down so that he could live again.

As Dad ministered to the stricken animal, out of the blue he said, "There are two kinds of religious people. Those who kick dirt and rocks into the faces of those who fall into a pit — and those who pull 'em out. I don't give a goddamn (ol' cowpoke talk here) for the religion of those who do the kickin' when they could have done the pullin'."

I have never forgotten what he said — nor the context in which he said it, pastorally caring for the fallen calf. Maybe Dad missed his calling and should have been a seminary professor instead of a cattle rancher.

Mom would have said it's not what you say that counts in religion — but what you do.

But Dad would be pleased to hear me report that through my *Trail by Fire* I learned that far more people have a pullin' religion than a kickin' one. And this is what Good News of the Gospel is all about. Hope still abounds!

✧

Five of the most productive years of my entire Episcopal priesthood followed.

My last set of wardens were gems. Jack Palma, the young lawyer and former parish chancellor, became my senior warden. Dick Waggener, my dear old friend from Green River who later moved to Cheyenne, took on the chores of junior warden. We met every week for lunch to compare notes and talk things over. They had contacts in the parish that I didn't have. I no longer felt isolated as if the battle was mine alone. We fully shared information and bounced ideas off one another.

I used a newly developed computer program to record my daily pastoral activities in fifteen-minute intervals — all day long, every day. Each interval was coded to identify such activities as study, visitations, administration, counseling, travel, and so forth. The computer then printed out a weekly total of the time spent in each category. The wardens reviewed it with me at our weekly luncheons and were most helpful in critiquing my use of time.

I was shocked to discover that I was consistently averaging over seventy hours per week. No wonder my family had complained for so many years about my absence from home. I vividly remembered my son, Barry, when he was about four years old, clutching my legs one evening as I was about to the leave the house for the tenth consecutive night of church meetings, begging me, "Daddy stay home and tell me another bedtime story about the time when you were a little boy."

But I couldn't because I had to be about my Father's business, which was calling me to another religious or civic responsibility. I realized now that the higher call of God might have been to have stayed home that night so that I could be about the business of being a better father to my own children. Whenever I was there at bedtime I would lie with them cuddled up against me in bed, in the soft glow of the night lamp, and tell them stories about the farm animals I knew as a child on my father's ranch. Fantasies they were, pure make-believe, about colts, calves, lambs, and dogs who talked to one another whenever people weren't around to hear the funny things they had to say about us. But they would let me listen because they were my friends and I was just a little boy with special ears for hearing animal talk.

Too many nights away from family on church work became the norm, and I was truly saddened with the revelation of how bad it had become — thirty-five years too late.

With renewed determination, I followed through on the absolute insistence of my counselors in Atlanta to take off one full day per week, totally free from all church responsibilities. Since Monday was my day off, I was to insist that no meetings be scheduled on Monday evening with an expectation that I attend. Not even a Monday-night vestry meeting. And if a three-day holiday extended into Monday, as it frequently does, I was to take Tuesday off.

I made the commitment to the Atlanta counselors and to myself that I would ask for this. With fear and trepidation I finally approached the vestry. They debated it approximately fifteen seconds and approved it unanimously.

I learned from this experience that the bondage of workaholism is both emotionally unhealthy and physically counterproductive. For the first time in the thirty-five years of my ministry, I was free to take Monday completely off — all day — and drive to Denver for a trip to a museum or art gallery and maybe have lunch at the Brown Palace. Or I could lollygag around Templeton House with a good book while listening to classical music. Or invite my grandchildren to join me at the pizza parlor. I even occasionally joined the Friday evening happy-hour crowd at the airport lounge, Governor Herschler's old hangout, to enjoy a drink and free hors d'oeuvres with friends.

I had finally learned that desperately trying harder and harder to usher in the kingdom of God, and cranking up better and better intentions of doing so, is not sufficiently trusting the Grace of God to let it happen — in spite of yourself.

Come to think of it, during my entire ministry I can't recall a single person making the deathbed confession, "I wish I had spent more time at the office." But I know hundreds of professionals, including ministers, whose chronic lament has been, "I wish I had spent more time with my family."

The ministry had become fun and challenging once again. And thus it was for the next five years as rector of St. Mark's Episcopal Church in Cheyenne. I believe that those who have faith, along with laughter and a persistent sense of humor, can survive almost anything.

✧

I am philosophical enough to realize that the congregational uproar was caused by something more than the persistent conspiracy of *Typhoid Mary*, as troublesome as that may have been — or the double whammy of a charge of lay sexual misconduct and the Billy Graham affair, which triggered it.

I had served as rector of that parish during twenty-two years of the most bitter turmoil the Episcopal Church has ever known in its history. There seemed to be a steady onslaught of controversy from one social revolution to the next. The civil rights movement and the Vietnam War divided America. Then came along the adoption of a new prayer book and liturgical changes which divided the church. Divorce became more prevalent and divided families. On top of this came the feminist movement and conflict over the ordination of women. This was followed by our discovery that homosexuality was still around in spite of our frantic efforts to deny its existence. To our chagrin we learned that heterosexuality had its proverbial hang-ups as well and wasn't all that pure and simple. Social restraints were bursting at the seams. Women doffed their hats in church. Toss in the hippies and the peace marches — and Episcopalians finally reached the breaking point where they could no longer bear the many . . . *manifold and sundry changes of this mortal life*, using good prayer book language.

I cannot ignore the charismatic movement, which I introduced into St. Mark's, and the influential role it played in their holy war which engulfed me. I painfully learned that the charismatic experience can warm the heart — and burn a church to the ground.

The truth is, I had been warned not only by my layman, Fred, but also by other ministers not to precede with the charismatic experimentation at St. Mark's. In spite of their dire predictions I went ahead with it anyway. I'm sorry now that I didn't heed their warnings and, therefore, must assume responsibility for partly inviting the wrath of Armageddon upon the church and myself.

Add to all of this the human foibles of Gene Todd, which are many — and you have a situation which lends itself to accumulative unrest, if a congregation wishes to concentrate on the negatives and not on the positives.

A good way to avoid this dilemma is to have a clergyman move every two or three years and start afresh with a new congregation. (Rationalized among clergy as being *called of the Lord* to serve elsewhere.) The same could be said of marriage, if everyone changed partners every few years there would be a perpetual honeymoon of giddy marital bliss.

But there would be no maturity either.

As a student of history I have learned that any person in a leadership role, from the lowest to the highest, invariably confronts a leadership crises in his or her career. Jesus didn't do all that well with his vestry of twelve either. Betrayal, denial, and abandonment abounded. He rose above it.

When a priest and congregation commit to the long haul — they can either painfully grow into maturity toward the stature of Christ, or they can disintegrate and fall apart into the giddy honeymoon of a new relationship every few years. I chose the former.

Although I regret my failures and mistakes, I will never regret my ultimate choice for a long tenure at St. Mark's Episcopal Church in Cheyenne. I wish I could have been more perfect. But not too perfect. Perfection itself becomes a character flaw few people can tolerate in the ministry.

There are many advantages of a short-tenured ministry — but there's also something to be said in behalf of clergy, like myself, who stay aboard ship for the long voyage, ride out the ocean storms, and with the help of God and a loyal crew steer the ship into a safe harbor. Although battered and bruised, both congregation and priest manage not only to survive — but also to thrive from the education and edification of the common journey.

It has been said that we still live in the "Messiah Age." If only we elect the right president, or governor, or bishop, or priest — then we can all sit back and let God usher in anew His kingdom on earth. The tragedy is, God tried it once, and we nailed Him to a tree. What makes us think we would do it any differently if we had a second chance?

Chapter 20

A s I write these words, I fear the reader will falsely assume that when I faced a crisis or dealt with a specific issue of some magnitude in my life or ministry, about which I have written in previous chapters, that all my time and energy were totally consumed toward the resolution of that one situation.

Nothing could be farther from the truth.

Like the title of a popular song *As the Beat Goes On* — so does the beat go on with all the regular routine chores of any active ministry: pastoral calling, sermon preparation, and preaching, teaching, celebrating Mass — as well as the inevitable *hatchin'* and *matchin'* and *dispatchin'* duties of every priest.

I was always heavily involved in diocesan leadership in addition to my responsibilities at the local congregational level. During my thirty-one years as a parochial Episcopal priest in Wyoming, I think I was elected or appointed to serve in just about every elected diocesan position. Twice I served as the elected deputy from Wyoming to triennial national conventions of the Episcopal Church, one in New Orleans and one in Pasadena.

Burial of my older brother Luther on a mountainside overlooking the beautiful Paradise (ranching) Valley near Livingston, Montana, in 1984. I also buried Dad, Mom, and my brother-in-law Don Dexter in Sheridan, Wyoming.

I was president of the diocesan standing committee (statewide governing body comparable to the vestry of a local parish) when we elected a new Episcopal bishop for Wyoming in 1969 to succeed my beloved Bishop Hunter upon his medical retirement.

The Rt. Reverend David Thornberry was a good man at the wrong time. He was program chairman of the national General Episcopal Convention which met in Cleveland the same year as his election to the episcopacy of Wyoming. This particular national convention, during the height of the civil rights movement only one year after the assassination of Martin Luther King Jr. proved itself to be extremely controversial and divisive, when black clergy and laymen stormed the podium and commandeered the microphone away from the presiding bishop of the United States and proceeded to lay out before the solemn assembly of a thousand delegates their demands for racial reform.

Poor Bishop Thornberry, on his first round of visitations throughout his new diocese, was burdened with the responsibility of trying to explain the justification for some of these black caucus demands. Everywhere he went, he was bombarded with hostile questions about the Episcopal Church caving in to these civil rights rebel-rousers. He naively thought the questions deserved honest answers.

Actually the questions were disguised angry protests, and with each logical explanation he dug his grave just a little bit deeper. The Episcopalians of Wyoming in the early 1970s were no more prepared to hear the bishop's rational explanations about the need for racial reform than was Governor George Wallace, while blocking the entrance of a black student at the University of Alabama, willing to hear a lecture on constitutional law from a federal marshal. The civil rights movement was still in its infancy of raw emotion before logic eventually prevailed.

Then why was he elected the bishop of Wyoming when we didn't know him any better than that?

His father.

His father, David W. Thornberry, was the beloved dean of St. Matthew's Cathedral in the 1930s who everyone remembered with great love and affection. Surely it would be a case of *like father — like son —* if "little David" was elected bishop of Wyoming.

I liked Dave and his wife, Ginney, very much and enjoyed many intimate conversations with him in particular. But I never believed that his Wyoming episcopacy was a happy time in the life of the Thornberrys.

I served on the search committee in 1977 when we elected a successor to Bishop Thornberry. Justice Richard Thomas of the Wyoming Supreme Court, a parishioner at St. Mark's and close personal friend, and I spent so many nights away from home attending meetings in Casper, and sharing motel rooms — that our wives accused us of sleeping with each other more than with them.

It is the common contention that our election of Bobby Jones as the new bishop of Wyoming was contingent upon the personal tragedy of his wife, Judy, who as the former wife of an Episcopal missionary in northern Alaska lost her husband and all three children when the oil heater of their Quonset hut malfunctioned, turning their home into a fiery inferno. She alone escaped with her life although severely burned.

Both Bishop Thornberry and Bishop Jones were good men with entirely different leadership styles. Thornberry working closely with associates in his compasionate commitment to social reform — and Jones distancing himself from others by maintaining a persistent adversarial relationship with his clergy.

I would like to think that the Episcopal Church of Wyoming has reached sufficient maturity that hereafter, whenever an election to the episcopacy occurs — we'll elect our new bishop on the merits of his or her own personal achievements, spirituality, and leadership potential, and not on that of a highly respected relative.

✧

Bishop Herbert Newell, of the Catholic Diocese of Cheyenne, called on me in 1966 to assist him in organizing the first combined worship service for both Catholics and Protestants which would be authorized by the Catholic Church in the state of Wyoming. A few years earlier he had invited me to be the first Protestant speaker at a Catholic women's convention in Kemmerer, and on the basis of that pleasant encounter, felt that I would be a friendly partner in planning this first ecumenical service for Catholics in Cheyenne.

It doesn't seem possible now, as I write these words, how strained were the relationships between Catholics and Protestants thirty years ago in comparison to the warm and cooperative spirit which now prevails. I remember Bishop Newell telling me that this first service of ecumenical worship must be held in the gymnasium of the Catholic high school because Catholics would be too shocked and affronted to have such a service in St. Mary's Cathedral.

"Then maybe next year," he said, "we can try it in the cathedral with a Catholic preacher. Then the year after that in the cathedral with a Protestant preacher. And then, finally, in the fourth year Catholics might be willing to participate in a joint venture of worship in a Protestant church."

He laughed at my suggestion that it sounded like a series of decompression chambers. But the bishop was right, we could not ignore the 500-year history of bitter animosity which had been perpetuated by both the Catholics and Protestants. Consequently, it was imperative that we move cautiously, and with religious sensitivity, as we made our plans for the cooperative venture. Between the two of us we decided that the service should have a purpose beyond simply bringing Catholics and Protestants into a common worship service. After some deliberation, we decided that it should be called an Interfaith Service of Prayer for World Peace and Unity.

This service has become an established tradition on Palm Sunday evening for Cheyenne churches of all denominations. Eventually the service became so well attended that it had to be moved to the Civic Center in order to accommodate the large crowd.

Two more ecumenical ventures of faith involving St. Mark's Church are worth mentioning here. One was our yearlong cooperative relationship first with the Jewish community in Cheyenne and then a year later with the Greek Orthodox Church. Both experiences were positive and meaningful not only to me, but also to the parishioners of St. Mark's as they became spiritually connected to these two great religious traditions.

Rabbi Myron Movsky became a dear personal friend. When his wife died, he called me to teach his courses in religious studies at the community college during his ritualized time of mourning. Later we entertained him, along with a congenial mix of Jews and Episcopalians, at a dinner party in Templeton House. I was honored to be invited as preacher at one of their synagogue Sabbath services on Friday evening and then, at another time, to celebrate the Passover dinner with the entire Jewish community in their large reception hall. They were always the most congenial hosts and delightful people.

Rabbi Movsky helped me write a script for a Passover celebration at St. Mark's on Maundy Thursday evening. With an array of all the customary Jewish dishes on the table, including roast lamb and matzo, we re-enacted the ceremonial dialogue telling the ancient story of the first Passover feast, interspersed with the traditional drinking of wine. It was a marvelous experience.

Upon Myron's second retirement from the active rabbinate, he gave me some of his ceremonial vestments which I wore when I preached at the synagogue.

Our yearlong special relationship with the Greek Orthodox community was another experience of religious enrichment for all of us at St. Mark's. What made this experience especially relevant to us was our church sponsoring an Ethiopian refugee couple for resettlement in the United States. Soloman and Ababa were members of the ancient Ethiopian Orthodox Coptic communion. They lived in our home for about six weeks before our church found them an apartment to rent along with a job so that they could both support themselves. Later we purchased a car for them.

I must give due credit to my wife, Rosemary, who so wonderfully opened our home to numerous situations such as this and always handled these extra social demands so graciously. All this while she was working nearly ten hours a day as a public health nurse.

The highlight of our whole year with the Orthodox people was their invitation for me to join them for their elaborate celebration of Holy Week and Easter, which usually occurs one week later (Gregorian calendar) than the date of Easter in western Christianity. I joined their Good Friday street procession for several city blocks carrying the crucified form of Christ before returning to the church. Three days later I participated in one of the most glorious celebrations of Easter that I have ever experienced. A divine liturgy which lasted for hours. Past midnight I joined them for a sumptuous roast lamb dinner followed with traditional Greek circle dancing until the sun rose on their Easter Sunday morning. Exhausted, they all went home to rest from the night of joyful festivities — and I barely made it to St. Mark's in time for our eight o'clock Sunday morning eucharist, without one wink of sleep all night long.

But I felt as if I had personally witnessed the Resurrection of Christ!

✧

I never abandoned my love of radio broadcasting, which I first acquired when I was six years old listening to Franklin Delano Roosevelt at our one-room country school at Ucross, Wyoming.

I established an early association with KUUY, a 10,000-watt CBS affiliate in Cheyenne, which began broadcasting our annual Frontier Day Worship Service. In addition, the station began live broadcasts of our Christmas and Easter services and any other special event at the church.

We did these broadcasts from St. Mark's with first-class radio professionalism. First of all, we installed a highly professional sound system in the church, and I carefully trained every participant in a worship service always to be on microphone. Therefore, the sound quality was first-rate. Second, we had a control room from which Jim Parrish, a parishioner and experienced radio announcer, would monitor the broadcast signal and "voice over" his own description of everything that was happening in the service. Hence, the radio listener not only heard the wonderful sound of the pipe organs and choral music but also was blessed with Jim's colorful commentaries.

In fact, Jim and I became so professional as a team that the radio station would simply bring down their remote broadcasting van, mount and zero-in their antennas toward the signal tower south of Cheyenne, and then disappear, leaving it up to us. I must say, in all honesty, that the production quality of these broadcasts equaled or exceeded that of any church service I've ever heard on national networks. Terrell Metheny from KUUY, who has been in radio management all his life at stations all over America, commented that our live broadcasts from St. Mark's came as close to perfection as anything he had ever heard.

I will never forget a letter we received from a sheepherder who listened to our Christmas Eve midnight broadcast in his lonely sheep wagon near Lusk, Wyoming (nearly 200 miles away), on a bitterly cold night. He wrote that the quality of sound with Jim's running commentary made him think that the whole service was especially beamed to him.

I have good news for him — it was!

Often I thought of that isolated and lonely sheepherder in later years, while our Christmas Eve services were in progress, and wondered if our choral anthems and Christmas carols from St. Mark's, through the miracle of radio, were coming down to him out of the darkness of the heavens as clearly as the angelic chorus would have sounded to the shepherds of Bethlehem when Christ was born.

I was pleased when KUUY invited me to begin my own weekly radio program, known as the *Rector's Study*. It was appropriately titled, because the broadcast was actually done from my own broadcast studio, which I built in the large basement study of Templeton House. Since radio is both my hobby and passion, I designed a studio made out of solid cherry wood with built-in sound mixers and high-quality microphones.

Broadcasting the "Rector's Study" from my own professional broadcasting-recording home studio — over radio station KUUY in Cheyenne. Note photos on back wall of my two fathers: my natural father, Fred Todd, and my "father-in-God," Bishop Wilson J. Hunter.

The hour-long program used an interview format; there was no provision for listeners to call the radio station and add their questions or comments. But it was more than just a talk show. Singing troubadours and small musical groups frequently appeared on these broadcasts, which gave the program an appealing freshness and originality, something like the radio of a bygone day in comparison to the canned artificiality of today's computerized, prerecorded broadcasting.

I made certain it was not billed as a "religious program," avoiding that label like the plague, because such programs are often dismissed as irrelevant to the real life of real people.

At first I simply invited the most interesting people I could find to appear on the show. After the program became firmly established, however, I began receiving requests from many people, representing various causes, wanting to make an appearance, sometimes six months in advance. I tried hard to be fair and selective. Periodically I would schedule a "living history" series of interviews with old-timers: pioneer ranchers, retired federal judges, broken-down rodeo cowboys, burned-out politicians, and the like. Many of these tapes I turned over to the living history collection at the Wyoming State Library.

One of the more interesting broadcasts was an interview with Mr. Cliff Harris, a former cook on the Union Pacific dining car. A kindly black man with a delightful sense of humor, he described what it was like living and working five or six days at a time on a railroad streamliner, broiling steaks over beds of red-hot coals and preparing gourmet cuisine as the train rocked and clipped along at seventy miles an hour, headed for California across the desert of Nevada.

The *Rector's Study* was broadcast on both the AM and FM stations of KUUY, and the FM signal was extended through a series of remote translators that stretched from Cheyenne to Casper. Consequently, the program developed a broad listening audience. My radio voice is not particularly good in comparison to the deep, smooth-sounding radio voices of today's professional radio personalities. But apparently my voice is different enough, perhaps because of my peculiar accent, to sound rather unique. A speech peculiarity, good or bad, results in voice recognition. To this day, I can enter a busy restaurant or strike up a conversation in a bank lobby, and someone will invariably come over to me and say, "You're Father Todd, aren't you? I can tell by the sound of your voice. I listened to your *Rector's Study* every week and wondered what you looked like."

Radio broadcasting has been a fascination of mine since childhood. I feel very comfortable speaking into a microphone. Weekly broadcasts of my "Rector's Study" developed a large listening audience.

A rancher north of town once told me, after introducing himself, "I mounted speakers on the cab of my truck so I could listen to country music while feeding cattle in the wintertime. But I always turned it to the *Rector's Study* because, frankly, I never knew what to expect." When I asked him what he meant, he answered, "Sometimes you interviewed the damnedest people I've ever heard. But you always asked 'em the kind of questions I wanted to ask 'em. Sometimes they were weird, but they were always so interesting. I especially liked it when you had live musicians singing away, and sometimes making human mistakes right on the air, like we all would do. I like live radio, even when it ain't always the best, because it's more personal than all that canned stuff you hear on commercial radio anymore."

Twice the *Rector's Study* went international.

One broadcast consisted of an interview with a young physician who charged that the government had downplayed the devastating long-range effect that a nuclear strike at Cheyenne would bring upon the whole Rocky Mountain region. (Cheyenne's missile base surely made it a first-strike target.) This show was picked up by the BBC and rebroadcast over much of Europe.

Another time I interviewed, through an English interpreter, a Spanish concert organist who was performing in our St. Mark's Noon Concert Series. Seeing my collection of western Americana albums, he asked if I would record a tape of "cowboy songs" for him. When I began the recording I realized that many of these classic old cowboy ballads would make no sense at all to a foreigner who didn't know what a *doggie* was, for instance, or what it meant to be a *night rider* along a cattle trail, or what a *chuckwagon* was all about. So I provided a little extemporaneous explanation to accompany each of the recording tracks. Before sending the tapes to the priest-organist in Spain, I decided to share them with my *Rector's Study* listening audience over KUUY. It proved to be one of my most successful broadcasts, because many people hungered to hear these old western classics again.

A couple of months later, I received a request from a public broadcast network in Spain asking permission to rebroadcast that tape for the Spanish listening audience. Apparently, the priest-organist in the famous cathedral of Seville somehow shared it among university friends, where it came to the attention of the public radio officials.

It was fun to think that something originating in my little studio in the basement of Templeton House eventually made its way to the radio networks of Europe.

A pleasant side benefit of my association with KUUY was the special invitation arranged by Terrell Metheny, station manager, for me to sit on stage for a Saturday-night broadcast from Nashville's famous Grand Ole Opry. Only very special guests of the performers are allowed backstage, where you mingle freely among the country stars as they drink coffee or soft drinks in a little snack bar located directly behind the backdrop curtains. Their casual camaraderie resembled that of an intimate family reunion. My clerical collar made me stand out enough that Roy Acuff introduced himself and invited me into his private dressing room to see the hundreds of framed photographs that lined the walls.

It was fun to watch the hand signals used by the backup singers and musicians while on stage. Off in the wings, technicians at huge mixing consoles seemed pleased that I was interested in how they blended all the microphone signals into a pleasant mix for the WSM radio listeners and the people in the packed auditorium.

While watching it all, I was as delirious with excitement and curiosity as when as a kid I lingered all day in the broadcast studios of KWYO in Sheridan, Wyoming. It's great to know that there's still a child within, even if we let him out to play only once in awhile.

✧

The *St. Mark's Noon Concert Series*, to which I have earlier referred, was one of the most innovative creative-artistic services which any church could offer its community.

The guiding genius of this community outreach was Edgar Young, our director of music at St. Mark's Church. I call him genius because the funding of this concert series was not in our church program-budget, yet Edgar ingeniously researched every source of public funding (city, state, and federal) of the creative arts, along with private endowments, and prevailed upon them all, separately and sometimes collectively, to fund these musical concerts.

The downtown location of St. Mark's in the governmental center of Wyoming's capital city made it ideal as a place for attracting connoisseurs of the arts for these noon concert series. Accomplished organists, like the Spanish priest-organist from Seville, along with chamber groups, soloists, balladeers, and instrumentalists were scheduled a year in advance. A few were local performers but the vast majority were professional classical musicians on a concert swing across America and welcomed a stopover in Cheyenne for a little lunch money along the way.

Overnighters were lodged as guests of the Todds in Templeton House. One performing couple with two children stayed nearly a week with the mother privately tutoring the youngsters in the rectory. This is what I mean when I say Edgar employed *creative financing* to lure artists to appear in the *St. Mark's Noon Concert Series*.

Once the Cheyenne Symphony Orchestra performed the music of Bach (for organ and orchestra) at St. Mark's, with our having to remove all the pews from the chancel to accommodate the musicians.

But what a gift our church made to the community with these monthly noonday concerts — especially enhanced by the natural acoustics of the grand old Gothic church building. Business and governmental workers brought their sack lunches and ate in the pews while listening to an hour of beautiful music by an infinite variety of performers from all over the world. St. Mark's provided free coffee and tea which I paid for from my rector's discretionary fund. A collection was always taken which, of course, helped with the overall expenses of bringing a prestigious performer to Cheyenne.

But eventually we had to give it up. Edgar's creative financing inevitably exhausted even his own ingenuity. In my opinion, his talent in life is not primarily that of a successful attorney, but in becoming a program director for a well-endowed museum, art gallery, or concert hall in a large city somewhere. Cheyenne simply wasn't big enough to sustain the dream of what he wanted our *St. Mark's Noon Concert Series* to become.

But it was so great while it lasted.

✧

Historic St. Mark's as a downtown church has many prestigious advantages. A major disadvantage was that it was easily accessible to professional con-artists who exploited legitimate charity normally provided to transient and homeless people. They could sweep the downtown churches with desperate hard-luck stories and collect duplicate donations for gas, bus tickets, and meals. The take of several hundred dollars was possible after only a few hours of successful panhandling.

I told the Reverend Warren Dierks at the First Methodist Church, located only one block away, that more "lifelong Methodists" were confirmed into "lifelong Episcopalians" in their walk along that one city block between us than had been confirmed by all the bishops of Wyoming.

The typical pitch of a professional scam artist would be, "Father, I've been an Episcopalian all my life. My uncle was a priest and my grandfather a bishop. My family has given their whole life to the Episcopal Church and now, by God, its time for the church to give me something . . . because I'm desperately in need of a hotel room for tonight, with dinner and breakfast, and a bus ticket to San Francisco tomorrow."

All day long, my parish secretary was constantly besieged with fraudulent scams like these — along with many legitimate requests coming from those sincerely seeking food, shelter, and clothing. It became obvious to me that the downtown churches needed to coordinate our charity to provide a semblance of consistency in services to those in genuine need as distinguished from those who would exploit the system. Otherwise, our duplicity was making ourselves a part of the problem.

I invited all the downtown clergy to meet with me to see if we couldn't pool our charitable funds and set up a system which would eliminate duplicate services to the same person. They quickly agreed. But it was necessary to coordinate our efforts with a much larger maze of public social service agencies also dealing with similar requests: Red Cross, health and public welfare, Salvation Army, law enforcement, Goodwill Industries — to name only a few. And it was imperative that we establish one central clearing office through which all claims for charity could be processed and monitored.

Thus began our Cooperative Ministry of Emergency Services in Cheyenne which I named COMEA. For over eighteen years I pulled together representatives of all the churches and social agencies for monthly meetings. Over morning coffee and doughnuts, provided by St. Mark's, we coordinated all our activities into a unified program of emergency assistance which embraced almost every conceivable situation of human need. It constantly needed refining to keep abreast with unusual circumstances where unfortunate individuals fell through the cracks of the welfare system.

The result was that people who sincerely needed legitimate assistance — got it. Those who were out to con the system were immediately detected and sent on their way. The word got out along the highway network that COMEA worked for those who genuinely needed help in Cheyenne, and you couldn't crack it if you were out to con it.

Finally, COMEA evolved into a locally and federally funded program for the homeless, including a "warmth" shelter for overnight lodging, meals for the hungry, employment counseling, medical attention for the indigent, and so forth. No longer was a hitchhiker compelled to sleep under a highway bridge during a winter night; or a child deprived of milk, blankets and diapers; or a family forbidden a tank of gas to move on toward its destination; or someone denied medical attention — simply because they didn't have the funds to pay for it.

The "warmth" shelter is staffed with volunteer help. Only the director and a few others in supervisory positions are salaried. The program works. Without doubt, the establishment of COMEA has been one of my proudest achievements as rector of St. Mark's Episcopal Church.

I have always felt that Christianity is two-dimensional. The vertical relationship is between man and God. The horizontal relationship is between man and man. Both relationships must exist simultaneously. Where they intersect is the cross of Christ.

✧

On Saturday evenings St. Mark's sponsored a young people's coffeehouse. It was housed in the youth room of the new addition I helped design. The kids turned down the overhead lights and lit candles on each card table. The candlelight reflecting shadows on the stone walls gave it the eerie appearance of a medieval castle. Coffee, tea, hot cider, and soda were sold along with fresh doughnuts.

It proved to become such a popular gathering place for teenagers, who really didn't have many other places to go in Cheyenne, that adult sponsors sometimes had to block entrance to newcomers to keep the room within its 200-person capacity. In fact, the coffeehouse experiment worked so well that eventually we had to close it down because it was becoming too successful for us to manage effectively.

One of the adult sponsors was an unlikely candidate to be managing teenagers. Frank Perkins, in his late sixties, had fairly old-fashioned views when it came to dealing with youngsters. He couldn't see any incongruity in his trying to enforce our no-smoking ban upon the kids while he, himself, insisted on smoking his pipe in their midst. He reasoned that young people should understand that adults are privileged to do things forbidden to teenagers. Smoking, he contended, was one of the bad habits that was an adult privilege.

He also volunteered to learn the intricacies of our church alarm system so that he could lock up the building every Saturday night. The adult volunteers were pleased that Frank took this responsibility upon himself, because most of them did not relish the spooky job of checking out the darkened, cavernous building with its many levels of rooms. However, it bothered me that Frank insisted on remaining behind for the final lock-up procedure, manipulating the sequential controls of the electronic alarm control panel, after he and I had checked out the building together. I wondered why we couldn't both leave at the same time.

Frank Perkins soon became an enigma to all of us.

He called himself a professional salesman. That is to say, he sold things — anything that was up for sale. "A salesman sells himself first and then his product second," was his familiar line. But it became apparent to those of us who knew him that he was having an increasingly difficult time scratching out a living at selling himself. He moved through a rapid succession of marginal sales jobs, lasting usually no longer than the probationary training period. In other words, new employers quickly learned something about Frank that the rest of us knew all too well — there was something wrong. "His brain seems to be short-circuited some way," is how one layman expressed it.

Indeed, something was wrong, but no one could put a finger on what it was. He lived alone in a tiny little apartment on the second floor of an old Cheyenne home. Twice I tried calling on him and both times he edged himself through the door into the hallway, where he took me by the arm and led me to the Frontier Hotel, only a few blocks away, for a cup of coffee. I resolved right then, with shades of Alfred Hitchcock's *Psycho*, that I didn't really want to see the interior of his apartment for fear of what I might find lurking there.

Frank never *looked well done up* — using a quaint expression borrowed from my father in reference to how people looked at their wedding or in their casket. He was just a wisp of a man, weighing no more than 130 pounds. His clean-shaven face was more wrinkled than a dried-up potato peel. The most noticeable things about Frank were his faded blue eyes, sunken into their sockets, which seemed to reflect enormous psychic pain — as if they concealed deep anguish, self-loathing, or massive denial. He could send a haunting chill down your spine when he looked directly at you.

Yet he was a loyal churchman, preferring the externals of high church ceremonials without ever satisfactorily explaining where this liturgical preference came from.

He never talked about his past. In fact, people learned not to ask Frank about his life to spare him the acute embarrassment of having to evade the question. His unadorned existence, pitiful hopelessness, and general ineptitude made it apparent that somewhere along the way Frank had slid into chronic dysfunctionalism. But he always bore a plastic smile and would always put the best spin on his latest sales job.

However, I learned more about his past than he realized. A dear old friend from my Vermillion days, Father Bob Crawford, stopped over in Cheyenne during one of his cross-country trips on the Union Pacific. Out of the blue one evening, while we were sipping brandy at Templeton House, he asked, "Have you ever come across a nut here in Cheyenne by the name of Frank Perkins?"

After I recovered from my shock, he told me that Frank had been a street urchin, probably a runaway from a family ranch, back in the days of Father Crawford's tenure at a high Anglo-Catholic parish in Omaha. A Mr. Dowling, a devoted churchman and a man of considerable means with high connections in Omaha society, took Frank into his home, cleaned him up, encouraged him to finish high school, got him a good job as a sales representative for an optical company, and even arranged a socialite wedding for the kid. Two sons were born. His wife divorced him in despair. One son died in a motorcycle accident; the other had become a successful young professional living in California, permanently estranged from this weird father whom he never really got to know.

That was all that Father Crawford could remember of Frank's distant past. But he said, "You ought to ask Frank about the positive influence of Mr. Dowling on his life. I'd be anxious to know how much of it he would acknowledge."

I did ask.

Frank's limp answer: "Dowling and I once were business associates."

My hunch is that he was so out of touch with his deeply repressed feelings — probably for most of his miserable life — that he couldn't express a legitimate emotion even if he desperately tried.

But Father Crawford's explanation helped explain Frank's Anglo-Catholic background and his obsession with the externals of liturgical worship and why he was always bugging me to use more incense. "Let the incense roll," he would say, "until it gets so thick that the congregation can't see nothing except the Lord lifted high upon his throne surrounded by the seraphim at his feet"— imagery borrowed from Isaiah 6.

He was always lonely at Christmastime. He would attend both Christmas Eve services and be there again for the final service on Christmas morning, after which he would invariably ask, "Father Gene, please allow me to buy you a piece of cherry pie and a cup of coffee out at the truck stop as a Christmas gift to my faithful priest?" I knew that he was desperately begging for companionship on what otherwise would have been a lonely Christmas Day for him. But having already required my family to delay our holiday celebration until after the last Christmas morning service, I had to decline his offers. The last thing I wanted to do on Christmas morning was leave my family waiting longer than it had already waited while I ate soggy pie at a dismal truck stop with Frank Perkins.

But I atoned for my guilt by inviting Frank to share Christmas with us instead. Usually I would drive him home with me on Christmas Eve, between the two large services, so that he could join my family for oyster stew and fruitcake by the fireplace for the hour or two before the midnight service. Eventually, we came to include him in our Thanksgiving dinners as well.

Old age descended upon Frank as his sales opportunities slowly slipped away. Unfortunately for my church staff, his home away from home became St. Mark's Church. There he would come and sit all day in the church office smoking his pipe, munching on overripe fruit, and napping in the afternoon. Although his presence didn't interfere with office routines and activities, it became an irritant to many.

Once the sexton came to me and said, "Father Todd, I don't know what's this thing with Frank Perkins and the church. But I keep bumping into him late at night and sometimes early in the morning when I'm down here checking things out. I'll bump into him in a darkened furnace room when I'm least expecting someone to be there, or behind the heavy curtains on the empty stage of the parish hall. It scares the hell out of me, and I'm afraid I'm gonna punch him out, not because I'm mad at him — just out of reflex action."

When we confronted Frank about his sudden appearance from out of nowhere, he would casually remind us that a big church like St. Mark's had many entrances, with many people and groups coming and going. Which was true. I installed wide-angle mirrors to better cover the main entrance to the office area, but still he surprised us with his sudden appearances. I ordered the locks changed and new keys issued.

Late one evening when I happened to drop by the church to pick up something I had forgotten, I overheard Frank talking on the telephone. I geared up my courage and dashed to all four extension phones along the darkened corridors and found Frank nowhere. It was spooky and I hurried away.

The next morning I asked him about it. His answer was evasive but plausible. "It couldn't have been me you heard, Father Todd. Your own investigation revealed that I was nowhere to be found in the building. And I have no telephone at home. It had to have been the crossed circuits of the telephone company in their building just across the alley here . . . and you were listening to someone else's conversation and just thought it was me."

Maybe so, but I was convinced that I recognized Frank's voice.

When we updated our telephone system we had privacy lines installed to protect the confidentiality of callers and could no longer monitor extension telephone conversations. Very late at night, however, I would often see a button light up, which indicated a circuit was open. Again I would dash to all extension telephones, only to find nothing but spooky silence and shadowy darkness.

I was mystified. The phone company, at my request, checked out the possibility of electrical shorts in the line and could find none. However, there were never any unauthorized long-distance telephone calls charged to our account — so I let it pass as part of my own paranoia.

We soon learned not to ask Frank to perform even the most simple tasks, because it quickly would become a complicated mess. Even the mundane chore of emptying the trash was too much. He would paw through it and tote half of it back and secretly stash it away in some hidden corner of the church.

Once he had been a good usher in church — until he began taking the morning offerings home to count the cash collection and then faithfully return it. We had no choice but to demand that the offerings be counted by two ushers, on the church premises, who both must sign the cash receipt. Furthermore, I had to ask parishioner Bill Haley, a skilled machinist, to weld us a steel money vault, bolted to the marble floor under heavy lock, into which the offerings were deposited to make certain the offense was never repeated. Even ushering had now become a complicated mess with him involved.

Sandy Jones, my parish secretary, came to me one morning and said, "Father Todd, we've got to do something about Frank Perkins spending all his time here in the church office and eating his lunch here. He brings in sacks of discarded fruit he finds in the trash bins behind Safeway and keeps trying to pawn them off on people coming into the office. They don't want that rotten old stuff because they know where it comes from."

Sandy was right.

I told Frank he would have to eat his lunch in the parish kitchen like the rest of us did. I showed him the women's dire warning pasted on the refrigerator that no surplus food was to be stashed there. Then I took him by the arm, led him out into the parish hall, pointed to the high overhead beams, and said, "Frank, up there is where the women will hang us both by the heels if we violate their warning. And while hanging there for three days and nights the only thing they will let us drink will be vinegar on a sponge hoisted up to us on a long bamboo pole."

He caught the humor of my warning and stashed nothing in the refrigerator.

A month later Sandy came to me again and said, "Father Todd, we've got to do something about Frank Perkins sitting out here in the front office all day long — every day. He's in on every conversation and hears everything I say to people on the phone when they call about personal and confidential matters. Every time I look up from my typewriter, there sits Frank Perkins just staring at me. He's getting on my nerves."

Sandy was right again.

Reluctantly, I told Frank that he must move to a very pleasant sitting area just inside the parish hall in very close proximity to the church office. He could still drink our coffee and would find this grouping of leather upholstered wingback chairs, with nice reading lamps, a far more comfortable place to sit and read. And on the coffee table was a large assortment of church periodicals and good reading material. He could even stretch out on the sofa and take an afternoon nap if he wanted to. He was very congenial, habitually so, and he abided by my requests.

Then he complained of not feeling well. In spite of his general contempt for doctors, I took him to one anyway. Later he showed me a large assortment of outdated vitamins and medications, which I'm sure he found in a trash barrel behind a drug store, and informed me that his regimen of self-medication was far more effective than the expensive prescriptions ordered by the doctor.

His health continued to deteriorate. One bitterly cold day he shuffled late into the office, almost noon, and I noticed that when he slumped into the wing chair his eyes appeared dazed, and he was rocking his body back and forth while swinging his head side to side. I remembered animals on the ranch doing the same thing when in excruciating pain. Over his verbal objections and physical resistance, I had the sexton help me load him into my car and drove him directly to the doctor's office. I instructed him to remain in the lobby there until I returned from a ladies guild luncheon in the parish hall.

During the luncheon I received a phone call that Frank had collapsed in the doctor's office and was rushed to the hospital, where he died. I couldn't resist imagining the chaos that surely would have erupted in the parish hall had I not driven him to the doctor's office when I did. Having a man drop dead in the middle of a luncheon is not usually on the ladies guild's agenda. But knowing good Episcopal women as I do and their faithfulness to duty, they probably would have proceeded with their agenda anyway as soon as we had carted his body away.

Frank's lone surviving son arrived from California. Tom Perkins bore no physical nor psychological resemblance to his dad. He was a college graduate, well dressed, professionally employed, and happily married to a beautiful wife. He kept telling us that he could not understand this bizarre dad of his. He said, "You know he told us that although he didn't have a telephone he nevertheless had access to a phone. And he told us that we were never to call him except after midnight. Only when you called me, Father Todd, about the death of my father did I learn that your church telephone number was the number he instructed us to call. What was he doing in your church past midnight every night? Was he your night watchman or something?"

I didn't answer.

Tom and his wife eventually received a key to his dad's apartment and were appalled at what they found. He called me on the phone. "Father Todd, this place is packed from floor to ceiling with stacks of neatly organized large brown manila envelopes — containing nothing but trash. I can hardly squeeze my way through the narrow passages of it all. The bedroom is packed so solidly that the bed is completely inundated. The bathroom is packed so solidly that we can't even gain entrance to it. Please tell me, where in the world did my father sleep and have access to a bathroom?"

By this time I knew the answer.

I planned the burial service for Frank Perkins at St. Mark's Church. With the incense so thick you couldn't see across the altar, it was to be a requiem Mass so liturgically high that it would be a downward slide into heaven.

Cremation was to follow.

Several days later the funeral director brought me a cardboard box containing the ashes of Frank Perkins with the instruction that Tom, who had since returned to California, wanted his father's cremains held in the church temporarily until such time as a place of permanent interment could be selected.

I placed the box on the top shelf of the cabinet above the sink in the outer office of the church. A few weeks later, Sandy Jones, my faithful parish secretary, came to me and said, "Father Todd, you're gonna have to do something about Frank Perkins. Every time I open the cabinet above the sink to make a fresh pot of coffee there's Frank Perkins looking down on me. Every time I look up from my typewriter, there he is again. You're gonna have to find him another place to stay because he's beginning to get on my nerves again."

Sandy was right.

But where was I to put him? Carrying the urn, I walked around the church looking for a safe place. After all, these were the sacred remains of a human being, a Christian soul, who by this time had made an indelible impression on all of us at St. Mark's. I finally decided on a large steel storage cabinet in the shadowy corner of the parish hall. It was about seven feet high, with doors that could be securely locked. It contained our year's supply of paper products. I reverently tucked Frank away in the corner of the top shelf and promptly forgot about him.

Several weeks later I heard a muffled scream from Sandy Jones, who came running into my study and gasped, "Father Todd, I'm reaching up into the storage cabinet for paper supplies and I suddenly bump into Frank Perkins hiding away up there in the darkened corner of the top shelf. Scares me to death. Can't you find a better place for him to hide than that?"

Again, Sandy was right. I needed to do something about Frank Perkins.

This time I put him in my study on the library shelves — between the section of books marked *Biographies* and *Mysteries*. After all, he was a biographical mystery to us all.

A year later, the sexton asked me to accompany him to an isolated storage room immediately adjacent to the stage off the parish hall. He handed me a leather bag and said, "Look what I found here. A bag filled with all the little tools of a locksmith and a ring of copied church keys. And a dirty little shavin' kit. Look, here's a towel wrapped around a bar of soap. Here's a bunch of half-empty bottles of shavin' lotions, junk that people throw away. And inside this bag, tucked away down here along the floor under the bottom shelf, is a telephone with alligator clips on it. The kind that telephone repairmen use when they clip into a line they're workin' on. Why do you suppose these crazy things are all stashed away in here?"

I looked around the cramped quarters of the supply closet, and my eyes froze on a large telephone circuit box mounted on the wall. The cover had long been removed, exposing what seemed like hundreds of little colored wires, all neatly crimped into an orderly design of coded connections. Above the frame of wires were several terminals — to which were attached the exterior telephone cables coming in from the outside alley.

"My God," I shuddered.

In my wildest imagination, it never once occurred to me that Frank could have used locksmith tools to access any room in the church. He certainly knew the alarm system network sufficiently to avoid triggering it with the accidental opening of a wired door. And here in this isolated storage room, to which only the sexton had a key, he could easily have attached the alligator clips of his repairman's phone to access the telephone lines to the outside world. And here he waited — hour after hour, long past midnight, for a chance call from his estranged son, Tom, from California.

I turned to the sexton and said, "Let's see if back behind this deep shelf, heaped high with junk stored away for a hundred years, we find anything resembling a sleeping bag."

We found it in ten seconds.

How many times have parishioners been up on that parish hall stage at night having no idea that just through that heavily locked door was hiding a desperately lonely man, anxiously awaiting his phone calls? How often did he sleep throughout the remainder of a feverish night, curled up on the floor in a flimsy sleeping bag, before rising early to wash and use the restroom before slipping out of the church before dawn so that no one would see him? How many times had I come within a few feet of him, concealed behind an open door, as I made my constant rounds through the empty building?

How often have I dreaded the spooky feeling of being alone in that church late at night, thinking I heard creaking floors, the groaning of overhead wooden beams, doors coming ajar then quietly clicking shut again — sounds I convinced myself were caused by nothing more than the normal contractions and settling of a drafty old stone building in the quiet coolness of the night?

I shuddered to think that maybe he was constantly watching my every movement from behind the drawn stage curtains before slinking into his darkened closet hideaway.

What would have happened had we accidentally found the poor soul hiding there?

Or dead there?

"Father Todd, you're trembling. Are you not feeling well?"

I didn't answer.

"Let's get the hell out of here if it's botherin' you all that much. You know it's kinda chilly in here. Maybe you're comin' down with a cold or somethin' — let's go get ourselves a cup of hot coffee. That'll make you feel better."

With only a few have I shared this tragic story. It has been a secret I've carefully sheltered within my own personal conscience, combined with overwhelming guilt. For a long time I had harbored a sixth-sense intuition of an *evening phantom* haunting the shadowy chambers of the church. Why didn't I pursue it more thoroughly? How could I have been so blind?

✧

If the cremains of Frank Perkins were the first to rest at St. Mark's Episcopal Church, they would not be the last.

Ever since visiting the catacombs under Rome where for 300 years the Christians had worshipped, surrounded by the tombs of the dead, during the intense Roman persecution — I had become convinced that we needed to install a columbarium at St. Mark's Church.

The concept was so new at first that parishioners didn't even know that a columbarium was a place of interment for the ashes of those who had been cremated. Once they learned what it was, many objected to it because it sounded morbid and goulish. Furthermore, it sounded contradictory to the Christian doctrine of the Resurrection.

It was obvious that I needed to do a lot of educating.

In my sermons and in my weekly newsletter, *The Messenger,* I began a series of teachings that Christianity was born in a cemetery because it was there that the resurrection of Christ was first discovered and announced to the world. I showed my colored slides, taken inside the Roman catacombs, to explain that it was here, among the dead, where the early Christians celebrated *Communion of the Saints* — past, present, and future. Furthermore, cemetery churchyards were a common tradition of all churches until the turn of the century when the value of urban land necessitated a separation of a church from its cemetery. Let's face it, it takes a lot of land to maintain a cemetery.

But with a growing trend toward cremation within the past twenty-five years, all that has changed. Not only can you bury many cremains within an area of only a few square feet, but it also can be less expensive for the family of the deceased. And selling columbarium spaces, called niches, can become a good money-making project for the local church. Most of all, theologically and emotionally, there is tremendous satisfaction in knowing that your final resting place is in a holy place where God is worshipped and in close proximity to where all the sacred rites and ceremonies of the church are celebrated.

Although there was considerable objection at first, the idea eventually caught on and enthusiasm began to build toward the construction of a beautiful bronze columbarium, mounted directly below the large *Good Shepherd* stained-glass window along the back wall of the church. Then we encountered a legal roadblock that no one expected. It seems that Wyoming had an archaic statute which forbid columbariums apart from public cemeteries.

I realized then that the possibility of St. Mark's ever having a columbarium demanded much more of me than simply convincing the local congregation of its desirability. I now had the more awesome task of convincing the state legislature to change the statute and persuade the governor to sign it into law.

To make a long story short, I had a lot of professional help.

Cheyenne has many lawyers who long have established an expertise as registered lobbyists, who know exactly how to get a bill introduced in the state legislature and then follow that bill through every step of the laborious process of committee hearings before its final vote on the floor of both houses. Otherwise it will get pigeon-holed in some committee wastebasket and never be heard from again. I remained constantly "on call" to dash up to a hearing room somewhere in the state capitol to speak in behalf of its passage.

I must admit that I had a little inside help as well. As house chaplain I had easy access to the speaker of the house who assured me that he would do everything he could to make certain the bill was approved by committee and brought back to the floor for debate and final passage.

It passed and Governor Mike Sullivan signed it into law. Now it was possible for St. Mark's to install the first church columbarium in the state of Wyoming.

Again, I had the architectural services of one of the very best. Claire Davis, a former junior warden, designed a large wooden framework which perfectly matched the natural antiquity of the century-old church to encase an exquisite bronze columbarium shipped to us from a foundry in New York. Fortunately, we had the skilled handiwork of Max Albert who was much more than an excellent carpenter, but truly an artisan in wood craftsmanship, to do the building for us. Indeed, the whole project became a work of art.

Even the marble baseboards were redesigned in such a way that the finished product was not only a thing of architectural beauty, but also looked as if it had been built there in 1886 when the original building was first constructed.

We had a magnificent *New Orleans*–style dedication of the new St. Mark's Columbarium on All Saint's Day of 1989. A Dixieland jazz band led the whole congregation in a slow and mournful gait down the long aisle of the church toward the columbarium as we sang the plaintive *Just a Closer Walk With Thee.* Following the dedication the band broke out into a spirited *When the Saints Go Marching In* — as it led the whole congregation, dancing and swaying, back up the aisle of the church and then over to the parish hall for cake and brandy.

What a day of celebration!

All Saints Columbarium installed along back wall of St. Mark's. It took an act of the state legislature to secure statutory permission to build the first church columbarium in Wyoming. Beautiful wood cabinetry encasing the bronze burial niches truly made it a work of art.

A year later, in early December 1990, while greeting a larger-than-usual congregation at the end of the morning service, Senior Warden Jack Palma kept telling me to hasten over to the parish hall. I couldn't understand the rush. When I entered the room I discovered a beautifully decorated reception table loaded with banquet food. Using the sound system which earlier I had installed in the parish hall, he called me to the microphone, while the whole congregation circled around, and announced that the congregation was celebrating my twenty-fifth anniversary as rector of St. Mark's Church.

Then Jack informed me that in grateful appreciation for my leadership in inspiring the congregation toward the installation of the beautiful new columbarium, the vestry was gifting me with two niches, worth $1000 each, so that Rosemary and I someday could be buried there, "And in this way, we'll have you with us here forever."

It was a total surprise!

The truth is, I had not yet made the decision that I personally wanted cremation for myself when I died. I never advocated cremation over traditional cemetery burials when I pushed for a columbarium at St. Mark's — *only that parishioners could now freely exercise this new option.*

However, having accepted the gift of love, there is no question now that cremation is what I want for myself. Whenever I visit St. Mark's, now that I'm retired, I take great comfort in seeing our names engraved on the brass plates marking the bronze niches which someday will be the final resting places for Rosemary and me (alongside all the other people of St. Mark's that we knew and loved). And I like it when I think of all the future baptisms performed no more than a few feet away from our burial vaults — symbolizing that birth and death, and everything between, are all under the watchful reign of

Another view of columbarium showing the towering Good Shepherd above and the fanfare herald trumpet organs mounted on back wall. I baptized my little grandson Riley Voycheske here in 1992, using the baptistry shown in foreground.

a loving God. Yes, it's comforting to think that I'll never be far away from everything that happens in that great ol' church in ages to come — because I deeply believe in *Communion of the Saints.*

We designated all columbarium sales to the Centennial Trust Fund which earlier I had established at St. Mark's, patterned closely to the one I instituted at University Baptist Church in Vermillion. This trust had already accumulated a considerable sum of money from previous endowments and is destined for several hundred thousand dollars yet to come from future columbarium sales. Income from the Centennial Trust investments are specifically designated for only historical preservation and renovation of St. Mark's Church, major capital improvements, or Christian outreach into Cheyenne and the world — which are beyond the ordinary operating budget of the local church. If ever a church trust such as this is violated by invading its funds for operational costs and program perks, not only will its principal soon be depleted, but also sources of future funding will dry up as well. Donors whose confidence have been shattered will not and should not be expected to contribute to any charitable trust fund, not alone a church trust, which only lightens the load of those whose Christian stewardship should be generously supporting it in the first place.

I mention this only because I think people would like to believe that even their purchase of a columbarium burial niche can also become an investment in the long-term benefit of their church.

✧

I've learned that many people don't like speaking of death. We're perfectly willing to talk about anything else in life at great length but not about the one event that is guaranteed to engulf us all. But the clergy are required to talk about it, not as the final defeat, but as the ultimate victory.

It takes courage to face death head-on. However, the most remarkable courage in dealing with death was shown to me by a group of teenagers.

A pediatrician called me one evening and told me about his young patient, Brad, only fourteen years old, suffering from terminal brain cancer. "We've done everything we can," Dr. Prentice said, "including chemotherapy and radiation, but to no avail. The tumor is growing so fast there's nothing more we can do. Brad's got only a few months to live. Even he knows now that he's dying. He asked, and we had to tell him. His family is unchurched, and they need spiritual direction and support. Especially Brad, who's asking questions that no one can answer. I have their permission to ask if you'd be willing to go by and see them."

Brad was sprawled out on a small cot in the basement recreation room of the family home, wearing only a pair of shorts because he felt feverish in the hot summer afternoons. He was exceptionally large for his age, which the doctor said may have been a response to pressure on the brain by the growing tumor. He looked especially pale, his body drained of all color, which because of his youthfulness I failed to recognize as the typical pallor of approaching death.

Here was just a junior high kid, who had never been religiously exposed to the church, asking me serious existential questions that few adults will openly discuss.

"Who is God? Where is he? How do we know he's real? If he's real, how come he lets people die?"

Profound questions they were. I gave answers that reflected the basic teachings of Christianity. I tried to speak slowly and thoughtfully and, above all, simply.

Each time he spoke, his face expressed a desperation for some answers about life and death. It was obvious to me that he knew death was going to be a solitary journey, which he alone would take. His mom and dad and sister would be with him for awhile, but eventually he would leave them behind and venture into the great unknown — all by himself. Naturally, he was scared.

We talked about the difference between empirical evidence and faith, how the latter transcends the former when it comes to things unseen. We talked about the love of God and triumphs of the human spirit. I was determined that there was to be no Pollyanna preaching to a fourteen-year-old on his death bed. You don't bullshit a dying kid with flip answers and trite promises. If I couldn't answer a question directly, I honestly told him so. When he asked me whether there really was a heaven, I told him I didn't know for sure because no one had been there who had come back to tell us about it. But I told him what Christ is reported to have said and what millions believed.

I called on him several times a week. I read to him short stories out of the Bible and told him stories of my own. He asked to be baptized. He took his baptism as seriously as a parachutist taking instruction on how to prepare for his first solo jump. This wasn't kid stuff to him anymore. He had become a young soldier preparing for life's greatest journey.

After lighting his baptism candle and letting it burn for awhile beside his bed, I told him he could now blow it out if he wanted to.

"Why?" he asked.

"Only to save it for another time," I answered, stupidly.

"Couldn't you give me another one then? I just like to watch it flicker and burn. Something like my life, isn't it . . . as it slowly burns down?"

I was too choked up to answer.

I continued my calls and I noticed he was failing fast. He asked me once in a weakened voice, "Father Todd, what's it like when you die? I mean, what's it really like?"

The ultimate question of all mankind.

I told him that I honestly didn't know because Christ and a few biblical characters were the only persons on earth who could have told us about that phenomenon — and they never revealed what death was really like. But I shared with him the near-death experiences Elizabeth Kubler Ross had written about in her book *Death and Dying* and shared stories about the tunnel of light and magnificent peace that were so frequently reported.

But he related most of all to my retelling of the story that the famed Dr. Peter Marshall, chaplain to the U.S. Senate, is reported to have told West Point cadets when he preached in their chapel at the beginning of World War II.

The story is about a dying boy who asks his father the same question: "Dad, what's it like to die?" And the father answers, "Son, do you remember when you were just a youngster how you used to crawl in bed with your mother when I was away at work late at night? And you didn't even remember that after you had fallen asleep, that I came home and carried you into your own bed in your own room now flooded with the morning sunlight."

"Brad," I said, "I would like to believe that this is the way it's going to be for you. You'll go to sleep here some evening — and in the morning, when you awaken, you'll joyfully discover that during the night God gathered you up in his arms and carried you over to the other side — to your own new room flooded with heavenly sunlight."

"Yeah, I like that," he smiled. "My own new room. And I can run outside into the sunshine and not be sick anymore."

The will to survive is the primary instinct of all humans and animals. We could hardly expect a fourteen-year-old to rationalize an understanding and acceptance of his own imminent death. However, I could see that Brad was making a progressive reconciliation with the reality that his short life was nearly over. Still, letting go was going to be tough on him as well as his family.

The hospice social worker called me one day and asked if I would be willing to meet with some of Brad's junior high friends, who had virtually stopped seeing him now that he was in the final stage of his illness. "Brad misses them," she said, "and we think it would be nice if we could persuade them to drop by and see him occasionally. He seems to be surrounded only by adults, and we think he still needs personal contact with friends his own age every once in a while."

It was a good thing we pulled Brad's young friends together, because they were outraged at the medical profession. "How come the doctors told Brad that he needed to take chemotherapy so he could get well again? And when he does, after vomiting all day long, every day, and losing all his hair, then they tell him he's gonna die anyway. What's going on here with lies like that?"

A good question. Theoretically, there's a logical medical explanation for this last preventive measure in the treatment of cancer. But many adults ask the same question with the same outraged skepticism.

"What can we talk about if we go see him?" they asked. "Won't it make him feel worse if we tell him about the fun things we're doing?"

Another good question. We admitted, honestly, that maybe it would make him feel sad in some ways. But we explained that he might feel worse if he thought they didn't want to see him because they were no longer his friends.

Sitting there among them was a little runt of a kid they nicknamed Pee Wee, who resembled the cartoon character of Charlie Brown. The bill of his baseball cap hung down over the side of his head, covering his ear. He never looked up. Never said a word. Seemed visibly shaken by it all.

"I'm worried about that little one," the social worker said as the boys left the room.

The next morning I had a phone call from Pee Wee's mother. "Please excuse my son from the expectation that he visit Brad. Even though he's the same age as Brad and the other boys, you can see that he's being left behind physically. His friends have suddenly shot up in height, and their voices are changing. Maybe next year he'll catch up in his puberty. But in the meantime, he's too immature physically and emotionally for something like this. He seems real moody and troubled, lost in his thoughts, ever since you all had that conference with the boys."

She hesitated for a moment and then added, "If he wants to go see Brad on his own, that's all right with me. But he won't. He's still just a little boy, you know?"

I respected the mother's opinion.

Two days later, however, the doorbell rang at Templeton House, and there standing on the stoop was Pee Wee, with his bicycle laid over on its side on the lawn. He had looked up my address and pedaled over six miles across Cheyenne to my home.

"Pee Wee, what in the world are you doing here?"

He handed me a large manila envelope. "Here, I want Brad to have this," he said, nervously rocking back and forth on his two feet, trying to conceal a tight little nervous grin. "I want you to give this to Brad. It's a picture I've drawn. I like to draw pictures. My teacher says my drawings are good. She thinks maybe someday I can be a commercial artist if I keep working at it."

He nervously withdrew the manila folder from my hand and pulled out a drawing. "This is a picture I drew about last summer when all of us went on a picnic out at Granite Lake. About ten miles out of town. And we were all ridin' our bicycles out there. See? And Brad came coastin' down that steep hill and didn't know that the bank dropped straight down into the water.

See? And he flew out into the air — holdin' onto his bike with one hand and holdin' his big floppy hat in the other — before he splashed down."

As Pee Wee told me this, he giggled, his face radiating the rare delight of a small kid telling a funny story.

"See here," he said, as he proudly held up the drawing to me, "this is my drawing of that."

"Pee Wee, this is wonderful," I exclaimed.

And it was. It was all there — Brad flying off into space, wearing Levi's and boots, long curly hair streaming behind him, bicycle and floppy hat in hand, with a perfect artistic expression of pure terror on his face as he prepared for splashdown into the lake.

"Again, Pee Wee, this is marvelous," I said again as a sincere compliment. "You're a very good artist. I think Brad would love this picture. But instead of my giving it to him — why don't you? I'll go with you."

We loaded his bike into the trunk of my car and headed over to Brad's home. By this time, I was visiting Brad every day. Brad's mother propped his head up on a pillow, and he took the drawing.

By the expression on his face, I could see that for a fleeting moment Brad forgot all about being sick — about dying — and saw himself, instead, as the carefree youngster of the summer before. A summer picnic with all his buddies. Sailing off into space with his bike and floppy hat, with the breeze in his face and the sun to his back. Back in the days when he was blessed with a full head of long hair, not bald as he was now. Splashing down into the water while his pals howled with laughter. Climbing out of the lake, drenched to the skin, and dragging his bike behind him. Joining everyone afterward in damp clothes for a wiener roast. Proud that he had been the life of the party, with a story he could brandish all year.

All this without even a hint that it would be his last carefree summer on earth. Already ballooning in his brain was the tumor that would end his life.

Brad continued smiling at the drawing, studying its details and quietly chuckling under his breath.

Pee Wee, pleased with himself but nervous as to what he was to say next in the face of death, turned and sprinted up the stairs of the tri-level home. He stopped on the landing and stood there, looking down at the floor as if consumed in thought. He remained there for almost a minute, with the bill of his baseball cap slid down over one ear.

Slowly he turned, descended down the stairs and returned to Brad's bedside. He nervously pulled off his cap and began twirling and bouncing it in his hands, then rocking to and fro on his feet while, with a quivering voice, he said, "Brad, I want you to know that I drew that picture and brought it to you here — not because my mother told me to or because someone made me do it. I came here, Brad, to let you know that you have always been my very special friend. I'm so sorry, man, that this is happening to you. I'm going to miss you, pal. And, Brad, I've come to tell you good-bye."

Tears welled in the eyes of both boys as Pee Wee leaned over and kissed Brad on the forehead.

Then he turned and leaped up the stairs. Through the garden-level window we could see him as he raced down the sidewalk as fast as his legs could carry him.

A pivotal moment!

We all have pivotal moments when we surprise everyone by suddenly rising beyond the expectations of others, and even ourselves, by doing something extraordinarily courageous, tender, and beautiful — because it is the right and honorable thing to do.

It was incredibly moving for me to watch the transformation, this little boy voluntarily doing something that few grown men could muster the emotional maturity and stature to do.

A few days later, Brad died.

While planning the funeral, his mother said, "I knew the end was near when Brad asked me to light his baptism candle beside his bed. He wouldn't take his eyes away from it."

✧

In 1990, I asked that the original wooden high altar at St. Mark's be detached from the front wall of the sanctuary and moved outward a few feet so that a priest could celebrate Mass by standing behind the altar, directly facing the congregation. This was in accordance with the new liturgical preference for what we called a "free-standing altar."

Again Claire Davis did the architectural design. She and I were in agreement that nothing done at St. Mark's should vary from the original decor of the building, constructed in 1886. And again we hired a superior wood craftsman for the job, Max Albert, who also worked on the columbarium. He was a short and stocky man, balding, who seemed to have no neck but only a series of double chins. His head appeared to be directly attached to his massive shoulders. His torso looked as solid as an oak tree.

Invariably, I would check on Max at least a dozen times a day as he worked away on both the columbarium — and now on the new altar configuration. Sometimes I would hold a piece of wood as he gently tapped it into place, fitting so tightly that it felt like polished glass. Other times, I would help make decisions if we encountered a problem Claire had not anticipated. For example, I wanted to make certain that new microphone cables were strung inside the altar to ensure that every word spoken there would be amplified and clearly heard by every single soul sitting in the pews — even those with hearing impairments. Worship is sadly diminished if the congregation must strain to hear the spoken *word* of God.

But once the historic old altar was detached and pulled away from the wooden structure (reredos) that towered above it, it became rather unstable. We had to crawl back into the altar shell and do some minor repair work on some loosened corner joints. My slender build made me better suited for work in cramped quarters than the bulky Max. As I pried and hammered away, I came across a yellowed piece of an old Cheyenne newspaper dated 1886. It was nothing more than the faded advertisement of a hardware store. Penciled in its margins was a shopping list of a few needed hardware supplies: nails, bolts, brushes, and linseed oil.

Obviously, as the carpenter worked away on this altar back in 1886, he penciled in these hardware needs, then shoved the list into a crevice, where it was forgotten and finally enclosed when the altar was mounted to the wall.

Being a student of history, I felt an overpowering personal link with that unknown carpenter of 1886. When the altar was stabilized, Max and I sat on the altar steps drinking coffee and discussing what it must have been like to have been a carpenter back then. As we talked, we could hear the howling of a Wyoming blizzard raging outside the church. We imagined how tough it would have been a hundred years ago to drive a horse-drawn buggy to work at the church site on such a stormy day as this. How about that horse, standing out there in a blizzard all day long. Would the carpenter have brought his lunch in a dinner pail? Of what food would it have consisted?

Max and I wished this carpenter had written something about his personal life and had left it there for us to find. Was he married? Happily so? Children? Or would his social life that evening consist of hitting the infamous dance hall bordellos of old Cheyenne? What would his health concerns have been? Did he belong to a church? Maybe St. Mark's? What were his worries about the past, and what were his dreams for the future?

Max said, "You know anything he would have written down, even the most mundane, would have been terribly fascinating to us today, wouldn't it?"

"Yes," I answered, "totally apart from any of the momentous historical things that were happening in 1886. Remember, this was only ten years after Custer's disastrous defeat at Little Big Horn."

Then I added, "Max, why don't we write down some mundane things that are going on in our lives today? And then enclose them in a sealed envelope and tack them to the interior wall of this altar? Maybe someone will discover them a century from now and find our musings of today to be just as fascinating to read in the year 2090 as we would have found such casual thoughts of this carpenter written back in 1886."

I got a pad and we began scribbling down our thoughts. He talked about his wife, Carol, suffering from emphysema and being on oxygen. He had no children. He was proud of his German ancestry. He loved his work. I don't remember what else he said.

I wrote down how I envied Max and his wood craftsmanship. He can stand back at the end of a day and see exactly what he accomplished. The beautiful curved molding, fitting so perfectly you can barely detect its seam. The finish so perfect you can't differentiate the old patina of 1886 from that applied just today. With the ministry, I reflected, you work all day at sowing seeds, and you seldom have the satisfaction of knowing whether they took root in good soil and flowered into maturity or whether they withered away in the rocks. I will never know if a sermon I've preached touched anyone's life in a truly significant way.

I wrote that I was pleased about my excellent health — but that heart disease and cancer were still the greatest causes of death in America, in spite of our incredible health care system. And now the ugly spectre of AIDS on the American social scene. Would these killers be all eliminated a hundred years from now? Instead of a horse and buggy, I described my brand-new Buick sitting outside the church. And I mentioned that on that particular evening I was meeting the families of my son, Barry, and my daughter Sheri in a popular restaurant for Italian pizza and a pitcher of beer. I commented on how much I loved my grown children, who now are doing a great job as parents, and how thoroughly I enjoyed being a grandfather. While eating pizza that night, each of the younger grandchildren would surely make their way to my lap for a little hug and some intimate talk.

I wrote that I was happily married to a beautiful person and that I was looking forward to retirement from the Episcopal ministry in only another year or so.

The scribblings were barely decipherable, so I typed them into my computer for a good printout. Before stuffing them into the envelope, I wrote in longhand at the bottom of the sheet:

Whoever you are that finds this message inside this altar from Max and me, I want to tell you: Treat this beautiful old altar with loving reverent care. If you have any thoughts about replacing it with some new-fangled fad that's sweeping the country, I beg you to think twice and please reconsider. A lot of love has gone into the building of it by skilled woodcarvers in 1886 and a gifted craftsmen in 1990 by the name of Max Albert. A lot of love has been celebrated across the top of it with the eucharistic Body of Christ. Carved in bold letters on the front of it are the words: SANCTUS — SANCTUS — SANCTUS. Treat it as something holy.

PS And if you don't, I promise to come back and haunt the devil out of you!

Eugene F. Todd
Rector — 1991

Chapter 21

I think many people assume the ministry is filled with only somber, holy events, punctuated with occasional bursts of an intangible something we might call spiritual joy. I'm here to tell you that members of the clergy also have done things so out of character and ridiculous that it becomes ludicrous — and sometimes, hilariously funny. Things can become so crazy and risqué that you dare not risk personal humiliation by telling anyone about them.

Since I'm now retired, I have nothing to lose in telling a few stories about myself, or involving myself, that I was too embarrassed to reveal during my active career. These revelations support the perennial accusation that Gene Todd, theologically, subscribes to a *High Doctrine of Fun*.

One year the county sheriff, facing a tough re-election campaign, desperately needed to bolster his sagging popularity. Under these circumstances, nothing works better than championing public morality. Condemning sexual immorality is always a good rallying cause. As I have previously written, many a gold-plated Cadillac has been delivered to the front gates of an evangelist's estate after only one sermon on the evils of sex.

The sheriff didn't have far to look for sexual immorality in Laramie County. He found it at the Clown's Den, a striptease joint located just outside Cheyenne on the old highway to Denver. Many drivers passed this roadside dive every day, but totally ignored it. No one thought this desolate little place was corrupting the morals of the entire county and bringing ruination to the capital city of Wyoming.

It took the incumbent sheriff, running for re-election, to tell us this.

But the sheriff discovered, much to his chagrin, that striptease artistry is not against the law in Wyoming. Pretty girls and handsome boys, twenty-one years and older, can strip to their G-string as much as they want, providing they don't go any further. A rash of letters appeared in the paper to that effect. The sheriff contended that something more was going on, which justified his entry into the fray.

Smarting from the scurrilous charge that he had overstepped his authority by setting himself up as the county moralist, he decided to select a team

511

of professional moralists to independently investigate the notorious den of inequity. That's when he contracted the services of Jim Clark, senior pastor of Cheyenne's First Presbyterian Church — and me. Representing two of the older and more prestigious churches of the city, we were to become the secret ace up his sleeve to silence his critics and safely reassure his landslide re-election as the county sheriff.

Deputy Lou Perna, my good friend and parishioner of St. Mark's, picked up Jim and me on a Friday night and drove us to the Clown's Den. We were carefully instructed to wear clothing no highly respected clergymen would wear in public. My disguise included a big-brimmed white straw hat, the kind everyone wears at Cheyenne's Frontier Days rodeo, along with my fanciest western shirt, tight-fitting Levi's, and a pair of borrowed shiny cowboy boots. I even brought along a pack of Marlboros to add authenticity to my disguise. Jim wore a brightly colored Hawaiian tourist shirt, loose-fitting white golf pants, and white sport shoes.

What a pair we were — beyond all suspicion.

The Reverend Dr. James Clark was not only a special colleague of mine in the ministry but also a brilliant scholar and gentleman. His doctorate was no honorary divinity degree but a genuinely earned Ph.D. from the University of Denver. He read the scriptures in Greek and mastered Hebrew and German. Ask Jim the time of day, and he would tell you Einstein's theory of relativity in determining atomic time, then give you a quick history of linear time-keeping in Western civilization. And it would all be accurate from the most encyclopedic memory of any man I've ever known. He was always ready to offer voluminous commentary on every conceivable subject.

Also, he was so completely bald that his head mirrored traffic along the highway — even on a cloudy day.

As Lou and another deputy drove us out to the Clown's Den, we were advised to maintain our disguise at all costs. We were never to reveal our identities or where we were from. "Above all," we were told, "don't tell anyone why you are there. That'll blow our cover sky high."

Whatever misgivings Jim and I had about the venture were confirmed when Lou pulled his car onto a side road, where we met another van of deputies. They told us they were in radio contact with other vans of deputies who were parked strategically on the surrounding hilltops. It became evident to Jim and me that they were fully prepared to raid the place that night.

I protested, "Look, this wasn't in the bargain. If you raid this place tonight, regardless of how you try explain it, it's gonna come out in the newspapers that the Clown's Den was raided — and caught in that raid were the Reverend Father Eugene Todd and the Reverend Dr. James Clark."

"We've got you covered so well, Father," the deputies said, "that if a raid takes place, we'll whisk you and Doctor Clark out a back door into a concealed car already waiting there for you. You'll have deputy Lou Perna sitting directly behind you, and we've got another undercover agent directly in front of you. They'll be your private bodyguards should anything break loose."

It was too late, we had been framed.

"Don't worry, Father," the deputy reassuringly said. "The sheriff is gonna make damn sure nothing happens to the two of you. Now here's your money for the cover charge, and cash for all the drinks you wanna order. Enjoy yourselves and don't worry about a thing. Just keep your eyes open as to what's going on."

Jim and I walked in and sat beside one another in the dimly lit, seamy place. Lou quietly took his seat behind us at another table. Our private bodyguard in front of us winked his assurance that we were covered. The air was so thick with cigarette smoke you could cut it with a knife. We both ordered a beer and settled in for our night of high espionage.

"Our first dancer this evening is Fi-Fi from Brazil," the loudspeakers announced.

Out she came, lavishly dressed in her sequined outfit. She was not bad-looking at all, with bouncing boobs the size of limp basketballs pumped full of silicone. The place was packed with noisy young men, most in their twenties with military haircuts, who cheered and applauded Fi-Fi on and on. First she peeled off her flimsy see-through blouse and tossed it over a chair. She made her flirtatious rounds on an elevated stage, mounted as if it were a giant table, bordered on all four sides by spectators sitting up to it, casually sipping their drinks. Back and forth she paraded. Finally, she unsnapped her tights and tossed them to the chair. Other articles of clothing followed, until she was down to her G-string, behind which men were stuffing dollar bills. Her admiring throng of fans cheered and howled. She made her grand exit and disappeared behind the curtains.

"Our next dancer is the vivacious Tootsie from Venice."

A flaming redhead, she gave much the same performance. To this day Jim and I disagree as to which gave the better performance. I say Fi-Fi, and he sticks loyally to his redhead, Tootsie.

After about the sixth dancer, the whole thing had become terribly boring.

Basking in our anonymity, Jim and I relaxed and ordered another round of beers — on the county, of course. This really wasn't a bad job after all. Free porno shows, free drinks, free private bodyguard protection— pretty good for a couple of jaded preachers. If ever we failed in the ministry, we mused, here was the possibility of a second career for both of us. We could serve God and country as undercover vice agents — snooping out the county morals. The God squad!

After the first cadre of dancers had done their thing, they began mingling with the male customers, still wearing their skimpy outfits, hawking exotic drinks from the bar. The "mother superior of the striptease sisterhood," as she called herself, took center stage and tried her hand as a sex comedian. She explained that she had allowed both her age and weight to remove herself from further consideration as only a "sex object."

Her attempt at comedy was terrible. She tried keeping the audience interested by asking the men to list all the different names they had for parts of the female anatomy — to see how they differed from state to state, she said. Not a very objective survey, I might add. Mostly they were old names, but then there were a few I had never heard.

Suddenly, pointing directly at me, she shouted into the microphone, "Hey, you back there, the cowboy wearing the big white hat — what state are you from?"

I remembered the solemn admonition from the deputy — *whatever you do, don't tell anyone who you are or where you're from.*

"Montana," I shouted back. Partly true, our northern Wyoming ranch was located near the Montana border.

"What town in Montana?" she shrieked.

"Billings," I hollered back. Again, partly true — everyone in northern Wyoming shops regularly in Billings. Dad trucked our cattle to the livestock auction there.

"What do you cowboys call it up there in Billings, Montana?"

I shouted back my word.

"Jesus Christ," she mutters into the microphone. "Clinical! You're not a cowboy but some goddamned doctor or something. Cowboys don't talk like that."

Then turning to the crowd, "Do you think that's how Montana cowboys talk to their sweethearts using clinical medical words like that?"

"Hell NO!" — came the loud choral response from the noisy horde of men. She had something going now with the crowd, and she was playing it to the hilt. She wanted to keep up the momentum.

Pointing to Jim next, she called, "Hey, you back there — the guy with the shiny bald head, sittin' beside the cowboy with the big hat — what state are you from?"

Jim's bald head turned as red as a lighted Christmas ornament.

Without looking up, staring into his beer, he held up his little finger and softly mumbled, "Same state."

"You mean Montana?"

Jim nodded, still looking down.

"What town in Montana?"

Jim held up the one little finger and again softly mumbled, "Same town."

"You mean Billings, where the cowboy's from?"

Jim nodded, without looking up.

"What do you call it up there?"

Jim held up the same little finger, gulped, and muttered, "Same thing."

I punched Jim in the ribs and whispered, "Jim, you have a Ph.D. and Ph.D.'s are supposed to be more original than that."

After all, my lie was half true — if you stretched it a bit. But his was mopped up right off the barroom floor. Copycat plagiarism is unethical for any Ph.D. — even if it's bravado from a striptease joint.

Let's face it, for a learned scholar with an encyclopedic memory and a Ph.D., it was a very dumb answer — and a royal cop-out. One would think that if an ordained Presbyterian minister has been pre-destined by God (stemming from the theological *doctrine of pre-destination* which Presbyterians formerly believed back in the days of John Calvin) — to tell a lie for a noble cause — it should at least be intelligent and convincing. His lie was neither. Even his favorite Tootsie slapped her forehead in disbelief over that one. He's got to do better than that, I thought, or he's gonna blow our sting operation sky high.

And it did.

The oversized mistress of ceremonies had the crowd in the palm of her hand now. She grabbed the mike and bellowed, "Hey, everyone here — take a good look at those two birds sittin' back there. The cowboy in the big white hat and that kook with the shiny bald head sittin' beside him. Do you know who them guys are? Take a good look at 'em back there by the exit door. Does anyone here recognize them two dudes?"

Every eye became focused on the two of us. More people in that striptease joint on that Friday night than the combined congregations of St. Mark's Episcopal Church and First Presbyterian Church on any Sunday morning — except Easter. Even Fi-Fi stood up to get a better look over the sea of heads all turned our way.

"Well, I know who they are and I know why they're here," she squealed. "Do you want me to tell you why them two bastards are here?"

The place turned deathly silent. Had some snitch tattled?

I saw our private bodyguard, sitting in front of us, stiffen and slowly extend his hand inside his jacket toward his concealed holster. The riot was about to begin.

"They are here because . . . " she screamed, pointing her arm straight toward us, wagging her finger. My blood froze. Jim's bald head flushed crimson.

"They are here because . . ." she hesitated, holding everyone in suspense.

". . . because," she screamed, "THEY ARE BOTH SEX PERVERTS!"

She scored her biggest laugh of the evening. And we got out of there, telling Lou something he already knew — that although the show was lewd and obscene, it was no worse than what you can watch on late-night television. Its most grievous sin was frivolous sexuality and licentious boredom, neither of which were against the law.

Shortly thereafter, Jim resigned his pastorate at First Presbyterian to pursue private research for the writing of a book. Even though he was my friend and colleague, I never had the nerve to ask him what kind of private research he was doing because I feared what he might tell me.

And I labored on faithfully in the vineyard of the Lord — as the only publicly proclaimed sex pervert in the Cheyenne ministry.

The poor sheriff lost the election — bungled by his perverted God squad!

✧

Ginger had a lot of spunk.

She was a working mother with three kids at home. She brought them regularly to Sunday school. She could manage any adversity with an unlimited capacity for hard work and remarkable emotional maturity. She was the kind of a woman who could have traveled the Oregon Trail in 1854, who, after the oxen gave out, would have pulled the covered wagon all by herself with her husband laid up inside with a sprained ankle.

With more an air of practicality than emotion, she told me that her husband, Wade, was having an affair with Allie, his best friend's wife. At least, she strongly suspected they were having an affair. When she confronted Wade, he denied it. When she confronted Allie, she denied it. She went to Ralph, Wade's best friend and Allie's husband, but he preferred to look the other way.

"So everyone is in denial but me," she said. "Wade and Allie tried to convince me that I'm the one who's crazy. Maybe I am. But I don't think so."

Ginger told me she was committed to this marriage with Wade and was determined to hold their family together. She admitted that they needed marriage counseling. "But how can we succeed with marriage counseling when Wade says there's nothing wrong except my unfounded suspicions? That I'm the only one who's crazy?"

It was apparent to Ginger that the only way she could break the deadlock would be to actually catch Wade and Allie in bed together. "Until that happens, nothing will change," she steadfastly maintained.

I didn't see her for a good long while. Then early one morning she called, breathless. "Is there any way you can squeeze me in to see you this morning, within the next hour if possible? I know this is short notice, but this is an emergency and I need to see you as quickly as possible."

As soon as she took her seat in my study, she blurted, "Well, I did it! I caught 'em. Boy, did I catch 'em!"

I'll let her tell the story — exactly the way she told it to me.

"I happened to be driving downtown early last night when I spotted Wade driving our camper west on Nineteenth Street. I wondered why in the world he was heading out that way. So I just followed him to the outskirts of town and sure enough, he pulled up into an open lot beside a parked car. I immediately recognized that it was Allie who climbed out of her car and slid into the seat with Wade — and off they drove, continuing west until they left town and were headed out into the open country.

"I flipped off my lights and trailed them, keeping far enough behind that they couldn't tell a car was following, and yet close enough that their taillights kept me posted as to where the road twisted and turned. I soon realized they were headed out toward Granite Lake. Damn them, I thought. After about ten miles, I saw Wade pull his camper off the highway and down a road leading into a campsite just down over the ridge. I knew now where they were headed. It was to a campsite where we often camped overnight with the kids. Damn him.

"Finally, they stopped. They shut off their lights. I stopped my car and shut off the ignition. All was quiet. I saw them climb out of the front seat and go around to the back door of the camper — and in they went. Damn them.

"I waited a little while. Then I slowly got out of my car and tiptoed down the road — Indian style, like a cat sneaking up on a mouse nibbling cheese, but so carefully and quietly that I couldn't even hear my own footprints in the dirt road."

By this time, I was sitting on the edge of my chair.

She continued, "Finally, I made it up to the cab. I could hear them inside the camper. But I took no chances. Slowly, ever so slowly, I opened the door on the driver's side. The keys were left in the ignition. Gradually, I lifted myself up into the driver's seat. I braced myself. Then I took a deep breath and hit it!"

"You hit it?"

"I hit it," Ginger repeated. "Boy, did I ever hit it. All in one motion, I switched on the ignition, threw it into gear, and away we went. I took a big loop in the flat beside the lake and headed back toward the road. I shifted into high gear and shoved the gas pedal to the floor. I was hittin' nearly sixty when I swerved onto the highway and then I shoved it up to as fast as that ol' Chevrolet could go. I also kept swervin' it back and forth, slammin' them up against one wall and then the next.

"I could hear 'em pounding on the cab, but I wasn't about to stop. I roared into Cheyenne and picked up my first cop car, a highway patrolman, after I ran two stop signs. When I raced through my first red light downtown, a police car joined up with the highway patrolman. When I raced through my third red light a second police car joined the chase. Now there were three cop cars in hot pursuit. But I knew better than to slow down or come to a stop because Wade and Allie would have jumped out. I wasn't gonna give 'em that chance 'til I got where I was headin'."

"My Lord, Ginger, where were you heading?"

"To Ralph's house! Finally, I swerved into his driveway and slammed on the brakes. Out of the house came Ralph, running and shouting, 'What in the hell is going on here?' I leaped out of the cab and raced toward the back of the camper and yanked open the door.

"Out tumbled Wade and Allie wrapped only in sheets and blankets! There they were, in the blinding glare of the headlights of three police cars, with sirens still whining away and their red and blue lights flashing. Talk about getting caught with your pants down. Both of 'em. Boy, did they look sheepish.

"And you should've seen poor mortified Ralph. He cupped his hands over both ears, with his mouth wide open in shock, and kept turning from Wade to Allie and then to the police, all the while shouting, 'Will someone please tell me what in the hell's goin' on here?' Of course, with hands cupped over both ears he couldn't hear the answer he didn't want to hear. So I hollered extra loud to him, 'Just what I've been tellin' you what was goin' on between my husband and your wife. Ralph, does this make a believer out of you? Or are you gonna keep your eyes closed and ears covered so that you can't see what's goin' on right under your nose?'

"By this time the officers grabbed me by the arms and whisked me back to the patrol car and down to the police station. Thank God for that. They got me away from Wade and Allie and Ralph — all wildly confronting each other, in full view of half the neighborhood, who came pouring out of their houses to see what was happening."

I was spellbound as I listened to the unfolding drama.

Ginger rose from her chair and moved to the window of my study and stood there, looking out for only a moment, without saying a word. Soon she whirled around, facing me, and said rather calmly, "Well, no one's in denial anymore."

And then with a mischievous look on her face she asked, "Tell me, Gene, what do you think of what I've done?"

"Ginger, that is the most astonishing story I have ever heard — or read about — or have seen in the movies. Please give me permission to tell this story if ever I write a book."

"I will," she laughed nervously, "as long as you don't use our real names."

We talked a little while about where she went from here with her life and marriage. Counseling was definitely in the works now that the game of denial was over. "Now maybe we can quit being ridiculous and get serious about working on our marriages," she said while leaving.

I stood in front of the window, looking out onto Central Avenue as I watched her drive away. On sudden impulse, I put on my coat and cap and headed out for the police station. There I met the arresting officers. And for the first and only time in my life, I arranged to have a traffic ticket "fixed." It can be done, you know, especially when a crime is so extraordinarily ingenious that the offender deserves a court award instead of a fine. Catching her husband in his adulterous affair, then chauffeuring the pair into town, still trapped in their camper bed, accompanied with a three-car police escort — is high drama destined for the silver screen. I'll admit that someone could have been hurt. But as it turned out, no one was harmed except the guilty culprits, who deserved their public humiliation.

I took the officers to lunch. After their dutiful lecture, they joined me in hilarious laughter and admitted that in their entire police career they had never seen anything quite like this.

To this day, whenever I see Ginger and Wade — who did preserve their marriage, by the way, because counseling was cheaper and more practical than a divorce — I say to myself, *Ginger, how I admire you. That was truly an original first-class act.*

After hearing hundreds of priestly confessions, I also commend Ginger's zest for living. She'll never have to confess the sin of boredom.

✧

One of the few privileges of an Episcopal rector is the selection of a new communion wine in conjunction with his altar guild. These good ladies, week in and week out, keep the church a place where people can worship the Lord in the beauty of holiness. Yet the congregation, as a rule, never sees the good work they do, because they perform their reverent duties faithfully before and after each service, when there's no one around.

Selecting a new communion wine is serious business in most Episcopal churches. It certainly was at St. Mark's.

A liquor store that carried a broad selection of high-quality wines sent six red wines to us at St. Mark's, from which we were to make our final choice. The altar guild director and her six team captains met with me in the guild room for a wine-tasting party late in the afternoon. We carefully opened each bottle and passed it around, first sniffing each one's vintage aroma. Some wines are quite fragrant. Then we gingerly poured a little sample into each of our miniature glasses for the taste test. Around and around the room we went until most of the bottles were almost half empty. With six bottles and six women, plus myself, this meant that each of us had consumed nearly half a bottle. However, we were still sober enough to make our final selection, a full-bodied red wine that was mellow and rich tasting. This wine was destined to become the sacramental Presence of Christ in our future services of Holy Communion.

The liquor store delivered a large case containing four one-gallon jugs of the newly selected port wine. One jug was kept in the sacristy for active use of the Altar Guild in setting up for Holy Communion; the rest were stored away in the original case.

A month later, Elsie, the altar guild director, asked where I had stored the extra case of wine. I told her I hadn't. I thought she had taken care of that. She hadn't. So we both went looking and we couldn't find it. The church sexton hadn't seen it either. Puzzled, we ordered a second case of port.

A month later, the second case turned up missing.

Exasperated, Elsie and I decided to order a third case and store it in a specific location in the inner storage room of the sacristy. We even marked the event on the calendar. But three weeks later the altar guild team came to me and said that when it went to get another jug of wine from the reserve supply that only one bottle was left in the case. What had happened to the other two?

No one knew.

Furthermore, Elsie determined that the active jug was lasting no more than a week, when it should have provided all the communion wine for a month. She requested that the altar guild teams mark each bottle, which they did. But then the communion wine miraculously diluted itself from a deep dark red to a blushed rosé and finally to white Chablis, which was nothing more than pure water. This was the reverse of the first miracle that Christ performed, at a wedding in Cana of Galilee.

We knew by now that someone was nipping at the jug. But who? That was the question.

Elsie and I carefully went over the list of altar guild members. Alice was a recovering alcoholic and perhaps in relapse. Elsie ordered the team captain to keep close tabs on her. But the wine kept disappearing at an ever-increasing rate, even when Alice was in the hospital, so we concluded we had a secret boozer in our midst who obviously was needing intervention.

I asked the sexton to change the locks on both the outer and inner door of the sacristy. Elsie distributed the new keys only to the team captains, with instruction that they alone were to unlock the inner sacristy and lock up after each celebration of the eucharist. I couldn't even access that inner sanctum where the wine was stored.

But this didn't work either. We were losing wine faster than we could buy it. So I ordered the sexton to construct a simple strong box, made of heavy wood planking, secured with a padlock with its key hidden in a place known only to Elsie.

Elsie and I went over the list of altar guild members for a second time, and she reported that morale was slipping, with all the good ladies suspecting one another and a few suspecting me. This I could understand because, by now, I was beginning to suspect Elsie. As a matter of fact, I thought she was reacting defensively, a little off-center, whenever we discussed the mystery of the disappearing wine. After all, she was the only one who knew where the secret key was hidden.

The sorry debacle was rapidly getting out of hand.

I remembered Joseph Cook, the founding father of St. Mark's Church, writing in his 1868 diary of arriving late to a meeting and discovering his vestry drunk. What would I do, I wondered, if I came to church some Saturday morning and found my altar guild in the same maudlin condition? I don't ever remember a seminary lecture on how a priest is supposed to handle a boozin' altar guild that was pickled, plastered, smashed, and soused to the gills.

And then the mystery was solved.

Whenever I have a wedding rehearsal, I take great pride in rehearsing every detail with ushers, musicians, bridal party, groom, groomsmen — even parents and grandparents. It has always been my philosophy that if you anticipate everything that could go wrong you could keep it from happening. Then everything goes perfectly, like clockwork, at the wedding itself.

The sexton was instructed, and paid extra, to open all the church doors two hours before a scheduled wedding so that everyone in the bridal party had plenty of time to dress and get ready for the nuptial rites. There was no need for me to be around, because we had thoroughly rehearsed every detail the night before. Normally, I would appear at the church about twenty minutes before the bridal procession down the aisle. Twenty minutes was usually plenty early.

However, at this particular wedding, when I arrived at the church at my regular time, only twenty minutes before it was scheduled to begin, I saw to my horror that everyone was standing out on the street — bride and groom, attendants, parents and grandparents, musicians and wedding guests, all in a state of acute anguish.

They were locked out of the church!

I quickly opened the doors, through which everyone thronged like sheep three days without water.

I raced through the church, flipping on lights, apologizing every step of the way. When I entered the hallway off the chancel I noticed that my altar guild had done an extraordinarily sloppy job in setting up the altar. There were even empty wine bottles lined up outside the sacristy door. I trashed the bottles as I dashed to the telephone the absent sexton. I'd deal later with my errant altar guild.

"Where in the hell have you been, Tim?" I shouted into the phone when he finally answered my frantic call. "We've got a wedding down here and you didn't unlock the church two hours ago like you were instructed and paid in advance to do."

"But I did," he meekly protested.

"What do you mean, Tim? The place is locked up tighter than a drum. The wedding party and guests were all standing out on the street when I arrived here only a few minutes ago. And you're supposed to be here on the premises, you know that. Everyone is as mad as hops, and I don't blame them. I'm angry too, Tim."

There was a long awkward pause and then . . .

"Geezus Chrisht, Fahsher Todd," he slurred, "I mush't have unlocked sche wrong goddamned schurch. *Hic!* Da'y all kinda look alike . . . ya know, dem' downtown schurches do. Geezus Chrisht . . . I didn't schink that priest looked musch like you when he told me I could juz leave and go home . . . 'cause, ya see, I juz ain't feelin' so good right now!"

I knew the mystery of the missing wine had been solved. But I also knew I was in deep trouble with my altar guild.

In all our deliberations with the altar guild, it never once occurred to Elsie or me that the sexton was the only person on the church staff who had a key to both the outer and inner sacristy doors. We had set him up like a fox guarding the chicken house, with instructions to keep an eye on my devout altar guild ladies, many of whom were avowed teetotalers. He watched them, all right — and learned exactly where everything was stored — including the hidden key to the strongbox.

How humiliating!

I later learned that he had been at the church earlier that morning when the altar guild was setting up for the afternoon wedding. After the women left, he dipped into what had now become his private cache of our excellent, carefully selected, sacramental communion wine. Then he staggered into St. Mary's Cathedral a block away, where he was kindly told it was "all right for him *just to leave*." Needless to say, I told him the same thing — but not until after we got him into an alcoholic treatment program.

I treated the altar guild to a lovely luncheon and tried to make my amends with a belabored apology. Being the gracious church ladies that they always are, they said they forgave me. But I really don't think they ever did.

I can't say I blame them.

✧

Right after the pope made another one of his famous denunciations of women being ordained into the Catholic priesthood, I received an invitation to address a small study-discussion group in Cheyenne. This group was committed to serious intellectual analysis of major world issues. Its membership cut across all social, political, and religious stratifications of Cheyenne society and consisted mostly of progressive Catholics, Protestants, Unitarians, and Jews — who prided themselves as being intellectually liberated in their religious pursuits.

I was honored with the invitation but burdened with the assigned topic of "What's the Objection to Ordination of Woman All About Anyway?" I was instructed to first deliver a short lecture on the subject and then lead a discussion.

Since this prestigious group represented the intelligentsia of Cheyenne, I knew I had to be well prepared. I began my research in the public library but had to move it to the theological libraries of both Iliff (Methodist) and St. Thomas (Catholic) seminaries of Denver.

I appeared before the auspicious group gathered in the spacious living room of a lovely Cheyenne home. I had far more material than what I needed for a forty-five-minute lecture-presentation and the discussion to follow. I knew most of these people or certainly knew about them, and I highly respected their intellectual curiosity. It was important that I do a good job.

I announced outright that most biblical scholars deny the existence of solid scriptural evidence which expressly forbid the ordination of women. Instead, objections to the priesthood of women essentially are within the invariable mix of the cultural, traditional, and historical vortex of Catholic Christianity. Add to this a heavy dose of the emotional reaction of men who feel their religious authority threatened — and you get the picture.

First, *tradition*. I had no more than introduced the topic when they interrupted me with the loud protest, "Gene, don't dwell on tradition. Tradition changes. At one time it was traditional for women to wear long dresses and to ride stagecoaches. Then it was trains. Now women fly in supersonic jets wearing miniskirts. Simply because it was traditional at one time for only men to be priests doesn't mean that it must remain this way forever."

They were right, of course.

Next, *culture*. Again I was interrupted by a chorus of objections, "Culture changes. It once was cultural for blacks to be slaves of white people. But that cultural attitude was dead wrong and it was rightfully changed. Past culture doesn't justify the future."

Of course, they were right.

Well, as a last resort, let's try *history*. Again a chorus of objections the moment I mentioned the word. They shook their heads and said, "History simply explains the past — it doesn't predict what the future should be. It was a historical fact that women were not allowed to vote, own property, or even earn their own salary until the Wyoming Territorial Legislature changed all that back in 1868. No one in their right mind would justify denying woman suffrage today simply because it was historically forbidden since the dawn of civilization."

Of course, they were right again.

The only problem was, my carefully prepared lecture was wiped out. There was nothing more I could say to these intellectual snobs, so I gathered up my notes from the podium and plopped myself into a chair.

Noting my irritation, they pleaded, "Gene, if objections to the priesthood of women are not rooted in holy scripture — it certainly has to be grounded in something more profound than the cultural, historical, and traditional practices of the past. History tells us that all those things change on a rather predictive pattern either by evolution or revolution, wouldn't you say?"

I nodded.

"Well, then what is it? There must be a profound theological or philosophical reason, perhaps psychological, why women cannot function as priests as authentically as men. Why God wouldn't call a woman into the priesthood as genuinely as a man?"

I shrugged my shoulders — still miffed at their outright dismissal of my magnificent lecture. After all, I was invited there to explain objection to the ordination of women — not to justify and defend it.

"Come on, Gene," they pleaded, trying to soothe my aggravation. "Don't be offended. We highly respect your intellectuality and spirituality. Yet you're a clergyman with a lot of common sense and a terrific sense of humor. We invited you here because we thought you were uniquely gifted to enlighten us on a topic we simply don't understand. Pray tell, what is it that makes people so adamantly opposed to the ordination of women? The real reason is that it's some big psychological thing about women, isn't it? Come out with it. Tell us the bottom line."

They had me. Not only had they shredded the thesis of my presentation, but had pushed me into a corner of no logical retreat. Even I was curious as to where I could possibly go from there with their final ultimatum.

I fidgeted with my teacup for a moment and finally said, "Well, you've pushed me into a corner on this one. You say you really want to know the bottom line, right?"

They all nodded and shifted forward in their chairs to hear my words of wisdom on the subject — now that I had accepted their challenge.

"If you really want to know, as you say you do, then I will tell you why it is that women can't be priests and men can."

The place turned very quiet. I had suddenly become the latest male authority defining the universal role of womanhood, not only to women themselves, but also for the church and human society. Even for God. Men have been adept at pontificating on this topic for 5000 years — including patriarchs, emperors, popes, and village clerics. Why shouldn't I have my crack at it now?

"No, you're wrong. It's not a big thing about women at all, as you've suggested." I answered. "Actually, it's a little thing about men!"

"Pray tell, what?" they gasped.

"You see," I began, "it all has to do with a little thing we call a penis. If you have a penis you can be anything you want to be in the kingdom of God on earth or in heaven beyond. You can be a priest, bishop, archbishop, cardinal, and pope. You can head up any religious institution or movement in the world. You see, it's not your brain or even your immortal soul that becomes the determinative factor — it's whether you have this little thing we call a penis. If you don't have that, regardless of your qualifications — you ain't gonna make it. It's just that simple!"

There wasn't a smile in the room. Only faces of serious intent.

I went on. "Now we've had many enduring symbols in Christianity but mostly the sign of a fish and the cross. Maybe it's time for a new one. We can put the immortal phallic symbol atop our church spires and hang it above our altars, not as an object of worship but as a public announcement to the world of our holy reverence for the spiritual supremacy of the male human form when it comes to deciphering the ultimate will of God and channeling His sacramental grace to His people of the earth. That only the male human form can validate an intermediary role between God and His creation. That only the male human form can determine whatever is truly religious in the affairs of humankind. Let's face it, God knows that the female human form is simply missing something very important which only the male has — to make all these holy things happen."

The place was strangely quiet.

"The only problem with all of this, as we approach the twenty-first century, is the modern world of incredible medical advances. Surgical sex changes, with hormonal therapy, are becoming more prevalent and more successful. So it's surely bound to happen, sooner than later, that a whole convent of nuns will acquire penile implants and then present themselves to the bishop as candidates for the male order of the holy priesthood!"

Absolute silence prevailed. They were hanging on every word.

"And that would be enough," I concluded, "to cause any good bishop to piss his pants."

The place exploded with laughter and applause.

Needless to say, they got the point. They poured themselves another round of coffee and tea, cut the cake, and we had a wonderful discussion. After all, prevention of ecclesiastical incontinence is as good a reason as any for rabid objection to female priests.

Absurdity aside, during the following conversation, I seriously stated that I found it exceedingly odd for male priests to argue that women, by virtue of their gender, can't present the sacramental Presence of Christ to the world in the Mass — when, to begin with, God Himself chose a woman (Mary) to present the physical Presence of Christ to the world in the flesh at his birth in Bethlehem. Conceivably our heavenly father, in His infinite wisdom, could certainly have had Jesus descend to the earth fully formed in His mature personhood, without benefit of an earthly mother and father, fully asexual, at the beginning of Christ's ministry — as easily as God had Him ascend to the heavens following His resurrection at the close of His ministry.

However one might want to discuss the issue, the group came to see that although objections to the priesthood of women are usually justified on intellectual grounds, the base objection is more emotional than theological. It doesn't do much good to argue the question rationally because it's primarily an emotional issue to begin with, which by definition means that it defies logical reasoning.

It was a wonderful evening — in spite of the fact that my lecture was wiped out at its very beginning, causing me to go home and throw away all my written notes with the resolution that I would never accept an invitation to speak on this subject again.

A week later I received a phone call from a woman with a sweet soft voice, who spoke with collegiate articulation, "Father Todd, this is Sister Rose Marie from Denver. You don't know me. But one of my dearest friends in Cheyenne attended the study-discussion group the other night where you spoke on the priesthood of women. They said you gave a most interesting presentation . . ."

"I most certainly did not, Sister," I said, interrupting her. "They yanked the rug right out from under me and I had nothing left to say. They are a bright bunch."

"My friends, who are devout Catholics, but progressive Catholics, nevertheless, were very impressed with what you had to say. They said you had a most interesting theory as to why women should not be ordained to the holy priesthood. Please tell me, Father Todd, what it was you said?"

"Sister, I really don't think you want to know."

"But really I do, Father Todd. They said you stated it had something to do with human anatomy. Is that right?"

"With male anatomy," I said, trying to be a bit more precise without playing my full hand until I found out where she was coming from. I was feeling pressed. I hunched that she knew exactly what I had said and was pushing me to repeat it. What I didn't know was what her particular angle of attack was going to be once I came out with it.

"It had everything to do with the male genitalia," I explained, "If you had the genitals of a male you could become anything in the kingdom of God that you were qualified to become."

I felt myself blushing because never before have I had such a frank conversation with a nun.

"Well, Father Todd, you are exactly right. When everything else has been said and done, when every theological tome has been fully explored, and every biblical exposition thoroughly plumbed, and every historical tradition hung out to dry — it all boils down to whether you have a penis. You hit it right on the head."

I wondered if the pun was intended but decided to ignore it.

After all, this was Sister Rose Marie, a Roman Catholic nun, on the other end of the line. Someone I didn't know but whose religious vocation I highly respected. Many nuns are on the new cutting edge of feminism within the Catholic Church. These articulate women are intellectually assertive and doctrinally liberated — who dismiss the traditional timeworn arguments against ordination of women as Jesuit casuistry at its worst.

But I didn't have long to think about it because Sister Rose Marie asked, "Father Todd, are you familiar with the old cowboy ballad entitled "Laredo"? The part that goes, *I can tell by your outfit that you are a cowboy?*"

Yes, I was very familiar with it.

"Here's my version of that old classic," as she softly chanted into the phone the old western tune with her new version of words:

I can tell by your outfit that you can be a bishop
You can tell by my outfit I can't be one, too.
But if us gals all get implants, then we can all become bishops
My O my, what will the Holy Mother do?

Tell me, what do you think of our new song?"

Silence on my end of the line was soon interrupted with peals of background laughter — and then I knew that apparently the whole sisterhood was listening in on the conversation through the use of a speaker phone.

In retrospect, some of my dearest and closest Episcopal friends don't like the idea of women priests either. Even my wife, Rosemary, isn't convinced she likes it all that much. But they openly admit that their objections primarily are emotional and not theological. I have great respect for their strongly held position even though I may disagree with it. A feeling is neither right or wrong by itself. Honestly admitting an emotional feeling is honorable and therapeutic. But masking our emotional position by convoluting it into a commandment of God and parading it around as the rationale of the Almighty instead of our own concealed irrationality is playing God both with others and ourselves.

I believe that the surrender of celibacy and the priesthood of women within the Catholic Church is a *historical imperative* — meaning by that, its time in history is coming soon and nothing on earth can stop it. The time warp will automatically adjust itself.

As I've written earlier, I have never equated celibacy with holiness of life or purity of spirit. Nor with gender, I now hasten to add.

However, I must admit that after this conversation with Sister Rose Marie, I always smile whenever I hear that immortal line from the old "Laredo" classic — *I can tell by your outfit that you are a cowboy.* For some reason, it conjures up a whole new image for me which I never had before.

✧

I retired from St. Mark's early in 1992. However after living in church-owned housing all my ministry, I came to the end of my career with no established equity in a home. Rosemary and I decided to purchase a townhome on the northern edge of Cheyenne, where all the new commercial and residential growth was occurring. Furthermore, we purchased the townhouse before it was even built so we could custom-design its interior to accommodate a formal dining room, solid cherry wood kitchen cabinets, marble gas fireplace in the living room, and a rather large master bedroom and double baths. Although our new townhome was smaller than Templeton House, we were determined that it would be every bit as elegant.

Jerry Plumley did much of the finish carpentry work, and I was his continual sidekick. How lucky I was to have Jerry around; I could describe what I wanted done, and he had the skilled expertise to do it perfectly. In this manner I designed and helped Jerry build me a new library-study in the basement and a room to accommodate my broadcast-recording studio.

When it came to painting the newly finished basement rooms, I contacted Job Services, a state employment agency. Throughout the years I've had exceptionally good luck using spot labor from Job Services to help me with many physical tasks. Remembering a lesson learned from my father in dealing with hired men or the German POWs on our ranch, I always treated these temporary workers respectfully and made certain they had coffee breaks, sandwiches for lunch, and snacks in late afternoon. And always I worked alongside as well as eating with them.

Job Services lined me up with a man living in a skid row hotel who was between alcoholic binges and needed a little extra cash before he embarked on his next one.

"I am a Polack," John said, rather proudly. "It's okay to call ourselves Polacks, we just don't like it when others call us that. But I was born and raised in a solid Polack neighborhood of old Chicago where everything was Polish, including the Polish Catholic Church."

Early on I sensed that John assumed I was a Roman Catholic priest, since Job Services always referred to me as Father Todd.

"Yes, *Fahtha*, whatever you say, *Fahtha*, I will do. I do everything my good priest tells me to do, *Fahtha*," he'd say, always giving the word *Fahtha* a soft *reverential* pronunciation.

No Episcopalian would be caught dead talking reverentially like that to his Anglican priest.

I could tell that John was baiting me for a discussion on religious matters, which I was avoiding, because I wasn't paying him good wages by the hour to discuss religion. Not even if he paid me was I going to waste valuable work time discussing religion. I hired him to help me paint the basement. That was it, no more and no less.

John had a personal tic: In response to anything you said, he would reflexively say, "What the hell why not." He would run all the words together as if they were one long hyphenated word with many syllables: *What-the-hell-why-not.*

"John, we're going to paint today," I would say.

What-the-hell-why-not.

"We're going to apply flat paint to the walls and gloss on the ceiling."

What-the-hell-why-not.

"And I'm going to start you out in the far bedroom while I take the study-library room, and we'll eventually end up painting our way toward one another in the long hallway that connects the two."

What-the-hell-why-not.

At first, his nervous tic was more an irritant to me than anything else. But as the day progressed it became increasingly amusing because it was so repetitive.

"John I've made you a cheese sandwich."

What-the-hell-why-not.

"How about a Coke or a cup of coffee?"

What-the-hell-why-not.

Sometimes I would have to turn my head and chuckle to myself. It was a perfectly harmless nervous tic but the kind you have to look out for — if you don't watch it, you'll end up doing it, too.

By late afternoon, we both had finished our respective rooms and were now painting toward one another in the connecting hallway. Now that we were in close range of one another, he started in on religion again.

"*Fahtha,* I just gotta tell you that there's a lot of things I don't like that's goin' on in our church these days. And there's a lot of things I do like. But mostly the things I don't like — like all these changes since Vatican II."

I decided to play along with it as if I were a Catholic priest, which he was still assuming, just to see where the conversation might lead us.

"Tell me, John, what don't you like?"

"*Fahtha,* back in our Polish neighborhood of Chicago the old priest ruled that parish with an iron hand. If you tried sneaking in to receive Holy Communion without being to confession the night before, he remembered because he could tell by the sound of your voice in the confessional, and he not only passed you by, but would shake his finger at you in full view of the whole congregation and say, 'Shame on you.' These days, we don't have priests like that anymore."

"Is that right?" I was trying to play it safe.

"*Fahtha,* the Polish Catholic Church is the elite branch of Roman Catholicism in the whole world today. *What-the-hell-why-not.* No wonder they chose a Polish pope when the cardinals decided to elect a non-Italian pope for the first time in centuries."

"Is that right?"

"Of course I'm right, *Fahtha.* You know that yourself. *What-the-hell-why-not.* As a boy I would go to Mass in that old Polish neighborhood parish church, and it would all be in Latin. The sermon would all be in Polish. We couldn't understand a damn word that was said — either in Latin or in Polish. But — *what-the-hell-why-not* — we went to church anyway. There was a holy mystery to it all. Incense rising up so thick you couldn't see the altar. Murals painted up the wall and across the ceiling. Addressing God in sacred foreign languages. The strait-laced old Polish priest, tottering back and forth, telling us everything we were supposed to do with our lives. The old way of doin' things, *Fahtha.* Now don't get me wrong, *Fahtha,* I like some of the new changes, *Fahtha* — but the old way of doin' things was the best, *Fahtha.*"

Right then the wall phone rang. He couldn't avoid overhearing my private telephone conversation. It was Rosemary wanting to know how late we would be working so she could plan dinner. I told her, "Give us two hours here to finish up. Rosemary, instead of your cooking dinner why don't we just go out and eat somewhere? And then, honey, let's go home and go straight to bed. I'm beat!"

I hung up the phone.

Without missing a single stroke of his brush, John casually asked, almost as if it were an aside, "Your housekeeper, *Fahtha?*"

I thought —*What-the-hell-why-not!*

So I answered, "Yes, she is my housekeeper and my cook. She is also my lover and my wife. By now we have eleven grandchildren."

John's brush froze to the wall. Out of the corner of my eye I watched him. His jaw dropped wide open. His face drained ashen. Not a muscle of his body flinched. I could see that he was running the tape of my words back and forth in his head, trying to process this startling new byte of raw information.

He stood there like a statue, fully a minute it seemed — then relaxed, dropped his arm to his side, still holding the brush, turned to me, shrugged his shoulders, and with a devilish grin winked his eye and said, "*What-the-hell-why-not, Fahtha!*"

He flipped the brush into his bucket of paint and wiped his hands.

"Now that's a change I like in our church today," he eagerly explained. "Celibacy is for the birds. Every good Catholic knows that. Why do you suppose we Catholics have these big Catholic families if we all thought celibacy was such a good thing?"

Warming up to his cause, he further expounded, "The only ones who say they believe in celibacy are the popes and bishops and priests. And the only reason you guys keep talking about it all the time is because you're just trying to convince yourselves it's such a good thing. No one else believes all that nonsense anymore."

He hesitated for a moment and then chided, "You priests delude yourselves into believing that since you're celibate we laymen think you're extra holy. Wrong. We just think you're a little queer."

Seeing that I was almost ready to crack up, John added, "Celibacy is priestly fanaticism, *Fahtha*. Really it is. All us Catholics are too busy making a living and supporting our families to pay any attention to it anymore. We've got more important things to do. *Fahtha*, I'm glad you went ahead and married your housekeeper. *What-the-hell-why-not*. Everyone knew you were sleeping with her. *What-the-hell-why-not*. I wish more priests would do that."

By this time I was doubled over with laughter. The poor guy could not see why it seemed so funny, so I invited him up into the kitchen for a Coke and explained that I was an Anglo-Catholic priest, not a Roman Catholic priest.

After thinking it over, he found it funny, too.

However, he still signified the inevitable tension facing not only modern-day Catholicism, but indeed all of Christendom — clinging to the past while embracing the necessity of change for the future — with a paradoxical attitude, in between, of *what-the-hell-why-not*.

And Polack John gave me a new working definition of religious fanaticism: *A religious fanatic is one who's only trying to convince himself that something is true while everyone else is too busy with more important things to pay serious attention to it.*

It has been said that religious sentimentality is loving something (anything) more than God does. Likewise, I would say, religious fanaticism is believing (or condemning) something even more than what God would believe or condemn.

Chapter 22

Getting ready for retirement involves far more than building a retirement home and finalizing your pension income. You must decide what creative things you're going to do in retirement. Above all, you must prepare yourself emotionally for another serious leave-taking in your life.

The first leave-taking that I remember was my slipping through the gate and heading for Piney Creek, where I nearly drowned. One more minute in the swirling floodwaters and it would have become my permanent leave-taking. Fortunately, I had many more leave-takings after that — leaving home to ride the school bus for the first grade, standing in that exact location on the highway twelve years later and catching the Burlington bus to head out for college. Graduate school, seminary, marriage, and four churches that I pastored all involved a series of leave-takings.

My most dramatic one, however, and potentially the most traumatic, was my dual leave-taking in 1992, when I retired as rector of St. Mark's Episcopal Church after a ministry there of twenty-seven years in Cheyenne — and accumulatively ending forty years in the active parochial ministry.

In preparation for retirement, I attended two training seminars in Seattle on doing interim ministry, both sponsored by the prestigious Alban Institute headquartered in Washington, D.C. This new form of ministry has become quite essential today in mainline denominational churches because of the lengthy search process involved in selecting a new minister.

At the Alban Institute, retiring ministers were asked to write out, in detail, our final farewell service at the churches we were serving. I honestly had never thought of this. Thinking it over, however, I finally decided on something that was uniquely different, yet appropriate, I thought, for this former Wyoming ranch kid. I wrote that following a typical worship service, I would walk down the long center aisle of St. Mark's behind the choir, as I've done hundreds of times before. Nothing unusual about this routine. But when I reached the church entrance, instead of greeting worshippers at the door as I normally do, I would hop on a horse borrowed from Jena Carey and gallop down Nineteenth Street. Just before I disappeared from view down the slope of the hill, I would whirl my horse around and wave my tasseled bieretta (clergy headgear) in fond farewell to a cheering congregation, glad to see the ol' parson leave — then do a Lone Ranger *Hi Ho Silver* routine and gallop off into the sunset, never to be seen again.

"Get serious," they shouted. "The art of saying good-bye is serious business and obviously you don't do it very well."

They were right.

(I still thought, however, my original idea would have been a memorable departure from historic St. Mark's Church.)

Seriously though, I realized that I have avoided good-byes most of my life. When I left the Piney Creek ranching valley, I never felt I had to say good-bye. The creek, winding down the narrow alluvial valley, would always be there. So would the willows and cottonwood trees along its banks. The peaked hills crested with twisted rock formations were eternal. So were the long draws leading up into those hills, filled with wild plum and chokecherry trees, where I played as a kid.

Girding oneself for retirement after forty years in the ministry takes some interior and exterior doing, as I discovered. But upon serious reflection — I decided that I was ready to step out and get on with other important things in life that I still wanted to do.

Years later, when I returned, everything was still there, as I had predicted — the winding creek, the beautiful trees, and picturesque hills. But gone were the ranching families I knew and loved, who worked the land and built a remarkable community. Gone were Dad and Mom and all their neighbors. Gone — and I never really told them good-bye.

After being at St. Mark's Church for twenty-seven years, for once, I needed to do my leave-taking right and boldly say good-bye.

During my last year at St. Mark's, I met every week with my two wardens, Jack Palma and Dick Waggener. With their prodding, I would talk about nothing else but emotionally wrapping up a forty-year ministry, with twenty-seven of those years spent exclusively in

Cheyenne. I cannot describe how invaluable these sessions were to me therapeutically. Jack and Dick were magnificent facilitators, helping me plumb out emotional feelings I never knew I had. These dedicated laymen became my spiritual directors.

More than that, however, they made a unique commitment to absolute confidentiality. We met for a whole year before anyone in St. Mark's or the Cheyenne community had any inkling that I was planning to take early retirement.

When the big day came on January 6, 1992, I stood before my congregation of beloved people at St. Mark's and tearfully told them good-bye. I wrote a Litany of Farewell in which both the congregation and I confessed our failures to be all that we should and could have been to one another for the twenty-seven years that our lives were intimately linked in the ministry of that great church — and we both offered forgiveness to one another. We also had a prayer of thanksgiving for all the good times we shared together and extended to each other our mutual blessings for a great future in the years ahead.

Then the choir sang once more the theme song of my entire ministry — the words more hauntingly appropriate now, at my retirement, than ever before.

My God and I go in the field together
We walk and talk as good friends should and do
We clasp our hands, our voices ring with laughter.
He tells me of the years that went before me
When heavenly plans were made for me to be
When all was but a dream of dim conception
This earth will pass, and with it common trifles
But God and I will go unendingly.

It was a wonderful service, followed with a gala reception in the parish hall and an open house in our new townhome that afternoon. Immediately following the morning service, however, I had one more pastoral call to make. Although I made it abundantly clear that I would not accept an invitation for any pastoral duty in the church — no funerals, weddings, baptisms, or pastoral calls of any kind — I did feel that I must make one more pastoral call on Joe and Margaret Steneck, parishioners both in their nineties, confined to a nursing home.

I tried telling them good-bye and they kept asking me where I was going. When I told them I was moving nowhere, but retiring in Cheyenne, they kept saying, "Oh well, then you'll keep calling on us just like you always have. And you will take care of us when we die, won't you?"

I couldn't make them understand that even though I would be retiring and living in Cheyenne, I would not be their pastor anymore. I would not even make a social call as a friend on a former parishioner, lest it be perceived as pastoral interference from a former rector. That's how determined I was not to become a detriment to the ongoing ministry of that congregation and its new rector. I even voluntarily surrendered all my keys to the church wardens so that I no longer would have physical access to the building. I was severing all ties.

As usual, Rosemary's open house that afternoon was as elegantly done as a White House reception. Old college roommates showed up, Jim Shadoan from Montana and Don Lagerlef from Oklahoma. Stan Fluharty from my first church in Padroni, Colorado, was there. Dear radio broadcasting friends from Minnesota, Terrell and Carol Metheney, helped with the table decorations and serving.

Photo taken of me with my three children at my retirement party in 1992. Barry, Lorilee, and Sheridan. The greatest satisfaction in life, I think, is to see your children mature into gracious adulthood — who bestow the gift of love and laughter to their own children and to the world around them.

All my children were there with the exception of one stepdaughter, Kim. Someone took a picture of me with my three children Lori, Barry, and Sheri.

On Monday evening the church sponsored a retirement banquet-dance at the Hitching Post. Jim Parrish put together a video on my life, which was fun to watch. Governor Mike Sullivan and Secretary of State Kathy Karpan were after-dinner speakers. A *women's choice* country dance followed (one more fling in behalf of women's rights). Following the example of my eighty-eight-year-old father at his last Todd reunion, I danced with every female in my family, first with Rosemary, then my daughters and stepdaughters, and finally my granddaughters, including my youngest, Hailey,

only two years old, who placed her stocking feet on my shoes and clung
to my legs. Around and around the floor we waltzed. After midnight we
all went home exhausted.

The next morning — a typical Wyoming blizzard! Roads were closed,
traffic was snarled, and everything shut down. I switched on our new gas
fireplace and watched men, hired by the townhouse association, trying to
shovel snow off our sidewalks. The wind drifted them shut almost as fast
as they shoveled them out. But I was safely inside with my wife and family where it was warm and cozy — looking out upon the raging storm. For
the first time that I could remember in forty years, I didn't have a sermon
to prepare, a committee meeting to attend, hospital calls to make, or an
appointment to keep.

That evening Rosemary and I relaxed in a large Jacuzzi tub installed
in our modern bathroom just off the master bedroom of our new townhome. The pressurized hot-water jets and swirling steam made us feel like
privileged courtesans of the ancient Roman baths.

This was retirement!

But not for long. Almost immediately I began teaching American history
at Laramie County Community College (LCCC), where I immensely enjoyed
the intellectual stimulation of class preparation and my contact with college
students. It was rewarding to put my M.A. degree in history to good use in
a college environment where the average student was thirty-three years old,
married with three children, and highly motivated to study and participate
in classroom discussion. Not so with the traditional student, fresh out of high
school, who looked upon reading assignments as corporal punishment.

Another historical challenge for me was the invitation to edit a manuscript by Evelyn Livingston Furman about Augusta Pierce Tabor, the pioneer
wife of the famous H.A.W. Tabor — the "Silver King of Colorado." My
interest in the fascinating Tabor legacy was sparked back in my college days,
especially the tragic story of Tabor's second wife, the beautiful Baby Doe,
who because of her fortuitous marriage became the wealthiest woman in
the state. But the enormous fortune disappeared overnight following the
Silver Panic of 1893, and she lived out the remainder of her life in abject
poverty, making her home in an abandoned tool shed near the mining shaft,
where her frozen body was found in 1935.

I wrote the preface for the Tabor book and it contains a photograph of
Mrs. Furman and me standing in front of her historic, and beautifully
restored, Leadville home.

In 1994 I accepted an appointment from the Bishop of Colorado, the
likable Rt. Reverend William J. Winterrowd, to become interim rector of

My ministry came full circle — beginning with a rural church in Padroni and ending, forty years later, with my interimship at the country church near Sedalia, both in Colorado.

St. Philip-in-the-Field Episcopal Church near Sedalia. (Proving once again the timeworn adage that old priests don't retire — they're just turned out to *pastor*.) The historic little country parish church sits on a bench of land looking out upon the ascending Front Range of the Rocky Mountains. It was a picturesque frame building, constructed in 1872 by the ranch people of Plum Creek valley, surrounded by a community cemetery.

It was a homecoming of sorts for me. The surrounding countryside was remarkably similar to our Piney Creek ranching valley near the Big Horn Mountains of northern Wyoming, quiet and peaceful. The rural scenery was spectacular. I spent the first hour in my tiny new office unpacking vestments and a few books when I suddenly looked out my window — and there, no more than six feet away, stood a beautiful buck deer, poised like a statue, his head held high and ears pitched forward, watching my shadowy movement through the glass.

Where else in this world would a buck deer become the first caller on a new rector? I named him Buck, and we became friends. He would often appear when I was outside sipping tea, where he'd find me quietly sitting alone on a meditation bench in the backyard. Even when he missed his teatime visitations, I knew he came later, because the potato chips I left for him on the fence post were gone.

The Canon of the Mass is sacrosanct — that is to say, the wording is never to be changed at the whim of the priest except for rare and extreme circumstances. You can imagine the congregational shock one morning when, during our liturgical thanksgivings, they heard from me at the altar, "And we offer thee our thanksgivings for the beautiful buck deer peering through the window this very moment as we worship thee. Give us just a moment to look out upon him and honor thee for these beautiful creatures of the good earth."

One day he brought his wife, Doe, and later their Bambi to the church yard. I asked the bishop for permission to confirm this new family into the Episcopal Church.

I frequently called on my extended congregation out in the cemetery. These people became more to me than names upon their tombstones. Early one Sunday morning I discovered that a young man had committed suicide there. His Jeep was parked nearby, the door left open with a suicide note on the front seat. I knelt into the deep snow beside his emaciated body, blood still oozing from his ear and freezing. A pistol lay between his legs. His unseeing blue eyes were wide open and staring up at me. When I anointed his forehead during my prayer, his eyelids blinked — only reflex action, the coroner said.

I differed with the coroner on his age. He called him an "older fellow." I said he was still a young man who obviously had been very sick. The coroner rifled through his billfold and discovered he was only thirty-three years old — and there was an appointment card with an AIDS specialist.

At the ten o'clock worship service I reminded the congregation that our church has AIDS — just like it has cancer and heart disease. We can no longer ignore this grim reality. We might like to delude ourselves into thinking that AIDS exists only in the big city, but here it is — just outside the door of our little country church.

I called the grieving father in Denver and asked him to tell me about his boy, who was roughly the age of my son, Barry. "He was a wonderful photographer," the father said, "who had a large photo collection of old historic Colorado churches. I'm sure you'd find a color slide of St. Philip-in-the-Field in that collection."

"I'm sure that's right," I said, "and the quiet peaceful dignity

A good place to meditate and study while looking out upon the foothills of the majestic Rocky Mountains. It was here, at teatime, that my friend "Buck" frequently called on me — sometime accompanied by his beautiful wife, Doe, and their little "Bambi."

of this country setting is such that he chose this holy ground as the place where he wanted to die."

An interim ministry is not supposed to be a time when anything significant happens; you leave those issues for the new minister when he or she comes aboard. Not so with Gene Todd. The basic pattern of my forty years in the ministry quickly reasserted itself. We acquired twenty-five acres of valuable real estate surrounding the church and began drawing up long-range building plans for a larger church and parish center. As at Padroni back in the 1950s, we sketched out plans for a new bell steeple.

Once again, Gene Todd became the subject of another congregational petition — this one, that I stay for another year. And then the bishop encouraged another year after that.

But it would be incorrect to say that the membership of my little pastoral church consisted of country people in the traditional sense of the word. To be sure, descendants of the original pioneer homesteaders and valley ranchers were still there: the Curtis clan and families of Esme Couch and Louise Christiansen. All remarkable people and loyal church members. (Esme as a young woman raced horses at Cheyenne's Frontier Days back in the 1920s when beautiful ladies didn't do tomboy things like that.)

But the beautiful and peaceful ranching valley had now become an area of explosive residential growth out of south Denver with homesite lots (acreages only) selling for hundreds of thousands of dollars. These affluent corporate executives and professional people preferred country living. Hence, they became my new parishioners providing gifted leadership to our little country church. My excellent wardens, Dr. Ben Contreras and Dan Sherer, were good examples of this leadership potential. Another example would be Craig and Mary Ewing, both young lawyers, whose large Gothic horse barn would make a beautiful Episcopal church.

Also in my little parish were space scientists, associated with prestigious Lockheed Martin Astronautics, who helped engineer our national ballistic defense system, as well as design booster rockets for launching satellites, manned space crafts, including *Atlantis*, and other vehicles used in interplanetary explorations. Some of these men had Ph.D.'s in physics and space science, like Ben Contreras and Dale Neal. Others like Lad Curtis were top-rate aeronautical engineers who helped design the landing modules for Mars and Venus. Steve Wilson was proud that part of his engineering hardware was permanently mounted on the lunar surface.

Having such talented professionals in my congregation prompted me to organize an Adult Forum for Sunday-morning discussions so that these ingenious laymen could share their life work with fellow parishioners and engage us in open conversation as to the possible theological meaning of their vocational endeavors.

During one of our warden luncheons, when discussing our $75,500 church budget, Senior Warden Ben Contreras told me that he had difficulty keeping figures relative. With the merger of Lockheed and Martin Marietta, Ben was to present to the presidents of both corporations a five-year aero-space project that would cost a cool $19.2 billion. I suggested that if he just knocked off the zeros and simply compared 75.5 to 19.2 it might be easier to maintain a balanced perspective. Besides, the institution of the church was much older and larger than either of the institutions he represented, and our heavenly aerospace program extended far beyond the universe and was designed to stay aloft eternally. He allowed that my words of wisdom were truthful — but not all that helpful.

The rector of St. Philip-in-the-Field during our annual homecoming celebration. I'm wearing a clergy outfit that would have been worn by an Episcopal priest in 1872, the year the little country church was built by neighboring ranchers.

And then there was Tweet Kimball who truly lived in a stone castle perched high upon the ponderosa butte, surrounded with a panoramic view of the Rockies, a 200-mile sweep from Longs Peak to Pikes Peak, including the cities of Denver and Colorado Springs. More legendary than the castle, with its turrets outside and vaulted rooms inside, was the personage of Tweet Kimball herself. It was she who hosted HRH the Princess Anne of Great Britain during her historic visit to Denver in 1981. Since I was a temporary bachelor, Tweet often invited me to the castle for elegant dinner parties and black-tie formal gatherings where I had the privilege of becoming acquainted with the shakers and movers of corporate Colorado and Denver society. One evening of sparkling conversation in her home among the cultural and intellectual elite, from all over the world, equaled a year of multicultural study at Oxford University. (Small world, indeed. One of her uniformed butlers was born and raised in Cheyenne, Wyoming!)

And I will never forget the immortal Catie Sinclaire whose family was well connected to the good fortune of Corning Glass, who at ninety-four daily swam twenty laps in her private pool. Try as hard as I could, I could never keep up. But she had an unfair advantage — she wore fins. My consolation prize was Scotch on the rocks, served in the adjoining "Dip & Nip" club room, using smoky malted barley whiskey direct from Scotland. She was deeply religious, a delightful storyteller and a fun-loving person.

The original plan Rosemary and I worked out was that we would alternate weekends — one weekend she would join me in Sedalia, and the next weekend (Sunday afternoon, Monday and Tuesday) I would drive to Cheyenne. It didn't quite work out that way. It ended up with my spending less than one weekend a month in Cheyenne. Fortunately, Rosemary's two daughters and families also lived in Denver, which made it possible for her to visit grandchildren far more frequently than ever before.

My ministry had come full circle — from my beginning at the little country church in Padroni to a little country church in Sedalia, with Vermillion, Green River, and Cheyenne in between. It seemed appropriate that my country roots would place me among country people, and the urbanites who preferred country living — communicants I loved so dearly.

Rosemary and me in Aspen attending the Colorado Clergy Conference in 1994. What a wonderful setting for a clergy gathering.

❖

While at St. Philip-in-the-Field, I began writing this book. I knew that my life by itself had very little interest to anyone, not even for my family. Certainly nothing beyond a few introductory pages. But the six decades of my life have brought me in touch with scores of the most interesting people you'd ever want to meet. On the surface they would seem to be ordinary people who lived ordinary lives. Not so. When you got to know them they were ordinary people who lived extra ordinary lives.

The stories of these people danced in my head and I decided to write them down. I realized that my childhood habit of carrying a notebook and pencil up into the Wyoming ranch hills for solitary writing continued into my adulthood where I mentally carried a pad and pen, always looking for a story waiting to be told. My biggest challenge was selecting which stories I would tell — from those that I didn't have room to write about. Believe me, I have many other stories I would like to tell.

My mother said she would like to have written a book about all the hired men that worked on our family cattle ranch. What a story that would have been. I've thought that maybe someday I'll write a book containing the stories I've heard pallbearers recall about the deceased — while riding in a mortuary limousine to the cemetery. You wouldn't believe them.

I discovered that writing the story of my life was very therapeutic. You get a better perspective on things once you begin writing it down. Things you failed to notice about yourself because you were too busy trying to survive in a world not given to serious self-reflection.

Born into humble circumstances on a Wyoming ranch made an indelible mark upon my self-identity and the way I perceived God and the world which He created. I couldn't shake it even when I tried. The transition from a small country school to college in the big city was traumatic. My liberal education at the University of Denver, seminary training at the Iliff School of Theology, graduate study at the University of South Dakota, and later at the Virginia Theological Seminary only sharpened and enhanced the intellectual curiosity which first stirred within me as a kid out in the peaceful solitude of those Wyoming hills.

At these great institutions of higher learning, I learned the absolute necessity of constant questioning in the pursuit of knowledge and understanding. Wisdom is never directly achieved — but becomes a by-product of the pursuit. But the pursuit is a lifelong journey to be continued beyond the fleeting eight years of formal education where it only began. Those who embrace the solitude of study and quiet reflection must at some time confront the world with a life of public service.

My life of public service was serving God and His people within the vocational calling of the Christian ministry. I discovered that its rigors pounded me hard into the person that I've always been in the process of becoming.

I have come to appreciate anew the importance of family — the good and bad influences which shape a personality. I remember visiting the grave of my great-grandparents in Iowa, who died forty years before I was born, and wondering what kind of people would they have been. How have their thoughts and genes affected me? Conversely, wouldn't they like to know what eventually happened to this large farming family that they raised?

When I returned to my hotel room that night I decided to write them a letter and tell them about their descendants who left Iowa and migrated to a new territorial frontier of America called Wyoming. That letter was expanded into a published book entitled *The Todd Legacy* which I read to nearly 200 Todds assembled at a Todd reunion in 1985.

As I wrote that book I was astounded as to how little we knew about these ancestors of ours. When I sifted through countless unmarked photographs I wondered who these people were who posed there in their best Sunday garbs — almost begging someone to identify them, call out their names, and say something about them as the wonderful human beings that they surely were.

Even more to the point, what about the importance to me of my immediate family — my own biological descendants? I developed a new perspective on this as well.

My oldest daughter, Lorilee, who we called Lori, born in 1955, was a vivacious child, fair complexioned with blonde hair that turned golden in the sunlight. She wouldn't sleep at night, preferring to crawl out of her bed and pad around the house in the darkness of the night. We finally had to tie her into the bed because a child loose in the house at night was a danger both to herself and others. Because she was the oldest, she became the little caretaker of her younger brother and sister. She became a gentle person with a lot of compassion for the unfortunates of our society. Little wonder that she resumed her college education after marriage and the birth of two children and graduated cum laude from New York University. She became a social worker with the placement of neglected children into foster homes. And on weekends she worked as a counselor in a home providing a sheltered environment for the retarded and dysfunctional. Lori is the social activist and reformer, interested in the political process so that it can bring about changes our society needs.

I have always loved Lori the most because she was my first little bouncing daughter.

Sheridan, who we called Sheri, was my youngest daughter born in 1960. Physically, she was the opposite of Lori, being a dark-complexioned brunette with dark eyes and a little dimple in her cheek which melted the heart of everyone, but particularly her daddy. We affectionately called her our little Indian because, like me, she easily tanned into a dark shade of brown in the summertime. Whenever we drove through the streets of Sheridan, Wyoming, where many Crow Indian people gathered along the sidewalks, we told Sheri to duck her head lest they think we had kidnapped one of their beautiful little Indian girls. She enjoyed the joke and proudly told her little friends that she was partly Indian. She couldn't compete with the gentle spirit of her older sister, so she became the mischievous one in the family. At the same time, she was a sensitive child who suffered the most, I think, from the divorce of her parents which occurred when she was only thirteen years old. I was too caught up in my own depression to more adequately help her cope with hers. She is now the working mother of three lovely children, who with her husband is building a summer home all by themselves, along the shore of Hawk Springs Lake, where they enjoy water sports to the fullest.

I have always loved Sheri the most because she was my youngest baby girl.

In the middle was my son, Barry, born in 1957. He was a sweet and affectionate little boy who loved his toy trucks and bedtime rituals. When he became older, he would take encyclopedias to bed with him — just to skim through the articles and look at the pictures. Although a vociferous child at home during his years in elementary school, he became pleasant and congenial as he moved into adulthood — with an infectious sense of humor, always smiling alluringly when he talks. He has the gift of storytelling. Vocationally, he didn't take after his father when it came to the world of ideas, preferring to work manually with his hands, and loving the outdoors for hunting and fishing. A pediatrician friend told me that Barry was one of the finest fathers he had ever encountered in his medical practice. A father who always got up with his two babies during the night to bring them to their nursing mother, then caring for them and rocking them back to sleep. He is a better father to his two children than I was to him.

I have always loved Barry the most because he was my only son — the affectionate little boy caught in the middle between two sisters.

As any parent knows — you can love each of your children the *most* — each in a unique and wonderfully different way.

A college education was so monumentally important to me that I just assumed my three children would naturally gravitate to it as well. I couldn't understand why, at first, they didn't when they graduated from high school. Maybe it was because I also believed that a college degree isn't everything. It doesn't assure integrity of character or meaning in life. Honest work by one's hands, hard manual labor, is noble and satisfying if this is what people choose to do with their lives.

Later, of course, Lori did go to college and is now pursuing a graduate degree in sociology. Barry reads western history and is more of an authority on the Indian wars of Wyoming than I — and I teach college history. For Christmas and birthdays I subscribe for him the *National Geographic* and *Smithsonian* which he devours from cover to cover. I'm convinced that someday, maybe in retirement from US West, Barry will go to college. Not in response to my expectation for him, or for any other ulterior purpose imposed upon himself — but only for the best reason of all, his own personal intellectual enrichment. And Sheri is working her way up through the managerial ranks of the corporate world — a world totally unknown to her father.

✧

But my immediate family is more than my biological family. When Rosemary and I were married in 1975 I acquired three new step-daughters, all in their teens and getting ready to leave home for college, children from Rosemary's previous marriage to Colonel Doug Adamson. Mary, Becky, and Kim have been a wonderful addition to my extended family life.

Although they are not my biological daughters, and I never knew them as small children, our adult relationship has become emotionally close. Following the death of Dr. Adamson, their natural father, I am now the only person who plays the father role in their lives.

I am also the only functioning maternal grandfather their five children have — the last count as of this writing. These grandchildren know me only as Granddad and would have difficulty in having it explained any other way. I feel as affectionately related to these grandchildren as I do to my biological grandchildren.

Between both sets of children, Rosemary and I are Nanna and Granddad to twelve grandchildren and we love almost every minute of our grandparenting. I say *almost* because there are times when it becomes too much, particularly with too many around in a townhome much smaller than the spacious Templeton House, but such moments are few and far between.

There's always the cookie jar with a *Granddad Cookie* awaiting the arrival of every grandchild, from the youngest (Riley) who as of this writing is two, to the oldest (Danny) who is in the army. I've heard howls of protests from anxious parents that these cookies absolutely ruin a child's appetite for a scrumptious family dinner which immediately was to follow. But when I ask these grandkids, after they became teenagers, if they felt terribly deprived for missing a family dinner because of a ruined appetite due to munching a *Granddad Cookie*, not one of them has yet confessed.

✧

Now in conclusion to this book, I ask myself the ultimate question: What have I learned from forty years in the ministry?

I can best answer the question by revealing what I would say if ever I'm invited to deliver a guest lecture in an Episcopal seminary, or any seminary for that matter, on how to succeed in the ministry.

The Gospel of Success

Rule # 1. *Don't stay put in one place very long.* Upward mobility is essential in the corporate world, and since the church has pretty much accepted the corporate model for itself — keep moving.

When you arrive at a new church, while the moving van is unloading, update your resume and let it be known you're interested in relocating within a couple years. A short stay in one church is much easier on the nerves, too. If you stay for the long haul, when the honeymoon is over, you'll get bogged down with insurmountable parish problems that require painful resolution. Avoid this pitfall if you can.

The more tenures you have at multiple churches and different jobs, the better it looks on a resume as a well-rounded experienced clergy person. Depth of experience is not a skill that's highly marketable in the ministry anymore. Breadth is in — and depth is out.

Rule # 2. *Don't schedule junior choir rehearsal in the chancel of the church at the same time on Saturday morning when the altar guild is setting up for Sunday services.* The divine destiny of each group is diametrically opposed to the other. It's a volatile mix. (Audrey in chapter 15.)

Rule # 3. *Don't become involved in social action, regardless of how justified it may seem by the Gospel you profess.* Always tell people you're quietly working behind the scene — soothing troubled waters — putting out fires — until the whole situation becomes resolved either in the courts or by hard political action of others. Then jump on the bandwagon and claim it as your idea all along. This works beautifully and you escape without getting your hide tanned.

Rule # 4. *Don't become involved in congregational controversy.* Avoid it like the plague, using the same technique and rationale found in Rule #3. If the controversy resolves itself, let it be known that it was due to your hard work in the background. However, if the controversy festers and worsens, immediately activate Rule #1 and hastily heed God's calling elsewhere.

Rule # 5. *Don't bare your soul to your congregation.* Let traveling evangelists and religious celebrities tell their maudlin stories of depravity to salvation, rags to riches, sin to glory — and allow them to *wow* your congregation. Encourage your congregation to share their personal testimonials as much as they want, but don't do it yourself. You'll make yourself vulnerable for emotional blackmail.

During the Billy Graham flap at St. Mark's, I was told that my mountaintop story (chapter 14) was being used against me by the dissidents as proof that I was unfit for the ministry. Fortunately, their gossip could never defile my personal relationship with God, because that was beyond their reach. Nevertheless, in retrospect, it was unwise of me to have shared the story. I should have played it safe and kept it to myself.

Rule # 6.   Don't barge in with too many changes for the choir or the altar guild. Being good and reasonable people, they can be gently persuaded to make changes as long as they're convinced the change was their idea in the first place. But they will rebel at any perception of dictatorial interference. When they do — you're through.

I read the history of a little Episcopal church in Nebraska celebrating its centennial anniversary. One hundred years ago a young priest took control away from the choir director and tried to force his liturgical changes. But on Sunday morning, the choir members, instead of heartily singing their newly taught choral responses, broke out in hysterical giggles. In full view of the congregation, the priest ripped off his vestments in disgust, stormed out of the church in a rage — and was never seen or heard from again.

One might ask how could a priest in a little Nebraska town simply vanish without anyone ever seeing him again? Following church the choir probably dragged him down to the Platte River and drowned him. Choirs can get away with that, you know.

In 1994, an Episcopal rector in Denver didn't like what the choir was doing and sold their electric organ to a flea market. The following Sunday, when they discovered what he had secretly done, he went the same way as the organ — only worse, they sold him into Roman slavery. The bishop and canon law were powerless to save him.

To mess with both the choir and the ladies guild is suicidal — with a torturous fate far worse than a merciful drowning.

Why? It's more than the fact that the altar guild director is a black-belted karate martialist and the choir director a trained guerrilla terrorist. You're dealing with bonded groups here who meet every week in the service of the Lord. Nothing invigorates a bonded group as much as a common enemy, real or imagined. Since the rector always makes a good enemy he needs to become an expert at persuading these groups that you're not out to change anything. Instead, you're simply allowing them to persuade you to reluctantly accept *their* wonderful ideas for change which were originally envisioned by you in the first place. It works!

Rule # 7.   Don't preach sermons that are too relevant to the daily needs of your parishioners, regardless of how idealistic this seems in theory. Confine them mostly to what the Bible says about ancient time, because that's safely removed from the complexities of modern times.

My mother used to say that unless a sermon helped her cope with all the vicissitudes of life, it had no practical value to her. She cautioned me to always ask *So What?* about every sermon I intended to preach. I believed her, and I still think she was right. But my mother lived on an isolated cattle ranch thirty miles from the nearest organized church. There's no way she could have known that such sermon relevancy is *Not preachin', brother, but meddlin'* — and it will get you in serious trouble.

Play it cool. Stick to the Bible, because no one will argue with that. Generally oppose sex and you'll be handsomely rewarded. Rally the crowds with rabid homophobia. (Remember: If it nets gold-plated Cadillacs for the TV evangelists it will, at least, produce a new Chevy for you.) Keep your preaching focused 2000 years ago and you're safe — and richer.

Rule # 8.   Don't use Jesus Christ as your role model in the ministry — too seriously. Talk about it, yes, but don't actually do it. Jesus was in constant conflict with the political and religious authorities of His day and didn't mesh well with the established power structure. He had too many unconventional ideas. He associated with the wrong people. Too many women tagged along after him. He wasn't very successful with his vestry of twelve either. These vestrymen, although handpicked by Jesus, never seemed to catch on to what he was about. His teachings confounded them. Denial, betrayal, and abandonment abounded. When He got nailed to a tree, with the exception of one, they were long gone.

Sometimes a clergy person must look reality straight in the eye — and deny it. Get practical with what the modern ministry demands, and make that your only goal. If you do, you'll be a success.

✧

On the other hand, if you aren't concerned about being successful in the ministry, as the world views it, and hope to do only the best job you can, serving God and people, the rules are much more simple.

The Gospel of Grace

Rule # 1.   Go into the ministry for the right reasons.

Don't enter the ministry thinking you're going to find Christ there. He's there, to be sure. But no more than you'd expect to find Him in the home, workplace, or marketplace. He's in these places every bit as much as in the church.

Don't think He's more available simply because you're in a holy place.

In 1985 Rosemary and I spent five weeks in Jerusalem. We attended lectures at St. George's College and then drove out to visit all the famous archeological sites of biblical times. I was overwhelmed with the historicity of it all far more than the religiosity of that ancient land in its modern setting of civil strife and military conflict.

In our St. George classes, we learned about secret entrances into parts of the famous Church of the Holy Sepulcher which enshrines the tomb of Christ — entrances not commonly known to tourists. (Unquestionably the most hallowed site of all Christendom.)

One Sunday afternoon, while shopping in the crowded bazaar along the narrow street corridors surrounding the church, I brazenly went behind a candy counter, and there, just as the archeologist had told us, I found a little trapdoor. I opened it and dropped five feet into the cavernous chamber below.

Terror struck me, however, when I realized the place was empty. I could hear the echo of my footsteps as I cautiously moved forward through the shadowy labyrinthian passageways deep within the bowels of the ancient church. The fear of a terrorist slipping into a holy shrine, as I had just done, is a real and present danger in the Middle East. I felt that at any moment my intrusive entry would be detected and I would be surrounded by armed guards with drawn guns.

But nothing happened. Several monks in black habits, sitting on the floor, waved at me as I passed by. Others were napping by a pillar. I penetrated deeper into the interior shadows of the church.

I slowly approached the tomb of Christ and was shocked to discover that there was not one single person around, contrary to the normal queue lines that are three to four hours long, amid the babbling throngs of Christian pilgrims from everywhere, patiently waiting to visit the holy shrine. Instead, the place was totally abandoned. (Later I learned that on Sunday afternoons everyone takes a Sabbath siesta.)

With fear and trepidation, I slipped inside the darkened tomb. I knelt there, realizing that of the millions of Christians the world over, only one of that vast number had the tomb of Jesus Christ completely to himself — and that person was Gene Todd of Cheyenne, Wyoming.

I prayed. Nothing happened. I prayed harder. Nothing. I was determined to make something happen. I stayed longer — five minutes, then ten.

Just cold, dank, empty nothingness.

It was time to go. I arose and stepped outside. What went wrong? Here was my one great moment, in the most holy sanctuary of Christendom, and nothing was happening.

I began to weep, which was truly out of character for me, letting go of my emotion like this. But there was no one around. Why not weep?

Suddenly, over my shoulder, out of the distant biblical past, I heard a clarion voice: "Are you looking for Jesus? You won't find Him here. He arose from the tomb. See . . . it's empty in there. He's gone out into the world. If you want to see Him you'll find him in Jerusalem, Rome, London, New York, Cheyenne. He's out there in that world. Not here."

I will never know why I was expecting to find the living Christ in the one place on earth where the Bible clearly tells us that He was not present — in his tomb! But I learned from this memorable experience that you'll find the resurrected Christ *out* there in the nitty-gritty of the real world where you live and work. Not just in the church. Wherever you find Him — it's a holy place!

Rule #2. *Humbly live the faith you teach and preach as best you can.* No more — no less. If it's more, it's sanctimonious. If it's less, it's hypocritical. If you reach a healthy spiritual balance somewhere between the two extremes, consider yourself lucky and don't worry. At least it's an honest place to begin, and God's grace will sustain you.

Rule #3. *Take care of yourself physically, emotionally, and spiritually.* Clergy wellness has become a new thing in the ministry within only the last ten years. A healthy lifestyle of physical exercise, emotional moderation, intellectual study, and prayerful spirituality doesn't just happen. It must be deliberately cultivated or the gift of joy and wonder will totally evade you.

Rule #4. *Follow the advice of Polack John: Don't delude yourself into believing that simply because you're in the ministry you're extra holy.* You're not. Tremendous heartache awaits anyone who is beckoned by God into the ministry for the best of reasons — when many don't survive it. Seeking a holiness boost through the ministry will guarantee your failure.

There can be tremendous satisfaction in the ministry, too. Once in a while you'll see someone like Maggie find faith and meaning in her sordid life, or a little Pee Wee rise up to greatness of courage and character when no one expects it of him.

Like watching people genuinely shielding the joy of others. Like baptizing the babies of the babies I originally baptized as I was regularly doing at St. Mark's after being there for twenty-seven years. Like drinking wine with people you love while hearing the wonderful tales of life they tell you if you're willing to listen and cry and laugh with them.

As I believe it is a mortal sin to bore people, so do I believe it is a sublime gift of God to cultivate a genuine sense of humor even in the midst of the most trying circumstances. Ninety-year-old Frances Haley told me in her final days that she would move from her chair to the bed only when she knew she was dying. Knowing this, I expressed surprise when I called one day and found her in bed.

"Oh," she said, with a twinkle in her eye, "whenever I see my minister coming, I always jump in bed. I get more attention that way."

This, a deathbed scene?

A gallant sense of humor like that will make the angels sing with laughter.

Occasionally, you'll get a compliment. Like the beautiful letters I received in Atlanta, especially the one from Maggie. Like dining in the elegant rectory of the Catholic Cathedral Basilica in Denver with the assistant rector who was formerly a Mormon who I instructed for confirmation into the Episcopal Church. He eventually became a Roman Catholic priest who studied in Rome. While munching on our salad in the papal suite which Pope John Paul used during his historic visit to Denver in 1992, Dave Stahl said, "Gene, you always impressed me with the beautiful way you read and conducted the liturgy. It converted me to Catholicism."

I'm glad. Dave will make a good priest.

✧

In retrospect, my overall perspective on the forty-year ministry of Gene Todd can best be summarized by saying — it was a mistake!

Not because my ministry wasn't fruitful. I firmly believe that according to all the critical standards of evaluation in determining a productive ministry, my pastorates at Padroni, Vermillion, Green River, and Cheyenne — even my interim ministry at Sedalia — would be considered successful.

But not productive enough for me to believe that the ministry was the right vocational choice for me. I've often wondered what might have happened if I had carried my law books to my first Denver University School of Law course in torts and contracts, instead of attending a class in the Old Testament at the Iliff School of Theology?

I probably would be a practicing attorney or a retiring judge in Colorado.

On the other hand, I think I could and would have become a successful professor of history at a major university. Or a successful college administrator. I believe I would have made a good layman as a liberal on social issues, as an Anglican traditionalist, as a conventional Christian — but never a fundamentalist.

When I review the forty-year span of my ministry, I realize that my opposition to racism, the Vietnam war, gay-bashing, and hate-mongering religious fundamentalism was confrontive and divisive. But in the long view, I believe that my opposition was right, for all the right reasons — but at the wrong time. Not to have taken the controversial stands I did would have made me a wimp. The fact that I felt compelled to make these choices and suffer the consequences proved that my personality was not cautiously well suited for the ministry within that historical time frame.

Although I take God seriously and have a healthy respect for religious authority and theological speculation, I lack the reverential solemnity of a professional cleric. The inherent frailty and myopia of the human condition prevents me from taking too seriously the institutions of religion and its hallowed leaders who presume to pontificate in the name of the Lord — whether they be popes, bishops, prime-time evangelists, lamas, rabbis, caliphs, or country parsons like myself.

The 102nd Archbishop of Canterbury and me attending the Anglican Institute in 1996. Lord Robert C. Runcie, a titular head of worldwide Anglican communion, also served as official pastor to the British royal family and officiated at the state-church wedding of Charles and Diana. He deeply regrets the marriage breakup and "silly antics" of the younger royal generation. He is a very warm and congenial person with a delightful sense of humor.

In fact, I find it terribly amusing. I simply shake my head and smile: *This too shall pass and with it common trifles.*

My abiding sense of humor, most of all, prevents me from taking myself too seriously. Hence, I'm always on the border of irreverency — which has become the story of my life and theme of this book. Another good reason why I should have stayed out of the ministry.

As the honky-tonk tune suggested, I should have been a *doctor or lawyer 'n such.*

But the ministry is not the full measure of my life.

More important to me and to God, I believe, are the priorities of becoming a warm and sensitive human being; a creature of the earth who relishes

spirituality of soul and sensuality of body; a man of integrity and courageous conviction; a person of hope and ingenuity; a loving husband; an
affectionate father and grandfather; a good friend and neighbor; a dedicated
citizen of the world whose resources he helps to conserve — and last, a
passionate and compassionate priest of the church. Not because I think the
priesthood is least important, but because anyone thinking they can succeed in the ministry without first pursuing the more basic qualities of
human excellence — is courting unmitigated disaster.

Have I achieved all these goals? Of course not.

The Bible advises us to press on toward perfection (Hebrews 6). This
means we must never achieve it. We always allow ourselves at least a one
percent margin of failure. It takes courage to be imperfect, and more so to
humbly admit it. Working on that one percent margin of imperfection keeps
me right out there on the raw cutting edge of life where, at times, I'm not
certain I'm gonna make it.

But as long as I keep working on it with humor, awe, and wonder,
then I'm a member of the human race, joyfully continuing the journey
of life for meaning and purpose — striving for wholeness and maturity
of mind and heart. If I breathe deeply of this pursuit, my spirit shall surely
transcend it — and I can laugh with the angels.

✧

My final revision of this chapter was completed at seven o'clock on
Sunday evening, August 13, 1995. I poured myself a frosted glass of iced
tea with a sprig of mint and leaned back in my easy chair for a night of
quiet celebration.

Two hours later I received a phone call that my youngest grandchild, Riley
Thomas Voycheske, had drowned along the shores of Hawk Springs
Reservoir near Torrington, Wyoming. His parents, Tom and Sheri, were
momentarily distracted while closing down the lake cottage, which they
had been building all by themselves, and packing up camping equipment
after another pleasant weekend of water sports and summer recreation. Little
Riley, two years old, loved splashing and wading in the warm water lapping upon the sandy beach. Suddenly, they discovered he was missing. When
they found him it was too late.

Immediately, our family was plunged into the depths of unbearable
anguish and darkest despair. We all knew, of course, that someday Riley
would die — as must we all. But this?

The burial of a child is diabolical, because it reverses the natural order
of life and death. It assaults the core of our ancestral inheritance and vio-
lates every fiber of our human existence.

I affectionately called him "My Little Riley Todd" (I have pet names for most of my grandchildren). I was his beloved "Gran-ka." The tragic loss, already overwhelming to us all, was all the more heartbreaking to me personally when I helplessly witnessed the gut-wrenching pain it inflicted upon my youngest daughter, Sheri, and her husband, Tom. As a helpless bystander, there was nothing ol' Dad could do to fix anything.

I took some comfort in the thought that God was with us in the depth of this horrendous loss as we remembered that He, too, lost a Son and knows the heartrending grief which every parent feels when you bury a child.

Riley Voycheske, my youngest grandchild and the first among my descendants to die. A delightful child, he loved splashing along the warm sandy beach of a lake where his parents and sister were vacationing. He suddenly turned up missing — but it was too late.

When I saw how compassionately Lori and Barry gently ministered to their younger sister — and how both Sheri and Tom seemed to set aside their own overpowering grief to comfort their young daughters — I had renewed hope in the grace of the second generation to carry on with life in a tender and loving way. The world forever needs the healing balm of those who deeply care.

All the Voycheskes and Todds gathered for Riley's funeral at St. Mark's Episcopal Church, where I assisted the Reverend "Skip" Reeves, my very capable successor at St. Mark's, with the burial rites. Riley's two older sisters, Kristin and Hailey, tenderly helped me place his ashes into the All Saints Columbarium at the back of the church, under the massive *Good Shepherd* stained-glass window towering above us. The rays of the bright afternoon sun, bursting through the dazzling collage of colored glass, flooded the interior shadows of the church with a mingled hue of shimmering light — and resurrection hope.

The service was attended by 300 people. How ironic that I began this book with a story about the near-drowning of a little two-year-old-boy — me — and I conclude, sixty-five years later, with another story about the tragic drowning of a two-year-old-youngster — my adorable little grandson. One cannot deny that the full circle of life has its bitter and poignant dimension.

Even more ironic to me is that the youngest child in my family would become the first to be interred in the elegant columbarium which I helped fashion with my spirit and hands — when I naturally expected to be the first to be buried there.

One of my prized possessions in our home is a handsome grandfather's clock upon which I have inscribed, on a brass plaque, the full name and birth date of each of my twelve grandchildren. Countless are the times Rosemary and I have checked the spelling of these precious names and hallowed dates for birthday remembrances. It is unbearable to think that the last child's name recorded there would be the first among us all to die.

My final prayer before the benediction, as we stood in front of the beautiful bronze columbarium, aglow in its warm soft lighting, was one that I prayed each night with my three children as I tucked them into bed. Sheri taught it to her three children — Kristin, Hailey, and Riley — and it became their bedtime prayer as well.

Jesus, tender shepherd hear me
Bless thy little lamb tonight
Through the darkness be thou near me
Keep me safe 'til morning light.

It remains a beautiful prayer. The inner strength we so desperately try to create for ourselves during a lifetime of character-building, spiritual development, and graceful maturing ultimately rests not upon our own efforts alone, as gigantic as this may seem, but upon the blessings of a Greater Power beyond ourselves, a "tender shepherd" who guides us through the valleys of darkness until we step out into the sunlit meadows of the hills on the other side.

I realized anew that when I finally reach the lofty summit of my final Lookout Mountain, and from that perspective take a grand view backward upon the full sweep of my life, with all its shadowed valleys and airy peaks, once again I hope to sing my favorite anthem:

My God and I
Go in the fields together
We walk and talk as good friends should and do
We clasp our hands
Our voices ring with laughter
My God and I
Will go unendingly.

Casual photo taken at a typical family gathering in 1996 showing all the Todd children and grandchildren at a steak fry in our back patio. Behind me is my oldest daughter, Lori, flanked by her two children, Leah and Daniel. Sitting at the table is my son, Barry, with his two children, Shaylyn and Jonathan, standing behind him. My youngest daughter, Sheri, is flanked by her two youngsters, Kristin and Hailey. (Missing here is grandson Riley who tragically drowned the summer before.)

EPILOGUE

Maybe some day, like Mr. Barnhill (chapter 18), I can sit on the back porch of my life and "live to remember" the sights and sounds and emotions of the vivid past.

To remember that farm boy who tromped across a cold and snowy windswept field late one Christmas Eve, behind a bunch of sauntering milk cows, asking himself what might become of his life when — in a moment of discovery — he learned that he had the freedom to make that choice.

To remember the years of college lectures, libraries crammed with books and educational seminars — reminding him that life is a never-ending pursuit of learning new skills and embracing more knowledge.

To remember God's creative gift of passion and lovemaking which brings incredible joy to the mystery and meaning of life.

To remember the tender cradling of his newly born babies, so perfectly formed that even their toenails needed clipping, and wondering what might become of their lives in the years that lay before them.

To remember the infectious laughter of our children outside at play with Taffy, our dachshund, and her five puppies — and later, their school graduations and their weddings. And then the laughter of their own children, my grandchildren, outside at play, like their parents before them.

To remember congregations of the faithful at Padroni, Vermillion, Green River, Cheyenne, and Sedalia — fervently singing their hymns and saying their prayers.

To remember the transient moments of triumphant victory and bitter defeat, the ecstasy of faith and the agony of doubt — and the constant reassurance that this too shall pass.

To remember a lifelong obsession with the written and spoken word — reading, writing, teaching, preaching, and broadcasting.

I am this boy.

I am this man.

As Mr. Barnhill said, when you "live to remember — you remember to live."

I have much to remember and I hope to invite the participants in my life to join me, up on the porch, so that we can talk and laugh about it awhile — as we enjoy the sunset and watch the evening stars come out.

As I write these words, my doctor tells me that I am in perfect health for a man forty-five years old. But I'm sixty-seven. In my entire life, never have I felt more healthful in body, mind, and spirit. I've slimmed down to 160 pounds through daily exercise and simple nutrition. Never an ache or pain, not even a headache. Never in my lifetime have I suffered a broken bone or intrusive surgery. I'm on no medication except for one little bedtime Mevacor pill, a nuisance prescribed over my objection, to further reduce my cholesterol count. Although I'm extremely health conscious, gourmet food and good wine at Rosemary's table will keep me on a perpetual diet.

A vegetative state for me would be the terrifying loss of both my physical health and the mental stimulation of my lifelong avocation with the written and spoken word — of man and God. Consequently, I stoke my spirituality with daily meditation. Every day I spend time in my library-study with the world of books and ideas to keep myself intellectually engaged. College teaching, interim preaching, working at my computer, socializing among intimate friends, and loving a wonderful family will keep me emotionally involved and incredibly busy throughout the remainder of my life.

In my spare time, I have written this book.

What more could a person ultimately need or desire in the retiring years of one's life than creative Living — Loving — Worshipping— and Dying — only to rise up and repeat the cycle all over again at a new level of one's existence? I dread impending old age only because it may force the gift of celibacy upon those of us who still don't want it.

As a whole, life has been . . . oh, so very good to me.

I've struggled in the faith but have been abundantly blessed by the journey and I'm deeply grateful.

But I also know, in spite of my good fortune, that my name is in the hat and the lottery continues until every name is drawn. I'm only one doctor's office visit removed from the solemn verdict. Wouldn't it be perfectly awful if everyone else got to go — and you were left behind? When my time comes, I pray that my going can be a first-class act. If not, at least, a demise with grace and dignity.

But if it can be neither, and I'm reduced to a vegetative state, then I make this formal request of my family — a fervent request which is both benevolent and profoundly religious, an act of mercy on your part which surely you can do — if truly you care. Secure for me a medical doctor who is more than a body technologist — one with enough human wisdom and spiritual compassion — that he will help me shut off the lights so I can peacefully go to sleep.

Otherwise I will miss the early dawn and beautiful sunrise of an exciting new day of my continuing journey.

To order this book for a friend

ORDER FORM

Tales & Irreverencies of a Country Parson

Eugene F. Todd

(Cloth hardbound, 584 pages, 90 photos, ISBN: 0-9654090-7-4)

Total Quantity Ordered   _____

Subtotal at $29.95 each $_____

Tax
Wyoming residents add 5% sales tax $_____

Shipping
Add $4.00 for first book,
$1.00 each additional book on same order $_____

TOTAL   (Enclosed check or money order) $_____

(Retail discount available upon request)

Western Americana Publishing
P.O. Box 20444
Cheyenne, WY 82003-7011
FAX (307)-778-6447

****

SHIP TO: (Please Print)

Name: _____

Address: _____

City: _____

State: _____ Zip: _____

Telephone: (_____) _____